Die at the Right Time!

Die at the

Right Time!

A Subjective Cultural History of the American Sixties

Eric v.d. Luft

>> North Syracuse, New York <<
<< Gegensatz Press >>
>> 2009 <<

Cataloging-in-Publication:

Luft, Eric v.d. (Eric von der), 1952-
    Die at the right time! : a subjective cultural history of the American sixties / Eric v.d. Luft.
    p. ; 26 cm.
    Includes bibliographical references and index.
    ISBN 978-0-9655179-2-8
    1. United States — History — 1961-1969. 2. Youth — United States — Political activity — History — 20th century. 3. Subculture — United States — History — 20th century. 4. Popular music — 1961-1970. 5. United States — Social conditions — 1960-1980. 6. Vietnamese Conflict, 1961-1975 — Protest movements — United States. 7. United States — Social life and customs — 1945-1970. 8. United States — Civilization — 1945- . 9. Radicalism   United States. 10. United States — Politics and government — 1963-1969. 11. Nineteen sixties. I. Title.
    E846.L83d 2009   973'.923 — dc22   AACR2
Library of Congress Control Number 2006934637

First edition, first printing. Printed in the United States of America by United Book Press, Baltimore, Maryland.

Front cover photograph by Associated Press, May 25, 1968. Used by permission of AP / Wide World.
Back cover photograph by the author, August 6, 1967.

The guillemets, or two pairs of opposing chevrons, dark on the lower cusps and light on the upper, are a trademark of Gegensatz Press.

Distributed to the trade worldwide by:
Gegensatz Press
108 Deborah Lane
North Syracuse, NY 13212-1931
<www.gegensatzpress.com>

Designed by the author.
Printed on acid-free paper. ∞

Contents

I dedicate this book to a beloved person, born late, but a true child of the sixties, whom I named after Grace Slick. Go on, kid, find your roots!

Preface and Acknowledgments

The purpose of this book is not to memorialize yesterday, but to inspire today and tomorrow. If it helps any present or future leftists, war resisters, or young visionaries to avoid past mistakes or to improve on past successes, then it will have achieved this purpose.

First conceived around 1978, it grew out of my conviction that the message of the sixties was already mostly misunderstood and would someday be lost unless someone wrote down what it was all about. That conviction has only strengthened over the years as I have ruminated on my adolescence, read books about the era, and noticed the way of the world since then.

I probably could have written *Die at the Right Time!* as early as about 1975, but it would have been a much different book. That was still too close to the events to allow putting them in their appropriate historical perspective. Certain milestones, including the death of Lyndon Johnson in 1973, the resignation of Richard Nixon in 1974, and especially the death of John Lennon in 1980, all had to occur before clear signals could be received that the sixties were finally over in spirit. In the famous "Owl of Minerva" passage in the Preface to the *Philosophy of Right*, Georg Wilhelm Friedrich Hegel wrote that teaching what the world ought to be requires distance in time. Philosophy, the judge of all things, must naturally always arrive on the scene too late to affect the unfolding of events in history, but when it finally arrives, it alone is capable of evaluating the significance of these events. Thus it may influence future events. The older, the more remote, and the more fixed things are, the more cogently philosophy can deal with them. Philosophy cannot hit a moving target. The sixties are old enough now to warrant Hegelian philosophical analysis. That is among the features of this book.

The title derives from the "On Free Death" chapter of Friedrich Nietzsche's *Thus Spake Zarathustra*, in which the title character proclaims: "Many die too late, and a few die too early. Yet the doctrine rings strange: 'Die at the right time!' (*Viele sterben zu spät, und Einige sterben zu früh. Noch klingt fremd die Lehre: 'stirb zur rechten Zeit!'*)." It alludes to all kinds of thought about proper and good death, from Socrates in Plato's *Apology*, *Crito*, and *Phaedo* to Epictetus's *Enchiridion* to Montaigne's "Custom of the Island of Cea" to a famous line in Pete Townshend's song, "Pure and Easy," which suggests that modern civilization, despite easy and instantaneous worldwide communication, seems obsessed with finding new ways to die, including stupid wars, counterproductive assassinations, useless recreational drugs, nuclear events, and random violence born of boredom.

The presentation is chronological, the focus — for reasons explained herein — is on the period from 1964 through 1970, and the exposition is genetic. Contrasted to systematic exposition, which explains in detail what a phenomenon is; historical exposition, which simply tells a story or grounds analysis in a narrative; and deductive exposition, which explains what a phenomenon entails; genetic exposition explains how a phenomenon came to be. This one is organized the way our lives were structured: fall semester, spring semester, summer vacation.

Some of the people with whom I shared growing up deserve to be mentioned here with love and gratitude: Heidi, Albert, Mace, Sue, Betsy, MBM, Pam, Drew, Amy C., Amy D., John B. (who turned me on to Hendrix), the Church of the Advent Youth Group, the late PJF ("I can dig the culture but not the politics"), Strumerino, Doug and Naomi from Hamorton, Cathy from Unionville, Linda and Dale from New Hampshire, and Roe the friendly chick ("Hello, Person!") from Yeadon whom I met while hitchhiking to Philadelphia. Also, I am forever indebted to members of the Society of Friends who embodied the power of nonviolent resistance, especially Helen H. Corson, Robin Harper, and Pennock J. Yeatman.

Part of the prologue is rewritten from "Thomas Szasz, M.D.: Philosopher, Psychiatrist, Libertarian," the cover story of the Summer 2001 SUNY Upstate Medical University *Alumni Journal*.

Earlier versions of portions of the "Summer 1966" and "1968" chapters were presented together as a paper, "The Mutual Influence of Rock Music and Antiwar Politics in 1968," at the "1968: Global Resistance / Local Knowledge" conference at Drew University on November 3-4, 2006. I wish to thank all the fine people who made that conference a success, especially Jeremy Varon, Aaron Pedinotti, Cheryl Oestreicher, Rich Greenwald, Rich Lee, Zach Lechner, David Allen, Madera Edwards, Dan Berger, Christopher Van Houten, Robert R. Goldberg, Andrew Hannon, Caitlin Casey, Melanie Brazzell, Astra Taylor, and Mark Rudd. Several conservations with Mark have deepened my understanding of the era.

The learned, talented people who have been most effective over the last fifty years in teaching me how to write deserve to be thanked: Fred Gilfillan, Sue Waltz, Ed Fitzkee, Albert Santora, the late Ed Pols, Kay Sherman, Bill Geoghegan, Bob Nunn, Duane Paluska, Al Wright, Scott Davis, Deborah Boe, George L. Kline, and Rebecca Garden. Of course, any problems that remain with my writing are my fault, not theirs. They tried! I particularly want to thank Joel Potash, Lisa Kaufmann, Leah Caldwell, and Rebecca for insightful comments on parts of the "Fall 1969" chapter.

I also wish to thank Diane Davis Luft (*uxor clarissima*); my daughter Sarah, who facilitated my research and recollection with Netflix; Prof. Jerry Farber of San Diego State University; Dr. Thomas S. Szasz of SUNY Upstate Medical University; Michael Tearson and Pierre Robert of WMMR-FM, Philadelphia; Genya Ravan; Melanie Safka Schekeryk; Richie Havens; Robert Alan ("Al") Haber; Muhammad Ahmad; Jennifer Hamlin-Navias; Ruth E. Kanost; Jentri Anders; graduate student assistant Stacie Mickens of the Mills Music Library, University of Wisconsin, Madison; various present and former librarians at Bowdoin College, Bryn Mawr College, Princeton University, Onondaga County Public Library, Liverpool Public Library, and Syracuse University; and rockers everywhere; all for their valuable help.

Philosophical Introduction and Prologue

Don't ask why, just do it!

Historical changes do not just happen. They have reasons and sometimes even causes. Transitions from each definable era to the next are not haphazard, but are prompted by what are sometimes called "historical forces." To call the fifties a decade of conformity, the sixties a decade of rebellion, the seventies a decade of hedonism, the eighties a decade of greed, the nineties a decade of indulgence, and the "aughts," as they seem to be unfolding, a decade of anger and fear, is all accurate but insufficient. These stark labels do not explain how or why these changes occurred, what drove them, or why, especially, given certain historical conditions, they were inevitable.

This book suggests some answers to why the sixties evolved logically out of the fifties and into the seventies. The word "logically" here does not have its usual honorific connotations. Rather, it means only that, given the psychosocial conditions of the fifties, the sixties were inevitable. Ditto for the inevitability of the seventies, given the sixties. The conclusion follows from the premises. Just as the adolescent necessarily grows out of the child, the child into the adolescent, the adult out of the adolescent, and the adolescent into the adult, so do historical eras necessarily — or "logically" — grow out of and into each other. Time moves only one way and will not be denied. The past is our data. The future does not yet exist to be known.

The data of the past can be described, but any such description is colored by the viewpoint and personality of the describer, by the distance in both space and time from each actual event being described, and by the natural limits of memory. The events of the past each only happened one way, but, if they are ever described, then they are necessarily described in many different ways, even by the same describer. Each description understands, interprets, interrelates, and uses the data in its own way, with or without ulterior motives. The data of history are absolute; so history itself, the chain of events, is objective; but historiography, the writing of history, is necessarily subjective. Hence the use of the word "subjective" in the subtitle of this book, not as a Kierkegaardian boast, but as a frank admission that what is stated here is — and can be — only one person's opinion. Any claim to objectivity in historiography is pretense. The objectivity of history is gone and unreachable.

Because history is dialectical in the Hegelian sense, this book resembles Hegel's *Phenomenology of Spirit* in that it tries to understand the "logical" interconnectedness of events by imposing a certain rationality on them according to their intrinsic features. Yet, against Hegel, this imposed rationality is unavoidably subjective. It is the imposition of only this particular historiographer. It can only *suggest* why phenomena grow out of and into each other.

Hegelian dialectic is not the familiar "thesis / antithesis / synthesis" caricature. That is, it is not the idea that a certain state of affairs in history meets its equally powerful opposite, and that the ensuing clash between them results in a new state of affairs, that will eventually meet its equally powerful opposite ... and so on. The problem with this caricature is that it does not explain where the "equally powerful opposite" comes from. The "thesis / antithesis / synthesis" myth is thus based on a *deus ex machina*.

In truth, Hegelian dialectic is the "logical" blueprint or flowchart for the evolution of each single state of affairs in history. Each defined or circumscribed state of affairs (*Satz*) contains at least one *internal* contradiction that defines an alternative state of affairs (*Gegensatz*). This contradiction will eventually manifest itself and threaten the *Satz*. The *Satz* will respond, and perhaps will be destroyed in the process, or perhaps it will survive, sadder but wiser. But somehow the contradiction will be addressed, since it cannot be ignored and will not go away, and somehow the inconsistency will be resolved by some compromise or agreement between the *Satz* and *Gegensatz*. This resolution of contradiction cannot be by the absolute victory of either side over the other, because in that case the *internal* contradiction would persist, and the conflicting process at this level would have to start all over again. There must be an integral part of both the *Satz* and the *Gegensatz* combined in any viable resolution. Both sides must be satisfied.

By this strictly internal conflict and resolution, each original *Satz* in history is simultaneously preserved in its essence, cancelled in its existence, and raised to a higher level which no longer contains that particular contradiction. In this way, history is analogous to ordinary human growth: The child, as she grows, is preserved as a human being, cancelled as a child, and raised to a higher level as an adolescent and eventually to an even higher level as an adult. Just as the adolescent is not possible without first the child, and just as the adult is not possible without first the adolescent, so the French Revolution was not possible without first the *Ancien Régime*, and so the Napoleonic Empire was not possible without first the French Revolution. Similarly, the psychosocial facts of the American sixties were not possible without first the psychosocial facts of the American fifties, and those facts of the seventies were not possible without first those of the sixties.

This Hegelian view of history owes much to philosophical anthropology, i.e., the belief that, given the respective predispositions, goals, and ethical characters of certain individuals, thus certain actions, events, and even outcomes in history become predictable, or "logical" in the sense above defined. Liberals act like liberals, conservatives act like conservatives, hypocrites act like hypocrites, and honest folk act like honest folk. Human nature is clear. Each person serves only his own particular interests and follows only his own particular motivations, even if those interests are daydreamy and even if those motivations are altruistic. Identify anyone's basic interests and motivations, and you will have gone a long way toward understanding and even predicting that person's actions. The paradigm practitioner of such keen prediction is the title character in *Njal's Saga*.

Our topic is the cultural sixties, not the chronological sixties. To speak of the sixties as a calendrical decade is arbitrary and deceptive. But to speak of the finite spirit which characterized the period that we call "the sixties" is no fabrication, for this spirit did indeed have definite limits. It did not exist much before 1963, and it has not existed for some years, certainly not since 1974. Difficult though it may be to determine just when this spirit died, we can surely now assert that it is dead, and not immediately likely to find new life. It had a romantic freshness which predestined it to a classically short Achillean life, and, like the death of Achilles, its passing (or more properly its "fading away") did not produce anything either worthy or remarkable. Its worth was in its life.

The spirit of which we speak did not arise spontaneously at the start of the decade or vanish suddenly at its end. Perhaps, then, to call the period of this cultural spirit "the sixties" is a little bizarre. But because this label has become widespread, largely through its use by those very people who fostered the spirit, and who juxtaposed this period with the dull, detested fifties and the selfish, contemptible seventies, there is no convenient way to avoid or improve their designation.

So, the decade that we conveniently call "the sixties" did not begin on either January 1, 1960 or January 1, 1961 and end on either December 31, 1969 or December 31, 1970 (considering rival mathematical biases toward the constitution of the calendar). The designation "sixties" is neither mathematical nor calendrical, but cultural. As such, one could argue that the sixties began with either the murder of John F. Kennedy on November 22, 1963 or the first appearance of the Beatles on *The Ed Sullivan Show* on February 9, 1964 and ended with either the last day at Woodstock on August 18, 1969, the debacle at Altamont on December 6, 1969, the street violence of May 1971, the gradual defeat of George McGovern in 1972, or on June 18, 1972, when the Watergate conspiracy that defined and dominated the seventies first gained public attention. A little bit of the sixties died at each of these times, so the actual result was that the era only faded away. But trying to give dates for the cultural sixties is endlessly controversial.

The first few mathematical/calendrical years of the decade were culturally still part of the fifties, despite the influence of JFK, Bob Dylan, Pete Seeger, Mort Sahl, and a few others.

In America, 1962 was culturally closer to 1945 than to 1965. Children obeyed commands, generally shared their parents' values, and did not yet prefer loud music. If they rebelled at all, it was only a "James Dean" rebellion, i.e., just perfunctory teenage bravado with no real reason or substance and no serious challenge to the established order. It was a phase of growing up within the fold, not a nascent commitment to growing out and away.

To assert that the murder of JFK was the main catalyst for the youth rebellion of the sixties would be simplistic, yet it was a very important factor. We had been raised to accept whatever sense our parents had imposed on the world and imparted to us— and by and large we did accept it — but the murder of JFK was a senseless death that called into question all the sense that all our ancestors had so far imposed and imparted. The world immediately became just as senseless as the senseless event that had rendered it senseless, and within a few years we came to see that Lyndon B. Johnson was a senseless president. Those bullets in Dallas overturned the whole world. Their most significant effect was to destroy whatever sense had characterized the world up to that point. They contributed materially to undermining our trust in our parents. The murder created two opposing worlds: our parents' and our own. The murder of JFK was a product of their world, not ours. Their world had produced Lee Harvey Oswald. He was not one of us.

Of course, this bifurcation of worlds was not due only to the murder of JFK. That was only the immediate cause. There were pre-existent underlying psychosocial causes, mostly grounded in our suppressed individuality, without which the mere killing of a president could not have had such a profound impact on us. JFK was more than a president; he was a symbol of hope, the very living breath of hope. Recovering our hope and optimism after his death was hard work — and that work became our task, our duty, for the sixties.

In the wake of World War I, the world correctly saw itself as absurd. That absurdity found expression in Dada, Surrealism, Tristan Tzara, Salvador Dali, Franz Kafka, Gertrude Stein, and perhaps most eloquently in T.S. Eliot's "The Wasteland." In the wake of World War II, the world correctly saw itself as even more absurd. That new absurdity arrived in the form of Jean-Paul Sartre, Albert Camus, Samuel Beckett, Eugène Ionesco, and all kinds of existentialists. In the wake of the murder of JFK and especially in the midst of LBJ's investment in Vietnam, the world again correctly saw itself as supremely absurd — and that even newer absurdity was expressed as *us*!

Ω

If you do not understand the French Revolution, then you do not understand history. Once and for all it defined the gulf between the right (conservatism) and the left (liberalism). In the protracted and tragic conflict among the ultraroyalists, clergy, constitutional monarchists, Chouans, fédérés, landowners, urban bourgoisie, Communards, peasants, homeless, Cordeliers, Girondins, Feuillants, Montagnards, Marais, Indulgents, muscadins, ouvriers, philosophes, Jacobins, Sansculottes, tricoteuses, and Enragés, we can understand the whole dynamics, logic, and illogic of class struggle, economic injustice, oppressive intolerance, repressed human spirit, religion's essence as bondage, and explosive sociopolitical anger.

Above all, the French Revolution should teach the left how *not* to conduct a revolution. During that whole period, the right remained fairly united, but the left squabbled constantly within itself and even killed many of its own most talented partisans. But, to be historically fair to those leftists of 1789 to 1795, they were inventing class-based revolution, and they did not know how best to do it. Thus comes the main lesson that we of the latter-day left must learn from that primal left. Unity! This does not mean forcing one another to agree with any standard party dogma or shunning or expelling comrades who disagree with the prevailing revolutionary opinion. Such purges, that we do to ourselves, are as bad as anything that the right does to us. We should not be our own enemies. Unity among revolutionaries does not mean that any of us should have to sacrifice our integrity. Rather, it means finding peaceful and productive ways to incorporate everyone's well-reasoned beliefs into the political synthesis. We must tolerate and respect all revolutionary views whether we agree with them or not, unless they promote violence, which, after all, is just the extreme manifestation of intolerance. That is our revolution's message: Tolerance! Intolerance is the province and weapon of the right. We tolerate anything except intolerance.

Both the September Massacres and the Reign of Terror were abominable. Nothing like either of them should ever be allowed to recur. Nevertheless, we could justify the September Massacres on the grounds that we were killing *them*, but we cannot justify the Reign of Terror, because then we were killing *ourselves*. Che Guevara, despite his innumerable faults, was correct that the true revolutionary is motivated by great feelings of love. To that I would add tolerance. Neither love nor tolerance dwelt in the soul of Maximilien Robespierre. Even as much as I remain a Jacobin at heart, I must say that Robespierre is exactly the kind of revolutionary leader that all future revolutions need to avoid. Rather than violent, cruel, opportunistic savages like Robespierre, Lenin, or Che, we need gentle but pragmatic guiding lights, who lead by example, like Gandhi and Martin Luther King.

A story circulates that Henry Kissinger asked Mao Zedong in the seventies to evaluate the impact of the French Revolution. Mao is supposed to have replied, "It's too early to tell." Mao nailed it! It is indeed much too early to tell. Totalitarian regimes — including the one that Mao himself founded in China — continue to oppress the majority of everyday people the world over. Until those people are free, the French Revolution will have had little effect. But it was the first step of a long journey in the true direction. To be a dictator in a free state is a crime.

Happiness and fulfillment as experienced by conservatives and liberals is essentially different. The happiness of conservatives is the gloating over defeated enemies, the rubbing-of-hands-with-glee following windfalls of good fortune, or the thrill of realizing that oneself, one's family, friends, peers, or chosen closed group are better than everyone else. The happiness of liberals is the serene and perhaps smug rejoicing at the betterment of society, the enhancement of civilization, the wider availability of common benefits such as education, the improvement of general health and welfare, the comeuppance of oppressors, the realization of human similarities amid the celebration of human differences, and the solidarity of the human spirit.

Similarly, the right and left have quite different concepts of freedom. For the right, freedom means being free to run roughshod over whomever or whatever they please; while for the left, it means freedom from poverty, hunger, oppression, and insecurity — all of which the rich right tends to take for granted. The "Four Freedoms" that President Franklin D. Roosevelt articulated in his January 6, 1941 speech to Congress — freedom of speech, freedom of religion, freedom from want, and freedom from fear — well express the liberal ideal.

While the left believes in freedom for everyone, the right promotes freedom only for those at the top of the hierarchy. Everyone else is relegated to some level of servitude or even slavery. The right — as any oligarchy must do — divides people from each other in order to maintain control over them. It uses race, age, nationality, ethnicity, socioeconomic status, political affiliation, religious conviction, musical taste, and any other divisive criterion it can conceive, exaggerate, emphasize, and exploit. The paradigm clash between the left and the right on the question of freedom is the American Civil War between Northern liberals, who wanted to impose on the entire nation their modern quasi-egalitarian ethical standards of human dignity, and Southern conservatives, who wanted to preserve their slaveholding heritage.

Conservatism is wrong. It runs fundamentally counter to the human spirit by restricting freedom and exercising control. The left would let the human spirit be free to grow and develop as it will, to chart its own path, and to follow its own desires. This freedom would be fun but dangerous. The human spirit needs some control, but just not as much as the right would prefer. So conservatism is indispensable. Without the right to check and balance the left, liberalism would fly off into anarchy.

Liberals and conservatives need each other. If the world from the dawn of humankind had been populated exclusively by conservatives, we would all still be preliterate primitives in trees and caves, and any attempt to break beyond that status would be met with swift and violent retribution. Conservatives have no incentive to change anything in the basic structure of their environment. If, on the other hand, the world had been populated exclusively by liberals, then innovation and society would have self-destructed in a whirlwind of chaos. Some measure of order is needed, but not too much.

The liberal / conservative cycle is oversimply as follows: Liberals detect something rotten in the status quo. They change it, approve of what they have done, and therefore seek to protect their new reality. Thus they become conservatives. Their wonderful new reality stagnates and putrefies. A new crop of liberals arises to detect this, and the cycle begins again. The Aristotelian sociopolitical mean is this interplay between left and right. The natural oscillation or pendulum-swinging between the two is Hegelian. If one tries to deny the dynamism of the dialectic and steer straight and narrow along the middle way without such interplay, then the result is the triumph of the right. The left, as natural critics, must remain always active in a gadfly role.

Thomas Hobbes is the model philosopher of the right. Everything in his political system, Leviathan, tends toward the standard rightist ideals of order, stability, conformity, and obedience. But who is the model philosopher of the left? That is a bit harder to say. John Locke? On the true path but does not go far enough.

Jean-Jacques Rousseau? Too wimpy. François Marie Arouet de Voltaire? Too unsystematic. Karl Marx? His economic theory in general does not work. Sartre? Too morose. Friedrich Nietzsche? Individualistic enough but with a cruel streak. Socrates? Obnoxious enough but too reluctant to disobey laws. John Stuart Mill? Too sloppy. Hegel? Too conciliatory. Immanuel Kant? Too didactic. Noam Chomsky? Too complicated. Peter Singer? Too flaky. John Rawls? Quite possibly, but rather early to tell. Simone de Beauvoir? Too narrow. And so on. And so on. And so on. This problem of picking a single leftist thinker to juxtapose to Hobbes highlights the familiar phenomenon of the ease with which the right unifies itself versus the difficulty with which the left manages its natural diversity.

In general, the motto of the right is, "Whatever is, is good"; while that of the left is, "Whatever is, could be better." Conservative Catholic Alexander Pope wrote in the First Epistle of *An Essay on Man*, "Whatever is, is right." Fabian socialist George Bernard Shaw wrote for the character of the Serpent in *Back to Methuselah*, "You see things, and you say, 'Why?' But I dream things that never were, and I say, 'Why not?'" This divergent attitude toward the status quo does not mean that the right is inherently satisfied while the left is inherently dissatisfied. The right is dissatisfied when things change too fast or too uncontrollably, but satisfied when things are under control and change at a predictable, manageable pace, especially when the rich get richer and more secure. The left is dissatisfied when things do not change fast enough, or worse, when things revert to old ways of being, but satisfied when things show evidence of moving toward liberty and justice for all, especially when the formerly poor, oppressed, and fearful find wealth, freedom, and security.

The founding of the United States of America in 1776 was a giant step in the proper direction away from monarchy, oligarchy, and tyranny. Unfortunately the plutocrats have had plenty of opportunity since then to hijack America, and by and large they have been successful. We have to take America back from them!

Countries that guarantee regular, free elections and extend the vote to large percentages of their citizens are fortunate in that they are capable of producing real, nonviolent revolutions at predictable intervals. In the United States, we can have a small revolution every two years and a large one every four — if the people want it. The trick is get them to want it, to inspire them to be politically active. America had leftist revolutions in 1932, 1960, and 2006; and rightist revolutions in 1980 and 1994. With greater voter involvement in the political process and greater turnout at elections, America could have more, better, and deeper revolutions.

There is nothing fundamentally wrong with the constitutional structure of the United States of America. Anyone who advocates overthrowing or redesigning the American government by either violent or nonviolent force is a rank ignorant fool — and a dangerous one at that. The American government, even with fascist bastards at the helm, is not the French *Ancien Régime*, which tried to prevent revolution and thus thoroughly deserved to be overthrown, even by the most violent force. But America, insofar as it continues to incorporate its revolutionary principles and allows revolution every two years, is laudable. It deserves to be preserved and further improved. The American Constitution is a liberal document, designed to ensure the freedom of the people. It deserves, on that account and especially on account of its Bill of Rights, to be honored, defended, and protected.

But America was not the home of the free. Some Americans were free, but not most. Women, children, blacks, employees, renters, debtors, homosexuals, and anyone who was different from whatever the "norm" was were not as free as financially independent, adult, white, short-haired, well-dressed men with their mortgages paid off. America had become an overabundant, interdependent plethora of corporations, and only the guys at the top were free. It was essentially a feudal system. Corporate America was unassailable, even by federally enforced antitrust laws. The Truman administration in 1948 had begun antitrust litigation to force du Pont to divest itself of its controlling influence on General Motors. This initiative finally succeeded during the JFK administration, by virtue of a federal court order in 1962 ordering du Pont within three years to get rid of 63 million shares of General Motors common stock worth 3.5 billion dollars. But Congress passed a special law to ease du Pont's tax burden and save it from antitrust penalties. Du Pont's formal control of General Motors ended in 1965, but the intimate business relationship remained intact. The feudal network was undamaged. Business went on as usual. The litigation was a zero sum game, a waste of everyone's time and money. For the everyday workers at both companies, nothing of consequence changed, certainly not for the better. By about that time we had come to realize that genuine personal freedom is not possible for employees or supporters of the corporate business world. Because we wanted freedom more than riches, we eschewed corporate America and all it stood for — including the war in Vietnam.

We were taught in church that pride is evil. As soon as we got out of church, and for the rest of the time until next Sunday morning, we were taught to take pride in our country, in its flag, in our appearance, and in a myraid of other socioeconomic and sociopolitical inventions. We were not supposed to understand, investigate, or even acknowledge this obvious contradiction. We were expected to believe whatever our elders told us was true, without question. If we did not understand, well, that was only because we were too young and immature to understand. They patted us on the head and promised us that we would understand when we grew up. Condescending to their children was their way of life, their way of protecting themselves from the danger of having to ask those very questions. Blame the inexperience of youth. Suppress adult illogic by ignoring childish logic. Just accept the given. Trust those who told it to you to accept it. Do not try to understand it yourself.

Popular author and TV host Art Linkletter actually made a business out of making fun of children. If we loved his TV show, *House Party*, or laughed at his book, *Kids Say the Darndest Things*, at the beginning of the sixties, by the end of the sixties we had come to recognize how exploitative, humiliating, and even cruel his schtick was and had come to regard both him and his enterprise as despicable and irredeemable. We were *people*, damn it, not the convenient laughingstock of our elders. We were to be raised and respected, not mocked for their amusement. If we were going to be freaks, it would be on our own terms, not theirs.

Our parents' generation was fanatically hung up on clothes, hair, and personal appearance — and not mainly their own, but other people's. They meddled with others' superficialities and judged others' whole human worth by these superficialities at least as much as they preened their own selves. For them, rules of etiquette, conventions of dress and "grooming" (ugh, I hate that word in that context — it reduces humans to the level of dogs), and gender-based and race-based social roles all had the status of laws of nature. To violate any of them would cause an intolerable upheaval. They cared so much about each other's appearance that they would even get gussied up in suits and ties and party dresses just to play bridge. Their standard of attractiveness exalted tall, elegant, short-haired, suavely groomed, faultlessly dressed, rich-looking white men of about thirty-five or forty, fresh from the barber, or five-foot-five, fashionable, done-up-haired, perfectly groomed, tastefully dressed, rich-looking white women of about twenty-five or thirty, fresh from the beauty parlor. They greeted almost any other appearance except a military uniform (in its proper setting) or work clothes (in their proper setting) with their appropriate measure of socially required contempt.

Positivism is the belief that whatever is given to sober experience — whether originating from nature, God, or humans — constitutes reality and that this reality is hard, fast, and incontrovertible. A major difference between our generation and our parents' generation was their positivist attitude toward rules. It seemed to us that, for them, rules of all kinds enjoyed the same solid ontological status as any given natural fact, the rock with which Samuel Johnson refuted Bishop Berkeley, or the laws of physics. All kinds of rules, including laws, social customs, etiquette, conventions of dress, roles of gender and race, and expectations of class, were simply to be obeyed and never questioned. Boys wore pants and short hair, girls wore skirts and long hair, the earth revolved around the sun, and that was that. That was just the way it was. We were allowed to try *within the system* to change any law or rule that we perceived as bad, but in the meantime we had to obey it as usual, and if in the end we failed to change it, then we were obliged to obey it forever. Everyone's hair always had to be slicked down.

Mostly because of what we so easily perceived as the obtuseness of our elders, in their support of the Vietnam War, their apparent disinclination to grant equal civil rights to all Americans, and their various hang-ups with social rules and norms — and because, thanks to the "baby boom" of kids too young too remember World War II but old enough to remember JFK, there were more of us than there were of them — by 1968 we were in open revolt. We did not have to either accept their culture or have none. There were enough of us to create our own culture — and that is just what we did. We did not all have what psychologist Dan Kiley in 1983 called "Peter Pan syndrome," the refusal to grow up, but we sure loved being young! We later came to agree with Pete Townshend about hoping to die before we got old.

To us family rules, school rules, and governmental laws were only suggestions. We sought solid rational ground for whatever we were told to obey. If we did not find it, then, and only then, we disobeyed. To obey a family rule, just because the oldest male in the house decrees it, is silly. Neither age, parenthood, nor gender is sufficient ground for authority. Only reason is. If, after our analysis, he turned out to be right, then we obeyed, not because he said so, but because he was right. If he turned out to be wrong, then we disobeyed, and our consciences were clear. We were not intimidated by threats of spanking, grounding, or other punishments. We were defenders of reason against the irrational. Similarly, to obey a school rule, just because an administrator or teacher says so, is silly. We either obeyed or disobeyed according to our own analysis, uncowed by threats of detention, expulsion, or other punishments. We were even less worried about school punishments than about family punishments. We were the "brightest and best"; they could not throw us out. Finally, to obey the law, just because it is the law, is silly. There were, are, and probably always will be a lot of ridiculous laws. Our self-appointed task was to ferret them out and bring them to public attention by disobeying them, again unhindered by fear of arrest, fine, imprisonment, or other punishments. Civil disobeyers like Henry David Thoreau, Mahatma Gandhi, and Martin Luther King were our heroes. We were not "juvenile delinquents," spoiled brats, or nihilistic disobeyers; on the contrary, we sought to create a better world by superseding stupid ideas.

If any rule or law was bad or nonsensical, then we were morally obligated to disobey it. Conventions of dress would always be trumped by what was comfortable, convenient, and personally expressive for each individual. Roles of gender and race were null and void. Social customs were archaic constructs in need of re-examination because their original rationale had been forgotten. Etiquette was to be superseded by common heartfelt human decency. Expectations of class were exposed as systematically oppressive.

Positivism would always have to answer to critical scrutiny. Our parents' standard positivist credo was succinctly expressed in any conflict with us as, "Because I said so, that's why!" They figured that this or similar dicta should end discussion right there. But that was never good enough for us. We wanted reasons.

How can anyone with any self-respect endure being told, "Don't ask why, just do it!"? Real humans, as rational beings, and having that rationality as the one thing that differentiates them from mere animals, demand to be satisfied with clear and logical answers to all their "why?" questions before they do anything that anyone else wants them to do.

Family situation comedies on TV in the fifties and early sixties, such as *Father Knows Best* and *Leave It to Beaver*, were based on "Don't-ask-why-just-do-it!-ism" and thus were worse than fantasies — they were lies. They were presented as reality, not as fantasy, and that is why they were lies. If they had been presented as fantasy, like *The Addams Family* or *The Munsters* in the mid-sixties, then they would not have been pernicious at all. We would have laughed at them for entirely different reasons — and that would have been OK. Jim Anderson, Ward Cleaver, Gomez Addams, and Herman Munster had quite a lot in common as comedic father figures in the paternalistic universe. They were all bumbling idiots. But Jim and Ward were expected to be obeyed without question, despite their bumbling idiocy, just because of their status as male heads of household; while Gomez and Herman were expected to reveal and augment their bumbling idiocy at every turn, and to be contravened constantly, despite their status as male heads of household.

In this regard, *The Addams Family* and *The Munsters* were more realistic than *Father Knows Best* and *Leave It to Beaver*. In fifties family sitcoms, the only character who approached being realistic was Eddie Haskell on *Leave It to Beaver* — and he was a complete shit. Probably grew up to be a prowar politician.

Jim Anderson was abrupt, self-righteous, sexist, and often just plain mean. Ward Cleaver was a bit mellower, and *Leave It to Beaver* was more fun to watch because it was full of *double entendres*.[1] For example, when June says, "Ward, I'm worried about the Beaver," which of the following should Ward reply?

> A. What's the matter this time?
> B. Where is he? I'll talk to him.
> C. What is it? Another yeast infection?
> D. Well, drop trou and let me have a look at it.

Despite the general dreariness of the fifties, we must acknowledge that this was a highly intellectual era, particularly in view of America's perceived need of scientific understanding in order to wage the Cold War, and especially in the wake of the Soviet launch of Sputnik on October 4, 1957. The Roosevelt, Truman, Eisenhower, and JFK eras all celebrated brainpower. That is to their credit — as not celebrating it to such an extent is to the discredit of every American era since then. TV shows such as *Sunrise Semester*, which ran on CBS from 1957 to 1982, and *General Electric College Bowl*, which ran on CBS and NBC from 1959 to 1970, exemplified the value that the American fifties and early sixties placed on intellectual achievement, even if ultimately not in its own right but rather for the sake of winning the Cold War. Later brain-oriented TV shows, such as *Jeopardy*, were just pale reflections.

In this Cold War context it was no accident that the first serialized episode of one of the most astute TV cartoon satires of all time, *Rocky and Bullwinkle* in its various incarnations, had secret rocket fuel as its central plot device. From 1959 through most of the sixties, *Rocky and Bullwinkle* matched and sometimes outdid such gems of sharp-witted, multivalent political comedy as Al Capp's *Li'l Abner*, Walt Kelly's *Pogo*, and the Marx Brothers' *Duck Soup*. With the whole world as its stage, its surrealistic geography was a hoot. Pottsylvania, home of Cold War villains Boris Badenov and Natasha Fatale, owed a lot to Capp's Lower Slobbovia, but was more an amalgam of the Soviet Union (the general motif), Imperial Germany (the planes and submarines), and Nazi Germany (Fearless Leader's uniform). The dialogue was laced with puns and topical allusions. The minimalist drawing contained subtle side humor for sharp-eyed viewers. A pretty clear indicator that *Rocky and Bullwinkle* was not intended just for kids is that one of the books in the library of Gidney's and Cloyd's moonship was *Sex on Planet "X."* The censors of the 1959-1960 season were not sharp-eyed enough to catch that one!

Concomitant with this atmosphere of national braininess was plenty of marvellous, uproarious, and often very subtle satire in addition to *Rocky and Bull-*

---

[1] This hilarious aspect of the show is explored in a satirical work: Will Jacobs and Gerard Jones, *The Beaver Papers: The Story of the "Lost Season"* (New York: Crown, 1983).

winkle. In the fifties Tom Lehrer was occasionally a graduate student in mathematics at Harvard University and a teacher of mathematics at Harvard, the Massachusetts Institute of Technology, and Wellesley College. Also a talented pianist, songwriter, and lyricist, he recorded and pressed in 1953 at his own expense 400 copies of *Songs by Tom Lehrer*, a ten-inch album of twelve parodies, including "The Old Dope Peddler," "Fight Fiercely, Harvard," "My Home Town," "The Irish Ballad," and "I Hold Your Hand in Mine." The pressing sold out without promotion, and news of his wit spread by word of mouth as Harvard students dispersed nationwide. A commercial live album, *An Evening Wasted with Tom Lehrer* (LP), followed in 1959 with eleven songs, including "Poisoning Pigeons in the Park," "Oedipus Rex," "It Makes a Fellow Proud to be a Soldier," and the brilliant "We Will All Go Together When We Go" — about nuclear war. In 1960 his *Revisited* album made the 1953 songs available commercially. Even more brilliant was *That Was The Year That Was*, his 1965 album of fourteen songs from his contributions to the NBC TV show, *That Was The Week That Was* (*TW3*), including "National Brotherhood Week," "Smut," "Pollution," "So Long, Mom: A Song for World War III," and "The Vatican Rag." The sharpest moment of his career was probably in 1973 when he remarked that giving the Nobel Peace Prize to Kissinger made political satire obsolete.

TW3 originated in England on the BBC in 1962. An outgrowth of the pioneering 1961-1962 BBC political satire show, *Beyond the Fringe*, *TW3* was produced not by the BBC's entertainment division, but by its news division. The British version centered around David Frost, Millicent Martin, and Kenneth Cope. In America the cast included Frost, Alan Alda, Nancy Ames, Henry Fonda, Buck Henry, Henry Morgan, Phyllis Newman, Elliot Reed, and many others. The American *TW3* was the first prime time show that was both truly irreverent and trenchantly funny. It ran only eighteen months, from November 1963 to May 1965, but in that time managed to drop precipitously from dazzling to stale. It was not missed when it ended.

Some TV shows in the early sixties were, at first look, just fluff; but upon deeper analysis could be seen as incisive social commentary. Foremost among such shows was *The Beverly Hillbillies*, which ran through most of the decade. Jed's, Jethro's, Elly May's, and Granny's bumpkin ways were patronizingly depicted as foolish, but were no less foolish than those of the rich, pompous, ass-kissing bank president, Mr. Drysdale. The only character who consistently made any sense was Drysdale's frequently discouraged secretary, Miss Hathaway. The villain of the series was Drysdale's insufferably snobbish wife, Margaret.

Greed and its naturally attendant social disruption was also the theme of a very funny, but again, at first look, very fluffy movie, *It's a Mad, Mad, Mad, Mad World*, which held any number of American customs, conventions, traditions, and prejudices up to ridicule.

Among the funniest comedians of the JFK era were satirists Mort Sahl, Lenny Bruce, and Vaughan Meader. Sahl would just bring the day's newspaper on stage, read it, and ad lib his act. Bruce was among the first comedians to talk bluntly about sex, drugs, and other sleazy but intrinsically funny topics, using the appropriate four-letter words. Meader brought his comedy to bear on the Kennedy family itself. Meader's and Sahl's careers collapsed after the murder of JFK. Meader ran out of material and Sahl could not get over his heartbreak. Bruce died in 1966 of a morphine overdose.

In 1962 Johnny Carson began a nearly thirty-year reign over the *Tonight Show*, rescued it from the turgidity that had been its hallmark since Jack Paar took over in 1957, and returned it to the fine miscellany of high and low comedy that Steve Allen had established for it in 1954.

Allan Sherman's odyssey from his first album, *My Son, The Folk Singer*, in 1962 to his hilarious book, *The Rape of the A*P*E**, in 1973 is analogous to ours from the Beach Boys to the Jefferson Airplane or from Elvis Presley to Jimi Hendrix, i.e., from mere entertainment to entertainment with a purpose. Sherman's early albums were funny as hell, but insubstantial. His book about sex more than made up for those albums in substance. "A*P*E*" stood for "American Puritan Ethic," which he lambasted with gusto.

A bright new star blasted into the comedy scene in 1963 with his first and arguably his best album, *Bill Cosby is a Very Funny Fellow, Right*. His dialogue between God designing and Noah building the ark was not only enough to make us bust our guts laughing, but also a harbinger of much future comedy. Cosby was not afraid to tackle religion. He was irreverent, but good-naturedly irreverent.

Another charismatic black man who captivated us with humor was Cassius Clay. A few months before he changed his name to Muhammad Ali, he released *I Am The Greatest!*, a comedic *tour de force* of narcissism in verse and proto-rap. Our elders mostly hated him because he was brash, black, and arrogant; but to us, brashness was cool, negritude was cool, and arrogance was not arrogance if one could deliver on one's boasts. He delivered. Everything he said he would do to Sonny Liston, he did. So his insolence was not bragging; it was accurate prediction. We loved him! Even those of us who did not like boxing loved him.

But the keenest satirist of the JFK, LBJ, and Nixon eras, and perhaps of the entire American twentieth century, was a gentle, self-effacing folk singer, Pete Seeger, the ever underlying presence of the sixties, never rising to prominent visibility, but always a powerfully active force, like Moriarty in Arthur Conan Doyle's Sherlock Holmes stories. Not at all evil like Moriarty, but at least as pervasive in his particular domain.

Seeger's natural domain was politics. He popularized "We Shall Overcome," the rallying song of the civil rights movement; recorded Malvina Reynolds's "Little Boxes," a landmark mockery of middle class conformity; and, with Lee Hays in 1949, co-wrote "If I Had a Hammer," which was covered by a slew of folk acts in the early sixties. From 1960 to 1963, as the number of American troops in Vietnam went from 900 to 16,300 "noncombatant military advisers" and as the racial and economic injustices that were woven deeply into the American fabric became more and more apparent and troublesome, Seeger became more and more active. His activism sparked other folkies.

The folk scene of the early sixties was thoroughly charged with politics. The Kingston Trio led the way. Moving from pop folk hits like "Tom Dooley" in

1958 to antiwar laments like "Where Have All the Flowers Gone?" in 1962 and satires like "Greenback Dollar" in 1963, they created the climate that enabled the emergence of Joan Baez in 1960, the Highwaymen and Judy Collins in 1961, and Bob Dylan and Peter, Paul, and Mary in 1962.

An ABC TV series, *Hootenanny*, tried in 1963 to present sanitized folk music without politics for a bland prime time audience. Impossible! The show banned Seeger, thus guaranteeing its lack of credibility with anyone who knew or cared about folk music. Most major folk artists boycotted the show in protest. The best that *Hootenanny* could thereafter book was the inanely commercial Serendipity Singers.

In 1963 Dylan's second album, *The Freewheelin' Bob Dylan*, established him as a formidable songwriter with six protest songs that quickly became leftist anthems and pop standards: "Blowin' in the Wind, "A Hard Rain's A-Gonna Fall," "Don't Think Twice, It's All Right," "Masters of War," "Talkin' World War III Blues," and "I Shall Be Free." After Peter, Paul, and Mary successfully covered "Blowin' in the Wind," other artists, not only folkies and leftists, became increasingly eager to cover his songs. Throughout the sixties his lyrics would be in everyone's ears, seldom via his own raspy little voice, but via much more melodic and evocative voices, like Roger McGuinn's, Sam Cooke's, or Joan Baez's.

With the exceptions of a few songs from a few blacks and a few folkies, such as "Blue Moon" by the Marcels, "Quarter to Three" by Gary U.S. Bonds, "Hit the Road, Jack" and "Busted" by Ray Charles, "Moon River" by Jerry Butler, "Duke of Earl" by Gene Chandler, "Twist and Shout" by the Isley Brothers, "He's a Rebel" by the Crystals, "South Street" by the Orlons, "Heat Wave" by Martha and the Vandellas, and Seeger's, the Kingston Trio's, Collins's, Baez's, and Dylan's stuff, the popular music from 1960 to 1963 was sappy, lackluster, and inconsequential. It did not rock. The best music was black music. Butler's "Moon River" was much more powerful than its composer Henry Mancini's version, released around the same time. Joey Dee and the Starliters' cover of the Isleys' "Shout" was hot, but could never reach the energy of the original.

Following criteria that Bing Crosby and his cohorts established in the thirties, listeners expected songs to be soft and pleasant, not hard or raucous. Melodic, beautifully sung, insincere love songs with fluffy lyrics dominated the airwaves. The same radio stations that played Elvis, Jerry Lee Lewis, and Chubby Checker also played Mantovani, Bert Kaempfert, Hugo Winterhalter, and other soporific murmurs.

Aside from some musical pearls like Del Shannon's "Runaway," Roy Orbison's "Running Scared," Patsy Cline's "Crazy," or Johnny Cash's "Ring of Fire," the most interesting non-folk music of the JFK era consisted of nutty things like "Big Bad John" by Jimmy Dean, "Walk Right In" by the Rooftop Singers, "Tie Me Kangaroo Down, Sport" by Rolf Harris, "Wipe Out" by the Surfaris, "Sugar Shack" by Jimmy Gilmer and the Fireballs, "Dominique" by the Singing Nun, and the immortal, unfathomably controversial "Louie Louie" by the Kingsmen. Undercurrents of frivolity, unrecognized sexism, and teenage angst characterized this music. It did not contain much serious protest — or serious lyrics at all. To find any meat in the lyrics of rock and pop songs before 1964 required either the listener's keen natural interpretive sense or the scholar's deliberate analysis.

In 1961 Dion, formerly the Bronx doo wop king in Dion and the Belmonts and later reinvented as sensitive singer-songwriter Dion DiMucci, had a huge solo hit with "Runaround Sue" and three months later with "The Wanderer." Our keen natural interpretative sense should have leaped into action, but remained asleep for years until the whole pre-Beatles rock-pop music era came under intellectual scrutiny. "Runaround Sue" attacked women who have multiple romantic or sexual partners. So far so good. No big problem with that, really. But "The Wanderer" threw "Runaround Sue" into stark relief by *glorifying* men who have multiple romantic or sexual partners. Few people would recognize the fundamental injustice of typical heterosexual relationships until the word came from feminist consciousness raising (CR) groups in the late sixties. But in Dion's heyday the ideal of the "great American romance" was defined by asymmetry, inequality, possessiveness, jealousy, and suspicion, with always the woman getting the short end of the deal. In such a relationship each owned the other, but while the man's ownership of the woman made her unfree, the woman's ownership of the man meant nothing more than that she expected him to be faithful to her. He retained his essential freedom. If he strayed, he would suffer no social consequences except losing that particular woman. But if she strayed, she would be branded a slut and would have difficulty finding another steady lover.

Dion's double standard between these two songs disgusted anyone who actually thought about it. But how many bothered to think about it? Sometimes sleeping people need reality to hit them in the head to wake them up.

Thomas Szasz did that. His 1961 book, *The Myth of Mental Illness*, claimed that there is no such thing, and that what we call "mental illness" is really a contrivance of the medical community, government, and organized religion to control, oppress, and manipulate people. Reaction to this book was swift and multifaceted. Traditional psychiatrists and psychologists were mostly aghast, but the future guru of psychedelia, Timothy Leary, still on the Harvard psychology faculty and two months short of his first LSD trip, wrote in a letter to Szasz on July 17, 1961:

> *The Myth of Mental Illness* is the most important book in the history of psychiatry. I know it is rash and premature to make this early judgment. I reserve the right later to revise and perhaps suggest it is the most important book published in the twentieth century. It is great in so many ways — scholarship, clinical insight, political savvy, common sense, historical sweep, human concern — and most of all for its compassionate, shattering honesty. I have already contacted several of my colleagues and intend that everyone I meet will be exposed to your work. I am in charge of the first year graduate training at this Center and while I don't believe in "required" reading I shall certainly "suggest" with enthusiasm that this book be read and reread. Your text states most eloquently, convincingly, systematically what a group of us here have been attempting to communicate.

Even during his sixties zenith, Szasz's views on mental illness were always part of a small minority opinion. His influence on psychiatric and social theory has diminished since then. When challenged in the nineties about his persistent disbelief in the reality of mental illness, despite medical imaging showing physical evidence of schizophrenia, he said, "Show me 100 brain CAT scans, blind, that will show which patients have mental illness as reliably as 100 leg x-rays, again blind, will show which patients have fractures, and then I will believe that there is mental illness." He contends that mental "illness" does not exist because the medical criterion for illness is the physical lesion, which the mind, not being a material object equatable with "brain," is not capable of having.

Szasz believes that some people are just plain "nutty" or even "mad," but that does not mean that they are diseased, or indeed, that anything at all is wrong with them. The concept of mental illness evolved in Europe in the sixteenth and seventeenth centuries. Many cultures, such as the Native American, have no such concept, and would regard as divinely inspired or specially insightful those whom regular Western medicine would classify as sick.

Szasz cites historical examples of ethical lapses in medical practice. Before the American Civil War, physicians classified "drapetomania," the tendency of slaves to run away; "dysaesthesia Aethiopis," the lethargy of black slaves; and "negritude," the very condition of having dark skin; all as diseases. Both "masturbatory insanity" and "homosexuality" were considered legitimate diseases when Szasz was in medical school in the forties. In the former U.S.S.R., the desire to emigrate was officially designated "schizophrenia." The pervasiveness of Ritalin in the nineties implied that American society regarded "hyperactive" boys as "diseased"; but, Szasz observes, high levels of activity are normal for boys.

"Psychiatry," Szasz frequently reminds us, "does not deal with diseases, but with conflicts between people." Psychiatric "treatment," because it deals with unwanted behavior rather than "disease," is not "medical" treatment, but a personal service if voluntary and a method of social control if involuntary. Psychiatrists should assume that people each have good reasons for behaving the way they do; that is, psychiatrists should feel professionally and morally obligated to respect the autonomy of each patient, rather than hastily judge that there is something "wrong" with the patient. Yet whether, on the one hand, to help the actual patient, or, on the other hand, to help society by integrating the patient, remains each psychiatrist's own decision. The systematic classification of diseases as entities is artificial and does not advance the cause of medicine, but allows physicians to pigeonhole and depersonalize patients, and assists physicians only in underserving or malserving their patients. Worse, it provides means for societal or governmental oppression of some kinds of patients, notably the young, the old, the poor, the politically "undesirable," and the socially "offensive." Such people, Szasz says, "tend to be abused by society, but when doctors do it, it is called 'treatment'." He urges abolishing both the insanity defense because it excuses the guilty and involuntary hospitalization because it punishes the innocent.

For Szasz, there is only one way to understand ethics, and that is by asking the classic Roman question: *Cui bono?* Whom will this action benefit? He agrees with the ancient Roman Stoics that even suicide is a question for each individual alone to decide, without influence or coercion from any external agent. His life's mission has been to wrest artificial controls on natural individual freedom away from politicians, clergy, physicians, lawyers, insurers, bureaucrats, etc., and return that freedom to individuals. In this quest, he shares ground with several prominent philosophers, such as Socrates, who was always willing to listen to what others had to say while guiding them gently toward the truth; Rousseau, who lamented that we are born free, but are everywhere in chains; Edmund Burke, who warned of the danger of liberty being gradually "nibbled away" by evil governments while duped citizens stand by and watch; Max Stirner, the "anarchist individualist" of the Young Hegelians; Mill, the liberal utilitarian author of *On Liberty*; Thoreau, the champion of civil disobedience in defense of individual liberty; Nietzsche, who urged us to use our own legs if we want to rise high and not allow ourselves to be carried on the backs of others; and Ludwig von Mises, the libertarian economist.

People must each be free to chart their own course. That means, among other things, the abolishment of censorship.

La Dolce Vita pushed the limits of censorship. The fact that it was obviously high art made any attempt to censor it ridiculous. It seemed to have very little plot, but just a lot of bizarre, decadent, and sexy episodes strung together in a nearly inscrutable way. It marked one of the first times that American audiences could see disinterested cinematic depictions of womanizing, orgies, homosexuality, or transvestitism. We Americans found ourselves hard pressed to grasp upper-class Italian culture sufficiently to understand the film. Whatever sense we managed to impose on it surely was wrong. We did not understand it, yet it fascinated us. Because we could not follow its plot, we had only impressions; but Federico Fellini the pessimist, the cynic, came through clearly enough. We perceived only that "the sweet life" was not sweet at all. The beautiful was ugly, the safe was dangerous, the musical was discordant, the sophisticated was stupid, the spiritual was superstitious, the clean was polluted, the sagacious was gullible, the powerful was impotent, and the abundant was barren. Fellini's irrational, Schopenhauerian universe infiltrated American popular culture, not only through the sixties, but permanently. The name of one of the film's main characters, the hounding photographer Paparazzo, soon entered the pejorative anglophone vernacular. Europe, through film, began to influence our world view.

Along with *La Dolce Vita*, plenty of other movies in the Eisenhower and JFK eras depicted the sleazy side of life. *The Hustler* was instrumental within this genre in developing the concept of the antihero, which would dominate serious films throughout the sixties. Paul Newman's Fast Eddie Felson was a "born loser" because he lacked self-control. His impulsiveness, self-importance, easily erupting anger, impudence, inability to hold his liquor, subconscious defeatism, and other contributing factors to his chronic failure all derived from this one basic character flaw. His natural talent and finely honed skill alone could not sustain him. His resurrection began after Piper Laurie's Sarah Packard showed unrequited faith in him and when he allowed the scuzziest scumbag in the film, George C. Scott's Bert Gordon, to be his guide to self-discipline. This mentoring gave Eddie the temperament to make him a winner by reinforcing his instinctive coldness, yet at the same time revealed that no one can be truly human who equates financial or material gain with winning. To live only for money is, as Eddie told Bert, to be able to live only by killing everything else. Sarah's suicide, if seen for what it really was, i.e., Bert treacherously murdering her, underscored this point. The main message of the film was that absolute heartlessness reigns wherever big money is the ultimate focus, but to be a real winner is to learn to love and be loved, without regard for money. Sarah and Eddie got this message from each other — tragically too late — but Bert never got it at all. There could be no redemption for Bert, as there was for Eddie, because Bert was consumed by greed.

As Bud Stamper, his first starring role, Warren Beatty earned instant credibility among young moviegoers by throwing a tantrum in the first scene of *Splendor in the Grass* because Natalie Wood's character, Deanie Loomis, refused to fuck him. She already had substantial credibility of her own from playing Judy in *Rebel Without a Cause* in 1955. The two of them would hold much sway over their young fans, both on and off screen, throughout the sixties. She in *Rebel Without a Cause* and both in *Splendor in the Grass* played good kids whose frustration under their elders' tyranny, self-righteousness, hypocrisy, and refusal to listen drove them over the edge — in Deanie's case, almost literally, as she attempted to throw herself over a waterfall. One memorable exchange from the earlier film just about summed it all up: James Dean's character, Jim Stark, complained, "Nobody talks to children," to which Judy replied, "No, they just tell them." Bud's father, the villain of *Splendor in the Grass*, was the past master of telling. He dictated to everyone, disrespected Bud's mother, sister, and women in general at every opportunity, cared only for money and status, and never took notice of any word that Bud or his sister ever said. Bud's stress from meekly resigning himself to the will of this arrogant, domineering, single-minded bastard made him short-tempered, uncommunicative, and thwarted his natural inclination to respect womankind. As the direct result of not defying his father, Bud nearly ruined the only life he cared about, Deanie's, and killed any chance they had for eventual married happiness. Only Bud's father's suicide after the 1929 stock market crash allowed Bud to overcome his alienation and build a happy life for himself. Unfortunately, by then it was too late to build it with Deanie.

Natalie Wood's star rose even higher with *West Side Story*, despite the fact that she was miscast as the Juliet-character, Maria. The catchy music and stunning choreography interwove almost flawlessly with the rehashed Shakespearian narrative of Capulets as Puerto Rican punks, Montagues as white American punks, and the streets of Verona as the slums of Manhattan. The result was similar to but not quite as a good as a Wagnerian *Gesamtkunstwerk*, "a complete work of art" that blended music and visuals into a seamless whole. Ernest Lehman's screenplay was contrived, but at least it gave a lot of us naive white suburban kids our first exposure to the injustice, stupidity, and hopelessness of inner-city ethnic prejudice.

Unconventional social and romantic relationships were a recurrent theme in films of the JFK era. François Truffaut's *Jules and Jim* sympathetically portrayed two men as tender friends, both in love with the same woman, yet as devoted to each other as Damon and Pythias. Their homosexual love, spiritually consummated but physically not, only grew deeper as the prospect of their sharing this woman, Catherine, for the rest of their lives gradually unfolded. The envisioned permanence of this male-male-female love triangle was depicted as reasonable and healthy. Though mocked by villagers, who called them a threesome of lunatics, they were not condemned by anyone else. The spanner in the works was Catherine, whose mercurial, narcissistic caprice proved to be their undoing. The men's tragic character flaw in the classic Aristotelian sense was that, despite knowing full well her utter unpredictability, they trusted her. On a whim Catherine killed herself and Jim together, leaving Jules to grieve, one presumes more for Jim than for her.

Truffaut was not alone in depicting the female element as the cause of rottenness in human relationships. In *Lolita*,[2] both author Vladimir Nabokov and director Stanley Kubrick blamed Humbert's obsession on her, not him. Moreover, because of the insufferable mother, Charlotte, the moviegoer can almost — almost — forgive middle-aged Humbert and teeny bopper Lolita for their mutual attraction. Yet there can never be any rationale to forgive Quilty the pornographer for seducing Lolita. He earned his execution at Humbert's hand, whether Lolita led him on or not. The idea that women, not men themselves, create evil in men's lusty hearts is at least as old as the Genesis myth. It has produced such persistent illogic as that rape victims cause themselves to be raped just by being women and that battered wives cause themselves to be beaten just by being wives. The ridiculousness of blaming the victim began to become generally apparent only after the publication of such books as Simone de Beauvoir's *The Second Sex* in 1953 and Betty Friedan's *The Feminine Mystique* in 1963. By the mid-sixties liberal women and men were beginning to believe that the time had come to do something about this pervasive and fundamental injustice.

Injustices, both overt and subliminal, abounded in that uptight society of the fifties and early sixties. Gender-based, race-based, money-based, class-based, age-based, affiliation-based, politics-based, hair-based, you-name-it-based — there they were. Through the rest of the sixties our job gradually became to try to eliminate the overt injustices and to bring the subliminal ones into the light so that they also could be eliminated. Movies helped.

Racial injustice was the theme of *To Kill a Mockingbird*. Gregory Peck's Atticus Finch, the widower father of two elementary school imps, was a humble, honest, small-town lawyer forced into a lose-lose situation, defending an obviously innocent black man in a capital case against the predetermined guilty verdict of ignorant Alabama country folk. His few allies in town, including the sheriff, the judge, and several of his neighbors, were powerless against this ingrained, illogical, anti-logical racism. But Atticus did not give up the fight. Even though his client died, he remained able to go through life with a clear conscience, kept his dignity in the face of temptations to descend to the barbaric level of the white racists, set a wonderful example for his kids to emulate, and won the respect of the local black community. A real hero!

---

[2] Oddly enough, Helen Hessel, who inspired the character of Catherine in *Jules and Jim*, translated Nabokov's *Lolita* from English into German in 1955.

On the opposite end of the spectrum of heroes from the unassuming, down-to-earth Atticus Finch was the glamorous superspy, James Bond, whose impact on the culture of the American sixties cannot be overestimated.

From 1953 until his death in 1964, former British spy and journalist Ian Fleming published one James Bond book each year. This series — *Casino Royale* (1953), *Live and Let Die* (1954), *Moonraker* (1955), *Diamonds Are Forever* (1956), *From Russia with Love* (1957), *Doctor No* (1958), *Goldfinger* (1959), *For Your Eyes Only* (1960), *Thunderball* (1961), *The Spy Who Loved Me* (1962), *On Her Majesty's Secret Service* (1963), *You Only Live Twice* (1964), and, posthumously, *The Man with the Golden Gun* (1965) — was extraordinarily popular. In the early sixties it spawned not only the Sean Connery movies but also comparably popular and more realistic spy novels such as John Le Carré's *The Spy Who Came in from the Cold* (1963) and Len Deighton's *The Ipcress File* (1962). The Cold War was the perfect milieu for spy fiction escapism. Fleming's Bond novels, despite their sensationalism and gadgetry, actually stand the test of time as period literature. His *Thunderball*, *On Her Majesty's Secret Service*, and *You Only Live Twice* form an especially well crafted trilogy of psychological thrillers.

The Bond books were as natural to be made into movies as any series ever written. *Dr. No* was not just a mindless, shoot-'em-up action movie. Bond's utter coolness and Connery's flawless repartee were at least as entertaining as the sexual innuendo, stylized violence, and action gimmicks, and ensured a diverse audience for *Dr. No* and subsequent Bond films. Yet, even despite Fleming's presence on the set in Jamaica, the movie was markedly less believable than the book. The first fourteen of the last sixteen minutes were weak and cartoonish, and, for me at least, ruined what would otherwise have been a great film. The book's torture maze terminated logically at the "killing ground"; the movie's absurdly at the most vulnerable point of Dr. No's operation. Worse than a typical Hollywood contrivance, that was a *deus ex machina* such as Fleming would never have put into any of the books. The hokey labels throughout Dr. No's control room, obviously for the sake of no one there, but only for the theater audience, added to the cartoon effect. Yet the 94 before and the two after those fourteen anomalous minutes were exquisite. The characters were smartly drawn and convincingly acted. Dr. No, as a member of S.P.E.C.T.R.E. (Special Executive for Counterintelligence, Terrorism, Revenge, and Extortion), rejected both East and West as equally stupid. By implication, we took this as a comment on the Cold War. Indeed East and West should have united in real life to fight their common enemy: international crime.

The stupidity of the Cold War took many forms, few stupider than McCarthyism. For many of us, our first brush with McCarthyism came via *The Manchurian Candidate*. We were mostly too young to have experienced the absurd circus of Senator Joseph McCarthy, who was censured in December 1954 and died in May 1957. James Gregory played Senator John Iselin in the movie to resemble McCarthy in every plausible way. We came away from the theater incredulous that such an obnoxious buffoon could ever have been a U.S. senator. But those few of us who bothered to do the research into the early fifties realized that Iselin was in fact a fairly accurate portrayal of McCarthy and that — yes — such an obnoxious buffoon really did represent the state of Wisconsin as a Republican from 1947 to 1957. The similarities did not end there. The movie contained plenty of fodder for nerds with too much time on their hands who wanted to find even the most tenuous links to real life. For instance, Raymond, the first name of the fictional brainwashed Sergeant Shaw in *The Manchurian Candidate*, was also the historical McCarthy's middle name. As ridiculous and fanciful as the plot was, with such devices as the wife of a U.S. senator being actually a high ranking and particularly machiavellian Soviet secret agent, it seemed less fanciful the more we realized how ridiculous the real Cold War and its two main rival governments were. Anti-Kremlin, anti-communist madness in Washington and anti-Pentagon, anti-capitalist madness in Moscow were equally stupid. The more we learned about the actual fifties and sixties, the more we realized that the arms race, the intrigue, the posturing, the saber-rattling braggadocio, the calculated fear of "duck-and-cover," and the blunt refusal by both sides to "peacefully coexist,"[3] were all at least as goofy as anything we saw in *The Manchurian Candidate*.

Fellini's *8½* explored in a chaotic way the relation between the true and the false. The moviegoer had difficulty telling the difference between depicted dream and depicted reality. Perhaps the film's message was that there is no absolute reality, only private fantasy. Art may be truer and more real than reality, because it forthrightly depicts reality as fantasy; while reality itself, unavoidably untrue to itself, pretends that it is reality when in fact it is only fantasy. Then what does "in fact" mean? Can there be any touchstone to determine what is real and what is not? Or perhaps such a line of interpretation is nonsense! The film may not be about the unreality of reality at all, but only about the main character Guido's multifaceted and purely personal problem of trying to create surreal cinematic art out of mundane realities such as traffic jams, childhood memories, church doctrine, nuclear war, spaceships, and love affairs. It may be just that simple. It may be just a quasi-autobiographical statement about the ordeal of directing movies. The title supports this face-value interpretation, as eight-and-a-half was the number of films that Fellini had made up to that point in his career. Perhaps we puzzled American viewers of Italian films tried to read too much philosophy, symbolism, and meaning into them when "in fact" their philosophy was incoherent and lopsidedly existential, their symbolism parochial and cryptic, and their meaning inaccessible to anyone except directors and others closely associated with these films — and perhaps not even to them. Yet, despite the apparent insanity of *8½*, we could take seriously its motto that happiness is being able to tell the truth without making anyone suffer.

Film-making in actual practice could be as insane as what was fictionalized in *8½*. Along with the magnificent, 15-million-dollar, Oscar-winning *Lawrence of Arabia* and the 19-million-dollar, historically inaccurate *Mutiny on the Bounty*, the biggest blockbuster of the JFK era was the 44-million-dollar *Cleopatra*. It was one of the most extravagant movies of any era. Pre-release scandals about mismanaged

---

[3] Nikita Khrushchev coined the term "peaceful coexistence" in 1957 as a catchphrase for the officially promulgated aims of post-Stalinist Soviet foreign policy. Seldom has any slogan been so cynically applied.

finances and disorganized production, lurid off-camera antics of Elizabeth Taylor and Richard Burton, and ubiquitous flashy hype made the movie itself seem anti-climactic. The career it helped the most was, ironically, that of *New York Herald Tribune* film critic Judith Crist, who famously hated it. *New York Times* critic Bosley Crowther's career went downhill after he praised it. Reviews nationwide were likewise mixed. In retrospect, however, and forgetting the real-life "Liz and Dick" soap opera, *Cleopatra* was not a bad film. Queen Cleopatra's railing at Caesar for burning the Alexandrian Library was alone in itself worth the price of admission. She mockingly allowed him to order his Roman "barbarians" to burn cities, tear down buildings, rape, murder, pillage, and "play conqueror" all they wanted, but insisted that no one had "the right to destroy one human thought."

A much better and cheaper film won the Best Picture Oscar for 1963, the one-million-dollar *Tom Jones*, a rollicking comedy full of slapstick and sight gags, but also a multivalent social commentary, remarkably keen in pointing out the vicious hypocrisy and avarice of the clergy, the rich, the privileged, and their dupes and lackeys. Its success, in contrast to the relative failure of *Cleopatra*, should have taught Hollywood once and for all that low budget does not mean low quality and high budget does not mean high quality.

Ω

World War II was everywhere. From the end of the war through the JFK era, Americans sincerely and fittingly celebrated it as a just war. It was constantly in our consciousness as one of America's finest triumphs. JFK himself had been a war hero. On ABC, *Combat* ran from 1962 to 1967, *McHale's Navy* from 1962 to 1966, and *The Gallant Men* from 1962 to 1963. Excellent — and I mean really excellent — films were made in the late fifties and early sixties about World War II, including *Heaven Knows, Mr. Allison* (1957), *The Bridge on the River Kwai* (1957), *The Enemy Below* (1957), *Sink the Bismarck!* (1960), *The Guns of Navarone* (1961), *The Longest Day* (1962), *PT 109* (1963), and *The Victors* (1963). The war movie trend also involved some outstanding films about World War I, such as *Paths of Glory* (1957) and *Lawrence of Arabia* (1962), and the Korean War, such as *Pork Chop Hill* (1959). We were steeped in war movies. The best of them all was *The Great Escape*, a not quite true story about captured Allied flyers in a high-security Nazi camp near what is now Żagań, Poland. Steve McQueen's character, the ever upbeat Captain Virgil Hilts, "The Cooler King," was the epitome of coolness, as in this exchange: Colonel von Luger: "Are all American officers so ill-mannered?" Hilts: "Um, about 99 per cent." This film underscored the maleness of war in that it had not even one female speaking part.

Thanks to Mitch Miller and his Sing-Along Gang, the catchy main themes from the soundtracks of *The Bridge on the River Kwai*, *The Guns of Navarone*, *The Longest Day*, and *The Great Escape* were on the radio and in the record stores.

Some may have wished to extend our national fascination with World War

II and — in its centennial years of 1961 to 1965 — the American Civil War into a celebration of war in general. But others were too sensible for such hawkishness in the current international political climate. They realized that atomic and hydrogen bombs were bigger threats than the Soviet Union and Red China and that global annihilation was a more likely possibility than either side winning World War III. Accordingly, peace movements, conciliatory movements, internationalist workers' movements, human rights movements, antinuclear movements, and other counter-establishment initiatives sprang up worldwide in the late fifties and early sixties. Among these were the Southern Christian Leadership Conference (SCLC) in 1957, the Direct Action Committee Against Nuclear War (DACANW) in 1958, Students for a Democratic Society (SDS) and the Student Nonviolent Coordinating Committee (SNCC) in 1960, and Physicians for Social Responsibility (PSR) in 1961.

Dag Hammarskjöld in the United Nations was a peacenik too. Losing him to a plane crash in 1961 was a major setback for progress toward world harmony. The leaders of these other movements, Bertrand Russell, Robert Alan Haber, Tom Hayden, Dave Dellinger, Stokely Carmichael, Bernard Lown, and even Martin Luther King himself, could not hold a candle to Hammarskjöld.

The JFK era was a curious mixture of unbridled hope from white students, black activists, and JFK himself, and despair from the blunt facts of the Cold War, racism, the systematic oppression of nearly everyone except rich white males, and the constant threat of nuclear annihilation. Birth control pills become available, but still men would tell women how, when, and whether to use them. King proclaimed, "I have a dream that my four little children will one day live in a nation where they will not be judged by the color of their skin but by the content of their character," but Ku Klux Klansman Byron De La Beckwith had shot Medgar Evers in the back only two months earlier. The 1962 SDS manifesto, the Port Huron Statement, expressed this paradox of hope and despair:

> The United States' principal goal should be creating a world where hunger, poverty, disease, ignorance, violence, and exploitation are replaced as central features by abundance, reason, love, and international cooperation. To many this will seem the product of juvenile hallucination: but we insist it is a more realistic goal than is a world of nuclear stalemate. Some will say this is a hope beyond all bounds: but is far better to us to have positive vision than a "hard headed" resignation. Some will sympathize, but claim it is impossible: if so, then, we, not Fate, are the responsible ones, for we have the means at our disposal. We should not give up the attempt for fear of failure.

The SDS embraced the ideals of education and declared that all New Left activists must have "real intellectual skills," that is, the philosophical ability to analyze, think critically, and synthesize.

The times in history when hope is most justified are when philosophy takes to the streets. Because these times are the most hopeful, they are also the most exciting. Witness fifth-century-B.C.E. Athens, Jesus's Palestinian ministry, the 1770s in America, the 1780s in France, the 1840s in Germany, and the 1960s worldwide.

Philosophy is pretty useless inside the ivory tower. It has to get out into the world to do any good. Cloistered philosophy, that is, academic philosophy as usual, is just the shortest tittle of the pen away from pedantry, chop logic, and sycophantic, idolatrous, incestuous scholarship. Karl Marx was quite correct in his "Eleventh Thesis on Feuerbach" that "philosophers have merely *interpreted* the world, but the point is to *change* it." Marx was then writing against Hegel, who had famously claimed in the Preface to his 1821 *Philosophy of Right* that philosophy cannot actually *do* anything, but can only *understand* events after the fact: "One more word about *teaching* what the world ought to be: Philosophy always arrives too late to do any such teaching. As the *thought* of the world, philosophy appears only in the period after actuality has been achieved and has completed its formative process." But there was more to Hegel than that. He was not so naive. He wrote the *Philosophy of Right* under great stress in 1820-1821, worried about the threat of harsh Prussian censorship mandated by the 1819 Carlsbad Decrees. He had to be careful not to be too prescriptive in print, although he was a bit more relaxed about expressing his political views in his lectures at the University of Berlin. For example, contrary to the interpretation of some scholars who would brand him a conservative, Hegel wrote "The actual is rational" in the *Philosophy of Right* to mollify the censors, but in his unmonitored lectures to his Berlin students, he said "The actual becomes rational." Hegel was never more in tune with reality than when he wrote in Paragraph 11 of his 1822 Foreword to Hermann Hinrichs's *Religion in its Internal Relation to Systematic Knowledge*: "Against ... the sterile erudition of orthodoxy, the better sense has a divine right."

Ω

Every Friday afternoon in sixth grade our teacher took us to the school library for an hour right after lunch. We were all lazily shuffling back from the cafeteria expecting just another episode in this routine. We were not looking forward to the library, but to the subsequent traditions: the weekly swim in the nearby college pool, then dismissal, the weekend, the *raison d'être* for most of us. Very poor planning it was to have the library hour on Friday afternoon. But who cared? For prep school sixth-graders we were already remarkably jaded. As it was now November we had all fully settled into the mechanical sameness to which we were obligated. We shuffled toward it, resignedly, toward maturity and consummated conformity, everything we were taught to be but never really wanted to be.

We were just assembling in line, two-by-two, for the march halfway down the hall to the library — **WHAT!?! NO!!** The fifth grade teacher, utterly frantic, crying real tears, not even trying to maintain any facade of composure in front of the students, burst into our room and shattered our apathy forever. He had been listening to the radio during lunch. President Kennedy had been shot and killed by a sniper in Dallas. Lyndon Johnson was President. We listened to the radio in the library and we still went for our swim. But forget the weekend! Forget the *raison* *d'être*! By the time the flags returned to the top of the staff thirty days later a new era had begun. Now we had come alive! No longer jaded, mechanical, lazy, or resignedly shuffling. That was all in the past.

In less than an instant we had all become aware of the perversity, corruption, and sickness in the very fabric of our time, our country, our attitudes, our traditions, our parents, our teachers, and ourselves. In less than an instant we came to know that this order, which had produced such atrocities, this system of mere prejudices, which had only been given to us, thrown at us, inflicted on us, but not even partially created by us, could not be allowed to continue to exist. Their values, which had enabled and abetted this murder, would have to be replaced by our values, which could never contribute to any such thing. We were going to make good and sure that the new era would be our era, defined by our attitudes, our priorities, and our power!

The National Football League played its full schedule of games that Sunday. Dave Meggyesy, then a linebacker with the St. Louis Cardinals, recalled:

> Probably one of the moments that politicized me and a number of my teammates was when we had to play the New York Giants the weekend after President Kennedy was killed. Athletes tend to hold their political views to themselves. But guys were really pissed about that. We all felt out of respect for the president, we should never have played. But the order came down from Pete Rozelle that we had to play to save the country, that football games would bring everyone together. The players heard that and said, "This is a bunch of bullshit."[4]

Perhaps the Episcopal bishop of the Diocese of New York from 1972 to 1989, Paul Moore, who had known JFK since they were teenagers, expressed our common feeling most eloquently:

> I was in bed with the flu in Indianapolis when Jenny called out: "The President's been shot!" Then followed those awful, agonizing moments when it became more and more clear that the wounds were fatal. I cried as much in anger as in grief. Our hope, our generation's leader, was gone. The family gathered in my bedroom to watch the dreadful unfolding coverage of the blow the nation and indeed the world had sustained. In retrospect, we are more aware of Jack Kennedy's faults, of his macho posture on foreign policy issues, of the dalliances in his personal life. But at the time he was the king of Camelot, and, even with all his faults, I believe the world would now be a far better place had he lived. He had begun the war on poverty, he had stood down Khrushchev in the Cuban missile crisis without a shot being fired. He had brains and a sense of history. Now all that was gone. Thank God we did not yet know of the tragedies still to come.[5]

---

[4] Dave Zirin, "Sports & Culture: An Interview with Dave Meggyesy," *ZMag*, 17, 2 (February 2004): online at <zmagsite.zmag.org/Feb2004/zirin0204.html>.

[5] Paul Moore, Jr., *Presences: A Bishop's Life in the City* (New York: Farrar, Straus and Giroux, 1997), p. 166.

For the next six or seven years, fundamental social and cultural change would occur in America with unprecedented speed.

It is no accident that this book appears forty years after 1969, the hopeful year that put the exclamation point on 1967, the rather naive year whose Summer of Love introduced widespread altruistic anarchy into American culture, and on 1968, the epic year that epitomizes the sixties. *Die at the Right Time!* celebrates 1967's, 1968's, and 1969's accomplishments, studies their failures, and laments their yet unfulfilled promises.

The serene spirit of 1967 in San Francisco, Monterey, and Montréal; the confrontational spirit of 1968 in Chicago, Prague, Resurrection City, and many other revolutionary sites; and the hypnotic spirit of 1969 as shown in the altruistic anarchy that made Woodstock a success, in the subdued turbulence of the November 15 March on Washington, and in the egoistic anarchy of Altamont that undermined the accomplishments of Woodstock and emboldened our detractors — are all aspects of the same spirit that animated 1775 in Lexington, 1776 in Philadelphia, 1789 in Paris, 1830 and 1848 on the barricades, and 1989 in Tiananmen Square. It is the spirit of Mario Cavaradossi in Giacomo Puccini's *Tosca*. That spirit will never die. People will eventually be free.

Ω

Chronology of the American Sixties

Understanding the development of any era, or any object of inquiry, requires knowing the order in which phenomena appeared. This chronology of significant events, singles, albums, books, movies, and TV shows from the sixties cannot be comprehensive, mainly because subjectivity has determined the "significance" of its entries. Yet the list is authoritative and its selections are credible. The author, at least, believes that no one can understand the too-young-to-remember-World-War-II-but-old-enough-to-remember-JFK generation without immersion in the items on this list: listen to this music, study these events, see these movies, watch these TV shows, and read these books, preferably in the same order as they were originally experienced.

Dates for events are as exact as possible; for movies, theatrical release date; for TV shows, first airing; for albums, date of release; for singles, first chart appearance; for books, date of publication.

For most media, finding dates as specific as a month or even a day was usually possible. I encountered two exceptions: First, without access to publishers' records, pinning books down to a date more specific than a year proved too difficult to be worthwhile. Second, Pete Seeger's discography is notoriously elusive. He released literally hundreds of recordings, but seldom made the charts. He was a constant and compelling undercurrent in the music of the fifties and sixties, with profound influence on the development of folk protest, folk pop, and folk rock.

58 March: Bertrand Russell and the Direct Action Committee Against Nuclear War (DACANW) devise the symbol later known as the "peace sign" by superimposing the semaphore codes for "N" and "D" (i.e., "nuclear disarmament") inside a circle, representing the unity of the world.

59 January 5: *General Electric College Bowl*, hosted first by Allen Ludden then by Robert Earle, runs on CBS until 1962, then on NBC until 1970.
59 July: Tom Lehrer: *An Evening Wasted with Tom Lehrer* (LP), with "We Will All Go Together When We Go."
59 November 19: Jay Ward's cartoon *Rocky and his Friends* runs on ABC until June 10, 1961, then as *The Bullwinkle Show* and other titles on NBC from September 24, 1961 to June 28, 1963 and ABC from 1964 to 1973.

60: Maximum number of U.S. troops in Vietnam = 900.

60 January: Robert Alan Haber and Tom Hayden found Students for a Democratic
   Society (SDS) in Ann Arbor, Michigan, breaking away from the League for
   Industrial Democracy.

60 April: Shaw University students create the Student Nonviolent Coordinating
   Committee (SNCC).

60 July: Tom Lehrer: *Revisited* (LP), with "The Old Dope Peddler."

60 October 16: Mort Sahl on *The Ed Sullivan Show*.

60 December: Birth control pills become available.

61: Maximum number of U.S. troops in Vietnam = 3,200.

61 (early in the year): Cardiologist Bernard Lown and several other doctors
   opposed to nuclear bomb development found Physicians for Social
   Responsibility (PSR) in Cambridge, Massachusetts.

61 January 20: JFK is inaugurated.

61 February 4: Lenny Bruce performs at Carnegie Hall.

61 March 11: Marcels: "Blue Moon."

61 March 18: Del Shannon: "Runaway."

61 April 19: *La Dolce Vita* (movie).

61 April 22: Roy Orbison: "Running Scared."

61 May: Thomas Szasz: *The Myth of Mental Illness* (book).

61 May 27: Gary U.S. Bonds: "Quarter to Three."

61 June 24: Highwaymen: "Michael."

61 July 17: Timothy Leary writes in a personal letter to Thomas Szasz: "*The Myth
   of Mental Illness* is the most important book in the history of psychiatry."

61 August: Pete Seeger: *Sing Out With Pete* (LP).

61 September: Michael Hollingshead introduces Timothy Leary to LSD.

61 September 9: Ray Charles: "Hit the Road, Jack."

61 September 23: Dion: "Runaround Sue."

61 September 25: *The Hustler* (movie).

61 September 30: Jerry Butler: "Moon River."

61 October 7: Jimmy Dean: "Big Bad John."

61 October 7: Henry Mancini: "Moon River."

61 October 10: *Splendor in the Grass* (movie).

61 October 18: *West Side Story* (movie).

61 October 21: Patsy Cline: "Crazy."

61 November: Judy Collins: *A Maid of Constant Sorrow* (LP).

61 December 16: Dion: "The Wanderer."

62: Maximum number of U.S. troops in Vietnam = 11,300.

62 January 6: Gene Chandler: "Duke of Earl."

62 January 13: Kingston Trio: "Where Have All the Flowers Gone?"

62 January 23: *Jules and Jim* (movie).

62 February: First issue of *Broadside* magazine, publishing lyrics of political

songs, appears in New York and runs until July 1987.

62 March: Bob Dylan: *Bob Dylan* (LP), with "In My Time of Dyin'."

62 March 24: Joey Dee and the Starliters: "Shout," cover of 1959 song by the Isley Brothers.

62 June 2: Isley Brothers: "Twist and Shout."

62 June 13: *Lolita* (movie).

62 June 15: SDS releases its manifesto, the Port Huron Statement.

62 August 11: Peter, Paul, and Mary: "If I Had a Hammer."

62 September 15: Crystals: "He's a Rebel."

62 September 26: *Beverly Hillbillies* runs on CBS until 1971.

62 October: Allan Sherman: *My Son, The Folk Singer* (LP).

62 October: Cuban Missile Crisis.

62 October 2: Johnny Carson hosts *The Tonight Show* on NBC until May 22, 1992.

62 October 24: *The Manchurian Candidate* (movie).

62 November: Vaughan Meader: *The First Family* (LP).

62 December: Allan Sherman: *My Son, The Celebrity* (LP).

62 December 10: *Lawrence of Arabia* (movie).

62 December 25: *To Kill a Mockingbird* (movie).

62 December 29: Rooftop Singers: "Walk Right In."

63: Maximum number of U.S. troops in Vietnam = 16,300.

63: Pete Seeger: *Broadside Ballads, Volume 2* (LP), with "Little Boxes" by Malvina Reynolds.

63 January: Pete Seeger: *The Bitter and the Sweet* (LP), with "We Shall Overcome."

63 February 2: Kingston Trio: "Greenback Dollar."

63 February 9: Orlons: "South Street."

63 March 16: Peter, Paul, and Mary: "Puff the Magic Dragon."

63 April 6: *Hootenanny* runs on ABC until September 9, 1964, but dooms itself to failure from the start by blacklisting Pete Seeger, thus earning boycotts from Peter, Paul, and Mary, the Kingston Trio, Bob Dylan, Joan Baez, and most other important folk acts of the time.

63 May: Bob Dylan: *The Freewheelin' Bob Dylan* (LP), with "Blowin' in the Wind, "Masters of War," "A Hard Rain's A-Gonna Fall," Don't Think Twice, It's All Right," "Talkin' World War III Blues," and "I Shall Be Free."

63 May: Harvard University fires Timothy Leary for giving drugs to students.

63 May 8: *Dr. No* (movie).

63 June: Allan Sherman: *My Son, The Nut* (LP).

63 June: Bill Cosby: *Bill Cosby is a Very Funny Fellow, Right* (LP).

63 June 8: Johnny Cash: "Ring of Fire."

63 June 8: Rolf Harris: "Tie Me Kangaroo Down, Sport."

63 June 8: Surfaris: "Wipe Out."

63 June 12: *Cleopatra* (movie).

63 June 12: Medgar Evers is murdered.

63 June 25: *8½* (movie).

63 June 26: *Tom Jones* (movie).

63 July 4: *The Great Escape* (movie).

63 July 6: Peter, Paul, and Mary: "Blowin' in the Wind."

63 July 27: Martha and the Vandellas: "Heat Wave."

63 July 27: Trini Lopez: "If I Had a Hammer."

63 August 28: Martin Luther King's "I Have a Dream" speech at the Lincoln Memorial in Washington, D.C.

63 September 7: Ray Charles: "Busted."

63 September 21: Jimmy Gilmer and the Fireballs: "Sugar Shack."

63 September 21: Peter, Paul, and Mary: "Don't Think Twice, It's All Right."

63 (fall): Pete Seeger: *We Shall Overcome: The Complete Carnegie Hall Concert, June 8, 1963* (LP), with "Little Boxes" by Malvina Reynolds.

63 October: Cassius Clay: *I Am The Greatest!* (LP).

63 October: Martin Luther King: *Great March to Freedom* (LP).

63 November: Joan Baez: *In Concert* (LP), with "We Shall Overcome" and "With God on Our Side."

63 November 2: The Singing Nun: "Dominique."

63 November 7: *It's a Mad, Mad, Mad, Mad World* (movie).

63 November 9: Kingsmen: "Louie Louie."

63 November 10: *That Was The Week That Was* (*TW3*) starring David Frost runs on NBC until May 4, 1965.

63 November 22: JFK is murdered.

63 December 7: Trashmen: "Surfin' Bird."

63 December 28: Lesley Gore: "You Don't Own Me."

64: Maximum number of U.S. troops in Vietnam = 23,300.

64: Herbert Marcuse: *One-Dimensional Man* (book).

64: Pete Seeger, Bob Dylan, Tom Paxton, Sam Hinton, Bob Davenport, the Freedom Singers, Jim Garland, Ed McCurdy, Phil Ochs, Peter LaFarge, and Joan Baez: *Newport Broadside 1963: Topical Songs at the Newport Folk Festival* (LP recorded in July 1963).

64: Richard Brautigan: *A Confederate General from Big Sur* (book).

64 January: Beatles: *Introducing the Beatles* (LP).

64 January: Beatles: *Meet the Beatles* (LP).

64 January: Bob Dylan: *The Times They Are A-Changin'* (LP), with "With God on Our Side" and "Only a Pawn in Their Game."

64 January 11: Beatles: "I Saw Her Standing There" / "I Want to Hold Your Hand."

64 January 18: Pete Seeger: "Little Boxes."

64 January 25: Beatles: "She Loves You."

64 January 29: *Dr. Strangelove, or: How I Learned to Stop Worrying and Love the Bomb* (movie).

64 February: Cassius Clay announces that he is a Muslim and changes his name to

Muhammad Ali.

64 February 1: Beatles: "Please Please Me."

64 February 7: Beatles arrive in the U.S.

64 February 9: Beatles on *The Ed Sullivan Show*.

64 February 15: Dave Clark Five: "Glad All Over."

64 March 7: Beatles: "Twist and Shout."

64 March 8: Dave Clark Five do "Glad All Over" on *The Ed Sullivan Show*.

64 March 11: *Becket* (movie).

64 March 20: *The Pink Panther* (movie).

64 March 28: Beatles: "Can't Buy Me Love."

64 March 28: Beatles: "Do You Want to Know a Secret."

64 April 4: Beatles: "Love Me Do."

64 April 10: Beatles: *The Beatles' Second Album* (LP).

64 April 27: John Lennon: *In His Own Write* (book).

64 May: Buffy Sainte-Marie: *It's My Way* (LP), with "Universal Soldier."

64 May: Rolling Stones: *Rolling Stones* (LP), with "Not Fade Away."

64 May 2: Beatles: "P.S. I Love You."

64 May 9: Rolling Stones: "Not Fade Away."

64 May 22: LBJ proclaims "The Great Society."

64 May 23: Serendipity Singers: "Beans in My Ears."

64 May 25: First issue of the *Los Angeles Free Press*, which runs until April 3, 1978.

64 May 27: *From Russia With Love* (movie).

64 May 30: Chuck Berry: "No Particular Place to Go."

64 June: Beatles: *A Hard Day's Night* (LP).

64 June 5: Rolling Stones begin their first American tour.

64 June 27: Dean Martin: "Everybody Loves Somebody."

64 July: Beatles: *Something New* (LP).

64 July: Mason Williams: *Them Poems* (LP).

64 July 2: LBJ signs the Civil Rights Act.

64 July 4: Rolling Stones: "Tell Me."

64 July 11: Beatles: "A Hard Day's Night."

64 July 25: Rolling Stones: "It's All Over Now."

64 August: Bob Dylan: *Another Side of Bob Dylan* (LP), with "All I Really Want to Do," "Chimes of Freedom," "I Shall Be Free, No. 10," and "My Back Pages."

64 August 2: North Vietnamese torpedo boat allegedly attacks *U.S.S. Maddox* in the Gulf of Tonkin.

64 August 5: LBJ asks Congress to pass Gulf of Tonkin Resolution.

64 August 7: Congress passes Gulf of Tonkin Resolution.

64 August 8: Animals: "House of the Rising Sun."

64 August 10: LBJ signs Gulf of Tonkin Resolution.

64 August 11: *A Hard Day's Night* (movie).

64 August 22: Gale Garnett: "We'll Sing in the Sunshine."

64 August 29: Roy Orbison: "Oh Pretty Woman."

64 September: Berkeley Free Speech Movement begins.

64 September: *The Lloyd Thaxton Show* goes into national syndication from Los Angeles.

64 September 5: Manfred Mann: "Do Wah Diddy Diddy."

64 September 16: *Shindig* replaces *Hootenanny* and runs on ABC until January 8, 1966.

64 September 18: *The Addams Family* runs on ABC until April 8, 1966.

64 September 22: *Fiddler on the Roof* runs on Broadway until July 12, 1972.

64 September 22: *The Man from U.N.C.L.E.* runs on NBC until January 15, 1968.

64 October: Allan Sherman: *For Swingin' Livers Only* (LP), with "Pop Hates the Beatles."

64 October: Animals: *The Animals* (LP), with "House of the Rising Sun."

64 October: Jack Weinberg warns, "Don't trust anyone over thirty."

64 October: Simon and Garfunkel: *Wednesday Morning, 3 A.M.* (LP), with bare-bones version of "Sounds of Silence."

64 October 3: Kinks: "You Really Got Me"; Ray and Dave Davies invent power-chord rock.

64 October 10: Shangri-Las: "Leader of the Pack."

64 October 17: Rolling Stones: "Time Is On My Side."

64 October 18: Animals on *The Ed Sullivan Show*.

64 October 25: Rolling Stones on *The Ed Sullivan Show*.

64 October 25: *Woman in the Dunes* (movie).

64 October 31: Marianne Faithfull: "As Tears Go By."

64 November: Bill Cosby: *I Started Out as a Child* (LP).

64 December: Beatles: *Beatles 65* (LP).

64 December: Rolling Stones: *12 x 5* (LP).

64 December 5: Beatles: "I Feel Fine"; John Lennon is the first to use feedback in a rock song.

64 December 5: Beatles: "She's a Woman."

64 December 25: *Goldfinger* (movie).

65: Maximum number of U.S. troops in Vietnam = 184,300.

65: Peter Max invents the "Cosmic" style of line and bold color prints.

65 January: B.B. King: *Live at the Regal* (LP).

65 January: Pete Seeger: *I Can See a New Day* (LP).

65 January: Pete Seeger: *Songs of Struggle and Protest, 1930-1950* (LP), with "What a Friend We Have in Congress" and "Joe Hill."

65 January 2: Kinks: "All Day and All of the Night."

65 January 9: Rolling Stones: "Heart of Stone."

65 January 12: *Hullabaloo* runs on NBC until April 11, 1966.

65 January 20: Kinks and Rolling Stones on *Shindig*.

65 February: Rolling Stones: *Now* (LP), with "Heart of Stone."

65 February 13: Animals: "Don't Let Me Be Misunderstood."

65 February 20: Beatles: "Eight Days a Week."

65 February 20: Junior Walker and the All-Stars: "Shotgun."

65 February 20: The Who: "I Can't Explain."

65 February 21: Malcolm X is murdered.

65 February 25: *Lord Jim* (movie).

65 March: Bob Dylan: *Bringing It All Back Home* (LP), with "Subterranean Homesick Blues," "Maggie's Farm," "115th Dream," and "It's Alright, Ma (I'm Only Bleeding)."

65 March: Kinks: *Kinks-Size* (LP), with "Tired of Waiting for You."

65 March: Pete Seeger: *WNEW's Story of Selma* (LP).

65 March: Phil Ochs: *All The News That's Fit To Sing* (LP), with "One More Parade," "Talking Vietnam," "The Power and the Glory," "Too Many Martyrs," and (on some copies) "Knock on the Door."

65 March 8: First U.S. combat troops (i.e., 4000 Marines) arrive in Vietnam.

65 March 13: Kinks: "Tired of Waiting for You."

65 March 27: Rolling Stones: "The Last Time."

65 March 27: Seekers: "Another You."

65 April: Yardbirds, Kinks, Beatles, and Brian Jones experiment with sitar.

65 April 3: Bob Dylan: "Subterranean Homesick Blues."

65 April 3: Sam the Sham and the Pharaohs: "Wooly Bully."

65 April 3: *Secret Agent*, a repackaging of the British series, *Danger Man*, runs in America on CBS until September 10, 1966.

65 April 17: Beatles: "Ticket to Ride."

65 April 17: Beau Brummels: "Just a Little."

65 April 17: SDS leads 25,000 antiwar demonstrators in Washington.

65 April 23: Sam and Dave: "Hold On! I'm a-Comin'."

65 May 8: Byrds: "Mr. Tambourine Man"; first hit in the folk rock genre.

65 May 8: Donovan: "Catch the Wind."

65 May 8: Yardbirds: "For Your Love."

65 May 9: Richard Pryor on *The Ed Sullivan Show*.

65 May 22: Jackie DeShannon: "What the World Needs Now is Love."

65 May 22: Them: "Gloria."

65 May 22: Them: "Here Comes the Night."

65 June: Beatles: *Beatles VI* (LP).

65 June: Pete Seeger: *Strangers and Cousins* (LP).

65 June: Them: *Them* (LP), with "Here Comes the Night" and "Gloria."

65 June 12: Kinks: "Set Me Free."

65 June 12: Rolling Stones: "Satisfaction."

65 June 24: John Lennon: *A Spaniard in the Works* (book).

65 June 28: *Where the Action Is* runs on ABC until March 31, 1967.

65 July: Kinks: *Kinda Kinks* (LP), with "Something Better Beginning."

65 July: Rolling Stones: *Out of Our Heads* (LP).

65 July 3: Byrds: "All I Really Want to Do."

65 July 17: Sonny and Cher: "I Got You Babe."

65 July 17: Wilson Pickett: "In the Midnight Hour."

65 July 25: Bob Dylan is booed for playing an electric guitar at the Newport Folk
   Festival.

65 July 28: *Ship of Fools* (movie).

65 July 31: Beatles: "Help!" (single) and *Help!* (LP).

65 July 31: Bob Dylan: "Like a Rolling Stone."

65 July 31: Turtles: "It Ain't Me Babe."

65 July 31: Yardbirds: "Heart Full of Soul."

65 August: Bill Cosby: *Why is There Air?* (LP).

65 August: Bob Dylan: *Highway 61 Revisited* (LP), with "Ballad of a Thin Man,"
   "Desolation Row," and "Like a Rolling Stone."

65 August: Byrds: *Mr. Tambourine Man* (LP), with "Chimes of Freedom."

65 August: Phil Ochs: *I Ain't Marching Anymore* (LP), with "Draft Dodger Rag"
   and the title track.

65 August 2: *The Ipcress File* (movie).

65 August 11: *Help!* (movie).

65 August 13: First issue of the *Berkeley Barb*, which runs until 1980.

65 August 13: Six days of burning, looting, and murder begin in Watts,
   California.

65 August 14: Animals: "We Gotta Get Out of This Place."

65 August 14: Barry McGuire: "Eve of Destruction."

65 August 14: McCoys: "Hang On Sloopy."

65 August 28: Lovin' Spoonful: "Do You Believe in Magic?"

65 September: Country Joe and the Fish: *Rag Baby Talking Issue No. 1* (EP), with
   "I Feel Like I'm Fixin' to Die Rag."

65 September: First issue of *Tiger Beat* magazine.

65 September: Fred Crippen's cartoon *Roger Ramjet* is nationally syndicated.

65 September: Tom Lehrer: *That Was the Year that Was* (LP), recorded live in
   July, with "National Brotherhood Week," "So Long, Mom (A Song for World
   War III)," "Who's Next?" and "The Vatican Rag."

65 September 15: *I Spy* runs on NBC until April 15, 1968.

65 September 18: Barbarians: "Are You a Boy or Are You a Girl?"

65 September 18: Beatles: "Yesterday."

65 September 18: Donovan: "Universal Soldier."

65 September 23: Yardbirds on *Shindig*.

65 September 25: Bob Dylan: "Positively 4th Street."

65 October: First issue of the *East Village Other* (New York), which runs until
   February 20, 1972.

65 October 2: The Who do "I Can't Explain" on *Shindig*.

65 October 9: Rolling Stones: "Get Off My Cloud."

65 October 9: Silkie: "You've Got to Hide Your Love Away."

65 October 23: Byrds: "Turn! Turn! Turn!"

65 October 30: Yardbirds: "I'm a Man."

65 November: Fugs: *The Village Fugs Sing Ballads of Contemporary Protest,
   Point of Views, and General Dissatisfaction* (LP).

65 November: Kinks: *Kinkdom* (LP), with "A Well Respected Man."

65 November: Rolling Stones: *December's Children* (LP).

65 November 3: *Juliet of the Spirits* (movie).

65 November 6: Animals: "It's My Life."

65 November 20: Simon and Garfunkel: "The Sounds of Silence."

65 November 27: Kinks: "A Well Respected Man"

65 December: Beatles: *Rubber Soul* (LP), with "Think for Yourself," "The Word," "Norwegian Wood," and "In My Life."

65 December: Donovan: *Catch the Wind* (LP), with "Keep on Truckin'."

65 December 11: Stevie Wonder: "Uptight."

65 December 12: Byrds on *The Ed Sullivan Show*.

65 December 18: Beatles: "Day Tripper" / "We Can Work it Out."

65 December 18: The Who: "My Generation."

65 December 21: *Thunderball* (movie).

65 December 22: *Doctor Zhivago* (movie).

65 December 25: Rolling Stones: "As Tears Go By."

66: Maximum number of U.S. troops in Vietnam = 385,300.

66 January: Mamas and Papas: *If You Can Believe Your Eyes and Ears* (LP), with "Go Where You Wanna Go."

66 January: Pete Seeger: *God Bless the Grass* (LP), with liner notes by U.S. Supreme Court Associate Justice William O. Douglas.

66 January 1: Mamas and Papas: "California Dreamin'."

66 January 29: Bobby Fuller Four: "I Fought the Law."

66 January 29: Nancy Sinatra: "These Boots Are Made for Walkin'."

66 January 29: Staff Sergeant Barry Sadler: "The Ballad of the Green Berets."

66 February: Animals: *Best of the Animals* (LP).

66 February: Byrds: *Turn! Turn! Turn!* (LP), with "He Was a Friend of Mine."

66 February: Simon and Garfunkel: *Sounds of Silence* (LP), with "I Am a Rock," "A Most Peculiar Man," and an orchestrated version of the title track.

66 February 6: Simon and Garfunkel on *The Ed Sullivan Show*.

66 February 7: First issue of *Crawdaddy* magazine, which runs until December 1978.

66 February 12: Simon and Garfunkel: "Homeward Bound."

66 February 26: Outsiders: "Time Won't Let Me."

66 February 26: Rolling Stones: "19th Nervous Breakdown."

66 March: Fugs: *The Fugs* (LP), with "Group Grope" and "Kill for Peace."

66 March: Kinks: *Kontroversy* (LP), with "Till the End of the Day."

66 March: Rolling Stones: *Big Hits: High Tide and Green Grass* (LP).

66 March 4: Maureen Cleave in the *London Evening Standard* quotes John Lennon: "Christianity will go. It will vanish and shrink. I needn't argue about that; I'm right and I will be proved right. We [i.e., the Beatles] are more popular than Jesus now; I don't know which will go first, rock 'n' roll or Christianity. Jesus was all right but his disciples were thick and ordinary. It's them twisting it

that ruins it for me." Five months later Americans will learn of this statement.

66 March 5: Beatles: "Nowhere Man."

66 March 10: Jefferson Kaye replaces Joey Reynolds from 7:00 p.m. to midnight on WKBW-AM, Buffalo, which reaches the entire eastern half of North America after dark and dominates the rock music airwaves until Kaye's replacement, Bud Ballou, leaves KB for WMEX-AM, Boston, on June 14, 1968.

66 March 12: Johnny Rivers: "Secret Agent Man."

66 March 12: Yardbirds: "Shapes of Things."

66 March 12: Young Rascals: "Good Lovin'."

66 March 19: Paul Revere and the Raiders: "Kicks."

66 March 19: Shadows of Knight: "Gloria."

66 March 28: *The Avengers* runs on ABC until September 15, 1969.

66 April: The Who: *The Who Sings My Generation* (LP).

66 April 2: Byrds: "Eight Miles High."

66 April 6: The Who: "Substitute," with lyrics censored in America.

66 April 8: The cover of *Time* magazine asks: "Is God Dead?"

66 April 16: Bob Dylan: "Rainy Day Women # 12 & 35."

66 April 16: Dutchess County (New York) Assistant District Attorney G. Gordon Liddy (later of Watergate notoreity) leads local police and FBI agents in a raid on the Millbrook estate to arrest Timothy Leary for possession of marijuana.

66 April 23: Them: "Gloria," re-release of 1965 song.

66 April 30: Simon and Garfunkel: "I Am a Rock."

66 April 30: Standells: "Dirty Water."

66 May: Bill Cosby: *Wonderfulness* (LP).

66 May: Phil Ochs: *In Concert* (LP), with "Love Me, I'm a Liberal."

66 May: Stokely Carmichael becomes chairman of SNCC.

66 May 1: James Brown on *The Ed Sullivan Show*.

66 May 7: Lovin' Spoonful: "Did You Ever Have to Make Up Your Mind?"

66 May 14: Dusty Springfield: "You Don't Have to Say You Love Me."

66 May 14: Kinks: "Dedicated Follower of Fashion."

66 May 14: Rolling Stones: "Paint It, Black."

66 May 16: Bob Dylan: *Blonde on Blonde* (LP), with "Leopard-Skin Pill-Box Hat" and "Stuck Inside of Mobile with the Memphis Blues Again."

66 May 21: Cyrkle: "Red Rubber Ball."

66 May 25: *The Russians are Coming! The Russians are Coming!* (movie).

66 May 27: *Time* magazine tells how Unionville (Pennsylvania) High School persecuted honor student Alan T. Miller for having long hair.

66 May 28: Ray Charles: "Let's Go Get Stoned."

66 June: Beatles: *Yesterday and Today* (LP), with "We Can Work It Out."

66 June: Rolling Stones: *Aftermath* (LP), with "Paint It, Black," "Stupid Girl," "Lady Jane," "Going Home," and "Under My Thumb."

66 June: William H. Masters and Virginia E. Johnson: *Human Sexual Response* (book).

66 June 10: Big Brother and the Holding Company debut their new singer, Janis

Joplin, at the Avalon Ballroom, San Francisco.

66 June 11: Beatles: "Paperback Writer" / "Rain."

66 June 18: Troggs: "Wild Thing."

66 June 21: *The Blue Max* (movie).

66 June 22: *Who's Afraid of Virginia Woolf?* (movie).

66 June 25: Yardbirds: "Over Under Sideways Down."

66 June 30: Betty Friedan and twenty-seven other delegates to the Third National Conference of Commissions on the Status of Women found the National Organization for Women (NOW) in Washington.

66 July: Kinks: *Greatest Hits* (LP).

66 July 2: Mamas and Papas: "I Saw Her Again."

66 July 9: Lovin' Spoonful: "Summer in the City."

66 July 9: Rolling Stones: "Lady Jane" / "Mother's Little Helper."

66 July 16: Stevie Wonder: "Blowin' in the Wind."

66 July 23: Donovan: "Sunshine Superman."

66 July 23: Lee Dorsey: "Working in the Coal Mine."

66 July 23: Napoleon XIV: "They're Coming to Take Me Away, Ha-Haaa!"

66 July 30: Wilson Pickett: "Land of 1000 Dances."

66 August: Beatles: *Revolver* (LP), with "Taxman" and "Eleanor Rigby."

66 August: Donovan: *Sunshine Superman* (LP), with "Fat Angel," "Season of the Witch," "The Trip," and "Celeste."

66 August: Frank Zappa and the Mothers of Invention: *Freak Out* (LP), with "Hungry Freaks, Daddy," "Who Are the Brain Police?," "Wowie Zowie," "You're Probably Wondering Why I'm Here," "Help, I'm a Rock," and "Return of the Son of Monster Magnet."

66 August: Jefferson Airplane: *Takes Off* (LP), with "It's No Secret."

66 August: Pete Seeger: *Dangerous Songs!?* (LP), with "Draft Dodger Rag" and "Die Gedanken sind Frei [Thoughts Are Free]."

66 August 2: Beatles: "Yellow Submarine."

66 August 6: Simon and Garfunkel: "The Dangling Conversation."

66 August 13: The Who: "The Kids Are Alright."

66 August 13: Kinks: "Sunny Afternoon" / "I'm Not Like Everybody Else."

66 August 20: Beatles: "Eleanor Rigby."

66 August 20: Jimmy Ruffin: "What Becomes of the Brokenhearted?"

66 September: Byrds: *Fifth Dimension* (LP), with "5D," "Mr. Spaceman," and "Eight Miles High."

66 September: Simon and Garfunkel: *Parsley, Sage, Rosemary, and Thyme* (LP), with "A Simple Desultory Philippic (or How I Was Robert McNamara'd Into Submission)," "Poem on the Underground Wall," "The Dangling Conversation," and "7 O'Clock News / Silent Night."

66 September 3: Frank Sinatra: "Summer Wind."

66 September 10: Count Five: "Psychotic Reaction."

66 September 12: *The Monkees* runs on NBC until March 25, 1968.

66 September 17: Byrds: "Mr. Spaceman."

66 September 17: Johnny Rivers: "Poor Side of Town."

66 September 24: Bobby Darin: "If I Were a Carpenter."

66 October: Buffalo Springfield: *Buffalo Springfield* (LP), with "For What It's Worth" and "Nowadays Clancy Can't Even Sing."

66 October: First issue of *Hullabaloo* magazine, which, renamed as *Circus* in March 1969, runs until September 28, 1978, then resumes in 1979.

66 October: In response to the increasing illegality of LSD and other drugs, Timothy Leary founds the League of Spiritual Discovery as a religion with the use of lysergic acid diethylamide as one of its sacraments.

66 October: Monkees: *The Monkees* (LP).

66 October 8: Mitch Ryder and the Detroit Wheels: "Devil with a Blue Dress On / Good Golly Miss Molly."

66 October 8: Rolling Stones: "Have You Seen Your Mother, Baby, Standing in the Shadow?"

66 October 17: *Georgy Girl* (movie).

66 October 22: Beach Boys: "Good Vibrations."

66 October 22: Mamas and Papas: "Look Through My Window."

66 November: Huey Newton and Bobby Seale found the Black Panther Party for Self-Defense, blending the revolutionary theories of Malcolm X, Mao, Marx, and Engels.

66 November: Judy Collins: *In My Life* (LP), with "Pirate Jenny," "Sunny Goodge Street," "Liverpool Lullaby," "Marat/Sade," and the title track.

66 November: Rolling Stones: *Got Live If You Want It* (LP).

66 November 5: Simon and Garfunkel: "A Hazy Shade of Winter."

66 November 12: Donovan: "Mellow Yellow."

66 November 12: Frank Sinatra: "That's Life."

66 November 14: *Fahrenheit 451* (movie).

66 November 19: Wilson Pickett: "Mustang Sally."

66 November 26: Aaron Neville: "Tell It Like It Is."

66 November 26: Blues Magoos: "We Ain't Got Nothin' Yet."

66 November 26: Seeds: "Pushin' Too Hard."

66 November 26: Yardbirds: "Happenings Ten Years Time Ago."

66 December 1: Critic Dwight MacDonald praises Barbara Garson's anti-LBJ play, *MacBird*, in the *New York Review of Books*.

66 December 10: Monkees: "I'm Not Your Stepping Stone."

66 December 10: Royal Guardsmen: "Snoopy vs. the Red Baron."

66 December 10: The Who: "I'm a Boy."

66 December 11: Mamas and Papas on *The Ed Sullivan Show*.

66 December 12: *A Man for All Seasons* (movie).

66 December 17: Electric Prunes: "I Had Too Much to Dream Last Night."

66 December 18: *Blow-Up* (movie).

67: Maximum number of U.S. troops in Vietnam = 485,600.

67 January: Cream: *Fresh Cream* (LP), with "I Feel Free," "I'm So Glad," and

"Toad."

67 January: Donovan: *Mellow Yellow* (LP).

67 January: Doors: *The Doors* (LP), with "Light My Fire," "Break On Through," "Crystal Ship," "End of the Night," and "The End."

67 January: John Mayall: *Bluesbreakers* (LP).

67 January: Kinks: *Face to Face* (LP), with "Sunny Afternoon."

67 January: Rolling Stones: *Between the Buttons* (LP), with "Let's Spend the Night Together" and "Ruby Tuesday."

67 January: Youngbloods: *Youngbloods* (LP), with "Get Together."

67 January 7: Senator Bobby: "Wild Thing."

67 January 14: Buffalo Springfield: "For What It's Worth."

67 January 14: Sonny and Cher: "The Beat Goes On."

67 January 14: "Gathering of the Tribes for a Human Be-In," Golden Gate Park, San Francisco, during which Timothy Leary advises "Tune in, turn on, drop out."

67 January 15: Rolling Stones censor "Let's Spend the Night Together" as "Let's Spend Some Time Together" for *The Ed Sullivan Show*.

67 January 19: *Macbird* opens at the Village Gate Theater in New York.

67 January 21: Fifth Dimension: "Go Where You Wanna Go."

67 January 21: Rolling Stones: "Ruby Tuesday."

67 January 22: Lovin' Spoonful on *The Ed Sullivan Show*.

67 January 28: Byrds: "So You Want to Be a Rock 'n' Roll Star."

67 February: Jefferson Airplane: *Surrealistic Pillow* (LP), with "Somebody to Love," "White Rabbit," and "Plastic Fantastic Lover."

67 February 4: Donovan: "Epistle to Dippy."

67 February 5: *The Smothers Brothers Comedy Hour* runs highly rated on CBS until cancelled on June 8, 1969 because of political pressure.

67 February 11: Tommy James and the Shondells: "I Think We're Alone Now."

67 February 12: Larry Miller invents underground album-oriented rock (AOR) broadcasting at KMPX-FM, San Francisco.

67 February 25: Beatles: "Penny Lane" / "Strawberry Fields Forever."

67 March: Bob Dylan: *Greatest Hits* (LP).

67 March: Grateful Dead: *Grateful Dead* (LP).

67 March: Velvet Underground: *Velvet Underground and Nico* (LP), with "I'm Waiting for My Man" and "Heroin."

67 March 1: Nancy Sinatra and Lee Hazlewood: "Summer Wine."

67 March 3: Jerry Farber's "The Student as Nigger" appears in the *Los Angeles Free Press*, vol. 4, no. 9, issue 137, pp. 8, 18-19.

67 March 11: Simon and Garfunkel: "At the Zoo."

67 April: Byrds: *Younger Than Yesterday* (LP).

67 April: Spring Mobilization to End the War in Vietnam (Spring Mobe) organizes nationwide activities.

67 April: The Who: *Happy Jack* (LP), with "Boris the Spider," "Cobwebs and Strange," and "A Quick One While He's Away."

67 April 1: Byrds: "My Back Pages."

67 April 7: Six veterans participate in an antiwar march in New York City and found Vietnam Veterans Against the War (VVAW).

67 April 7: Tom Donahue begins broadcasting rock on KMPX.

67 April 8: Animals: "When I Was Young."

67 April 8: Jefferson Airplane: "Somebody to Love."

67 April 8: The Who: "Happy Jack."

67 April 24: Pink Floyd: "Arnold Layne."

67 April 28: Muhammad Ali resists the military draft, declaring, "I ain't got no quarrel with those Vietcong."

67 April 29: Aretha Franklin: "Respect."

67 April 29: Mamas and Papas: "Creeque Alley."

67 April 29: World Boxing Association (WBA) strips Muhammad Ali of his heavyweight championship title.

67 April 30: Paul Revere and the Raiders on *The Ed Sullivan Show*.

67 May: Bill Cosby: *Revenge* (LP).

67 May: Country Joe and the Fish: *Electric Music for the Mind and Body* (LP), with "Not So Sweet Martha Lorraine" and "Death Sound."

67 May: First issue of *Guitar Player* magazine.

67 May: Frank Zappa and the Mothers of Invention: *Absolutely Free* (LP), with "Plastic People" and "America Drinks and Goes Home."

67 May: H. Rap Brown becomes chairman of SNCC.

67 May 3: PBS affiliate WGBH-TV, Boston, films a debate on drugs between Timothy Leary and MIT professor Jerome Lettvin.

67 May 13: Every Mother's Son: "Come on Down to My Boat."

67 May 14: Turtles on *The Ed Sullivan Show*.

67 May 20: Janis Ian: "Society's Child."

67 May 27: Bee Gees: "New York Mining Disaster, 1941."

67 May 27: Bob Dylan: "Leopard-Skin Pill-Box Hat."

67 May 27: Doors: "Light My Fire."

67 May 27: Scott McKenzie: "San Francisco (Wear Some Flowers in Your Hair)."

67 June: Rolling Stones: *Flowers* (LP).

67 June: Fugs: *Virgin Fugs* (LP), with "Saran Wrap," "Coca Cola Douche," and "New Amphetamine Shriek."

67 June 1: Beatles: *Sgt. Pepper's Lonely Hearts Club Band* (LP).

67 June 11: Richard Pryor on *The Ed Sullivan Show* does his bit on African-Americans in U.S. Navy submarines.

67 June 13: *You Only Live Twice* (movie).

67 June 16: Monterey International Pop Festival runs until June 18, with landmark performances by Jimi Hendrix, Janis Joplin, and the Who.

67 June 16: The Association, the Paupers, Lou Rawls, Beverley, Eric Burdon and the Animals, Johnny Rivers, and Simon and Garfunkel play at Monterey.

67 June 17: Canned Heat, Big Brother and the Holding Company, Country Joe

and the Fish, Al Kooper, the Paul Butterfield Blues Band, Quicksilver Messenger Service, the Steve Miller Band, the Electric Flag, Moby Grape, Hugh Masekela, the Byrds, Laura Nyro, Jefferson Airplane, Booker T. and the M.G.s with the Mar-Keys, and Otis Redding play at Monterey.

67 June 18: Ravi Shankar, the Blues Project, Big Brother and the Holding Company (again), the Group With No Name, Buffalo Springfield, the Who, the Grateful Dead, the Jimi Hendrix Experience, Scott McKenzie, and the Mamas and Papas play at Monterey.

67 June 19: *The King of Hearts* (movie).

67 June 20: Federal court in Houston convicts Muhammad Ali of draft evasion, fines him $10,000, and sentences him to five years in prison.

67 June 24: Procol Harum: "A Whiter Shade of Pale."

67 July: Vanilla Fudge: *Vanilla Fudge* (LP).

67 July 1: The Who: "Pictures of Lily."

67 July 1: Vanilla Fudge: "You Keep Me Hangin' On."

67 July 8: Bee Gees: "To Love Somebody."

67 July 22: Monkees: "Pleasant Valley Sunday."

67 July 24: Pink Floyd: "See Emily Play."

67 July 29: Beatles: "All You Need is Love" / "Baby, You're a Rich Man."

67 July 29: Simon and Garfunkel: "Fakin' It."

67 July 29: Soul Brothers Six: "Some Kind of Wonderful."

67 August: Kinks: *Live Kinks* (LP).

67 August: Pete Seeger: *Waist Deep in the Big Muddy and Other Love Songs* (LP), with "Last Night I Had the Strangest Dream."

67 August: Procol Harum: *A Whiter Shade of Pale* (LP).

67 August 2: *In the Heat of the Night* (movie).

67 August 5: Eric Burdon and the Animals: "San Franciscan Nights."

67 August 5: Jackie Wilson: "Higher and Higher."

67 August 6 (Hiroshima Day): Grateful Dead opens for Jefferson Airplane twice in Montréal, afternoon at Place-Ville-Marie, evening at Expo 67.

67 August 12: Donovan: "There is a Mountain."

67 August 13: *Bonnie and Clyde* (movie).

67 August 24: Abbie Hoffman and Jerry Rubin use guerrilla theater to point up American greed by throwing dollar bills from the balcony of the New York Stock Exchange, thus starting a mad scramble on the floor.

67 September: Arlo Guthrie: *Alice's Restaurant* (LP).

67 September: Beach Boys: *Smiley Smile* (LP), with "Good Vibrations."

67 September: *Big Brother and the Holding Company* (eponymous LP).

67 September: Jimi Hendrix Experience: *Are You Experienced?* (LP), with "Purple Haze," "Third Stone From the Sun," and the title track.

67 September: Van Morrison: *Blowin' Your Mind* (LP).

67 September 2: Jefferson Airplane: "Ballad of You and Me and Pooneil."

67 September 2: Jimi Hendrix Experience: "Purple Haze."

67 September 2: Lulu: "To Sir, With Love."

67 September 9: Rolling Stones: "We Love You" / "Dandelion."

67 September 9: Sam and Dave: "Soul Man."

67 September 9: Youngbloods: "Get Together."

67 September 17: Jim Morrison of the Doors defies Ed Sullivan by singing the word "higher" on live TV in "Light My Fire."

67 September 17: The Who on *The Smothers Brothers Comedy Hour*.

67 September 23: Doors: "People Are Strange."

67 September 23: Strawberry Alarm Clock: "Incense and Peppermints."

67 October: Buffalo Springfield: *Again* (LP), with "Broken Arrow."

67 October: Byrds: *Greatest Hits* (LP), with Dave Swaney's liner notes.

67 October: Doors: *Strange Days* (LP), with "People Are Strange," "Horse Latitudes," "When the Music's Over," and the title track.

67 October: Mamas and Papas: *Farewell to the First Golden Era* (LP).

67 October: Pete Seeger: *Greatest Hits* (LP).

67 October 7: Miriam Makeba: "Pata Pata."

67 October 7: The Who: "I Can See For Miles."

67 October 14: Fantastic Johnny C: "Boogaloo Down Broadway."

67 October 17: James Rado's and Gerome Ragni's *Hair* opens at Joseph Papp's New York Shakespeare Festival Public Theater, off-Broadway.

67 October 21: Procol Harum: "Homburg."

67 October 21: Student Mobilization Committee (SMC or Student Mobe) leads antiwar march on Washington and the Pentagon.

67 October 23: *How I Won the War* (movie).

67 October 31: WNEW-FM, New York, changes format to progressive rock.

67 October 31: Richard Brautigan: *Trout Fishing in America* (book).

67 November: Beatles: *Magical Mystery Tour* (LP).

67 November: Country Joe and the Fish: *I Feel Like I'm Fixin' to Die* (LP), with "The Fish Cheer and I Feel Like I'm Fixin' to Die Rag."

67 November: First issue of the *Distant Drummer* (Philadelphia), which runs until September 24, 1970.

67 November: Fugs: *Tenderness Junction* (LP), with "Hare Krishna," "Turn On / Tune In / Drop Out," "Exorcising the Evil Spirits from the Pentagon, October 21, 1967," and "War Song."

67 November: Rolling Stones: *Their Satanic Majesties Request* (LP).

67 November: Tim Buckley: *Goodbye and Hello* (LP).

67 November: Tom Donahue brings progressive rock to KPPC-FM, Pasadena, California.

67 November 1: *Cool Hand Luke* (movie).

67 November 2: LBJ's advisors suggest that the American public would support the war if they heard more encouraging reports about it.

67 November 4: Human Beinz: "Nobody But Me."

67 November 4: Stone Poneys with Linda Ronstadt: "Different Drum."

67 November 9: John Lennon on cover of first issue of *Rolling Stone* magazine.

67 November 11: Small Faces: "Itchycoo Park."

67 November 18: John Fred and his Playboy Band: "Judy in Disguise."

67 November 18: Johnny Rivers: "Summer Rain."

67 December: Abbie Hoffman and Jerry Rubin co-found the Youth International Party (Yippies).

67 December: Bob Dylan: *John Wesley Harding* (LP), with "All Along the Watchtower."

67 December: Cream: *Disraeli Gears* (LP), with "Strange Brew," "S[he] W[as] L[ike] A B[earded] R[ainbow]," and "Sunshine of Your Love."

67 December: The Who: *The Who Sell Out* (LP), with "Armenia City in the Sky," "Mary-Anne with the Shaky Hands," "I Can See for Miles," "Relax," "Sunrise," and "Rael."

67 December 2: Beatles: "Hello Goodbye" / "I Am the Walrus."

67 December 2: Donovan: "Wear Your Love Like Heaven."

67 December 2: Doors: "Love Me Two Times."

67 December 12: *Guess Who's Coming to Dinner* (movie).

67 December 16: Eric Burdon and the Animals: "Monterey."

67 December 21: *The Graduate* (movie).

67 December 23: Impressions: "We're a Winner."

67 December 30: Rolling Stones: "She's a Rainbow."

68: Maximum number of U.S. troops in Vietnam = 536,100.

68: Pete Seeger: *Pete Seeger Now* (LP).

68: Pete Seeger: *Pete Seeger Sings and Answers Questions at the Ford Hall Forum in Boston* (LP).

68: Pete Seeger: *Pete Seeger Sings Leadbelly* (LP).

68: Richard Brautigan: *In Watermelon Sugar* (book).

68: Richard Brautigan: *The Pill Versus the Springhill Mine Disaster* (book).

68: Tom Paxton: *Morning Again* (LP), with "Talking Vietnam Potluck Blues."

68 January: Firesign Theatre: *Waiting for the Electrician or Someone Like Him* (LP), with "Temporarily Humboldt County."

68 January: Frank Zappa and the Mothers of Invention: *We're Only in It for the Money* (LP), with "Are You Hung Up?" "Who Needs the Peace Corps?" "What's the Ugliest Part of Your Body?" "Absolutely Free," "Flower Punk," "Hot Poop," "Let's Make the Water Turn Black," and "Take Your Clothes Off When You Dance."

68 January: Jefferson Airplane: *After Bathing at Baxter's* (LP), with "Last Wall of the Castle," "The Ballad of You and Me and Pooneil," "Rejoyce," "Two Heads," and "A Small Package of Value Will Come to You Shortly."

68 January: Judy Collins: *Wildflowers* (LP).

68 January: Phil Ochs: *Pleasures of the Harbor* (LP), with "Outside of a Small Circle of Friends."

68 January: Spirit: *Spirit* (LP), with "Fresh Garbage."

68 January: Steppenwolf: *Steppenwolf* (LP), with "Born to Be Wild," "Your Wall's Too High," "Desperation," "The Ostrich," and "The Pusher."

68 January: Velvet Underground: *White Light / White Heat* (LP).

68 January 1: Bill Cosby's persona, Captain Oh Wow, answers listeners' letters on syndicated radio until September 9, 1968.

68 January 6: Cream: "Sunshine of Your Love."

68 January 13: Fireballs: "Bottle of Wine."

68 January 14: Vanilla Fudge on *The Ed Sullivan Show*.

68 January 22: *Rowan and Martin's Laugh-In* replaces *The Man from U.N.C.L.E.* and runs on NBC until May 14, 1973.

68 February: Blue Cheer: *Vincebus Eruptum* (LP), with "Summertime Blues."

68 February: Bonzo Dog Doo-Dah Band: *Gorilla* (LP), with "Jollity Farm" and "The Intro and the Outro."

68 February: First issue of *Zap Comix* (No. 0) appears underground in San Francisco.

68 February: Kinks: *Something Else* (LP).

68 February: Ten Years After: *Ten Years After* (LP).

68 February 3: Kenny Rogers and the First Edition: "Just Dropped in (to See What Condition my Condition Was in)."

68 February 10: Blue Cheer: "Summertime Blues."

68 February 10: Blue Cheer on *American Bandstand*.

68 February 11: Pat Paulsen announces his candidacy for President of the United States on *The Smothers Brothers Comedy Hour*.

68 February 17: Sly and the Family Stone: "Dance to the Music."

68 February 25: Pete Seeger sings "Waist Deep in the Big Muddy" on *The Smothers Brothers Comedy Hour*.

68 March: Byrds: *Notorious Byrd Brothers* (LP), with "Wasn't Born to Follow."

68 March: Eldridge Cleaver: *Soul on Ice* (book).

68 March: Jimi Hendrix Experience: *Axis: Bold as Love* (LP), with "Spanish Castle Magic," "Little Wing," and "If Six Was Nine."

68 March: Moody Blues: *Days of Future Passed* (LP).

68 March: Pink Floyd: *Piper at the Gates of Dawn* (LP).

68 March: Traffic: *Mr. Fantasy* (LP), with "Dear Mr. Fantasy" and "Dealer."

68 March 2: Manfred Mann: "The Mighty Quinn."

68 March 9: Donovan: "Jennifer Juniper."

68 March 15: WBCN-FM, Boston, breaks its classical format by playing Cream's "I Feel Free."

68 March 16: My Lai massacre of civilians in Vietnam; cover-up would hide this event from the public until November 1969.

68 March 23: Beatles: "Lady Madonna."

68 March 23: Doors: "The Unknown Soldier."

68 March 23: The Who: "Call Me Lightning."

68 March 31: LBJ declares: "I shall not seek, and I will not accept, the nomination of my party for another term as your President."

68 April: Laura Nyro: *Eli and the Thirteenth Confession* (LP).

68 April: Simon and Garfunkel: *Bookends* (LP), with "Hazy Shade of Winter,"

"America," "Fakin' It," "At the Zoo," and "Mrs. Robinson."

68 April: Tom Rush: *The Circle Game* (LP), with "Urge for Going."

68 April 3: *2001: A Space Odyssey* (movie).

68 April 4: Martin Luther King is murdered.

68 April 23: Mark Rudd leads the SDS in taking over Columbia University to protest its alliance with the defense industry.

68 April 27: Byrds: "You Ain't Going Nowhcrc."

68 April 27: Simon and Garfunkel: "Mrs. Robinson."

68 April 29: A revised version of *Hair* opens on Broadway at the Biltmore Theater and runs until July 1, 1972.

68 April 29: Dave Herman begins the Marconi Experiment on WMMR-FM, Philadelphia.

68 May: Quicksilver Messenger Service: "Pride of Man" (single) and *Quicksilver Messenger Service* (LP), with "Pride of Man."

68 May: Tom Donahue and his entire staff desert KMPX and bring underground rock to KSAN-FM, San Francisco.

68 May 4: Friend and Lover: "Reach Out of the Darkness."

68 May 4: Merrilee Rush and the Turnabouts: "Angel of the Morning."

68 May 4: Richard Harris: "MacArthur Park."

68 May 11: Status Quo: "Pictures of Matchstick Men."

68 May 12: Rev. Ralph David Abernathy and Rev. Jesse Jackson lead Poor People's Campaign in a march on Washington, where they build a shanty town called Resurrection City.

68 May 17: Catonsville Nine destroy draft office records.

68 May 18: Animals: "Sky Pilot."

68 May 19: Gylan Kain, David Nelson, and Abiodun Oyewole create the Last Poets in New York City on Malcolm X's birthday to spread the Black Panther message.

68 May 25: Tiny Tim: "Tip-Toe Through the Tulips With Me."

68 May 26: An AP wirephoto of LBJ giving a Nazi salute the day before at the International Ladies' Garment Workers Union convention in Atlantic City appears on the *Philadelphia Sunday Bulletin* front page — above the fold.

68 May 29: *Wild in the Streets* (movie).

68 June: Captain Beefheart and His Magic Band: *Safe as Milk* (LP).

68 June: Cream: *Wheels of Fire* (LP), with "White Room," "Politician," "Deserted Cities of the Heart," and "Toad."

68 June: Fairport Convention: *Fairport Convention* (LP).

68 June: The Nice: *The Thoughts of Emerlist Davjack* (LP).

68 June: Tom and Raechel Donahue bring progressive rock to KMET-FM, Los Angeles.

68 June 1: Fifth Dimension: "Stoned Soul Picnic."

68 June 1: Shorty Long: "Here Comes the Judge."

68 June 1: *The Prisoner* runs on CBS until September 21, 1968.

68 June 3: Valerie Solanis shoots Andy Warhol.

68 June 5: Robert F. Kennedy is murdered.

68 June 8: Rolling Stones: "Jumpin' Jack Flash."

68 June 10: *Petulia* (movie).

68 June 15: Donovan: "Hurdy Gurdy Man."

68 June 15: Pigmeat Markham: "Here Comes the Judge."

68 June 24: District of Columbia police shut down Resurrection City.

68 June 26: Keith Emerson of the Nice burns an American flag onstage at the
  Royal Albert Hall while performing Leonard Bernstein's "America."

68 June 28: Frank Zappa's "The Oracle Has It All Psyched Out" appears in *Life*
  magazine.

68 June 29: Doors: "Hello, I Love You."

68 July: The Band: *Music From Big Pink* (LP), with "The Weight," "Chest
  Fever," "This Wheel's on Fire," and "I Shall Be Released."

68 July: Big Brother and the Holding Company with Janis Joplin: *Cheap Thrills*
  (LP), with "Combination of the Two," "Summertime," "Piece of My Heart,"
  "Turtle Blues," and "Ball and Chain."

68 July: Donovan: *In Concert* (LP), with "Celeste," "Fat Angel," and "Rules and
  Regulations."

68 July: Doors: *Waiting for the Sun* (LP), with "Hello, I Love You," "Love
  Street," "Five to One," and "The Unknown Soldier."

68 July: Electric Flag: *A Long Time Comin'* (LP), with "Killing Floor."

68 July: Iron Butterfly: *In-A-Gadda-Da-Vida* (LP).

68 July: Ten Years After: *Undead* (LP), with "I'm Going Home."

68 July 13: Steppenwolf: "Born to Be Wild."

68 July 20: Rascals: "People Got to Be Free."

68 August: Fleetwood Mac: *Fleetwood Mac* (LP).

68 August: Grateful Dead: *Anthem of the Sun* (LP).

68 August: *Hair* (original Broadway cast LP recording).

68 August: Nazz: *Nazz* (LP), with "Open My Eyes."

68 August: Tom Wolfe: *The Electric Kool-Aid Acid Test* and *The Pump House
  Gang* (books published simultaneously).

68 August 3: Canned Heat: "On the Road Again."

68 August 3: Ray Stevens: "Mr. Businessman."

68 August 10: Deep Purple: "Hush."

68 August 10: The Who: "Magic Bus."

68 August 24: Chambers Brothers: "Time Has Come Today."

68 August 28: Hosted by Howard K. Smith, Gore Vidal calls William F. Buckley
  a "crypto-nazi" during their live ABC TV commentary on the Democratic
  National Convention in Chicago.

68 September: Jefferson Airplane: *Crown of Creation* (LP), with "Lather,"
  "Triad," "If You Feel," "Greasy Heart," and the title track.

68 September: Jimi Hendrix Experience: *Electric Ladyland* (LP), with "And the
  Gods Made Love," "Voodoo Chile," and "All Along the Watchtower."

68 September: Mike Bloomfield, Al Kooper, Stephen Stills: *Super Session* (LP),
  with "His Holy Modal Majesty" and "Season of the Witch."

68 September: Moody Blues: *In Search of the Lost Chord* (LP), with "Legend of a Mind," "Departure," "The Best Way to Travel," and "Om."

68 September: Pink Floyd: *Saucerful of Secrets* (LP).

68 September: Procol Harum: *Shine On Brightly* (LP).

68 September: The Who: *Magic Bus* (LP), with "Pictures of Lily."

68 September 7: Big Brother and the Holding Company with Janis Joplin: "Piece of My IIcart."

68 September 7: James Brown: "Say It Loud — I'm Black and I'm Proud."

68 September 7: The Crazy World of Arthur Brown: "Fire."

68 September 14: Beatles: "Hey Jude" / "Revolution."

68 September 21: Creedence Clearwater Revival: "Susie Q."

68 September 21: Mary Hopkin: "Those Were the Days."

68 September 28: Cream: "White Room."

68 September 28: Max Frost and the Troopers: "Shape of Things to Come."

68 September 29: Jefferson Airplane performs "Crown of Creation" and "Won't You Try / Saturday Afternoon" on *The Ed Sullivan Show*.

68 October: Country Joe and the Fish: *Together* (LP).

68 October: Fugs: *It Crawled Into My Hand, Honest* (LP).

68 October: Holy Modal Rounders: *The Moray Eels Eat the Holy Modal Rounders* (LP), with "The Bird Song."

68 October: Pentangle: *Pentangle* (LP).

68 October: Phil Ochs: *Tape From California* (LP), with "White Boots Marching in a Yellow Land" and "The War is Over."

68 October: Steve Miller Band: *Sailor* (LP), with "Living in the U.S.A."

68 October: Traffic: *Traffic* (LP), with "Forty Thousand Headmen."

68 October: Walter [i.e., Wendy] Carlos: *Switched-On Bach* (LP).

68 October 3: Abbie Hoffman is arrested for wearing an American flag shirt to his House Un-American Activities Committee (HUAC) hearing.

68 October 10: *Barbarella* (movie).

68 October 12: Steppenwolf: "Magic Carpet Ride."

68 October 16: Tommie Smith and John Carlos, winners of gold and bronze medals in the 200 meter dash at the Mexico City Olympics, raise their fists in the black power salute during "The Star Spangled Banner."

68 October 19: Dion: "Abraham, Martin, and John."

68 October 19: Supremes: "Love Child."

68 October 20: Henry Fonda narrates "Pat Paulsen for President" special episode of *The Smothers Brothers Comedy Hour*.

68 October 27: Mary Hopkin on *The Ed Sullivan Show*.

68 October 30: *The Lion in Winter* (movie).

68 November: Beatles: [*The White Album*] (LP).

68 November: Byrds: *Sweetheart of the Rodeo* (LP).

68 November: Frank Zappa and the Mothers of Invention: *Cruisin' With Ruben and the Jets* (LP).

68 November: Kinks: *Four More Well Respected Gentlemen* (LP).

68 November: Neil Young: *Neil Young* (LP), with "The Loner."

68 November: Rolling Stones: *Beggars Banquet* (LP), with "Sympathy for the Devil," "Street Fighting Man," and "Salt of the Earth."

68 November: Ten Years After: *Stonedhenge* (LP).

68 November: The Who: *Direct Hits* (LP), released in U.K. but available underground in U.S.A.

68 November: Van Morrison: *Astral Weeks* (LP).

68 November 9: Steve Miller Band: "Living in the U.S.A."

68 November 10: *The Producers* (movie).

68 November 16: Bob Seger System: "Ramblin' Gamblin' Man."

68 November 16: Temptations: "Cloud Nine."

68 November 30: *One Plus One* (movie) premieres at London Film Festival.

68 November 30: Canned Heat: "Going Up the Country."

68 December: Captain Beefheart and His Magic Band: *Strictly Personal* (LP).

68 December: Judy Collins: *Who Knows Where the Time Goes* (LP).

68 December: The Nice: *Ars Longa Vita Brevis* (LP).

68 December: Spirit: *The Family That Plays Together* (LP).

68 December 7: Sly and the Family Stone: "Everyday People."

68 December 14: Tommy James and the Shondells: "Crimson and Clover."

68 December 14: Bee Gees: "I Started a Joke."

68 December 15: *Greetings* (movie).

68 December 19: *If ...* (movie) premieres in New York, but does not appear widely in American theaters until after its release on March 9, 1969.

68 December 20: Abbie Hoffman is convicted for wearing American flag shirt to HUAC.

68 December 26: *Monterey Pop* (movie).

68 December 28: Doors: "Touch Me."

68 December 29: Sly and the Family Stone on *The Ed Sullivan Show*.

68 (late in the year): Abbie Hoffman: *Revolution for the Hell of It* (book).

69: Maximum number of U.S. troops in Vietnam = 475,200.

69: Jaime Brockett: *Remember the Wind and the Rain* (LP), with "Legend of the U.S.S. Titanic" (Capitol release of 1968 LP on local Boston label, Oracle).

69 January: Beatles: *Yellow Submarine* (LP).

69 January: Buffalo Springfield: *Retrospective* (LP).

69 January: Cream: *Goodbye Cream* (LP).

69 January: Creedence Clearwater Revival: *Bayou Country* (LP).

69 January: Donovan: *Greatest Hits* (LP).

69 January: Fleetwood Mac: *English Rose* (LP).

69 January: Jethro Tull: *This Was* (LP).

69 January: Led Zeppelin: *Led Zeppelin* (LP).

69 January: Pentangle: *Sweet Child* (LP).

69 January 1: Barry Kramer founds *Creem* magazine in Detroit.

69 January 12: Chambers Brothers on *The Ed Sullivan Show*.

69 January 25: Creedence Clearwater Revival: "Proud Mary."

69 January 25: Spirit: "I Got a Line on You."

69 February: Byrds: *Dr. Byrds and Mr. Hyde* (LP), with "Drug Store Truck Drivin' Man."

69 February: John Lennon and Yoko Ono: *Two Virgins* (LP).

69 February: Mike Bloomfield and Al Kooper: *Live Adventures* (LP), with introductory speeches and "Dear Mr. Fantasy."

69 February: Philip Roth: *Portnoy's Complaint* (book).

69 February 15: Temptations: "Run Away Child, Running Wild."

69 February 22: Edwin Starr: "Twenty-Five Miles."

69 March: Jefferson Airplane: *Bless Its Pointed Little Head* (LP), with "Fat Angel," "Somebody to Love," and "Plastic Fantastic Lover."

69 March: Kinks: *The Kinks are the Village Green Preservation Society* (LP), with "Johnny Thunder."

69 March: MC5: *Kick Out the Jams* (LP).

69 March: Steppenwolf: *At Your Birthday Party* (LP).

69 March 1: Steppenwolf: "Rock Me."

69 March 8: Fifth Dimension: "Aquarius / Let the Sun Shine In."

69 March 9: Creedence Clearwater Revival on the *Ed Sullivan Show*.

69 March 10: *I Am Curious (Yellow)* (movie).

69 March 15: Isley Brothers: "It's Your Thing."

69 March 16: Janis Joplin on *The Ed Sullivan Show*.

69 March 20: John Lennon and Yoko Ono marry in Gibraltar, then spend their honeymoon in the Amsterdam Hilton, Room 902, in bed, publicly advocating for peace.

69 March 22: Cowsills: "Hair."

69 March 22: Frank Sinatra: "My Way."

69 April: Bob Dylan: *Nashville Skyline* (LP).

69 April: Chicago: *Chicago Transit Authority* (LP), with "Prologue, August 29, 1968," "Someday, August 29, 1968," and "Liberation."

69 April: Frank Zappa and the Mothers of Invention: *Uncle Meat* (LP).

69 April: Joe Cocker: *With a Little Help From My Friends* (LP).

69 April: Joni Mitchell: *Clouds* (LP), with "Both Sides Now."

69 April: Moody Blues: *On the Threshold of a Dream* (LP).

69 April: Nazz: *Nazz Nazz* (LP).

69 April: Procol Harum: *A Salty Dog* (LP).

69 April: Sly and the Family Stone: "Stand!" (single) and *Stand!* (LP).

69 April: Traffic: *Last Exit* (LP).

69 April: Velvet Underground: *Velvet Underground* (LP).

69 April: Youngbloods: *Elephant Mountain* (LP), with "Darkness Darkness."

69 April 5: Friends of Distinction: "Grazing in the Grass."

69 April 5: Simon and Garfunkel: "The Boxer."

69 April 5: The Who: "Pinball Wizard."

69 April 12: Donovan: "Atlantis."

69 April 26: Three Dog Night: "One."

69 April 26: Black Economic Development Conference (BEDC) approves James
  Forman's Black Manifesto, calling for reparations of "15 dollars per nigger."

69 April 27: Joe Cocker and the Grease Band on *The Ed Sullivan Show*.

69 May: Crosby, Stills, and Nash: *Crosby, Stills, and Nash* (LP), with "Pre-Road
  Downs," "Wooden Ships," and "Long Time Gone."

69 May: Joan Baez: *David's Album* (LP).

69 May: John Lennon and Yoko Ono: *Life With the Lions* (LP).

69 May: Neil Young: *Everybody Knows This is Nowhere* (LP), with "Cinnamon
  Girl," "Down by the River," and "Cowgirl in the Sand."

69 May: Phil Ochs: *Rehearsals for Retirement* (LP), with "I Kill Therefore I Am"
  and "Another Age."

69 May: The Who: *Tommy* (LP); the first rock opera.

69 May 1: James Forman and BEDC begin demanding that white churches
  support the Black Manifesto and pledge reparations.

69 May 3: Beatles: "Get Back."

69 May 3: Creedence Clearwater Revival: "Bad Moon Rising."

69 May 3: Elvis Presley: "In the Ghetto."

69 May 4: James Forman disrupts communion at Riverside Episcopal Church,
  New York City, to present BEDC's demands.

69 May 25: *Midnight Cowboy* (movie).

69 May 26: John Lennon and Yoko Ono begin their second "bed-in for peace" in
  suite 1738-1740-1742, Queen Elizabeth Hotel, Montréal.

69 May 26: *The Dick Cavett Show* runs sporadically on ABC until 1974.

69 June: Fugs: *The Belle of Avenue A* (LP).

69 June: Grateful Dead: *Aoxomoxoa* (LP), with "St. Stephen."

69 June: With the Revolutionary Youth Movement (RYM) resolution as its
  manifesto, the Weather Underground ("The Weatherman Faction") splinters
  from the SDS.

69 June 1: John Lennon, Yoko Ono, Tommy Smothers, Timothy Leary, Derek
  Taylor, Petula Clark, Rabbi Abraham Feinberg, Paul Williams, and many others
  record "Give Peace a Chance" during the bed-in in Montréal.

69 June 7: Sly and the Family Stone: "I Want to Take You Higher."

69 June 10: *Last Summer* (movie).

69 June 14: Beatles: "The Ballad of John and Yoko."

69 June 14: Jackie DeShannon: "Put a Little Love in Your Heart."

69 June 22: Cuyahoga River catches fire near Cleveland, Ohio.

69 June 28: Youngbloods: "Get Together" (re-release).

69 July: Jethro Tull: *Stand Up* (LP), with "Bourée" and "Nothing Is Easy."

69 July: Mountain: *Mountain* (LP).

69 July: Spirit: *Clear* (LP).

69 July: Spooky Tooth: *Spooky Two* (LP), with "Evil Woman."

69 July: Ten Years After: *Ssssh* (LP).

69 July 3: Brian Jones drowns.

69 July 7 and September 9: Jimi Hendrix on *The Dick Cavett Show*.

69 July 10: *Putney Swope* (movie).

69 July 12: The Who: "I'm Free."

69 July 14: *Easy Rider* (movie).

69 July 18: Janis Joplin on *The Dick Cavett Show* and again on June 25, 1970 and August 3, 1970.

69 July 19: Rolling Stones: "Honky Tonk Women."

69 July 26: Creedence Clearwater Revival: "Green River."

69 July 26: John Lennon and the Plastic Ono Band: "Give Peace a Chance."

69 July 26: Johnny Cash: "A Boy Named Sue."

69 August: Blind Faith: *Blind Faith* (LP), with "Do What You Like."

69 August: Creedence Clearwater Revival: *Green River* (LP).

69 August: *Easy Rider* (LP soundtrack), with Fraternity of Man: "Don't Bogart Me" and the Byrds: "Wasn't Born to Follow."

69 August: Jerry Farber republishes the widely pirated "The Student as Nigger" in *The Student as Nigger: Essays and Stories*.

69 August: John Mayall: *Turning Point* (LP), with "The Laws Must Change."

69 August: Kinks: *Arthur* (LP), with "Shangri-La" and "Victoria."

69 August: Rolling Stones: *Through the Past Darkly* (LP).

69 August: Santana: *Santana* (LP), with "Evil Ways" and "Soul Sacrifice."

69 August 1: About 110,000 attend the Atlantic City Pop Festival, which runs until August 3.

69 August 1: Procol Harum; Joni Mitchell; the Chambers Brothers; Blood, Sweat, and Tears; Lighthouse; Iron Butterfly; Miles Davis; Mother Earth; and Chicago play at Atlantic City.

69 August 2: Nilsson: "Everybody's Talkin'."

69 August 2: Sly and the Family Stone: "Hot Fun in the Summertime."

69 August 2: Three Dog Night: "Easy to Be Hard."

69 August 2: American Dream, Tim Buckley, the Byrds, Booker T. and the M.G.s, Hugh Masekela, Paul Butterfield Blues Band, B.B. King, Creedence Clearwater Revival, Jefferson Airplane, Dr. John the Night Tripper, and AUM play at Atlantic City.

69 August 3: Sir Douglas Quintet, Santana Blues Band, Canned Heat, Three Dog Night, Joe Cocker, Frank Zappa and the Mothers of Invention, Lothar and the Hand People, Buddy Miles, Janis Joplin, and Little Richard play at Atlantic City.

69 August 15: On Max Yasgur's farm near Bethel, New York, the Woodstock Music and Art Fair runs until August 18, one day longer than scheduled, attracting at least 300,000.

69 August 15: Richie Havens, Country Joe McDonald, John B. Sebastian, Sweetwater, Bert Sommer, Tim Hardin, Ravi Shankar, Melanie, Arlo Guthrie, and Joan Baez play at Woodstock.

69 August 16: Thunderclap Newman: "Something in the Air."

69 August 16: Quill, Keef Hartley, Santana, the Incredible String Band, Canned Heat, Mountain, Creedence Clearwater Revival, the Grateful Dead, Janis Joplin,

Sly and the Family Stone, and the Who play at Woodstock.

69 August 17: Jefferson Airplane; Joe Cocker; Country Joe and the Fish; Ten Years After; the Band; Blood, Sweat and Tears; Johnny Winter; Crosby, Stills, Nash, and Young; the Paul Butterfield Blues Band, and Sha-Na-Na play at Woodstock.

69 August 17: Steppenwolf on *The Ed Sullivan Show*.

69 August 18: Jimi Hendrix closes Woodstock.

69 August 19: Jefferson Airplane do "We Can Be Together" uncensored on *The Dick Cavett Show*, probably the first time the word "fuck" is heard on network TV.

69 August 20: *Alice's Restaurant* (movie).

69 August 27: *Medium Cool* (movie).

69 September: Country Joe and the Fish: *Here We Are Again* (LP).

69 September: Fleetwood Mac: *Then Play On* (LP), with "Oh Well."

69 September: Rod Stewart: *The Rod Stewart Album* (LP).

69 September: Sons of Champlin: *The Sons* (LP), with "You Can Fly."

69 September: The Band: *The Band* (LP), with "Up on Cripple Creek."

69 September 6: Smith (with Gayle McCormick): "Baby, It's You."

69 September 24: Chicago Eight trial begins, becoming Seven on November 5 because of the removal of Bobby Seale.

69 September 27: Peggy Lee: "Is That All There Is?"

69 October: Beatles: *Abbey Road* (LP), with "Come Together" and "The End."

69 October: Byrds: *Ballad of Easy Rider* (LP), with "Jesus is Just Alright."

69 October: Doors: *Soft Parade* (LP), with "Touch Me."

69 October: Firesign Theatre: *How Can You Be in Two Places at Once When You're Not Anywhere at All?* (LP).

69 October: Frank Zappa and the Mothers of Invention: *Burnt Weeny Sandwich* (LP) and Frank Zappa (solo): *Hot Rats* (LP).

69 October: Joe Cocker: *Joe Cocker* (LP), with "Delta Lady."

69 October: John Lennon and Yoko Ono: *Wedding Album* (LP).

69 October: Led Zeppelin: *Led Zeppelin II* (LP), with "Moby Dick."

69 October: Pentangle: *Basket of Light* (LP).

69 October: Steppenwolf: *Monster* (LP), with "Draft Resister."

69 October 3: *Oh! What a Lovely War!* (movie).

69 October 4: Crosby, Stills, and Nash: "Suite: Judy Blue Eyes."

69 October 8: *Bob and Carol and Ted and Alice* (movie).

69 October 8: Four days of riots, the "Weatherman Days of Rage," begin in Chicago.

69 October 15: "National Moratorium Day," peaceful work stoppages, demonstrations, and teach-ins to protest the war.

69 October 18: Beatles: "Come Together" / "Something."

69 October 18: Blood, Sweat, and Tears: "And When I Die."

69 October 19: Smith (with Gayle McCormick) sings "Baby, It's You" on *The Ed Sullivan Show*.

69 October 24: *Butch Cassidy and the Sundance Kid* (movie).

69 October 25: Creedence Clearwater Revival: "Down on the Corner" / "Fortunate Son."

69 November: Creedence Clearwater Revival: *Willy and the Poor Boys* (LP).

69 November: Jefferson Airplane: *Volunteers* (LP), with "We Can Be Together," "Hey Fredrick," "Eskimo Blue Day," and the title track.

69 November: King Crimson: *In the Court of the Crimson King* (LP).

69 November: Pink Floyd: *Ummagumma* (LP), with "Astronomy Domine."

69 November: Rolling Stones: *Let It Bleed* (LP), with "Gimme Shelter," "You Can't Always Get What You Want," and "Midnight Rambler."

69 November 1: Merle Haggard: "Okie from Muskogee."

69 November 2: The Band on *The Ed Sullivan Show*.

69 November 7: Boston Eight destroy draft office records.

69 November 15: Led Zeppelin: "Whole Lotta Love."

69 November 15: New Mobilization to End the War in Vietnam (New Mobe) and SMC lead the biggest antiwar march on Washington to date.

69 November 23: Rolling Stones do "Gimme Shelter," "Love in Vain," and "Honky Tonk Women" uncensored on *The Ed Sullivan Show*.

69 December: Allman Brothers: *The Allman Brothers Band* (LP).

69 December: Country Joe and the Fish: *Greatest Hits* (LP).

69 December: David Frye: *I Am the President* (LP).

69 December: Fairport Convention: *Liege and Lief* (LP).

69 December: John Lennon and the Plastic Ono Band: *Live Peace in Toronto* (LP), with "Give Peace a Chance" and "Cold Turkey."

69 December: Moody Blues: *To Our Children's Children* (LP).

69 December 1: First draft lottery, with September 14, 1950 "winning."

69 December 4: Janis Joplin sings duet of "Raise Your Hand" with Tom Jones on his ABC TV show, *This is Tom Jones*.

69 December 4: Chicago police murder Black Panther Fred Hampton in cold blood.

69 December 5: *Life* magazine prints Ronald Haeberle's My Lai massacre photos.

69 December 6: Hell's Angels murder a fan during Rolling Stones free concert at Altamont, California.

69 December 18: *The Damned* (movie).

69 December 18: *On Her Majesty's Secret Service* (movie).

69 December 27: Sly and the Family Stone: "Everybody is a Star" / "Thank You Falettinme Be Mice Elf Agin."

69 December 29: Princeton University Triangle Club's *Call a Spade a Shovel* enrages conservative alumni in Grosse Pointe, Michigan.

69 (late in the year): Abbie Hoffman: *Woodstock Nation: A Talk-Rock Album* (book).

70: Maximum number of U.S. troops in Vietnam = 334,600.

70 January: Captain Beefheart and His Magic Band: *Trout Mask Replica* (LP).

70 January: Grateful Dead: *Live Dead* (LP), with "Turn on Your Love Light."

70 January: Simon and Garfunkel: *Bridge Over Troubled Water* (LP), with "The Boxer" and the title track.

70 January: Turtles: "We Ain't Gonna Party No More" is released as the B-side of "Who Would Ever Think That I Would Marry Margaret?"

70 January 17: Temptations: "Psychedelic Shack."

70 January 24: Creedence Clearwater Revival: "Travelin' Band" / "Who'll Stop the Rain?"

70 January 25: *M*A*S*H* (movie).

70 January 31: Santana: "Evil Ways."

70 January 31: Simon and Garfunkel: "Bridge Over Troubled Water."

70 February: Beatles: *Hey Jude* (LP), with "Rain."

70 February: Doors: *Morrison Hotel* (LP), with "Peace Frog."

70 February: Fugs: *Golden Filth* (LP), with "Saran Wrap."

70 February: Mountain: *Climbing* (LP), with "Mississippi Queen."

70 February: Van Morrison: *Moondance* (LP), with "Into the Mystic."

70 February 4: *Patton* (movie).

70 February 9: *Zabriskie Point* (movie).

70 February 18: *What Do You Say to a Naked Lady?* (movie).

70 February 21: John Lennon: "Instant Karma."

70 February 28: Marmalade: "Reflections of My Life."

70 March: Crosby, Stills, Nash, and Young: *Déja Vu* (LP), with "Almost Cut my Hair," "Carry On," "Teach Your Children," and "Woodstock."

70 March: James Taylor: *Sweet Baby James* (LP), with "Fire and Rain."

70 March: Jethro Tull: *Benefit* (LP), with "Teacher."

70 March: Ten Years After: *Cricklewood Green* (LP).

70 March 11: *Fellini Satyricon* (movie).

70 March 14: Beatles: "Let It Be" (Apple 2764) as recorded in 1969.

70 March 14: Rare Earth: "Get Ready."

70 March 15: Jerry Rubin: *Do It! Scenarios of the Revolution* (book).

70 March 21: Guess Who: "American Woman."

70 March 17: *The Boys in the Band* (movie).

70 March 21: Crosby, Stills, Nash, and Young: "Woodstock."

70 March 25: *The Adventurers* (movie).

70 March 26: *Woodstock* (movie).

70 March 27: CBS censors Abbie Hoffman's American flag shirt on *The Merv Griffin Show*.

70 March 28: Ray Stevens: "Everything is Beautiful."

70 April: Joni Mitchell: *Ladies of the Canyon* (LP), with "Big Yellow Taxi."

70 April: Turtles: *More Golden Hits* (LP), with "We Ain't Gonna Party No More."

70 April 1: Richard Brautigan: *Rommel Drives on Deep into Egypt* (book).

70 April 18: Creedence Clearwater Revival: "Up Around the Bend."

70 April 18: Melanie, with the Edwin Hawkins Singers: "Lay Down (Candles in the Rain)."

70 April 24: Grace Slick and Abbie Hoffman try to attend Tricia Nixon's Finch College alumnae party at the White House and spike the drinks with LSD.

70 April 26: *One Plus One* released as *Sympathy for the Devil* (movie).

70 May: Beatles: *Let It Be* (LP), with title track remixed by Phil Spector.

70 May: Rod Stewart: *Gasoline Alley* (LP).

70 May: The Who: *Live at Leeds* (LP), with "Summertime Blues," "Young Man Blues," "Substitute," and extended versions of "My Generation" and "Magic Bus."

70 May 2: Blues Image: "Ride, Captain, Ride."

70 May 4: National Guard murders four students at Kent State University, Ohio, prompting nationwide student and faculty strikes.

70 May 13: *Getting Straight* (movie).

70 May 15: Mississippi police murder two students at Jackson State University.

70 May 16: Beatles: "The Long and Winding Road."

70 May 16: Pipkins: "Gimme Dat Ding."

70 May 23: Temptations: "Ball of Confusion."

70 May 23: Three Dog Night: "Mama Told Me Not to Come."

70 June: Black Sabbath: *Black Sabbath* (LP), with "The Wizard."

70 June: Deep Purple: *Deep Purple in Rock* (LP).

70 June: Delaney and Bonnie and Friends: *On Tour with Eric Clapton* (LP).

70 June: Last Poets: *The Last Poets* (LP), with "Niggers Are Scared of Revolution," "Wake Up, Niggers," and "When the Revolution Comes."

70 June: Marmalade: *Reflections of my Life* (LP).

70 June: Michael Tearson becomes music director at WMMR-FM.

70 June: Traffic: *John Barleycorn Must Die* (LP), with "Freedom Rider."

70 June: *Woodstock* (LP soundtrack).

70 June 6: Crosby, Stills, Nash, and Young: "Teach Your Children."

70 June 6: Sly and the Family Stone: "I Want to Take You Higher" (re-release).

70 June 8: Bob Dylan: *Self Portrait* (LP), with "Like a Rolling Stone."

70 June 15: *The Strawberry Statement* (movie).

70 June 20: Crosby, Stills, Nash, and Young: "Ohio."

70 June 23: *Kelly's Heroes* (movie).

70 June 24: *Catch-22* (movie).

70 July: Creedence Clearwater Revival: *Cosmo's Factory* (LP), with "Who'll Stop the Rain?" and "Long as I Can See the Light."

70 July: Dave Mason: *Alone Together* (LP), with "World in Changes."

70 July: Doors: *Absolutely Live* (LP), with "Petition the Lord with Prayer," "Celebration of the Lizard," "When the Music's Over," and "Five to One."

70 July: Grateful Dead: *Workingman's Dead* (LP), with "Dire Wolf."

70 July: Moody Blues: *A Question of Balance* (LP), with "Question."

70 July 1: Second draft lottery, with July 9, 1951 "winning."

70 July 3: Atlanta Pop Festival, despite Georgia Governor Lester Maddox's attempts to ban it and all future festivals, runs successfully for three days.

70 July 4: The Who: "Summertime Blues."

70 July 11: Edwin Starr: "War."

70 July 11: Mungo Jerry: "In the Summertime."

70 July 15: *Joe* (movie).

70 July 30: Authorities prohibit Powder Ridge Festival in Middlefield, Connecticut, which had been scheduled from July 31 to August 2, but Melanie plays there anyway.

70 August: Frank Zappa and the Mothers of Invention: *Weasels Ripped My Flesh* (LP), with "My Guitar Wants to Kill Your Mama."

70 August: Joe Cocker: *Mad Dogs and Englishmen* (LP).

70 August: King Crimson: *In the Wake of Poseidon* (LP).

70 August: Melanie: *Candles in the Rain* (LP), with "Lay Down (Candles in the Rain)," "Leftover Wine," "Ruby Tuesday," and "What Have They Done To My Song, Ma?"

70 August 3: *Performance* (movie).

70 August 4: A six-day festival in Harmonyville, Chester County, Pennsylvania, was supposed to begin, but was cancelled several weeks before.

70 August 8: Creedence Clearwater Revival: "Lookin' Out My Back Door."

70 August 15: Kinks: "Lola."

70 August 15: Melanie: "Peace Will Come."

70 August 22: Free: "All Right Now."

70 September: Allman Brothers: *Idlewild South* (LP).

70 September: Black Sabbath: *Paranoid* (LP), with "War Pigs."

70 September: Byrds: *Untitled* (LP), with "You All Look Alike."

70 September: Firesign Theatre: *Don't Crush that Dwarf, Hand Me the Pliers* (LP).

70 September: Hot Tuna: *Hot Tuna* (LP), with "Death Don't Have No Mercy."

70 September: Neil Young: *After the Gold Rush* (LP), with "Southern Man."

70 September: Pink Floyd: *Atom Heart Mother* (LP).

70 September: Rolling Stones: *Get Yer Ya-Ya's Out* (LP).

70 September: Santana: *Abraxas* (LP), with "Black Magic Woman."

70 September 12: *Five Easy Pieces* (movie).

70 September 18: Jimi Hendrix dies.

70 September 26: The Who: "See Me, Feel Me."

70 October: Bob Dylan: *New Morning* (LP), with "If Dogs Run Free."

70 October: Country Joe and the Fish: *CJ Fish* (LP).

70 October: Frank Zappa: *Chunga's Revenge* (LP).

70 October: Led Zeppelin: *Led Zeppelin III* (LP).

70 October 4: Janis Joplin dies.

70 October 4: Melanie sings "Peace Will Come" on *The Ed Sullivan Show*.

70 October 5: *Trash* (movie).

70 October 10: Quicksilver Messenger Service: "Fresh Air."

70 November: Canned Heat: "Let's Work Together."

70 November: George Harrison: *All Things Must Pass* (LP).

70 November: Grateful Dead: *American Beauty* (LP), with "Box of Rain."

70 November: Kinks: *Lola Versus Powerman and the Moneygoround* (LP).

70 November: Nazz: *Nazz III* (LP), with "Loosen Up."

70 November: Spirit: *The Twelve Dreams of Dr. Sardonicus* (LP).

70 November: Velvet Underground: *Loaded* (LP), with "Sweet Jane."

70 November 7: Santana: "Black Magic Woman."

70 November 28: Bee Gees: "Lonely Days."

70 December: John Lennon: *Plastic Ono Band* (LP), with "Working Class Hero" and "God."

70 December: Melanie: *Leftover Wine* (LP), with "Peace Will Come."

70 December: Paul Kantner and Jefferson Starship: *Blows Against the Empire* (LP), with "Mau Mau (Amerikon)," "Let's Go Together," "A Child is Coming," "Sunrise," "Hijack," and "Starship."

70 December: Quicksilver Messenger Service: *What About Me?* (LP).

70 December 5: Melanie: "Ruby Tuesday," validating the Rolling Stones.

70 December 6: *Gimme Shelter* (movie).

70 December 23: *Little Big Man* (movie).

71: Maximum number of U.S. troops in Vietnam = 156,800.

71: Pete Seeger: *Young vs. Old* (LP).

71: Richard Brautigan: *The Abortion: An Historical Romance 1966* (book).

71 January: Mountain: *Nantucket Sleighride* (LP).

71 January 30: Creedence Clearwater Revival: "Have You Ever Seen the Rain?"

71 February 20: Marvin Gaye: "What's Going On."

71 March: Crosby, Stills, Nash, and Young: *4 Way Street* (LP), with "Triad," "Long Time Gone," "Pre-Road Downs," "Southern Man," "Carry On," "49 Bye-Byes / America's Children," "Ohio," "Chicago," and "Find the Cost of Freedom."

71 March: David Frye: *Radio Free Nixon* (LP).

71 March: The Who record Townshend's "Pure and Easy," but this version is not released until *Odds and Sods* in 1974.

71 March 28: Last new episode of *The Ed Sullivan Show*.

71 March 29: Court-martial convicts Lieutenant William Calley of murder in My Lai massacre.

71 April: Doors: *L.A. Woman* (LP), with "The Changeling."

71 April: Last Poets: *This Is Madness* (LP), with "Related to What," "Black Is," "Mean Machine," and "White Man's Got a God Complex."

71 April 3: Doors: "Love Her Madly."

71 April 3: John Lennon: "Power to the People."

71 April 9: *Summer of '42* (movie).

71 April 23: Rolling Stones: *Sticky Fingers* (LP), with "Wild Horses."

71 April 24: Rolling Stones: "Brown Sugar."

71 April 24: National Peace Action Coalition (NPAC) non-violent march on Washington against the war draws about half a million demonstrators.

71 April 26: Violent antiwar activities in Washington until May 6.

71 May: *A Child's Garden of Grass: A Pre-Legalization Comedy* (LP).

71 May: Rod Stewart: *Every Picture Tells a Story* (LP).

71 May: Spooky Tooth: *Tobacco Road* [i.e., *It's All About Spooky Tooth*] (LP).

71 June: Allman Brothers: *At the Fillmore East* (LP), with "Whipping Post."

71 June 13: *New York Times* begins publishing the "Pentagon Papers," secret files on the Vietnam war stolen by Daniel Ellsberg.

71 June 19: Rolling Stones: "Wild Horses."

71 June 27: Bill Graham closes the Fillmore East.

71 June 28: U.S. Supreme Court overturns Muhammad Ali's draft evasion conviction.

71 June 30: *Carnal Knowledge* (movie).

71 July: Moody Blues: *Every Good Boy Deserves Favor* (LP).

71 July 3: Doors: "Riders on the Storm."

71 July 3: Jim Morrison dies.

71 July 10: The Who: "Won't Get Fooled Again."

71 July 17: Creedence Clearwater Revival: "Sweet Hitch-Hiker."

71 August: Jethro Tull: *Aqualung* (LP), with "My God," "Hymn 43," and "Wind Up."

71 August: The Who: *Who's Next* (LP), with "Won't Get Fooled Again."

71 August 5: Third draft lottery, with December 4, 1952 "winning."

71 September: Frank Zappa and the Mothers of Invention: *Fillmore East, June 1971* (LP).

71 September: Grateful Dead: [*Skull and Roses*] (LP).

71 September: John Lennon: *Imagine* (LP), with "How Do You Sleep?"

71 September: New Riders of the Purple Sage: *New Riders of the Purple Sage* (LP).

71 September 11: John Lennon and Yoko Ono on *The Dick Cavett Show* and again on September 24.

71 October 3: *The Last Picture Show* (movie).

71 October 16: John Lennon: "Imagine."

71 October 30: The Who: "Behind Blue Eyes."

71 November: Led Zeppelin: *Led Zeppelin* [*IV*, i.e., *Zoso*] (LP), with "Stairway to Heaven."

71 November: Youngbloods: *Good and Dusty* (LP), with "Hippie from Olema."

71 November 27: Don McLean: "American Pie."

71 December 4: Grateful Dead: "Truckin'."

71 December 20: *Harold and Maude* (movie).

72: Maximum number of U.S. troops in Vietnam = 24,200.

72 February 2: *A Clockwork Orange* (movie).

72 February 2: Fourth and last draft lottery, with March 6, 1953 "winning."

72 April 12: *Fritz the Cat* (movie).

72 June 17: Nixon's supporters burglarize Democratic Party facilities at the Watergate building.

72 September 13: *The Ruling Class* (movie).

72 October: Pete Townshend: *Who Came First* (LP), with solo version of "Pure and Easy."

72 November 7: Nixon defeats McGovern.

72 December: *Life* magazine ceases publication.

$$\Omega$$

Spring 1964

Beatlemania!

Something had to be done. The world as we had known it — the masterful brink-manship with which JFK had handled the Cuban missile crisis, the age when blacks would passively suffer white assertiveness, the bogus rebellion with which teenagers had heretofore typically confronted their parents' values while always tacitly accepting these values — was gone. That rebellion had now, almost over-night, become genuine. Our parents' values were, at last, actually being challenged — and our parents were nervous, not only by the increasing thoughtfulness and sincerity of what they had always considered just a normal phase of adolescent growth, but also, and especially, by the truth that they all knew, but that few would admit, that it was their world, their generation, that had killed our president. Our parents were worried because they must have suspected, deep in their hearts, that we, over against them, might be right. Not extreme right like Barry Goldwater, but absolutely right.

The man who, as we had believed in our dazed Cold War innocence, could have done something, was gone. His eternal flame was no guiding torch or rallying point. JFK was part of the old era too, and for that reason it was just as well that he was dead. We were not survivors so devoted to our fallen leader that we forgot or lost ourselves. We were survivors for whom the falling of our leader enabled us to remember and find ourselves. The young white radicalism of the sixties never could have happened if there had been a two-term Kennedy presidency. The figure of JFK never could have engendered such an uprising, because he was, as we saw him, too conciliatory, too benign, too humanly lovable, in short, too understanding, to be able to spark the kind of mass opposition that Lyndon Johnson and Richard Nixon inflicted upon themselves. The setting of the young against the government in the sixties was almost entirely because of LBJ. Without him there would have been little or no challenge to basic federal authority. But through him we saw clearly that something had to be done. We believed that, with JFK gone, we were the only ones who could do it.

In the new year 1964 the mood of the country, though shocked, was still complacent, conservative, obtuse. There was some latent revolutionary talent — so latent that it was barely noticeable. But it was there. It dared not show, announce, or assert itself, even hint at itself, because it had no direction. Every revolutionary person in the land felt lonely and unsupported. As discretion had yielded to concealment, the underground had grown. But those who were underground craved the fresh air above and the powerful, free, indiscreet companionship and unity with their fellows. So a few of these would-be Nietzschean individuals poked their mole noses out from under the ground. A few brave heralds experimented with indiscretion. But what did they find? An atmosphere fetid with complacency, conservatism, and obtuseness. The stench drove them back underground. They lacked three things to clear the air: numbers, communication, and leadership. Little did they recognize at that time that numbers were really no problem at all; for a few good leaders would soon rally and generate sufficient numbers. The nation was gravid with legions of revolutionaries. Communication would soon be facilitated through music and the underground press. All they lacked were leaders. SDS-ers Haber and Hayden were unknown and neither was especially charismatic. Malcolm X only led blacks.

There are two things that few born before, say, 1940, can understand about the generation that characterized the sixties: first, our complete, undiluted hatred of Lyndon Baines Johnson; and second, the unqualified, integral, and absolute importance of music in our lives. Regarding the second, Pete Townshend once said that if the Who did not go on stage as scheduled, then it would not be just a case of disappointing the fans; it would be a case of the kids having nothing to live for.[6] That might have been overstating it, but the point was well made.

We hated LBJ as much as we had loved JFK, and for the same reasons. JFK was a visionary liberal who nevertheless exercised fiscal responsibility and diplomatic restraint. Johnson was a sociopolitical conservative, a fiscal loose cannon, and an unrestrained Cold Warrior who used the civil rights movement, the issue of poverty, and the demand for health care funding reform opportunistically, without conviction, to aggrandize himself. The so-called "Great Society" was a sham from when he first proclaimed it on May 22, 1964 — and we knew it.

A fit subject for debate is whether the Beatles would have been so fanatically received in America if JFK's death had not traumatized the nation just two-and-a-half months before. We were sickened. We wanted little of the old order. We were desperately in search of something, anything, that we could clutch, cherish, and call our own, that we could be proud of, hold up before the world, and defend with all our hearts and souls. We wanted a substitute for the inspiration that JFK had provided, the inspiration that we now realized had always been false, for it had died with him, and is still buried at Arlington.

If, on the other hand, this inspiration had truly been rooted in our own

---

[6] Pete Townshend, interviewed in his home in Twickenham, Middlesex, October 1977, for the BBC-1 TV show, *Tonight*; excerpt included in the movie, *The Kids Are Alright*, Chapter 40, "Final Words": "It's not people just saying, 'Listen, you'll disappoint your fans if you don't go on. The show must go on. You know, you must go on, otherwise all those people will be so upset.' It's, 'You've gotta go on, man, otherwise, all those kids, they'll be finished. They'll have nothing to live for.' That's rock-and-roll."

hearts, as we had assumed it was before November 22, 1963, then it would have lived in us after him. But this was not the case. The moral spirit that guided the sixties was not the moral spirit of JFK, although, to be sure, the moral spirit that guided the sixties would never have been possible without JFK's special life and death to awaken it. The moral spirit that guided the sixties was born, like a Nietzschean tragedy, out of the spirit of music.

Each item on the agenda of what became the sixties subculture from 1964 to 1970 was expressed in music, which for us had promptly become, after the Beatles arrived in the United States, not so much a take-it-or-leave-it form of entertainment but an essential means of communication, almost a private language shared among us but an enigma to our parents, who mostly remained willingly deaf and scornful. Among these agenda items were, in no particular order:

The natural equality of all races.

Opposition to the subjection, oppression, and commodification of women.

Respect on their own terms for women and oppressed minorities.

De-emphasis on money as the primary cultural value.

Opposition to all forms of hypocrisy.

Opposition to power in families determined by accident of birth or social status, e.g., parenthood, guardianship, or age, instead of by reason. That is, if we were to obey at all, we would obey because the command made sense in its own right and context, not because we heard along with the command: "Because I'm your mother" or "Because I said so" or "Because I'll beat the crap out of you if you don't" or something similarly illogical.

Opposition to spanking and other forms of violence as means of punishment in families.

Opposition to conformity, babbitry, and materialistic culture.

Preference for religion based on ethics rather than on doctrine.

Personal freedom, including the freedom to use — or not to use — the recreational drugs of our choice.

Rebelliousness and irreverence in general, and especially the refusal to give blind obedience to anyone or anything.

Sexual liberation, i.e., anything is permissible between consenting adults.

Preference for the intellectual life over the life of action.

Elevation of the values of the mind and heart above those of the body.

General suspicion of authority.

Self-determination, or freedom from our parents' expectations to be able to mold us as they saw fit.

Opposition to the Vietnam War, but not necessarily to war in general.

Indulgence in fantasy.

General preference for anything funny over anything serious, i.e., a Nietzschean willingness to laugh at stuffed shirts rather than aspire to be, become, or emulate those stuffed shirts.

The belief that our status as human beings trumps our status as citizens of any country or as members of either gender or of any race, ethnic group, social organization, tribe, clan, family, club, army, or any other subset of the set of all human beings.

Dedication to learning how to think critically, weighing all the facts, not treating received opinion or tradition as if it were fact, and refusing to learn how to fit into a pre-existent, imperfect, unnatural system whose flaws are obvious and remediable.

Opposition to violence, unfairness, bullying, and injustice.

Unselfishness.

Belief in heterosexual, interracial, transclass, and intergenerational friendships, rather than the Aristotelian belief — and American societal prejudice — that true friends must be pairs of the same sex, race, and class, and ideally also of similar age.

The belief that might seldom makes right, and if it does, then whatever is right is right not because of might, but because of some other intrinsic factor that would make it right with or without might to support it.

The centrality of music as an indispensable element of a well-lived life.

Music did not suddenly become socially conscious or politically outspoken after the death of JFK. There had long been undercurrents of deeper meaning, mostly in the acoustic guitar music of such songwriters as Woody Guthrie, Pete Seeger, Tom Paxton, Phil Ochs, Buffy Sainte-Marie, and Bob Dylan. Indeed, those who took the time to listen carefully to the lyrics of either Seeger or the pre-electric Dylan got a fairly thorough leftist political education. But the death of JFK instantly cleared the air for such heavily message-laden music to flourish for nearly a decade in the mainstream of popular culture. Political content such as that in the multi-artist album, *Newport Broadside 1963: Topical Songs At The Newport Folk Festival*, would no longer be unfamiliar to all except initiated folkies, but would soon be presented for general scrutiny. Thanks to Dylan and the Byrds, who would soon electrify folk music — and piss off the initiated folkies in the process — this content would become part of the everyday consciousness of rock-and-rollers. Folk rockers would fill the role of "town criers" to young political activists for the rest of the sixties. Folk rock, enjoying a bigger audience than plain old folk music ever had, would reap tremendous political benefit for the left. By covering Buffy's "Universal Soldier," Donovan would bring her song into the mainstream and thus create one of the most widely sung and dearly cherished antiwar anthems. Similarly, by covering Seeger's "Turn! Turn! Turn!," the Byrds would publicize to a huge audience some basic leftist ideals as insinuated by the biblical book of Ecclesiastes.

Music does not change the attitudes, beliefs, or behavior of any listener, but reflects and confirms them, or brings them to the surface if they are latent, or to consciousness if they are subconscious. Music becomes popular when it resonates with people as they already are, or with beliefs that its listeners already hold. It articulates what people may have felt previously to have been unarticulated. It may wake people up, but they were already themselves when they were still asleep.

No one can understand any person or group of people without understanding their music. We thought we understood Lesley Gore well enough after her first three songs, but she completely surprised us with her fourth. Unlikely as it may seem, this teenage pop star who sang "It's My Party," "Judy's Turn to Cry," and "She's a Fool" sacrificed her girly-girl image to record the first feminist anthem: "You Don't Own Me." Apparently she was singing from the heart. She came out to the world as a lesbian in 2005, rather anticlimactically, for her sexual orientation was already well known inside the music community and to anyone who had followed her career from the late sixties on.

As is usual in matters of culture, music, and art, England was several giant steps ahead of America at this time. Already the British kids had rebelled — and in earnest — the mods in the vanguard and the rockers not far behind, all proving it in their music. With very few exceptions, American pop music was stuck in doldrums amid hot rod music; party music; California surf music; wacko landlocked pseudo-surf music like "Surfin' Bird" by the Trashmen, a pretty good four-man garage band from Minneapolis; whiny neo-crooning crap spewed out by Bobby Vinton, the Four Seasons, and their ilk; and ridiculous ditties like "Beans in My Ears" by the Serendipity Singers, nine clean-cut pop-folkies from the University of Colorado. Most of it was meaningless. About the best American song that spring was "No Particular Place to Go" by Chuck Berry, one of the true founders of rock-and-roll — and one its greatest and most underrated guitarists.

American kids desperately needed an infusion of fresh music. The Beatles provided it.

In December 1963 small stories hit the American press and airwaves about a long-haired rock-and-roll band who were then an extraordinarily popular fad in their native England. As yet we had heard none of their music, and we wondered why their hair should be long.

Authorized by EMI Parlophone, the Beatles' official British record label, Capitol Records released the Beatles' first American album, *Meet the Beatles*,[7] in January 1964. Not to be outdone, Vee Jay Records slapped together a melange of old and new cuts and released them the same month as *Introducing the Beatles*.[8] These two albums, along with the singles "My Bonnie" / "The Saints," "From Me to You" / "Thank You Girl," "I Saw Her Standing There" / "I Want to Hold Your Hand," "She Loves You" / "I'll Get You," "Please Please Me" / "Ask Me Why," and "Please Please Me" / "From Me to You," comprised all the Beatles music that we Americans could have heard before the Beatles came to the United States. But the fact was that most of us heard little of it. Aside from places like New York City

---

[7] The tracks were "I Want to Hold Your Hand," "I Saw Her Standing There," "This Boy," "It Won't Be Long," "All I've Got to Do," "All My Loving," "Don't Bother Me," "Little Child," "Till There Was You," "Hold Me Tight," "I Wanna Be Your Man," and "Not a Second Time."

[8] This existed in two versions, the earlier containing "Love Me Do" and "P.S. I Love You" instead of "Ask Me Why" and "Please Please Me." The other tracks were "I Saw Her Standing There," "Misery," "Anna (Go to Him)," "Chains," "Boys," "Baby It's You," "Do You Want to Know a Secret," "A Taste of Honey," "There's a Place," and "Twist and Shout." Capitol would release most of these tracks in March 1965 as *The Early Beatles*.

with "Murray the K" Kaufman[9] on WINS-AM, Washington with Carroll James on WWDC-AM, and Philadelphia, St. Louis, and Chicago with other innovative and sharp-eared DJs championing them early, there were few areas in the United States where the Beatles could be heard on radio before late January. Just about the only other American exposure to the Beatles then was Jack Paar running a few British clips on his NBC TV show, Friday evening, January 3.

So, except for "I Saw Her Standing There" / "I Want to Hold Your Hand," which hit number one on the *Billboard Hot 100* on February 1, most of us never heard a Beatles song until Sunday, February 9, when, motivated more by curiosity than foreknowledge, 73,000,000 Americans watched *Ed Sullivan* to see what this British phenomenon was all about. They played "All My Loving," "Till There Was You," "She Loves You," "I Saw Her Standing There," and "I Want to Hold Your Hand," thus inaugurating their six-year reign over popular music in America.

You can imagine what school was like the next day! It was like that all week. Kids were ecstatic; teachers were either appalled, scornful, bewildered, or disinterested. Friday was Valentine's Day. Girls did not want Valentine cards from boys who did not love the Beatles. Boys whom girls had previously ignored now suddenly found themselves popular as soon as they declared their devotion to the four Liverpudlians — and moreover, their newfound popularity was directly proportional to their level of devotion.

Such intoxication could not last. Adolescent and pre-adolescent social relations returned within a few months to what they had been before the Beatles factor temporarily redetermined them. Frenzy and infatuation gradually settled down into lasting, but lower-keyed, admiration. The screaming diminished, the trappings disappeared, but the heart of the matter — the music — not only survived but flourished. To our parents, Beatlemania was just a passing fad that would burn itself out by the summer. They did not understand the importance of the music.

The Beatles wrote their own songs. We could trust them as human beings on account of that. They covered some songs also, but the Beatles were not, like most of the acts on the music charts, primarily mercenaries singing other people's songs for hire, regardless of whether they believed the meanings of those songs. This added measure of sincerity and credibility enhanced their appeal for those of us who were desperate to find some kind of honesty somewhere in our post-JFK lives. In this regard the Beatles were more like Dylan than like Bing Crosby, Frank Sinatra, or Elvis.

Their lyrics at first were not much to brag about — just "silly love songs," as Paul McCartney later put it — but wow! Did their music ever rock! Songs like "I Want to Hold Your Hand," "She Loves You," "Please Please Me," "Can't Buy Me Love," "It Won't Be Long," and "All My Loving" were the heaviest, edgiest rock songs we had ever heard up to that point. We fell in love with the Beatles!

The implied juxtaposition between their self-written single, "Can't Buy Me

---

[9] On the basis of this early and strong promotion, some called Murray the K "The Fifth Beatle," which was quite unfair to more legitimate contenders such as George Martin, Stuart Sutcliffe, Brian Epstein, and later, Billy Preston.

Love," praising the carefree life, and their cover of Janie Bradford's and Berry Gordy's "Money (That's What I Want)" on *The Beatles' Second Album*, praising avarice, presented a contradiction of meanings that we had to unravel. We knew immediately which one they meant. They would always believe their own words before anyone else's. In later years we would be faced with having to resolve contradictory meanings between — or among — songs that they wrote themselves. Such quandaries would throw the individual personalities, characters, and agendas of the three songwriting Beatles into stark relief over against each other. But that was still to come. For the time being the Beatles were a unity — at least in our eyes.

But why did they cover "Money"? Why, after they became huge, did they cover anything at all? Why, after they had established themselves as songwriters *par excellence*, did they continue to release some of their earlier recorded covers, even great songs like the Isley Brothers' "Twist and Shout"? We quickly learned not to put much stock in the lyrics of their covers.

Their covering Chuck Berry's "Roll Over Beethoven" did not suggest to us white kids who had been raised on *Swan Lake* and Beethoven's *Fifth Symphony* that classical music was stuffy. We knew it was not. Rather, we began to think that many of the people who played and preferred classical music were stuffy, and that they needed to have a bit more fun in their lives, not taking things quite so seriously. Such people believed that good music should be subtle and decorous; but we were beginning to realize that good music, including the classics, had to be wild and free. That budding realization about the best possible constructive relationship between orchestral and rock music would a few years later be confirmed by Procol Harum, *Sergeant Pepper's Lonely Hearts Club Band*, the Moody Blues, King Crimson, and especially by the Nice's first two albums, *The Thoughts of Emerlist Davjack* and *Ars Longa Vita Brevis*.

The Beatles' Second Album was not nearly as exciting as *Meet the Beatles*. Six of its eleven songs were covers. That was disappointing. Its five originals each had the word "you" in the title and were just "silly love songs," although "You Can't Do That," a Lennon song, showed a jealous boy threatening a girl whom he accused of being a flirt. Off that album, ditties like "Love Me Do," "Do You Want to Know a Secret," and "P.S. I Love You" were about as deep as the Beatles got in those early days. Beatles songs with real meaning were still some time away.

Other British acts soon presented themselves in America as rivals to the Beatles. The earliest of these was the edgier, less melodic Dave Clark Five, whose hard-driving "Glad All Over" and "Bits and Pieces" won a substantial, if ephemeral, fan base within a crowd rougher than those who typically became Beatlemaniacs. American DJs, record distributors, and music executives were quick to capitalize on the fact that, at least for the time being, any hairy British pop group, however it looked, played, or sounded, was likely to sell tunes in the States. Consequently, a lot of fluffy, insignificant British groups followed the Dave Clark Five to America that spring and summer. These groups, such as Gerry and the Pacemakers, Peter and Gordon, the Searchers, the Swinging Blue Jeans, and Chad and Jeremy, were eminently forgettable, but profitable for the suits who engineered this first wave of the so-called "British Invasion." Step by step, however, higher quality British bands appeared, usually as good as and sometimes better than the Beatles. In essence this meant the Rolling Stones late that spring, the Animals that summer, and the Kinks that fall. The Stones hooked us right away with that chunky Bo Diddley beat in "Not Fade Away." We knew they were out of the ordinary and were likely to last. The Dave Clark Five faded away. Thereafter for American ears the main rivalry among British bands was between the Beatles and the Stones.

Despite the best efforts of Lennon/McCartney, Jagger/Richards, Dylan, and the Brill Building, the most enduring, broadly appealing, and just plain beautiful music of the decade, even for our generation, was written by — Henry Mancini. The composer of "Moon River," "The Pink Panther Theme," and "The Peter Gunn Theme" enjoyed such wide exposure through his film and TV scores that he was automatically a big part of our everyday lives. His best work was in collaboration with director Blake Edwards, and Edwards's best was in collaboration with him. Their superb comedy, *The Pink Panther*, spawned several well known franchises, including one for Peter Sellers, who is rightfully identified with Inspector Jacques Clouseau just as much as Sean Connery is with James Bond, Basil Rathbone with Sherlock Holmes, or Bela Lugosi with Dracula. Sellers was such an immediate and huge hit in this role that the sequel, *A Shot in the Dark*,[10] was released just three months later, on June 23. The first Pink Panther animated cartoon, "The Pink Phink," was released on December 18. These pantomime cartoons, which were played mostly in theaters as preludes to feature films, soon became very popular. Sound effects and Mancini's music provided their only "dialogue."

Ω

Three landmark films in early 1964 dealt with authority's abuse of its powers.

Kubrick's *Dr. Strangelove, or: How I Learned to Stop Worrying and Love the Bomb* was the first antiwar movie that many of us ever saw. Whether our first or not, it was certainly one of the best. It laid bare the absolute madness of the Cold War, the nuclear arms race, and, by implication, all wars and all arms races. The obvious madness of Brigadier General Jack D. Ripper, the renegade U.S. Air Force base commander who singlehandedly started World War III by ordering his B-52s to drop hydrogen bombs on the Soviet Union, seemed at the beginning of the film to be in contrast to the everyday military world; but as other characters came into the plot and each revealed their own particular madnesses, the everyday military world seemed madder and madder, so that we gradually saw that Ripper was right at home in it, a symptom, not an anomaly. The only major characters who were not insane were Group Captain Lionel Mandrake and President Merkin Muffley, both played to comic perfection by Peter Sellers. The film's message appeared to be that the military cannot be trusted to preserve peace, however much they may

---

[10] This excellent comedy is not to be confused with the pitiful 1935 murder mystery of the same title.

brainwash themselves with the actual motto of the Strategic Air Command (SAC): "Peace is Our Profession." Scratch any career military officer and you find a war-lover like General Buck Turgidson, who was more impressed by the skill of American pilots than by the possibility of global nuclear annihilation. In this scene he seemed to prefer that, instead of one of our planes being shot down and thus saving the planet, our expert flying would cause a glorious universal *Götterdämmerung*.

The most poignant aspect of the film was the British "Forces' Sweetheart," Vera Lynn, singing her popular torch song of World War II, "We'll Meet Again," as the finale. We all knew the song already. Even those of us who did not remember World War II heard it frequently on the radio. It was a song of hope. For all its horror, World War II was a war of hope from the Allies' point of view, and its outcome by and large justified that hope. But the Cold War and its relentless nuclear threat, in contrast, held no possibility of hope for either side. As the hydrogen bombs exploded in the final scene, there was no possibility that anyone would ever meet again. Lynn's inspiring promise had become empty. Kubrick's inversion of her song's original meaning was brilliant. It would not be the only time that he would jolt us with an ironic upset of familiarity.

The movie *Becket*, based on Jean Anouilh's play, was rife with historical errors, some glaring, such as Becket's Saxon ancestry and Eleanor of Aquitaine's relative powerlessness. In fact, Becket was of the Norman family Becquet and Eleanor was among the most powerful women in English and French history. Neither of these errors was incidental; but both, especially the former, were key to Anouilh's plot, with its interwoven themes of class warfare and the oppression of conquered people. Edward Anhalt's screenplay reproduced Anouilh's errors and introduced a few of its own. Given the fundamental historical inaccuracy that undergirded the entire presentation, it would be best to regard it as fiction, not even as historical fiction.

Peter O'Toole played King Henry II as a boorish, arrogant, elitist fool, bigoted against all his underlings, but in particular the Saxons, whom he habitually called "pig" or "dog." Richard Burton played Thomas Becket, the king's partying buddy and eventual foil, as a subtle collaborator in search of honor and love. Becket felt a strong solidarity with the common people, and plotted when necessary against the king for their sake. He outwitted Henry to prevent him from raping a peasant girl. The turning point in their friendship may have occurred when Henry, cashing in his end of the bargain that Becket had made with him to save this girl, attempted to have his way with Becket's own lover, Gwendolen, who killed herself rather than submit to the king's lust. Yet Becket remained at least ostensibly loyal.

Henry wanted to tax the churches to fund his wars and aimed to curtail the power of ecclesiastical courts to try priests in civil and criminal cases. Becket, as Chancellor of England, was Henry's most useful ally in these wrangles. While in Henry's service, he upheld secular over ecclesiastical authority and supported the king's worldly attempt to control spiritual concerns. But he had no strong ideological convictions beyond being a good servant.

When Theobald, the aged Archbishop of Canterbury, died, Henry thought to win final victory in his battles with the church by making his closest personal friend, most loyal servant, most intelligent advisor, and most proficient operative, Becket, the new head of the English church, even though Becket was yet only a deacon. To Henry's "I think there is a man we can rely on," Becket, before he knew that Henry meant him, replied, "No matter who it is, once the archbishop's mitre is on his head, he will no longer be on your side." When he learned that Henry intended to make him Archbishop of Canterbury, he tried — sincerely, almost as if precognizant of the future — three times to dissuade him. The first time, "My Lord, don't do this," was practically hissed as a threat. The second, "My Lord, this frightens me," was an attempt to reason with the king. The third, "I beg of you, do not do this," was abject and desperate. Yet the king, as kings will, prevailed.

In his one day of priesthood between his deaconhood and his consecration as archbishop, Becket obeyed Matthew 19:21, Mark 10:21, and Luke 18:22 by selling all his luxuries and giving the proceeds to the poor, but in a showy performance of generosity such as Jesus might have condemned according to Matthew 6:1-8. Yet he took his new role seriously. Ever the good servant, Becket fully transferred his loyalty from king and country to church, pope, and God. For the first time in his life he felt fulfilled. As he explained to Henry, "I do not seek power, my prince. It is only that I finally discovered a real honor to defend." So Henry branded him a traitor and engineered his death. Altogether this movie remains a powerful argument for the strict separation of church and state.

The third of these films, *From Russia With Love*, was the most nearly believable James Bond film, and for that reason arguably the best. It continued the disparagement of the Cold War that the movie series had begun in *Dr. No*. In the book Klebb, Kronsteen, and Grant all worked for SMERSH (*Smert' Shpionam* = "Death to Spies"), the actual Soviet assassination and revenge agency of the fifties. Thus the conflict in the book was strictly within the two-sided context of the Cold War. But in the movie these three villains were all operatives of the fictitious S.P.E.C.T.R.E., which was, as its leader Blofeld put it, the third Siamese fighting fish, who would wait until the life-or-death battle was over between the first two, then finish off the weakened victor. S.P.E.C.T.R.E. secretly provoked both the Soviets and the British in Istanbul, so that they and their allies blamed and killed each other while remaining ignorant of S.P.E.C.T.R.E.'s presence in Turkey. Bond survived S.P.E.C.T.R.E.'s multifaceted plot primarily by his resourcefulness, quick reflexes, and brute strength, and only secondarily by gadgets. Indeed, by the lavish standards of subsequent Bond films, the fancy spy gadgetry in *From Russia With Love* was almost non-existent. The only gadget that figured in the plot was the booby-trapped attaché case that concealed tear gas, a sniper rifle, a throwing knife, extra pistol ammo, and fifty gold sovereigns. Fans who respected Bond's ingenuity must have believed that he would have found a way to kill Grant on the train even without his attaché case.

Each of these three films contributed in its own way to undermine whatever faith we had left in the old order.

Ω

Summer 1961

Finding our feet in the Great Society

> There were no flies on Frank that morning — after all why
> not? He was a responsible citizen with a wife and child,
> wasn't he? It was a typical Frank morning and with an
> agility that defies description he leapt into the barthroom
> onto the scales. To his great harold he discovered he was
> twelve inches more tall heavy!
> — John Lennon, "No Flies on Frank," *In His Own Write*

Do not underestimate the importance of Lennon's first book, *In His Own Write*.
The singers of our parents' generation were empty shells with beautiful voices. A
few of them, such as Frank Sinatra, Bing Crosby, and Elvis — Yes, I put Elvis in
our parents' generation! His world view was much closer to theirs than to ours. —
supplemented their singing triumphs with successful acting careers and some, like
Sinatra, were even fairly good actors. But they did not write their own songs. They
apparently did not have that much intelligence. They had nothing of their own to
express, and could only reshape and enhance someone else's cutesy tunes and fluffy
lyrics. But Lennon! Not only did he write his own tunes and lyrics, and sing them
from the heart rather than from formality or mannerism; and not only was he a fine
actor; he also wrote irreverent, witty, multivalent prose and poetry! He had brains!
He had something to say and was able to say it well in several different ways. *In
His Own Write* was a revelation to us that entertainment both could and should be
intellectual. McCartney nailed it in his introduction:

> "Is he deep?" He wore glasses so it was possible, and even without them
> there was no holding him. ... Again I think — "Is he deep?" "Is he arty, with
> it or cultured?" There are bound to be thickheads who will wonder why some
> of it doesn't make sense, and others who will search for hidden meanings.
> ... None of it has to make sense and if it seems funny then that's enough.

Those of us who had already studied Edward Lear and Lewis Carroll in school immediately recognized Lennon's genius. Much of *In His Own Write* is just puns and other kinds of word play, but the text is also rich in allusions to cultural, historical, political, literary, and artistic phenomena — albeit most of these allusions are rather obscure or cryptic. It was hilarious and that was enough.

The sixties were a great era for nonsense writing, deep or not.

Mason Williams's "Them Poems" were not great art, but they grew ever more popular from 1964 through the rest of the decade and added much to the unrestrained spirit of fun and creative chaos that characterized the sixties. They were catchy, mirthful, and bluntly formulaic. Each them poem, written in mock hick dialect, consisted of five four-line stanzas with the second and fourth line of each stanza rhyming and the whole thing having a strong beat. The first line was always, "How about them ..."; the second always, "Ain't they ..."; and the seventeenth always, "How to be a ..." Titles included "Them Toad Suckers," "Them Lunch Toters," "Them Moose Goosers," "Them Yodel Yellers," "Them Tummy Gummers," "Them Dog Kickers," "Them Duck Pluckers," "Them Hog Liver Likers," "Them Ewe Doers," "Them Sand Pickers," "Them Sticker Gitters," "Them Banjo Pickers," "Them Hors D'Oeuvers," "Them Surf Serfs," "Them Stamp Lickers," "Them Beaver Cleavers," "Them Whisker Flickers," and "Them Doodle Dashers." They were so easy to imitate that doing so became one of our favorite pastimes. Here are four that my girlfriend and I wrote together in 1969:

"Them Math Teachers"

How about them math teachers?
Ain't they slick?
Teachin' that math
And makin' us sick

Some come bald
Some come hairy
Some come pigeon-toed
But they all come scary

Spoutin' 'bout trig
Yellin' out logs
Barkin' out formulas
Just like dogs

Them mean old math teachers
Sweatin' for they lives
Tell us all 'bout calculus
Then say two and two is five

How to be a math teacher?
Here's how to reach it
Go to school for ninety years
If you're still alive then teach it.

"Them Real Dumb Be-ers"

How about them real dumb be-ers?
Ain't they scum?
All over ever'where
Bein' real dumb

Ya sees 'em in the subway
Ya sees 'em in the street
But mosta them's in Washin'ton
Tryin' to act sweet

Them real dumb be-ers
None o' them's a hero
They's dumb and they's dumber
But the dumbest one is Spiro

Some folks think they's smart
But if you's one who do
Then we is gonna tell ya this:
You's a real dumb be-er too

How to be a real dumb be-er?
Tell ya how it come
Just git ya'self in polly-tix
And be real dumb.

"Them Pig Punchers"	"Them Cop Macers"
How about them pig punchers? Ain't they sweet? Roundin' up pigs Punch 'em in they meat	How about them cop macers? Ain't they tops? Runnin' down the street Macin' them cops
Punchin' them sow-hogs Beatin' them boars Punch 'em when they's wide awake Punch 'em when they snores	Macin' them city cops Macin' them feds Gassin' them state fuzz In they heads
Windin' up they fisties Sock 'em in they gut Haul off at them piggies Left hook to they butt	Shootin' that tear gas Fillin' fuzz with mace Watch 'em burn they eyes out Watch 'em pick they face
Hit 'em in they pigtails Hit 'em in they snout Hit 'em in they bacon Tryin' to knock 'em out	Gonna git each cop in town Ever' pig around Gonna watch 'em scream in pain Writhin' onna ground
How to be a pig puncher? If ya wanna crunch it Findy self a hog-beast Make a fist and punch it.	How to be a cop macer? Git a can o' mace Steal it from a piggy-fuzz Squirt him inna face.

The big news of the summer was the enactment of the Civil Rights Act, a monumental piece of progressive legislation designed to "enforce the constitutional right to vote, to confer jurisdiction upon the district courts of the United States to provide injunctive relief against discrimination in public accommodations, to authorize the Attorney General to institute suits to protect constitutional rights in public facilities and public education, to extend the Commission on Civil Rights, to prevent discrimination in federally assisted programs, to establish a Commission on Equal Employment Opportunity, and for other purposes." LBJ tried hard to take credit for it, but it had been JFK's baby. On November 27, 1963, in his first speech as president to Congress, LBJ had asked that the bill be passed as a memorial to our murdered leader. LBJ could not have cared less about civil rights in principle, but he was a consummate political opportunist who quickly recognized and acted upon any prospect for enhancing his prestige and solidifying his nationwide base, even if alienating some racist whites. The House of Representatives passed the bill 290 to 130 in February — clearly it was the will of the people. If the vote had been closer, one wonders whether LBJ would have expended so much energy squeezing it through the Senate, which was hamstrung by his filibustering Southern cronies. For whatever reason, LBJ successfully twisted a lot of senatorial arms. After an eighty-three-day filibuster, the Senate passed the bill 73 to 27. The House voted 289 to 126 to accept the Senate's amended version. LBJ signed it immediately.

Among the non-Southern senators who joined the Southern bloc in voting against the Civil Rights Act was Barry Goldwater, who would soon lose the 1964 presidential race to LBJ by 43 million to 27 million popular votes, 61 to 39 per cent, 486 to 52 electoral votes, and 44 to six states. The ultra-conservative vs. the crypto-conservative. What a mess!

Ω

The liner notes to *Another Side of Bob Dylan* consisted of just of one long series of Dylan's beat poems, "Some Other Kinds of Songs." A few excerpts:

> lenny bruce shows his seventh
> avenue hand-made movies, while a
> bunch of women sneak little white
> tablets into shoes, stockings, hats
> an other hidin places. ...
> ... in east berlin
> renata tells me that i must wear
> tie t get in t this certain place
> i wanna go. back here, literate
> old man with rebel flag above
> home sweet home sign says he won't
> vote for goldwater. "talks too
> much. should keep his mouth shut" ...
> ... people pound their
> chests an other people's chests an
> interpret bibles t suit their own
> means. respect is just a misinterpreted word
> an if Jesus Christ himself came
> down through these streets, Christianity
> would start all over again. ...
> an dean martin should apologize
> t the rolling stones
> ho hum ...
> ... an' i say that every question
> if it's a truthful question
> can be answered by askin' it ...
> ... all is lost Cinderella
> all is lost

Bob's Dean Martin remark referred to the crooner's gratuitous denunciations of the Rolling Stones' long hair during the band's first American tour. The Stones were earthier, guttier, sexier, and nastier than the Beatles — and so, to our parents' generation, even more threatening. Martin's stupid insults clumsily revealed our parents' inability to deal with the likes of the Stones.

However, Martin had a "bully pulpit." His "Everybody Loves Somebody" blunted the British Invasion that summer. After the Beatles held the number one position on the *Billboard Hot 100* for fourteen consecutive weeks with "I Want to Hold Your Hand," "She Loves You," and "Can't Buy Me Love," the lead shifted among black Americans like Louis Armstrong, Mary Wells, and the Dixie Cups; young white Americans like the Beach Boys and the Four Seasons; and Britons like the Beatles and Peter and Gordon until Martin's "Everybody Loves Somebody" hit it for one week, August 15-21. Martin was the first white male of our parents' generation to capture number one on the pop chart since Steve Lawrence with "Go Away Little Girl" in January 1963. Martin, slick drunken boor that he was, became their "Great White Hope." Insulting the Rolling Stones was at that point just the next logical step in his career. It sure highlighted his hypocrisy.

On their first American tour, the Stones played mostly rocked-up blues covers. Mick Jagger and Keith Richards would not hit their stride as songwriters until 1965. "Tell Me" was their own, but their other early hits, "Not Fade Away," "Route 66," "I'm a King Bee," "Carol," "It's All Over Now," and "Time Is On My Side," were all covers.

Complementing the Stones in sleaze and grit was another new British band, the Animals, whose "House of the Rising Sun," a cover of Georgia Turner's and Bert Martin's thirties white blues lament about drinking, whoring, and gambling — three subjects that Dean Martin knew well — sat at number one for three weeks. Driven by Alan Price's landmark organ riff and Eric Burdon's growly vocals, this song conveyed all the urgency of downtrodden people suffering on the wrong side of life.

Dylan similarly concerned himself with the plight of the poor and oppressed. He had covered "House of the Rising Sun" on his first album in 1962, and now, on *Another Side*, he addressed basic issues of human well-being, as indeed he had also done on his three previous albums and would continue to do throughout his career. "Chimes of Freedom" was a hopeful song of soldiers looking for peace, refugees looking for sanctuary, abused women looking for safety and justice, and everyone else looking for any kind of relief. "I Shall Be Free, No. 10" followed the same theme, but in a humorous way. It parodied Muhammad Ali's poetry, mocked bigotry by declaring that he would not let Goldwater move into his neighborhood or marry into his family, ridiculed country club exclusivity, and proclaimed in no uncertain terms the absolute equality of all human beings. "Motorpsycho Nightmare" used a bizarre twist on the old travelling salesman joke motif to attack political intolerance. The lyrics of "My Back Pages" were obscure, nearly inscrutable, but the refrain was clear enough. It meant that breaking out of traditional conservatism, denying its mythology, and refusing its promises can rejuvenate a person. Psychologically, a sixty-year-old leftist is younger than a twenty-year-old right-winger, because the leftist has a mind open to fresh ideas, respects and tolerates all people instead of using them, and may even love them for their own sake. The Byrds would reprise this theme in early 1967 when they covered "My Back Pages" on the very appropriately titled *Younger Than Yesterday*.

Also on *Another Side*, "All I Really Want to Do" suggested that relationships between men and women do not have to be asymmetrical, sexually charged affairs between unequals, but that a man and a woman can actually be just plain friends. Not only equals, but friends. In a similar vein, "It Ain't Me Babe" was not only Dylan's rejection of a particular woman, but also a rejection of the whole idea of a traditional "great American romance."

Gale Garnett's "We'll Sing in the Sunshine" supported a new, liberating direction for women in heterosexual relationships. She celebrated the woman who was free to enjoy a man for whatever he was worth, and then walk away, unscathed. The idea was beginning to creep into the mainstream consciousness that for women, as well as for men, freedom was more important and more desirable than either the asymmetrical tradition or the "great American romance." As women became more free, men became more respectful of them. Society began to encourage men to stop objectifying women as sexual instruments, and gradually pushed them toward regarding women as real human beings, rightfully equal to themselves in every way.

Roy Orbison's "Oh Pretty Woman" was a very respectful song. Compare it with the 1982 Van Halen version and note how David Lee Roth changed the lyrics to fit his leering, lecherous, misogynist personality. Orbison promised to treat her right, but Roth replaced that phrase with a blunt restatement of how much he needed her that night. Orbison's focus was on her; Roth's was on himself. Roy showed genuine sensitivity and human concern for man and woman together as equal partners in love and sex, but selfish Dave seemed interested only in his own instant physical gratification, at the lowest common level of male experience, not caring at all about the woman as a fellow human being. Orbison sounded genuinely surprised and thankful that she decided to walk back to him, but Roth sounded like he simply expected it.

The difference between these two versions of "Oh Pretty Woman" typifies the deterioration of rock's general attitude toward women from the era of the mid-sixties until the late seventies to the era from the early eighties until at least the time of writing this sentence, early 2007. Since the eighties there has been in popular music a deliberate and nearly total rejection of the highest political and social ideals of the sixties, as seen in the resurgence of the most mindless crypto-fascist heavy metal and rockabilly music written and sung in praise of brutish power, random violence, fistfights for fun, and callous exploitation of women. Coincident with this phenomenon, and not unrelated to it, is the fact that, in the eighties, to a degree not seen since the thirties and forties, style replaced substance as the main ingredient in successful pop songs.

Ω

Of the eleven songs on *Something New*, only two, "Slow Down" and "Matchbox," were covers. One of the others was a German translation of "I Want to Hold Your Hand." The eight new originals were mostly just the "silly love songs" that we had already come to expect of the Beatles, yet some of the lyrics were beginning to get a bit deeper. "I'll Cry Instead" dealt with resentment, loneliness, and dreams of petty revenge, and suggested that maybe jilted lovers would be happier if they talked things out with their friends instead of brooding in solitude. "If I Fell" was about maturing in a new relationship despite the fact that the guy had failed to move on after being dumped, and therefore still wished misery on his old girlfriend. "Tell Me Why" depicted a boy trying to apologize to his girlfriend for whatever offense she may have suffered at his hands. "When I Get Home" expressed impatience at not being with one's lover, while "Things We Said Today" anticipated growing blissfully old in harmony with her. "Anytime At All" represented a boy promising unconditional devotion to his girlfriend. "And I Love Her," which was probably the most romantic song that Lennon/McCartney ever wrote, softly idealized from the male standpoint both the woman and their shared love. "I'm Happy Just to Dance With You" articulated a similar sentiment, but from a more juvenile perspective.

We knew that some of these songs would be in the Beatles' forthcoming movie, *A Hard Day's Night*. Besides what was available on *Something New* and in previous releases, the rest that would be in the film were all on the soundtrack, *A Hard Day's Night* ("The Red Album"), which appeared almost two months before the movie. Its twelve songs included "Can't Buy Me Love," five of the eight originals on *Something New*, four George Martin instrumentals, and two new tunes: "A Hard Day's Night," a hymn to domestic tranquility in what was probably a traditional, asymmetrical marriage, and "I Should Have Known Better," a rosy picture of a new love infatuation.

Rather than being confused by the apparently cryptic title, "A Hard Day's Night," we knew exactly what it meant. It derived from an *In His Own Write* story, "Sad Michael": "He'd had a hard day's night that day ..." It simply meant a long, hard stretch of work, which was quite apt, because the movie was to be about a typical, hectic day in the life of the Beatles. We later learned that the phrase was coined, not by John, but by Ringo Starr, who intended to say "It's been a hard day's work," but, upon noticing halfway through speaking that darkness had fallen, accidentally substituted "night" for "work." In any case, as soon as we heard the song's magnificent opening chord on George Harrison's twelve-string Rickenbacker guitar,[11] we loved it all. That chord rang like the harbinger of everything good that was ever to come. It was loud, jarring, and some might have called it dissonant, but to us it was the encapsulation in a single harmonic sound of everything that

---

[11] The Beatles were responsible for two of the most famous chords in rock, the opening chord of "A Hard Day's Night" and the closing chord of "A Day in the Life." No one knows exactly what these chords were. The primary instrument in the former was George's twelve-string Rickenbacker, but with John playing the same notes on his six-string, Paul playing a high D on his Hofner bass, Ringo diddling lightly on his snare drum and cymbals, and George Martin playing a low D - G - high D chord on a grand piano all thrown together into the mix. The latter was created by five players on three pianos: John, Paul, Ringo, George Martin, and Mal Evans simultaneously each banging out two E major chords, which Martin then sustained beyond belief with studio tricks.

we had been waiting for. That chord gave us hope, like a temple bell summoning us to the most sacred of devotions.

The prospect of seeing our beloved Beatles in their own feature film made the August opening of *A Hard Day's Night* the most eagerly anticipated event of the summer. We knew that it had been filmed in March and April. With its soundtrack album having appeared in June and its title song as a single in July, we could not wait to see it, but we were not expecting much. With beach movies, Elvis movies, hot rod movies, and other such schlock dominating the teenage market in the early sixties, even we Beatlemaniacs assumed that *A Hard Day's Night* would be just more of the same — but we knew that at least the music would be great. Moreover, already knowing the title song and most of the other songs by heart before we walked into the theater was a big advantage.

The distribution patterns of movies in America differed in the sixties from what is standard in the early twenty-first century. Gigantic chains of multiplex theaters now permit the nearly simultaneous appearance of each new release nationwide and each movie remains among the offerings of multiplexes as long as it is making money, though local managers may relocate it to smaller screens. But in the sixties, when even twin or quad theaters were rare, when chains tended to be regional rather than national, and when most theaters were owner-operated entities, each new movie would run for about a week, regardless of how much money it brought in, then give place to the next one. Holdovers were infrequent, were very well publicized in the local media — and always indicated real blockbusters. Movie schedules for each particular theater were usually available weeks or even months in advance. With the unevenness of negotiations and contracts between individual theater owners and movie distributors, any given movie might not appear in a certain town until long after its theatrical release date. There were so-called first-run, second-run, and (usually drive-in) third-run theaters. A moviegoer who wished to see a new movie as soon as possible after its release might have to travel many miles, even to a major city, to do so. Going out to the movies was a special event for rural, small-town, and even mid-size city residents, and typically involved much logistical planning.

Accordingly, those of us who lived off the bus or subway lines and who were too young to drive wheedled our parents into taking us to see *A Hard Day's Night* as soon as possible in a first-run theater. This meant that many more parents saw *A Hard Day's Night* than saw most beach, hot rod, or Elvis movies. And guess what! A lot of them liked it! Well, why not? They had some measure of discernment, and *A Hard Day's Night* was a much, much better film than anyone had imagined. It was not the usual teenage schlock; it was a comedic masterpiece.

Unlike Frankie Avalon, Annette Funicello, Paul Petersen, Elvis, or others of that late fifties and early sixties rock-and-roll movie ilk, each Beatle could really act. Playing oneself is the hardest acting job to do, but each did it with aplomb. Their natural good humor shone through in every scene. Screenwriter Alun Owen had for a large part used the Beatles' own banter among themselves as the basis of his screenplay. From this point forward, there could be no doubt that the Beatles were intelligent, witty, exuberant, unpretentious, and appealing. Even people who did not like them could no longer dismiss them as simian moptops. They were the romantic epitome of youth, a clear vision of the best possible future.

Ten minutes into *A Hard Day's Night*, the Beatles' assistant Shake was reading one of the *Mad* books, *Son of Mad*, on the train from Liverpool to London. This product placement was quite in keeping with the film's irreverent, happy-go-lucky spirit. For intelligent print satire in the sixties there was only one reliable source: *Mad* magazine. *Mad* sent everything up, but nothing so often or so adroitly as crass commercialism. Being both crass and commercial itself, it attacked these targets as only an insider could. The July 1964 issue contained marvelous lampoons of *Cleopatra*, Little League, political campaigning, TV cop shows, and the tobacco industry's response to the six-month-old report of the Surgeon General's Advisory Committee on Smoking and Health — plus the expected mean-spirited jab at the Beatles. The creators of *Mad* were, after all, members of the older generation. But the funniest section of that issue was "Comics for Publications That Don't Have Comics," delicious parodies of *Blondie*, *Pogo*, *Peanuts*, *Dennis the Menace*, *Little Orphan Annie*, and a few others. Subsequently, and in some cases not long after, a few of those publications, notably the *Wall Street Journal*, began including comics.

Comedy was very important to us. We loved to laugh. Life itself would have been unthinkable without laughter. Adults mystified us in this regard. They gave the impression of being not too interested in laughing. They were serious to the point of unintentional self-parody. They chuckled and tittered, but did not roar or guffaw, as we did whenever we got the chance. They seemed to be more concerned with maintaining their proper decorum than with actually enjoying their lives. They were too consumed with business and its demands to allow pure mirth to intrude on their affairs. Moreover, they wanted their comedy just plain silly and light rather than multivalent, meaningful, or somehow relevant to sociopolitical matters. Plus, they expected us to become humorless like them when we grew up. That was a disincentive to grow up if there ever was one.

A great actor of their generation, Gary Cooper, known for his solemnity, said on the December 14, 1947, episode of *The Edgar Bergen and Charlie McCarthy Show* that he liked good jokes as much as anyone, sometimes, as long as they were not too funny. This remark just about summed up our parents' attitude toward comedy.

For us the best comedians were those with strong sociopolitical messages, like Lenny Bruce, Bill Cosby, Tom Lehrer, and even old-timers like Bob Hope, Groucho Marx, Phil Silvers, Jack Benny, Spike Jones, and Bugs Bunny, who could each be taken as sociopolitical if we listened between their lines. Among our favorites were the Three Stooges, who appealed to our Marxist sensibilities because they played bumbling, stupid, but honest workers striving against all odds to make a living in the world of social snobs, military martinets, and bullying bosses — and to our Nietzschean sensibilities because they spent a great deal of their time and energy pricking holes in stuffed shirts.

Nothing was worth shit if we could not laugh at it. Furthermore, if anything, like the church, prohibited anyone from laughing at it, then on that account alone it was worth even less than shit. To comedy nothing should ever be forbidden. Comedy is the epitome of free speech and the essence of the human spirit.

Ω

The Vietnam War began in earnest in August 1964 with the Gulf of Tonkin Resolution. American troops had already been in Vietnam for several years, but this enabled the first major escalation into unrestrained combat.

I want to make very clear that I personally did not turn against the Vietnam War until late 1966 or maybe even early 1967. I do not remember exactly when that change in my fundamental thinking occurred, but I am sure that I was already solidly in the antiwar camp by the time of the Spring Mobe in April 1967. My point is that I was never a kneejerk antiwar, anti-government, or anti-LBJ activist. Despite — or perhaps because of — my conservative Republican parentage, I was already a leftist in social and domestic issues by about age ten, but I did not turn from being a young Cold Warrior in foreign policy until I was about fourteen. I came upon my new antiwar ideology slowly, cautiously, and even reluctantly.

I never liked LBJ, but in the first year of his presidency I believed his Cold War rhetoric and accepted the logic of the "domino theory," which held that if South Vietnam fell to communism, then all of Southeast Asia would likely fall too. I campaigned for him against Goldwater in the 1964 election. I believed, correctly or incorrectly, that Goldwater was a warmonger whose pro-rich, anti-welfare domestic policies would create horrible rates of unemployment and throw millions of Americans into poverty.

Compare and contrast four demonstrably parallel events: the Reichstag fire on February 27, 1933; the Japanese attack on Pearl Harbor on December 7, 1941; the North Vietnamese attack on an American gunship in the Gulf of Tonkin on August 2, 1964; and the great crime of September 11, 2001.

Hitler, in power only about a month, reaped tremendous political benefit from the partial destruction of the Reichstag. Whether Dutch communist Marinus Van der Lubbe or the Nazis themselves set the fire will probably never be known. The next day President Paul von Hindenburg, at Hitler's request, suspended freedom of speech and several other basic rights. By May 1933 Hitler was able to convert the German republic into a military dictatorship. In August 1939 he started a war by unilaterally invading a sovereign nation on flimsy pretenses.

Franklin D. Roosevelt, recently elected to his third term with 54.7 per cent of the popular vote, 449 to 82 electoral votes, and 38 of 48 states, did not need and did not reap any benefit, political or otherwise, from the attack on Pearl Harbor. He reluctantly reacted to the Japanese having unilaterally started a war. He asked Congress to declare a just war, which they quickly did. He did not thereby seek or gain any powers beyond what he already had.

LBJ, in power only about eight months, reaped tremendous political benefit from the attack on *U.S.S. Maddox* in the Gulf of Tonkin. Hanoi was certainly responsible, but may have been provoked. On August 5, LBJ presented the Gulf of Tonkin Resolution to Congress. They passed it on August 7 and he signed it on August 10. It granted him the power to wage war unilaterally as he saw fit in Southeast Asia without a formal congressional declaration of war. He and Defense Secretary Robert McNamara immediately began implementing plans to escalate the conflict.

George Dubya Bush, in power only about eight months, reaped tremendous political benefit from the total destruction of the World Trade Center towers and the partial destruction of the Pentagon. Whether Osama bin Laden and Al Qaeda acted alone or with the complicity of the Bush-Cheney circle will probably never be known. On October 24, 2001, Congress passed the USA-PATRIOT ("Uniting and Strengthening America by Providing Appropriate Tools Required to Intercept and Obstruct Terrorism") Act, which dramatically reduced basic human and civil rights for ordinary, innocent Americans and just as dramatically increased the power and authority of the president. By 2002 Dubya could confidently expect Congress to rubber stamp any and all of his aggressive anti-rights policies. In conducting his so-called "War on Terror," he suspended *habeas corpus*, set up secret prisons, instituted torture as a means of interrogation, ignored the will of the United Nations, insulted America's allies, and defied the Geneva Conventions. In March 2003 he started a war by unilaterally invading a sovereign nation on two flimsy pretenses: that Iraq was in collusion with Al Qaeda and that Iraq was acquiring weapons of mass destruction, both of which would be proved categorically false by 2005.

The similarities between LBJ's Vietnam War and Dubya's Iraq War are conspicuous. The following satirical checklist, "Vietnam II: Pre-Flight Check," circulated widely on the Internet beginning around March 10, 2003, a week and a half before the invasion:

☐ Cabal of oldsters who won't listen to outside advice?
☐ No understanding of the ethnicities of the many locals?
☐ Imposing country boundaries drawn in Europe, not by the locals?
☐ Unshakable faith in our superior technology?
☐ France secretly hoping we fall on our asses?
☐ Russia secretly hoping we fall on our asses?
☐ China secretly hoping we fall on our asses?
☐ Secretary of Defense pushing a conflict the Joint Chiefs of Staff never wanted?
☐ Fear we'll look bad if we back down now?
☐ Corrupt Texan in the White House?
☐ Land war in Asia?
☐ Right unhappy with outcome of previous war?
☐ Enemy easily moves in/out of neighboring countries?
☐ Soldiers about to be dosed with our own chemicals?
☐ Friendly fire problem ignored instead of solved?
☐ Anti-Americanism up sharply in Europe?

☐ B-52 bombers?

☐ Helicopters that clog up on the local dust?

☐ Infighting among the branches of the military?

☐ Locals that cheer us by day, hate us by night?

☐ Local experts ignored?

☐ Local politicians ignored?

☐ Locals used to conflicts lasting longer than the U.S.A. has been a
        country?

☐ Against advice, Prez won't raise taxes to pay for war?

☐ Blue water navy ships operating in brown water?

☐ Use of nukes hinted at if things don't go our way?

☐ Unpopular war?

Ω

Fall 1964

Don't trust anyone over thirty!

> Language ... becomes itself an instrument of control even
> where it does not transmit orders but information; where it
> demands, not obedience but choice, not submission but
> freedom. This language controls by reducing the linguistic
> forms and symbols of reflection, abstraction, development,
> contradiction; by substituting images for concepts.
>   — Herbert Marcuse, *One-Dimensional Man*
>   Chapter 4, "The Closing of the Universe of Discourse"

We may not have especially liked our parents' favorite singers, instrumentalists, arrangers, composers, or lyricists, but we never impugned their musicianship. Jo Stafford, Bing Crosby, Frank Sinatra, Louis Armstrong, the Andrews Sisters, Patti Page, Perry Como, Duke Ellington, Irving Berlin, Ella Fitzgerald, Johnny Mercer, and _____ (fill-in-the-blank) _____ and his Orchestra were all fine musicians. We all knew that. We just happened to prefer rock.

But 1964 was rife with attacks, slurs, and cheap shots from their generation against our favorite singers and musicians — and, by extension, against us too. This prolonged assault was not merely their expressed dislike of our music. That would have been OK. It was also their vicious, mostly ignorant condemnations of every recorded sound that we loved to hear on the radio. Every comedian of their generation got into the act. Bob Hope, Martha Raye, Jack Jones, and Tony Randall portraying "Sukiyaki Ringo Hope and his Japanese Beatles" on Bob's April 17, 1964, NBC TV *Comedy Special* was about as good-natured as these slaps got. Comedy and satire are one thing; unfounded smears are another.

Allan Sherman was a wonderful parodist who had already garnered quite a few fans in my generation with *My Son the Folk Singer*, *My Son the Celebrity*, and *My Son the Nut*. Hilarious! But when he released "Pop Hates the Beatles," I for one felt like screaming, "Et tu, Brute!" Those lyrics stated quite plainly that the

Beatles' guitars were out of tune and that Ringo could not keep a beat. All false! We could only conclude that such gratuitous lies were motivated by the same level of abhorrence of our music that had ruined Stan Freberg for us. They were not comedy. They were not funny. They were just plain mean, stupid, and wrong.

Why should our parents and their heroes have directed such vitriol against us? We began to suspect that it was because they did not like us very much. They, who valued conformity and sameness above all else, could see right away in 1964 that we did not resemble them and probably would not grow into resembling them anytime soon — despite their best efforts. What best efforts? They did not know how to persuade or foster, but only how to insult, mock, belittle, and spank. Winning World War II did not prepare them to raise families.

We did not create the so-called "generation gap." They did. We only wanted to be accepted for what we really were, both by each other and by them. They tried to pull us kicking and screaming into their stupid conformist black-and-white world. When we resisted, they punished, rejected, belittled, humiliated, and hated us, even though our resistance had arisen only because we had envisioned something better than what they had to offer, not because we harbored any personal hatred for them. What choice did we have then but to band together and build our own culture?

They would not even let us talk. "Children should be seen and not heard!" was their watchword. They seemed to us to convey that anyone under the age of twenty-one could not possibly have anything important to say. Their very way-of-life declared: "They are not yet well-informed enough about the world. Once they finish school they will be like us and then they will be worth listening to. Little kids are merely cute and teenagers are merely annoying. Why should we take anything any of them say seriously?"

Why — on the other hand — should we have put up with such demeaning condescension? They had put up with it from our grandparents when they were kids. They obviously expected us to put up with it too. Why shouldn't we? Why didn't we? Well, for whatever reason, we did not. Perhaps we felt emboldened by what was so easy for us to see as the gargantuan mess they had made of the world. We thought that we could do better.

Because our elders generally hated music that we knew was good, we naturally began to ask ourselves what other attitudes of theirs were screwed up. The list of answers to that question turned out to be pretty long. They had given us Jim Crow laws, segregationist mentality, hypocritical commitment to the principles of equal rights laid out in the Declaration of Independence, unfairly overpaid owners and managers and unfairly underpaid employees and workers, might-makes-right authoritarianism, stupid anti-marijuana laws, age-based condescension, sex-based condescension, artificial social roles, and of course, the Vietnam War. We knew that we could do better on all these counts. We only needed to speak out.

The problem was that they did not want to let us speak out!

So, in September 1964, the time was ripe, if not perfect, for the onset of the Berkeley Free Speech Movement. If ever Hegelian historical forces sparked a new development, this was it. That the basic impetus for full freedom of speech, freedom of assembly, and due process rights for young people should have started in California was not surprising, given that California was a relatively liberal state. A false perception persists that the Berkeley Free Speech Movement pitted students and outside agitators against the University of California faculty, administrators, and regents, plus the governor and the legislature. The fact is that the students, agitators, most of the faculty, and some of the administrators were on our side; and the regents, politicians, voters, and most of the administrators on the other. But that is an oversimplification. It may be more accurate to say that the movement pitted mostly liberals, mostly young, against mostly conservatives, mostly old.

The issue was straightforward: freedom. Freedom is not something that people in power give at their discretion to other people. Freedom is everyone's birthright, that may be taken away and must be guarded. We guard it best, not by fighting for it, but by using it. "Just do it!" as Jerry Rubin would later say.

Mario Savio was not a radical. He was just a twenty-one-year-old philosophy major at Cal Berkeley who felt a keen inclination toward natural morality, human rights, political fairness, and social justice. For many years the university administration had prohibited political activity in the center of campus, but had allowed it on the perimeter. On September 14 the administration banned leafleting, pamphleteering, and any other politicking anywhere on campus.[12] Students were furious. They correctly felt that a fundamental American constitutional right of free expression had been unilaterally and arbitrarily taken away from them. Even some students who supported Goldwater for president sided with the free speech advocates against the administration. Savio led the student protests. Outside activists, true radicals, poured into Berkeley to support the students, who set up political leafleting tables around the administration building itself, Sproul Hall. On September 28 the administration suspended Savio and seven other students indefinitely. Indefinite suspension had neither precedent nor written justification in the university rules.

On October 1 Jack Weinberg, a twenty-four-year-old Cal Berkeley alumnus and an experienced nonviolent civil rights activist, was staffing the Congress of Racial Equality (CORE) table on campus. He was arrested for refusing to show identification. Savio and other protesters surrounded the police car in which Weinberg was held and prevented the cops from driving it away. They made speeches from its roof and sang "We Shall Overcome." The standoff lasted over thirty hours. Weinberg recalled for James Ricci's education column in the November 29, 2006 *Los Angeles Times*: "This was not a hostile scene, in any way. ... This was different from the later time when hostility to police was a theme of activism. Nobody had any beefs with the campus police. They had a not very pleasant task, but they did

---

[12] This battle for freedom of political expression has mostly been won at private colleges and universities, but not at public institutions. For example, in 2000 a top administrator at the State University of New York (SUNY) Upstate Medical University told me that as an Upstate employee I was not allowed to show support for Bill Bradley's presidential candidacy on my personal faculty Web site. He had the letter of university regulations on his side, but not the spirit of America. Any American should be allowed to show support for any legitimate presidential candidate anytime, anyplace. It was not as if I were using university facilities to advocate the violent overthrow of the republic.

it in good spirits. I was not fearful in the slightest." Easily noticing the age divide between the pro-free-speech and anti-free-speech factions, Weinberg coined the pithy motto that would haunt leftists throughout the sixties: "Don't trust anyone over thirty!" It became especially problematic when Dr. Benjamin Spock, the Berrigan brothers, and other "untrustworthy" oldsters showed up on our side.

The Los Angeles Free Press, one of the nation's first underground newspapers, covered the Berkeley Free Speech Movement extensively. On March 19, 1965, it ran a famous editorial on page 3 about the Berkeley situation and free speech everywhere: "What's in a Word? 'Phuque' Won't Do." Indeed it won't! "Phuque Senzorship!" won't do as a slogan. No shit!

Controversy around free speech generally concerns three types of discourse: political, blasphemous, and obscene. No rational citizen would claim that one has the right to endanger others by falsely yelling "Fire!" in a crowded theater. That fourth type is not an exercise of free speech; it is just plain sick. Such reckless and perverse uses of the vocal equipment are not at issue in free speech debates.

But each of the other three should be protected as everyone's absolute right. First, the sociopolitical world will not advance unless everyone always feels free to express any political opinion at all. Stagnation in the well of ideas is not an option, even in the name of tradition, orthodoxy, or upholding the current regime. Second, the whole idea of blasphemy is ridiculous. It should have disappeared from history along with the Spanish Inquisition, the Salem witch trials, stoning for adultery, and burning so-called heretics at the stake. If God really is the loving, forgiving, compassionate creator of imperfect beings that all three major Western monotheistic religions say God is, then God would not give a shit about how we imperfect beings, acting only according to our created nature, use the divine names. But if, on the other hand, God is a cruel tyrant, unworthy of worship, then of course God would expect mortal creatures to grovel, genuflect, pray, chant, sacrifice, kowtow, prostrate themselves, and reverently kiss the divine ass at every opportunity. Reverence is no more a virtue than obedience is. Both countermand human self-respect. Third, as for obscenity, well ... [heh heh heh]

Words, words, words! Word swords! We did not care if "damn" and "hell" were blasphemous or that "shit," "fuck," "cock," and "cunt" were vulgar. If they fit the context, we used them in everyday speech and openly tolerated anyone else using them. Why not? Why be hypocritical about it? Some objected that words like "fuck" were so overused that they had become practically meaningless. Moreover, they reasoned, if these words had become meaningless, then why use them? These people had a valid point about the disappearance of denotation, but no word works better than "fuck" to intensify a phrase or to express anger, frustration, sheer joy, or any strong emotion. Some also objected that these words are naturally brutal and degrading. That is a very good point. Yet it is context-specific. It does not mean that we should not use these words; it only advises us to be careful how, when, where, and why we use them, to ensure that we do not hurt any feelings that we would rather not hurt. For example, calling a vulva a cunt is neutral, but calling a woman a cunt is a vicious insult that few women ever deserve. Calling your best friend a dumb fuck in jest is OK, but throwing that epithet at a new acquaintance in an otherwise peaceful gathering is usually not wise.

If politics is the art of building civilization, then all speech is political. That is, if politics is the neverending act of creating the *polis*, the city-state in which all citizens enjoy full rights, security, opportunity, and freedom, then anything that is ever said, written, or otherwise expressed has bearing on that development. It contributes toward producing the climate in which the *polis* may or may not succeed.

The focus of politics that fall was on the presidential election. The recent passage of the Civil Rights Act, which the electorate overwhelmingly supported, and the promise of a "Great Society" made LBJ a very popular man. The full, horrific consequences of the Gulf of Tonkin Resolution were not yet apparent.

The common people do not have to be cajoled into voting for the left. It is in their best interest. But the right, if it is ever to prevail in a republican democracy, needs to cajole them into voting for the right, i.e., the rich need to convince the poor that what is good for the rich is also good for the poor and the controlling minority needs to convince the controllable majority that what is good for the too powerful few is also good for the less powerful many. Since this cajoling is sometimes successful, the left sometimes needs to uncajole or countercajole the electorate and bring them back to the party that can really help them. Hence the left often appears defensive in elections. If the left were more articulate *ab initio*, then such defense against the moneyed interests would seldom be necessary.

The problem was that neither of the candidates in the 1964 presidential election were leftists.

Barry Goldwater was a plain, blunt, honest man. A good man. He was no cajoler. He was an extreme but conscientious conservative who advertised himself as exactly that. Up against LBJ, one of the arch-cajolers of all time, and bucking a gigantic sympathy vote for the Democrats in the wake of JFK's murder, he never had a chance of winning. The sneaky crypto-conservative masquerading as a progressive liberal beat him in a landslide.

Ω

As natural anti-conformists, we loved anything weird. So, just as naturally, when we first heard Vic Mizzy's finger-snapping theme announce the bringing of the Charles Addams cartoons from *The New Yorker* to life, we were enthralled. The casting and naming of the characters — John Astin as the manic paterfamilias Gomez, Carolyn Jones as his ghoulish but gorgeous wife Morticia, Jackie Coogan as fat bald dumb Uncle Fester, Blossom Rock as Grandmama the witch,[13] Lisa Loring as spooky six-year-old Wednesday, Ken Weatherwax as chunky eight-year-old Pugsley, and Ted Cassidy as the looming butler Lurch — were all perfect. The family was always at home. Their house itself was a character. As Wednesday said to the truant officer, Sam Hilliard, "We like it. It's so nice and gloomy."

---

[13] A witch is a "<u>W</u>oman <u>I</u>n <u>T</u>otal <u>C</u>ontrol of <u>H</u>erself."

The first episode of *The Addams Family*, "The Addams Family Goes to School," may have been the funniest and best crafted of the series. Arguing with Hilliard, Gomez defended keeping Wednesday and Pugsley out of school: "Why have children just to get rid of them?" When the children finally went, they were traumatized on their first day by Grimm's fairy tales of a knight in shining armor killing a "poor, defenseless dragon" and of "little juvenile delinquents," Hansel and Gretel, "pushing sweet old ladies into hot ovens." Gomez tagged the content of these stories as "atavistic cruelty, perverse barbarism." He and Morticia would not tolerate their children being exposed to it and insisted that Hilliard tell the school board that such violence should not be part of the curriculum. Hilliard gradually came around: "You know, I'm beginning to think you've got something. ... I'm beginning to see your point. Something must be done. From dragons to toy guns to real guns to bombs to atom bombs! You know what? Thinking like yours can save the world. I must confess I misjudged you people completely."

The Addamses deeply loved one another, eschewed corporal punishment, respected their children, genuinely enjoyed one another's company, and were a close-knit family. They did not take anything too seriously. They made their own lifestyle decisions and did not rely on custom. Outside the Addams home seemed dull and flat; inside was fun and exciting. As Morticia said, "Every day is a party with us." We recognized much of ourselves in the Addamses and much of our parents in the outside world. Better to be weird, happy freaks than common, sad, normal people. The best trait of the Addamses was their dogged independence:

> Grandmama: I remember the first time I voted, nineteen-hundred-and-six.
> Fester: Grandmama, you know there was no woman suffrage in nineteen-oh-six.
> Grandmama: [indignantly] That didn't stop me.
> Fester: Ah, a real Addams!

They were cleverly eccentric first and subtly monstrous second. Their main TV rivals, the Munsters,[14] by contrast, were crassly monstrous first and bluntly eccentric second. Where the Addamses were witty, fresh, and disarming, the Munsters were stock, schlock, and tacky shock. The characters were lowbrow comic stereotypes of standard thirties and forties movie monsters: Dracula, Frankenstein's monster, Dracula's daughter, Wolfman, mad scientist, etc. Any parallels drawn between the two shows only made the Addams show seem even better than it already was.

Those few of us who saw *Woman in the Dunes* saw the weirdest movie we had yet seen. Much weirder than Fellini. Compared to *Woman in the Dunes*, Ingmar Bergman's films seemed like Walt Disney's. Its strident, screaming, creepy, percussive score alone was enough to make us realize that.

A Tokyo entomologist hunting insects in a vast area of dunes ruminated on "men and women enslaved by suspicions that the other is holding back." Odd camera angles, ultra close-ups, and bizarre, nearly abstract images worthy of Salvador Dali made the entomologist himself seem an insect in the sand. When he missed the last

---

[14] *The Munsters* series began on CBS a week after *The Addams Family* debut in 1964 and ended a month after *The Addams Family* finale in 1966.

scheduled bus back to the city, a local villager promised him overnight lodging. But the villagers tricked him. He ended up kidnapped, consigned to a giant sand pit that functioned as an oubliette. A middle-aged widow lived alone in the pit in her half-buried cottage. She never came out of the pit — or wanted to. Her job was to shovel sand out of the pit to prevent both her own home from being buried and the nearby cottages of other villagers from being undermined. In exchange for her work, the villagers gave her subsistence rations. They needed another worker to help her excavate, and perhaps also to be the man to replace her sand-killed husband — hence the kidnapping.

The film was obviously an allegory — but of what? It was sharply critical of both human tradition and human innovation. In the entomologist vs. the villagers we saw themes of individualism vs. collectivism. At first, naturally, he resisted, but gradually gave up, domesticated himself, and the two prisoners became like an old normal married couple:

> Man: Doesn't this fill you with emptiness? Are you shoveling to survive, or surviving to shovel?
> Woman: Well, it's not as fun as Tokyo.
> Man: I'm not talking about Tokyo! How can you stand being locked up like this?
> Woman: But it's my home.
> Man: More reason to assert yourself. For me, it's a matter of time until help comes.
> Woman: Help?
> Man: Of course. If I'm out for a week, someone will come by. Then they'll see an open book ... My disappearance will seem strange. For you, this could be for life.
> Woman: But the bones are buried here.
> Man: Bones?
> Woman: Bones of my husband and daughter.
> Man: Then we can ... dig them up. Then you can leave. I'll help. You must know how to get them to let down the ladder.
> Woman: It's not like I'll have anything to do outside.
> Man: You could walk around.
> Woman: Walk around?
> Man: It's great to be able to walk around freely.
> Woman: [laughing] Won't you get more tired, just walking around?
> Man: [angrily] Stop joking! Even dogs go crazy, chained up all day. You are a human being.
> Woman: But if it weren't for the sand, nobody would bother with me, Isn't that right? Even you, mister ...

He wanted to solve — and probably could have solved — the shifting sand problem once and for all with technology rather than continue indefinitely and ineffectively to hold it at bay with tradition. He reasoned that he could teach the villagers the technology and then they would let him go. He nearly escaped once, but fell into quicksand and was recaptured. As part of the treachery of traditionalists against civilization, the demonic villagers offered him his freedom if he would rape the woman in public for their pleasure. He succumbed to this temptation, and tried it, but she succeeded in fighting him off. Even if he had done as they demanded, they would not have freed him, even for ten minutes to look at the sea.

Civilization is the peaceful maximization of freedom, security, art, leisure, and music, with adequate food, water, and other necessities for all. It is the optimal human condition. Yet few of us are willing to help to build it. Are we so attached to our homes and traditions that, even though they are demonstrably stupid and readily improved, we stick to our old ways against all reason? Why do people freely choose to continue to live in shifting sand dunes, in swamps, below sea level, on the slopes of active volcanoes, in the frozen north, or on frequent flood plains? Why do they not just move into friendlier, more pacified, more accommodating, more civilized environments? Why do humans apparently prefer to live as insects in a forbidding universe of relentless sand bounded by sea on one side and quicksand on the other, rather than try to improve their fate?

A somewhat kinder look at tradition was the hit Broadway play, *Fiddler on the Roof*, about a benevolent Jewish widower in late tsarist Russia, Tevye, who had three and only three missions: to be a good milkman and keep his community well supplied with kosher dairy products, to study the Torah as often and as carefully as possible, and to marry off his three daughters.

Tevye was a fool. He gradually reconciled himself to his first daughter choosing to marry someone he just plain did not like. He even managed to endure his second daughter choosing to marry a revolutionary. But he could never stomach his third daughter choosing to marry a goy! What an idiot! To place dogma and insular prejudice above the love and happiness of his daughter! Lousy father!

Tradition sometimes seems a euphemism for "oppression," "ignorance," or "narrowmindedness." Not that we cannot learn from the past. The past is a rich and wonderful source of insight into the present and future. It deserves to be studied and respected. Civilization cannot advance unless we do so. But tradition just accepts the past uncritically. Nothing should ever be accepted uncritically!

A young person can apprehend the world in either of two ways: either uncritically, by receiving opinions and attitudes from elders as if they were facts; or critically, by accurately discerning genuine facts and creating new opinions and attitudes based on one's own reception of these facts. To put statements such as "Jesus is Lord" or "Short hair looks good on boys" or "Aristocratic people are very nice" on par with "2 + 2 = 4" or "Steel is harder than talc" or "Meade defeated Lee at Gettysburg" is ill-advised, since the former three are only matters of opinion and vary from culture to culture, while the latter three are facts on which all rational minds can and should agree. The second way, insofar as it is grounded in reality, is the better and more constructive means to encounter the world. The time is sad when the young are uncritical.

We need to read books. Good books. Maybe even some not-so-good books if they bring us new ideas. Banned books are the best to read. Only conservatives ban books. If they ban any particular book, then it is worth our while to find out why. That means we have to read it.

Conservatives hated Herbert Marcuse. Even leftists realized that he paled beside Hegel and Marx; but his *One-Dimensional Man: Studies in the Ideology of Advanced Industrial Society* soon became a key document of the New Left. His writings were sometimes historically inaccurate and philosophically sloppy, but his imaginative analysis of modern technological, hierarchical, capitalist society won many converts. Some even called him "Father of the New Left" for his advocacy of constant social critique, unfettered dissent, and perpetual revolution. This designation embarrassed him because he knew that he did not deserve it. Even though fragmented and undirected, the New Left had existed long before *One-Dimensional Man*.

Marcuse had been Martin Heidegger's student at the University of Freiburg, where he had written his doctoral dissertation on Hegel's philosophy of history in 1922. A Jew, he had immigrated to America in 1933 to escape the Nazis. At the time of *One-Dimensional Man* he was teaching at Brandeis University, but moved to the University of California, San Diego, in 1965. Among his students were Abbie Hoffman at Brandeis and Angela Davis at both Brandeis and San Diego. Earlier books that prepared his way toward writing *One-Dimensional Man* were *Reason and Revolution: Hegel and the Rise of Social Theory* in 1941, *Eros and Civilization: A Philosophical Inquiry into Freud* in 1955, and *Soviet Marxism* in 1958. The Freud book laid out many of the values that utopian leftists would adopt in the sixties. The Marx book argued that twentieth-century communist governments were too nationalistic and thus untrue to Marx's collectivist principles.

To be "one-dimensional" was to be a cog in the industrial, commercial, economic machine and to have no life outside that. Middle-class white-collar and even blue-collar workers became one-dimensional as they became better paid and began to acquire and take for granted luxuries that would have been reserved for the uppermost classes as recently as the late nineteenth or early twentieth century. As they grew ever more dependent on ever speedier and more complicated technological advances for their wealth and luxuries, technology enslaved them. But they did not mind. They loved being rich in the luxuriant modern world and did not care that they had in the process lost their freedom, individuality, and dignity. They had succumbed to what Nietzsche called "despicable ease."

Marcuse argued that a one-dimensional person not only would not, but in fact could not think outside the domain of discourse established by the prevailing socioeconomic and sociopolitical system. This was even true in academia. Students, teachers, and professors who believed that they were coming up with new ideas were really just reinterpreting the system. Their criticisms did not threaten it at all. On the contrary, their criticisms actually strengthened the system, because their ideas could be expressed only within the context of the system; because giving thinkers the illusion of true freedom by protecting their free speech increased the system's measure of control over potential troublemakers; and because of what Marcuse would call in 1965 "repressive tolerance," the system's built-in defense mechanism against new ideologies. Thus these academics, despite whatever may have been their own deepest intentions, were really doing doctrinal theology, not speculative, open-ended philosophy, and their god was technology. The system, having institutionalized and routinized freedom itself, perverted the very concept of freedom and in so doing rendered the actualization of true freedom impossible.

Science and technology instrumentalized nature. That is, they modified the human planet so that the very act of staying alive was no longer a daily struggle. Things that did not even exist in the nineteenth century became everyday necessities in twentieth-century industrialized societies. This was the "pacification of existence," the key premise of *One-Dimensional Man*. The technological pacification of existence enabled a worldwide plutocratic oligarchy to control nearly the whole human race by the economic domination of the lower classes, the creation of a permanent underclass through the welfare system, the exploitation of the third world and its raw industrial materials, and the constant warring in third-world countries that ensured peace at home for first- and second-world countries while providing them with a dependable permanent market for arms sales. As soon as the powers-that-be discovered that nearly everyone was willing to sell freedom for comfort and to give up almost every aspect of human dignity if well paid, then those powers began investing heavily in technology in order to implement and solidify this new, invincible, and so far foolproof means of social control. Any white man in any country was free to join the oligarchy if he played the game, conformed, and embraced greed as his primary virtue.

These features of the pacification of existence were all essential components of the technological and industrial progress by which humankind was gradually and inexorably reduced to the comfortable status of well-fed cattle, or to what Marcuse called the "happy consciousness." Material luxuries penetrated modern life to the extent that the "loss of conscience due to the satisfactory liberties granted by an unfree society [made] for a *happy consciousness* which facilitate[d] acceptance of the misdeeds of society. It [was] the token of declining autonomy and comprehension."[15] In other words, modern happiness was shallow. By implication — and Hegel's analysis concurred — the "unhappy consciousness" was deep. For Hegel in the *Phenomenology*, the unhappy consciousness emerged from recognizing the "inverted world" in which the expected natural positions of the sensible and the supersensible were reversed, from consequent stoicism, then from consequent skepticism. It led to doubt, despair, and eventually religion. Thus, seen under the aspect of the entire dialectic, it was really a perverse kind of hope. But Marcuse's happy consciousness contrasted sharply with Hegel's unhappy consciousness by being hopelessness itself — albeit not recognizing itself as hopeless. It was — and remains — the grand delusion.

Marcuse's book was not entirely coherent, but resonated with intellectuals who, like the beats of the fifties, felt alienated from mainstream American society and did not know why. Few people agreed with *One-Dimensional Man*, but many college students knew it and talked about it. It made us think about ways we might

---

[15] Herbert Marcuse, *One-Dimensional Man: Studies in the Ideology of Advanced Industrial Society* (Boston: Beacon, 1964), Chapter 3, "The Conquest of the Unhappy Consciousness: Repressive Desublimation," p. 76 (Marcuse's italics).

develop to make sure that our social criticism would be heard by the warmongers, segregationists, traditionalist bosses, technocrats, stuffed shirts, money-grubbers, ass-kissers, phonies, Babbitts, and anyone else who needed to hear it. We at least took Marcuse more seriously than the system took us.

Comedy is also a good way to learn how to be critical. Listen between the comedian's lines. A trove of sociopolitical information lies there. Most comedy, and almost all good comedy, is born of *pathos*, even the gentle humor in the fifteen bits on Bill Cosby's *I Started Out as a Child*.

The October 1964 *Mad* contained, again, the expected mean-spirited jab at the Beatles, but also several gems, such as "If Celebrities Ran for Political Office" and "Etiquette." The targets of the month were phoniness, snobbishness, and hypocrisy — just the things we noticed every day in our parents and loved to see satirized, mainly because we were powerless to do anything about them at home. The December 1964 issue continued jabbing at the tobacco industry, TV, movies, advertising, and the oppression of the poor by the rich; but its best bit was a six-page conjecture, "When Today's Celebrities Become Tomorrow's Historical Heroes."

Richard Brautigan's first novel, *A Confederate General from Big Sur*, was, like his subsequent nine, a quirky mélange of incongruous juxtapositions, mellow humor, bizarre observations, even more bizarre interpretations, absurdity, nonsense, streams-of-consciousness, free associations, abrupt breaks, and just plain fun. His main goal seems to have been to write books that would be fun to read. A brief sample from the first chapter demonstrates the typical Brautigan:

> I've heard that the population of Big Sur in those Civil War days was mostly just some Digger Indians. I've heard that the Digger Indians down there didn't wear any clothes. They didn't have any fire or shelter or culture. They didn't grow anything. They didn't hunt and they didn't fish. They didn't bury their dead or give birth to their children. They lived on roots and limpets and sat pleasantly out in the rain.
>
> I can imagine the expression on General Robert E. Lee's face when this gang showed up, bearing strange gifts from the Pacific Ocean.
>
> It was during the second day of the Battle of the Wilderness. ...
>
> When Lee got to the rear of the lines, there were the 8th Big Sur Volunteer Heavy Root Eaters reporting for duty. The air around them was filled with the smell of roots and limpets. The 8th Big Sur Volunteer Heavy Root Eaters reported like autumn to the Army of Northern Virginia.
>
> They all gathered around Lee's horse and stared in amazement, for it was the first time that they had ever seen a horse. One of the Digger Indians offered Traveller a limpet to eat.
>
> When I first heard about Big Sur I didn't know that it was part of the defunct Confederate States of America, a country that went out of style like an idea or a lampshade or some kind of food that people don't cook any more, once the favorite dish in thousands of homes.

You can see why we loved this stuff! Brautigan's poetry and prose contributed heavily toward defining the wacko California and especially San Francisco mystique that by 1967 had come to characterize the sixties. Somehow — who knows how? — it made us think.

Ω

On the strength of just one song, "House of the Rising Sun," the Animals were huge that fall. The Rolling Stones, already with a whole slew of great songs to their credit, were not yet quite that big. Both groups appeared on *Ed Sullivan* that October, but the Animals, at least for the time being, seemed to have the bigger impact. The Stones' second album, *12 x 5*, — twelve songs by five dudes, get it? — began to change that, began to establish them as the group that would be universally acknowledged by the time of *Beggar's Banquet* at the end of 1968 as "The Greatest Rock-and-Roll Band in the World."

12 x 5 had seven covers and five originals. Two of the originals, "Empty Heart," a blues number about contemplating suicide, and "2120 South Michigan Avenue," an instrumental referring to the Chicago address of the legendary blues label, Chess Records, were credited to Nanker Phelge. This name was Brian Jones's pseudonym for the whole group. "Nanker" was a crasis of two British slang terms, "nankie," a pompous or officious little man, and "wanker," a masturbator. In Brian's terminology, a "nanker" was a particular grimace he made to mock the upper class by pushing up the tip of his nose with his middle finger while pulling down his lower eyelids with his first and third fingers. "Phelge" was from James ("Jimmy") Phelge, who roomed with Mick, Keith, and Brian at 102 Edith Grove, Chelsea, in the early sixties.

The three songs written by Jagger/Richards were omens of future achievement. Their "Good Times, Bad Times" may have been the first explicitly antiwar song to come out of the British Invasion. Its last verse proclaimed that, without worldwide trust, there was no alternative except war. "Congratulations" was a sarcastic sneer at the girl who just dumped the singer. "Grown Up Wrong" told of a girl losing her childhood too soon. These were not the "silly love songs" that Lennon/McCartney were churning out. Stones lyrics were full of innuendos, raunchiness, and just plain sleaze. The Stones were beginning to cultivate their bad boy reputation.

One of Mick's girlfriends, Marianne Faithfull, "covered" the alleged Mick Jagger / Andrew Loog Oldham / Keith Richards composition, "As Tears Go By," which the Stones themselves would not release for over a year. She would later claim to have written it herself. Maybe she did; maybe not.

Almost as big as the Animals and the Rolling Stones that fall was another new British band, the Kinks.

"You Really Got Me" was as much a milestone in rock history as "Heartbreak Hotel," "I Want to Hold Your Hand," *Sgt. Pepper's Lonely Hearts Club Band*, *Tommy*, or "Stairway to Heaven." It only went as high as number seven on the *Billboard Hot 100*, but the song introduced the power chord. Kinks co-founders

Ray and Dave Davies invented power-chord rock. "Invent" is not too strong a term. They really did invent it. No one had done it before, but nearly every rock band has done it since. Power-chord rock is music based on a two-note electric guitar chord, either a perfect fifth or, if inverted, a perfect fourth, played extra loud with a hard downstroke and with the living crap distorted out of it. Other guitarists, notably Link Wray, had used heavy two-note chords earlier, but the extreme distortion was the Kinks' innovation. Ray and Dave came up with it in the front room of their parents' house, as Ray described in his "unauthorized autobiography":

> Once David brought home a little 8-watt valve amplifier that he got in a secondhand shop. It became known as "the green amp." ... David took some of Mum's knitting needles and stuck them into the speakers of the little green amp. He christened it the fart box. ... I sat down in the front room one day and started to write a song on the old upright. ... Then I called Dave in ... and he picked up his guitar and plugged into the green amp. He started playing along with the riff I was punching out with my left hand. As the amp warmed up I heard that wonderful distorted sound. It was a perfect representation of my anger, and yet beautiful at the same time ... I had written "You Really Got Me," and it had happened in the front room because all important things happened there.[16]

Until 1966 and from 1969 all through the seventies we would gradually discover that Ray was a popular music genius, perhaps one of the most self-deprecating yet also one of the most inspired popular music geniuses of all time. Along with Pete Townshend, Jagger/Richards, Lennon/McCartney, Paul Simon, Joni Mitchell, and Neil Young, Ray became one of a handful of truly marvelous non-Brill-Building songwriters of the sixties and beyond.

Another rock music milestone at the end of 1964 was the Beatles' "I Feel Fine," which was mostly a Lennon product. It was the first recorded instance of deliberate feedback in a commercially released song. John, who had inserted the feedback, famously defied anyone to find an earlier instance. Perhaps even more significantly, it also marked a surge in the popularity of riff-driven, guitar-oriented rock songs. A riff is a short, catchy, repeated melodic phrase. Its shortness, usually no longer than a bar or two, its typical heaviness, and its stubborn recurrence provide the basic rhythm of the song. Music purists call it by its Italian name, *ostinato*. "I Feel Fine" was by no means the first riff-driven, guitar-oriented rock song — "You Really Got Me," slightly earlier, was another — but it paved the way for the greatest classics of that genre, such as "Satisfaction," "Sunshine of Your Love," "Smoke on the Water," and most of the Led Zeppelin catalog.

The flipside of "I Feel Fine," "She's a Woman," featured Paul on lead vocal suggesting that a woman's greatest asset would be her loyalty to her man. Another "silly love song," but maybe just a tad deeper than his earlier ones. Even deeper was his "I'll Follow the Sun." Beatles lyrics were starting to get interesting. Of the other eight songs besides these three on the *Beatles 65* album, five (John's

---

[16] Ray Davies, *X-Ray* (Woodstock, N.Y.: Overlook Press, 1995), pp. 32-33, 62-63.

"No Reply," "I'm a Loser," and "I'll Be Back"; John's and Paul's "Baby's in Black"; and Ringo's cover of Carl Perkins's "Honey Don't") were about lost or tenuous loves. The rest were covers. John covered Roy Lee Johnson's "Mr. Moonlight" and, as what was obviously a heartfelt tribute, Chuck Berry's "Rock and Roll Music." Just for fun, George did Perkins's "Everybody's Trying to Be My Baby."

As the Beatles had given the entire rock-and-roll industry a gigantic boost, demand increased in 1964 for more teen music on TV than just *American Bandstand*. Two new shows that responded to this demand were *The Lloyd Thaxton Show* and *Shindig*.

Lloyd Thaxton was a Dick Clark clone, a bit wackier, but, if possible, less adventurous in his musical taste. His local Los Angeles teen music and dance show on KCOP TV immediately became very popular nationally when it went into syndication. Yet Lloyd was stuck in a time warp. He never progressed beyond a Pat Boone / Everly Brothers / Connie Francis soft rock mentality. He was slick but goofy, nattily dressed but old-fashioned in his outlook, a confirmed adult hooked on teen idols, surf music, and beach movies. His show was fun but fluffy.

Shindig had fewer gimmicks, less comedy, and better music. It was a key venue for showcasing British Invasion acts in America. Among the musicians that appeared on *Shindig* in its first few months were the Beatles, the Dave Clark Five, the Supremes, the Righteous Brothers, the Isley Brothers, Roy Orbison, Johnny Rivers, Gale Garnett, Manfred Mann, Sam Cooke, the Newbeats, Aretha Franklin, Marvin Gaye, Mary Wells, the Everly Brothers, and the Beach Boys. Before it ended its eighty-five-episode run just over a year later it would have the Rolling Stones, the Who, the Kinks, the Yardbirds, the Moody Blues, the Animals, Johnny Cash, Herman's Hermits, Petula Clark, the Beau Brummels, the Standells, the Four Tops, Ray Charles, Howlin' Wolf, the Zombies, Jackie DeShannon, the Byrds, the Sir Douglas Quintet, Donovan, Bo Diddley, James Brown, the Turtles, Booker T. and the M.G.s, the Lovin' Spoonful, Barry McGuire, the Hollies, the Kingsmen, and the Mamas and the Papas. We watched it every chance we got and we missed it when it was cancelled.

Despite our search for authenticity in songwriting and our growing distrust of cover tunes, the Brill Building continued to contribute mightily to our culture. Its Jeff Barry and Ellie Greenwich penned "Do Wah Diddy Diddy," a huge hit for South African - British keyboardist Michael Lubowitz and his five-piece band, Manfred Mann. With Shadow Morton, Barry and Greenwich also wrote and produced the Shangri-Las' "Leader of the Pack," one of the weirdest and most durable in the "teen death rock" genre that had been popular since the late fifties.

From 1955, when they were fourteen, until 1963 two soft-spoken guys from Queens, New York, made music under the pseudonyms Tom Graph and Jerry Landis ("Tom and Jerry"). In 1957 they had a minor hit with "Hey Schoolgirl" and did a gig on the November 22, 1957 *American Bandstand*. They continued sporadically in music as Tom went to Columbia University to study mathematics and Jerry went to Queens College to study English literature. In late 1964 they recorded an acoustic folk album, *Wednesday Morning, 3 A.M.*, consisting of three traditional songs, one Dylan song, three other covers, and five of Jerry's original songs. Released under their real names, [Paul ("Jerry")] Simon and [Art ("Tom")] Garfunkel, this album made almost no impact.

Ω

Spies kept creeping into our consciousness. On September 22 we were first permitted access to Del Floria's Tailor Shop somewhere in Manhattan's east forties, the main of several secret entrances to the New York headquarters of U.N.C.L.E. (United Network Command for Law and Enforcement). As did S.P.E.C.T.R.E., the U.N.C.L.E. organization transcended the Cold War, but on the good side. Its usual foe was a S.P.E.C.T.R.E.-like bunch of baddies, T.H.R.U.S.H. (Technological Hierarchy for the Removal of Undesirables and the Subjugation of Humanity). *The Man from U.N.C.L.E.* was a subtly satirical, borderline campy series. The witty exchanges among the two top U.N.C.L.E. agents, Napoleon Solo, Robert Vaughn's suave Bond-like American, and Illya Kuryakin, David McCallum's cheeky Russian with the blond Beatle haircut, and their British chief, Leo G. Carroll's venerable Alexander Waverly, were as funny as Connery's repartee in the Bond films or the Beatles' banter in *A Hard Day's Night*. The plots were farfetched, but no more so than those of the Bond stories that they parodied with uncanny precision. In a TV world that would soon become awash in spy shows ranging from the sophisticated (*The Avengers, I Spy*) to the suspenseful (*Secret Agent*) to the asinine (*Get Smart*), *The Man from U.N.C.L.E.*, at least through its second season, remained the standard of quality against which the others were measured.

The best Christmas present we got in 1964 was *Goldfinger*, the third James Bond movie. It was more entertaining, but much less plausible than *From Russia With Love*, particularly the 60,000-person death pantomime complete with phony car crash. It had funnier jokes but duller characters than its two predecessors. It was the first Bond film to go hogwild with gadgets, gizmos, and doohickeys, thus shifting the emphasis on Bond from his wits to his arsenal. Both the Cold War and S.P.E.C.T.R.E were absent. Auric Goldfinger, with no national, organizational, or ideological loyalties, was just a common criminal writ large.

Those of us who knew the books immediately thought that Gert Fröbe — fine actor though he was — was miscast as Goldfinger. With his big, grotesque, red body, he would have made a perfect Hugo Drax in *Moonraker*. Even Fröbe's portrayal of Goldfinger as a boorish lout reminded us of Drax. To present Goldfinger as Fleming created him, Harry Saltzman and Cubby Broccoli would have done better to introduce a short, thickset Latvian character actor who could have dyed his hair red and affected a British accent.

James Bond, perpetually thirty-five, was a link between our parents' generation and ours. No one did not love him. He was something that the two opposing generations could enjoy together. He was plainly a member of their generation, a Cold Warrior, a vicious, violent killer. Not quite amoral, but certainly ruthless. Not quite Nietzschean, but still a complex, unique individual. Not quite emotionless, but certainly in control. His character showed us that through self-mastery it was possible not to make mistakes. That was enviable. To err is human; not to err is superhuman. Certainly he had more of Ian Fleming's and Broccoli/Saltzman's aesthetic sensibilities than ours. In *Goldfinger* he insulted the Beatles. To love him was a living contradiction for our generation. Yet we did love him — in spades. He was debonair, worldly, deadly, sexy, even elegant — all the things that we dowdy kids were not, and never really aspired to be. He was not a role model for us, but the epitome of our deepest, keenest sociosexual fantasies. He supplied the daydreams and appealed to the bruised egos of the frustrated lover, the frustrated winner, the frustrated hero, the frustrated everyone. For us white heterosexual males, young or old, rich or poor, he could do everything. We wanted to have his resourcefulness, but not in his line of work. We wanted his level of success with women, but with homegrown chicks, not his exotic beauties. Oh, how we envied him! But why? He really was kind of a shit.

Spring 1965

Not by any means, but by any means necessary

1965 was the year that rock music got serious. Two completely different influences dominated this transition: from London, the Rolling Stones, who made black music palatable to a diversified white audience; and from Los Angeles, the Byrds, who made Dylan and folk music palatable to a mainstream, rock-oriented audience.

Whenever musicians and listeners take each other seriously, music ceases to be mere entertainment and instead assumes the power of a driving social force. But when does such mutual respect occur? When the lyrics carry some weight and relate directly to what the listeners care about most deeply in their everyday lives. When the tunes are not only catchy, but also innovative, accessible, and powerful enough to make the listeners want to forget everything else — at least for the time being. Above all, when the listeners are the musicians and the musicians are the listeners, i.e., when the music comes from the people, not from hack songwriters in Tin Pan Alley.

For example, songs like "Don't Let Me Be Misunderstood," "We Gotta Get Out of This Place," and "It's My Life" by the Animals sounded gritty, plebian, and honest. They spoke to life as we knew it and they stayed with us. Even though the composers and lyricists of these three songs (respectively: Bennie Benjamin / Sol Marcus / Gloria Caldwell; Barry Mann / Cynthia Weil; Roger Atkins / Carl D'Errico) all had Tin Pan Alley or Brill Building connections, they definitely did not sound like it when the Animals recorded their stuff. Eric Burdon had a knack for bringing music and lyrics down to earth. By contrast, when Frank Sinatra released a song in a similar thematic vein, "My Way" in 1969, he still sounded more like a rich bastard than a Hoboken slum kid. Sinatra was false to his working class roots; but Burdon and, later, Bruce Springsteen, were consummately true to theirs.

Black music, which had been sanitized for white audiences in the fifties, now arrived raw, clean, and powerful, not only through American blacks such as Wilson Pickett, James Brown, and B.B. King, but also indirectly via British groups, especially the Stones. American white performers were Johnny-come-lately in this regard. But once we young whites heard this magnificent black music in all its strength, how could we not admire the remarkable race that originated it? Music is not only the universal language, but also the great human unifier. Through our love of black music, we learned to treat blacks as our equals. Different human groups can never appreciate each other until and unless they appreciate — and even love — each other's music.

Yet America remained a deeply racist society. On February 21 we lost Malcolm X. Despite the fact that three or five black men from the Nation of Islam (the "Black Muslims") killed him, it can still be seen as a racist killing, because its motives were grounded in conflict within the civil rights movement. The FBI and the KKK must have been delighted. A week earlier unknown thugs, likely from the Nation of Islam, had firebombed his home. The Nation of Islam had marked him for death since he split from it in March 1964, criticizing its leader, Elijah Muhammad, partly on issues of civil rights strategy and tactics. A rising Black Muslim honcho, former calypso singer and violinist Louis Farrakhan,[17] had denounced Malcolm, his mentor, as a heretic — and this denunciation may have led directly to the murder. The Nation of Islam was a militant, defiantly separatist group, but Malcolm was beginning to move in several promising new directions toward a more inclusive approach that would be more accepting of whites and less accepting of violence. He had not turned this corner yet, but he was on his way. His April 1964 pilgrimage to Mecca had opened his eyes to what he considered "true Islam." Upon his return, he founded the Organization of Afro-American Unity (OAAU), a secular group with higher, more universalist ideals than the Nation of Islam had. When he died, he was still on this spiritual, psychological, and political journey to overcome his harsh midwestern origins and the typical indignities he felt as a black American in white America.[18] His OAAU soon thereafter fell apart. Who knows what heights of socioracial progress he would have achieved if he had lived?

In January 1965 *Mad* magazine continued its attacks on phoniness, advertising, and racism, and included a feature that replaced dialogue in modern situations with quotations from Shakespeare. The racism bit suggested that other nations might see our justice system as dominated by the KKK. The next issue, March 1965, pushed this theme further by showing foreign visitors to America victimized by crime, rudeness, and bigotry. That issue also included scathing views of advertising, status-seeking, hypocrisy, and children's TV. The April issue sent up James Bond, home study courses, pop psychology, and of course, advertising. Racism and advertising, advertising and racism, went together like hand and glove. Did we

---

[17] Farrakhan gave up music for religion. The Nation of Islam Web site <www.noi.org/ mlfbio.htm> reports: "Although music had been his first love, within three months after joining the Nation of Islam in 1955, Minister Malcolm X told the New York Mosque and the new convert Louis X that Elijah Muhammad had said that all Muslims would have to get out of show business or get out of the Temple. Most of the musicians left Temple No. 7, but Louis X, later renamed Louis Farrakhan, chose to dedicate his life to the Teachings of the Honorable Elijah Muhammad."

[18] For example, his estate's official Web site <www.cmgww.com/historic/malcolm/about/ bio.htm> contains this passage: "He graduated from junior high at the top of his class. However, when a favorite teacher told Malcolm his dream of becoming a lawyer was 'no realistic goal for a nigger', Malcolm lost interest in school."

see any people of color plugging products on network TV or in mainstream magazines? Ah well, it was our parents' world, not ours. If we had been writing the ads, things would have been different. Ray Charles and Chuck Berry would have been right up there with Bob Hope and Jack Benny selling cars and cigarettes.

Our parents were about to become the victims of their self-created paradox. Hoist on their own petard. On the one hand, they had taught us to be strong, proud, resourceful, and independent. That was, after all, the American way. They were not only bound by religious and patriotic duty, but also honored and gratified, to teach us these values. But on the other hand, they had also planned our lives for us. They had unilaterally decided how we would dress, how we would wear our hair, which youth clubs we would join, which forms of speech we would use in company, whom we would befriend and whom we would shun, which schools and colleges we would attend, which careers we would follow, how much money we would make, which values we would hold, and sometimes even which ethnic or religious groups we would hate. Their decisions in this regard were strictly arbitrary, because they did not respect us as persons, but treated us only as pups, as extensions of themselves, as young bodies and minds to be molded into predetermined shapes. In their view, the job of parenting was no more and no less than this process of molding us to fit their expectations.

Our parents taught us to think for ourselves, but because they believed that our opinions did not matter before we turned twenty-one, it was no wonder that we rebelled.

Our parents beat us. They called it spanking, but it was beating. "Spare the rod and spoil the child" was their watchword. They seldom used actual rods, but they used belts, hairbrushes, rulers, flat hands, fists, and fingernails. As they had taken this violent shit from our grandparents, and had been eventually grateful for it, the idea apparently never occurred to them that we should not likewise take it from them and be likewise eventually grateful. Our parents beating us might have made some of us obedient, but it also made us cold and mean — just like them. It also made us resentful, unlike them. They had not resented our grandparents for beating them, but we certainly resented them for beating us. I do not know why this should have been so, yet that was the fact. While they had meekly submitted to our grandparents abusing them, believing that they deserved it; we resisted, ran away, and sometimes even fought back when they tried to abuse us. We knew that we did not deserve it. Thank God that a few of us in the mid-sixties began to see the need to break forever this cycle of parents' physical violence toward children. To avoid growing up to be cold and mean, we had to get away, break away, do whatever was necessary — and we did it. We had to teach our parents that unspoiled kids could be raised without using violent punishments, threats, or bribery, but only such measures as groundings, time outs, denials of privileges, and plain, simple reason. In the seventies, with the anti-spanking battle mostly won, we would turn our attention to the even larger problem of husbands beating wives, boyfriends beating girlfriends, etc.

Why did we give more credibility to rock musicians than to our parents? The musicians did not order us around. They looked like us, dressed like us, thought like us, dreamed like us. They were us! Our parents, on the other hand, were the ultimate "them"! They set themselves up against us, trying to pull us into their world. That older world was alien, humorless, hierarchical, and frightening, but our (brave) new world, the musician's world, was familiar, comforting, colorful, hopeful, joyous, egalitarian, and fun.

But musicians did drugs. Lots of drugs.

The sixties have the reputation for being a drug-crazed era, but in reality people then used intoxicating substances neither more nor less than in any other era. This undeserved reputation derives from three factors:

1. New drugs became available and older drugs became better known. For example, LSD, first synthesized in 1938, became well known as a hallucinogen in the sixties through the efforts of Timothy Leary, Owsley Stanley, Ken Kesey, Tom Wolfe, John Lennon, *et al.*
2. Our parents harbored a lot of just plain wrong information about drugs, except benzedrine and alcohol. This *Reefer Madness* mentality dominated their generation.
3. The press gave way too much hyperbolic, sensationalist publicity to drugs.

The typical intoxicant-of-choice for kids who did not think about life or politics and only cared about parties and pleasure was beer. At some further point, when circumstances forced them to confront life and politics, they simply adopted whatever choice in sociopolitics seemed easiest, usually whatever beliefs their parents and peers shared, because they had not given and would not ever give these serious issues any serious thought. As these straight kids grew to be like their parents — and ours — they may have moved on to stronger liquor, but would more naturally stick with beer, the ultimate elixir of sociopolitical conservatives.

To use marijuana at all, on the other hand, at least until it becomes legal, requires already a certain willingness to defy the status quo, to distance oneself from one's parents, or simply to be different.

Marijuana was everywhere. It was cheap — dirt cheap. Throughout the latter half of the sixties and well into the seventies we could safely buy mediocre marijuana for $10, $12, or $15 an ounce and really excellent marijuana for $20 or $25. The most common deal was $20 an ounce. One quarter of this (a "nickel bag") cost $5. We could roll a lot of joints from an ounce.

Other drugs were scarcer and more expensive. Even a confirmed "head" who smoked marijuana every day could easily go for years without encountering LSD, mescaline, peyote, cocaine, opium, or even heroin. These other drugs got more publicity than they probably deserved. Many of them, such as methedrine, were dangerous. Marijuana did not lead to them.

The fact is that, except for the possibility of respiratory system damage from the smoke, marijuana is safer than beer and no more dangerous than tobacco. It is so benign that it should hardly count as a drug at all.

Reefer Madness, originally called *Tell Your Children*, was a low-budget, 66-minute, anti-drug, Hollywood propaganda film made in 1936. It was intended seriously; our parents took it seriously; but we laughed our asses off at it. It was false! We knew perfectly well that marijuana does not cause incurable insanity or create killers, libertines, and jazz aficionados out of ordinary people, as this movie would have had us believe. Mid-sixties college students discovered it in the redistribution vaults and began showing it in campus theaters and fraternity houses as a comedy. Shortly after R. Keith Stroup founded the National Association for the Reform of Marijuana Laws (NORML) in 1970, NORML began plugging the film like crazy. Its very absurdity made it one of most rational pro-legalization tools.

We experienced drugs through music, took advantage of musicians' almost natural inclination to indulge in drugs, and shamelessly used these musicians as our stand-ins and guinea pigs. If they did it, and communicated the experience to us accurately in their songs, then we did not have to do it. Like Jesus on the cross, they did it for us. Thus we got all the enjoyment with none of the risk. Watching our favorite musicians burn out on drugs — Brian Jones, Janis Joplin, Jimi Hendrix, Jim Morrison, Keith Richards, Ozzy Osbourne — was for some of us a sufficient warning, but for others of us it was a dare. While the vicarious experience of drugs through musicians was enough to satisfy the curiosity of many of us, their music tempted others of us to experiment, even as dangerously as, or more dangerously than, our druggy musician heroes did. Of course it was the risk-taking minority, not the sufficiently warned majority, who got the lion's share of the publicity. That is why the perception persists of the sixties as a drug-crazed era and of us as drug-crazed wackos.

There was a synesthesia of music, theater, literature, and the plastic arts, all influenced by drugs, that blended into one another, bolstered one another, and expressed the drug experience for non-users, less experienced users, and ultra-experienced users alike. Into this synesthesia came Peter Max, whose cartoonish surrealism defined visual psychedelia with bright primary colors in unexpected positions and juxtapositions. His so-called "Cosmic Art" found frequent commercial application, which provided more ammunition for his detractors, but we welcomed seeing his prints whenever we could. They brought much-needed color into a gray world.

Snobs differentiated between entertainment and art. We did not. Art was art and entertainment was entertainment, but if entertainment was good entertainment, or if it had meaning, then it was art. It required skill to produce it; thus it was art. For them Peter Max, Andy Warhol, rock music, etc., were (bad) entertainment and not art; for us they were art and (good) entertainment.

Ω

When *Hullabaloo* began on NBC in January, we recognized right away that, musically, it was not as good as *Shindig*, but better than *Lloyd Thaxton* and *American Bandstand*. Each episode had a guest host, mostly crooners. The hosts of the first few months were Jack Jones, Paul Anka, LBJ's daughter Lynda Bird's actor boyfriend George Hamilton, Frank Sinatra, Jr., Gary Crosby, Frankie Avalon, Annette

Funicello, Sammy Davis, Jr., Trini Lopez, Bobby Vinton, and so on in that vein. You get the idea. Not exactly edgy rockers!

Nevertheless, *Hullabaloo* had some good acts. The Zombies and the New Christy Minstrels were on the first show; the Nashville Teens, Marianne Faithfull, and Johnny Rivers on the second; the Supremes on the third; Marvin Gaye on the fourth; Judy Collins, the Shangri-Las, and Herman's Hermits on the fifth; the Kinks on the sixth along with the Beatles' manager Brian Epstein interviewing the Stones' manager Andrew Loog Oldham; the Beau Brummels and the Searchers on the seventh; Lesley Gore on the eighth; and so on. These acts were mostly shown in small bits among the likes of Liza Minnelli, Joey Heatherton, and the Hanover, New Jersey, High School Marching Band — I kid you not! *Hullabaloo* was altogether very middle-of-the-road, a poor attempt to be both intergenerationally appealing like *Ed Sullivan* and at the same time "hip," "with it," or whatever else could be described by whatever other terms the pseudo-hepcats were using as honorific adjectives in those days. Generally it was just plain slick and phony.

Yet serious rock was booming. The Kinks' music was becoming more complex. "All Day and All of the Night" was pretty much just a hard rock imitation of "You Really Got Me," but "Tired of Waiting for You" was a gentle, melancholy minor key tune built on a simple but evocative eight-note riff: B-D-G-B-A-C-F-A. Moreover, the lyrics affirmed that one's life is one's own, even in matters of the heart. That flew in the face of Dion and his ilk who believed in the "great American romance." Like "Stop Your Sobbing" on their first album, "Tired of Waiting for You" on their second foreshadowed Ray Davies's eventual songwriting brilliance. Also on *Kinks-Size* was "I Gotta Move," a riff-driven song about love and fashion among London's mods, and "Come On Now," a Beatlish number whose riff sounds sort of like that in "I Feel Fine."

Early 1965 was kind of a lull for Beatles music. All they released of consequence were "Eight Days a Week" and "Ticket to Ride," both solid rockers but neither especially groundbreaking. We knew that they were filming their second movie, *Help!*, so we were willing to wait.

The Stones, on the other hand, were breaking a lot of ground. "Heart of Stone" was about the heaviest blues we had heard up to that point. Brian Jones's ringing guitar riff in "The Last Time" pushed riff-driven rock up a notch. Many years later we would discover that the Stones (and the Yardbirds and Led Zeppelin and any number of other white blues bands) had been ripping off black blues and gospel artists, but at the time we had not yet heard any of that wonderful black music. In early 1965, as far as we were concerned, the Stones were the blues incarnate. The music dated back to the fifties, forties, and even thirties, but it was new to us. We white kids then knew nothing of the Delta or Chicago blues traditions. We had no idea who Robert Johnson was. But we knew what we liked.

The American debut of the Who came in February with "I Can't Explain," but, even though this was one of their greatest singles, hardly anyone noticed. They would not appear on *Shindig* until October 2, December 9, and December 30, would never appear on *Ed Sullivan*, and would not tour the United States until 1967. Until they hit with "Happy Jack" early in 1967, few Americans knew about them.

The Yardbirds' first American hit, "For Your Love," was also the last time that Eric Clapton would play guitar for the group. He believed that this song, with its harpsichord and other un-blues-y touches, was too commercial. He wanted to play genuine blues, and so deserted the Yardbirds to play with John Mayall's Blues-breakers. The irony is that Clapton in the seventies became more commercial than the Yardbirds ever were.

Black music — i.e., real, gritty, down-to-earth black music, not just Mo-town — was beginning to become better known and to get airplay on white radio, particularly on top forty AM stations. Thanks to the Animals, Kinks, and Stones, previously placid white kids were demanding heavier music — and that generally meant black music. Songs like "Shotgun" by Junior Walker and the All-Stars and "Hold On! I'm a-Comin'" by Sam and Dave began to educate white audiences as to what soul music was all about.

B.B. King and his Gibson six-string, Lucille, had been entertaining black audiences since the forties. They generally acknowledged him as the greatest living bluesman. But whites did not know about him. His breakthrough to interracial appreciation came in early 1965 with the release of *Live at the Regal*, recorded at his November 21, 1964 performance at the Regal Theater[19] in the heart of southside Chicago's black ghetto. This magnificent album contained tight rhythms, tasty horns, heartfelt singing, sad stories, and B.B.'s precise, mellow, guitar licks. His seven-piece band was absolutely solid. The set ranged from old blues numbers like his and Jules Taub's "Sweet Little Angel," John Lee Hooker's "It's My Own Fault," Victoria Spivey's and Noble Floyd's "You Done Lost Your Good Thing Now," and Jane and Leonard Feather's "How Blue Can You Get" to newer tunes like Joe Josea's and Maxwell Davis's "You Upset Me Baby" and Charles Singleton's "Help the Poor." Within a few years he would be playing in Bill Graham's Fill-mores, Las Vegas nightclubs, and on national tours with major white rock acts like the Stones.

Black assertiveness was starting to show in stand-up comedy for white audiences. On May 9, those of us who were lucky enough to see the first of Richard Pryor's thirteen appearances on *Ed Sullivan* witnessed the first national exposure of the black Lenny Bruce. Of course, he did not do any of that sort of material on Ed's show; but we could see right away that he was proud of his blackness, that he was raunchier than Bill Cosby and at least as funny, and that he might be dangerous. We were not surprised when his first comedy albums came out in the late sixties with warning labels for language because he used words like "nigger" and "motherfucker." His eponymous debut album in 1968 showed him dressed in only a loincloth with a bone through his nose and other Stone Age jewelry, holding a primitive bow and arrows, squatting in front of a cave, and looking like a typical

---

[19] Built in 1928 and demolished in 1973, the Regal was at 4719 South Parkway, i.e., 4719 South King Drive. In August 1968, just before the opening of the Democratic National Convention, Mayor Richard J. Daley, one of Martin Luther King's most fervent enemies, in a typical display of hypocrisy, insincerity, cynicism, and political opportunism, renamed it Dr. Martin Luther King Drive.

sullen black savage on a *National Geographic* cover. Tracks on that album included "Super Nigger," "Farting," "Prison Play," and the classic "Army Life." His tagline was, "That nigger's crazy!" He was too. And funny as shit.

Ω

"The Mad, Mad Tea Party Affair," the eighteenth episode and probably the most interesting of the first *Man from U.N.C.L.E.* season, ran on February 1. Nearly all the action occurred inside U.N.C.L.E. headquarters. The plot was more cerebral than most, and even the usual repartee was perhaps a tad sharper. Two infiltrators, one a real enemy from T.H.R.U.S.H., the other a slippery fellow hired by Waverly to detect flaws in the security of the building, were roaming headquarters at will. Solo and Kuryakin had to find out which was which and what they were up to. As spy shows on TV and spy movies in the theaters ran the gamut from mostly ridiculous to occasionally sublime, we welcomed the sublime — such as this episode — whenever they popped up. Neither James Bond nor U.N.C.L.E. were dependable sources of the sublime, but *Secret Agent* was.

The anglophilia that we had been nursing ever since the Beatles landed in America in February 1964 got a huge boost when Ralph Smart's erudite British spy series, *Danger Man*, renamed *Secret Agent* for American audiences, made its CBS TV debut in April. With Patrick McGoohan starring as John Drake, the show featured subtle humor, understated action, complex plots, plausible Cold War situations, excellent acting, mod clothes, and intelligent, multivalent dialogue. Johnny Rivers's hard-rocking theme song, "Secret Agent Man," of the American version made an interesting contrast to the subdued harpsichord jazz instrumental theme song of the British version (for those of us who knew both).

Danger Man had begun as a series of thirty-minute ITV shows on September 11, 1960, with John Drake working for NATO. It ran thirty-nine episodes in Britain until January 20, 1962 and in the United States twenty-four episodes on CBS from April 5 until September 13, 1961 as the Wednesday night summer replacement for *Wanted: Dead or Alive*. CBS then had no further interest in it — until 1965.

In 1964, with *Dr. No* and *From Russia With Love* both big hits and the spy fad taking hold of both Britain and America, Smart revived *Danger Man* in a one-hour format. This time Drake was working for the British Secret Service. Unlike both James Bond and Napoleon Solo, Drake relied on cunning rather than gadgets and weapons. Drake seldom carried a gun and did not indulge in much violence. He enjoyed women, gambling, alcohol, and fine food, but was not a womanizer, gourmet, or in general a glamorous spy like Bond or Solo. Drake was a thinking person's Bond at a time when TV was not ashamed to air fiction that entertained people by making them think.

Thinking was the main task of the audience of Richard Brooks's movie adaptation of Joseph Conrad's novel of psychological realism, *Lord Jim*. Its theme, the disoriented, unbalanced man in search of himself, would be revisited many times throughout the sixties, in movies, plays, books, songs, and poems. Jim, a promising young merchant ship's officer, an aloof, introverted romantic, but a man of action, exuded the nineteenth-century British attitude of natural superiority to anything non-British, particularly the squalid, teeming Asian masses. As first officer of *S.S. Patna*, an ill-captained, rusty tub en route from Java to the Red Sea, Jim fancied himself a hero, in charge of her cargo of 800 Muslims on the Hajj. Yet the voyage was to prove him overconfident in his own abilities, unstable in the face of danger, and deficient in self-knowledge. In a storm, convinced that the *Patna* was sinking, Jim's long-suppressed dread of the unpredictable turned to panic. He deserted his post and jumped for his life along with the captain and two others. Yet the *Patna* survived and even reached port ahead of Jim's lifeboat. He spent the rest of his thereafter miserable, guilt-ridden life roaming Southeast Asia and its nearby seas, trying to prove that, even if he was no hero, he was at least no coward. He fell in with gun-runners for oppressed locals, performed some heroic deeds, but could never quite purge his shame. At last he engineered his suicide as atonement for his sins and recovery of his honor.

If the movie taught us anything constructive, it was that white imperialists seeking danger and adventure would do better than to meddle in the indigenous affairs of Southeast Asia.

The satire, "Lord Jump," in the October 1965 *Mad* concentrated on the film's pessimism, mystifying existential philosophy, lack of faithfulness to the book, and — unfairly — on what it judged to be Peter O'Toole's monolithic performance in the title role.

Ω

Not coincidentally, the rise of folk rock coincided with the first deployment of American combat troops in Vietnam. Visionaries like Bob Dylan and Roger McGuinn foresaw electrifying folk music as a way to reach a wider audience with antiwar messages. The first folk rock album was an antiwar album, Dylan's *Bringing It All Back Home*, in March 1965. The first folk rock single — as well as one of the earliest examples of proto-rap — was Dylan's "Subterranean Homesick Blues," in April. The first folk rock hit on the *Billboard Hot 100* was a cover of a Dylan tune, "Mr. Tambourine Man" by McGuinn's band, the Byrds, in May. It reached number one in June.

The first American combat troops arrived in Vietnam in March. Reinforcements arrived steadily in waves for the next several months. B-52s on June 17 dropped the first American bombs in Vietnam. By the end of June 125,000 American troops were there. Altogether in 1965 LBJ added 161,000 troops to the Vietnam escalation, an increase of 691 per cent over 1964 levels.

Bringing It All Back Home was revolutionary in many ways besides being just the first folk album to use electric instruments. The cover art was weird and novel, not just the usual straight-on shot of the artist(s), but a fisheye view of Sally Grossman, Dylan's manager's wife, in a sexy red dress, smoking and lounging with Dylan in the Grossmans' cluttered living room. The liner notes, another of Dylan's beat poems, read in part:

erotic hitchhiker wearing japanese
blanket. gets my attention by asking didn't
he see me at this hootenanny down in
puerto vallarta, mexico/i say no you must
be mistaken. i happen to be one of the
Supremes/then he rips off his blanket
an' suddenly becomes a middle-aged druggist.
up for district attorney. he starts screaming at me you're the one. you're the one
that's been causing all them riots over in
vietnam. immediately turns t' a bunch of
people an' says if elected, he'll have me
electrocuted publicly on the next fourth
of july. ...
... the fact that the white house is filled with
leaders that've never been t' the apollo
theater amazes me. why allen ginsberg was
not chosen t' read poetry at the inauguration
boggles my mind/if someone thinks norman
mailer is more important than hank williams
that's fine. i have no arguments an' i
never drink milk. i would rather model harmonica holders than discuss aztec anthropology/
english literature. or history of the united
nations. i accept chaos. I am not sure whether
it accepts me. i know there're some people terrified
of the bomb. but there are other people terrified
t' be seen carrying a modern screen magazine. ...
... I am about t' sketch You
a picture of what goes on around here sometimes. though I don't understand too well
myself what's really happening. i do know
that we're all gonna die someday an' that no
death has ever stopped the world. my poems
are written in a rhythm of unpoetic distortion/
divided by pierced ears. ...
... some
people say that i am a poet

The first cut on *Bringing It All Back Home*, "Subterranean Homesick Blues," was arguably one of the most important songs of the decade and certainly one of the most innovative. The title simply referred to the nostalgia for a safe life, the social alienation, and the general paranoia that the lone activist against the government typically felt. Conformity, acquiescence, and the ordinary life, for all their faults, nevertheless offered comfort, security, and a degree of protection. Anyone who chose not to conform, not to acquiesce, or not to live an ordinary life, even if only a dissenter and not a criminal, had to expect and even welcome discomfort, insecurity, and persecution. That was the price that had to be paid for living underground. The song evoked visions of leftist Jean-Paul Marat, sick and hounded throughout the French Revolution until murdered by a "centrist," Charlotte Corday, and of fictional antiheroes such as Fedor Dostoevskii's underground man.

"Subterranean Homesick Blues" remains, however all that may be, most famous for the second verse's last two lines, which eventually provided a name for the violent splinter group from the SDS, the Weather Underground.

"She Belongs to Me" celebrated a particularly strong and independent woman, Joan Baez. The very idea of her "belonging" to anyone was incongruent and inexplicable. Had Dylan lapsed into "great American romance" syndrome?

"Maggie's Farm" was the singer's declaration that he was going to be true only to himself from then on, and not be anyone else's slave, servant, employee, stooge, lackey, or clone. Who was Maggie? We had no idea. Subsequent archaeological research on Dylan's career speculated that the song referred to his performance at Silas Magee's farm in Greenwood, Mississippi, on July 6, 1963, but we knew nothing about that. The identity of Maggie remained a mystery, but, as far as we were concerned, the song could have been called "Lyndon's Farm," "McNamara's Farm," or even "Uncle Sam's Farm." Opponents of ultraconservative British Prime Minister Margaret ("Maggie Snatcher") Thatcher in the eighties revived "Maggie's Farm" to their advantage.

"Love Minus Zero / No Limit" seemed like a description of an ideal woman, principled, vulnerable, but with a dogged, independent streak.

"Outlaw Blues" suggested that interracial love affairs and even interracial marriages were perfectly OK.

"On the Road Again" seemed at first like nonsense, but quickly revealed the intolerability of the traditional life of the extended family and strongly defended the need of any self-respecting freethinker to escape the ordinary, domestic life of theft, hypocrisy, crazy habits, stupid religion, and oppressive stunts.

"Bob Dylan's 115th Dream" really was just nonsense. Its main value was in being funny.

Like most of Dylan's lyrics, the words to "Mr. Tambourine Man" were difficult to understand. We suspected that it might be a drug song, because the word "trip" occurred in it, but that was rather tenuous reasoning. Maybe it was about music's unique ability to rescue us from the trials and tribulations of this world. That interpretation seemed more plausible, plausible enough to use for a hypothesis. But who knew what it was really about? We just liked the tune. Q.E.D.

"Gates of Eden" contrasted the warlike secular world with the religious fantasy of paradise. There seemed to be no communication between these two camps, i.e., those who understood the world could not believe in a sinless, totally free paradise, and those who believed in this paradise could not fathom worldly priorities and perversions.

"It's Alright, Ma (I'm Only Bleeding)" was a cryptic attack on hypocrisy, blind obedience, social posing, political arrogance, saber rattling, and the threats of war, random violence, and nuclear holocaust. Maybe Dylan tried to accomplish too much in this song. Musically, it was noteworthy; but its lyrical result was rather chaotic. Trying to decipher whatever meaning may have lurked in most of Dylan's lyrics was like panning for gold. Most of your hard work would be for nothing and most of what you found would be useless sand and rocks, but every once in a while you would find a twenty-four karat nugget. Listening carefully to "It's Alright, Ma (I'm Only Bleeding)" or "Gates of Eden" were perfect examples of such prospecting.

The last cut on *Bringing It All Back Home*, "It's All Over Now, Baby Blue," expressed a frequent theme in Dylan's lyrics: the bewilderment of straights at the changes in what they had thought was their society. As he had already done in "The Times They Are A-Changin'" and would soon do again in "Ballad of a Thin Man," he described the upheaval in the life of a traditionalist who discovered that the world had moved beyond what had been a comfortable, conformist niche. Because Baby Blue's old world was gone, she or he would do best to accept that fact and learn how to become comfortable in the new one. Who was Baby Blue? We did not know, but the tag seemed to be a condescending pet name for someone so mired in the past that he or she could not get hip to whatever was happening now. In that light, it could even have referred to traditional acoustic folkies like Pete Seeger.

Seeger opposed electric music, but he reaped quite a lot of benefit from folk rock anyway. The enhanced popularity of Dylan and the Byrds spilled over into folk music in general, not only making Seeger's own name better known, but also enabling the rise of other true folkies and folk rockers alike, such as Donovan, Phil Ochs, Judy Collins, the Youngbloods, the Turtles, Barry McGuire, the Mamas and the Papas, the Lovin' Spoonful, Simon and Garfunkel, Tom Paxton, Joan Baez, and Arlo Guthrie.

Seeger was busy that spring. Born in 1919, he had dropped out of Harvard in 1938 during his sophomore year and never looked back. A banjo picker and a sympathizer with the communists and the Wobblies since the thirties, blacklisted and muzzled in the McCarthy era, and a longtime peacenik and activist, Seeger found himself in his true element in the mid-sixties. Essentially and consummately political, he seemed to derive new energy from the civil rights and anti-Vietnam War movements, like the mythical Antaeus, who gained new strength from each of his defeats. He released three albums in three months, two on the Folkways label, *Songs of Struggle and Protest, 1930-1950* and *WNEW's Story of Selma*, and one on Columbia, *I Can See a New Day*. These three albums contained labor organizing songs, political satires, just plain angry protests, and old standards. Among the titles were "What a Friend We Have in Congress," "Bourgeois Blues," "I Don't Want Your Millions, Mister," "Joe Hill," Woody Guthrie's "This Land is Your Land," "Follow the Drinking Gourd," "The Bells of Rhymney," and "How Can I

Keep from Singing?" On the Selma album, a quasi-documentary about the famous marches for voting rights from Selma to Montgomery, Alabama, March 7 to 25, 1965, Seeger teamed up with the Freedom Voices and black folkie Len Chandler to do such tunes as "Hold On (Keep Your Eyes On The Prize)," "Oh, Wallace," "Murder on the Roads of Alabama," and "Ain't Gonna Let Nobody Turn Me 'Round."

The focus of protest, at least white activism, began to shift away from civil rights and toward the war. The SDS was in the forefront. It led the first major antiwar demonstration of the Vietnam era, as 25,000 marched on Washington on April 17. Folkies and folk rockers — not yet real rockers — took up the protest theme. Phil Ochs was in the forefront. His debut album, *All The News That's Fit To Sing*, showed him as a bright new force, one of the left's most brilliant satirical lyricists — much more accessible than Dylan and just as trenchant. Like Mort Sahl, Ochs drew his inspiration from the daily news and, also like Sahl, when the news was not working for him, he was a dud. His "One More Parade" described the folly of young men embracing war as their means to honor and glory and lamented the old war widows' inability or unwillingness to check this folly. In a similar vein, "The Power and the Glory" proclaimed the greatness of America, but argued that this greatness was properly based on the freedom of its citizens and the wealth of its poor, not on the warmongering of its rulers or the wealth of its rich. "Talking Vietnam" compared Southeast Asia with Dixie, asserting that the evils that the mainly Christian American government was perpetrating against the mainly Buddhist Vietnamese people, such as murder, disenfranchisement, burning, and exploitation, were analogous to those that white Southern racists were perpetrating against Southern blacks. "Too Many Martyrs" was a eulogy for Medgar Evers. "Knock on the Door" recounted the long history of the terror that governments have always inflicted on their own citizens.

Another auspicious American debut that spring was that of the Scottish folk singer Donovan, whose "Catch the Wind" immediately invited comparisons with Dylan. These comparisons were ill-founded, superficial, and — well, frankly I could never figure out why anyone ever compared those two at all. Perhaps it was because, with his mop of curly dark hair, Donovan looked a bit like Dylan. But similarities ended there. Dylan, five years older, influenced Donovan, not the other way around, and not mutually. Both were folk musicians, but Dylan was a folk rocker and Donovan was a pop star. Dylan had a hardass, shitkicking image, but Donovan had the soft, dreamy, psychedelic image of what in a few years we would call a "flower child." Dylan went through a lot of phases, but soft psychedelia, the essence of Donovan, was never one of them.

The entertainment scene was getting heavier and entertainers were getting more resolute. Some of this shift was attributable to undiluted and unsanitized black music and black stand-up comedy becoming more generally available to white audiences, but most of it was due to the urgency of the two most important sociopolitical issues of the day, racial injustice and the Vietnam War, and the need to communicate about these issues. Not every new song dealt with race, the war, or some other manifestation of correctable injustice, but a significant number of them dealt with themes and topics more important, more down-to-earth, or more widely familiar than would have been typical ten, five, or even two years earlier. Even some of the pop ditties now showed some substance. "Another You" by the Seekers was on one level just a love song, but on a higher level it was a hymn to hope. "Wooly Bully" by Sam the Sham and the Pharaohs was superficially just a nonsense lyric, but closer scrutiny revealed sexual innuendo. "Just a Little" by the Beau Brummels only lamented lost love, but broke our hearts with its exquisitely gloomy guitar break between the second and third verses.

Perhaps the most uncanny harbinger of times shortly to come was when crossover country singer Jackie DeShannon had a big hit with "What the World Needs Now is Love." This song, written by two middle-of-the-road songwriters from our parents' generation, Hal David (born in 1921) and Burt Bacharach (born in 1928), soon became a soft rock peace anthem. Citizens were beginning to unify — across generations, tastes, and styles — against the war.

Summer 1965

Help!

His brow is wet with honest sweat,
He earns whate'er he can,
And looks the whole world in the face,
For he owes not any man. ...

Toiling, — rejoicing, — sorrowing,
Onward through life he goes;
Each morning sees some task begin,
Each evening sees it close;
Something attempted, something done,
Has earned a night's repose.

Thanks, thanks to thee, my worthy friend,
For the lessons thou hast taught!
Thus at the flaming forge of life
Our fortunes must be wrought;
Thus on its sounding anvil shaped
Each burning deed and thought.

— Henry Wadsworth Longfellow, "The
Village Blacksmith" (1840), lines 8-12, 37-48

Much of what we wanted was grounded in the American dream of the nineteenth century: to own one's own land and home, to be neither anyone's employee nor anyone's boss, to earn an honest living, to deal fairly and to be dealt with fairly, to be dependable but not dependent, and to bend the knee to no one. These are worthy ideals, but the nineteenth century was tainted by ingrained patriarchy, paternalism, sexism, ageism, racism, and all sorts of other iniquities that together entailed that only white Christian men should ever have any opportunity to achieve the American dream. So the American dream itself unjustly received some of this taint. If we could have the individual self-reliance of the American nineteenth century, without these iniquities, coupled with the universal egalitarianism that we envisioned to begin in the late twentieth century — or in other words, if everyone, regardless of gender, color, or any other discriminatory factor, had equal access to the American dream — then we would truly have a Great Society! Our ideals were much higher than LBJ's — and more sincere.

But these were radical ideas.

By 1965 the proportion of young people who considered themselves "radical" had grown considerably since the JFK era. Why? What did it mean to be "radical"? How did one come to be "radicalized"?

In the first place, we had by now realized that we had been lied to. All our lives. We resented it. Our elders had unilaterally undermined our trust in them. They had lied to us about Santa Claus, the tooth fairy, and countless other childhood myths; so what else could we not trust them about? More to the point, did anything remain that we could trust them about? Vietnam? Race relations? Capitalism? Social roles? Music? America itself?

Being radical meant simply using one's own mind, and not being, as Kant said in "What Is Enlightenment?", in a state of tutelage:

> Enlightenment is [our] release from [our] self-incurred tutelage. Tutelage is [our] inability to make use of [our] understanding without direction from another. Self-incurred is this tutelage when its cause lies not in lack of reason but in lack of resolution and courage to use it without direction from another. *Sapere aude!* [Dare to know!] "Have courage to use your own reason!" — that is the motto of enlightenment.[20]

Radicals had to learn how to eschew the positivism that took human constructs for natural facts; how to avoid succumbing to the informal logical fallacies of relevance, especially *ad hominem, ad misericordiam, ad verecundiam, ad baculum, ad populum*, and *ignoratio elenchi*; and how to treat sacred scripture like any other book. The Bible was just one set of propositions to be considered impartially in comparison with other sets of propositions. It was, after all, even if divinely inspired, a human construct. As such, its contents were open to question, interpretation, reasoned acceptance, or reasoned rejection, and were on no account to be taken as absolute or revealed facts.

Radicalism was something to which we open minds aspired, and which we approached asymptotically. To become radical we had to study opposing points of view, and then distill an objective point of view from among them. We had to go to the root of any issue, problem, or situation, so as to be able to see it as it was in itself, apart from preconceptions imposed on us by our parents, religion, ethnicity, country, personal prejudices, status, or any other irrelevant factor. The very word "radical" derives from the Latin *radix*, which means "root."

Being radical entailed refusing to "belong." People naturally feel a need to

---

[20] Immanuel Kant, *"Foundations of the Metaphysics of Morals" and "What is Enlightenment?"* translated by Lewis White Beck (Indianapolis: Bobbs-Merrill, 1959), p. 85.

belong. They want to be accepted by some group. They really do not care which group as long as it satisfies this need. But radicals had to learn how to do away with this need. More good could be accomplished in solitude than as a member of any group, even a team. That did not mean that radicals had to be lonely and could not love, be loved, or feel sympathy. On the contrary, doing away with the need to belong to a circumscribed group freed us to love and be loved freely, without pressure or guilt. Belonging to a family or a country felt good, but it separated us from the rest of the world, compromised loyalty to principles, and created innumerable ethical dilemmas. We radicals thus declared ourselves members of no particular family, but sons, daughters, sisters, and brothers of all humanity; and citizens of no particular country, but citizens of the whole world as if it were one country. Only in that way could we see issues *sub specie aeternitatis* (under the aspect of eternity), untainted by the biases of our families of origin or our native lands.

Americans had to learn to see the Vietnam War as the Vietnamese saw it. White people had to learn to see racism as people of color saw it. Rich people had to learn to see prices and wages as poor people saw them. Nationalists had to learn to see issues *sub specie humanitatis* (under the aspect of humanity) rather than from the standpoint of their country, which was, after all, even if it was America, Red China, or the Soviet Union, relatively small. To the extent that such learning occurred, those people became radical.

Above all, being radical meant thinking for oneself, respecting oneself as an individual, and daring to buck the tides of fashion, public opinion, received wisdom, and authoritarian pronouncements. All true radicals are individualists.

Producer Harry Saltzman's and director Sidney J. Furie's film of Len Deighton's novel, *The Ipcress File*, was serious philosophy disguised as a spy thriller. Not much like the book, it was one of those few films that were better literature than their corresponding books. Bill Canaway's and James Doran's screenplay not only explored the psychological phenomena of individualism, but also made a solid philosophical case for individualism in the face of the hegemony of society.

The realistic antihero of *The Ipcress File*, Michael Caine's Harry Palmer, was a plainclothes army sergeant, a sarcastic, brazen, but mundane working-class spy whose only similarity to James Bond was his taste for gourmet food. But, unlike Bond, he cooked it himself. Palmer relished his natural insubordinate streak and was something of a joker.

Colonel Ross, Palmer's commanding officer in the spy network, forced him to do his bidding by blackmailing him with the threat of two years in military prison for defrauding German soldiers while stationed in Berlin. Ross transferred Palmer to Major Dalby's unit, for reasons known only to Ross. Palmer immediately showed Dalby the same determination that he had always shown Ross, to do things his own way. But only his insubordination allowed him to crack the assignment. If he had followed orders, rules, and standard procedures like his colleagues did, then he, like them, would never had gotten anywhere with it. Individuality bred in him the kind of creative thinking that enabled such breakthroughs, while conformist, obedient, procedural thinking was essentially sterile. Yet at the same time Palmer entangled himself in a web of intrigue that would not have materialized for him if he had been a conforming, obedient, procedural thinker. Through this intrigue Palmer discovered that either Ross or Dalby was a traitor, but he could not tell which one.

Palmer was kidnapped from a train heading out of London, thrown into solitary confinement in a cold, gray brick cell, and told that he was in Albania. His kidnappers, using sleep deprivation, starvation, freezing, harsh metallic and electronic noise, hypnotic visual stimuli, and other forms of induced psychological stress, tried to break his will and make an automaton of him. Only his natural disinclination to obey, his strong sense of self, and his willingness to inflict great pain on himself rather than submit to anyone else's will saved him. He secretly dug a bent tenpenny nail into his palm, so that the pain would distract him from the brainwashing and work against it like an antidote.

The Ipcress File continued in the individualistic tradition of *The Great Escape*. In some ways Palmer was reminiscent of Frank Sinatra's Major Ben Marco in *The Manchurian Candidate*. That is, both resisted brainwashing by the sheer force of their individuality. Any conformist would have succumbed. The step from conformist to apparatchik is tiny. Likewise, the step from rebel individualist to hero is tiny.

Sound and music played a gigantic role in *The Ipcress File*. John Barry's haunting score heightened the film's psychological tension and even suggested the alienation of the true individual from society.

The Ipcress File won the British equivalent of the Best Picture Oscar, i.e., the British Academy of Film and Television Arts (BAFTA) award for Best British Film of 1965. It also won the *palme d'or* at the Cannes Film Festival. But that year the Academy Award for Best Picture went to *The Sound of Music*, the worst choice alongside the other four nominees: *Doctor Zhivago*, *Darling*, *Ship of Fools*, and *A Thousand Clowns*. As usual, Hollywood chose to reward style over substance. *The Ipcress File* was not even nominated for a single Oscar. In 1965, at least, the British and French had much better taste in films than the Americans did.

The taste of America's rock audience also still had a long way to go. On their initial releases, two of Them's best songs made hardly any impact. "Gloria" did not break into the top forty and "Here Comes the Night" only reached number twenty-four. Other, comparably innovative, British bands were more fortunate in 1965, notably the Yardbirds and the Rolling Stones.

The Yardbirds' second American hit, "Heart Full of Soul," was supposed to have featured a sitar played by an Indian session musician and inspired by the band's new guitarist, Jeff Beck. Several versions were recorded, but the released version had no sitar, just Beck imitating the sitar with his guitar. This was because, as Beck later revealed, the session man could not play in 4/4 time. If he had, then this song, not the Beatles' "Norwegian Wood" five months later, would have been the first rock song to use a sitar.

"Satisfaction" was the song and *Out of Our Heads* was the album that made the Stones the giants that they were. Of the twelve songs on the LP, five were covers, three were by Jagger/Richards ("The Last Time," "Satisfaction," and "One More Try"), and four were by Nanker Phelge. Jagger's leering, cynical voice was at its plebeian best in "The Spider and the Fly," a hymn to promiscuity, infidelity, and seduction. Sleazy sexuality was Jagger's specialty, both in his music and in his personal life.

What can we say about "Satisfaction"? It has become a cliché since the nineties, but in its own time it was the most powerful tune in rock. The lewd and scornful innuendo of the lyrics was straight away classic. Jagger's persona in the song hated advertising and apparently the entire economic establishment. He could not get laid until next week because the only woman who would give him any kind of reaction was having her period. And that riff — that thundering, omnipotent riff that Keith literally dreamed up in a Florida hotel — that magic, distorted permutation of only three notes: B - C# - D — that simple riff that anyone could play — God, how it charged us up!

The flipside of "Satisfaction," Nanker Phelge's "The Under-Assistant West Coast Promotion Man," pushed further the theme of hating the economic establishment in general and the record business in particular. As rich as the Stones eventually got, they keenly felt early in their careers how professionally and thoroughly they and almost all other commercially viable musicians were being ripped off by the record companies.

Notwithstanding "Summertime, Summertime," the 1958 ditty by the Jamies, the first real rock song to use a harpsichord was the Stones' "Play With Fire," a Nanker Phelge tune that appeared both as the flipside of "The Last Time" in March and on *Out of Our Heads* in July. Not Brian Jones, but Jack Nitzsche, the song arranger who would later marry Buffy Sainte-Marie, added the harpsichord to this mix. Brian would, however, be the main harpsichord player on future Stones songs that used it, such as "Ride on Baby" in 1965, "Yesterday's Papers" in 1966, and "Sittin' on a Fence" in 1967.

Many Nanker Phelge and Jagger/Richards lyrics of the Brian Jones era (1962-1969) dealt with class struggle, class prejudice, class warfare. Apparently issues of classism struck these boys' nerves. "Play With Fire" in 1965 told of an upper-class woman who used to frequent rich neighborhoods in West London like St. John's Wood and Knightsbridge but for whatever reason now hung out in lower-class slums like Stepney in East London. The message of this song was not unlike Bob Dylan's in "Like a Rolling Stone" just a few months later. "19th Nervous Breakdown" in 1966 suggested that a privileged upbringing did not necessarily make a healthy psyche. "Miss Amanda Jones" in 1967 related the tension and inconsistency between a woman's divided loyalties to her loose, fun-loving friends and her straightlaced upper-class family. "Cool, Calm and Collected" in 1967 described a similar woman who chose to remain true to her uptight roots. "Backstreet Girl" in 1967 was sung from the point of view of an upper-class man who kept a boorish lower-class woman for sex but did not want his wife, his family, or any of his highfalutin friends to find out. "Sympathy for the Devil" in 1968 identified evil with the ruling class. Both "Salt of the Earth" and "Factory Girl" in 1968 honored the working class. The former, wishing incurable diseases on the bosses, was as vehement as a Wobbly anthem. "Street Fighting Man" in 1968 implied that sometimes the poor become so desperate that they have no option except violence, even to the point of revolution. It further suggested that all war is class war.

Class war also manifests itself as race war. When one race treats another as if lower class, then these two kinds of war become almost indistinguishable. So it was in August 1965 when black anger over years of systematic socioeconomic oppression erupted into six ultraviolent days in Watts, California. We onlookers from afar could not figure out why the rioters burned their own homes, looted their own stores, and murdered their own people. Was it only logistics? Could they not organize or redeploy well enough to attack rich white neighborhoods? Were local targets simply more convenient? Did desperation blind them to better strategies? Or was it that they wanted to create ashes from which they could rise as a phoenix?

Not only whites, but also Martin Luther King and other, more "moderate," more circumspect black leaders, were frustrated by the shameless "Burn, baby, burn!" attitude of the down-and-out desperados of Watts. It seemed that utter hopelessness had taken over the civil rights movement, at least temporarily, for one insane summer. But who could guarantee that the insanity would be temporary? Who could keep violence born of desperation from escalating? How could anyone keep hope alive among people who were convinced that hope was not worth keeping alive? Even though written by whites and recorded by a white group, the Animals' "We Gotta Get Out of This Place," a razor-sharp howl of socioeconomic desperation, coincidentally provided apt and valid theme music for these riots. There was a bit of hope in that song, but not much. In Watts there was none.

Into this tense milieu came one of the most important leftist periodicals of the sixties, the *Berkeley Barb*. Inspired by the Berkeley Free Speech Movement and wishing to lend a fresh voice to the antiwar, civil rights, sexual liberation, and drug legalization movements, wacko middle-aged Marxist Max Scherr (sometimes misspelled "Scheer") founded the *Barb* in August 1965. He quickly built its circulation up to the tens of thousands. Its underground content appealed not only to students at Cal Berkeley and the wider radical community in the San Francisco Bay area, but also to "prurient interests." The *Barb* ran some of the nation's earliest sexually explicit and deviant personal ads. Scherr made a lot of money from them.

The radical left is often seen as angry and — especially by its detractors — negative. Indeed, the radical left often is angry and negative. Its anger is partially because many people become radicalized when they realize that the right has lied to them all their lives. They naturally resent having been duped for so long and thus are naturally angry, not only at the right for duping and exploiting them, but also at themselves for not figuring out the truth sooner. Similarly, their negativity arises from their disillusionment with the established order. Such negativity, along with, in many cases, desperation, further feeds their anger. Yet anger is poisonous and counterproductive. We must each guard against harboring it. We must each fight our own baser natures to eliminate anger from our psyches, even such blameless anger as the left typically feels. Probably the best way to fight anger is to learn to laugh at whatever makes us angry. In 1965 that meant reading and sharing *Mad*.

The June 1965 *Mad* was arguably its best issue ever. Alongside sharpwitted spoofs of beach movies, *Ripley's Believe It or Not*, salon hairstyles, hunting, and

Peyton Place were two absolute classics: "43-Man Squamish" and a parody of Alfred Noyes's "The Highwayman." The premise of the former was that college athletics denied all but the most talented jocks the opportunity to participate. But squamish was "a brand new sport that promises to provide good, clean amateur fun for all." The rules, conditions of contests, uniforms, and terminology were all hilarious. Colleges across North America, including Rensselaer Polytechnic Institute, Marquette University, and the University of Alberta, formed squamish teams. A good idea goes a long way. As for "The Highwayman," we all had to read the wretched original in junior high, so it invigorated us to see the modern highwayman as a greasy hot rodder, the inn as a cheap burger joint, Bess the landlord's daughter as Shirley the obese white trash, Tim the ostler as Clyde the dishwasher, and King George II's ale-drinking men as coffee-drinking cruiser cops. The July 1965 *Mad* was not generally as good, yet it included "The Man from A.U.N.T.I.E. (Association for Unbelievably Nauseating Television and Idiotic Entertainment)," a trenchant satire of *The Man from U.N.C.L.E.*

Another comedy highlight of the summer was Bill Cosby's third album, *Why is There Air?* Cosby's humor was clean. He generated laughter out of hyperbole, sound effects, and unusual juxtapositions from everyday situations in school, sports, relationships, and driving up and down those dizzying hills in San Francisco. So, why is there air? The Temple University philosophy major with the IQ of 300 thousand did not know, but every Temple physical education major knew that it was to blow up volleyballs, basketballs, and footballs.

We also fought our inner anger with music. Heartfelt songs are cathartic.

On July 25 at the Newport Folk Festival Bob Dylan learned the hard way not to play a gig without first doing a proper sound check:

> Dylan told no more people than necessary about his plans ... He relished the dramatic departure. He couldn't envision a backfire. ... At the festival, the Butterfield Band and The Chambers Brothers this year, and Muddy Waters the year before, had shown that amplified-electric instrumentation and heavy rhythm were not taboo. It was, to Dylan, "all music, no more, no less." ...
>
> Dylan told [Al] Kooper he wanted to bring the "Rolling Stone" sound onstage. Three members of the Butterfield Band were recruited: guitarist Mike Bloomfield, drummer Sam Lay, and bassist Jerome Arnold. ... Dylan completed his band with pianist Barry Goldberg. ... They kept their plan secret until they walked onstage, Dylan, in a matador-outlaw orange shirt and black leather, carrying an electric guitar. From the moment the group swung into a rocking electric version of "Maggie's Farm," the Newport audience registered hostility. As the group finished "Farm," there was some

reserved applause and a flurry of boos. ... The microphones and speakers were all out of balance, and the sound was poor and lopsided. For even the most ardent fan of the new music, the performance was unpersuasive. As Dylan led his band into "Rolling Stone," the audience grew shriller ... Dylan began "It Takes a Train to Cry," and the applause diminished as the heckling increased. Dylan and the group disappeared offstage, and there was a long, clumsy silence. Peter Yarrow urged Bob to return and gave him his acoustic guitar. ... To shouts for "Tambourine Man," Dylan said: *"OK, I'll do that one for you."* The older song had a palliative effect and won strong applause. Then Dylan did "It's All Over Now, Baby Blue," singing adieu to Newport, good-bye to the folk-purist audience.

Backstage, there had been almost as much excitement as out front. At the first sound of the amplified instruments, Pete Seeger had turned a bright purple and begun kicking his feet and flailing his arms. (A festival official said later: *"I had never seen any trace of violence in Pete, except at that moment. He was furious with Dylan!"*) ...[21]

Despite his disappointment at being unable to attract initiated folkies to folk rock, 1965 was, in many ways, the year of Bob Dylan. His *Highway 61 Revisited* was far superior to anything he had done before. During the JFK era and even early in the LBJ era his lyrics may have seemed at worst meaningless and at best prophetic, but now, deep in the midst of the LBJ morass, many of them hit their mark squarely as comment on the present situation. As a tunesmith, few could match him; but his obscure, cryptic, and probably often nonsensical allusions might have led some of his detractors to consider him a charlatan as a lyricist. For anyone, fan or not, to call him a poet was beyond the pale. He often reached for rhymes with any word that happened to fit, regardless of whether it meant anything in the context of the song. Or maybe not. Maybe all his rhymes held deep, deep meanings that none of us could ever hope to fathom. [Smirk!] Yeah, right!

The test of a poet is whether probing the connotations of the mysterious words will eventually reward the mind or heart of the listener or reader. The value of any poetry is directly proportional to the depth of this reward. The skill of the poet is the ability to create in the listener or reader the desire to do the research to reap this reward. By these criteria Homer, Dante, Shakespeare, Basho, Schiller, Pope, Keats, Goethe, Mörike, Wordsworth, Heine, Baudelaire, Verlaine, Eliot, Frost, Ginsberg, and Plath are all consummate poets. But Dylan? Well, maybe. Maybe once in a while. He certainly was not consistently a rich source of poetic insight.

Be that as it may, and admitting that his poetry was not really as wonderful as his most devoted fans believed it was, many of his words proved to be uncommonly perceptive. "Ballad of a Thin Man," certainly among his greatest lyrics, took to a higher level of consequence the themes of intergenerational angst, younger-

---

[21] Robert Shelton. *No Direction Home: The Life and Music of Bob Dylan* (New York: Beech Tree, 1986; Cambridge, Mass.: Da Capo, 2003), pp. 301-303.

generational hipness, and older-generational ignorance that had characterized "A Hard Rain's A-Gonna Fall" in 1963 and "The Times They Are A-Changin'" in 1964. His Mr. Jones became a symbol of the bewilderment with which the older generation met us. Locked into their own gray world of business-as-usual, they either could not or would not see the emergent color in the streets. Some of us recognized our fathers in Mr. Jones, and we were not amused.

The first cut on *Highway 61 Revisited*, "Like a Rolling Stone," took a singularly unsympathetic view of a pampered, sheltered, spoiled rich bitch who could not manage real life once her riches were gone. "Serves her right!" Dylan seemed to say. But with Dylan, who could tell for sure? Maybe he liked her.

On one level, "Tombstone Blues" was a simple albeit cryptic meditation on mortality, but on higher levels of allusion contained some scathing comment on contemporary American life, culture, government, and politics. One verse told of the "king of the Philistines" (i.e., LBJ), who honored dead soldiers, silenced people who would advocate saving lives by ending war, praised and rewarded the most subservient soldiers, then ordered them to Vietnam to fight and die for nothing.

The title of "It Takes a Lot to Laugh, It Takes a Train to Cry" means that there is not a lot to laugh about if you are homeless and bumming rides on trains. In such desperate situations, crying is easy, laughing is hard, especially in winter.

Continuing the theme of the hardscrabble life, "From a Buick 6" depicted the car-oriented culture of the rural poor. In the tradition of Robert Johnson's Hudson Terraplane, Jackie Brenston's and Ike Turner's Oldsmobile Rocket 88, and countless big Cadillacs and Fords, this six-cylinder Buick, probably second- or third-hand, served as a metaphor of the freedom that remained always just beyond the struggling driver's reach.

Conservatives are more likely than liberals to twist themselves into knots in order to fit into the world. Liberals are more likely than conservatives to twist the world into knots to make it fit them. This distinction is especially true of cultural conservatives and liberals, and hinges on the relationship of each to positivism. Cultural conservatives, being positivists, receive and respect the world as it is, and see their moral obligation to learn how to function in it, whether it makes sense or not, without changing it. Liberals, both cultural and political, being anti-positivists, see the world as something to be molded to accommodate human needs, and recognize their moral duty to change it for the better by improving social conditions. Political conservatives like Hitler and Stalin were changers too, but the difference between them and either cultural or political liberals was that they each sought to return to an imagined world of nationalistic and militaristic glory, a goal which is anathema to all leftists. Dylan's Mr. Jones in "Ballad of a Thin Man" was a model of the cultural conservative in this regard. He apparently could function perfectly well in the world as it was when he was young; but the world had changed now, and he could no longer understand it, be at home in it, or deal with it. He had twisted himself into knots once; he could not do it again. Tough shit!

"Queen Jane Approximately" was a very personal song. No one except Dylan himself seemed to know who or what it was about. Speculations have included: Jane was a woman going through a moral crisis and the singer offered comfort;

Jane was a woman with highfalutin notions who had just been knocked off her pedestal; Jane aspired but failed to be queenlike (hence the word "approximately); Queen Jane was not a woman at all, but a gay guy (i.e., a "queen"); and "Queen Jane" = marijuana (i.e., "Mary Jane"). None of these interpretations was immediately plausible.

U.S. Route 61 was not just any old road. It ran from northern Minnesota, where Dylan was born in 1941 as Robert Allen Zimmerman, through St. Louis and Memphis to the Delta Blues Country around New Orleans. It was the Blues Highway on which Bessie Smith died and Robert Johnson sold his soul. "Highway 61 Revisited" thus allegorized Dylan's lifelong journey from his traditional Jewish roots toward the music he loved. As usual with Dylan songs, the lyrics are nearly impossible to unravel, but we may speculate that the Abraham in the first verse referred not only to the biblical father of Isaac, but also to Dylan's own father.

"Just Like Tom Thumb's Blues" told a fairly straightforward story of a visit to Ciudad Juárez, Mexico, across the Rio Grande from El Paso, Texas, and the attendant hassles with the cops and the locals, especially the women.

"Desolation Row" asserted that erudition will not save you from depression or despair. Knowledge is not sufficient for happiness. Shared suffering is also necessary for any human to emerge from such stultification. The song's many literary and historical allusions — to T.S. Eliot, Ezra Pound, the Bible, Shakespeare, Victor Hugo, Albert Einstein, the *Titanic*, etc. — suggested that Dylan himself was more knowledgeable than happy, at least when he wrote it.

Dylan's extensive liner notes for *Highway 61 Revisited* were less like the beat poems printed in previous albums and more like plain stream-of-consciousness nonsense — and even more inscrutable. Surely some diehard fans spent hours of fruitless mental masturbation trying to decipher that Joycean mess — but not I.

Covering and/or imitating Dylan became almost *de rigueur* for folk rockers. The Byrds covered him profusely — and well. A Dylan tune sung by McGuinn was easier on the ears than when sung by Dylan. The Byrds dramatically expanded the audience for the important message of Dylan's "Chimes of Freedom." The Turtles covered "It Ain't Me Babe," also sounding better than Dylan. Phil Ochs's "Draft Dodger Rag" and Barry McGuire's "Eve of Destruction" were Dylanesque.

"Eve of Destruction" was the first so-called "protest song" to reach number one on the *Billboard Hot 100*. This development signalled two things: first, that antiwar feeling was becoming mainstream; and second, that the left now had a real, reliable channel for getting its word out — the AM airwaves, which, until 1965, had not played much of our stuff. Dylan, for example, got very little airplay; and Seeger, almost none. But now that folk music was rocking, it was acceptable to an AM top forty radio audience.

The Byrds' cover of "All I Really Want to Do" from *Another Side of Bob Dylan* emphasized for a broader audience the important social points about sexual equality and fairness that Dylan had made a year earlier. Traditional rules for dating were null and void because they oppressed, objectified, and trivialized women and made men into cardboard caricatures of chivalry. Positivist etiquette was null and void because it made no sense in the free modern world. The "great American romance" was, because of its moral asymmetry, a holdover from the anti-feminist and ultimately anti-human fifties. From now on, lovers would be friends first and lovers second, so that when or if the love affair ended or cooled, the two people could still be friends. People are, after all, human first but either male or female second — and equal naturally but unequal unnaturally. We wanted to be real, not artificial. If that meant being funky rather than suave, sophisticated, or elegant, then we would embrace funk.

If Sonny and Cher had done "I Got You Babe" in the fifties, the *Zeitgeist* of sexual inequality would have demanded that he sing "I got you," to which she would have had to respond, "you got me. But to reflect its meaning more accurately in 1965, it should perhaps have been called "We Got Each Other Babe." It really was a song of two equals expressing their fair and reciprocal devotion. The lyrics presented them as friends first and lovers second. As it should be.[22]

In a similar vein was Wilson Pickett's "In the Midnight Hour." He was willing to wait until his anticipated sex partner was ready for it. He intended to look her in the eye to fathom her level of commitment to him before he made any moves. He was not going to rush the relationship or push her into impulsive intimacy. He seemed to know that women who initiate heterosexual action themselves are better lovers than those whom he might have to seduce. So, even though he was respecting her, he was at the same time best serving his own interests.

The McCoys' "Hang On Sloopy" remains difficult to categorize. On one hand, it harked back to the possessiveness and asymmetry of the "great American romance" era. On the other hand, it transcended and even obliterateed class distinctions, proclaiming that lower-class women were every bit as good as anyone else. The singer was obviously obsessed with sex, but wanted to do things on Sloopy's terms. The song was really a tribute to jazz singer and pianist Dorothy Sloop, but we did not know that then. Some of us thought "sloopy" was a dirty word; others thought it was a mispronunciation of "Soupy" (Sales) or "Snoopy," the beagle in *Peanuts*. We had no idea what it meant, but we loved its sleazy feel and funky riff.

Kinks lyrics continued to get more complex. Ray's songs were starting to tell interconnected stories in relation to one another, at least implicitly. His soon-to-be-well-known neuroses crept into his songwriting: Is a new love affair just a set up for eventual heartbreak or is it "Something Better Beginning"? "Who'll Be the Next in Line" for heartbreak? Perhaps "You Shouldn't Be Sad," you should be in love instead, or at least rejoice that some people are in love. Maybe "Ev'rybody's Gonna Be Happy" someday. Ray was so neurotic that we had to wonder, if he ever got his "Set Me Free" wish, would he really be free thereafter or would he continue to obsess over his lost loves and supposed inadequacies.

The Beatles continued their lull from the spring. Lennon's second book, *A Spaniard in the Works*, was not as clever or as much fun as *In His Own Write*, but was still a gold mine of puns — if you like puns. Likewise, *Beatles VI* was not much

---

[22] Life imitated art. Sonny Bono and Cherilyn Sarkisian LaPiere remained friends even after their divorce in 1975, and even after she became a pop diva and he a Republican congressional representative. Again, as it should be.

of an album. With five covers, six Lennon/McCartney songs, and one Harrison song, it broke no new ground. Far more exciting later that summer were the Beatles' single "Help!", album *Help!*, and movie *Help!*

The Beatles' second movie was a wacky extravaganza, more absurd and less believable than *A Hard Day's Night*, which had at least some verisimilitude. *Help!* had almost none. Its surreal use of space and time foreshadowed *The Monkees* TV show that would debut on NBC a little over a year later. *Help!* had more of an illogical Three Stooges, Marx Brothers, or even Wile E. Coyote vs. Road Runner quality to it than did *A Hard Day's Night*. It was chock full of religious, political, social, and cultural stereotypes, all of which fell victim to scathing satire, mostly from John. Its plot was loosely based on Ringo's penchant for wearing large rings and on the Hindu Thugs' tradition of human sacrifice to the goddess Kali. Mostly, however, *Help!* was an extended spoof on the James Bond movies, particularly the most recent one, *Goldfinger*, with sight gags referring to Oddjob's hat and Goldfinger's laser. The score included not only Beatles songs, but also clever insinuations of excerpts from Monty Norman's "James Bond Theme," Beethoven's *Ninth Symphony*, Rossini's *Barber of Seville Overture*, Wagner's *Lohengrin*, and Tchaikovsky's *1812 Overture*. John indulged in brazen self-promotion, displaying *A Spaniard in the Works* and reciting "I Sat Belonely" from *In His Own Write*. Victor Spinetti's and Roy Kinnear's respective characters, the mad scientist, Professor Foot, and his assistant, Algernon, skewered the technological basis of the military-industrial complex. Algernon complained of Foot: "He's out to rule the world, if he could get a government grant." Foot lamented: "MIT was after me, you know. Wanted me to rule the world for them."

Stanley Kramer's film of Katherine Anne Porter's *Ship of Fools* depicted the voyage of a German liner from Veracruz, Mexico, to Bremerhaven, Germany, via Tenerife in January 1933. In a plotless series of disheartening vignettes, it implied the world in microcosm populated with stereotypes of social climbers, bigots, functionaries, lonely hearts, dreamers, losers, boors, phonies, sluts, lechers, rabble rousers, addicts, artists, fugitives, workers, pimps, bums, psychotics, deportees, fanatics, cynics, plain folk, self-righteous hypocrites, rich narcissists, class warriors, spoiled brats, sadists, masochists, victims, animal lovers, manipulators, fascists, socialists, cowards, cheats, teasers, and deniers all exhibiting various kinds and degrees of racial, religious, social, and ethnic prejudice. That world was ugly and hopeless. Hitler came to power while the ship was at sea. With the film arriving as it did in the middle of America's civil rights movement, with Malcolm X recently dead and Martin Luther King still alive, were we to wonder whether our winning World War II in Europe had actually solved any of the deep-seated social and racial problems that had brought Hitler to power and caused the war in the first place?

The title track of Phil Ochs's second album, *I Ain't Marching Anymore*, had a message almost identical to that of Buffy Sainte-Marie's "Universal Soldier." His lyrics recounted from a soldier's-eye view many of the most famous wars and battles in American history — then declared them futile, evil, and misguided. The last verse told in disgust how both organized labor and business management profit from constant war. The persona of the song, representing "Joe Average," finally declared that, even if he were charged with treason, he would not participate in any such belligerence again. Phil reprised his standard character of the "typical American boy" in "Draft Dodger Rag," which underscored the difference between those who evaded or "dodged" the Selective Service and those who resisted it. The former were gung ho for American militarism, conservatism, fundamentalism, and anti-communist mania, yet felt that they were personally privileged enough that they did not have to fight. The appropriate label for such "patriots" is either "hypocritical cowards" or "cowardly hypocrites." Take your pick. Those who support militarism should be willing to join the military.[23] But the latter, the resisters, on the other hand, refused to serve in the military because of their sincere and conscientious objection to either that war in particular or war in general. They were not hypocritical at all and, in the face of threats of jail, persecution, or assault, were supremely brave. We scorned and shunned the former and loved and abetted the latter. Hawks in the Vietnam era tried to use the terms "draft dodger" and "draft resister" synonymously, but we doves knew the difference — and acted on it.

In 1965 there seemed to be more dodgers than resisters. That would change in a few years. The anti-draft revolution was just beginning.

Strangers and Cousins, Seeger's summer 1965 album — (he released one every few months) — was a true internationalist effort, with songs in several languages. Its fourteen tracks were his "Oh, Had I a Golden Thread"; Matt McGinn's "Manura Manyah" in Scottish Gaelic; Tom Botting's English translation of Arkady Ostrovsky's and Lev Oshanin's Soviet Russian children's song, "May There Always Be Sunshine"; Fadhili William Mdawida's "Malaika" in Swahili; a lament of prisoners in Nazi concentration camps, "Peat Bog Soldiers"; an Indian prayer, "Ragaputi," in Hindi; the traditional Appalachian "Sourwood Mountain"; his "All Mixed Up"; "Kevin Barry," a celebration of a martyr in the War of Irish Independence; "Shtille di Nacht" in Yiddish; Dylan's "Masters of War" with spoken Japanese translation; Vern Partlow's "Talking Atom Blues (Old Man Atom)"; Jaime Robert Robertson's "Uh, Uh, Uh"; and his and Lee Hays's classic "If I Had A Hammer." We assumed that the good-tempered Pete did not stay mad at Dylan long. He may even have begun to realize that rock was the new folk and that electric music had greater natural power and appeal than acoustic, because it went more quickly and more vigorously to the gut.

Seeger was not the only well-meaning member of the older generation who missed the big point about sixties rock. That big point was that popular music was no longer just entertainment. Rock had in effect replaced folk music in Western

---

[23] Note how many of the conservative warmongers and supporters of the second Bush administration's Iraq War — including Dick Cheney, Rush Limbaugh, Donald Rumsfeld, Newt Gingrich, Karl Rove, Paul Wolfowitz, John Ashcroft, Clarence Thomas, Trent Lott, Dan Quayle, Dennis Hastert, Tom DeLay, Rudy Giuliani, Bill Kristol, Pat Buchanan, George Will, and Dubya himself — skillfully evaded military service in Vietnam or Korea. They are aptly called "chicken hawks." Contrast this to the fact that at least two of the foremost liberal antiwar politicians in the first decade of the twenty-first century, John Kerry and Albert Gore, volunteered for military service in Vietnam.

culture as the political voice of the common people, and was now serving as the social conscience of our generation. The older generation either did not try to understand rock at all, or if they did, they failed to understand it because they did not distinguish sufficiently between pre-Beatles and post-Beatles rock, i.e., between fluffy, meaningless, sanitized Pat Boonish stuff and the real, honest, unabashed, dirty, filthy, gutsy rock. The worst offender in this regard, who would have been pernicious if he were not so transparently ridiculous, was Dick Clark, who never ceased to lump doo woppers and booner crooners together with real rockers as if they were all part of the same genre.

Created, written, and produced by Clark for ABC after-school TV, *Where the Action Is* was a pitiful black-and-white weekly thirty-minute attempt to roll American rock back to the values and attitudes of the pre-Beatles era. Even with Freddy ("Boom Boom") Cannon's theme song and Paul Revere and the Raiders as hosts, the show was an even bigger turkey than *Hullabaloo*. Washed-up teen idol Steve Alaimo and sappy bubblegummer Tommy Roe as co-hosts saw to that. Even the occasional appearance of great guests like the Mamas and the Papas, Ike and Tina Turner, Barry McGuire, Dusty Springfield, the Byrds, the Supremes, the Turtles, Sam and Dave, the Who, Percy Sledge, Joe Tex, Donovan, Junior Walker and the All-Stars, the Sir Douglas Quintet, James Brown, Sonny and Cher, the Zombies, Aretha Franklin, the Kinks, Mitch Ryder and the Detroit Wheels, the Yardbirds, the Outsiders, Otis Redding, the Temptations, Edwin Starr, the Animals, Them, the Spencer Davis Group, the McCoys, and the Lovin' Spoonful could not save it. Most of the performers were of the Frankie Avalon / Neil Sedaka ilk.

The band name, Lovin' Spoonful, must have seemed innocent and maybe even whimsical to our parents. If they had known the wealth of its allusions, they might have been upset. It could have referred to cocaine, which is snorted out of a tiny little spoon — or to the typical volume of semen in a male orgasm — or to Willie Dixon's song, "Spoonful," and all its allusions — or to Mississippi John Hurt's song, "Coffee Blues," and all its innuendos — or, well, use your imagination. Anyway, the band was harmless. Yet the lyrics of its first hit, "Do You Believe in Magic?", were very important toward the development and theoretical foundation of sixties youth culture. The song praised music as a magical force that can free the oppressed, enlighten the perplexed, gladden the morose, and serve as the basis of a well-lived life. In our hearts we knew this was all true.

$$\Omega$$

Fall 1965

Turn! Turn! Turn!

For everything there is a season, and a time for every
matter under heaven:
a time to be born, and a time to die; a time to plant, and a
time to pluck up what is planted;
a time to kill, and a time to heal; a time to break down,
and a time to build up;
a time to weep, and a time to laugh; a time to mourn, and
a time to dance;
a time to cast away stones, and a time to gather stones
together; a time to embrace, and a time to refrain from
embracing;
a time to seek, and a time to lose; a time to keep, and a
time to cast away;
a time to rend, and a time to sew; a time to keep silence,
and a time to speak;
a time to love, and a time to hate; a time for war, and a
time for peace.
What gain has the worker from his toil?
— Ecclesiastes 3:1-9 (RSV)

Among my cohorts when I was working against the Vietnam War in 1969 or 1970
was an elderly Quaker, Helen Corson, who had marched against World War I and
every war since. Serene and full of wisdom, she would say to us young whipper-
snappers, "You know, World War I was supposed to have been 'The War to End
All Wars,' but we must have done something wrong, because it wasn't." She believed that the only way to end war once and for all was to teach people not to
want it. That was our purpose and duty as demonstrators, to educate them in this
way. We agreed with her that the only possible solution was to persuade people,
especially young men, just to say no. She was glad to learn two songs from us that

expressed that thought, Buffy Sainte-Marie's "Universal Soldier" and Phil Ochs's "I Ain't Marching Anymore." In late 1965 both songs had just recently come into our consciousness — the former mainly through Donovan's cover — and they would be among our mainstay antiwar anthems for the rest of the era.

We had lots of anthems. i.e., "message songs" that we actually sang rather than just listened to: "We Shall Overcome," a nineteenth-century black freedom song; Hays's and Seeger's "If I Had a Hammer" from 1949; Seeger's "Where Have All the Flowers Gone" from 1956; his "Turn! Turn! Turn!" from 1962, which the Byrds covered in 1965; Dylan's "Blowin' in the Wind" from 1963; "Universal Soldier" from 1964 and 1965; "What the World Needs Now is Love" and "I Ain't Marching Anymore" from 1965; Buffalo Springfield's "For What It's Worth" from 1966; Lennon's "All You Need is Love" from 1967 and "Give Peace a Chance" from 1969; the Youngbloods' "Get Together" from 1967 and 1969; the Rascals' "People Got to Be Free" from 1968; Jefferson Airplane's "We Can Be Together" and "Volunteers" from 1969; and Melanie's "Peace Will Come" from 1970 were just a few.

Even though Country Joe and the Fish released their own landmark antiwar anthem, "I Feel Like I'm Fixin' to Die Rag," in September 1965 on *Rag Baby Talking Issue No. 1*, most of us did not know about it until it came out on its own LP in November 1967, and a few stragglers among us did not hear it until 1970 when the *Woodstock* movie and soundtrack appeared. A perception persists that the original version of the cheer that preceded the song was "F-I-S-H" and that Country Joe McDonald changed it to "F-U-C-K" at Woodstock. In fact, it was the other way around. The band was doing "Gimme an F! — Gimme a U! — Gimme a C! — Gimme a K!" right from the beginning in little clubs and bars in San Francisco, before it had a recording contract. The record company made them clean it up for vinyl, so they substituted "Gimme an F! — Gimme an I! — Gimme an S! — Gimme a [sic] H!" At Woodstock Joe just reverted to the original.

Things were still clean and slick in 1965. The "let-it-all-hang-out" funkiness that characterized the sixties did not really take hold until 1967 or 1968. Gray suit wearing hypocrites who used "damn" and "hell" in their everyday discourse still wanted to censor "fuck," "shit," etc., at every opportunity. Free speech pioneers like the Jefferson Airplane, Frank Zappa, the MC5, and John Lennon would eventually break through the recorded music censorship barrier at the end of the sixties and the beginning of the seventies.

Yet, despite censorship, incisive satire was rampant.

The September 1965 *Mad* attacked the rich for raising their kids to be lifelong spoiled brats, continued its usual assaults on hypocrisy and snobbishness, and speculated on what Walter Cronkite's newscast would be like if he imitated Ed Sullivan's approach. The Cronkite bit included a razor-sharp portrayal of LBJ as Señor Wences the ventriloquist, Vice President Hubert Humphrey as his puppet, and Republican Senator Everett Dirksen as Pedro, the disembodied head in the box. Just like real life! Even sharper was the political satire depicting an interview with a burly police officer whose first duty was to the John Birch Society.

In October *Mad* went directly for LBJ's jugular with "The Mad United

States Foreign Policy Primer," which implied that he did not understand the ramifications of his own policy; that because of him citizens of enemy, neutral, and friendly nations all hated the United States; that relations with Arab nations were corrupt; that American policy toward Africa was hypocritical, given the racial problems at home; that America propped up unpopular and illegitimate military governments, such as the one in South Vietnam; that the Vietnamese did not want Americans in Vietnam; that the spoils system tainted ambassadorial appointments; that Americans were ignorant of foreign cultures, languages, and literatures; that the Kremlin understood American foreign policy better than America did; and that American citizens and foreigners alike were each righteously angry at LBJ's regime.

The December issue contained a speculative bit, "When Politicians Do TV Commercials," with Nixon hawking Close shaving cream, Generalissimo and Madame Chiang Kai-shek chowing down on Gung-Ho foods to prevent communist takeover of their metabolisms, LBJ getting his cabinet drunk on Pecos beer so that he could railroad his policy through them, Khrushchev selling Tinkle mouthwash, Goldwater plugging Muleburro cigarettes for right-wing smokers, and George Wallace bragging about how All-White detergent, "a product of W.A.S.P. Enterprises," gets sheets white enough for night-ridin', demonstration-bustin', lynchin', and even sleepin'. That issue also included a brilliant, pure fun parody of Coleridge, "The Rime of the Modern Surfer."

Tom Lehrer's long-awaited new album, *That Was the Year that Was*, contained fourteen hilarious, no-holds-barred attacks on American culture, politics, and government. He introduced "National Brotherhood Week" by reminding his live audience that this year Malcolm X had been murdered on the first day of that special week, which just went to show how "effective" (his term) the very idea of it was. The song expanded a theme that he had used in one verse of "A Christmas Carol" in 1959 on *An Evening Wasted*, namely, that with certain times officially designated for treating each other with loving kindness, we become even more free the rest of the year to hate each other as much as we want.

"MLF Lullaby" ridiculed the notion of a Multi-Lateral Force, including ex-Nazis, to deter the U.S.S.R. from starting a nuclear war.

"George Murphy" paid mock tribute to the singer-dancer-actor who had just been elected U.S. senator from California. The song, perhaps with dreadful prescience, mentioned Ronald Reagan.

"The Folk Song Army" suggested rather seriously that perhaps more action than just singing protest songs is required to establish peace and justice in the world.

"Smut" was an anti-censorship march.

"Send the Marines" directly assailed LBJ's strongarm diplomacy and militaristic arrogance.

"Pollution" was an environmentalist warning about urban water and air.

"So Long, Mom: A Song for World War III" well depicted the folly of any further wars.

"Whatever Became of Hubert?" deplored that Hubert Humphrey, who as a senator from Minnesota had deserved his reputation as "a fiery liberal spirit," had now been effectively silenced as LBJ's vice president.

"New Math" tackled faddish and unnecessarily complicated methods of teaching arithmetic in elementary school.

"Alma" eulogized Alma Maria Schindler Mahler Gropius Werfel (1879-1964), the Viennese *femme fatale* who either loved or married most of the luminaries in the Austrian upper-class art world.

Taking up one of Lehrer's most frequent themes, the nuclear arms race, "Who's Next?" wondered which jurisdictions after the U.S., the U.S.S.R., France, and Red China would be next to get the bomb: Indonesia? South Africa? Egypt? Israel? Luxembourg? Monaco? Alabama? The song prompted memories of Leonard Wibberley's 1955 novel, *The Mouse that Roared*, in which the tiny Duchy of Grand Fenwick found itself able to blackmail the whole world because it had accidentally acquired the bomb.

"Wernher von Braun" noted the American hypocrisy of using ex-Nazis as rocket scientists in NASA.

Quite simply the funniest mockery of Roman Catholicism in particular and organized religion in general that we had ever heard, "The Vatican Rag" speculated on the pop culture shapes that church rituals might eventually assume as the Vatican II reforms played themselves out.

Among the so-called "clean" performers, Lehrer was the best — i.e., the most dangerous and least inhibited — satirist of his era.

Others, equally or even more funny, were not quite so clean.

The Fugs consisted of Greenwich Village beat poets Tuli Kupferberg and Ed Sanders backed by drummer Ken Weaver and two real musicians from the Holy Modal Rounders, Peter Stampfel and Steve Weber. Sanders was mainly an author and publisher ("I'll print anything!"). From 1962 to 1965 he edited all thirteen issues of the beat mineograph journal, *Fuck You: A Magazine of the Arts*. Kupferberg was a forty-two-year-old wacko anarchist poet. Their entire mission with the Fugs was to be as obscene and controversial as possible. The name "Fugs" derived from Norman Mailer's euphemism for "fuck" in his 1948 novel, *The Naked and the Dead*. Thanks to Mailer and the Fugs, softening consonants grew into a faddish enunciation game among college students in the late sixties and early seventies: "t" became "d"; "p" became "b"; "k" became hard "g"; "f" became "v"; "j" became "zh"; "s" became "z"; and "tch" became "dge." Zo, Duli Gubverberg and Ed Zanderz zdarded the Vugz in Greenwidge Villazhe in ninedeen zixdy-vive. Yeah, zome of uz really talged lige thad, my vriend Philib, vor egzamble.[24]

The Fugs preferred to play for free at protest events and other happenings rather than at regular paying gigs. Few promoters outside New York would book them, given that they usually tried to provoke hostility in their audiences. They were, however, beloved in several clubs in the Village. Some of the songs on their first album, *The Village Fugs Sing Ballads of Contemporary Protest, Point of Views, and General Dissatisfaction*, were "Slum Goddess," "I Couldn't Get High," and "Boobs a Lot." Naturally they were on the Broadside label of Folkways, the

---

[24] See R. Crumb's "Deep Meaning Gommigs" in *Motor City Comics* (San Francisco: Rip Off Press, 1969), p. [14].

only record company that would tolerate them. They were a censor's nightmare but the perfect outlet for anyone's filthy absurdist fantasies. Only an open mind was required.

Somewhat lighter satire appeared in *Roger Ramjet* and *I Spy*.

Fred Crippen created *Roger Ramjet* in the image of Jay Ward's *Rocky and Bullwinkle*. Ramjet was a bumbling but well-meaning fool like Dudley Do-Right. Ace pilot and superhero at the constant beck and call of the Pentagon's Counter Bad Guy Division in the person of General G.I. Brassbottom, Ramjet led the American Eagle Squadron, a sort of all-purpose special forces team whose other pilots were all prepubescent boys: Yank, Doodle, and Dan. There was also a girl, Dee, but apparently she did not fly. (At about six years old, did she already just do the secretarial work and make the coffee?) American patriotic symbolism was unrestrained. Ramjet flew a red plane with white and blue markings. His squadron flew blue planes with white and red markings. The opening titles showed Ramjet within the frame of a dollar bill. Juvenile voices sang the theme song to the tune of "Yankee Doodle."

Ramjet was unabashedly the minion — or dupe? — of lily-white, moneyed, nationalistic interests, as when he saved the Nouveau Riche Regatta from the pirates Red Dog and Long Joan Silver. His super power, like a *deus ex machina*, got him and the country out of illogical scrapes. That he did it with a drug was not lost on us. What hypocrisy for the older generation to deny us drugs by both law and prejudice, but then give us an afternoon cartoon doofus superhero whose "proton energy pills" provided him with the strength of twenty atomic bombs for twenty seconds.

Satire, not art, not social consciousness, and certainly not ethnic or gender sensitivity, was the key to the show's success. It sent up a few movies, notably *The Treasure of the Sierra Madre* and *High Noon*. Arguably the two funniest episodes concerned the fictional Latin American country of San Domino: "Revolution" featured the supercilious American ambassador, Henry Cabbage Patch, and the junta of the Enchilada Brothers, Beef and Chicken, and their comrade, Tequila Mockingbird; while "Coffee" satirized LBJ, Señor Wences, and Yankee imperialism. The triangle of Ramjet, his girlfriend, selfish manipulator Lotta Love, and his archrival for her affections, Lance Crossfire, provided material for several episodes. Sexism was blatant, and sometimes gender identity was bent, as when Ramjet foiled the Solenoid Robots and won the Miss America Contest, hosted by Bart Perks. Besides the Solenoid Robots, frequent villains were Noodles Romanoff and the National Association of Spies, Traitors, and Yahoos (N.A.S.T.Y.). The plots were inane, the animation was minimal, and the repartee, asides, puns, and innuendos were hilarious. The overall effect was quite Rocky-and-Bullwinklish — but never quite up to that high standard.

For three seasons on NBC from 1965 to 1968, *I Spy* presented TV's first significant positive image of cooperation between the black and white races — as equals. With Robert Culp as the white CIA spy, undercover as globetrotting tennis player Kelly Robinson, and Bill Cosby as the black CIA spy, undercover as Kelly's manager, Alexander Scott, *I Spy* was like an interracially rather than internationally integrated *Man from U.N.C.L.E.* Its plots were as unlikely, its actions were as improbable, its repartee was as clever, and its approach was as lighthearted. Yet the ugly reality of the Cold War and other brutality was never far below the surface.

Ω

Meanwhile the squeaky clean pop teeny bopper world was likewise alive and well. The teen magazine genre that had originated in the forties had now grown to be almost respectable journalism with regard to the kind of popular music that appealed to girls from fifth or sixth grade through high school. Much of the credit for this improvement in the quality of teen mags was due to Gloria Stavers, editor of *16* from 1958 to 1975. She was over thirty but still thought like a teeny bopper. She kept well away from serious subjects, such as singers' political views, but was scrupulously accurate in whatever she did choose to include in *16*. She delegated little, writing most of the articles, doing many of the interviews, pushing much of the publicity, and taking many of the photographs herself. Her rapport with the feelings and desires of her readers quickly made her an authority on teen culture, with one result being that record companies would frequently consult her about how to promote new artists. She also deserved a lot of credit for helping to launch the American careers of several major British bands, such as the Kinks, the Who, and Herman's Hermits.

Until magazines like *Crawdaddy*, *Hullabaloo/Circus*, *Creem*, and *Rolling Stone* emerged to concentrate almost exclusively on rock and to appeal to boys, men, and twenty-somethings as well as to preteen and teenage girls, the only significant competition for *16* that arose in the sixties was *Tiger Beat*. *16* was based in New York, so *Tiger Beat* from the start emphasized its Los Angeles perspective. Capitalizing on the celebrity of its best-known co-founder, the first several issues were titled *Lloyd Thaxton's Tiger Beat*. His stamp was likewise on the content of the mag, which quickly established itself as a teen idol oracle and concentrated most of its promotional energy on California groups, such as the Byrds, the Turtles, Sonny and Cher, and later, the Monkees.

When we heard the Silkie's "You've Got to Hide Your Love Away" on the radio, we thought it was the Beatles. Little did we know that the Silkie were not just cover artists, but close associates of the Beatles. Brian Epstein managed both. For this song, John produced, Paul played guitar, and George played tambourine. But we did not know any of that. We did not know who the Silkie were or why they sounded so much like the Beatles.

Unlike other British bands such as the Beatles, the Dave Clark Five, the Kinks, the Animals, the Stones, and even the Yardbirds and Herman's Hermit's, the Who did not achieve immediate success in America. They released solid songs like "I Can't Explain," "My Generation," "Substitute," "The Kids Are Alright," and "I'm a Boy" in 1965 and 1966, but did not become well known to Americans until 1967, when "Boris the Spider," "Happy Jack," "Pictures of Lily," "I Can See

For Miles," and classic appearances at Monterey and on the Smothers Brothers TV show made their fame. Several theories exist as to why such a tremendous band as the Who was fated to take the slow road in America. The three most plausible are that their mod clothes and image were too alien for America — although the same argument would not apply to the equally moddish Kinks — that the four members of the Who were each too damn weird, and that their music was too far ahead of its time. Call these the clothes argument, the personality argument, and the music argument. None of them makes much sense. Was the world in 1965 and 1966 really not yet ready to rock as hard as the Who expected them to? Not yet ready to accept weird Londoners with weird lyrics, weird stage shows, and weird clothes? Perhaps. But the Kinks' "You Really Got Me" rocked as hard as any Who song; early Who lyrics were not very weird; their onstage microphone-swinging, guitar-smashing antics were not yet widely familiar; and in late 1965 their clothes were no weirder than, say, those of Sam the Sham and the Pharaohs, Sonny and Cher, or even, occasionally, the Stones.

Hair was getting longer and becoming an issue. Massachusetts proto-punks the Barbarians scored a hit, very minor nationally but fairly big in east and west coast cities, with "Are You a Boy or Are You a Girl?" The lyrics mentioned the Rolling Stones, alluded to the Beatles, and described a boy who, even in skin tight pants, looked like a girl. Hmmm? At first we thought that the song made fun of long hair, taking the side of short-haired tradition, but one look at the album cover early in 1966 dispelled that notion. The band, especially Victor Moulton ("Moulty"), the one-handed drummer, had wicked long hair for 1965. So the song really proclaimed that gender bending and androgyny were OK and, in defending a man's right to have long hair, anticipated Bob Seger's "Turn the Page" from 1973.

So, are you a boy or a girl? Interesting question! Maybe a little of both. Men may deny it, but they each have feminine qualities. Women likewise each have masculine qualities. This is cool. In 1965 we were just beginning to realize that maybe these opposite-sex qualities in each person were meant to be explored, understood, expanded, and even treasured, not suppressed, hidden, or denied.

Besides these rapidly developing (for us) sexuality and gender issues, the embryonic underground press dealt with the war, political injustice, drugs, music, and any other non-fluffy matters that would be of interest to the young, the left, and the restless. Almost as soon as the *East Village Other* (affectionately known as *EVO*) began its just-over-six-year life in late 1965, it became one of the three most influential underground newspapers, along with the *Berkeley Barb* and the *Los Angeles Free Press*. *EVO* was for many of us easterners our first introduction to underground comics. Even the *Village Voice* was not nearly so radical.

Ω

Robert Strange McNamara, LBJ's Secretary of Defense, may have been the most evil politician of the era. As soon as he published his memoir in 1995, I eagerly sought to read it, because the reviews and advance blurbs promised that, in it, he would apologize for the Vietnam War. So I read it — and was filled with anger! He apologized all right, but only for not winning the war. He did not repent his crimes. He did not regret the war. The only mistake he acknowledged was *not winning*!

On November 2, in conscientious imitation of the many Buddhist monks and nuns who were martyring themselves in Vietnam to protest both the American presence and the puppet dictatorship in the southern part of the country, Norman Morrison, a devout Quaker from Baltimore, got as close as he could outside Mc-Namara's office window at the Pentagon, gave his one-year-old Emily to a passerby, soaked himself in kerosene, and burned himself to death. McNamara tried to make him out as the would-be murderer of his little baby: "When he set himself on fire, he was holding his one-year-old daughter in his arms. Bystanders screamed, 'Save the child!' and he flung her out of his arms."[25] But this and other incidents, and the continuing escalation of the war, brought some tension between McNamara, on one side, and his family, associates, and friends, on the other: "Marg and our three children shared many of Morrison's feelings about the war, as did the wives and children of several of my cabinet colleagues. ... [Jackie Kennedy] erupted in fury and tears and directed her wrath at me. ... She had grown very depressed by, and very critical of, the war. ... She suddenly exploded. She turned and began, literally, to beat on my chest, demanding that I 'do something to stop the slaughter!'" (pp. 216, 257-258). Ordinary citizens got into it too: "My encounters with other protesters became louder and uglier. ... A man approached [in August 1966], shouted 'Murderer!' and spat on me. Then, during the Christmas holidays, while I was lunching with Marg ... a woman came to the table and in a voice loud enough to be heard across the room, screamed, 'Baby burner! You have blood on your hands!'" (p. 258). Bravo!

I wish we had known in the sixties the contemporary popular lament, "Emily, My Child," written by Vietnamese poet To Huu in the persona of Morrison, who, as "Mo Ri Xon," had instantly become a folk hero in Vietnam:

> Emily, come with me
> So when grown up you will know the way and not be lost.
> Where are we going, Daddy?
> To the riverbank, the Potomac.
> What do you want me to see, Daddy?
> I want you, dear, to see the Pentagon.
> O my child, with your round eyes,
> O my child with your golden hair,
> Ask me no more questions, darling!
> Come, I will carry you.
> Soon you will be home again with Mummy
>
> Washington ...

---

[25] Robert Strange McNamara, *In Retrospect: The Tragedy and Lessons of Vietnam* (New York: Random House, Times Books, 1995), p. 216.

Twilight ...
O souls
Living still or having gone before.
Blaze up. Truth, blaze up!
Johnson!
Your crimes are piling high.
All humanity is outraged.
You, the great dollar devil of our world.
You cannot borrow the mantle
Of Christ, nor the saffron robe of Buddha!

McNamara!
Where are you hiding? In the graveyard
Of your vast five-cornered house
Each corner a continent.
You hide yourself
From the flaming world
As an ostrich hides its head in the burning sand.

Look this way!
For this one moment, look at me!
Here you see not just a man with a child in his arms.
I am of Today.
And this my child, my Emily, is the life of all our Futures.
Here I stand
And together with me
The great heart of America.
To light to the horizon
A beacon of Justice.

You gang of devils! In whose name
Do you send B-52s,
Napalm, and poison gases
From the White House,
From Guam Island,
To Viet Nam?

To murder peace and national freedom,
To burn down hospitals and schools,
To kill people who know nothing but love,
To kill children who know nothing but going to school,
To kill with poisons fields covered with flowers and leaves all the four seasons,
To kill even the flow of poetry, song, music and painting!

In whose name
Do you bury our American youth in coffins?
Young men, strong and handsome,
Able today to release the power of nature
To bring happiness to men!

In whose name
Do you send us to thick jungles
Full of spike pits, of resistance swamps?
To villages and towns which become elusive fortresses,
Where day and night the earth quakes and the sky rocks ...?
O Viet Nam, strange land
Where little boys are heroes,
Where hornets are trained as fighters,
Where even flowers and fruit become weapons!

To hell, to hell with you,
You gang of devils!
And listen, O my America!
To this anguished voice, the never-dying voice,
Of this son of yours, a man of this century.

Emily, my darling!
The night is falling..
Tonight I cannot take you home!
After the flames have flared
Mummy will come and fetch you.
Will you hug her and kiss her
For me?
And tell her:
Daddy's gone gladly, don't be sad!

Washington ...
Twilight ...
O souls
Still living or having gone before!
Now my heart is at its brightest!
I burn my body.
So the flames may blaze
The Truth.[26]

This poem was required reading in Vietnamese high schools for three decades.

Ω

Folk rock marched on. Dylan's "Positively 4th Street" was one of his most accessible lyrics, a bittersweet vignette of soured human relations. It hit number seven on the *Billboard* chart in early October.

---

[26] Translated by Tran Van Chuong and "F.G." in *Winds of Peace: Newsletter for Madison Friends' Projects in Viet Nam*, no. 2 (January 2000): 5. I thank Christopher Van Houten of Northwestern University for drawing my attention to it.

Tom Wilson, the Columbia Records producer of Simon and Garfunkel's *Wednesday Morning, 3 A.M.*, reworked the original acoustic version of "Sounds of Silence" with drums and electric instruments and released it as a single in late 1965. He expected to make a quick buck by cashing in on the Byrds-inspired folk rock trend. The ploy succeeded even better than he had hoped. The song reached the top ten in December 1965 and hit number one in January 1966. Simon and Garfunkel themselves had already gone their separate ways, but reunited as soon as they learned that they had a hit record.

The Byrds snuck Pete Seeger into the mainstream with "Turn! Turn! Turn!" Yes, Pete took the words from the Bible, but he paraphrased them enough to make them his own. He wrote the song in 1959, and it was covered by several folkies, including Judy Collins in 1963, before the Byrds made it popular.

The Byrds' performance on the December 12 *Ed Sullivan Show* was a joke. First they did their new number one single, "Turn! Turn! Turn!", live, but then lip-synched their old number one single, "Mr. Tambourine Man." All five band members looked blasé, handsome, and "groovy" — McGuinn seemingly stoned behind his cobalt blue rectangular granny glasses, Crosby impish with his knee-length cape and sidelong glances, Mike Clarke and Chris Hillman each ostensibly trying to see which of them could more resemble Brian Jones, and Gene Clark appearing bored with the tunes and disgusted with having to lipsynch and be upstaged by Crosby. The general effect was to no one's lasting credit, least of all Sullivan's. That the Byrds' hearts were not in this TV gig was obvious. That Sullivan did not like them was equally obvious. We later learned that Crosby had argued with Sullivan's stage director earlier in the day. The Byrds were never invited back to the show.

Ed Sullivan did not take shit from anyone. He had a keen nose for talent and reached out to bring any act to his show that he thought might appeal to any sector of the public, but he ran his show like an autocrat and was not afraid to ban anyone, however popular, who pissed him off. He famously banned Bo Diddley in 1955 for playing "Bo Diddley" instead of "Sixteen Tons," Bob Dylan in 1963 because Dylan walked off when Sullivan would not allow "Talkin' John Birch Paranoid Blues," and the Doors in 1967 after not following his censorship rules. The Byrds learned all this the hard way.

Another folk rocker — if indeed a "rocker," then just about the softest on the Mohs scale of hardness in rock — Donovan, the guy whom the tie-wearing promoters obtusely wanted to dub as "Scotland's answer to Dylan," came on the scene with his first American LP, *Catch the Wind*. Its title track, last spring's single, was a simple song about the heartbreak of unrequited love, but its delicacy and his ethereal Celtic lilt together elevated it to almost iconic status, despite its relative lack of popularity compared with his future hits, such as "Sunshine Superman" and "Mellow Yellow." It was a great song, but it did not rock.

Also on *Catch the Wind* Donovan covered "Keep on Truckin'." The "Keep on Truckin'" motif in American music and folklore began with black bluesmen and jazzmen in the twenties. Using this tradition, Blind Boy Fuller wrote and recorded "Truckin' My Blues Away" in the mid-thirties. Around the same time arose the similar, anonymous, and slightly bawdier "Mandy Lane," also known as "Keep on Truckin' Mama." In Walt Disney's 1941 cartoon movie, *Dumbo*, the crows did the truckin' walk as they sang "When I See an Elephant Fly." After Donovan came the Grateful Dead with "Truckin'" in 1970, Hot Tuna with "Keep on Truckin'" in 1971, and Eddie Kendricks with a completely different "Keep on Truckin'" in 1973. These songs are all related, yet scarcely any two versions resemble each other. The whole idea of truckin' — i.e., walkin' slow with the head and shoulders back and the feet way out in front — got new life in 1967 from Robert Crumb's famous illustrations of the traditional lyrics in *Zap Comix*, No. 1.

On the opposite end of the Mohs scale from Donovan, the Yardbirds' new release was a cover of Bo Diddley's "I'm a Man." It really rocked! Beck's distortions and other innovations were incredible. He was beginning to invent for his fans the concept of a "guitar hero."[27] Blues-based British rock was becoming harder and harder and more and more complex, fascinating, and loud. The louder we played it, the more complex and fascinating it became; and the louder it was, the more we loved it.

The Animals' "It's My Life" was a tough song, a robust sociopolitical statement of dogged individualism, naked ambition, overpowering self-confidence, working-class pride, and macho swaggering, but it was fraught with misogyny. When they performed the song on *Hullabaloo* on October 11, the set included several women's heads mounted on the walls as hunting trophies. Ideologically, the lyrics resembled Lennon's "Run For Your Life," James Brown's "It's a Man's Man's Man's World" (which we would hear for the first time next spring), and even Dion's now detested "Runaround Sue." Yet it was difficult to discount Eric Burdon, because his music was so great, and those of us who were upset by the misogynist lyrics of this song could take some comfort in the fact that it was a cover, that its words were written, not by him, but by Roger Atkins and Carl D'Errico. Our distrust of covers continued. Burdon would later redeem himself with his own, more sensitive lyrics, such as "San Franciscan Nights"; as Lennon would later apologize for having written "Run For Your Life" and would supersede 1965's "Girl" with 1980's "Woman," and, to a lesser extent, 1965's "Run For Your Life" with 1971's "Jealous Guy." Lennon's ultimate public atonement for all his past male chauvinism, jealousy, and misogyny would come in 1972 when he and Yoko Ono co-wrote "Woman is the Nigger of the World."[28]

---

[27] Clapton had not yet been called "God" for his guitar work. That graffito appeared on an Islington underground station wall in 1966 when Clapton was with John Mayall's Bluesbreakers. No one in the general public knew of Hendrix yet.

[28] This special use of the word "nigger" will be explained below in the discussion of Jerry Farber's "The Student as Nigger" in the "Spring 1967" chapter. When John and Yoko appeared on the May 12, 1972 *Dick Cavett Show*, John illuminated the issue by quoting a co-founder of the Congressional Black Caucus, Ron Dellums (D-Cal): "If you define nigger as someone whose life style is defined by others, whose opportunities are defined by others, whose role in society is defined by others, then good news! — you don't have to be black to be a nigger in this society. Most of the people in America are niggers."

Kinkdom was the Kinks' most complex album to date. Ray was rapidly becoming one of the best songwriters and most poignant lyricists in rock. His solid verses fed perfectly into Peter Quaife's heavy bass riffs and allowed brother Dave a lot of room for wild experiments on the guitar and other instruments. At the time, even though Ray was no stranger to melody, the Kinks were laying down the most thundering music in rock. Relative to other rock bands in 1965 they were analogous to Blue Cheer in 1968, Led Zeppelin in 1969, Black Sabbath in 1970, the Who in 1971, AC/DC in 1979, or Metallica in 1986. Embryonic heavy metal! That's what the Kinks were. Of course, we did not yet have the term "heavy metal," but the unnamed concept was already firmly in our minds — and we loved it!

Most of the tunes on *Kinkdom* had sad lyrics and simple progressions. "Who'll Be the Next in Line" was a basic, unadorned song about heartbreak. "Wait Till the Summer Comes Along" was Ray's lament that these bright days would never come along for him. "See My Friends," one of the most evocative of Ray's many odes to loneliness, featured eerie reverberating guitars and despondent vocals almost like a dirge or a chant in E flat major. With his lover gone, the singer had only his friends left, and he did not even have them, for they were all having fun without him on the other side of the river. "Such a Shame" confessed that the singer had screwed things up, broken his promises, and generally done wrong. "I Need You" began with feedback, then proceeded into a Beatlesque love song with a stinging Dave Davies guitar solo. After disconnecting from a guitar intro that was reminiscent of "Tired of Waiting for You," "Never Met a Girl Like You Before" delivered an upbeat, almost joyful tune. "Don't You Fret" was even a bit more upbeat, a lilting little melody that sounded like it should have been sung around the campfire while roasting marshmallows, a song of hope that lovers would soon be reunited. "It's All Right" was also just an unpretentious lyric about the singer's eagerness to get home to his sweetie, but it had a tremendous bass line and a memorable harmonica solo.

Kinkdom contained only two covers, "Naggin' Woman" and "Louie Louie." Ray's clearly enunciated "Louie Louie" differed from the Kingsmen's version in that you could understand all the words. Whether the words that Ray sang were the same as those that the Kingsmen mumbled remains anybody's guess.

The gem of *Kinkdom* was their current single, "A Well Respected Man," a contemptuous lampoon of upper-class hedonism, shallowness, presumption, and highhandedness. It harked back to wonderful Depression-era movies like *It Happened One Night*, which clearly showed that the honest working person's enemies were not each other, competing for perks, breaks, jobs, influential associates, and enviable romances, but the upper-class bosses, heirs, snoots, and asskissers who, as part of their typical divide-and-conquer strategy, created and sustained this aura of competition and thus systematically kept working people from all these things. Anytime or anywhere that social or distributive justice is lacking, any attack on the status-seeking conformity, inhuman values, or squelching power of the conservative rich is most welcome.

At the age of fifteen, Little Stevie Wonder, Motown's juvenile pop soul phenomenon, who had scored a big hit in 1963 with "Fingertips (Part 2)," was becoming a man with a strong tenor voice and a wider repertoire. Dropping the word "Little" from his billing, he released "Uptight (Everything's Alright)," which he co-wrote with Henry Cosby and Sylvia Moy. This song was his breakthrough to mainstream respect. An upbeat, almost hard-rockin' tune, it celebrated a minor victory in the perpetual class war, the poor boy's elation at a rich girl's love for him. Some of us joked that the song sounded like a Tampax commercial — in the groove, uptight, outa sight — but all joking aside, this wonderful, extraordinarily talented musician was laying the groundwork for what would become his heyday in the 1970s, with songs like "Superstition" and albums like *Songs in the Key of Life*, opening for the Rolling Stones during their Mick Taylor period and playing every instrument on stage.

From about the time of *December's Children* (or maybe *Out of Our Heads*) and *Rubber Soul* until the end of the decade, our most eagerly anticipated events were each next Beatles song or each next Stones song. Their music had become supremely interesting — even to the extent that we believed that the next record from either of these two bands would surely contain some marvelous new sound like nothing we had ever heard before. Neither band ever disappointed us in this regard for the rest of the era. Each of their new albums from late 1965 until the Beatles broke up in 1970 really was quite different from anything that either had done up to that point.

December's Children (and Everybody's) was a modest follow-up to *Out of Our Heads*. It included the Stones' recent single, "Get Off My Cloud," a succinct and hard-rocking proclamation of their "We piss anywhere, man"[29] mentality; and the soft ballad, "As Tears Go By," which became their next single. Its other ten songs were six covers ("She Said Yeah," Chuck Berry's "Talkin' About You," "You Better Move On," Muddy Waters's "Look What You've Done," "Route 66," and Hank Snow's "I'm Moving On") and four originals ("The Singer Not the Song," "I'm Free," "Gotta Get Away," and "Blue Turns to Grey"). "Route 66" and "I'm Moving On" were live; the rest were studio recordings. The whole album gave the impression of a hodgepodge, like the band was just marking time, waiting to take the next step.

Rubber Soul marked the dawn of progressive rock. Other rock bands and other rock albums had previously included instruments beyond what was expected in typical rock songs, i.e., drums, guitar, bass, saxophone, piano and/or Hammond B-3 organ; but *Rubber Soul* was not just experimentation with new instruments. It also represented an entirely new approach to rock. It expanded the boundaries of rock into what could only be called progressive.

Progressive rock may be defined as rock that respects, suggests, and/or

---

[29] On March 18, 1965, Charles Keeley, working at a service station on Romford Road, Stratford, London, England, refused to give the men's room key to Bill Wyman, whom he called "a shaggy-haired monster." Several other people then emerged from the Stones' chauffeured Daimler, including Mick Jagger and Brian Jones, one of whom — (accounts differ) — told Keeley, "We piss anywhere, man." Bill, Mick, and Brian then pissed on the wall of the station, to the cheers of onlookers. Keeley pressed charges and won.

incorporates other forms and genres of music, especially classical and jazz, besides just the blues on which rock was founded. It would sound composed rather than merely written, would use a great variety of instruments, techniques, tempos, rhythms, harmonies, scales, themes, and formats, and would sometimes even border on the symphonic. In 1965 it was embryonic — we did not even have a name for it yet. The term, "progressive rock," may have been coined as early as 1966 or 1967, perhaps by some DJ, but it was certainly in the lexicon by 1969, when it was used to describe King Crimson.

Within a few years it would not be unusual to hear a violin, flute, sitar, or harpsichord in a rock song. Since last spring Brian Jones of the Stones, George Harrison[30] of the Beatles, Jeff Beck of the Yardbirds, and Dave Davies of the Kinks had been learning the sitar. Now we were hearing the first fruits of that study. "Norwegian Wood" was the first song to employ it to good effect, but George would add it to many Beatles songs, notably "Within You Without You" on *Sgt. Pepper's* in 1967. Brian would lend it to "Paint It, Black" in 1966.[31] Beck imitated it frequently on his guitar, in both the Yardbirds and his subsequent bands. Dave imitated a sitar on guitar for "See My Friends" in 1965 and used an actual sitar on "Fancy" in 1966.

In late 1965 the Beatles' music became exciting and innovative again. We can forget McCartney's "Yesterday" and "Michelle," which were just trivial ditties that made Beatles music more broadly appealing to a soft pop or even an easy listening audience — but *Rubber Soul* was a true milestone in the art of music, and legitimately remains one of the greatest albums of all time. Besides its instrumental advances and fascinating cover art, it was distinctive for its quantum leap in the depth of its lyrics. "Think for Yourself," "The Word," and "In My Life" on *Rubber Soul* were the Beatles' first "message songs" (although a case might be made for "You've Got to Hide Your Love Away" on the *Help!* album). George's "Think for Yourself" flipped the middle finger at officious bureaucrats, power-drunk cops, domineering bosses, and all the other arrogant bastards who tried to run our lives for us according to the conformist pattern. The lyrics of John's "The Word" seemed hortatory, didactic, almost liturgical. Preaching love in this way obviously did not refer to the kind of "love" (*erôs*) in the typical girl/boy love songs for which the Beatles were heretofore known. Was John becoming deeper, more abstract, more intellectual, a missionary for *philia*, *agapê*, or *karitas*? Probably. At least in his public image he was becoming much more literary. He wrote the words to "In My Life" as his first deliberately literary poem. He and Paul wrote the melody together. George Martin wrote and played the beautiful keyboard break. But the focus must

---

[30] George had learned about the sitar from Roger McGuinn, who, ironically, never used it on a recording himself. McGuinn may have been returning a favor, as he had learned about the twelve-string Rickenbacker by watching George play it in *A Hard Day's Night*.

[31] The first time many of us would actually see a sitar — or begin to know what it was — would not be until September 11, 1966, when Brian, dressed all in white and sitting cross-legged on a stage pedestal like a god among the rest of the Stones, played it for "Paint It, Black" on *Ed Sullivan*.

be on the lyrics. The tone of the piece was nostalgic, but the words went beyond mere wistfulness, all the way to an implicit comment on the nature of life, death, change, and how we either accept or refuse to accept them. Love is necessary if we are ever to reconcile ourselves to the way of the world.

"Wait" was one of very few 50/50 songwriting collaborations between John and Paul and, appropriately enough, was about reconciliation. "I've Just Seen a Face" was one of Paul's most finely crafted love songs, upbeat, bouncy, not at all sappy. "You Won't See Me" and "I'm Looking Through You" were his criticisms of his girlfriend, Jane Asher. They were not very bitter, but about as bitter as Paul ever got.

John wrote "It's Only Love" but always thereafter claimed to hate it because of its corny lyrics. He was right about the words, but the tune was catchy, and the echo and distortion on the guitars sounded great. Better lyrics indeed appeared in most of his songs, such as "Girl," which, despite its eventual supersession by "Woman," he always claimed to like. The significance of the viper inhalations that punctuated this song was not lost on us. They sounded exactly like smoking a joint. This gratuitous insertion of drug humor into a love song reminded us of when he pantomimed shoving a Coke bottle up his nose in *A Hard Day's Night*. John was certainly an opportunistic missionary for drugs.

John's "Norwegian Wood (This Bird Has Flown)" gave us sounds that we had never heard before — and not just the sitar. The lyrics were equally innovative. They seemed to operate on several levels. At its most basic, the song was merely a narrative of a brief romantic encounter. At the next level, it showed that the singer's relationship with this woman was just a tad unconventional. At another level it was cryptic — and whenever we heard cryptic lyrics we immediately suspected — Aha! — drugs. What the hell was Norwegian wood anyway? Marijuana? We did not know. Was the song about sex or drugs or both? Or did it transcend both? We just did not know. The mystery that was John Lennon was beginning to fascinate us.

Yet John's "Run for Your Life" was an embarrassment. It embarrassed us and it later embarrassed him — in the early seventies after Yoko Ono had straightened him out. Why did he write such hateful misogynist trash? Was there some evil secret about John that we did not realize? Or was he writing in a persona? The tune was cool but the words were awful. Threatening a woman with murder for cheating on her man was not something to be commended.

The Beatles' next single, the double-sided hit, "Day Tripper" and "We Can Work it Out," was like a coda to *Rubber Soul*.

The British colloquialism, "day tripper," means a tourist who prefers short, usually preplanned journeys or guided jaunts: day trips. But John's song, "Day Tripper," was not about that at all. That was just a symbol. John's actual topic — or rather, target — was the undependable friend, the phony, the pretender, the uncommitted drifter from idea to idea, cause to cause, fad to fad, the unworthy confidant, the hypocrite, the backstabber, the tease, or what we in America might call a "weekend warrior" or a "fairweather friend." Some said that the song was about "tripping" on LSD, but nothing in the words seemed to support that interpretation.

Yet, Lennon would not have been averse to a three-way play on the word "trip."

The lyrics of "We Can Work it Out" made it one of the most important Beatles songs. It challenged all sorts of basic assumptions about human relationships, mainly the idea that one party or the other in a bilateral relationship had to be the "boss" who made the decisions for both rather than allow dialogue, compromise, or consensus. Written mostly by Paul about his relationship with Jane Asher, it included four lines by John that extended Paul's argument to include all human interaction, not just heterosexual love affairs. John wrote that to fuss and fight was tantamount to crime against nature because human life was too short to waste with that kind of crap. He was absolutely correct.

Yet the United States of America seemed to honor fighting and conflict in all forms, from war itself to ordinary family dynamics.

In the sixties the family ideal, not the reality, but the ideal, was still that the husband/father would earn all the necessary money while the wife/mother would keep a perfect house and not work outside the home. Within these circumstances a typical pattern would be that the kids would aggravate the mother until, in sheer frustration, she would threaten, "Just you wait until your father gets home!" When he arrived, she would tell him what was what, he would explode, the kids would cower, God would return to His Heaven, and all would again be right with the world. Society regarded this pattern as normal.

Yet in this situation the father was not an object of love for his kids, but an object of awe and terror. He was to be feared and respected, and was not really interested whether his kids loved him or not. This governance of, by, and for father-figures was essentially fallacious. The patriarchal view of life was an extended *ad baculum* fallacy (appeal to force) just as the paternalistic view was an extended *ad verecundiam* fallacy (appeal to illegitimate authority). But why should "might makes right" be the ground of childraising and why should anger be the appropriate expression of this might?

Our parents' generation, earlier generations, and the less introspective members of our generation regarded anger as an acceptable, legitimate, natural expression of emotion, especially for men, who, after all, controlled things and made the rules. For many men, anger was the only emotion they ever expressed. They saw nothing wrong with that. Anger was manly. It led to forceful confrontation and was the mark of a winner. Our parents certainly saw no reason to control their anger toward us, although, in perfect hypocrisy, they expected us to control our anger toward them. Specifically, society both accepted and even encouraged parental anger as an appropriate response to any conflict that might arise between parent and child.

To be a parent without using anger as the primary resource would involve actually listening to one's kids, which, of course, being much too busy with more serious matters, most parents were not willing to do.

Ω

... what is proclaimed and practiced as tolerance today, is in many of its most effective manifestations serving the cause of oppression.

— Herbert Marcuse, "Repressive Tolerance," in: *A Critique of Pure Tolerance* (Boston: Beacon, 1965), p. 81.

... the virtue of a monarchy is loyalty, for the state is gathered into the person of the king, and the society is bound together by each subject's personal duty to him. ... The ideal nationalist democracy exhibits the virtue of patriotism, which is distinguished from loyalty by having the state itself as its object rather than the king.

— Robert Paul Wolff, "Beyond Tolerance," *ibid.*, pp. 3-4.

David Lean's masterpiece film of Robert Bolt's screenplay of Boris Pasternak's epic love story, *Doctor Zhivago*,[32] illustrated the folly of judging people's worth by how much money they have, how powerful they are, or how loyal or useful to the prevailing political climate they are; and instead suggested that individual dignity born of ethical character should be the only true measure of a human being.

Despite being made smack dab in the middle of the Cold War, *Doctor Zhivago* presented a judicious, non-propagandistic view of the Bolshevik Revolution. It depicted this early form of Russian communism as a system that depended for its survival upon meddling in citizens' private lives to the point of killing human feelings, but at the same time it blamed this loss of individual feeling and dignity not on the communist uprising against the tsar, but on the centuries of tsarist oppression that prompted the uprising. The tsars themselves created the murderers and monsters that overthrew their systematic terror and put a more chaotic terror in place of it, just as the *Ancien Régime* desensitized the Sansculottes to love and violence and instilled in them a lust for revenge even before the French Revolution began. Because the tsars and the French kings had never treated them fairly or humanely, the lowest strata of the Russian and French societies had never learned human integrity and had never come to expect human decency in anyone's dealings with them. In the name of equality Bolshevism reduced everyone except the military to the status of poor peasants. In the name of brotherhood everyone perfunctorily called everyone else "comrade." The military dictatorship of forced labor camps that ensued under Stalin meant that little progress toward freedom (свобода), the original stated goal of the revolution, was ever achieved. This was the concrete outcome of the lowest classes' revenge.

---

[32] In *Darling*, released earlier in 1965, and *Doctor Zhivago* we saw the first two major appearances of Julie Christie, one of the most beautiful and important stars of the sixties. She did not have many roles, but those she had, such as a dual leading role in *Fahrenheit 451* and leading roles in *Far From the Madding Crowd* and *Petulia*, she played to lyrical perfection.

The tsar's dragoons charging and sabering peaceful unarmed demonstrators did more to aid the nascent revolution than to quell it. They turned more people against the tsar by their brutality than they turned toward him by arousing fear. The tsar might have been wiser to employ a technique that Marcuse identified in the title of his 1965 essay, "Repressive Tolerance." That is, just ignore dissent and it will go away. A subversive element in society cannot grow to be a majority unless it is stimulated by events. If the government refuses to be baited, then these events will not occur. If it does not respond with cruelty to displayed dissent, then fence-sitters will be neither disgusted by its rough treatment of peaceful citizens nor inspired to rise up against it, either peacefully or violently. In such cases, not only revolution, but even internal reform, becomes less likely. The government just becomes stronger, more remote, and less responsive to the needs and pleas of its people. Rather than, as in the sixties, attack us with clubs, guns, cattle prods, tear gas, injunctions, and other blunt means of control, which all proved ineffective because they galvanized us, drew attention to us, and attracted more lovers of freedom to our side; the American government and their corporate media allies have learned since the early seventies to attack us with benign neglect.[33] Censorship by direct or violent intervention or censorship by peacefully ensuring that the speaker is simply ignored are equally authentic forms of tactical censorship, but the latter form is more effective in achieving the government's goal of preventing us from being heard.

Fellini's first color film, *Juliet of the Spirits*, was an in-depth psychological study of a prim, lonely, haunted, upper-class, middle-aged housewife who, although devoted to her cold, philandering husband, became progressively more alienated from him the more she became invested in the occult. She was so obsessed with her memories, fears, and delusions that neither she nor the audience could tell the difference between her visionary fantasy and her suppressed reality. When, at the end, she was finally able to recognize that difference, put her visions in their proper place, and confront ugly reality head-on, she decisively took control of herself so that her alienation became, paradoxically, her liberation. No longer living through him and suppressing her own life, she could now jettison not only him, but also her hypercritical mother, superficial friends, and ulteriorly motivated acquaintances to plot her own course thereafter. As surreal as any of Fellini's films, this film's symbols were abundant and inscrutable to the extent that watching it would have been utterly frustrating if the staging, costumes, sets, and photography had not been so alluring. Fellini was to film as Salvador Dali was to painting: His work was beautiful, but if you understood him, then there was something wrong with you.

---

[33] The powers-that-be have learned their lesson well. In the sixties American leftist activism received extensive coverage in the mainstream newspapers and on radio and TV. This publicity strengthened us. The mainstream media in the first decade of the twenty-first century mostly ignores leftist marches and rallies but instead is full of sordid celebrity gossip, such as in the sixties was relegated to sleazy tabloids that intelligent people scorned. Because intelligent people are now awash in non-news and other media fluff while real news of street actions goes unreported or underreported, we are weakened.

Thunderball, our 1965 Christmas present from Harry Saltzman and Cubby Broccoli, was even more outrageous with gadgets than its predecessor, *Goldfinger*. The personal rocket pack, the plastic surgery, and the various underwater doodads almost qualified it as science fiction. Verisimilitude was marginal, and considerably less than both the book and the previous three films. The parachuting U.S. frogmen were implausible. So close to shore, the Coast Guard could have put more of them into the water more quickly, more efficiently, and less flamboyantly with standard commando procedures. The final scene was idiotic. Such a sea-to-air rescue would have to be done with a helicopter — not a four-prop plane travelling two or three hundred miles per hour — to avoid killing, maiming, or at least further endangering Bond and Domino. How would that plane land with two humans dangling from its skyhook? Alternately, how would they get into the plane before it landed? Why pick them up from the rubber raft by air anyway? The Coast Guard had plenty of ships in the area.

We lovers of realism — and reality — began to lose faith in James Bond. With *Thunderball*, the series drifted from fantasy into self-parody.

Spring 1966

Anyone who thinks that individuality means being different need not apply

It is pretty much true that few twentieth-century American males had long hair until the Beatles appeared on *Ed Sullivan*. The upsurge over the next several years of men growing long hair was not only our slavish imitation of our favorite music stars. There was some of that mere copying, but more generally this upsurge was an overdue expression of our suppressed individuality. Short hair makes men look alike, despite its different colors, textures, etc., simply because there is less of it to notice; but long hair, in varying lengths, just by its sheer magnitude, flaunts its differences, emphasizes its colors, shows off its curliness, waviness, or straightness, and proclaims individuality. Long hair is the freak flag of freedom.

When we saw the Beatles, our reaction was not, "Wow! Those guys have long hair, colorful jackets, and pointy boots. They look cool. I want long hair, colorful jackets, and pointy boots too." Instead, our reaction was, "Wow! Those guys have long hair, colorful jackets, and pointy boots. They can dress any way they want. That's cool! I want to dress any way I want, too." Maybe dressing any way we wanted included long hair, colorful jackets, and pointy boots. Maybe not. That decision was entirely up to each of us. What it definitely did not include was trying to look like everyone else. June Harris wrote in her liner notes to *The Best of the Animals*:

> You'll never find the Animals on the night club or discotheque circuit. The regular kind of night life means nothing to them. And forget about the way they dress! That's according to the mood of the moment.
>
> On the morning the Animals left for England, I met Eric Burdon at Kennedy International. The rest of the group had already left, but he had a three hour stopover before catching his plane. He was dressed in suede from head to foot. He likes suede, also denim. He used to like leather, but then everyone started wearing it.

Bingo! That nailed it!

Would it be "reverse conformity" to allow others to dictate what you do *not* wear? Perhaps. If so, then Burdon — and all of us — were reverse conformists.

But be that as it may, we believed that our hair and clothes expressed our individuality. We only wanted to look natural and unforced instead of artificial and phony. Anyone else telling us, or even suggesting to us, how to wear our hair or clothes was tantamount to suppressing our individuality. What is individuality without its free expression? By stifling our expression of our individuality the authorities within the establishment intended to stifle our individuality itself. They figured that if they could make us look like them, then they could make us be like them. That tactic only made us more resentful and did not help their cause. On the contrary, it made them seem ridiculous.

Our parents took a positivistic approach to style. For us, style was arbitrary, purely a matter of personal choice — the most obvious outward expression of personal freedom. Their attitude toward style showed us that they were not free.

For us, the establishment was typified in the Babbitt-like smallmindedness of public secondary school administrators. As a case in point, consider this story, "Hairsplitting," from the May 27, 1966, issue of *Time* magazine:

> Somewhere deep in the psyche of many U.S. adults lurks a triggering device that raises hackles whenever a boy with long hair passes by. Public-school officials seem unusually susceptible to this reaction — and spend countless hours haggling over the length of a lad's locks.
>
> The silliest solution to one of these hairsplitting arguments is in effect at Unionville (Pa.) High School, where a school handbook proclaims that "in a democracy, dress and grooming are dictated by good taste and pride in one's appearance" and that "a child's behavior is most often a reflection of the way he dresses." To Superintendent LeVan P. Smith, democratic hair must not touch the eyes, ears or shirt collar. He suspended Alan T. Miller, 18, whose hair infringes upon his shirt but whose behavior somehow had not been adversely affected. Alan drew straight A's his entire junior year, missed only one day of school in three years, was never a disciplinary problem, and won Unionville High's only National Merit Scholarship.
>
> Smith argues that Alan's hair presented "a distraction to the rest of the class." Alan's parents took the dismissal to court, arguing in part that Alan, as a guitar player in a moneymaking five-piece rhythm and blues group, needed to wear his hair long. Superintendent Smith bent his rules and compromised, contending that "we have a responsibility to try to rehabilitate those who are defiant of regulations."
>
> Now Alan sits at home and attends class via a two-way telephone hookup, paid for by the school board. Teachers and students must speak loudly so that the apparatus, which is moved from room to room, can pick up the voices. A teacher writing on a blackboard must be sure to pronounce what she writes, and to explain diagrams. Alan, unable to get recognition by raising his hand, just interrupts by phone to recite. It's all rather distracting, but at least Alan will be able to take his final exams, graduate, and ...

Who was going to "rehabilitate" illogical morons like Smith who believed that Miller's hookup from home was less distracting to the class than the bit of hair on his collar? Who was going to remove from power those who equated democracy with obeying dictates, participating in a nationwide consensus on what constitutes good taste, and not defying regulations? Smith was neither fired nor even pilloried for his stupidity, but remained superintendent until his death in 1968.

Smith, our parents, and like-minded members of their generation — who were probably the majority — all told us that short hair for boys was normal, masculine, and attractive, and that for a boy's hair to touch his collar, ear lobes, or eyebrows was deviant, slovenly, and effeminate. Short hair for boys was the natural way of the world, positively, positivistically. But we saw George Washington on the dollar bill with his powdered wig of foofy hair puffed out over his ears — and Abe Lincoln on the five with his own hair luxuriantly curling over the tips of his ears and his cute little Cap'n Ahab beard — and Andy Jackson on the twenty with his wavy locks framing his grim military countenance. We questioned our elders about these dead presidents. Surely the Father of Our Country was not deviant? Of course the "Great Emancipator" (as we believed at the time before black history studies revealed the truth) was not slovenly? Most assuredly the Victor of New Orleans was not effeminate? Or so we argued. "That was then, this is now," they replied, "That was the style then, it is not right anymore." But, we wondered, how did style get from then to now? Did it just pop up *ex nihilo*? And how did it come to be accepted so positively as a positivistic fact rather than as a transient and mutable phase in the history of fashion? They apparently did not wonder such things. They were stymied. They retreated to their tried and true shibboleth of conformity, "That's just the way it is. Accept it!" Well, we were not about to accept *anything* that did not make sense — and male hairstyles that became popular just two or three generations ago now being touted as hard and fast facts of life, nature, and sexuality and as unquestionable standards of decency made no sense at all.

By 1966 standards Miller's hair was fairly long. But by standards of conformity to prevailing fashion that even rich, powerful, white-collar men followed in the mid-seventies, it was short. Arch-conservatives Dick Cheney and Donald Rumsfeld, as members of the Ford administration in 1975, had longer hair than Miller had in 1966. Conservatives are always followers.

The Unionville administration's main problem with Alan Miller was not his hair. It was his disobedience and lack of conformity. Nor was our parents' main issue with our appearance either our hair or our clothes. It was obedience and conformity. The hair and clothes clashes were merely symptomatic of the central issue: obedience and conformity.

Our elders demanded respect from us. But respect cannot be demanded; it must be earned. Ways not to earn it included — from positions of ignorance, obtuseness, stubbornness, or insensitivity — pontificating about drugs, bashing rock music, and insulting our hair.

At least seven possible reasons exist why men or boys might want to grow their hair long in a short-haired male society:

1. They might just like the way long hair looks.

2. They may be too lazy to cut it or too poor to get it cut.
3. Privileged whites may want to grow their hair long as a political statement, so that they will be persecuted, and thus will have some small measure of solidarity or shared experience with oppressed minorities, such as blacks.
4. They may wish to conform with their long-haired friends, so as to fit into a crowd or a clique.
5. They may, like Alan Miller, believe that they need long hair to create an image.
6. They may wish to make a political statement, to let their "freak flag fly," as it were.
7. They may just grow it for the sheer joy of pissing off uptight short-haired males and their equally uptight female associates.

Whichever of these reasons, or whichever combination of these reasons, or whichever other reason(s) any man or boy may have for growing long hair, these reasons all have one important aspect in common: They are no one else's business except the person's whose hair it is.

What we wear, how we do or cut or grow our hair, how we color or accessorize ourselves — these are all very small things really. So small that they ought to be left to each individual to choose for him/herself. ***They are no one else's goddam business!***

Legitimate questions about wearing clothes include: Are they warm (or cool) enough? Are they comfortable? Do they provide enough pockets? Do they cover the genitals? Are they clean? Does the person who is wearing them like them? Are they economical? Are they safe? Are they practical? These are all questions that can and should be answered only by the wearer. They are indeed no one else's business, not our parents', our teachers', our bosses', our peers', our so-called friends', or anyone else's. Let the wearer alone decide what to wear!

Exceptions are justified for protective clothing in certain occupations, such as firefighting. Anyone who wants to fight a fire barefoot, with untied long hair, and in a flammable Hawaiian shirt is a fool and should be sacked for the greater good of society. But if that person is, say, an accountant, and wants to go to the office barefoot, with free-flowing hair, and wearing a Hawaiian shirt — well, why not? It would liven up this dull world. Let it be.

But, these few reasonable exceptions aside, if other people can command you to wear a certain thing, to cut your hair a certain way, or to accept a certain fashion, then they own you. If they receive no complaint, smirk, or countersuggestion from you, then they absolutely own you. If they can get you do that, then they can get you to do anything, and they know it. If they cannot get you to do that, then they are unsure of what they might or might not be able to get you to do, and they know that too. So, they will force you to surrender your most personal token of your individuality before they will consider hiring, enrolling, enlisting, befriending, promoting, encouraging, defending, or trusting you.

School dress codes, and especially school uniforms, are loathsome. They accomplish nothing worthwhile. They serve only to demean the students, to stifle individuality, and to enforce the mindlessness of regimentation.

Obedience is not a virtue. It is an admission of inferiority and incompetence. Think for yourself! Thinking for yourself is not necessarily disobedience. It is simply taking charge of your own life. Disobedience for disobedience's sake is not to be encouraged, but when disobedience for the sake of preserving or enhancing one's personal integrity becomes necessary, then obedience becomes absolutely a vice.

Idiotic educational policies were not limited to secondary schools. Not only were all levels of education, both public and private, full of stupid rules irrelevant to the true mission of these institutions, but the high standards of education itself, which had been well established in the forties and fifties, were beginning to fall apart. High grades were becoming easier to achieve. Failures were becoming less frequent. Athletics were receiving too much emphasis relative to academics. Too many insufficiently talented students were being admitted to college. They had no reason to be there, and their presence diminished the whole intellectual atmosphere. Worthless and infantile courses were becoming more common in college curricula. Formerly rigorous liberal arts discussion courses were turning into bullshit seminars — and frustrated, powerless professors could do little about it.

None of this criticism is meant to agree with Allan Bloom's allegations in *The Closing of the American Mind* (1987) that pandering to students' interests in multiculturalism, moral relativism, and diversity was ruining America's colleges. Rather, it agrees with *Mad*'s March 1966 satire, "College Programs to Develop Masters of Mediocrity," which depicted eager, self-confident, diverse frosh deteriorating over four years into sullen, submissive, carbon copies of one another. The catalog of *Mad*'s Megalopolis State University College of Disillusion included courses such as "Introduction to Apathy," "Remedial Indifference," "Techniques of Scapegoating," "Contemporary Self-Acceptance," "Principles and Methods of Cheating," "Practical Materialism," "Human Selectivity," "Marrying for Money," "Progressive Underachievement," "Unprogressive Overachievement," "Basic Hypocrisy," "All-Purpose Opinion Formulation," "Contact Maintenance," "Studies in Egocentricity," and "Flaunting." This curriculum was designed to teach the skills that were needed to get ahead in the conformist, corporate business world, such as stabbing colleagues in the back, leeching off the parents, worshipping the almighty dollar, kissing the ass of authority, whining, slacking off, and watching television at every opportunity instead of reading.

Bloom said that the decline in American education was attributable to what was being taught. He was wrong. The decline was due mainly to the lackadaisical way in which all subjects were being taught. Any subject can — and should — be taught rigorously. Put intellectual rigor in front of students and force them to adhere to it in order to graduate, and they will rise to the occasion — and be all the happier for it. But make courses too undemanding for them, expect little of them, just try to make them content, and they will fall to the occasion. They will become anesthetized by Nietzsche's "despicable ease." They will be great consumers, but terrible citizens.

The so-called "dumbing down" of America from the sixties to the early twenty-first century has not been caused, as Bloom asserted, by leftist values sneaking into the fabric of society. It was not caused by the influx of black studies, women's studies, popular music studies, modern art studies, cultural relativism, the scientific world view of Thomas Kuhn, or the values of Nietzsche or Marx. On the contrary, it has been caused primarily by commercial interests modifying education so as to make society's most affluent members into less discriminating and more impulsive consumers. In other words, what has really been ruining higher education is its administrators pandering to some of the very values that Bloom himself cherished, namely, authority, wealth, obedience, patriotism, and cultural elitism. Granted, Bloom also cherished intellectual rigor, classical curricula, Greek philosophy, and moral absolutism, all most worthy, but he missed the boat on the rest of it. Leave education to the intellectuals!

Ω

A new vocal harmony group from Los Angeles, the Mamas and the Papas, did much to dispel that city's surf music image and bring it into the post-folk-rock era when southern California bands like Buffalo Springfield, the Byrds, the Doors, the Turtles, Love, and the Electric Prunes would be engaged in a sort of DJ-induced "rivalry" with "psychedelic" northern California bands like Big Brother and the Holding Company, Jefferson Airplane, the Grateful Dead, Quicksilver Messenger Service, and Moby Grape. But San Francisco had not yet become musically what it was, and, if there was any "rivalry" in American rock in 1966, then it was Los Angeles vs. New York City artists like the Lovin' Spoonful, Simon and Garfunkel, the Fugs, the Young Rascals, and Dylan.

The Mamas' and the Papas' "California Dreamin'" lent itself easily to metaphorical interpretation. The singer wanted a better life. He wanted to escape the cold and enjoy the warmth. Yet he remained under the yoke of the church. The priest preferred the cold, and knew that he could talk the singer into staying home. The cold of the familiar Northeastern United States represented tradition, rules, and stagnation. The warmth of the yet unknown California represented freedom, fun, and growth.

Some of the other songs on their debut album, *If You Can Believe Your Eyes and Ears*, were nearly as fascinating. "Got a Feelin'" told of an exploited lover who turned the tables and found new strength in having been used. "Monday, Monday" was a gentle poke at the nine-to-five everyday business world and how it can mess up one's love life. Not much there, really. "I Call Your Name" covered the Lennon/McCartney tune, slowing it down considerably and replacing the hard edge of Lennon's vocal with an antiphonal duet between (primarily) Cass and (secondarily) Denny, two softer voices that lent a dreamlike quality to the tune. But it was John Phillips's "Go Where You Wanna Go" that really hit the mark, transmitting the same important message as George Harrison's "Think for Yourself." Yet the lyrics were ambiguous. Was the persona of the singer, Michelle, a woman running her own life and calling her own shots, or was she at the mercy of her far-roaming man? Or was she trying to convince herself to stop crying and just let him go and do what he wanted to do? For a group that performed about half covers and half Phillips originals and did not even play its own instruments, the Mamas and the Papas were damn good!

Cool vocal harmonies, subtle messages, and engaging lyrics from the East Coast were provided mostly by Simon and Garfunkel. They were unmatched as troubadours of leftist social commentary for the rest of the decade — unmatched in this even by Dylan, because their lyrics, unlike Dylan's, were clear and intelligible. Also, they just looked so cool on the front cover of *Sounds of Silence* walking up that country path in their jeans, Beatle boots, and black coats, looking over their shoulders, suspiciously, at us. Two of the photos on the back cover showed Garfunkel with a copy of *Tiger Beat* — which was quite funny, because Lloyd Thaxton never understood S&G.

Their *Sounds of Silence* album contained only one song that Paul Simon did not write. Confusion surrounded it. "Angie" was credited on the back cover to Davy Graham but on the record itself to Bert Jansch, and it was spelled "A-n-j-i" on the front cover but "A-n-g-i-e" elsewhere. Anyway, back to the ten important songs:

The overarching themes of the album were loneliness, alienation, and death. The first two, at least, were very familiar to us; and as for the third, well, there was Vietnam, as well as newscasts full of various assassinations, suicides, murders, insurrections, and lethal riots to remind us. The title song, "The Sounds of Silence," was about communication — or rather, the difficulty and ultimate impossibility of fruitful or accurate communication among those who will not try, see, or listen. The singer had a terrifying dream in which he found that the truth he knew and felt was ineffable. The people to whom he tried to speak greeted him with only hostility and suspicion. The light of their post-industrial, unnatural, perhaps post-apocalyptic world was neon, not sunlight, nor even moonlight. They deified their neon idol as Aaron had deified the golden calf in the Sinai wilderness. The song ended with the bleak realization that these people would probably never notice the everyday truth that was written plainly all around them.

The album's most complex message was delivered in "I Am a Rock," an ode to willful withdrawal from society. Its central image of the singer's impregnable fortress in December recalled other poetic Decembers, such as that in Edgar Allan Poe's "The Raven." The fortress, of course, was only psychological, but powerful nonetheless, as the singer rationalized his loneliness and actually turned it to his apparent advantage. Through pure resolution, he made himself immune to pain, crying — and indeed, because he became incapable of any kind of human vulnerability, he thus became incapable of any human feeling at all. Yet the song made it seem like sitting in your room all the time and just reading and writing was not such a bad way to live.

"A Most Peculiar Man" was, in a sense, the logical extension of "I Am a Rock." Whereas the Rock derived a perverse, unholy strength from his solitude, isolation, loneliness, and alienation; the Peculiar Man, on the other hand, let these same factors drive him to a pathetic suicide. The difference between the two men was that the Rock had ideas and literature to feed and protect him; the Peculiar Man had nothing, no internal life at all, except despair. He allowed himself to become bored. Intelligent people should never be bored.

Simon adapted the words of "Richard Cory" from Edwin Arlington Robinson's poem about class struggle and the nature of true happiness. The superficial trappings of a rich socialite could not compare with the meager but genuine pleasures of an honest working man. The former was miserable and shot himself; the latter, even though he cursed his own impoverished life, was in fact happy, but could not figure out why he was — or especially why Cory was not.

"April Come She Will" expressed the intractable inevitability of the passage of time and its cycle of birth and death. "Leaves That Are Green" pushed this idea further, describing the sorrowful wisdom that comes as we accommodate ourselves to this cycle.

"Blessed" was a Jewish boy's attack on the deep-seated hypocrisy of Christianity, particularly the Christian promise to bless, comfort, and help the lowest dregs of society. That mainstream Christians in America did not give a shit about the poor, the junkies, the whores, the victimized, or the hopeless should already have been obvious.

"Somewhere They Can't Find Me" depicted a criminal on the run who, like most of his ilk, saw no need to take personal responsbility for his own actions. Instead, he attributed his crime to fate and considered himself merely unlucky, not guilty.

"Kathy's Song" mentioned all sorts of wonderful things — the mind, England, distraction, sleep, kissing, truth — but all in a melancholy, almost despondent way. The singer had given up on everything except love.

"We've Got a Groovy Thing Goin'" may at first have seemed like it was, as the liner notes said, "just for fun," a catchy little tune with a main riff reminiscent of Nat Adderley's "Work Song," but it really was a serious lyric about a dying love affair. The singer was warning the woman who was about to leave him that she risked falling into insanity if she went through with it. Typical male hubris!

Riding on the crest of sudden and huge popularity, they did "I Am a Rock" on *Ed Sullivan* and released "Homeward Bound" and "I Am a Rock" as singles.

Other singles out of New York included the Young Rascals' "Good Lovin'," which soon became a frequently and often very well covered tune — and later a standard concert piece for Bob Weir and the Grateful Dead. Brian Epstein managed and John Lennon named the Cyrkle, a band from Easton, Pennsylvania, who had a hit with "Red Rubber Ball." The Lovin' Spoonful's "Did You Ever Have to Make Up Your Mind?" celebrated a playboy having a great time juggling several women, including a pair of sisters. Thematically, this song seemed like the promiscuous male flipside of Dusty Springfield's desperate woman's cry for a monogamous relationship in "You Don't Have to Say You Love Me." Dusty was from London, and one of very few women to have any American success in the "British Invasion" of 1964 and 1965. We were not much into heavy make-up, but her deep black eye shadow looked cool. Apparently a Phoenix, Arizona, high school senior named Vincent Furnier — who in 1971 would gain fame as Alice Cooper — thought so too.

Just before the summer, Dylan put out one of rock's first double albums, *Blonde on Blonde*. It would be his last new material for a year and a half. He broke his neck in a motorcycle crash on July 29, 1966, and during his recovery lived as a recluse in Woodstock,[34] New York. Rumors consumed us. Neither he nor his publicists said anything. We did not know whether he was dead, crippled, vegetative, or on the way to full recovery. For all we knew, the crash itself might have been faked and Dylan might have been alive and well in Tahiti, chuckling at our gullibility. Would it be too cynical to say that his near-death helped the sales of *Blonde on Blonde*?

Side one began with his recent single, "Rainy Day Women # 12 & 35," instantly recognizable as an advertisement for marijuana. "Pledging My Time" was Bob's excursion into basic old harmonica-laced blues. "Visions of Johanna" was a slow, beautiful song with some of his most obscure lyrics ever — and that's saying something. Joan Baez claimed it was about her. Maybe it was. Who could tell? The last song on this side, "One of Us Must Know (Sooner or Later)," was much more accessible, a plain love song expressing a sentiment similar to McCartney's "We Can Work it Out."

The four songs on side two were all catchy and memorable. Even though full of typical Dylanesque allusions and mystifications, the general meaning of "I Want You" was clear enough. By contrast, the words of "Stuck Inside of Mobile with the Memphis Blues Again" seemed to be pure nonsense, with allusions more allusive, mystifications more mystifying, and thus more typical of Dylan's chronic reaching for rhyme and filling the lyric sheet with whatever words happened to pop into his head. "Leopard-Skin Pill-Box Hat" was a good-natured jab at fashion-conscious women who tried to look like Jackie Kennedy. "Just Like a Woman" condescended to a woman who was too fragile, immature, and drugged-up to succeed in a serious relationship.

Side three contained five mostly forgettable songs. "Most Likely You Go Your Way (and I'll Go Mine)" had such a strong beat that it was almost danceable, yet it broke no new ground and essentially was just a dull song of lost love. "Temporary Like Achilles" was an old-style piano blues number about a woman rejecting a suitor's advances — but what the hell could mentioning the short-lived Greek hero of the Trojan War have meant? "Absolutely Sweet Marie," an unusually upbeat and hard-rocking tune for this period in Dylan's career, expressed the longing of a desperate man for a woman, yet, shining through its — again — typically obscure and disconnected images, its main point seemed to contrast honesty to legality. Some said that "4th Time Around" was a dig at Lennon's "Norwegian Wood"; others said that it was a ripoff of "Norwegian Wood"; and still others said that "Norwegian Wood" was a ripoff of Dylan's songwriting technique and had pissed Dylan off so much that he attacked Lennon with the line about not asking for crutches — but we did not believe any of that. Each was just a song about a weird encounter with a woman — the connection ended there. Yes, Lennon went through

---

[34] In Ulster County; not to be confused with the site of the 1969 festival, which occurred in Bethel, Sullivan County.

a "Dylan period" when, as he later admitted, he was heavily influenced by Dylan — as many singers and songwriters were in the sixties — but Lennon never sounded a bit like Dylan and none of his songs ever sounded a bit like Dylan's. In "Obviously 5 Believers," a song that begs a woman to come home, nothing is "obvious" about who the five believers or fifteen jugglers are or why they are the singer's friends.

Dylan achieved something truly remarkable with *Blonde on Blonde*. One of its songs, "Sad-Eyed Lady of the Lowlands," lasted for an *entire album side!* The standard length for popular songs was then around three minutes, often less, seldom more. Marty Robbins's "El Paso" in 1959 at 4:44 was one of very few successful tunes to push that limit, which was dictated by radio airplay moguls. Those suits generally believed that no one in their listening audiences would want to hear a song longer than three minutes. As in most cases where ulteriorly motivated non-musicians make commercial judgments about music, they were dead wrong. There was indeed a hunger out there for long songs, a hunger that would not be satisfied until the late sixties and early seventies. Dylan was the guy who began to feed it. Even though side four of *Blonde on Blonde* was only 11:23, short by subsequent standards, it set the stage for such album-side masterpieces as Iron Butterfly's "In-A-Gadda-Da-Vida," the Allman Brothers' "Whipping Post" on *At the Fillmore East*, and the Byrds' "Eight Miles High" on *Untitled*, as well as long cuts like the Animals' "Sky Pilot," the Beatles' "Hey Jude," the album version of the Doors' "Light My Fire," extended Grateful Dead jams, and the long medley on side two of *Abbey Road*. Not even to mention the Who's "Won't Get Fooled Again" or Led Zeppelin's *Stairway to Heaven*.

Also in New York, the Fugs kept getting funnier and funnier. Their epony-mous second album contained "Group Grope," "Kill for Peace," "Coming Down," "Dirty Old Man," "Frenzy," and five other song poems that each delivered exactly what their titles suggested, with no holds barred: raw sex, free drugs, and intrepid antiwar agitation.

A major step toward establishing rock as a legitimate art form occurred this spring when Paul Williams, then a student at Swarthmore College, founded *Crawdaddy* magazine as a journal of rock criticism and shortly thereafter moved it first to Cambridge, Massachusetts, then to New York. More serious and literate than either *16* or *Tiger Beat*, and preceding *Hullabaloo*, *Circus*, *Creem*, *Guitar Player*, and *Rolling Stone*, *Crawdaddy* injected intelligent life into the discussion of the content and meaning of rock. Williams named it after the Crawdaddy Club in London, where, in 1962, the Rolling Stones played their first gig. At first it was essentially an "underground" publication, mimeographed, appearing irregularly, but mostly bimonthly. Only nineteen issues appeared from February 1966 to Octo-ber 1968, but they included pioneer reviews of important artists who as yet were receiving little or no radio airplay, such as the Butterfield Blues Band and the Blues Project in the first issue; the Spencer Davis Group, the Hollies, and Slim Harpo in the second; Them in the third; Jefferson Airplane in the seventh; Buffalo Springfield in the eighth; the Doors and the Youngbloods in the ninth; Moby Grape, Country Joe and the Fish, the Who, and the Grateful Dead in the tenth; and Jimi

Hendrix and the Mothers of Invention in the eleventh. *Crawdaddy* was a mag for connoisseurs.

Meanwhile, back in Los Angeles, the Byrds were emerging from folk rock into what would soon become psychedelia. They were credited by many then, and are still credited by some today, with having invented folk rock. But the inventor of folk rock was Dylan in early 1965 with *Bringing It All Back Home*. Ironically, the Byrds neither were nor are typically credited with having invented psychedelic rock — but they did. Some might argue that the first psychedelic song was "Norwegian Wood," and they might have a point, but the first *bona fide* psychedelic song was "Eight Miles High" a few months later. Of course, the Byrds did not invent psychedelic rock *ex nihilo* — no one ever invents anything *ex nihilo* — they had influences, including John Lennon, Brian Jones, Dave Davies, Indian music, and the drugs themselves. The archetypal psychedelic instrument was not McGuinn's jingly jangly twelve-string Rickenbacker, but, as we would learn in April 1967, Jorma Kaukonen's heavily electrified and feedbacky six-string Gibson hollowbody; the archetypal locus of psychedelia was not Los Angeles, but San Francisco; the archetypal psychedelic band was not the Byrds, but Jefferson Airplane; and the archetypal psychedelic tune was nothing that the Byrds ever recorded, but any of the heavier songs from any of the Airplane's second through fourth albums: *Surrealistic Pillow*, *After Bathing at Baxter's*, or *Crown of Creation*.

A British psychiatrist named Humphry Fortescue Osmond coined the term "psychedelic" in 1957 to describe the gentle or calming effects of some hallucinogenic drugs. It soon caught on with the users of such drugs, especially in America. The earliest musical application of the word may have been by the Holy Modal Rounders, a New York blues and folk band, precursors of the Fugs, in 1964. By the end of 1966 it was in common usage nationwide, mostly because of its currency among musicians.

We naturally all thought that "Eight Miles High" was a drug song. McGuinn said it was about a plane ride to London, not about drugs at all. If this is true, then that is one of the great ironies in the history of rock. In fact, it was probably about both. The words describing the plane ride were sufficiently ambivalent to allow their being interpreted plausibly as describing a drug experience.

The gem of the Byrds' second album, *Turn! Turn! Turn!* was "He Was a Friend of Mine," in which McGuinn reworked an old folk song to express what we all still felt about JFK. The love and sorrow we held for this departed spirit of hope would soon manifest itself in Bobby Kennedy's tragic attempt to challenge LBJ for the leadership of the Democratic Party. Bobby, once his brother's attorney general, now the carpetbagging senator from New York, would use his increasing opposition to the Vietnam War as his leverage against the White House. We would flock to Bobby as we had once flocked to Jack, conveniently oblivious to the fact that the younger brother could not hold a candle to the older.

The Standells scored a hit with "Dirty Water," a heavy, hard-beating song about the raunchy side of life in Boston. They sounded like a working-class garage band from one of of the tougher parts of that New England city. How were we to know that they were really a well-connected bunch of Los Angeles suburban kids, managed by a former member of the Four Preps, one of the cleanest cut of the clean-cut vocal harmony groups of the late fifties? Anyway, they fooled us — and their music was excellent. They followed "Dirty Water" promptly with "Sometimes Good Guys Don't Wear White," which snarled at listeners to "get a crewcut" if they did not like the singer's long hair and to "flake off" (i.e., fuck off) if they believed that men in white collars were better than he was. Again the Standells' chip-on-the-shoulder rock, even though completely phony, hit the mark spot on. They clearly expressed not only the primeval alienation of the blue-collar world from the white-collar world, but also the newly developing alienation of white-collar children from white-collar parents.

Several other excellent singles also came out of Los Angeles. The Bobby Fuller Four's "I Fought the Law" and Johnny Rivers's "Secret Agent Man," his theme from the TV series, rocked as hard as anything in 1966. Nancy Sinatra's "These Boots Are Made for Walkin'" contributed to the strong, independent woman persona that had begun with Lesley Gore's "You Don't Own Me" and Gale Garnett's "We'll Sing in the Sunshine"; would grow even more powerful through Grace Slick, Janis Joplin, and Genya Ravan; would eventually wither in self-parody with Helen Reddy's "I Am Woman" in 1972; and would not be revived until Patti Smith, Joan Jett, Chrissie Hynde, and Pat Benatar surfaced in the late seventies and early eighties.

"Kicks" by Paul Revere and the Raiders was usually heard as an anti-drug song, but could also be interpreted as a pro-conformity song. They were indeed just a rather middle-of-the-road group from Boise, Idaho. As for their preening, prancing, pompous lead singer, Mark Lindsay, well, we could smell a phony a mile away. "Kicks" rocked, but "Time Won't Let Me" by a grittier singles band, the Outsiders, from Cleveland, rocked harder. Too bad the Outsiders were not as lucky in Los Angeles as some lesser bands, such as Paul Revere and the Raiders, but soon great quantities of exceptional hard rock would pour forth from northern Ohio bands like the Human Beinz, the Raspberries, and the James Gang.

In England our favorite bands were really cranking it up!

The Yardbirds' apocalyptic and allusive "Shapes of Things," released early in 1966, is not to be confused with Barry Mann's and Cynthia Weil's "Shape of Things to Come," which, in the September 1968 version by Max Frost and the Troopers, provided incisive but didactic and fatalistic commentary on the present revolution. The Yardbirds' tune, by contrast, communicated not only both hope and fear for the future, but also uncertainty about it. The import of the lyric was not unlike that of Jaques's famous "seven ages of man" speech in Shakespeare's *As You Like It*, II, vii, 139-166. The singer found himself in the third age, the lover, wondering when and whether he would proceed to the fourth, the soldier.

Ray Davies's songs on *Kontroversy*, the Kinks' fifth album, were generally more introspective but less accessible than on the previous four. We would learn later that he had entered one of his frequent periods of ... — a clinical psychologist might call it "depression." Unlike others, such as Mick Jagger and Paul McCartney, Ray never really enjoyed being a rock star. Not much was "kontroversial" about *Kontroversy*, but songs on it like "You Can't Win," "Where Have the Good Times

Gone," "Till the End of the Day," and "What's in Store for Me?" revealed Ray's mood, as Dave's tune, "I Am Free," revealed his. Their new single, "Dedicated Follower of Fashion," was a bit brighter and continued the line of satire that they had begun with "A Well Respected Man." The thematic emphasis was on the word "follower," as all who hang their fortunes on anything as superficial as clothes must be nothing but mere followers. They allow their minds to be made up for them, and if in matters of dress, then surely in every other matter as well. They really are quite useless. The Kinks' message was clear: Dress the way you want. Be the way you want. Be neither a follower nor a leader, but just be yourself, an individual. Screw what anyone else thinks about you.

Ostensibly the Rolling Stones' new single, "19th Nervous Breakdown," was just a lament for a spoiled rich kid whose parents ruined her with indulgence, giving her money and toys and "things" and the whole lot else, except love, but it also contained an obvious reference to LSD that somehow escaped the censors. Rock lyricists had all by now learned from Dylan that, if they wanted to put meaningful or realistic words into a song, they sometimes had to do it obliquely or even cryptically. Jagger was getting very good at this. Moreover, as the Stones would do so often in the future, this song presented a paradox between sad, draining lyrics and happy, lively music.

Their sixth American album was a greatest hits compilation, *Big Hits: High Tide and Green Grass*. Yet it was more than just a collection of outstanding rock numbers. It was a mini-history of their evolution over the last two years, from gut-bucket blues band to innovative rock artists. A milestone in their career. A moment when we could reflect on what might come next from this variegated phenomenon: Charlie's cheeky reliability, Bill's sullen resoluteness, Mick's cocky posturing and graceful lyrics, Keith's heavy riffs and gentle melodies, and Brian's multifaceted instrumentation and dissipated life. By the time of *Aftermath*, only a few months later, they would truly be, as they were thereafter frequently billed, "The Greatest Rock-and-Roll Band in the World."

Their next single, "Paint It, Black," was their loudest, hardest rocking song to date — and perhaps ever. Over forty years later, it still deserves to be cranked up to full volume whenever it comes on the radio. It has stood the test of time much better than "Satisfaction," "Sympathy for the Devil," or even "Jumpin' Jack Flash." Maybe that is at least partially because of its theme: the singer's despair at the death of his young lover. Yes, there were other songs in this "death rock" genre, such as Mark Dinning's moronic "Teen Angel," J. Frank Wilson's sappy "Last Kiss," Jan and Dean's macho "Dead Man's Curve," and the Shangri-Las' cheesy "Leader of the Pack," but comparing "Paint It, Black" to any of them is like "Hyperion to a satyr," as Hamlet would compare his virtuous father to his perfidious uncle (I, ii, 142). The singer was so despondent that he could no longer enjoy colors or other simple pleasures of life. He tried to convince himself that her death was a natural, ordinary event, but that did not console him. He wanted the whole world to die, with her, with him. Odd though — again — that such demoralizing lyrics should be set to such upbeat music.

We did not hear anything new from the Beatles in early 1966 except their single, "Nowhere Man," which, as we learned later, had been recorded long ago and was included, along with "Drive My Car," "If I Needed Someone," and "What Goes On," on the fourteen-song British version of *Rubber Soul*. "Nowhere Man" criticized the effete dreamer for just sitting on his ass and doing nothing. Not that anything was wrong with dreaming, but action was required too. The complete human being must be balanced between mind and body.

The Who's fourth American single, "Substitute," was issued with Townshend's lyrics censored. The bowdlerizers believed that American kids were too sensitive and delicate to be allowed to hear that a white child had a black father. That line had to be changed. What an irony that the song was named "Substitute"! But these bowdlerizers were too unhip for their own good. They let other lines stay in the song that were more suggestive, more perverse, and thus naturally more cryptic. Bravo, Pete! Attaboy! Slipped in those sneaky lines about transvestism, cocaine, and incest. We got it!

Most of America, even members of my generation, did not know of the Who until after they played Monterey in June 1967, after they released "I Can See For Miles" in October 1967, after the Animals released "Monterey" in December 1967, or after the movie *Monterey Pop* appeared in December 1968. But a few of us around the big cities heard the minimal airplay that the single "My Generation" got in late 1965 and early 1966 and that the album *The Who Sings My Generation* got in the spring and summer of 1966. Even fewer of us thereby became instant and lifelong Who fans. We were the lucky ones! We got to share with British kids Townshend's declared obsession with power and volume, volume and power — an obsession that did not come to full fruition until *Live at Leeds*, *Who's Next*, and other post-*Tommy* projects — years before anyone else in America did.

Volume, as Townshend well knew right from the beginning of real rock in 1964, not only makes sound louder and harder to ignore, but also affects the quality or musicality of the sound. That is, volume adds a certain aesthetic power to music. Volume until then had been conceived mostly in terms of comfortable listening levels rather than as a component of music along with tone, timbre, rhythm, texture, melody, instrumentation, etc. To be sure, classical composers who wished to vary intensity had used the full dynamic range from *ppp* to *fff* to their advantage for centuries, but in their music even *fff* was not very loud. Townshend did not want his audience to be comfortable. In his music, while not denying the necessity or desirability of occasional changes in intensity, a song played soft is lousy, but the same song played loud enough to hurt your ears is irresistible. A song played at higher volume is not the same song only louder, but is in fact a different — and better — song.[35]

---

[35] Pete Townshend, interviewed in his home on Wardour Street, Soho, London, June 21, 1966, for the ABC TV show, *Where the Action Is*; excerpt included in the movie, *The Kids Are Alright*, Chapter 35, "Pete: The Power of Volume": "One of the reasons for having, sort of, music and things consistently loud is 'cuz you get so many people that just turn deaf ears to what you do. You know what I mean, they just won't listen to what you do, and it doesn't matter how good or bad it is. In fact, the bigger it is, normally, the

We did not want to be saying, "Hey, that song sounds pretty good, but I can hardly hear it. Crank it up!" Straining one's ears to hear a song created tension that prevented us from fully appreciating or enjoying the music. Making it loud rendered just the bare physical fact of hearing it unproblematic. It made listening easy, but it was not easy listening.

A real travesty is that the Shadows of Knight's cover of "Gloria," an inferior, slicked-down version, went into the top ten on the singles charts while Them's rawer, edgier, and generally better — original — version barely made the top 100. Now *any* version of "Gloria" is bound to be good. It is simply a great song, and Van Morrison deserves all the credit for that. Only those of us who, again, being lucky enough to live in big city radio markets, actually heard Them's "Gloria" when they first released it in May 1965 and when they re-released it (apparently to try to compete with the Shadows of Knight) in April 1966, could make an objective comparison. We thereby gained tremendous evidence that the best artist to record a song is its author, just because that person is the only one who really feels its meaning or truly knows its emotions. Covers tend to be stylized and contrived, even when they are technically superior; but original versions recorded by their own authors tend to be gutwrenching and honest, and therefore more fun, even when played or sung sloppily. In short, and relatively speaking, covers are unfelt; songwriters' originals are felt. There are a few exceptions, of course, notably the Byrds covering Dylan, but the Shadows of Knight were not even in the same league of heartfelt aesthetics with Them.

Plato's *Ion* tells of the way that poetry and music are transmitted from its creators to the people. The muse, the divine inspiration of all art, is like a magnet. Poets and composers hang on this magnet as if they were iron rings. Reciters and performing musicians, also like iron rings, hang on the poets and composers. Finally, the listeners, the audience, likewise iron, hang on the reciters and musicians, thus receiving only the thrice weakened power of the magnet. Plato's metaphor supports the idea that singer-songwriters, being closer to the source, are more worthy of our attention than cover singers.

For the next three years starting this spring, our anglophilia was enhanced by the imported British TV spy series, *The Avengers*, a whimsical interaction of English eccentricities, urbane style, crazy science, and Cold War paranoia. Patrick Macnee played John Steed, a stereotypical middle-aged English gentleman complete with bowler hat, neatly furled umbrella, and finely tailored clothes. Yet not far beneath this suave exterior Steed was lethal. His bowler was steel-brimmed, his umbrella was a weapon, and he was expert in all manner of martial arts, whether armed or unarmed. No less skilled was his partner in spying, Emma Peel, seductively portrayed by Diana Rigg in leather, Carnaby Street fashions, or tight, skimpy outfits that showed off to best advantage one of the most beautiful and athletic women on the small screen. The plots and action were preposterous — even more so than those of its closest American competitors, *The Man from U.N.C.L.E.* and *I*

---

more they'll close their ears to it, and so the louder you gotta work, you know. Volume's a fantastic thing. Power and volume. Power and volume!"

Spy — but the repartee between Steed and Peel was superior in pure wit to any other dialogue on TV at that time. Moreover, a subtle sexual innuendo thrived that was not possible between Napoleon Solo and Illya Kuryakin, Alexander Scott and Kelly Robinson, or even, despite the high camp of the *Batman* TV series, Adam West's Batman and Burt Ward's Robin.

Ω

The death of God was a theological and theistic concept — not an atheistic one. Whereas atheists such as Nietzsche would hold that God was never real in the first place and thus could not die, theists would take the death of God to mean the loss of transcendence, morality, sprituality, or godly values in the immanent, everyday world. In other words, the world has become too secular. Thomas J.J. Altizer, the theologian who invented the idea of the death of God as it was bandied about in the sixties, argued that the Christian God in a symbolic sense has been dead since the crucifixion but in an existential or historical sense gradually died at Auschwitz, in Vietnam, and in other situations where utter lack of human feeling, decency, or morality was evident. The death of God was tantamount to more and more people falling away from believing in God, from believing that the Christian message could save or redeem humanity, from accepting Christian principles as ethical, or from acting according to Christian morality. But God could be revived. We Americans could bring God back to life by — for example — getting out of Vietnam, treating all races and peoples as equals, and rediscovering the true significance of Jesus preaching nonviolent action and self-control. Altizer's "radical theology" was an attempt to reinterpret Protestant theology in terms of Nietzsche, Hegel, Paul Tillich, Rudolf Bultmann, and a few other thinkers. That this essentially academic endeavor should have become a hot topic among non-academics and even entered the main-stream via "Is God Dead?" on the cover of *Time* in the big red letters of either communism or Jell-O against the stark black blackground of either anarchy or extinction was bizarre at best and more probably just plain ill-advised. It was not newsworthy. It was comic. It was either ivory tower liberal theology airing its dirty laundry in public or conservative theology exposing liberal theology to the public to be chastised, ridiculed, and rejected. If the latter, then, that the idea of the death of God broke out into the profane world at all is evidence that conservative or fundamentalist churches, which obviously have a stake in such questions, have no sense of humor.

The whole question of God's living reality or dead unreality was pointless to us. We did not need God, Christianity, or Altizer to tell us that the Vietnam War, racism, and other systematic oppressions were wrong. Internal squabbles among various Christian denominations or between opposing Christian theological positions did not interest us. Our spirituality was beyond churchiness. It was grounded in thisworldliness and street action to bring true morality back to the world. Jesus would have approved of us.

"God and Country!", the conservatives proclaimed. Bullshit! The exclusive disjunction, God *or* country, would have been more accurate. If Jesus was ever clear about anything, he was clear about this: The aims of nations, states, and rulers, on the one hand, and the aims of God, morality, and righteousness, on the other, are not the same, and cannot ever be the same. "Give to Caesar what is Caesar's; give to God what is God's," he said in Matthew 22:21. This means obey the secular law whenever it does not conflict with true morality; but when the secular law does conflict with true morality, then obey your higher authority, your conscience, the conscience that God gave you. Moral authority always trumps secular authority. It was our moral duty to oppose the Vietnam War, to resist the draft, to end racism, to disobey immoral laws. To assert instead, as did the jingoistic slogan "God and Country!", that moral authority and secular authority are congruent, identical, or harmonious, is worse than stupid. It is false, dangerous, and — un-Christian.

As the number of American troops in Vietnam surged into the 300 thousands, Staff Sergeant Barry Sadler, a thrill-seeking high school dropout then recovering from a severe punji stick leg wound suffered in Vietnam, sat at number one on *Billboard* for five weeks with his jingo anthem, "The Ballad of the Green Berets," which glorified useless death, encouraged coldness in mothers and wives, and fortified the myth that patriotism = militarism.

The nationalistic zealots then included the Assistant District Attorney of Dutchess County, New York, a man who would later be sentenced to twenty years in federal prison for masterminding the Watergate burglary, and who, while working for President Richard Nixon, concocted schemes to kidnap, murder, defame, or otherwise neutralize those whom the ultra-paranoid Nixon perceived as "enemies," mostly just private citizens going about their legal, everyday business. This amoral ex-con, G. Gordon Liddy, blinded by the narrowest kind of patriotism, would still later become a successful conservative radio talk show host. But in the spring of 1966, believing every word of *Reefer Madness* as if it were gospel, he was obsessed with finding a way to prosecute Timothy Leary, who was then living in Millbrook, about halfway between Poughkeepsie and the Connecticut border. He led an armed midnight raid into the bedrooms of unarmed, peaceful citizens in Leary's home and arrested Leary and several others for possession of marijuana. This was our opponents' typical level of morality. All summer we followed news reports of the case, which we considered persecution and harassment. We rejoiced when, on September 23, all charges were dropped.

Such imperious far-right police were the target of the March 1966 *Mad*'s magazine-within-a-magazine, the December 1965 issue of *Badge & Billy: The Magazine for Law Enforcement Officers*, which portrayed cops as trigger-happy, sadistic, self-righteous, power-drunk bullies. In the light of recent street repressions in Alabama and Mississippi, this portrayal was fairly accurate. On the other hand, *Mad* might have been accused of having contributed to the stereotype of the boorish, moronic, racist, pig-headed, neo-fascist, and blatantly unjust Southern policeman. But no! Bull Connor established that stereotype himself, just by being himself.

Not all police, prosecutors, politicians, and judges supported or even tolerated the likes of G. Gordon Liddy, Bull Connor, or George Wallace. Our side obtained a strong imprimatur when William O. Douglas, the most prominent liberal judge in the U.S. Supreme Court, wrote the liner notes for Pete Seeger's latest LP, *God Bless the Grass*, which was about our stewardship of the earth and the environment. Its title actually referred to real honest-to-God lawn-type grass, not to marijuana — but we enjoyed seeing *double entendres* even where none were either present or intended. Even though the album did not advocate drugs, the fact that a U.S. Supreme Court justice would publicly affiliate himself with the notorious Pete Seeger, one of the main targets of the House Un-American Activities Committee (HUAC), was significant. Douglas was an avid outdoorsman, concerned with preserving wilderness areas and cleaning the air. His liner notes were a short inspirational essay on environmental conservation. *God Bless the Grass* was one of the first musical statements of the emerging environmentalist movement.

The other major protester among the folk singers of that era released a partially live album that spring, *Phil Ochs in Concert*. Ochs wrote all the songs. "I'm Going To Say It Now" asserted in no uncertain terms his First Amendment constitutional rights. "Bracero" attacked American immigration policy and the fruit and vegetable growers' exploitation of Chicano workers. "Ringing of Revolution" described typical upper-class ignorance of the plight of the poor and, in the spoken intro, likened Lyndon Johnson to the actor John Wayne, who was known for his simplistic cowboy shoot-'em-up roles. "Is There Anybody Here?" pointed out that the true purpose of a soldier is not to fight for freedom or to wear a fancy uniform, but to obey without thinking, to kill, and to die. "Cannons of Christianity" played off the pun on "canons" (ecclesiastical rules) to show how bellicose the bishops, priests, and missionaries have become, and how far away they have fallen from the message of the Prince of Peace, whom they pretend to serve. "There But For Fortune" decried the element of chance in deciding who would succeed or fail, live or die, or be rich or poor. "Cops of the World" and "(The Marines Have Landed on the Shores of) Santo Domingo" each in its own way condemned the United States for its arrogant, unilateralist, violent, and deceitful foreign policy. "Changes" was a pastoral lament for the madness into which the world has turned. "Love Me, I'm a Liberal" chastised the left and the center-left for its phoniness, hypocrisy, inconsistency, and opportunism. "When I'm Gone" was an existentialist statement of the singer's duty to oppose injustice here and now.

Meanwhile, back in the streets ...

Blacks were getting angrier — and with good reason. The reforms in race relations that were gradually being legislated into existence were so far having very little effect. Black leadership was increasingly divided about whether to pursue Martin Luther King's strategy of peaceful confrontation or the late Malcolm X's strategy of armed resistance. In May a great irony occurred when Stokely Carmichael replaced the more moderate John Lewis as chairman of SNCC (pronounced "Snick"), which was originally the "Student" "Nonviolent" Coordinating Committee, but now included few students and was beginning to shift toward advocating violent confrontation. Carmichael was King's ally until mid-1966; but after June 6, when Aubrey James Norvell used a 16-gauge shotgun to wound James Meredith, who four years earlier had broken the color barrier at the University of Mississippi,

Carmichael moved quickly away from nonviolent philosophy. When he was shot, Meredith had been leading a "March Against Fear" from Memphis, Tennessee, to Jackson, Mississippi, to register black voters. King, Carmichael, Floyd McKissick, and several other black leaders continued the march in Meredith's place. Their ranks swelled with the miles. Carmichael grew steadily angrier. On June 16 he delivered a fiery speech to the group, proclaiming "Black Power!" That slogan, from then on, was SNCC's rallying cry. Within a year SNCC would become known, fairly or not, as one of the prime instigators of ghetto riots and black attacks on both whites and blacks; and Carmichael himself would become known, again either fairly or unfairly, as an agitator for black separatism, a refuter of King's integrationism, and a herald of H. Rap Brown's "Burn, baby, burn!" mentality. After Brown succeeded him as SNCC chairman in 1967, Carmichael would affiliate with the Black Panthers, preach Pan-Africanism, marry Miriam Makeba, move to Africa, change his name to Kwame Ture to honor Ghanaian socialist Kwame Nkrumah and Guinean nationalist Ahmed Sékou Touré, then distance himself from the Panthers because of their willingness to accommodate whites among their radical supporters.

Even as this bitter racial violence was brewing, other blacks were trying just to go about their daily business. James Brown and the Famous Flames did an electrifying debut on *The Ed Sullivan Show* with a medley of "Papa's Got a Brand New Bag" and "I Got You / I Feel Good." Ray Charles's handlers snuck his "Let's Go Get Stoned" past the radio airplay censors. Maybe they told them that it was about getting drunk, not about smoking dope. Bill Cosby released his fourth album, the aptly titled *Wonderfulness*, a collection of whimsical stories, mostly, as usual, about his childhood and adolescence in North Philadelphia. Aside from classic hilarity like "Tonsils" and "Chicken Heart," Cosby's stand-up comedy in the sixties gave otherwise ignorant whites a gentle, fly-on-the-wall view of the humanity of inner-city black life.

Ω

The Russians are Coming! The Russians are Coming!, a multivalent comedy about mob psychology in the Cold War, showed a Russian Navy submarine aground by accident on a sandbar of a tiny Massachusetts island populated by only a few hundred rustics and summer people. Neither captain nor crew had any hostile intentions. They were frightened that, if they were discovered, the American Air Force would strafe the sub and kill them all. The captain therefore detailed a party of nine sailors to go ashore and borrow a motorboat to tug the sub off the sandbar, without raising any alarms or alerting any American military authorities. Initial sketchy reports of the Russian presence on the island quickly assumed Chicken Little proportions of mass hysteria. Everyone was frightened except the most innocent little children. Islanders armed with pistols, small caliber rifles, shotguns, harpoons, bows and arrows, fell in behind an American Legion blowhard who seemed itching to start World War III. Meanwhile, the tide floated the sub free. The human dimension of international tension at last gave way to simple human fellow feeling, as expressed best in the words of the impressionable young Russian sailor Alexei, "I wish not to hate anybody." Politics were forgotten and what could have ended tragically ended happily.

The movie can be comprehended as an essay on communication. The first American adult we see in the film does not listen to his nine-year-old son's truthful story of the Russian landing — and the moviegoer gets the idea that this father is not in the habit of believing his son about much of anything, of listening seriously to anything he says, or respecting him in general. Similar instances of missed opportunities for fruitful communication abound, some caused by the English-Russian language barrier, but most not. If the film had a message, it was that misunderstanding through poor communication is the root of all conflict. If there were a single worldwide *lingua franca*, and if people of all kinds were willing to listen to one another with respect and attention, then there might be fewer and less severe wars.

Summer 1966

It can't happen here!

Many of us first learned about airborne combat in World War I through Charles Schulz's *Peanuts* subcomic, "Snoopy vs. the Red Baron." The World War I flying ace, Snoopy's alter ego, inspired some of us to study the war more deeply. Surely by mid-1966, even before the Royal Guardsmen charted their three pop hits on this theme, we all knew who Manfred von Richthofen was. Fokker triplanes, especially red ones, were very cool.

Into this fertile milieu John Guillermin released his film of Jack D. Hunter's 1964 novel, *The Blue Max*. The screenplay was a free adaptation. Guillermin killed the "hero" off at the end as part of a sordid love triangle, but Hunter ended the book with him and Hermann Goering drinking a toast to the future Germany that they would create together. Using as its premise a German flyer's monomaniacal quest for the Kaiser's highest medal, the *Pour le Mérite*, the movie suggested that almost as vile as the physical horrors of war were the bankrupt morals of would-be war heroes who were more interested in personal glory than in doing their duty to their country. The irony was that while this flyer chased his perverse and superficial goal to show that he, a commoner, was as much a man as the aristocrats, he was being exploited and eventually sacrificed by imperial puppeteers who needed a working-class hero to propagandize the masses. Their behavior was even more unethical than his. War, for all its attractiveness in *Peanuts*, was ugly on every level in this film, from the trenches to the general staff office.

The Blue Max was more about class war than about World War I. It pointed up the hypocrisy and frivolity of the upper classes. The working-class antihero, Bruno Stachel, was a tragic figure because he rejected the values of his own class in favor of the values of the hereditary ruling class. He wanted to know what it meant to be a man, but he did not even know what it meant to be human. By accepting the upper-class definition of manhood, he thus precluded for himself any chance of becoming human.

Perhaps social morality shines most brightly in those times when the rich prefer the values and attitudes of the so-called lower classes to their own habitual values and attitudes. Similarly, it may be equally true that this morality shines least brightly in those times when the lower classes emulate and idolize the rich instead of remaining true to themselves. When the children of the rich desert the rich and reject the values of the rich — that is auspicious!

It may not be much of an oversimplification to claim that the higher the social class, the greater the traditional and expected concern with appearance, while the lower the social class, the greater the natural and unavoidable concern with reality. As the rich fret about politeness, fashion, decorum, protocol, and other contrivances of the spoiled human soul, the poor are forced to struggle with genuine daily human needs. It is a sign of perversity and self-delusion when the poor attach importance to style and convention, just as it is a sign of enlightenment and not mere condescension when the young rich actually kick their old families in the ass and run off to make their livings honestly in the streets and shops. In every generation, there are young rich whose crocodile pity for the starving masses moves them to become social workers or some such like, to lend helping hands. They are generally more a part of the problem than a part of any solution. They maintain their ties with their families, and they rob the poor of their dignity. But — for a child of a rich family to break those ties unilaterally, and to choose — not just to live among the poor like some sort of missionary — but actually to become poor, to leave one class and embrace a new one, like an immigrant, a self-exile, or, from the family's point of view, a traitor, takes great courage, great love, great self-knowledge, and great contempt. By these standards, our generation was the most enlightened, virtuous, and introspective of any in American history.

Contempt for the rich, either the poor person's spontaneous and rather shallow contempt, based on simple resentment instead of first-hand awareness of conditions among the rulers, or the more rare and more surprising rich person's contempt, so much deeper because it is so much more intimate, is healthy.

Contempt is always a creative emotion. What does it create? Love! One truly loves good if and only if one has contempt for evil — and one loves evil if and only if one has contempt for good. Antipathy toward anything pushes you toward its opposite. Love of one thing is forever inseparable from contempt for its opposite or for its enemy. Indeed, it is precisely contempt that engenders any sort of love in the first place. Warmth would not be loved if cold were not first hated. Friends would not be sought and loved if loneliness were not first recognized and hated. Peace would not be cherished as an ideal if war were not first hated as a reality. The Cro-Magnon people would never have been inspired to forsake their caves if they had not somehow hated life as they then knew it.

No progress is ever possible unless prevailing conditions are first hated. Such contempt serves as the immediate impetus to move away from these conditions toward whatever is perceived to be better. Contempt is the most powerful motivator. Alexander Graham Bell would not have invented the telephone if he had not held some measure of contempt for life without such a device. Edward Jenner would not have discovered his vaccine if he had merely tolerated smallpox instead of actively hating it. Tolerance does not promote change in the status quo; but hatred does, for the human spirit cannot abide remaining in a state in which it hates what it encounters. It will seek to destroy or to make ineffectual the object of its contempt. We would not have loved the blunt earthiness and honesty that we saw in the poor if we had not first hated the delicate prettiness and hypocrisy that we saw in the rich. We would not have been "nigger lovers" if we had not first become "honky haters." We would not have preached against the Vietnam War if we had not first hated it — and because of this, some of us would not have been so desperate to respond positively to opportunistic demagogues like Bobby Kennedy if we had not first hated LBJ.

Contempt is the quintessential Nietzschean emotion and Friedrich Nietzsche was the quintessential philosopher for the sixties. After I first read *Thus Spake Zarathustra* in July 1966, I always kept a copy close by. Everything we sixties radicals are, were, or ever aspired to be is in that book. Read it slowly if you want to understand us.

We took seriously the word of Nietzsche's character Zarathustra, "I love the great despisers, because they are the great admirers, and arrows of yearning for the far shore."[36] Without contempt first, there is no possibility of love. The true enemy of the creative, living, loving human spirit is not hatred or contempt, but apathy. One can neither hate nor love unless one first cares.

The rich pretend that character determines the worth of the individual, but in fact, they believe worth to be determined by the size of one's bank account. The poor pretend that one's worth is determined by the size of one's bank account, but in fact, they know that worth is determined by one's character. An anonymous Victorian moralist, probably thinking to praise the upper classes and insult the lower, declared: "Servants talk about People; Gentlefolk discuss Things." But the last laugh is on this moralist — for the rich would not be able to talk about people even if they wanted to do so — because they do not know anything about people except how to exploit them!

None of our avowed contempt for the rich, the war, the racial and social environment, our institutions, schools, or even our parents, violated the Christian principle of loving one's enemy. You must understand how we loved and how we hated. If we hated our parents, we hated them as social types and not as human beings. If we hated LBJ, we hated him as a politician and especially as the president, but not as a person, however evil a person he may have been. Unfortunately, neither our parents nor LBJ ever understood our peculiar contempt for them, and never figured out how we could be consistent in damning them and at the same time calling for universal human love and respect. Richard Wagner never understood that Nietzsche's attacks on him were not personal, but only philosophical criticisms in which Wagner stood as a symbol for a certain set of ideas. Nietzsche always loved Wagner the man, but gradually came to hate Wagner the artist. Similarly, our attacks in the sixties were always philosophical and never personal, and we used certain people only as symbols of certain postures, and not as the butts of simple insolence or unwarranted meanness. In the spirit of Gandhi and

---

[36] *Also Sprach Zarathustra*, Preface 4, 6: "Ich liebe die grossen Verachtenden, weil sie die grossen Verehrenden sind und Pfeile der Sehnsucht nach dem andern Ufer."

Martin Luther King, we always loved our enemies, or at least tried to love them — but, like Jesus when he was throwing the moneychangers out of the temple, when they confronted us as enemies, instead of standing by us as people, we treated them as enemies. We did not hit first, but when we were hit, we only very seldom turned the other cheek.

But how did we hit back? Ah, there's the rub — or at least there was the rub for our foes. We hit back hard, but we did not hit back in kind. We hit back with messages — and our main message was that each individual human being has a unique, intrinsic, substantial, and incontrovertible worth that is completely unrelated to race, religion, sex, sexual preference, ethnic or national origin, hair length, bank balance, private habits, clothing selection, or even political orientation. Our strategies and practices for hitting back with this message were not always effective, but they were always very interesting. They ranged from complex, premeditated acts of civil disobedience to unrestrained exuberances of sheer fun.

Parents and adults do not take the opinions of teenagers seriously — and sometimes for good reason, since many teenagers are only interested in fun. We were indeed interested in fun, but also in *so much more* than mere fun. We had to be. But we could not convince anyone outside of our immediate sphere that we were to be taken seriously. Our plight was that of a sane person in a lunatic asylum which is run either by the lunatics themselves or by the wicked.

In "Over Under Sideways Down" the Yardbirds bragged of their aspiration to become all the wicked, horrible things that their elders had proclaimed were wrong. They were singing about hedonism, but we recognized that their message in this song applied equally well to sociopolitical leanings, to creativity, to intelligent alternatives, to free-spirited madness.

Madness, madness, madness ...

It was no accident that, in the mad summer of this mad year, a ridiculous novelty song like Napoleon XIV's "They're Coming to Take Me Away, Ha-Haaa!" rose as high as number three on the *Billboard* chart. That would not have happened either two years earlier (when we were too wrapped up in the Beatles) or two years later (when we were too serious).

Madness, madness, madness ...

Mad followed its June 1966 "Hypocrisy Primer" with "Mixing Personal Politics with Careers" in the July issue. The ultra-liberal restaurant owner told the customer what to eat then charged twenty times its value to cover full employment, foreign aid, and Medicare. The John Birch Society exterminator destroyed a home while trying to kill non-existent termites. The ultra-conservative used car salesman would not sell to immigrants and would only deal in handcrafted, non-union, pre-World-War-I models "built to precision by honest workmen who were proud to do an honest 14-hour-day's work for an honest dollar." The communist surgeon removed the patient's intestine to liberate the inflamed appendix. The socialist laundryman divided all his customers' shirts into equal piles and returned them without regard to size, color, condition, or previous ownership. The anarchist quarterback literally threw the bomb.

Madness, madness, madness ...

Hugh Sidey referred to us on page 34D of the July 1, 1966, issue of *Life* as the "tidal wave of young people which already has inundated education, altered fashions and literature, affected morals and music, changed our economics [and] is now being felt in presidential politics." His article was about how Bobby Kennedy was sucking up to us, and in so doing was positioning himself for a successful challenge to either LBJ in 1968 or Hubert Humphrey in 1972. Indeed many of my generation adored Bobby Kennedy, but to me he was always an unprincipled opportunist who knew how to work a crowd and owed as much to P.T. Barnum's there's-a-sucker-born-every-minute philosophy as to his late brother's unconscionable elevation of him to U.S. Attorney General over better qualified and more ethical lawyers.

Damn it, we had principles!

There were still quite a few songs in the air about mistreating or objectifying women. We hated this. Even those of us males who were not quite yet feminists objected to objectifying anyone. Our whole ideology was grounded in the principle that no one deserved to be objectified. People were simply people. They were not tools to be used, niggers to be lynched, dupes to be cheated, enemies to be killed, cunts to be fucked, tits to be felt, asses to be grabbed, servants to be browbeaten, masses to be controlled, or resources to be depleted. The peace movement was all about fairness, good will, and camaraderie — local on the practical level and worldwide on the ideal level. The civil rights movement was all about treating people as ends in themselves rather than as means to some boss's, general's, owner's, rich man's, landlord's, or politician's ends. Following our duty to our own consciences as the ultimate moral law, we put ethics above custom and obeyed Kant's categorical imperative to think and act always so that we would treat persons as ends in themselves, never as means to anyone else's ends.

Our whole agenda involved making friends. There are just two main ways to get rid of your enemy: either kill him/her or make him/her your friend. There are just two main ways to deal with someone who refuses to be your friend: either make her/him your enemy or ignore her/him. We preferred, whenever possible, to choose the latter of each of these two alternatives. However we dealt with the world, we tried not to make enemies, to acknowledge enemies, to ally ourselves with anyone who expected us to help them fight their enemies, or to allow the government or the church to tell us who our enemies should be.

This uplifting Kantian message appeared over and over again in our music. The Beatles' "We Can Work it Out" is an outstanding example.

The purpose of government is to protect the people from the corporations and other moneyed interests, not to control the people or to make wars. Government fails when it is in cahoots with these moneyed interests and thereby aids and abets them in their inveterate ambition to rip off the people for their own aggrandizement. The government providing for the "welfare" of the people does not mean putting them on the dole or dictating their economic lives; rather, it means creating and sustaining the conditions under which the "common wealth" of all the people can be ensured. This does not entail establishing central control of the economy or restricting free enterprise, but it does entail regulating the moneyed interests and

avoiding war. Official suspicion of the rich is good public policy, necessary to ensure the people's rights and freedoms, to prevent the rich from leading the nation
to war for their own glory, and to promote human values worldwide. Extra-governmental organizations and the free actions of free people are often also necessary to
safeguard these basic human rights, freedoms, and values of peace, prosperity, and
equality. The American Civil Liberties Union (ACLU), the Southern Christian
Leadership Conference (SCLC), the original Students for a Democratic Society
(SDS), and — founded this summer — the National Organization for Women
(NOW), are all examples of such organizations. Moreover, if they stay true to their
respective purposes, then such organizations as private liberal arts colleges, labor
unions, local granges, the American Association of Retired Persons (AARP), and
even the United Nations (UN) itself, likewise serve this safeguarding function.

The ultimate premise of Kantian ethics is freedom. All rational beings,
even humans, are free. If they were not, they would be incapable of ethical action,
their choices not their own, but dictated by external powers.

Into this rarefied atmosphere of idealism, egalitarianism, disobedience,
freedom, and nascent social revolution strode two scientists: William H. Masters, a
physician, and Virginia E. Johnson, a psychologist. Since 1957 their joint research
had concerned the sexual behavior of the human animal. With federal government
funding they hired hundreds of volunteers and, under strictly controlled laboratory
conditions, watched pairs copulate and singles masturbate. Until then the standard
in sex research had been Alfred Kinsey's two reports, *Sexual Behavior in the Human Male* (1948) and *Sexual Behavior in the Human Female* (1953). But Kinsey
had relied on interviews, not observation. Masters and Johnson sought to supersede Kinsey's speculative and qualitative research with hard facts and quantitative
science. On April 18, 1966, they published their discoveries as a book, *Human
Sexual Response*, not in the medical press, but with a trade publisher, Little, Brown
and Company. Even though written in rigorously clinical terms, by June 1966 — to
everyone's surprise — it was a runaway bestseller. Apparently the average American's appetite for information about raw, basic sex was greater than anyone had
imagined. Well, why not? We were not just a nation of frustrated voyeurs and perverts. We all had reasonable sexual needs that should have been satisfied, or at least
accounted for. From the Victorian era through the fifties sex had been rendered
diabolical, but our repressed souls were now starting to bring this natural and beautiful function out into the open where everyone, not just horny men, could enjoy
it. Dependable birth control and more accurate and comprehensive sex education
helped women to enjoy it as much as men did, so that they could approach it freely,
no longer dreading it as a procreative duty or a male demand.

Sex, sex, sex ...

After *Cleopatra*, stormy on-again-off-again real-life lovers Richard Burton
and Elizabeth Taylor co-starred in ten more films: *The V.I.P.s*, *The Sandpiper*,
Who's Afraid of Virginia Woolf?, *The Taming of the Shrew*, *Doctor Faustus*, *The
Comedians*, *Boom*, *Under Milk Wood*, *Hammersmith is Out*, and *Divorce His —
Divorce Hers*. By far the best of the bunch was *Who's Afraid of Virginia Woolf?*,
especially insofar as it was a grim revelation of our parents' generation's middle-

class misery wrought by their typical lack of honesty, sympathy, and general human respect. Burton and Taylor were both members of our parents' generation, so, even though we paid them some attention — we could not avoid the pervasive media hype about them — we did not put a lot of stock in them. To us, they were good examples of how *not* to live. *Who's Afraid of Virginia Woolf?* seemed like just an extended metaphor of their actual lives, or a convincing characterization of their ugly reality.

In *Who's Afraid of Virginia Woolf?* playwright Edward Albee, screenwriter Ernest Lehman, and director Mike Nichols broke through the flimsy public facades, posing, and cultivated politesse of regular, well-educated, middle-class American adults to show their carefully hidden real personalities exposed only in alcohol-fueled bickering, cruelty, and derision. Quite familiar to us kids was the phenomenon of couples inviting other couples into their homes — what they called "entertaining" — not because they wanted to or because they liked the people, but because their social position demanded it. Such phony, contrived, protocol-driven, child-banishing social activities as our parents seemed to enjoy were marked by insincere and self-delusional conversations about superficial values. Only occasional excess of alcohol ever brought out the truth. Our parents pretended to be so good, so pure, so upright, but in reality they were just boorish, sex-obsessed schlumps like anyone else. We were boorish and sex-obsessed too — but, unlike them, we were not hypocritical about it. We wore our ugly, perverse nastiness on our sleeves. Not our goodness, but our honesty, made us better than they, at least in that regard. Albee's naming the two main characters "George" and "Martha" was a stroke of brilliance. The reference was to George and Martha Washington, "The Father of Our Country" and his wife, the first "First Lady." This latter-day George and Martha, this childless couple, were indeed the parents of latter-day America.

Ω

The Rolling Stones' *Aftermath* was the first of many masterpiece albums that this band would release. It was their darkest LP to date — and it was their first to contain no cover tunes. Whether deserved or undeserved, much of the Stones' reputation for misogyny derives from it, mainly from two cuts, "Under My Thumb" and "Stupid Girl." It also included their magnificent "Paint It, Black." But above all, it was characterized by the Stones becoming more melodic and experimenting with a greater variety of instruments, including dulcimer, marimba, and, thanks to Ian Stewart and Jack Nitzsche, several kinds of keyboards.

"Lady Jane," a melancholy love song for three women at once (the other two being Lady Anne and sweet Marie), was a clear example of this turn toward the melodious and variegated. The singer planned to marry Lady Jane because she was the richest among them, and he promised to be faithful to her, but the tone of the song led us readily to surmise that he would not. "Don'cha Bother Me" expressed the singer's distaste for someone who copied his hair, clothes, and general appearance, and consequently was a year behind in the fashions. In "Think" the singer chastised his lover for having become predictable, dull, and complacent. "Flight 505" was sung from the point of view of a passenger killed in a plane crash. Ironically, he was on the plane to try to get away from his present life. In "High and Dry" the singer, having been dumped by a rich woman who correctly deduced that he was mainly after her money, declared his resolve to glom onto a poorer woman next time, for the sake of feeling more securely in love. Adding to the theme of "High and Dry," "It's Not Easy" bemoaned the solitary life of the jilted lover. With its rhythm played on a harpsichord, "I Am Waiting" recounted the impatient thoughts of a lonely man eager for a new lover. "Going Home," an extended blues number, was the Stones' first contribution to feeding our new appetite for long songs.

The Stones' concurrent single, "Mother's Little Helper," attacked the hypocrisy of the older generation with regard to drugs. While our elders scolded us, while their cops arrested us, and while their judges jailed us for our recreational use of marijuana and LSD, they themselves relied every day on prescription and non-prescription tranquilizers, sedatives, analgesics, etc. — not to mention alcohol, caffeine, and nicotine.

But the protest song was not the Stones' forte. That domain continued to be ruled by Pete Seeger, Phil Ochs, Joan Baez, and Dylan. Seeger's newest LP, *Dangerous Songs!?*, was one of his best and longest, with eighteen cuts. The only "danger" lay in *not* listening to them, in ignoring his message, in keeping our thoughts along the narrow lines where those who did not want us to listen to Pete Seeger wanted us to keep them. Ever the internationalist, he sang "Thoughts Are Free," i.e., "Die Gedanken sind Frei," in its original German. Other songs on this album denounced the draft, the Vietnam War, union-busting, capital punishment, racism, Roman Catholic opposition to birth control, and — brought to mind a host of issues to which every competent and conscientious citizen should have been paying attention.

The Beatles' *Yesterday and Today* was a compilation album of eleven songs. Although we had not yet heard all the tracks, they had all previously appeared in Britain and some in America as singles or B-sides; so really it included no new songs and broke no new ground. This album, as such, never appeared in Britain. In America it just marked time between two major, innovative achievements, *Rubber Soul* in December 1965 and *Revolver* in August 1966. The only discussion it sparked concerned its cover art. The original cover showed the four smiling broadly in white butcher jackets with beheaded dolls and bloody joints of meat hanging all over them. Parents, censors, uptight DJs, and other humorless types who could neither recognize nor appreciate a joke naturally went apeshit. Capitol Records had manufactured 750,000 copies of the album with that cover, but recalled all distributed copies immediately as soon as the general public reaction against it became known. Capitol then destroyed some of the covers and pasted over the rest with a rather dreary photo of the straightfaced Beatles in ordinary clothes, Paul sitting inside a steamer trunk, John sitting on top of it, and the other two standing in back.

The five songs on *Yesterday and Today* that had not previously appeared in America were John's "I'm Only Sleeping," "Dr. Robert," and "And Your Bird Can Sing"; Paul's "Drive My Car"; and George's "If I Needed Someone." "I'm Only Sleeping" was a paean to laziness, to staying in bed in the morning, and articulated well the implicit motto of many creative or artistic people who are lucky enough not to have to work nine to five: "Never before noon!" The music lent a dreamlike quality to the song that connoted drugs to some of us, but — in this case at least — it was probably best to take Lennon's lyrics just at face value. He was known not to be a so-called "morning person." "Dr. Robert," on the other hand, was obviously a drug song, yet what its nuances were, we could not tell, not being familiar with the British National Health Service. "And Your Bird Can Sing" seemed to criticize those who relied too much on their material possessions, but it was open to a variety of interpretations and we never really understood what it meant. "Bird," as we all knew, was British slang for "girl," so maybe that had something to do with it. "Drive My Car" was a catchy tune with silly lyrics about a man and a woman bantering and haggling over sex. Typical McCartney! "If I Needed Someone" was apparently just a love song.

We were hungry for new sounds. Starving, in fact. *Rubber Soul*, *Kinkdom*, and *Aftermath* had whetted our appetites. The basic formulas and instrumentation for our parents' music had been established in the thirties (male and female vocal soloists, bandleader, orchestra full of brass and woodwinds), and for rock-and-roll in the late fifties (vocals, drums, bass, one or two guitars, maybe a saxophone, maybe a piano or a Hammond B-3). Both genres had remained essentially unchanged since their respective inceptions and had descended into mannerism, i.e., the emphasis on style rather than on substance or innovation. What we were listening to was no longer "rock-and-roll." We now used that term to refer only to the Elvis-inspired, mostly pre-Beatles-or-if-post-Beatles-then-only-minimally-affected-by-the-Beatles kind of music, including such acts as Little Richard, Chubby Checker, the Dave Clark Five, Eddie Cochran, the Everly Brothers, Chuck Berry, Carl Perkins, Gene Vincent, Duane Eddy, Bo Diddley, and such like. We had enjoyed — very much — listening to them in their own time, but their time was now past. We wanted to hear not only sounds that we had never heard before, but also *types* of sounds that we had never heard before. We wanted our musicians to reinvent music — and that is what they were doing, at least the ones we cared about. We now called this music just "rock."

Of course, different kinds of rock emerged, depending on their influences. First came folk rock. By the decade's end there would be literally dozens of kinds of rock, e.g.: progressive rock (music incorporating a wide variety of instruments and techniques, often with classical motifs — the Beatles, Procol Harum, the Moody Blues); art rock (subspecies of progressive rock, but more experimental, *avant garde*, often with synthesizers and extended instrumental lines — Pink Floyd); raga rock (music featuring the sitar and other Indian classical instruments — George Harrison); psychedelic rock (music influenced by and evoking psychedelic drugs — the Grateful Dead, the Doors, the Byrds); acid rock (subspecies of psychedelic rock, but more heavily electronic, typically distorted, with the focus on LSD — Jefferson Airplane, Jimi Hendrix, Iron Butterfly); jazz rock (rock based in jazz — Chicago;

Blood, Sweat, and Tears); blues rock (rock based in the blues — Cream, the Rolling Stones, John Mayall); and hard rock (heavy, the precursor of heavy metal, usually with power chords, often with a progressive feel — the Who, the Yardbirds, Deep Purple, Steppenwolf). Bringing sitars, celestas, harpsichords, all sorts of other instruments, as well as feedback, crazy amplifications, and electronic studio tricks into the mix had started progressive rock in 1965. Every subsequent subgenre of rock grew out of progressive rock.

We had a premonition of the new directions in which the Beatles were about to move when their double-sided single, Paul's "Paperback Writer" and John's "Rain," made the charts in June. Both songs were substantial and ground-breaking. The former was an upbeat, danceable tune whose words seemed to criticize pulp fiction authors who pander to their editors and readers. Or maybe not. Maybe it was not critical at all, but merely descriptive. The latter used tapes played backwards and other experimental maneuvers to build an eerie sonic presence that combined well with John's didactic lyrics. His lesson was that we do ourselves no good by allowing our mood to be determined by external factors, such as the weather. Rather, we should each act independently to set our own mood, regardless of the weather or, by extension, anything else in our surroundings.

Revolver marked the Beatles' transition into sounds created in the studio that could not be reproduced on stage. Recorded music used to be the recording of performed music. But much of the music on *Revolver* could not be performed; it was layered over many sessions, and would not have existed without the complex electronic manipulations of George Martin.

Despite its interesting sound effects and general *bonhommie*, "Yellow Submarine" was fluff, pure fluff, one of very few Beatles songs that could be criticized in this way. John, Paul, Donovan, and several others colloborated to write a little party tune that Ringo could sing.

"Eleanor Rigby" was Paul's essay on loneliness, mortality, despair, and futility. Despite Father McKenzie's and Eleanor's close connection to the church, religion does not seem to have made either of their lives any better. His "Here, There, and Everywhere" was a gentle love song, expressing the completeness that he felt when his lover was near him. It was one of Paul's most eloquent lyrics. His "Good Day Sunshine" was a merry song of a romantic couple's joy, plain and simple. His "For No One" was exactly the opposite, a heartbreaking song of a dead relationship, warmth gone cold, passion forgotten, nothing forgiven. His "Got to Get You Into My Life" seemed to have been the singer's self-encouragement to chase a certain woman, but Paul much later said that it was about marijuana. If it really was a drug song, then Paul hid its actual meaning too well. It sure sounded like a love song. It still does.

George contributed three tunes: "Taxman," "Love You To," and "I Want to Tell You." The first was a political statement and sounded surprisingly right-wing, but probably attacked right-wing greed as much as it did left-wing mismanagement. The next featured George's hard-rocking sitar, lamented the transitoriness and brevity of life, and identified love as the only ray of hope. The third recounted the singer's nervousness and awkwardness in the presence of his intended lover.

John's "She Said She Said" introduced some incoherent concepts and asked a few stupid, unanswerable, and not even particularly philosophical questions: What is it like to be dead? What does it feel like not to have been born? Whoever "she" might have been remained a mystery, but obviously she had some profound effect on the singer. The song's incoherence made us instantly suspect that it was about LSD. We were right. John confirmed this interpretation many years later. His "Tomorrow Never Knows," the last cut on the American version of *Revolver*, appeared to resolve some of the incoherence of "She Said She Said." Its mystical tones created an atmosphere of resignation and serenity that conveyed well the Hindu monism that was at the heart of its message. Drugs may have been involved too, but they did not seem necessary, or at least not as important as introspection and meditation.

The back cover of Donovan's breakthrough album, one of the first important psychedelic albums, *Sunshine Superman*, featured Donovan's unique way of listing his tunes:

> part one, sunshine super-duper man: a collapsed love affair no less. the legend of the girl-child linda: a tale for ageing children. twelve kingfishers: dive — a flash of turquoise-brilliants into the pool (summer — donoleitcho's island). the ferris wheel: from the kingdom of the green witch, a girl spoke of how she'd gotten her hair caught in a wheel of sorts. i've been looking through ice-blue shades: someday my princess will come (soon please).

> part two. the season of the witch: starring mr. plod in action with a daughter of the evil land of mordor. the trip: is a hub of life, a club of life in the vest coat of the americas. the lady guinevere: all of a sudden i was there, 400 a.d., hidding like a child watching. ... the fat angel: appeared to me on visit to los angeles. celeste is my name for the lady weaver of all the skies who weaves our fates on a silver loom in the silent room of eternal love.

We could make almost nothing of his cryptic references. We thought that the title cut, his current single, was a drug song, not a love song, the "sunshine" referring to a variety of LSD. Many years later we would learn that Jimmy Page had played guitar on that song. Linda was Donovan's then girlfriend, Linda Lawrence, Brian Jones's former girlfriend, but we did not know any of that yet. We did know, however, that Donovan and Brian were close personal friends and mutual musical influences. The next tune was called "Three King Fishers" even though it indeed mentioned twelve. "Ferris Wheel," a sitar piece rife with mystical images, many concerning hair, was one of two songs on this LP (the other being "The Fat Angel") to mention a silver bicycle. But who knew what that meant? The Bert of "Bert's Blues" was Bert Jansch, but we in America would not figure that out until Pentangle became popular here in 1969. "Season of the Witch" seemed to be about paranoia. Many of us who were not yet familiar with J.R.R. Tolkien's *Lord of the Rings* first learned of it from Donovan's reference to Mordor (above). Naturally we then had to go and read those wonderful books. We discovered a lot about literature by listening to song lyrics and reading liner notes. Exploiting a *double entendre*, "The

Trip" referred to both a real nightclub in L.A. and the LSD experience. "Guinevere," the imagined apotheosis of the queen of the early medieval British court, painted an idyllic picture of a particularly beautiful and mysterious woman. This song is not to be confused with David Crosby's "Guinnevere" (two n's), which would appear three years later on the eponymous debut LP of Crosby, Stills, and Nash.

"Celeste" accurately reflected the feelings of those of us who had not sold out and probably never would sell out. The utter sincerity of its lyrics was remarkable. The singer, being conscious of his acting and his silliness, thereby showed that he was in fact neither acting nor silly, but entirely true to himself, pure in his intentions, and deeply in love. His happiness derived from his authenticity. Even sharing his lover's sadness brought joy to them both. His honesty, optimism, and guileless joy brightened not only his own and his lover's lives, but the whole world. Such unassuming modesty was rare and refreshing in a rock ballad lyric.

"The Fat Angel" may have been Mama Cass Elliot — or maybe just a large jet airplane. Even as the Byrds' "Eight Miles High" may have been about a plane trip from L.A. to London, "The Fat Angel" may have been about a plane trip from London to L.A. — or it may have been mainly about drugs. Its drug references were more obvious than those alleged to have been in "Eight Miles High." It advertised Trans-Love Airways and Jefferson Airplane. But what were Trans-Love Airways and Jefferson Airplane?

With the exception of WKBW-AM listeners, very few people in the east noticed Jefferson Airplane's debut album, *Jefferson Airplane Takes Off*. It was still Marty Balin's band, not yet Paul Kantner's. Signe Toly Anderson and Marty were the lead singers. Jack Casady was on bass, Jorma Kaukonen on lead guitar, and Skip Spence, soon to be the founding rhythm guitarist of Moby Grape, on drums. Grace Slick was still in the Great Society, where she remained mostly unknown.

The tunes on *Takes Off* were bluesy, subdued, romantic. Marty wrote or co-wrote eight of the eleven songs and was, at that time in his career, thoroughly into ballads. Signe's roots were in folk music. Her covers of Chet Powers's "(Let's) Get Together," which the Youngbloods would soon make a folk rock standard, and Lester Melrose's "Chauffeur Blues" were powerful and entrancing. Likewise Marty's vocals on "Blues from an Airplane," "It's No Secret," the ultra-soft "Come Up the Years," "And I Like It," and "Don't Slip Away." Even though the album sounded pretty good loud, it did not really rock. It was not druggy or political in the least. Its big attractions were Marty's voice, Jorma's guitar, Jack's bass, and their unique harmonic and melodic progressions, all of which foreshadowed greater things to come.

Despite getting almost no radio airplay, the Mothers of Invention burst like gangbusters into the underground scene with their debut album, *Freak Out*. Their leader, Frank Zappa, was not only the consummate iconoclast and a singularly unrestrained political satirist, but also a fine musician, as both a guitarist and a composer/arranger. The titles alone of their songs were evidence enough that they were not "just another band from L.A." We marvelled at the album cover in the record stores before we ever heard a note of their music. The visual presentation of *Freak Out* bordered on Dada. It fascinated us. We had to hear whatever sounds were created by people who would allow their music to be enclosed in such a cover. Who was Suzy Creamcheese? What got into her? Why did she type on the back cover:

> These Mothers is crazy. You can tell by their clothes. One guy wears beads and they all smell bad. We were gonna get them for a dance after the basketball game but my best pal warned me you can never tell how many will show up ... sometimes the guy in the fur coat doesn't show up and sometimes he does show up only he brings a big bunch of crazy people with him and they dance all over the place. None of the kids at my school like these Mothers ... specially since my teacher told us what the words to their songs meant.

Suzy was uptight. The Mothers' music did not make us want to dance, but it certainly made us think. Zappa pulled absolutely no punches when writing about sex, hypocrisy, conformity, politics, phoniness, censorship, teenage superficiality, adult stupor, etc., and each of his songs dealt with one of more of these topics or with something at least as important. There was no fluff on this album — unless *avant garde* compositions are to be considered fluff. Aside from the lyrics, the music was progressive rock, influenced about equally by jazz percussion, fifties doo wop harmonies, and the work of Edgard Varèse. Altogether *Freak Out* was worthy of Zappa's boast that it had "no commercial potential."

"Hungry Freaks, Daddy" took the message of Dylan's "Ballad of a Thin Man" further — in a threatening, apocalyptic direction. The lyrics spoke of the inevitability of a revolt of the frustrated against the anti-intellectualism of LBJ's Great Society, of freethinkers against its ineffective, mind-numbing schools, of honest folk against the consumerism and babbitry of middle-class Americans, and especially of the sexually, culturally, and socially repressed against the pervasive lack of true personal freedom throughout America. This revolt might not be violent, but it would be authentic, powerful, broad-based, and quintessentially American. It would be the true pursuit of the American dream, in the face of the government that simultaneously promoted and obstructed the realization this dream. The great hypocrisy of the Great Society was that it pretended to be inclusive, but in fact systematically excluded freaks, i.e., non-conformists who thought for themselves, opposed America's fundamental shallowness and belligerence, sneered at money, and did not espouse mediocrity, but aspired instead to cultural, artistic, musical, and spiritual excellence.

"I Ain't Got No Heart" expressed the singer's disdain for sentimental love. Such cynicism was obviously the pose of a persona. Not that Zappa himself was not cynical. He was. Supremely. But not in this direction.

"Who Are the Brain Police?" The purveyors of artificiality and inauthenticity? Your neighbors? Your friends? Your parents? Your TV sets? Your plastic appliances? Your stupid little selves? That kazoo player in the background of this song? Your dependence on any of these?

"Go Cry on Somebody's Else's Shoulder" was a whiny doo wop parody sung in a stereotyped Chicano accent and laced with not-very-subtle sexual innuendos. Its satire on the leftover fifties teenage emphasis on cars, clothes, properly greased-back hair, and other meaningless status symbols was priceless.

"Motherly Love" was an unabashed and explicit call for any and all young, beautiful women to become groupies and get laid by the band. Of course, the lyrics claimed in typical male braggadocio that each Mother was gigantically endowed and incredibly proficient in bed.

"How Could I Be Such a Fool?" was just a straightforward love song in waltz time.

"Wowie Zowie" was a frank [pun intended] admission that the singer did not care whom he fucked or what she looked like, smelled like, or tasted like, or who her parents were, or how she dressed, or whether she practiced adequate personal hygiene, etc., etc., etc. — just as long as she put out.

"You Didn't Try to Call Me" was like chapter two of "Wowie Zowie." The high school girl was not attracted by the high school boy's specially pampered car, did not call, did not show up, and did not put out.

"Any Way the Wind Blows" ratherly bitterly attacked the woman whom the singer was leaving and rationalized their break-up.

"I'm Not Satisfied" showed the singer contemplating suicide over his perceived victimization at the hands of just about everyone. It was not an exercise in self-pity, but an eloquent if oblique statement of why self-pity should be avoided. All the singer's ventures had failed, his love life was in shambles, but instead of despairing, he should have become proud of his individuality and uniqueness. He should even have dared other people to like him, instead of caring whether they did or not. He alone, within himself, had the ability to turn his failure into success, but he allowed his failure to get the better of him.

"You're Probably Wondering Why I'm Here" attacked phony high school hipness based on clothes and cars rather than knowledge. Zappa could not endure anyone who claimed to be anything that they were not, and here he unleashed his vitriol not only against the obedient kids with fifties mentalities, who, like Wally and Beaver Cleaver, acted oh-so-good while in fact smothering their own natural human qualities and sexual inclinations, but also and especially against the pretentious teeny boppers of the mid-sixties, who acted oh-so-hip when in fact they were naive little twerps, annoying little brats, and mindless little copycats, just as mired in the plastic values of white suburbia as were Wally and Beaver.

Ashamed of how his white race treated blacks, Zappa wrote in the liner notes that "Trouble Every Day" "is how I feel about racial unrest in general and the Watts situation in particular. It was written during the Watts riot as it developed. I shopped it briefly all over Hollywood but no one would touch it ... everybody worries so much about not getting any air play. My, my." His main complaint was that mainstream America just watched racial injustice on TV but did not *do* anything about it. They merely absorbed the news as if it were the sports, the weather, a sitcom, or any other TV show.

"Help, I'm a Rock" was partially a spoof of Simon and Garfunkel's "I Am a Rock" but more cogently a comedic strike at the monolithic mentality of police and politicians.

"The Return of the Son of Monster Magnet" was a sonic montage of slogans, absurd noises, discordant harmonies, jazz breaks, instrumental incongruities, sexual propositions, and vocal novelties. Here we learned that the term "freak out," which we had believed referred only to having a bad experience on hallucinatory drugs, held for Zappa also a sociopolitical meaning akin to what Timothy Leary would soon signify by "Turn on! Tune in! Drop out!" That is, he was contrasting straight society to freak society, and encouraging the misfits of straight society to be true to themselves, to admit they were freaks, to drop out of straight society, and stop acting phony like Wally and the Beav. Naturally we identified with these freaks. We did not yet know that Zappa did not use — and was strictly opposed to his band members using — marijuana, LSD, alcohol, and the whole plethora of mind-altering substances. Of course, at this early stage, and given that he was so weird, we naturally assumed that he was a drug user — a huge, prolific drug user.[37] Ah well ... some of us don't need 'em.

Napoléon Bonaparte told the Conseil d'État on March 4, 1806: "Religion establishes a heavenly idea of equality that prevents the poor from slaughtering the rich."[38] Zappa wrote in the liner notes of *Freak Out* that he told tourists at the Whisky-a-Go-Go in Los Angeles in December 1965: "If your children ever find out how lame you really are, they'll murder you in your sleep."

For the profound effect it had on turning culture around, *Freak Out* was the most important album of the year, even more so than *Revolver*.

Freak Out was a revelation! The Mothers of Invention came across as angry young judges with a sense of humor — as opposed to the SDS and SNCC: angry young judges with no sense of humor.

Ω

Among singles, we enjoyed everything from ballads to folk rock to soul to harder and harder solid rock.

In "I Saw Her Again," the Mamas' and the Papas' third single, the singer pretended to regret leading a woman on, just using her for sex and to get back at another woman. It was not so blunt or blatant as the Stones' "Under My Thumb," but every bit as misogynistic. Simon and Garfunkel's "The Dangling Conversation" indicted superficiality and pretension among the educated classes and especially among neurotic urban snobs of literature, art, and theater. It was even more existentialistic than most of Simon's lyrics — but more erudite too, with apt references to Emily Dickinson, Robert Frost, and psychoanalysis.

---

[37] I think I know how Zappa must have felt. From the late sixties on, because I had long hair, bare feet, idiosyncratic clothes, and oddball ideas, people just assumed that I did marijuana, LSD, mescaline, and all sorts of similar drugs. But the fact is I did not do marijuana until 1976 and I never did any of the others. Three cheers for stereotypes!!!

[38] "La religion rattache au ciel une idée d'égalité qui empêche le riche d'être massacré par le pauvre."

In soul music, the wicked, wicked Wilson Pickett injected a ton of energy into "Land of 1000 Dances," thus making a big improvement over the relatively sleepy 1965 version by Cannibal and the Headhunters. Lee Dorsey's "Working in the Coal Mine" gave us a bit of insight into the social and personal problems caused by the persistent exhaustion of the working class. Stevie Wonder became the umpteenth artist to cover Dylan's "Blowin' in the Wind." Jimmy Ruffin, the older brother of the Temptations' David Ruffin, had a big hit with "What Becomes of the Brokenhearted?", one of Motown's most important songs, containing unusually poignant lyrics of hope hidden beneath despair.

The Troggs (short for Troglodytes) built "Wild Thing" around a simple, basic, I-IV-V-IV progression in A major. It was barely melodic at all, but it was raunchy as hell. In the seventies, bands like the Ramones would return to the simplest possible music to create punk rock, but let the punk rockers never forget that the Troggs were their godfathers. Other hard rock this summer included the Who's fifth American single, "The Kids Are Alright," in which the singer renounced jealousy and proclaimed instead that he wanted whatever would be best for his girlfriend, even if that would not involve him. Surprisingly, one of the hardest rocking and most fun songs of the season was from a folk rock group: the Lovin' Spoonful's "Summer in the City," which painted a vivid picture of hot, sweaty days and nights in New York.

Among this summer's most inspirational anthems was the flipside of the Kinks' ode to untroubled laziness, "Sunny Afternoon": the angry, defiant, yet sorrowful "I'm Not Like Everybody Else." The title spoke for itself and the lyrics did not disappoint. With its tearjerking pattern of A minor, D, and E minor chords and its low-end melody, it drove the point home that sincere, self-respecting individualism was the best way to live, even if such a life meant being miserable. Permanent self-respect on our own terms was more important than transient happiness on anyone else's terms, because it would eventually provide a higher, more secure form of happiness. None of us indeed was like anybody else. It was well about time that we each came to grips with that basic fact. If Ray Davies had never written another song, "I'm Not Like Everybody Else" alone would have made him a hero.

Ω

In August 1966 a bizarre, remarkable, and far-reaching chain of events arose from a five-month-old offhand remark and a few misunderstandings, mishandlings, or perhaps intentional manipulations in the American press.

On March 4 Maureen Cleave's tasteful, purely descriptive article, "How Does a Beatle Live? John Lennon Lives Like This," in the *London Evening Standard* contained the following paragraph:

Experience has sown few seeds of doubt in him: not that his mind is closed, but it's closed round whatever he believes at the time. 'Christianity will go,' he said. 'It will vanish and shrink. I needn't argue about that; I'm right and I will be proved right. We're more popular than Jesus now; I don't know which will go first — rock 'n' roll or Christianity. Jesus was all right but his disciples were thick and ordinary. It's them twisting it that ruins it for me.' He is reading extensively about religion.

Of course he was only making a blunt observation about the level of his band's success. At the time he said it, it may even have been true, at least in the English-speaking world. The British, quite sensibly, took the whole thing in stride. No big deal. A simple empirical statement, perhaps verifiable, perhaps not, and a simple prediction, not verifiable.

On July 29 *Datebook*, a cheapo teeny bopper magazine, published its September 1966 "Shout-Out Issue." Its cover had a very nice color photo of Paul McCartney and eight out-of-context quotations, including: "Paul McCartney: 'It's a lousy country where anyone black is a dirty nigger.' John Lennon: 'I don't know which will go first — rock 'n' roll or Christianity.' ... Dylan: 'Message songs are a drug!' ... Tim Leary: 'Turn on, tune in, drop out!' ..." The story itself, "The Ten Adults You Dig / Hate the Most," continued the out-of-context skewing. Lennon was thoroughly misrepresented.

Fundamentalist Christians surged out of the woodwork. Newspapers across the nation and the world glommed onto the story. Conservative preachers went apeshit. Never known for their subtlety in parsing non-biblical language or in understanding non-biblical logic, they took Lennon's innocent and rather serene comment as a blasphemous rant. They and everyone else mostly ignored McCartney's and Leary's more inflammatory quotes on the same cover of *Datebook*.

The first week of August saw anti-Beatle protests nationwide, but especially in the South and Midwest, the so-called "Bible Belt." These included death threats sent to not only Lennon, but also the other three, who had nothing to do with it. There were mass record smashings, stompings, and trashings of Beatles records; bonfires of Beatles merchandise of all kinds; burnings in effigy; solemn vows of true believers never to listen to Beatles music again; and all sorts of other overreactive lunacy. Even some radio stations, which had previously played the Beatles, organized anti-Beatles rallies. The Ku Klux Klan got into it too. Apparently any perceived danger to the eternal might of Jesus Christ is also a danger to pointy-headed white supremacy. Or so believe the sheep. Must be, because, on August 8, the Apartheid regime banned the Beatles and their music from South Africa.

August 1966 was a defining moment in the psychology of the polarization of America. Conservatives, fundamentalists, traditionalists, and their ilk retreated away from the Beatles and progressive rock toward Elvis, Jerry Lee Lewis, rockabilly, country-and-western, etc., i.e., the basic, sensual, driving, but non-political hard rock that would eventually become "southern rock" in the early to mid-seventies — the Allman Brothers notwithstanding. On the other hand, liberals, secularists, non-conformists, and our ilk rejected Elvis *et al.*, and embraced the Beatles, the progressive rockers, the freethinking *avant garde*, *et al.*, even more lovingly than before. We were the only people who bought *Revolver*. Rock had become political: the Beatles and their fans on the left, Elvis and his fans on the right. It is no accident that Elvis himself would later volunteer to be Nixon's narc.

When the Beatles conquered America on February 9, 1964, there were no discernible sociopolitical or religious differences among their new fans. Beatle-mania attracted rich kids, poor kids, white kids, black kids, conservative kids, liberal kids, religious kids, secular kids. This undifferentiated fan profile remained generally true for the next two-and-a-half years. The Beatles' music had united these millions of kids against older people — also of all sociopolitical and religious stripes — who just happened not to like that kind of music. The only issues originally dividing Beatlemaniacs from non-Beatlemaniacs were the music itself and issues closely related to the band's public image, e.g., hair, clothes, and drugs. Nothing substantially divided Beatlemaniacs from each other. Religion, politics, and socioeconomic class were not much at issue — yet.

Fall 1966

For what it's worth...

About this time the word "hippie" entered the general vocabulary. Please understand that we seldom called ourselves "hippies" — we called ourselves "freaks" — but we did not object to being called "hippies," at least not until much later, after the concept of "hippie" had become a caricature in the early seventies. "Hippies" was what those who did not understand us called us. Strictly speaking, a "hippie" was only someone who was "hip" to drugs. To our detractors we were no more than this; but in fact we were quite distinct from such cardboard cutout junkies, and with an entirely different set of goals. Thus we called ourselves "freaks." A "freak" is just that — a "freak." If they had only known.

But what was a hippie/freak? What did it mean to be a hippie/freak? Above all, the hippie/freak was political. The hair, the drugs, the clothes, and even the music were less important than the politics — and those other things all derived from sociopolitical ideology or sociopolitical gut feelings anyway. Hippie/freak politics was primarily nonconformist and secondarily socialist. The hippie/freak loved nothing as much as freedom. Ironically, the clearest and most accurate example of what it meant to be a hippie/freak was made over twenty years later by a non-hippie/freak, i.e., by the lone civilian who stood up to a column of tanks in Tiananmen Square in June 1989. That action was quintessentially hippie/freak.

Some say that — despite his long hair and scruffy, idiosyncratic appearance — Frank Zappa was not a hippie/freak because he did not do drugs himself, did not allow members of his band to use them, and had no tolerance for what he called the "cosmic debris" of fanciful, irrational, metaphysical speculation. But hippies/freaks were not defined by their love of recreational drugs, their astrological beliefs, their improbable sentiments, their occultic predilections, or even their clothes and hair. Rather, they were best identified by their steadfast love of complete personal freedom, their unrestrained irreverence, their firm refusal to follow any rules without first knowing why, and their belief in the natural and unbreakable link between music and politics. Thus Zappa, the creator of some of the best anti-establishment musical satire of the twentieth century, the author of "The

Oracle Has It All Psyched Out," the model for the "Phi Zappa Krappa" poster, the confidant of Václav Havel, and the anti-censorship nemesis of Tipper Gore and the Parents' Music Resource Center (PMRC), could easily be seen as the ultimate, archetypal hippie/freak.

Even though politics was paramount in hippie/freakdom, it was music that defined the hippie/freak. Musicians, like their listeners, had begun to ramify into hippie/freak and non-hippie/freak, or straight. Los Angeles, at least for the time being, was the epicenter of hippie/freak culture. Neither London, New York, nor even San Francisco were yet noteworthy in that regard.

The Byrds soon became known, again at least for the time being, as the pivotal hippie/freak band. Their "5D" was a hippie/freak anthem, a very important song for both its eerie, ethereal sound and especially its lyrics. The single had come out in July but went nowhere. Not until the LP appeared in September did people who did not listen to WKBW or other early progressive radio stations first become aware of it. McGuinn sang of how science and technology had advanced at a maddening pace, while progress in social justice, ethics, morality, and common human decency had lagged behind and had even been victimized by sci-tech progress. His message was to open our hearts to universal love, beauty, and harmony, not to restrict our aspirations to the cold and narrow world of mere analysis, logic, and discord. Resonance with William Blake, John Keats, and the rest of the English Romantic poets was obvious. Yes, it was a drug song, but primarily an exploration of the intellectual or introspective value of psychedelic substances.

Also on the LP, *Fifth Dimension*, besides "5D" and "Eight Miles High" was their current single, "Mr. Spaceman." At first listen it seemed just a comic interlude in the Byrds' *oeuvre*, but closer attention suggested that it held just as serious a message as any other McGuinn song, namely that, if we wish to expand our horizons, it would be best to treat other creatures, other species, even extraterrestrials, with respect. Its flipside, Crosby's "What's Happening?!?!," amid enthralling guitar effects expressed his general dismay with whatever he did not yet understand. The album *in toto* was noteworthy for its innovative arrangements, augmented by the performances of session keyboardist Van Dyke Parks.

Among the new hippie/freak bands, the most influential would prove to be a quintet of folk rockers from Los Angeles: Richie Furay, Dewey Martin, Bruce Palmer, Stephen Stills, and Neil Young — Buffalo Springfield. Either Stills or Young wrote each song, but Furay sang lead on half of them. Stills's masterpiece, "For What It's Worth," did not appear in the original monaural version of the debut album, but, to reflect its release as a single in January 1967, it replaced his "Baby Don't Scold Me" as soon as the LP came out in stereo. "For What It's Worth" told the story of a particular confrontation between police and protesters on Sunset Strip in Los Angeles, but, because Stills wrote its lyrics in general terms, it came to signify all contemporary protests and confrontations, whether related to the Vietnam War, racial injustice, labor vs. management, free speech, or any other issue that motivated its advocates to take to the streets.

Young's "Nowadays Clancy Can't Even Sing" was a poignant lyric about a free man repressed and prevented from realizing his most personal aspirations.

We all felt like that. Such (parental) repression became a common theme in rock. Perhaps its most eloquent articulation was in Pink Floyd's "Mother" on *The Wall*, released in 1979.

Of all the folkies, the most beautiful voice belonged to Judy Collins. She did not write very much of her own material, but her singing was so nearly perfect that we forgave her that little deficiency. She was as famous for her gorgeous blue eyes as for her lovely music. Concertgoers in the back rows of large halls, without binoculars, could see clearly the pair of faultless sapphires that Stills would a few years later celebrate in "Suite: Judy Blue Eyes."

Her sixth album, *In My Life*, revealed her radical sociopolitical leanings more distinctly than any of her previous five or subsequent dozens. Opening with Dylan's "Tom Thumb's Blues,"[39] a song about helplessness in an unfamiliar environment, Judy established the bittersweet, sometimes melancholy, sometimes comical tone of the album. In Richard Fariña's[40] "Hard Lovin' Loser" she lampooned phony macho posers. For Bertolt Brecht's and Kurt Weill's "Pirate Jenny," a key moment in *The Threepenny Opera*, Judy assumed the persona of a resentful scrubwoman drudging for pittance and occasional patronizing tips at an upper-class hotel. From her dream of killing the guests, Brecht and Weill intended us to infer the justice of the lowest classes inflicting the bloodiest possible revenge on their masters and bosses. Leonard Cohen's "Suzanne," the only non-sociopolitical song on the album, was an intensely private lyric about Suzanne Verdal, a dancer whom Cohen knew in Montréal. Jacques Brel's "La Colombe," translated as "The Dove" by Alasdair Clayre, was a didactic antiwar sermon that implicitly invoked Matthew 10:34, where Jesus proclaimed, "Do not think that I have come to bring peace on earth. I come not to bring peace, but a sword." The loss of hope, the adoration of weapons, the desensitizing of young men, the perverse aims of nations, and the eventual onset of war all combine to kill the dove of peace.

The focal point of *In My Life* was "Marat/Sade," a medley derived from Richard Peaslee's and Adrian Mitchell's musical version of *The Persecution and Assassination of Jean-Paul Marat as Performed by the Inmates of the Asylum of Charenton under the Direction of the Marquis de Sade*[41] by Peter Weiss, better known by its short title, *Marat/Sade*. The play achieved worldwide acclaim as soon as Peter Brook staged it in London in 1964. Brook would make it into a movie in 1967. Judy sang the medley as a revolutionary anthem. Her scene was France in mid-Revolution: early 1793. The king was dead, the queen was in prison, and power was uneasily divided between the moderate Girondins and the more radical Montagnards, which consisted mainly of two factions: Jean-Paul Marat's and Georges Jacques Danton's Cordeliers and Maximilien Robespierre's Jacobins. Many middle-

---

[39] On *Highway 61 Revisited* it is called "Just Like Tom Thumb's Blues."

[40] Joan Baez's brother-in-law. Her sister Mimi married him in 1963. He died at twenty-nine in a motorcycle crash on April 30, 1966, during Mimi's twenty-first birthday party.

[41] Written in 1963 as *Die Verfolgung und Ermordung Jean Paul Marats dargestellt durch die Schauspielgruppe des Hospizes zu Charenton unter Anleitung des Herrn de Sade*, translated in 1964 by Geoffrey Skelton.

class and lower-class groups and individuals had profited from the Revolution, but the Sansculottes, the lowest and poorest stratum of society, had gotten nothing. Their only advocate and only hope was Marat, who since 1789 had been publishing an underground journal, *L'Ami du peuple* (*The Friend of the People*). The Sansculottes called him also "the friend of the people." He voiced their hatred of all their oppressors: the royalty, the nobility, aristocrats, landowners, businessmen, the military, the priests, and the Girondins. He did not seek to quell their impatience, but encouraged them to rise up with as much violence as necessary to secure their rights. The "Marat/Sade" medley related his being hounded by the Girondins.[42] If this medley accomplished nothing else, it reminded us that all class-based revolution harks back to the French Revolution.

We did not believe that in any of this Judy was condoning violence, even revolutionary violence. Rather, she was only understanding that, given the harsh rule and demeaning conditions that the upper classes routinely impose on the lower, such violence is historically inevitable and such cruel attitudes as Jenny's and the Sansculottes' are at least predictable if not also sometimes justifiable.

Randy Newman's "I Think It's Going to Rain Today" lamented the fragility of the best human qualities and suggested that loneliness, indifference, and deceit always remained only a heartbeat away. Donovan's "Sunny Goodge Street" surveyed north London's mod, drug, music, and bar scene. Stan Kelly's "Liverpool Lullaby" grieved for the apparently neverending cycle of physical and psychological violence of parents against children. Cohen's "Dress Rehearsal Rag" showed a down-and-out actor contemplating suicide. The album ended with the title cut, Judy's wistful cover of the Beatles' masterpiece from *Rubber Soul*.

The tunes and lyrics on Simon and Garfunkel's *Parsley, Sage, Rosemary, and Thyme* were not as gloomy as those on *Sounds of Silence*, and the psychological import may have diminished, but the music was every bit as excellent, the harmonies were every bit as captivating, and the sociopolitical message was heightened. As Ralph Gleason wrote in the liner notes (lumping the non-writing Garfunkel in with the writing Simon):

> That Simon and Garfunkel — and the other representatives of the new generation's songwriters, an elite which includes Bob Dylan, Phil Ochs, John Sebastian, Marty Balin, Dino Valenti, Tim Hardin, Al Kooper, Smokey Robinson, Mick Jagger, John Lennon, Paul McCartney, John Phillips and others — have succeeded in putting beauty and truth and meaning into popular song, fractures the stereotyped adult view that the music of youth is at best only trivial rhymes and silly teen-age noise, and at worst offensive.
>
> This generation is producing poets who write songs, and never before in the sixty-year history of [recorded] American popular music has this been true. ...
>
> ... The references to Tolstoy and to Tinker Bell ... all assume a common experience and a common language, the international language of youth. ...

---

[42] The historical Marat was murdered on July 13, 1793 by a Girondin, Charlotte Corday.

... There are songs of alienation but there are songs of love, too, and they touch closely the prevailing philosophical current of the New Youth which is that of creativity AGAINST the machine and, thus, FOR humanity.

It is no accident that this album is dedicated to Lenny Bruce. As is becoming evident, he was a secular saint. His torture, like that of youth and of the new music, at the hands of the Establishment (remember when Congressional hearings deplored the state of popular music?) links them together.

An anonymous article called "The New Troubadours" in the October 28, 1966, issue of *Time* magazine discussed the newfangled rock music that had upset some kids because they could not dance to it. The author referred to the Lovin' Spoonful, the Beatles, Donovan, the Mamas and the Papas, and S&G:

Paul Simon and Art Garfunkel, both 23, are the most literate of the new troubadours. Their low-key harmonizing has sold nearly 6,000,000 records in the past year. They sing about man's failure, naturally, to communicate ... The team switched from folk singing to folk rock because "those mountain songs didn't say anything to the kids in the 22-story apartment house." Songwriter Simon, a short moonfaced lad whose lyrics are studied in a few high school English courses, does not admit to any big message. "We are just creating doubts and raising questions," he explains. Garfunkel, a Columbia University graduate student who sports a Dr. Zorba shock of electrified hair, says: "Pop music is the most vibrant force in music today. It's like dope — so heady, so alive."

Parsley, Sage, Rosemary, and Thyme contained ten tunes besides the already familiar "Homeward Bound" and "The Dangling Conversation." In "Scarborough Fair / Canticle" Simon and Garfunkel sang two songs at once, one an English Renaissance folk song about a man who set a woman a series of impossible tasks to win his love, the other Simon's melody with Garfunkel's antiwar lyrics, telling of the individual soldier's alienation or detachment from the generals' immersion in the joy of killing. Also serving as antiwar counterpoint was "7 O'Clock News / Silent Night," which juxtaposed the solemn Christmas hymn to a TV newscaster's dry reading of gloomy stories about LBJ's activities, Lenny Bruce's death, mass murders in Chicago, antiwar protests, and Nixon's hawkishness.

Continuing the antiwar theme, but in a humorous, multi-satiric way was "A Simple Desultory Philippic (or How I Was Robert McNamara'd Into Submission)." Making a verb out of the detested McNamara's name immediately told the whole story, i.e., the singer had been tricked, browbeaten, cajoled, harassed, bullied, misled, and perhaps even drafted into submission. Sometimes in concert Simon would change the lyrics quite a lot, and the subtitle to "How I Was Lyndon Johnsoned Into Submission." Same difference. McNamara and LBJ. Equally guilty. Anyway, the words complained about how the singer suffered sensory overload from so many uninvited influences on his daily life. These personified intrusions included Bob Dylan, Ayn Rand, Norman Mailer, the Stones, the Beatles, Phil Spector, Andy Warhol, Barry Sadler, etc., etc., etc., all of whom in their combined effect left him confused about the meaning of culture, society, and the world in general. A few lines may have suggested just smoking pot and forgetting about it all, but a more plausible interpretation would be that the song advocated just smoking pot and confronting it all. Don't give up! *Illegitimi non carborundum!*

S&G touted something called "The Big Bright Green Pleasure Machine" as a panacea, but what was it? Marijuana? A television set? A muscle car? What? As if any of our basic concerns could be solved just by buying another luxury! Surely the main problems which this song lamented, emotional pain and belittlement, could never be solved by any material means.

"The 59th Street Bridge Song (Feelin' Groovy)" was simply an ode to jauntiness, quite lighthearted.

An optimist's interpretation of "Flowers Never Bend With the Rainfall" might be that it recommended steadfast hope, even in the face of apparent hopelessness; a pessimist's might be that it preached resignation to one's fate, a Stoic *amor fati*. The optimist's view would be supported if we were to regard this song as thematically consistent with "Cloudy," which plainly stated that clouds, usually symbols of despair, inspired the singer to meditate, daydream, and cogitate, all in the most carefree way.

"For Emily, Whenever I May Find Her" was a singularly beautiful love song consisting only of Simon's finger picking and Garfunkel's vocal solo.

"Patterns," a creepy intonation of the morbid realities of life and death, left the listener with a feeling of being trapped like a rat, as if one's life were predetermined by forces outside anyone's control, and as if humans had no real freedom.

"A Poem on the Underground Wall" was an existential sketch of a lonely, frightened graffiti scribbler who dared to write only one word — probably "fuck" — deep in the New York subway.

S&G's new single, "A Hazy Shade of Winter," depicted an introspective, self-pitying malcontent desperately clinging to hope. He found coping with change difficult, but was unable to move freely or resolutely in any direction. The "snow" in his life bogged him down. Perhaps the "snow" was cocaine, or perhaps just a metaphor for the ordinary troubles of everyday life.

Preservation has its place, and is often defensible, but, without an underpinning of reason, is demeaning, contrary, and obfuscating to the human spirit. Change, on the other hand, is not always good, and must be adopted with prudence and, if possible, careful advance planning and a strong underpinning of reason. Haphazard, irrational change, i.e., change for its own sake, should yield to rational preservation, i.e., preservation for the sake of a higher ideal. Yet, even without the underpinning of reason, change for the sake of change is almost always better than preservation for the sake of preservation. Liberal adventure and willingness to experiment holds greater potential for human advancement than conservative fear of anything that is different. This tension between the value of change and its emotional danger was John Phillips's main message in the Mamas' and the Papas' new single, "Look Through My Window" (not to be confused with the Hollies' late 1965 early 1966 pop ditty, "Look Through Any Window").

When the Mamas and the Papas appeared on *Ed Sullivan*, my own father, who was overweight, exclaimed as soon as he saw Mama Cass, "She's a fat slob." The double standard was alive and well, not only for men and women, the old and the young, the white and the black, the rich and the poor, but also apparently for businessmen and singers. That was just one more bit of evidence that their generation was so hung up on appearance that they could not easily drill through the trappings of pop culture to get at its substance, which they probably did not care about anyway.

Donovan's new single, "Mellow Yellow," was a mystery, full of either nonsense or apparently deep cryptic messages. We could not tell which. We thought about it long and hard, trying to come up with possible meanings. Did it refer to getting high by smoking banana peels? Or to James Joyce's description of Molly Bloom's ass in *Ulysses*: "He kissed the plump mellow yellow smellow melons of her rump, on each plump melonous hemisphere, in their mellow yellow furrow, with obscure prolonged provocative melonsmellonous osculation." Was the electrical banana a dildo? Or was it Lowell ("Banana") Levinger, rhythm guitarist of the Youngbloods? Who or what was "Saffron"? What did "Fourteen" have to do with anything? Who knew? As we tended to do with any lyrics that we did not understand, we simply dismissed them as drug-induced. With Donovan's lyrics, such dismissal came naturally.

The Stones' "Have You Seen Your Mother, Baby, Standing in the Shadow?" was about alienation and social confusion. The singer, ostensibly self-assured, urged his interlocutor to spare no effort to step out of her shadowy, secret life into her proper place in the world, namely as his lover. Besides the single, it also appeared along with "Under My Thumb," "Get Off My Cloud," "Lady Jane," "The Last Time," "19th Nervous Breakdown," "I'm Alright," "Satisfaction," and four cover songs on *Got Live If You Want It*, the Stones' first live album.

The Who's "I'm a Boy" was probably rock's earliest favorable treatment of gay, transgender, or gender-bending issues. It sympathetically portrayed a young lad whose mother was disappointed that he had not been born a girl. She tried to remold him accordingly, dressing him in frilly clothes, making up his face, and not letting him play outside with other boys. He resisted. He wanted only to do the rough, tough, butch, macho things that boys normally do. He wanted to fit in — on his own terms. By extension, the song was about any kid who could not in good conscience accommodate his parents' preconceived notions of who or what he should be. Townshend's sensitivity to the emotionally oppressed was beginning to shine through.

"Happenings Ten Years Time Ago" was the most experimental single that the Yardbirds had released to date. Jimmy Page was usually on bass in those days, but with he and Jeff Beck playing joint lead guitar, and with session musician John Paul Jones playing bass, this song was the first foreshadowing of what would become Led Zeppelin. It was driving, hard, psychedelic rock with intelligent lyrics. The singer wondered about the reality of the past and its possible influence on the future. Like Salvador Dali's painting, "The Persistence of Memory," "Happenings Ten Years Time Ago" explored the boundary between facts and dreams, as well as the effect of time on all that we experience.

In 1966 most guitarists still kept their guitar straps short, so that the body of their instrument would lie rigidly across their chest or stomach and they would have to bend the elbow of their picking hand at a sharp angle. But when we saw the Yardbirds on television we saw something quite different — and incredibly sexy. Page had lengthened his strap and slung his guitar low, across his pelvis, so that the guitar became a free-swinging, complete phallic symbol. As his fretting hand went up and down the guitar neck, it seemed that he was fingering his dick, and as he picked, it seemed that he was diddling with his balls. How cool! How appropriate! Ever since Page invented that stance, there has been scarcely one rock guitarist who has not done likewise.

The hardest, heaviest rock of 1966 came from the Stones, the Who, and the Yardbirds; but, the Brits aside, the ultra-energetic medley, "Devil with a Blue Dress On / Good Golly Miss Molly" by Mitch Ryder and the Detroit Wheels was the year's hardest rocking tune. Even people who could not dance or did not usually want to dance had to dance to this thing. The double-time drums, the howling guitar, Mitch's authoritative voice, the lyrics that reeked raw sex —all of it. You just could not sit still!

Like its predecessors, "In the Midnight Hour" and "Land of 1000 Dances," Wilson Pickett's "Mustang Sally" delivered solid, vibrant rhythm and blues. It pointed up the folly of trying to buy love with cars and other expensive gifts. Yet to argue with anyone in 1966 who wanted a Ford Mustang would have been difficult. Introduced at the 1964 New York World's Fair, the earliest Mustangs were small, powerful, and sexy. Even people who did not care much about the differences between one model of car and another wanted Mustangs. "Mustang Sally" was free advertising for the Ford Motor Company, as well as a great song to crank up to full volume on the car radio, even if your car was a lackluster Ford Bronco, Chevy Corvair, or VW Bug.

Much of our love of music came from our excitement at hearing sounds and kinds of sound that no one had ever heard before. Classical music, jazz, so-called "easy listening," our parents' music, and even the blues all consisted just of new configurations of old sounds. Everyone knew what a violin, a trumpet, a guitar, or a drum sounded like. Merely rearranging their sounds was not very interesting.

But the new rock was all about new sounds and new kinds of sound: creating different and unique kinds of sound; identifying a band by its particular sound; inventing new ways to make sound. Within a few years, even in the case of a song that we had not yet heard, we would know, as soon as the song was played, who the band and guitarist were, just by the sound of the guitar. No other guitar sounded like Jorma Kaukonen's, or Neil Young's, or Eric Clapton's, or Roger McGuinn's. Special effects began to dominate rock. Individualized special effects became signatures. As we became familiar, for example, with the sound of Clapton playing his black Fender Stratocaster through a Leslie cabinet, we knew as soon as we heard any new song with that sound in it, even before the DJ announced the band, that it was Cream.

So it was with the Electric Prunes' only hit, "I Had Too Much to Dream Last Night," a hard, edgy bit of solid rocking psychedelia. Few songs were as full of sounds that we had never heard before. God, how we loved that stuff! But within a year the Prunes would become more famous for their Vox Wah-Wah Pedal radio commercial than for their tunes. Deservedly so. It was a peach of a pitch. The announcer yelled to be heard over the Prunes' instruments:

> Now, the Electric Prunes for Vox, bringing you the exciting new sound of the Vox Wah-Wah Pedal. Let the Electric Prunes demonstrate the difference. Play it, Prunes, first without the Wah-Wah Pedal. [The Prunes played an ordinary, rather dull guitar lick.] Now, listen to the difference when you push that Vox Wah-Wah Pedal down. [The Prunes played the same lick, but this time it sounded fantastic.] You can even make your guitar sound like a sitar. [The Prunes played a different lick. It did not sound much like a sitar, but still sounded good.] It's the now sound! It's what's happening! That's why the Electric Prunes, Animals, Herman's Hermits, Paul Revere and the Raiders, Stones, the Seeds, are all using the Vox Wah-Wah Pedal, and it works with any amplifier. If you're a professional musician, or wanna sound like one, get with the new Vox Wah-Wah Pedal at your Vox dealer — Now!

In the same subgenre of flash-in-the-pan hard-ass psychedelia were "Psychotic Reaction" by Count Five, "We Ain't Got Nothin' Yet" by the Blues Magoos, and "Pushin' Too Hard" by the Seeds. Count Five was a kitschy, affected bunch of Yardbirds clones from San Jose, California. The fact that they dressed in Dracula capes onstage was alone enough to consign them to oblivion. The Blues Magoos, from the Bronx, were probably the best musicians in this subgenre, but could not sustain their one-hit popularity beyond the lava-lamp image of their debut album, *Psychedelic Lollipop*. The Seeds, a Los Angeles garage band, self-destructed in 1967 when they attempted complex progressive rock beyond their talents. Lead vocalist Sky Saxon moved to Hawaii and became a notorious, burned-out, drug-crazed, wacko-religious recluse. Too bad. The freedom-loving message of "Pushin' Too Hard" was worth promulgating.

But there was a lot of abjectly phony, strictly commercial music out there too: bubble gum, sappy pop, antiquated crooning, so-called "easy listening," and of course the Beach Boys.

Despite the fact that "Good Vibrations" was pseudo-psychedelia, a shallow attempt to cash in on the wider instrumentation of the new sound of rock — despite the fact that it was the Beach Boys, the embodiment of all that remained meaningless in rock, the representative surf band which Zappa was already attacking and against which Hendrix would soon arise — despite all that, it was still a pretty good tune if you ignored its stupid lyrics and concentrated instead on the otherworldly sound of the theremin or glass harp or whatever it was.

Frank Sinatra sat up in his coffin for the umpteenth time and coughed up two typically frivolous, superficial, plastic hits: "Summer Wind" and "That's Life." The former was innocuous enough, a simple love song, but the latter — *Oy!* "That's Life" was an ode to nearly everything about mainstream America that was anathema to us: conformity, love of money and power, status-seeking materialism, dog-eat-dog competition, joyful participation in the corporate rat race, and conservative acceptance of the *status quo*. In celebrating these things even Sinatra, the lackey of big business, the consummate commercial prostitute, was probably, accidentally, sincere.

Not all mainstream crooners were big-business lackeys and commercial prostitutes like Sinatra. Some non-rocking pop songs, like Johnny Rivers's "Poor Side of Town" and Bobby Darin's "If I Were a Carpenter," attacked rich snobs for classism and sided with the simple, honorable aspirations of the poor to be able to love and marry whomever they pleased. Like "That's Life," "Poor Side of Town" was about climbing the economic ladder, but, whereas "That's Life" was about the rich trying to get richer, "Poor Side of Town" was about two desperate people just trying to escape from poverty. Hence Rivers's message was socially responsible while Sinatra's was not. Moreover, "Poor Side of Town" attacked the immorality of rich playboys seducing poor women with false promises of wealth. We presumed that Sinatra, on the other hand, would *be* one of those playboys.

Darin turned "If I Were a Carpenter," a folk song written by Tim Hardin, into a popular crooning number. Its main target was the pressure of class differences that divided people from one another and complicated simple human relationhips, especially romantic relationships. Such differences of occupation, finances, status, and genealogy made the lives of honest tradespeople, our most solid citizens, unnecessarily more difficult. The song also brought to the fore the harmful distinction between "women" and "ladies." The former were natural adult females; the latter were the phony, plastic, pretentious products of the conventions of high society. The former were free; the latter were the slaves of their social positions.

The nadir of plasticity was still television. Premises for sitcoms and even dramatic shows were getting phonier and cheesier and stupider and ...

Confronted with the steadily growing popularity of what they still considered a fad, post-Beatles rock, NBC TV executives tried to figure out new ways, besides just shows like *Shindig, Hullabaloo, Lloyd Thaxton, American Bandstand, Where the Action Is*, and *Ed Sullivan*, to tap into what they saw only as a market: impressionable teenagers. How about a musical sitcom? Sort of like *A Hard Day's Night*, only weekly, and in color? Anarchic? Absurd? Specious? Sounds great! Let's do it! The whole kit and kaboodle. TV. Records. Concerts. Promos. Personal appearances. Of course they'll be just pretty faces. We won't let 'em play their own instruments. We'll call 'em something really stupid, like "The Monkees."

At least at first, the Monkees were a teeny bopper ripoff of the heavier music that was happening in 1965 and 1966. Don Kirshner, a slick, middle-of-the-road record producer, manufactured the band out of three Americans and what he probably considered the obligatory Brit. Kirshner's admirers said that he had an ear for talent and his finger on the pulse of popular taste; but his detractors said that he was a pimp, a panderer, and an indulger of the lowest common denominator of eleven-year-old girls' syrupy fantasies. As he was later responsible for the Archies, it would seem that his detractors were right.

The Monkees' songs were straight out of the Brill Building. The group looked as phony as a three-dollar bill. Only Mike Nesmith, the guitarist, was a real musician. *The Monkees* TV show consisted mainly of ridiculous, quasi-surrealistic, disconnected bits that were often presented in choppy, speeded-up footage reminiscent of the skiing scene in *Help!* or the Who's video for "Happy Jack."

Rumors flew that the Monkees' first hit, "Last Train to Clarksville," was an antiwar song. Maybe it was, but if so, then that theme was well hidden. Tommy Boyce's and Bobby Hart's lyrics could be interpreted to refer to a draftee about to report to boot camp and scared that he will never come back, but other interpretations were equally plausible. The sociopolitical and antiwar protest meanings of some subsequent Monkees' songs were more obvious. "I'm Not Your Stepping Stone," for instance, was a direct attack on classism. Eventually they would grow away from Kirshner and gain some respect. But for the time being they were about as transparently phony as anyone in the music or television business ever got.

We needed someone, something — anyone, anything — who would simply tell the truth, or who, in the words of Aaron Neville, would "tell it like it is." His song was a plea not to be toyed with. We could to a large extent depend on each other for honest opinion and straightforward information, without propaganda, condescension, trickery, or commercial bullshit, but we could not trust the media, our elders, or especially the federal government, which would proclaim, for example, that the Vietnamese wanted American troops there, that America was winning the war in Vietnam, that LBJ was waging homefront wars against poverty, racial discrimination, and illiteracy, and that rock was just a fad. Whether these effluvia from Washington, D.C., were lies, mistakes, or some combination thereof, we neither knew nor cared. We only knew that they were false, wrong, and malicious; and we only cared to find and learn whatever was true, correct, and beneficial. This quest for truth and honesty inspired all sorts of innovations. We could not trust the mainstream media, not even the venerable Walter ("That's the way it is") Cronkite, so the underground media thrived, just as it had in the French Revolution. *Hullabaloo*, later known as *Circus*, joined *Crawdaddy* among premier rock mags. We could not trust the government, so some of us created substitutes, extra-governmental or quasi-governmental political organizations such as the Black Panthers. Among the ideas that moved Huey Newton and Bobby Seale to form their Black Panther Party for Self-Defense were plans to unify the urban black community against its oppressors, to provide armed resistance to police harassment of blacks, to serve in lieu of the police in the black community, to distribute free food and clothing to the urban poor, to improve access to health care in the ghetto, and generally to empower the disempowered by flying in the face of corporate America. Naturally the white capitalist power structure saw all this as subversive, treacherous, and un-American. Since the government fed us lies and inaccuracies about drugs too and tried with increasing zeal to interfere in what should have remained free, private, personal, individual decisions whether to use or not use hallucinogenic or psychedelic drugs, Timothy Leary countered by trying to use the federal constitutional guarantee of non-interference in religious matters to reassert his rights by setting up a "church" called the League of Spiritual Discovery (LSD) and, under that cloak, encouraging the use of lysergic acid diethylamide (LSD) as if it were a religious sacrament. He should have been allowed to do this. The government has a valid right to regulate substances, such as tobacco, that affect public health, but hallucinogenics and psychedelics have no direct bearing on public health, and thus should not have been made illegal.

Ω

Fred Zinnemann's exquisite film, *A Man for All Seasons*, picked up where *Becket* left off with regard to the neverending divergence between personal conscience and political duty, or between freedom and obedience. King Henry VIII believed that he needed a male heir to prevent return to the Wars of the Roses upon his death. He further believed that his mistress, Anne Boleyn, could provide this heir while his wife, Catherine of Aragon, could not. Thus for reasons of state, he sought to manipulate the Roman Catholic Church into allowing him to divorce Catherine so that he could marry Anne. When his chancellor, Cardinal Thomas Wolsey, asked Sir Thomas More to "explain how you, as a councilor of England, can obstruct these measures for the sake of your own private conscience," More replied, "Well, I think that when statesmen forsake their own private conscience for the sake of their public duties, they lead their country by a short route to chaos." The issue of the king's relation to the church was still burning when More was elevated to chancellor following Wolsey's death. Widely known as the only honest man in Henry's court, he remained true to himself and his religious beliefs rather than accede to Henry's wishes that matters regarding Catherine and Anne be made more convenient for the crown. At the king's command, More was persecuted, imprisoned, and eventually beheaded for refusing to subscribe to the 1534 Act of Supremacy and for refusing to tell anyone why he refused. How little is worth a king's friendship!

As More only reluctantly became chancellor and only reluctantly martyred himself to his conscience, just as we in the sixties only reluctantly came to oppose the LBJ regime; drawing the implicit analogy between ourselves as the honest, conscience-bound More and LBJ as the boorish, overbearing, self-righteous Henry VIII was not difficult.

Robert Bolt wrote the screenplay from his own play and won an Oscar for it. The Oscars do not always indicate quality, but this year they did. *A Man for All Seasons* won Best Picture, Zinnemann Best Director, and Paul Scofield Best Actor as Thomas More— all well deserved.

Michelangelo Antonioni's *Blow-Up* was a brilliant, savage, but inconclusive investigation of what we see and what we do not, of what is real and what is not, and of what is important and what is not. That is one side of it. When it came out, it was touted as a deep, serious, symbolic, powerfully meaningful film by a fascinatingly enigmatic Italian director, but a few of us saw it for what it really was — a comedy. As a cross-section of the jaded 1966 mod scene in London, it was incredibly funny, especially for those of us young Americans who had never been to London. In one scene, our hero, the profligate, tactless, slapdash photographer, apparently not even a Yardbirds fan himself, with spirit and adrenalin wrested Jeff Beck's smashed guitar neck away from crazed clubgoers, who had looked half-dead until Beck threw the potential souvenir into their midst. The effect was like chumming shark-infested waters. His battle won and his escape made, our hero casually tossed the prize onto the sidewalk and went back to his original concern. The scene in which the two teeny bopper wannabe models flashed full-frontal female pudenda for one of the first times[43] in a mainstream non-porn film was gratuitous but hilarious. Fuddy duddies may have been offended, but we easygoing people left the theater laughing our asses off.

Georgy Girl was a dark comedy about a prematurely frumpy virgin in her early twenties caught up in the wild life of mod London. On the one hand, she wanted to have fun, be invited to parties, be socially accepted; but on the other hand, she was not willing to sacrifice her self-respect to gain this or anything else. In other words, she was not willing to surrender her feisty natural self to be a phony. Her father, wanting Georgy to be a "lady" (i.e., a painted slut), did nothing to prevent his predatory boss, a repulsive, overbearing, legalistic sleazebag who claimed to be 49 but looked at least 60 and whose lechery was somewhat worse than that of Nabokov's Humbert[44] but not as bad as that of Nabokov's Quilty, from trying to coerce Georgy into becoming his mistress. In any case, Georgy was not the flirt that Lolita was — but that should not matter. Women are never the cause of their own rape, whatever they wear, however they act, or whoever their associates or family are, and any father who enables or abets the systematic rape of his daughter should never be forgiven, however fearful he may be of his boss's power.

Georgy's frivolous, manipulative, selfish bitch of a roommate's boyfriend-then-husband was lecherous too, but at least he was Georgy's age. As this husband gradually came to see the depth, worth, and essential humanity of Georgy and the shallowness, worthlessness, and essential inhumanity of his own wife, he seemed at first to grow deeper, more worthy, and more human himself, and to undergo a sort of rebirth. But no! He remained unsaved, even by Georgy's unselfish devotion to his baby daughter. As he abandoned his job, his baby, and Georgy, just as his wife had abandoned him, he remarked, "That's where you're a freak, Georgy, not by being big and ugly and all that, it's this wanting to save people." We certainly identified with Georgy then. We also were freaks, for wanting to save the world from callousness, exploitation, and moneyed interests, In the end, Georgy could not save her unfatherly father, his boss, her roommate, her roommate's husband, or any of the other villains, but she did save the baby! The whole message of the movie was summed up in a juxtaposing scene of Georgy tenderly holding the baby vs. the boss clutching the *Financial Times*.

The Seekers' theme music was incongruous with and inappropriate for the film. It was light, fluffy, and upbeat, giving the impression that *Georgy Girl* would be a light romantic comedy à la Cary Grant. But *Georgy Girl* was a serious film

---

[43] Some say that this was the first time. They overlook Hedy Lamarr (billed under her real name as Hedy Kiesler) swimming nude in the 1932 Czech film, *Ecstasy*, which was banned in Germany, the United States, and several other countries, but made her famous.

[44] Both Humbert in *Lolita* and the boss in *Georgy Girl* were played by the same actor, James Mason.

about real social problems. At the very least it was an indictment of the same mentality that the Kinks had recently lampooned in "Dedicated Follower of Fashion."

François Truffaut's film of Ray Bradbury's *Fahrenheit 451* was a vivid critique of conformity and an eloquent attack on censorship. Its premise was that a totalitarian government would need to instill team spirit in its citizens if it wished to survive and prosper. Even the benevolent totalitarianism that the film depicted was necessarily legalistic. It needed laws as well as customs, culture, and traditions to develop a level of conformity sufficient to protect its existence. Creating and maintaining conformity meant preventing citizens from thinking for themselves. Hence its law that all books must be burned, all reading banned, and all thoughts expressed only in either numbers or pictures. Education was entirely vocational and consisted just of the minimum required to produce bureaucrats, enforcers, and functionaries. Even adult students were not allowed to engage the subject matter critically, but were made to memorize and recite like nineteenth-century eight-year-olds.

Rulers can rule more easily and efficiently when citizens do not think, but only conform and obey. The *Fahrenheit 451* government filled its citizens' heads with sports, wide-screen TVs built right into home walls broadcasting the most mindless dreck, and other seductive, visual, but non-discursive stimuli that would engage only the organs of perception and basic understanding, hold the higher cortical operations at bay, and preclude deep thought. Thus the citizens were kept entertained and docile. All government officials, from the rulers themselves down to the lowliest public servant, were expected to enjoy and promote sports, as the Captain explained to Montag: "More sports for everyone, hmm? Strengthen the group spirit. Organize the fun. Hmm? Just keep them busy, and you keep them happy. That's what matters." Books cannot help to achieve that goal:

> Clarisse: Then why do some people still read them although it's so dangerous?
> Montag: Precisely because it is forbidden.
> Clarisse: Why is it forbidden?
> Montag: Because it makes people unhappy.
> Clarisse: Do you really believe that?
> Montag: Oh, yes. Books disturb people. They make them antisocial.

Montag is correct. Books do indeed make people antisocial. But he is mistaken that anything is wrong with that. Books make them antisocial in the best possible way. Books make people think before they disagree, disobey, or disrupt.

Maybe the producers of *Fahrenheit 451* expected us to see the Soviet Union in the depicted society. Maybe some of us did, but some of us saw our own as well. The imposed primary societal values of cheerful conformity, instant obedience, and superficial happiness were — in our yet adolescent experience — typically American. In view of the Vietnam War, this speech of the Captain to Montag seemed particularly to indict America: "... with the new amendment to the law, we must expect to be worked really very hard. Very hard, indeed, until we can arrange for new volunteers to be drafted."

The chief supporter of the Vietnam War and the draft, LBJ, was an easy target for satirists. His ambition was so transparent, his opportunism so blatant, his anti-intellectualism so thorough, his bullying so legendary, his boorishness so fitting, and his arrogance so compelling — plus, he was so ugly — that scarcely any aspect of his entire being was not ripe for lampooning. Among the satirists who rose to this occasion was Barbara Garson, a 25-year-old socialist who had been arrested with Mario Savio during the Berkeley Free Speech Movement. She first intended to write *MacBird* as only a fifteen minute skit to be performed during an antiwar rally in October 1965, but changed her mind and wrote it instead as a full-length, three-act parody of Shakespeare's *Macbeth*. LBJ was the title character, JFK Duncan, Bobby Kennedy a combination of Malcolm and Macduff, Ted Kennedy Donalbain, one of LBJ's sycophantic cronies Banquo, and Lady Bird Johnson Lady Macbeth. Chief Justice Earl Warren, United Nations Ambassador Adlai Stevenson, and Senator Wayne Morse were Scottish nobles. The three witches were a beatnik, a black agitator, and a labor activist. All these parts, especially the second witch, were written to comic precision. But Garson missed one trick. Macbeth's armor bearer in Shakespeare's play was named Seyton, pronounced "Satan." That could have been McNamara.

Though abridged, the plot of *MacBird* was analogous to that of *Macbeth* in all major respects. You get the idea.

MacBird spoofed Shakespeare as much as it did mid-sixties American politics, parodying, besides *Macbeth*, lines from *Hamlet*, *King Lear*, *Julius Caesar*, and several other of the bard's plays. Moreover, Garson brought it off with aplomb. As Dwight MacDonald pointed out in his review of *MacBird* in the *New York Review of Books*, it was a tribute to her flair as a playwright that she was able on the one hand to suggest that LBJ was, if not complicit in, then at least not much saddened by JFK's murder, and yet on the other hand construct the play to remain funny as hell and not at all in bad taste. Few of us got to see *MacBird*, but a lot of us read it. I, for one, laughed right out loud.

In December 1966 *Mad* returned to political satire after a hiatus of several issues. Its "Hello, Lyndon! or: My Fair Lady Bird" used the form of the Broadway musical to mock LBJ's boorishness, arrogance, showing off, bullying, sneakiness, corruption, Vietnam policy, favoritism, megalomania, crypto-conservatism, and other faults which by now we knew all too well to be true. The border under the first few panels was "LBJLBJLBJLBJLBJLBJLBJLBJLBJLBJLBJLBJLBJLBJLBJLBJ" but at one point it read "LBJERK." Subtle!

Ω

Spring 1967

Turn on! Tune in! Drop out!

The only obligation which I have a right to assume is to do at any time what I think right. It is truly enough said that a corporation has no conscience; but a corporation of conscientious men is a corporation *with* a conscience. Law never made men a whit more just; and, by means of their respect for it, even the well-disposed are daily made the agents of injustice. A common and natural result of an undue respect for the law is, that you may see a file of soldiers, colonel, captain, corporal, privates, powder-monkeys, and all, marching in admirable order over hill and dale to the wars, against their wills, ay, against their common sense and consciences, which makes it very steep marching indeed, and produces a palpitation of the heart. They have no doubt that it is a damnable business in which they are concerned; they are all peaceably inclined. Now, what are they? Men at all? or small movable forts and magazines, at the service of some unscrupulous man in power? ... It is not a man's duty, as a matter of course, to devote himself to the eradication of any, even to most enormous wrong; he may still properly have other concerns to engage him; but it is his duty, at least, to wash his hands of it, and, if he gives it no thought longer, not to give it practically his support. If I devote myself to other pursuits and contemplations, I must first see, at least, that I do not pursue them sitting upon another man's shoulders. I must get off him first, that he may pursue his contemplations too.

— Henry David Thoreau,
"Civil Disobedience" (1848)

What is courage? Are soldiers in battle truly courageous if they enjoy killing great numbers of the enemy? If they only shoot on impulse to save their own or their buddies' skins? If they only follow orders, even if "above and beyond" the most immediate "call of duty"? If they only act either to gain the favor or avoid the disfavor of their superior officers? If, as draftees, they resign themselves against their better judgment to submit to the demands of their new job? If they find themselves strictly controlled by allegedly higher moral agents when their own natural powers of moral decision have been methodically stripped from them so that they have become essentially no more than animals with particularly strong instincts for survival? Probably such soldiers are not courageous, for courage must be deliberate, freely attained, and must primarily involve general feelings but only secondarily specific actions.

If anything, we war resisters were supremely courageous, in the most positive sense — courageous like Jesus in Gethsemane and before Pilate, like Gandhi in South Africa and India, like Martin Luther King in Selma, like our anonymous hero in Tiananmen Square in 1989. It took tremendous courage to say: "We must not hate, and must not seek to be hated, but must be willing to be hated. We must love, but must not seek to be loved, and must be willing to be unloved."

We were not draft dodgers or draft evaders. We were draft resisters. There is a big difference. Draft dodging or draft evasion is done out of personal cowardice, a filthy and selfish desire to avoid one's duty. Draft resistance is done out of duty to one's conscience, requires great courage, and is grounded in ethical principles and in the sincerely held belief that the draft itself is evil. We believed that our highest God-given duty was not to submit to our country's military policy, but to resist the draft, to show where our country's government was acting immorally, and thus to try to make our country morally better. Draft resisters are open, free from anxiety, and unashamed. Draft dodgers are guilt-ridden rats, hiding under rocks and sneaking around in the dark.

The antiwar movement was bright and steamrolling in early 1967. The music was upbeat. We were full of hope.

Early 1967 was before any of us outside Larry Miller's KMPX-FM range in the San Francisco Bay Area had access to free-form "underground" FM progressive rock radio; but, after dark, those of us east of the Mississippi River from Georgia to Maine and well into Canada had "KB," WKBW-AM, 1520 in Buffalo, New York. For all we knew, KB was nearly as good as Miller's stuff. It was surely better than any other AM radio station. Jefferson Kaye and Bud Ballou, DJs from 7:00 p.m. to midnight, played an amazing variety of B-sides and album tracks beyond just the usual top forty hits. Ballou was the best! He called Jefferson Airplane "my group" and had the nerve to play the Doors' "End of the Night" as his closing theme. Plus, he had Stanley the Engineer: "Isn't dat AW-ful dere? Isn't dat WUN-derful dere?" And Chickenman! When Ballou left KB for WMEX-AM in Boston in June 1968 and was replaced by Sandy Beach, KB went directly to hell. Rock FM, with its clearer sound, was ascendant by then anyway. The handwriting for the demise of interesting rock on AM radio was on the wall.

On April 7, 1967, Tom Donahue revolutionized FM radio when he began playing just his own favorite songs on KMPX, mostly album cuts buried so deep that other radio stations would not even find them, let alone play them. Even though

Larry Miller preceded him by a few months and thus is legitimately called the inventor of underground rock radio, it was "Big Daddy" Donahue who injected real viability into the new format. He did exactly what he wanted, did not shrink from controversy, and often made political statements on the air. His support of obscure local bands helped to create the "San Francisco sound" that would soon become the soundtrack of the "Summer of Love."

Except for "Light My Fire," "For What It's Worth," "Somebody to Love," and "White Rabbit," which all got airplay on ordinary top forty AM radio stations, we in the east learned of the Doors, Buffalo Springfield, and Jefferson Airplane from KB. In late 1966, KB was already playing "Come up the Years" and "It's No Secret" while the rest of radio was ignoring *Jefferson Airplane Takes Off*. Also in 1966, KB was playing "Nowadays Clancy Can't Even Sing" while the rest of radio would not touch a song with the word "damn" in it. Ballou, fascinated by Grace Slick after the Airplane released *Surrealistic Pillow*, got behind the band with a passion, playing every song on the album in its regular rotation. In the same way, many of us first heard "Break On Through," "The Crystal Ship," "End of the Night," and the other tracks on the Doors' debut album on KB. I think that Ballou might even have played "The End" once or twice. But sons killing dads and fucking moms was dicey, even for KB.

The Doors' eponymous first LP opened, appropriately enough, with "Break on Through (to the Other Side)." Its lyrics and those of "The Crystal Ship" were, though pretentious and nearly inscrutable, the most transparently druggy that we had yet heard. The eleven songs on *The Doors* broke us on through to Jim Morrison's insane, morbid world of drugs, sex, perversion, and psychosis. His lyrics could be either incredibly stupid (e.g., "Light My Fire," and later, "Moonlight Drive," "Touch Me," "L.A. Woman") or incredibly fertile (e.g., "The End," and later, "People Are Strange," "Five to One," "Riders on the Storm"), but they were always interesting and, at least among male singers, his voice was the sexiest in rock. The album included only two covers — both well chosen — Bertolt Brecht's and Kurt Weill's lowlife anthem, "Alabama Song (Whisky Bar)," from their opera *The Rise and Fall of the City of Mahagonny* and Willie Dixon's blues standard about a woman's extramarital lover, "Back Door Man." Morrison delivered a haunting interpretation of the former and a raunchy, sex-crazed version of the latter. His performance of his own lyrics, even his stupid ones, was obviously heartfelt and even more haunting, raunchy, and sex-crazed. He was a consummate showman. A mesmerizer. A seducer. Perhaps a charlatan, but a captivating charlatan. Yet the guts of the band was Ray Manzarek's musicianship. What impressed us most about Manzarek was that his multivalent virtuosity on the keyboards made it possible for his rock band to exist successfully without a bass player. A remarkable feat!

Jefferson Airplane's breakthrough album, the amazing *Surrealistic Pillow*, featured the band's classic personnel: Grace and Marty on vocals, Paul on rhythm guitar, Jorma on lead guitar, Jack on bass, and Spencer Dryden on drums. Its first song, "She Has Funny Cars," instantly fulfilled what Marty had promised — but had not yet fully delivered — in Ralph Gleason's liner notes for *Takes Off*, where Gleason had quoted him:

We like to put the music down like a big hand and grab you and shake you. We like the excitement of the rock. ... When we play, we're involved and I think that really communicates to an audience ... something, the power of creating, you can feel it. To anyone who is involved, who really believes in what he's doing, it really comes across. Everyone in our group is very involved with what we're doing, enjoys doing it and really believes in it. No matter how many times we do it, we've never, ever, once been on stage when we didn't become one person. We're terrific fans of everything that happens and we experiment. ... I never have to explain my songs to my age group ... I feel like I'm talking. It's the greatest way to communicate.

Takes Off did not grab and shake, but *Surrealistic Pillow* certainly did. A lot of that new power was due, of course, to Grace, but also to the increased presence of Jorma's unique electric wizardry. It was Jorma, not Grace, who really hit you hard on "Somebody to Love." Jorma, electric not acoustic, was the quintessential psychedelic guitarist. In tandem with Jack Casady's evocative bass he was simply overwhelming.

Surrealistic Pillow opened with Spencer's funky Bo Diddley drumbeat on "She Has Funny Cars," co-written by Marty and Jorma, one of the band's frequent attacks on phony values and shallow materialism, and one with a particularly catchy riff. After the thundering "Somebody to Love," the tone altered for the rest of side one with three soft ballads: "My Best Friend," "Today," and "Comin' Back to Me." The Airplane's distinctive heaviness resumed on side two with the powerful "3/5 of a Mile in 10 Seconds," but then dropped into semi-softness with Paul's enigmatic "D.C.B.A.-25" and into total softness with "How Do You Feel?" Then the mood shifted yet again, this time into a folkish, almost Celtic ambiance with Jorma's wordless acoustic guitar solo, "Embryonic Journey," a virtuoso's memorable *tour de force*. Driven by Spencer's snares and Jack's bass, Grace's "White Rabbit" — which for many of us remains the ultimate drug song — was uniquely characterized by its Ravel's-*Boléro*-like crescendo. Marty's bitter "Plastic Fantastic Lover" concluded the experience.

Surrealistic Pillow was one of the most influential rock albums of all time. Its variety of textures was incredible. Its overall message was simply — love — whether sexual, familial, altruistic, whatever — all kinds of love.

Among the credits on *Pillow*'s back cover was, "Jerry Garcia, musical and spiritual adviser." In early 1967 we outside San Francisco had no idea who Jerry Garcia was, but we thought it was cool that a band would even have a spiritual adviser. Within a year we would all know very well who Jerry was and why he was eminently qualified to give this kind of advice.

A word about a few song titles: "3/5 of a Mile in 10 Seconds" is 216 miles per hour. Pretty fast, but not for a jet plane. The Airplane was an idiosyncratic, propeller-driven machine, as depicted on the cover of *After Bathing at Baxter's*. Marty's "Plastic Fantastic Lover" was his television set. Some thought that a plastic fantastic lover was a dildo, but that meaning came later, probably in the seventies.

The word "plastic" in the sixties meant "phony, artificial, contrived, unnatural," and was *always* pejorative. Plastic people were not to be trusted. "D.C.B.A.-25" was a typical Kantnerian cryptic message, the chord progression of the song combined with LSD-25, i.e., lysergic acid diethylamide, Lyserg Säure Diethylamid, the semisynthetic hallucinogenic organic crystalline compound, $C_{20}H_{25}N_3O$. We all caught the LSD reference, but at the time, a few of us figured that "D.C.B.A." must be a warning: "Don't Consume Bad Acid." Oh, how imaginative we were!

In "3/5 of a Mile in 10 Seconds," Marty attacked people who derived the greater part of their amusement from picking on others. He wanted people to leave him alone who would seize upon any little difference from themselves and, without even trying to understand that difference or its *raison d'être*, make a mockery of it. Such people were the brutish enforcers of conformity, the grown-up school bullies who never outgrew their love of bullying, and indeed, saw no reason to abandon it or to evolve into higher sentient creatures. Rather than laugh at anyone else because of their differences, and rather than keep a sharp eye out for any such differences in order to have something new and fresh to laugh at, intelligent people prefer to derive their amusement through less cruel, less reactionary, less opportunistic means. Intelligent people accept other people's differences, even when they cannot fathom them. They realize, for example, that the world is a richer place because some men have long hair while others wear it short.

Many of us were nerds in elementary school, junior high, and high school. We were smarter than our schoolmates and we knew it. So did our teachers and administrators. But tough kids beat us up with impunity. No one intervened. The subliminal message our parents' generation was thereby sending to us was: "Brains are not as important as brawn. Don't be different by being smarter. Be dumber and blend in. If you can't defend yourself physically, then you're not worth defending."

To them, success meant growing up, getting a high-paying job, wearing a suit, buying extravagant luxuries — "winning the race." To us, success meant staying youthful, loving our lives, having the freedom not to have to wear a coat-and-tie and instead to wear whatever clothes we pleased, earning just enough money to buy sufficient necessities to be comfortable without cheating anyone else out of the necessities they deserved — and not even entering the so-called "race." Their goal was to die with the most toys; ours was to identify the real problems of the world, each of us to isolate a small subset of these problems on which we could realistically work, to solve the problems in that subset, and thus to leave the world better than it was when we were born. For example, if we were born into a family that abused its children, and if we could break that cycle by refusing categorically to beat or insult our kids, then we would have achieved our goal. We could then die in peace, with clear consciences, knowing that we had improved humanity and had been constructive agents of genuine, concrete, and beneficial change.

Such good will was the motivating power behind the "Gathering of the Tribes for a Human Be-In" on Saturday, January 14, a peaceful afternoon and evening of poetry, philosophy, comedy, and music in Golden Gate Park, San Francisco, during which Timothy Leary famously advised, "Tune in, turn on, drop out."

Its ostensible purpose was to reconcile the various leftist factions in the Bay Area: the Berkeley radicals, the leftover fifties beats, the nascent sixties hippies, and other counterculture activists. Among the performers and participants were poets Gary Snyder, Lenore Kandel, and Allen Ginsberg, comedian Dick Gregory, spiritualist Baba Ram Dass (i.e., Leary's former Harvard University faculty colleague Richard Alpert), LSD-distributor Owsley Stanley, and embryonic versions of several soon-to-be-classic San Francisco bands: Jefferson Airplane, the Grateful Dead, and Quicksilver Messenger Service. Hell's Angels patrolled and, unlike later at Altamont, did not raise a fuss. We in the east did not hear much about the Be-In, but apparently it was renowned in California. What little we did hear about it only added to the mystique that was beginning to be San Francisco. Its vibes would pave the way for Monterey Pop and — ultimately — Woodstock.

Leary's "Tune in, turn on, drop out" slogan could just as well have been about government, straight society, or the rat race as about drugs, and that is how many of us took it: "Tune in" = "Pay attention; don't be apathetic." "Turn on" = "Become aware; find out what they are doing." "Drop out" = "Ignore them; disobey; follow only your conscience; be free; set your own course; don't follow established patterns that you had no part in creating; wash your hands of whatever wrongs that you perceive."

The first new songs we heard in 1967 were full of uplifting messages about freedom, freehandedness, freewheeling glee, freestanding souls, freeliving, free-loading, freefloating, and freethinking. Foremost was "I Feel Free," the first cut on the first side of the first album by the first supergroup — Cream, the power trio: jazz drummer Ginger Baker, blues guitarist Eric Clapton, and jazz-blues bassist Jack Bruce, who had started in music as a Scottish folkie. *Fresh Cream* gave us eleven songs that made the word "fresh" an understatement. "I Feel Free" and "I'm So Glad" each encouraged optimism, perseverance, and self-determination. "Sweet Wine" contained a particularly fine Clapton guitar solo and suggested that getting drunk in the happy-go-lucky country was better than worrying one's life away in the money-driven city. "Dreaming" showcased Bruce's distinctive high tenor voice, and "Spoonful" and "Rollin' and Tumblin'" his wailing blues harmonica. "Spoonful," "Sleepy Time Time," "Cat's Squirrel," "Four Until Late," and "Rollin' and Tumblin'" were all basic blues numbers, each in a different vein. "Toad" was our introduction to the exciting possibilities of the extended free-form drum solo. "N.S.U." was a cheery tune about the carefree life of a rich man who is nevertheless aware that money alone cannot buy him happiness. The term "N.S.U." actually means "non-specific urethritis," i.e., a British medical designation for any non-gonorrheal sexually transmitted infection of the urinary tract. It took some digging for us to figure this out, and most of us got it wrong, guessing such wild surmises as "No Such Union" or "New School University."

Another Clapton project appeared the same month: seven blues covers and five John Mayall blues compositions anchored by John McVie's heavy bass playing and presented with Clapton's terrific guitar work on *Bluesbreakers*.

On the same theme as "N.S.U.," the Kinks' "Sunny Afternoon," last summer's single repackaged on the otherwise nondescript album, *Face to Face*, was in the dead of winter a reminder of the glories of just being a warm-weather bum. Last fall's Donovan single, the baffling "Mellow Yellow," reappeared on the LP of the same name along with other upbeat ditties like "Sunny South Kensington," "Museum," and "The Observation."

As expected, messages of freedom from the Rolling Stones were entwined with songs of drugs and celebrations of sex. Their *Between the Buttons* was their druggiest, sexist, dirtiest album to date. Naturally we loved it — for just those reasons. That Ed Sullivan forced Jagger to sing "Let's Spend Some Time Together" instead of "Let's Spend the Night Together" raised both the song and its album — markedly — permanently — in our estimation. That Jagger capitulated to this censorship lowered him — slightly — temporarily — in our estimation.[45] The term, "between the buttons," could have referred to those two bright eye-shaped things in front of Charlie Watts's coat in the album's cover photo — and this was the interpretation that was officially put forth — but in fact it referred to the downish period in a junkie's life after the last pill and before the next one. The Stones were the masters of innuendo! We knew this and we looked for it in all their work, both musical and visual. A song like "My Obsession" could just as well have been titled "My Unbridled Lust," but Jagger/Richards had at least a modicum of subtlety.

On the basis of such songs as "Under My Thumb," the Rolling Stones had a perhaps deserved reputation for misogyny. Yet they wrote and recorded "Ruby Tuesday" and "Complicated," which should have dispelled that misogynist image. These two songs honored free women precisely because of their freedom. Considering that the Stones celebrated their own autonomy in any number of songs, it should not surprise us too much that in *Between the Buttons* they also celebrated the autonomy of very special women. The lyrics implied that the title character of "Ruby Tuesday" and the unnamed woman in "Complicated" could teach us all a lesson or two about how best to live.

Strong women were a frequent theme of singles in 1967. The Fifth Dimension covered the Mamas' and the Papas' year-old "Go Where You Wanna Go." Nancy Sinatra and Lee Hazlewood offered "Summer Wine," about a seductive trickster who gets her own way, ethically or not. But the most passionate statement in this vein was made by Aretha Franklin. Her "Respect" was a political song on many levels: racial, feminist, economic, sexual. It portrayed a tough black woman of independent financial means who called her own shots, both with her lover and presumably also with everyone else, even whites. In the tradition of Lesley Gore's "You Don't Own Me," it asserted in no uncertain terms that she was to be accepted

---

[45] The Stones were Sullivan favorites, appearing October 25, 1964 ("Around and Around," "Time Is On My Side"); May 2, 1965 ("The Last Time," "Little Red Rooster," "Everybody Needs Somebody to Love"); February 13, 1966 ("Satisfaction," "As Tears Go By," "19th Nervous Breakdown"); September 11, 1966 ("Paint It, Black," "Lady Jane," "Have You Seen Your Mother, Baby, Standing in the Shadow?"); January 15, 1967 ("Ruby Tuesday," "Let's Spend ~~the Night~~ Some Time Together"); and November 23, 1969 ("Gimme Shelter," "Love in Vain," "Honky Tonk Women"). Is it irony, progress, or ironic progress that Ed in 1969 allowed Mick to sing the even raunchier "Honky Tonk Women" uncensored?

as an equal in every way. By extension, it celebrated freedom in general, not only hers, but also women's, blacks', everyone's.

The freedom that we all sought and celebrated required universal human respect, a mutual "live and let live" attitude among all people. This was Jesse Colin Young's message in the Youngbloods' "Get Together," which later this year would become an anthem.

Proponents of American militarism always have the word "freedom" on their lips. They believe that freedom is won in wars, they exhort us to thank veterans for our freedom, and they equate our present freedom with the fruits of past military victories and the likelihood of our future freedom with continued military prowess and preparedness. They wave American flags everywhere and look with suspicion upon any citizen who does not. They believe that love of country means supporting it equally whether it is ethically right or ethically wrong — and moreover, that it would be disloyal, even treasonable, to try to find out in any particular case whether America's position is ethically right or ethically wrong, since the only ethical course for any American anytime is to support America's position, just because it *is* America's position. They remain fond of slogans like "Freedom Is Not Free" and "If You Want Freedom, You Have To Fight For It." What perfect examples of Orwellian doublethink! On its basis LBJ justified his escalation in Vietnam and Dubya his invasion of Iraq. Neither Vietnam nor Iraq threatened our freedom, and we did not gain or enhance anyone's freedom by conducting these wars.

The plain truth is that such people have no idea what freedom really is!

One had only to look at soldiers (whether volunteers or draftees), at LBJ, at Robert McNamara, at Barry Goldwater, at corporate executives, at stockbrokers, at American Legionnaires, at Veterans of Foreign Wars, at gung ho rednecks, at "Love-It-Or-Leave-It!" patriots, at Billy Graham, at fundamentalist churchgoers, or at any supporter of the Vietnam War, to see how unfree they all were. You could see in their eyes, in their faces, in their clothes, what slaves of the establishment they all were — and preferred to remain. They were the most slavish kind of slaves: voluntary, self-enslaving slaves. All that any of them would ever have to do to become, be, and stay truly free would be to tune in, to turn on, and especially to drop out. America was a slave-making machine. It decoyed new slaves from birth with the myth of the American dream of individual freedom, self-sufficiency, and personal economic power.

Political or national independence and to some extent even personal liberty — but not real freedom — can be achieved by fighting. The Allied victory in World War II rescued the world from Nazism, Fascism, and Japanese militarism; saved many people from death, torture, and imprisonment; was too late to save others; and in general had welcome results; but, even though it protected and restored liberty, it did not enhance anyone's freedom. Similarly, the American Revolutionary War gained America's independence from British colonialism, but the average American farmer was neither more nor less free either before or after that war. He gained certain rights from it, e.g., the right not to have soldiers quartered in his home, the right to keep and bear arms, and the right to petition for redress of grievances, etc., but these are political liberties, not instances of real freedom. Freedom is psychological, not sociopolitical or economic. It is an internal, not an external, condition. One important aspect of real freedom is the attitude that you can do whatever you goddam well please, whether the state, the church, the patriarchs, or any other authority allows it or not. Yet freedom is not hedonistic, selfish, or even particularly altruistic. It is simply "live-and-let-live." Freedom, in short, is the refusal to accept that any worldly, political, societal, or ecclesiastical authority has final sovereignty over the individual and the attendant recognition that the ultimate authority over each individual is only the Kantian conscience, the inner spiritual awareness of what is right and what is wrong, or the infallible intuition of what Kant in the *Groundwork of the Metaphysics of Morals* called the ethical duty of the rational being. Laws and governments can acknowledge and protect freedom, but cannot bestow or bequeath it. True freedom requires introspection, disinterested introspection, and the best path toward this kind of spiritual development is reading. Malcolm X knew this. He wrote of his time in Norfolk Prison Colony, Massachusetts: "Anyone who has read a great deal can imagine the new world that opened. Let me tell you something: from then until I left that prison, in every free moment I had, if I was not reading in the library, I was reading in my bunk. You couldn't have gotten me out of books with a wedge. ... months passed without my even thinking about being imprisoned. In fact, up to then, I never had been so truly free in my life."[46]

To be free, you only have to — *be free*. Just live it!

Despite the growing national and spiritual awareness that his aggressive foreign policies were antithetical to the true principles of individual freedom and even to the cherished American dream, LBJ increased American military strength in Vietnam by 100,000 troops.

It amazed us that so many supporters of the Vietnam War claimed to be Christians. F. Scott Fitzgerald wrote in "The Crack-Up," *Esquire* (February 1936), "The test of a first-rate intelligence is the ability to hold two opposed ideas in the mind at the same time, and still retain the ability to function." As usual, Fitzgerald, the establishment lackey, was wrong. Only a moron or an ignoramus could pass that "test." A truly "first-rate intelligence" would recognize the contradiction and move beyond it by either reconciling the differences or rejecting one side or the other. Only a moron or an ignoramus could profess to be a Christian and at the same time support military aggression — even for the supposed sake of "freedom." Any intelligent person with an objective knowledge of the ethical content of the New Testament would plainly see that the message of Jesus is as incompatible with American militarism as it was with the Roman variety — Matthew 10:34 (where Jesus was speaking descriptively, not prescriptively) notwithstanding.

Jesus said in Matthew 7:21: "Not every one who says to me, 'Lord, Lord', shall enter the kingdom of heaven, but he who does the will of my Father who is in heaven." In Matthew 5:22-24, 5:43-48, 22:37-40, 25:40, 25:45, Mark 12:28-34, and many other passages, Jesus was clear and explicit about what the Father's will

---

[46] Alex Haley, *The Autobiography of Malcolm X* (New York: Grove Press, 1965), pp. 172-173.

is: Express your love of God by treating all human beings as you would treat your brothers, your sisters, and yourself. This is the true essence of Christianity. Thus it may be said that Christianity reduces to ethics. But the Christian right, the "God *and* country" people, focus their religion on the fearmongering in the Gospel of John rather than on the ethical teachings of the Synoptics. They insist that saying "Lord, Lord" — and meaning it — is all they have to do to please Jesus and to fulfill the will of God. For them, Christianity reduces to fear. They are taught from birth to *fear* Jesus, who should never be feared, no more than Gandhi, Thoreau, Tolstoi, or Martin Luther King should be feared, but instead should be forever known as "The Prince of Peace," one of the gentlest exponents of nonviolence who ever lived. For them, the brotherly/sisterly love of all people and other legitimate, central principles of New Testament ethics fly out the window. They treat other people like shit, they grovel before their imagined God, they are terrified of hell, they eschew logic, they twist reason, and they meddle in our lives, trying to get us just to "believe." Whether we, they, or anyone ever actually live according to the nonviolent ethical principles of Jesus is of no importance to them. In fact, they frequently condemn in the name of Jesus those who live as Jesus taught us to live.

Just as the purpose of true religion is to promote peace, harmony, unity, nonviolence, and spiritual love (ἀγάπη) among all people, so the purpose of valid government is to secure the people's natural and political rights, and to protect the people from anyone or anything — including the government itself — that would take these rights away. In the words of the second paragraph of the Declaration of Independence: "... to secure these rights, Governments are instituted among Men, deriving their just powers from the consent of the governed." And further: "... whenever any Form of Government becomes destructive of these ends, it is the Right of the People to alter or to abolish it, and to institute new Government, laying its foundation on such principles and organizing its powers in such form, as to them shall seem most likely to effect their Safety and Happiness." We always had these quintessentally American revolutionary principles in mind, and were constantly vigilant to protect, not only our own rights and freedoms, but the rights and freedoms of all people, including the rights not to be drafted, not to be attacked, and not to be killed; yet the American right wing had the nerve to call us traitors. They had forgotten America's true principles, and instead had come to equate America with military might, patriotism with instinctive pride in this military might, and treason with failure to feel this pride.

The pervasive juxtaposition, painful contradiction, and obvious disjunction between militarism and freedom — and especially for us young Americans, between the reality of America's arrogant, ostentatious, quasi-fascist militarism and the big lie that America was the champion of world freedom, the beacon to all nations — was epitomized in the excellent visual satire of *Fresh Cream*'s cover art, which showed, in harsh red, black, and brown, scowling and wearing military clothes, three musicians who sang about true freedom. As we had come to expect, the British were way ahead of us.

American leftist political satire had a few bright moments too. A New York comedy troupe, the Hardly Worthit Players, pretending to be a band called Senator

Bobby, released a parody of the Troggs' "Wild Thing," a good-natured send-up of Bobby and Ted Kennedy's post-JFK mystique.

The Smothers Brothers Comedy Hour was not only an instant TV hit with very wide appeal, but also an irreverent young dissenter's dream. It got into trouble from the start with sanctimonious backbench censors. For example, CBS famously refused to allow Pete Seeger to perform "Waist Deep in the Big Muddy," because the lyrics obviously insinuated that LBJ was a big fool to pursue the Vietnam War. Despite its gigantic ratings, the show suffered constant attack from uptight religious fanatics, fuddy duddies, jingoists, prigs, and pigs — all sullen, judgmental types who were upset by dialogue such as:

> Dick Smothers: Do you know what Easter is actually all about?
> Tom Smothers: Sure. It's the day Jesus Christ rose from his tomb.
> Dick: That's right. I'm proud of you.
> Tom: And if he sees his shadow, he has to go back in again for six weeks.

With popular opinion and good humor on their side, Tom and Dick struggled against the humorless forces of self-righteous propriety and self-proclaimed decency until CBS finally caved in to the prowar, anti-irreverence bloc and cancelled their show two and a half years into its run. Their lost fight just went to show that being funny as hell did not mean shit in America if you ran afoul of the government, the church, or their corporate broadcasting lackeys. We were damned if we were going to let our country be run by people with no sense of humor. We were damned. They had none — and they were running the country.

The March 1967 *Mad* used news photos to reinterpret the Preamble of the United States Constitution in terms of labor unrest, vigilante justice, lynching, urban riots, poverty, neo-Nazism, and the durability of the Ku Klux Klan. Letters to the editor (printed in the June issue) about this piece fell into two distinct camps. Some excerpts: "exactly the kind of shocking satire needed to jog us Americans from our complacency and remind us of our lost ideals" — "should serve to remind us how noble a statement the Preamble is, and how far we must go to fulfill the noble ideals expressed in it" — "a work of art and expression of truth ... ingenious insight into our 'Great Society'" — "shows clearly what America is today, not what it was meant to be" — "ominous eye-opener ... will awaken many readers, but let's hope it activates them" — "I admire your courage and daring. *Mad*, more than any other magazine or newspaper, represents one of our most precious freedoms, that of the press" — "one of the most unusual pieces of classic satire ever published ... should be framed and hung in the Smithsonian" — "distressingly realistic and thought-provoking" — "deserves a Pulitzer Prize" — "the most disgusting article you have ever printed. You knock our great country in every respect and you don't seem to appreciate your being lucky enough to live in the United States which happens to be the greatest country to ever exist on this planet" — "Being a loyal American and a Southerner, I cannot help but take offense ... There are some things that should be treated with discreetness, rather than mocked in a satire magazine" — "shows disrespect for what our country stands for" — "an example of the type of 'hate literature' you've been turning out recently. I felt it was revolting." Also in the March issue, a cartoon showed a crime victim working with a police artist to create a composite sketch of the perpetrator — who ended up looking exactly like LBJ. Shall we just say, perhaps, that being a loyal American entails a willingness to engage openly in constructive political controversy — to keep one's sense of humor — and to rejoice that *anything* may be satirized.

Being a loyal citizen of any country does not mean embracing each and every little thing that one's country does, is, advocates, represents, or symbolizes. Nor does it mean defensively bristling whenever one's country is criticized. Nor again does it mean being a regionalist, like our Southern friend in the preceding paragraph, reacting with indignation instead of curiosity and concern whenever a negative and curable trait of his homeland is brought to his attention. Rather, being a good citizen means working hard to recognize faults and improve conditions, thinking about both domestic and international ethics, considering alternatives, listening with an open mind to criticism of one's country, and generally trying to make it a better place to live, a more equitable distributor of wealth and resources, and a more sporting constituent in the worldwide swarm of countries. This all requires keen vision, a universalist sense of justice, and a strong sense of fairness. Above all, it recognizes and even celebrates that one's own country is not, or ought not to be, a unilateralist tyrant, a uniquely privileged or special place on the globe, but just a part of the globe like any other country. This multilateralist view is not treason; it is humanism.

We recognized with crystal clarity that American armed forces had no more right to be in Vietnam than Vietnamese armed forces had to be in America. What would Americans have done if the Vietnamese had invaded the United States? They woud naturally have fought back against the invaders with as much tenacity as the American government and media now blamed the Vietnamese for using against those who had invaded their country. Hah! — and the arch-hypocrite LBJ claimed that he was fighting for Vietnamese "self-determination"! Well, they had already self-determined. They had chosen Ho Chi Minh and they did not want outside interference. What if some foreign country had merely decided that they did not like LBJ and had invaded the United States in order to depose him and install their own form of government in Washington? How would the world community have judged that? By analogy, how was the present Vietnam situation any different?

Militaristic patriotism always gets in the way of peace, human dignity, and honor. True patriotism is not militaristic, does not seek to make one's country a worldwide bully, but seeks to acclimatize one's country to the whole world community, as a good and equal neighbor.

Opposition to the Vietnam War was becoming broader, better organized, more partisan. Republicans in general and LBJ were for the war, Democrats in general and Republican Senator Mark Hatfield were against it. An *ad hoc* national coalition called the "Spring Mobe," i.e., the Spring Mobilization to End the War in Vietnam, promoted direct but nonviolent acts of radical pacifism nationwide. The six Vietnam War veterans who founded Vietnam Veterans Against the War (VVAW) and paraded their new organization in a New York City antiwar march were good, loyal American citizens, and so proved their true patriotism and loyalty by this very deed. Of course, the hawks called the Spring Mobe and the VVAW communists, heathens, and traitors. That was only to be expected. We tried not to become self-righteous in the face of it.

Ω

Middle-of-the-roaders Sonny and Cher had a fairly interesting single with "The Beat Goes On," whose thudding beat was quite appropriate for its rather sobering message of the inexorable momentum of time, the unchangeable process of change, and the episodic disconnectedness of everyday life. Should we despair, resign ourselves, or rejoice in the face of this fate? They did not say. Perhaps they did not know. In any event, we were suspicious of Sonny and Cher. They were obviously each trying much too hard to be hip — so we naturally suspected that neither of them really were. Sonny looked like he was trying, trying, trying to look like Ringo Starr, only stupider; and Cher, with all that gaudy make-up and those glittering designer clothes, looked more like Theda Bara or Lily Munster than a rock star. We preferred our stars to be unaffected. Sonny and Cher seemed to cherish affectation.

Another affected group who occasionally won our transient respect (with rocking tunes such as "Just Like Me," "Kicks," "Hungry," and "Good Thing") was Paul Revere and the Raiders. When they appeared on *The Ed Sullivan Show* playing worthy songs ("Good Thing," "Ups and Downs," "Him or Me, What's It Gonna Be?" and "Kicks") but prancing around in those hokey powder blue Revolutionary War uniforms — well, any good impression that their sound might have made was negated by their visuals. Yes, we entirely believed that anyone could wear whatever they wanted, but we could smell affectation, pretentiousness, phoniness, plasticity, and commercial ulterior motives ten miles away. They were not being themselves, their **natural** selves. They were allowing their handlers to mold them and package them as consumer products. Their humanity seldom shone through. They just looked and acted — plastic. Sort of like the Monkees in an eighteenth-century time warp.

There were no such incongruities between music and appearance when the Lovin' Spoonful did "Nashville Cats" and "Darlin' Be Home Soon" on *The Ed Sullivan Show* in January and "Bald Headed Lena," "Do You Believe in Magic?" and "Daydream" there in March. They were obviously wearing their own clothes. Their street clothes. Their personally chosen and preferred funky duds. Sebastian and company were honest musicians and the Spoonful was an honest band. What we saw was what we got. What we got was what we saw. We respected that. Yes, Sebastian looked a bit like Lennon, but he did not affect that resemblance. He really *did* look a bit like Lennon.

It is difficult to know what to make of Tommy James and the Shondells. On the one hand, they seemed to float above whatever middle ground they could find among hard rock, soft pop, garage rock, bubble gum, and psychedelic rock. On the other hand, they were not a fabricated or phony band like the Monkees or the Raiders, and Tommy James was a fine musician. Their first hit, "Hanky Panky," in 1966 really rocked. Their current single, "I Think We're Alone Now," was a catchy pop tune that carried a valuable message about the need for teenagers to rebel against condescending and overprotective parents. Their subsequent hits until 1969 would include "Mirage" (bubble gum / soft pop), "Mony Mony" (dance rock), "Crimson and Clover" (soft psychedelia), "Sweet Cherry Wine" (antiwar pop), and "Crystal Blue Persuasion" (counterfeit psychedelia).

Nine central metaphors constituted the import of Simon and Garfunkel's "At the Zoo," namely:

monkey = honesty
giraffe = dishonesty
elephant = kindness and stupidity
orangutan = skepticism, territoriality, and defensiveness
zookeeper = drunkenness
zebra = reactionary intransigence
antelope = missionary zeal
pigeon = sneakiness
hamster = habitual drug use

These correlations were rather difficult to understand, but we were sure that there had to be some meaning in it all. Damned if we knew what it was!

Since Dylan was still convalescing from his motorcycle crash and had released no new material, but only his *Greatest Hits* LP, the Byrds did their part to keep his work current by covering his "My Back Pages" on their *Younger Than Yesterday* and releasing it simultaneously as a single. The Byrds were now down to four from five, with Gene Clark officially gone. Indeed, only four had been shown on the cover of *Fifth Dimension*, but Clark had played on some of its tunes and had co-written "Eight Miles High." He had no presence at all on *Younger Than Yesterday*. Crosby, Hillman, and McGuinn now shared the songwriting, with Hillman emerging as a skilled writer and with Crosby's tunes moving ever further in different directions from the rest of the band. Some say that Crosby and McGuinn had a clash of egos, but in any case, Crosby and the Byrds would part ways just a few months later.

The most prominent of the other ten songs on *Younger Than Yesterday* was "So You Want to Be a Rock 'n' Roll Star," which satirized the corporate music machine and, as such, harked back to the Stones' "The Under-Assistant West Coast Promotion Man." Hillman's "Have You Seen Her Face?" was a rocking little number that sounded somewhat like a Kinks song. "C.T.A.-102" was the designation of a certain object that seemed to be emitting radio signals from deep space. McGuinn was apparently fascinated by space aliens. "Renaissance Fair" celebrated dreaminess and psychedelia in very general terms. Hillman's "Time Between" and "Thoughts and Words" were catchy but somewhat melancholy love songs. His "The Girl With No Name" was an upbeat tune depicting a free-spirited woman in a positive light. Crosby's "Everybody's Been Burned" and "Mind Gardens" were eerie, almost macabre songs that presaged some of his more downish work with

Stills, Nash, and Young. Co-written by Crosby and McGuinn, "Why?" was classic Byrds psychedelia.

The Mamas' and the Papas' new single, "Creeque Alley," was a cryptic autobiographical excursion through the early to mid-sixties lower Manhattan folk and folk rock scenes. It named a lot of names, most of which we recognized but some not. If it was meant to be informative, it failed, except for those who were already insiders. For the rest of us, it came across as self-indulgent.

Andy Warhol was an overrated schlock and kitsch artist in New York City. He seemed more interested in having his name bandied about than in creating anything of real substance. We were loath to call his stupid paintings of Campbell soup cans "fine art," as he expected us to do. He wanted to be worshipped as the god of art, but he was just a commercial artist with an ego. He epitomized all that was shallow about the New York clique of pseudo-sophisticates. The illustrator of Amy Vanderbilt's *Complete Book of Etiquette* was completely for sale.

Yet, he was a tremendous catalyst and facilitator. Because he knew nearly every celebrity, near celebrity, or wannabe celebrity in New York, he was important in bringing various people together who would then collaborate with each other to create valuable contributions to culture. In some cases, especially with women, he played the part of a Svengali, then discarded them. But in other cases, despite being an inveterate controller, he stepped back far enough to allow the other artists' own creativity to shine through. His most noteworthy achievement in this regard was the Velvet Underground.

In 1966, while planning his Exploding Plastic Inevitable (EPI) multimedia extravaganza, Warhol recruited a struggling band consisting of singer Lou Reed, guitarist Sterling Morrison, bassist John Cale, and drummer Maureen Tucker, and brought them together with a German singer, Christa Päffgen, known as "Nico." Delighted with their performance in EPI, he produced an LP for them and donated a drawing of a banana for its cover. The result, the uncanny teamwork of a bunch of down-and-out junkies and a conceited impresario, was one of most important albums in the history of progressive rock, *The Velvet Underground and Nico*. This and the other three Velvet Underground albums, *White Light / White Heat* (1968), *The Velvet Underground* (1969), and *Loaded* (1970), were commercial flops, at least at first. When Lou Reed forged a successful solo career in the early seventies, the now-extinct Velvets became much better known. Interest in Reed's roots generated a new market for these four LPs.

In the sixties the Velvets' audience was mostly gays, Warholites, and other musicians. The gay cult continued to follow Reed after the Velvets broke up. The Warholites were notoriously fickle, given to their leader's proclamation that no one gets more than fifteen minutes of fame. But the musicians were dedicated fans. Pioneers such as David Bowie, Brian Eno, Iggy Pop, Patti Smith, Mott the Hoople, and the founders of punk rock would not have been what they were in the seventies without the influence of the Velvet Underground in the late sixties.

Besides their raw, basic, but experimental musicianship, the Velvets were noted for Reed's gay voice and sleazy lyrics. The opening cut on *The Velvet Underground and Nico*, "Sunday Morning," was about paranoia and feeling down. "I'm

Waiting for My Man" described the singer's nervous anticipation of a drug deal. "Femme Fatale" was a not very flattering sketch of Warholite Edie Sedgwick. "Venus in Furs" presented a sympathetic view of sadomasochism. "Run, Run, Run" told of the desperate lengths to which drug users would go to get fixes. "All Tomorrow's Parties" depicted the hedonistic fascination with dress and appearance within Warhol's entourage. "Heroin" was a straightforward, non-judgmental account of a junkie's typical experience. "There She Goes Again" did the same for a prostitute's experience. "I'll Be Your Mirror" sounded like a love song, but probably it was not. "The Black Angel's Death Song" ridiculed the role of religion in the murderous conflicts among human beings. Finally, the lyrics of the dissonant, *avant garde*, jazzy "European Son" were inscrutable, but unmistakably bitter.

The Grateful Dead's eponymous debut LP went almost unnoticed in the East, despite its fascinating cover art, excellent tunes like "The Golden Road to Unlimited Devotion," and their almost constant touring. They got almost no radio airplay, not even on WKBW. They would not break through until 1969 with "St. Stephen" and "China Cat Sunflower" on *Aoxomoxoa* or maybe not until mid-1970 with "Uncle John's Band," "Dire Wolf," and "Casey Jones" on *Workingman's Dead*. They would not become huge until their sixth album, *American Beauty*, was released late in 1970. Besides the Airplane, the only San Francisco band that was even barely popular in the East as early as 1967 was Country Joe and the Fish, whose "Not So Sweet Martha Lorraine" from *Electric Music for the Mind and Body* and "The Fish Cheer and I Feel Like I'm Fixin' to Die Rag" from *I Feel Like I'm Fixin' to Die* would each get some airplay on KB later in the year.

Music from Britain was getting trippier and spacier, more psychedelic, even from hard-ass bands like the Who and the Animals. Not that the Brits were following America's musical lead in anything except the blues. On the contrary, they themselves were inventing this new music, these new sounds. If they were following any lead, it was that of the Beatles.

Of course, the Beatles just continued to amaze us. "Penny Lane" was a fairly typical McCartney song, but we had never heard anything before like Lennon's "Strawberry Fields Forever." This double-sided 45 satisfied every kind of Beatles fan. For those who preferred inconsequential pop ditties, "Penny Lane" provided a picturesque tour of a pleasant little suburban street on the southeast side of Liverpool, about two thirds of a mile from North Mossley Hill Road to the roundabout at Allerton Road, and offered a glimpse of its personalities, the barber, the banker, the fireman, the nurse, and the children, sort of like an upbeat, updated, expanded "Eleanor Rigby," without the death or morbidity. For those who took their music and its lyrics a bit more seriously, "Strawberry Fields Forever" was a multilayered psychedelic masterpiece, a meditative excursion, a soothing poetic invocation to inner peace or spiritual serenity. The place that John honored with his vague lyrics sounded like heaven to us, an oasis in the desert of earthly turmoil, an ideal, albeit druggy, destination to "get away from it all." We learned much later that Strawberry Field (singular) was an orphanage in Liverpool, on whose grounds, against his Aunt Mimi's wishes, John used to play with his friends when he was a small boy. But for the time being in 1967 it meant nothing like that — it was just an intriguing pastoral image. It suggested a place where nothing would matter, where, whether or not anyone else understood us, we would understand ourselves well enough to be perfectly happy.

Nevertheless, "Green, Green," the New Christy Minstrels' hit from the summer of 1963, our pre-Beatles years, our buoyant JFK infatuation years, with its implied admonitions against seeking greener grass, even ethereal greener grass, was still ringing in our ears.

The Who's second album, *Happy Jack*, began to reveal their extraordinary sense of humor as well as their refreshing musical innovation. Here were displayed the high, sometimes falsetto, harmonies that would characterize so many Who songs. Those few of us who already cared about the Who were beginning to get to know their four very different personalities. John Entwistle was the dark side of the band, exhibiting a wry, twisted, Karloffian perspective on all manner of things. His "Boris the Spider," which became his signature song, told a weird story of killing an apparently harmless household spider. His "Whiskey Man" was a disturbing collage of first-person impressions of alcoholism, schizophrenia, delirium, manic delusions, padded cells, and mistreatment of the insane. Keith Moon's "I Need You" was a relatively straightforward and subdued pop song, using a harpsichord, several other kinds of keyboards, and a jumble of spoken voices to commendable effect; but his circus-like instrumental, "Cobwebs and Strange," epitomized the ever whimsical, never serious about anything, ever puerile, wild clown drummer. Cobwebs were, well, just cobwebs, and "strange," as a noun, though we did not know it yet, but would soon find out, was another slang term for "pussy." What the juxtaposition meant, who could say? Roger Daltrey's "See My Way" did nothing to dispel his image as a mod poser, yet it was a beautiful little song.

Townshend's songs exuded his private tension that constantly threatened to explode in a neurotic blur of fantastic music. Indeed, Townshend and Ray Davies rivaled each other in neurosis, although Davies's was more low-key, melancholy, and perhaps self-pitying, while Townshend's was more high-key, uptight, stressful, and dangerous. "Run, Run, Run" was a simple rocker that sounded like it belonged on *The Who Sings My Generation* rather than on this more complex second album. Ditto — almost — for "Don't Look Away." "So Sad About Us" was an unadorned but eloquent lament over the irrevocability of breaking up a romance. "Happy Jack," their current single, was a bizarre portrait of a self-sufficient, friendly, but chronically abused loner. He had every reason to be bitter at his fate, but refused to forsake his essential happiness.

"A Quick One While He's Away" foreshadowed great things. It was Townshend's "mini-opera," a plain tale of loneliness, infidelity, and forgiveness, told with humor and panache. A nine-minute song in six parts, it was catchy, eclectic, and rather charming. First, "Her Man's Been Gone" introduced a lonely woman whose lover was a day late returning home, evidently from some sort of year-long out-of-town business. Then, "Crying Town" disclosed that the whole town was aware of her plight. Third, in "We Have a Remedy" the well-meaning townspeople brought her flowers and trinkets to help her pass the time, but to no avail. Fourth, "Ivor the Engine Driver" depicted how the eponymous friend of her absent lover offered her his comfort, his solace, and his dick, all of which she gladly accepted. Fifth, the sloggy, Roy-Rogersy "Soon Be Home" indicated that the lover was returning. Finally, "Forgiven" presented the happy ending. She confessed her faithlessness, but the returned lover was so pleased to see her, so thrilled to be reunited with his one true love, and so understanding of her loneliness, that he spontaneously and unconditionally forgave her all her sins. We naturally suspected that the reason he understood her so well was that he had had a few on the side while he was away, and perhaps even felt guilty about it. So, his forgiving her was a preemptive strike. Nevertheless, it was nice to know that Pete forgave *us* all *our* sins. Absolution from him was more welcome and sincere than from a priest, who would just go through the weekly rote.

Several of the songs, notably "Whiskey Man" and "Forgiven," had guitar riffs or codas that sounded like teasers, i.e., they seemed to evoke some sound that had not yet fully come into existence, at least not on that record. They would reappear in future Who songs, particular on *Tommy*.

The Animals had been mainly a cover band and Eric Burdon mainly a cover artist, but when he put his talents toward songwriting, many of the results were stellar. Co-writing with his new bandmates, guitarist Vic Briggs, guitarist John Weider, drummer Barry Jenkins, and bassist Danny McCulloch, he came up with four gems: "When I Was Young" in early 1967, "San Franciscan Nights" in mid-1967, "Monterey" in late 1967, and "Sky Pilot" in mid-1968. "When I Was Young" resembled his earlier working-class anthems in both theme and sound. Besides just celebrating youth, as expected, it also gave approval to such phenomena as interracial romance, humanistic faith, godless existence, early sexual activity, and the widest possible extremes of emotion. Its ominous introductory guitar, bass, and violin riffs heralded gloomy reminiscences of hard childhood and tough adolescence. The singer's persona grew up too fast. His father was away, fighting in World War II. His home had few comforts and, we presumed, his town suffered from Nazi bombing raids. For Burdon, born in 1941 in a northern English working-class town, the lyrics could have been autobiographical. Basically, the song was a lament. Its topic was the loss — not of innocence — but of opportunity. Its lyrics in some ways reminded listeners of Dylan's "My Back Pages," particularly regarding the reversal of the aging process: being older and wiser when we are young, and becoming younger and stupider as we grow old. If only we could recognize this transition, appreciate it fully, capture it, and exploit it to positive effect while we are still chronologically young!

As we had now come to expect from Donovan, his new single, "Epistle to Dippy," was full of allusions, mostly obscure, to gentle, idyllic sorts of things. The first line contained a reference to Tolkien's *Lord of the Rings*, but that did not help us much to interpret the song. The lyrics depicted a person, Dippy, apparently a woman, who affected the outward trappings of hippiedom, e.g., fancy glasses, but seemed to have no deep understanding of the culture that true hippiedom represented. Moreover, she seemed to have psychiatric problems, perhaps even multiple personality disorder or, at the very least, insufficient self-knowledge. No base. No firm foundation. No principles. We did not know who Dippy was, but the stereotype was clear enough: the phony hippie, such as Zappa had already lambasted on *Freak Out* and would soon do again even more vehemently on *Absolutely Free*. Donovan was much kinder than Zappa would have been with her. The Scottish balladeer only poked indulgent fun at her, not sarcasm or insults.

The spring of 1967 marked the debut of a British band who, in a quite different manifestation, would dominate album-oriented rock (AOR) from 1973 until the mid-eighties: Pink Floyd. Crucial to understanding Pink Floyd is to realize that the band who created *Dark Side of the Moon*, *Wish You Were Here*, *Animals*, and *The Wall* did not have Syd Barrett in it. Their first single, "Arnold Layne," was pure Barrett. The whole original concept of the band was Barrett's: the idea to combine San Francisco psychedelia with extended free-form jamming and London mod sensibilities. Barrett, whom his admirer and bandmate Roger Waters would later eulogize as the "Crazy Diamond," went irretrievably insane, perhaps because of LSD, in 1968, had to leave the band, and was replaced by David Gilmour. Thereafter, with mostly Waters setting Pink Floyd's musical direction, the tunes and lyrics became much darker.

"Arnold Layne" continued the themes of the Kinks' "Dedicated Follower of Fashion" and the Who's "I'm a Boy." All three songs, each in its own perverse way, celebrated radical individuality discernible as the freedom to be oneself in matters of dress or gender identification. The Kinks' song told us not to be followers, but just to dress any way we wanted. The Who's song related the woes of a boy whose mother treated him like a girl, but it also suggested obliquely that if the only way to be true to oneself was to lead a transgendered life, then a transgendered life was the life to lead. Barrett's song combined these ideas. Arnold Layne (who we later learned was a real person in Cambridge, England) was a transvestite who, apparently either too ashamed or too poor to buy women's clothes in stores, stole them from clotheslines. The lyrics did not condemn Layne's transvestitism, gender-bending, or even his thievery. They just painted a portrait of the drag queen, described his arrest and imprisonment, and let the listeners judge for themselves.

Ω

But al be that he was a philosophre,
Yet hadde he but litel gold in cofre;
But al that he mighte of his freendes hente,
On bokes and on lerninge he it spente,
And bisily gan for the soules preye
Of hem that yaf him wher-with to scoleye.
Of studie took he most cure and most hede.
Noght o word spak he more than was nede,
And that was seyd in forme and reverence,
And short and quik, and ful of hy sentence.

> Souninge in moral vertu was his speche,
> And gladly wolde he lerne, and gladly teche.
> — Geoffrey Chaucer,
> *The Canterbury Tales*, 297-308

Jerry Farber, who would later become professor of English and comparative lite-rature at San Diego State University, was teaching at California State University, Los Angeles, when he wrote "The Student as Nigger" and published it under-ground in the *Los Angeles Free Press* on March 3, 1967. Within the next two years it was republished across the continent in hundreds of venues, such as underground mimeographs and college newspapers, mostly for free distribution.

What surprised us was not the content of the essay — for we already knew, suspected, or felt most of its meaning — but the fact that a ***teacher*** — one of "***them***" — wrote it. In Farber we had a fifth columnist, an ally in their ranks, an eloquent spokesperson for our basic frustration with the whole education system. He gave us hope.

Farber's main point was that the structure, tradition, and ethos of education, contrary to its avowed purpose, actually prevented learning, bored students, made them hate school because it did not empower them or encourage them to think for themselves or even to enjoy thinking, reading, or exploring new ideas. It primarily taught them just to follow orders. It worked to close their minds. In other words, it made "niggers" out of them. The word "nigger," in Farber's special usage, did not refer to black people. Quite the opposite, his essay was aimed at all races.[47] A "nigger" was simply anyone who shuffled around, dejected, accepting the subservient role that others, having assumed positions of authority or dominance, had imposed. The ideal student, in the eyes of most administrators, was not necessarily a great athlete, a supergenius, a diligent achiever, or even a remarkable exponent of school spirit, but was simply ***obedient!*** Farber's idea was to get rid of this focus on obedience so that students might have fun in school, want to open their minds, care about learning, get excited about culture, and even begin to feel free — and alive.

"The Student as Nigger" did not mention or even allude to Hegel, yet it was thoroughly Hegelian in the sense that it presented the standard relationship be-tween student and teacher as analogous to Hegel's dialectic of master and servant. For Hegel, the archetypal social relationship was asymmetrical, defined by the out-come of a primeval life-and-death struggle between two equals. The winner of the fight gave the loser the choice of either death or servitude. A loser with self-respect would choose death; one without self-respect would chose servitude. Thus arose the basis of the class system. This master/servant relationship became instituted as a fundamental aspect of society, with hereditary succession of masters and servants and with roles assigned according to age, gender, race, etc. The entire political establishment was built upon this fundamental but artificial inequality. The paradox was that the established masters, as bosses and managers, did no real work, but only

---

[47] See footnote 28 above in the "Fall 1965" chapter.

bossed and managed, while the servants, as real workers, provided the masters with the necessities of life and thus became, in this sense, the *de facto* masters of the masters. In other words, servants could survive without masters but masters could not survive without servants. By the same token, teachers needed students in order just to be teachers at all, but students did not need teachers in order to live, eat, survive, enjoy themselves, learn, or develop their full, free, intellectual potential. We could, in fact, all gladly learn from one another, and all gladly teach one another, without the imposition of sociopolitical inequality upon the education process. We could improve society by seeing learned individuals, not as bosses, superiors, and dictators, but as sharers, equals, partners in the quest for knowledge and understanding. To respect anyone on whom you do not depend, who does not depend on you, and who does not give you orders is so much easier than to respect someone who depends on you but demands your obedience.

Along with the writings of Herbert Marcuse, which were more explicitly derived either directly from Hegel or indirectly from Hegel through Marx; the Port Huron Statement; Rachel Carson's *Silent Spring*; and several other texts, including, believe it or not, the U.S. Constitution; "The Student as Nigger" became a central document of the New Left.

In August 1969 the essay was the centerpiece of Farber's anthology, *The Student as Nigger: Essays and Stories*. He wrote in the preface to this book:

> At the University of Montana the article was used in a Freshman English class and was promptly attacked by an ROTC colonel, whose daughter was in the class. The colonel sent faculty members copies of the article, in which he had underlined all the objectionable words — all the way down to such modest vulgarities as "rat's ass." To my surprise the colonel even underlined "provo" (I suppose that, not knowing what it meant, he didn't want to take any chances). Interestingly enough, though the colonel's delicate sensibilities required him to underline "student-faculty lovemaking" and "goddamn school," it never occurred to him to underline "nigger." Before long the article became a major issue in a state-wide campaign to defeat a higher-education tax levy referendum. Thousands of copies were mailed to voters. Accompanying material urged citizens to vote down the referendum (it squeaked by) in protest and referred to "The Student As Nigger" as a "dirty, filthy source of moral poison," "degenerate writing" and "obscene pornographic smut" (the three biggies here in one memorable phrase). ...

> I have received scarcely any criticism from students on the article. In fact, it seems that there is little in "The Student As Nigger" that most students don't already know very well. Students, and a number of teachers as well, have welcomed it as an expression of their anger, their frustration and their growing desire for change. The outraged criticism has come primarily from administrators, parents and elected officials — and this outrage has centered not so much on the ideas in the article as on its "filthy language." There is little I can say in answer to this kind of criticism. I don't believe that any

words are filthy, not even words like "counterinsurgency," and certainly not words like "fuck," "pussy," "cock" and so on. In any case, I would never censor anything I wrote just as I would never censor my speech in the classroom. I don't go out of my way, as some persons have assumed, to use so-called taboo words but, on the other hand, I don't go out of my way to avoid them. They simply occur where they want to, as do other words in the language.

Summer 1967

All you need is love!

... love on earth is more excellent than praise in heaven ...
— Meister Eckhart, *Parisian Questions*, 3

Anything worth doing is worth having fun while you are doing it. This does not mean to practice hedonism, which is frivolous, unproductive, and demeaning. Nor does it mean to shirk your work in favor of play. Rather, it means to play while you work, to make your work into play, and to remember always that play is serious business. Whatever you do, make sure that it is worthwhile, that it enhances the human spirit — and above all, make sure that you enjoy it.

To achieve the perfect blend of play and work is a fine art. This year we did it! This was our high-water mark, the "Summer of Love."

It was called the "Summer of Love" because we lived out the message of our music. We loved, we gave, we celebrated, we simply became ourselves. We refused to be anything but free.

Ω

The second Mothers of Invention LP, *Absolutely Free*, opened with "Plastic People," which went instantly and directly for the jugular by lampooning LBJ in its first few lines. Then the song described a young woman who gobbed make-up on her face and depended on a fancy-schmancy and probably expensive shampoo to beautify her hair. Plastic people were phony people. We hated sophistication of style. What our parents considered neat, spiffy, and desirable we considered artificial and repulsive. We could trust scruffy people; they did not put on airs. What we saw was what we got. Zappa was scruffy, natural, and therefore trustworthy. He let his hair just hang out. LBJ, though boorish, was not scruffy, not natural, and certainly not to be trusted. Every single one of his thousands of carefully trimmed hairs had to be perfectly combed into place. The young woman was too concerned with her appearance and not sufficiently concerned with her reality. From around 1966 or 1967 until well into the seventies, to call anyone "plastic" was our lowest insult. At the same time, "natural" was our highest praise. We aspired to naturalness, art-lessness, honesty, transparency, trustworthiness, universal consciousness, mutual respect — and indeed, absolute freedom. Plastic people cared about nothing more than convention, conformity, and of course, money. If they spent so much time, effort, and, if they had it, money to disguise or embellish their physical nature, were they not also likely to disguise or embellish their inner nature as well? Yes, that was only an inductive generalization, but it was our experience of them.

Rightly or wrongly, we saw their generation as phony and affected and ours as sincere and natural. Theirs was the generation of appearance, ours the generation of reality. They each strived to create a public image or impression, but we each just let our unique natural selves hang out and each create its own individuality. Public appearance be damned! We each were only what we were and that was good enough for the public. We had better things to do than worry about what strangers thought of us. Time spent on one's appearance was so much less time spent on one's reality. No one could be both fastidious and honest. Anyone who was judgmental of anyone else's clothes and hair would likely also be judgmental of their whole lives and existences, their ideas, politics, private affairs, religious beliefs or lack thereof, attitudes, accents — every nitpicky little thing that was really none of the self-appointed judge's business. Important aspects of humanity would be neglected or even lost in such judgments. Even worse, such judges would live as if expecting others to be similarly judgmental of them, their whole lives and existences, ideas, politics, private affairs, religious beliefs or lack thereof, attitudes, accents — every nitpicky little thing that should really be no one else's business. But our individu-alistic clothes and hair proclaimed, "Live and let live! Judge not, lest you be judged! Respect each other for what they each are! Accept them! Learn from them! Love them!"

Their phoniness and affectation versus our sincerity and naturalness was reflected not only in hair, dress, and action, but also in music. Compare, for exam-ple, a supremely tactless and honest song like the Doors' "When the Music's Over" (released late in 1967) with any song that Bing Crosby ever recorded and you will know, negatively, what the motto "Be yourself!" means. Bing was never himself in public.

Zappa segued from condemning all social plasticity into two songs dealing with edible plants. Zappa was typically cryptic but honest. An important component of honesty was being blunt about sex — and he certainly was. There was no coy-ness in his sexual content. It was out there. In "The Duke of Prunes," various foods stood as metaphors for sexual organs, fluids, and activities. This song was quite fun to decode.

"Call Any Vegetable" made us wonder whether Zappa intended the vegeta-ble to be a metaphor for the passive, unthinking, plastic conformist, or whether he meant the word "vegetable" to be taken literally. Either interpretation was possible; each had its problems and its counterevidence. Yet the former was more likely. His suggestions that we might converse with vegetables, go to church with them, and do all sorts of groovy things with them, reminded us of our relationships with our parents.

"Big Leg Emma" was just a funny song about a zitty, overweight girlfriend. In a similar lighthearted vein, "Why Don'tcha Do Me Right?" depicted a horny guy begging a woman for sex.

"Status Back, Baby" lambasted the superficial values that permeated high schools in the fifties and somehow persisted into the sixties, values that were designed by parents, teachers, and administrators to keep kids dumb by giving them an overwhelming mix of dull, pointless activities to which they could conform. To get an idea of Zappa's target, read some old *Archie* comics, watch *Father Knows Best*, *Our Miss Brooks*, or *Leave It to Beaver*, or listen to *The Aldrich Family* or *A Date With Judy*.

"Uncle Bernie's Farm" had probably the most vitriolic lyrics on the album. Zappa's target here was a specific aspect of plasticity: the toy industry. Toys were not designed, manufactured, or sold by people who loved, respected, or cared about children. On the contrary, these designers, manufacturers, sellers, and their managers and executives were only out to make big profits, and they saw that the surest way to achieve this goal was to cultivate and exploit any inclinations that kids might have toward violence, selfishness, greed, narcissism, arrogance, cruelty, and other deleterious traits. So they produced and advertised toy weapons, toy monsters, toy make-up, toy money, and toys that would disgust, destroy, poison, distort, and deprave. These advertisements promoted the idea that kids should regard their parents, not as loving guardians, but only as bottomless sources of money, money, money to buy things, things, things. The simple fact that most toys in the late twentieth century were made of plastic served Zappa naturally as the perfect metaphor for the whole business.

In "Son of Suzy Creamcheese," the uptight high school girl character from *Freak Out* reappeared. She did not really have a son — this was just the sequel to her original story. She seemed to be slightly more hip now, and to have assumed some aspects of the phony hippie. We still did not know what Suzy was all about.

In "Brown Shoes Don't Make It," Zappa was not telling us that we could not wear brown shoes. Rather, he was merely reprising and amplifying his initial attack on plasticity, pointing out that sociopolitical ostracism was more subtle than simple judgments about what people wore. Furthermore, this song condemned the outward respectability and economic productivity that could serve as social invisibility and thus be an effective cover-up for such unforgivable sexual perversions as incest, pedophilia, and rape.

Zappa attacked nearly everything, but no target so skillfully or steadily as hypocrisy. Indeed, hypocrisy was under attack from all sides. In July 1967 *Mad* continued its campaign against hypocrisy with photos illustrating the Ten Judaeo-Christian Commandments:

I. Thou shalt have no other gods before me. — Photo: Young girls kneeling before the Beatles.

II. Thou shalt not make unto thee any graven image. — Photo: Actress kissing her Oscar.

III. Thou shalt not take the name of the Lord, thy God, in vain. — Photo: Lester Maddox preaching segregation.

IV. Remember the Sabbath Day, to keep it holy. — Photo: Golfers.

V. Honor thy father and thy mother. — Photo: The Mamas and the Papas.

VI. Thou shalt not kill. — Photo: A head-on car crash.

VII. Thou shalt not commit adultery. — Photo: Bob's Motel, a sleazy joint with $5.00, $6.50, and $8.00 rooms.

VIII. Thou shalt not steal. — Photo: Form 1040, U.S. Individual Income Tax.

IX. Thou shalt not bear false witness against thy neighbor. — Photo: Senator Joseph McCarthy.

X. Thou shalt not covet thy neighbor's wife. — Photo: Richard Burton ogling Elizabeth Taylor sitting in Eddie Fisher's lap.

In "America Drinks and Goes Home," using music reminiscent of thirties cabaret tunes, particularly "Cocktails for Two," Zappa underscored one of American society's most typical and prevalent hypocrisies: that the Sinatra generation swilled itself in alcohol, bragged about it, but then condemned the Beatles generation for taking recreational drugs.

Electric Music for the Mind and Body, the first important album by Country Joe and the Fish, was a trippy, easy-going accompaniment or substitute for the drug experience. It opened with "Flying High," which had a good backbeat; but Barry Melton's psychedelic guitar and Joe McDonald's spacy singing, not to mention its rather blunt lyrics, marked it for a drug song. "Not So Sweet Martha Lorraine" was a bitter love song about an intellectual woman who tried to remold any man who fancied her. The lyrics of the blues tune "Death Sound" were ambiguous about whether peace itself or a love affair had died. "Happiness is a Porpoise Mouth" was the weirdest song on the album, with inscrutable, yet vaguely sexual lyrics. Two years later, when Neil Young released his second solo LP, we would marvel at how much "Running Dry" sounded like "Porpoise Mouth." Not that we would accuse Neil of ripping off anyone. Surely it was just coincidence. The slow, slow, slow instrumental "Section 43" could have referred to a section of an auditorium or arena (although CJF were not playing such large venues) or to some part of some law, perhaps Section 43 of the Canadian criminal code, the so-called "Spanking Law," which explicitly permitted the corporal punishment of children: "Every schoolteacher, parent or person standing in the place of a parent is justified in using force by way of correction toward a pupil or child, as the case may be, who is under his care, if the force does not exceed what is reasonable under the circumstances." "Superbird" was an uptempo attack on LBJ; "Sad and Lonely Times" a simple country tune; and "Love" a raunchy piece of funk. "Bass Strings" unabashedly advocated marijuana and LSD with languid music and gentle lyrics. There was not a lot of bass in it, but quite a bit of high treble organ and other ethereal psychedelic sounds. "The Masked Marauder" was another instrumental (except for la-la-la-la), mostly organ-driven, but with some chunky guitar. The album's finale, "Grace," featured very visual lyrics, painting a colorful picture of love and serenity.

So much interest in electric stringed instrument innovation existed by this time that *Guitar Player* magazine could have its debut and be assured of a solid readership base.

Even on AM radio, some interesting stuff was going on. Dylan's handlers, seeing that he was either still incapacitated or just reclusive, released the year-old "Leopard-Skin Pill-Box Hat" from *Blonde on Blonde* as a single. A one-hit wonder band from New York City, Every Mother's Son, rocked with the sexually suggestive "Come on Down to My Boat." One of the best singles bands of all time, the Turtles, did their two current hits, "Happy Together" and "She'd Rather Be With Me" on *The Ed Sullivan Show*. With what would soon become their trademark reedy, wraithlike vocals, high harmonies, and weird, alluring lyrics, the Bee Gees made their debut with "New York Mining Disaster, 1941" and "To Love Somebody," two fantastic songs, far superior to the wildly popular disco crap that they would crank out in the seventies. The so-called "Prefab Four," i.e., the Monkees, somewhat uncharacteristically did "Pleasant Valley Sunday," a sarcastic tune that mocked shallow, middle-class values and the suburban generation gap.

Simon and Garfunkel's "Fakin' It" explored the difference between honest and phony behavior. The singer was impressed with the guileless way in which a certain young woman conducted her life, and at the same time was equally distressed with the insincerity of his own life. He was at his wit's end. For some obscure reason, he dreamed of a past life in which he was a tailor. Beverley Kutner, later Martyn, Paul Simon's British protégée who sang at Monterey, contributed the prim, cheerful, out-of-the-blue spoken line about "Mr. Leitch," plainly referring to Donovan, whose real full name was Donovan Philips Leitch. But what kind of reference was it? Paul had not established himself as a sardonic lyricist like Dylan, so this was probably not a slur against Donovan. Yet it was an unexpectedly difficult Simon lyric to interpret. Was it a compliment? Was the woman in the tailor shop a customer greeting the singer/tailor as Mr. Leitch, or was she a colleague greeting a newly entered customer as Mr. Leitch? Why did the song allude to Donovan at all?

Donovan's new single, "There is a Mountain," was a serene, pastoral, but upbeat meditation on transience, contingency, change, the natural impermanence of even the most seemingly permanent things, or the illusion that in Hinduism and Buddhism is called *samsara*. Such songs were catalysts for our intellectual development, this one prompting us to look up not only Hinduism and Buddhism, but also philosophers like Heraclitus, the first advocate of the concept of universal flux, in whose texts we would discover such reassuring ideas as: "Only in change can anything find rest."

Pink Floyd's second single, "See Emily Play," led us back again into the insane world of Syd Barrett. The lyrics obliquely suggested that playfulness, fantasy, and, by extension, human happiness in general, could be enhanced by insanity. Well, that argument might have turned out to be plausible in some cases, but, sad to say, not in Barrett's own, as we would learn within a few years.

Our daytime AM radio introduction to the Doors proved later to be atypical of their music: a catchy pop ditty called "Light My Fire." Its signature organ riff, not Jim Morrison's singing, was its highlight. It passed for a plain old love song, although some of its lyrics could be interpreted as druggy. We at first naively thought that the stupid name of this band, the Doors, referred to swinging, but we soon learned that Morrison had called it after the title of a book by Aldous Huxley, who had quoted from William Blake's "The Marriage of Heaven and Hell": "If the doors of perception were cleansed every thing would appear to man as it is: infinite." That confirmed the druggy interpretation of "Light My Fire" — and thus aligned it lyrically with the Beatles' "Norwegian Wood."

Consistent with with Blake's romantic mysticism, Huxley's thesis in *The Doors of Perception* was that mescaline could open the mind to seeing the world as it really is, rather than as it commonly appears to us. Huxley likened his seeing the world through mescaline to Adam seeing Eden upon opening his eyes for the first time. Even the most mundane objects were vibrant, pulsating, saturated with color. Huxley claimed to be seeing "naked existence," "eternal life," "pure Being," not just objects. But in fact he was only seeing the results of the drug's effects on his sense of sight; the rest of his heightened awareness was only his imagined interpretation, grounded in his prior knowledge of Eastern religions. He was so overwhelmed by seeing ordinary objects "glowing" that he became intoxicated with this new beauty and fooled himself into believing that these things then really were what they seemed now to be. His big mistake was to equate a distorted visual experience with a genuine mystical experience, which can come only from quieting the mind and moving beyond rationality after having first absorbed and accepted rationality. All the great mystics from Buddha to Plotinus to Eckhart knew this. Blake and Huxley apparently did not. That is why Blake and Huxley were self-deluding charlatans, not true mystics. They took shortcuts. True mystical experience will not allow shortcuts.

The Doors of Perception was an eloquent book, but Huxley was an idiot insofar as he willingly reduced intellection to intensified sensory awareness of merely existing objects shining from their own "inner light." By reducing knowledge to sensation, he, in typical British analytic philosophical fashion, implied the ridiculous argument that, because sensation puts us each in contact only with our own sense data, therefore all knowledge is only of our own sense data, but because the proper object of knowledge is what is real, or what really exists, and because we each know only our own sense data, therefore only sense data really exists, and therefore, as George Berkeley put it, "to be is to be perceived, *esse est percipi*." Huxley thus ignored the whole realm of the knowledge of the non-physical, i.e., the ideas or concepts of philosophy, religion, art, introspection, or subjectivity. He could have done better with a good dose of Plato, Descartes, or Kant than with a dose of mescaline.

With books like *The Doors of Perception* and music like that of the Doors, we did not need to take drugs. These authors and musicians took them for us. If these books and this music attracted some to drugs, they just as much repelled others from them. Not taking drugs did not make any of us any less a member in good standing of our generation. Our culture was not grounded in drugs, but in tolerance and universalism.

We were beginning to understand and internalize the difference between 45 RPM records (singles with B-sides) and 33 1/3 RPM long-playing (LP) albums. 45s cost just under a dollar and gave us only two songs each, but albums were about $3.00 and held ten, eleven, or twelve songs. So each song on a 45 was about 50¢ while each on an album was only about 30¢. But the 45 RPM ripoff was not just quantitative. There was a qualitative difference as well — and it was growing wider. The contrast between the single and album versions of "Light My Fire" underscored this fact. The single version, cut down to 2:52 for AM radio, lacked the impressive organ-led instrumental scherzo in the 6:30 album version. That feature alone saved "Light My Fire" from being just another pop song and made it into a real work of art. Ray Manzarek was indeed a fine musician, one of the best keyboardists in rock, along with Keith Emerson, Rick Wakeman, and Nicky Hopkins. But he was too much in awe of Morrison. He later became better known for kissing Morrison's dead ass that for his keyboarding. He should have just shut up and played. But we did not know any of that yet. We had only begun to appreciate long songs. The three-minute pop song had become a joke to us. We wanted art.

Before *Sgt. Pepper's Lonely Hearts Club Band*, the 45 RPM single was the basic unit of consumption for rock music. If the Doors had just begun to change that, the Beatles changed it definitively, decisively, and forever. *Sgt. Pepper's* was a unit in itself. It did not even *have* any singles — which, at the time, was unheard of. It not only kicked 45s out of our consciousness, it also paved the way for a slew of "concept albums" and sparked the idea of FM album-oriented radio (AOR).

Before 1967 FM radio had been the exclusive home of workaday relaxants, easy listening soporifics, and upper-class classics. Very few people ever listened to it. Popular radio was AM radio — and deservedly so, for AM radio presented, through the mainstream pop stations, country stations, black stations, news stations, etc., and especially through the top forty stations that dominated the early and middle sixties, as much variety in broadcasting as was possible up to that time. AM was king.

However, the top forty DJs, as well as the various rock-and-roll TV show hosts, were becoming increasingly alienated from the very music that they wanted to play, were expected to play, and that their listeners wanted to hear. While Dick Clark was quite at home with Fabian or the Beach Boys, he was bewildered and perhaps even ill at ease with Blue Cheer. While Lloyd Thaxton was able to interpret and use the music of Jay and the Americans in the spirit in which it was intended, he apparently could not understand either the motivation or the message of Simon and Garfunkel. Moreover, these AM DJs — with few exceptions, such as Murray the K and Bud Ballou — who learned the business in the age of Elvis, the Everly Brothers, and Chubby Checker, and who generally did well by such musicians, did not seem to know how to deal with Jimi Hendrix, Janis Joplin, or the Doors in any way that would do justice to them or their music. These promoters were faced with a dilemma: Their public demanded to hear a new, more seriously conceived, more complex, more subtle, more "underground" music, a music which they simply did not understand.

Sgt. Pepper's Lonely Hearts Club Band filled this need — in spades. The Beatles would later be inconsistent in affirming or denying that it was intended in the studio as a "concept album," but for us it was clearly a unified whole, because, even though the album was not unified in theme, each song on it presented sounds — and *types* of sounds — that we had never heard before. So much novelty all within just one LP was amazing!

Despite the "Billy Shears" segue, the contrast between the first two songs was stunning: Paul's "Sgt. Pepper's Lonely Hearts Club Band" was a simple Mc-Cartneyish ditty, but "With a Little Help from My Friends," which John and Paul had co-written for Ringo, was a Lennonesque message song, almost a sermon. Even more stunning was John's "Lucy in the Sky With Diamonds," which has already been analyzed to death, probably more than any other Beatles song except his "Strawberry Fields." Whether or not the title referred to LSD — and John later emphatically denied that it did — we all noticed this acronym immediately, and we believed that it could not possibly be coincidental. Both the words and the music sure as hell sounded like a drug song anyway. We had never experienced anything even remotely like it before. "Getting Better" and "Fixing a Hole," both Paul's, were a thematic pair, expressing optimism, contrition, and resolve. We all identified with the girl in Paul's "She's Leaving Home." We knew exactly how trapped she felt, how desperate she was, how clueless and hopeless her parents were, and why she had to force herself to tear up her roots in order to be free. She was a reluctant runaway. John's "Being for the Benefit of Mr. Kite!" was a meaning-less but entertaining tune more worthy of Paul. We had come to expect more serious or "heavy" lyrics from John.

Side Two opened with something almost completely unexpected, "Within You Without You," George's articulate, concise, hypnotic, sitar-driven statement of his mysticism. In a sense it continued the experimentation that he had begun on *Revolver* with "Love You To." Paul's rather fluffy "When I'm Sixty-Four" was followed by his otherworldly "Lovely Rita," perhaps his best song ever. "Good Morning Good Morning," John's straightforward description of the banality of everyday existence, thereby served as the thematic prologue to his "A Day in the Life," which would comment on this banality. "Sgt. Pepper's Lonely Hearts Club Band (Reprise)" was like the intermission between the penultimate and final acts of a very draining tragedy, relieving a bit of tension before the dénouement.

The final act, "A Day in the Life," really woke us up! Lennon succeeded in his proclaimed desire to turn us on. One of our favorite games was already trying to figure out the cryptic lyrics of Beatles songs, especially John's, but also Paul's — we had had a ball with "Eleanor Rigby." We did not know who had died in a car crash or what war movie John meant, or whether these references were all just fictitious, but we sure came up with some wild surmises. By 1969 we were won-dering if the dead guy was Paul and by the fall of 1967 we had learned that the film was probably Richard Lester's *How I Won the War*, in which Lennon himself had a bit part, but not until the 1970s did we learn who Tara Browne was or that he was the Beatles' 21-year-old aristocratic acquaintance who had driven to his death on December 18, 1966. The holes in Blackburn, Lancashire, were 4,000 potholes in the city's roads that needed to be filled. The story goes that John read about these potholes in the *Daily Mail* while he was writing the song. But the holes that filled the Royal Albert Hall were not potholes. His reference to the Albert Hall was not even related to his reference to Blackburn. That was just his trick, or a segue using the word "hole." The holes in the Albert Hall were assholes, i.e., the number of people who could attend a concert there. The capacity of the Albert Hall was then about 8,000 (and has since been reduced to 5,544). Rumor had it that the assholes were fans of the Rolling Stones, whose Albert Hall gig on September 23, 1966, supposedly outdrew the Beatles' two appearances there, April 18, 1963 and (on a double bill with the Stones) September 15, 1963. But that rumor never quite rang true. Who knows who the assholes were?

The June 16 issue of *Life* magazine contained "The New Far-Out Beatles," Thomas Thompson's richly illustrated account of the *Sgt. Pepper's* recording sessions. This article opened our eyes to how much more complex had grown in just three years not only their songwriting and recording process, but also they themselves. "Of the four, 26-year-old John's life is probably the most complicated. An awesome world of literature, art, philosophy and thought has opened up to him. He reads copiously — everything from Bertrand Russell to Paul Tillich to Allen Ginsberg, and he writes poetry which only he can understand" (p. 105). Of course, this made us want to read Russell, Tillich, and Ginsberg too — and we did, if we had not done so already. Thompson also wrote of "their droopy French mustaches, their bookwormish faces and their bizarre clothing" (p. 101), and of their homes, families, and habits. A photo showed Paul in a trance listening to a studio playback of "Lovely Rita." This is how music ought to be heard, we thought. Let it pour into your soul and take you over. Thompson's tagline testified to the Beatles' honesty and creative integrity: "Ever-wilder assaults on the ear — and fans can like it or not" (p. 106).

The *Sgt. Pepper's* cover was almost as interesting as its music — and would become even more interesting in 1969 when that stupid "Paul is dead" rumor arose.[48] We had lots of fun trying to identify all those seventy-odd people in the pictured group. We had fun trying to understand the lyrics. We had fun just listening to the music — which was about as complex as any we had ever heard. The Beatles were such a dependable source of fun. That is why we respected them so much.

Precedent existed for putting a lot of unconnected celebrities on the cover of an album. The Beatles did not invent this. The back cover of *Both Sides of Herman's Hermits*, released in August 1966, showed a caricature of the band performing to an audience of Elizabeth Taylor, Richard Burton, all four Beatles, Fidel Castro, Steve Allen, Ed Sullivan, Nikita Khrushchev, Barbra Streisand, Princess Margaret, Antony Armstrong-Jones, Lyndon Johnson, Harry Truman, Mao Zedong, and several others.

---

[48] For example, hold an unframed rectangular mirror perpendicular to the cover with its reflective surface facing the top of the album and its edge horizontally bisecting the word "HEARTS" on the bass drum. The result will read "HE DIE" with an arrow pointing to Paul.

The Beatles' double-sided psychedelic single, "All You Need is Love" / "Baby, You're a Rich Man," was a worthy follow-up to *Sgt. Pepper's*. Both songs were deep. A line in each of them said that what appeared to any beholder was what presented itself to appear, not what the beholder wanted to have appear. Both of these lyrics were John's, and we could infer their epistemological significance, describing his world as an objective reality to be explored by any means available, including imagination and drugs, not as a subjective fantasy to be imagined *ex nihilo* or created by drugs.

"All You Need is Love" began with a thematic quotation from "La Marseillaise," the French national anthem. Why should this be so, except that it was a consummate revolutionary song, celebrating the power of the people against the ultra-rightists? Recall the stirring scene from *Casablanca* in which Victor Laszlo and Rick Blaine (Paul Henreid and Humphrey Bogart) used it to defy the Nazis. Like most national anthems, "La Marseillaise" is a militaristic song, and John was not a militarist. Yet this quotation was a clever choice. He would not have used "The Star Spangled Banner," which is about war between two countries, not about class war, the perpetual struggle of the have-nots against the haves. John was a peaceful but steadfast soldier in the worldwide class war.

"Baby, You're a Rich Man" extended the premise of "All You Need is Love" to bring a sharper focus onto the idea of self-knowledge. Getting to know one's own self was the most important thing that one could ever do. The ensuing wealth would be not in money, but in spirit. Therein lay real power.

Both sides of the 45 were songs of hope!

Ω

We had never heard of Procol Harum until we heard "A Whiter Shade of Pale," the title song of their first album. What an extraordinary introduction to any band! — To be instantly transfixed by a brand new sound! It may have been a drug song. It was certainly, quintessentially psychedelic, but its mysterious lyrics somehow seemed more spiritual than druggy. We were told that the name "Procol Harum" was Latin for "Beyond These Things." That little tidbit of info sent us running for the *Latin Grammar* of Gildersleeve and Lodge. We learned there that "Procol Harum" was **bad** Latin for "Beyond These Things." The preposition *procol*, which means "beyond" or "far from" is really spelled *procul* and, to refer to "these things," it would have to take *his* (i.e., "these"), the common gender ablative plural of *hic / haec / hoc*, which means "this" in its many inflections. *Harum* is not ablative, but the feminine genitive plural of *hic / haec / hoc*. In any event, "A Whiter Shade of Pale" was a monumental, watershed tune in the history of rock, mainly because of its Bach-inspired organ riff on the Hammond M-102 (not the B-3 that was more typical in rock bands who used organs). It was a solid top-ten hit on the singles charts, which was quite unusual for a spacy, psychedelic song, even in 1967. As for its lyrics, well, just be very suspicious of anyone who claims to know what they mean, even today.

Two other tunes on Procol Harum's debut album caught our attention, "Conquistador," mainly for its antiwar, anti-imperialist lyrics, and "Repent Walpurgis," a trippy instrumental with fine guitar and keyboard solos. Walpurgis, we learned, is the "Night of Witches" or the "Witches' Sabbath," a Central European satanic or Roman Catholic festival held on May Day Eve, i.e., St. Walpurga's Day Eve, April 30. As such, the song may have referred to Goethe's *Faust*, in which Walpurgis Night figures significantly.

In their self-titled debut LP, the Vanilla Fudge slowed the rhythm of seven covers of pop tunes way down, leaving a lot of deep space between the notes. This was a gimmick, a schtick, but, thanks to the quartet's musicianship, it worked. The single from the album, a seven-minute-twenty-second cover of the Supremes' "You Keep Me Hangin' On," was a surprise hit. Trippy music was beginning to get regular radio airplay. Some would even argue later that Fudge, especially via bassist Tim Bogert and drummer Carmine Appice, had contributed to the invention of heavy metal, but such arguments fell short because Fudge's essential feature was soporificity and catatonia, not power or volume.

The new Stones album, *Flowers*, was partially a compilation of recent hit singles — "Ruby Tuesday," "Have You Seen Your Mother, Baby, Standing in the Shadow?", "Let's Spend the Night Together," "Lady Jane," and "Mother's Little Helper" — but also included "Out of Time," which had been on the British but not the American version of *Aftermath*, a cover of the Temptations' "My Girl," as well as five new tunes: "Backstreet Girl" was sung in the condescending persona of an upper-class twit who was ashamed of his lower-class girlfriend, and indeed, wanted her only for sex. In "Please Go Home," a solid rocker with a Bo Diddley beat, the beleaguered persona was trying to get rid of a clinging, annoying woman. The slow-tempo "Take It or Leave It" had him wallowing in self-pity, complaining to his lover about her unreliability. He took the next step in "Ride On, Baby," when, fed up with her antics, he resolved to kick her out of his life. The melancholy, chastened persona of "Sittin' on a Fence" sought to avoid failure and despair by surrendering instead to resignation, but with a possibly futile technique of Hamlet-like indecision.

Jagger had already practiced his androgynous strut for a couple of years, but the diaphanous clothes and effeminate make-up that he began wearing around the time of *Flowers* made us wonder, "Is he gay?" We immediately answered, "So what! What difference does it make one way or the other?" If he was gay, then gay was good.

Lyrics had become sleazier and, to avoid the puritanical censors, sneakier. Blatantly risqué bands like the Fugs could not get airplay except on college radio stations, but more devious bands like the Who could score a hit with "Pictures of Lily," about a father teaching his son to masturbate, 38 years after her death, with photos of British actress Lillie Langtry (1853-1929), the upper-class beauty who notoriously descended from her birth rank to become a popular but unskilled actress, the protégé of Oscar Wilde, and the mistress of the Prince of Wales.

The Fugs' third album — or second, depending on how you figure it, as Fugs recording history is chaotic, to say the least — *Virgin Fugs*, was a laff riot! "We're

the Fugs" introduced the band as horny antiwar survivors of the beat poetry movement of the fifties. "New Amphetamine Shriek" was, believe it or not, an *anti*-drug
song. We generally regarded amphetamines, "speed," as a nasty, dangerous, possibly lethal, and not particularly enlightening species of drugs. Conscientious heads
avoided them. "Saran Wrap" suggested using this Dow Chemical Company product
for makeshift condoms rather than for its commercially intended purpose of saving
food leftovers. Antiwar activists were then boycotting Dow because it manufactured
both napalm and Agent Orange for military use in Vietnam. "The Ten Commandments" recounted all of them but emphasized thou shalt not kill and thou shalt not
covet thy neighbor's ass. "Hallucination Horrors" was a catalog of drugs from caffeine to morphine that the Fugs apparently enjoyed. "I Command the House of the
Devil" attacked LBJ's government. "C.I.A. Man" depicted government agents as
subversive killers. "Coca-Cola Douche" claimed that this would make the pussy taste
better and the woman more exciting. The singer of "My Bed is Getting Crowded"
wanted at least six of his simultaneous sex partners to leave so that he could get
some work done. "Caca Rocka" was a pseudo-blues song of being down and out.
The album concluded with the Fugs' deliberately stupid harmonies over their buddy
Allen Ginsberg's "I Saw the Best Minds of My Generation Rot."

The *Live Kinks* album was eagerly anticipated but rather disappointing. At
that time they were much better in the studio than on stage, where Ray typically
seemed ill at ease. They would not become a great live act until the seventies.

Pete Seeger's summer 1967 album, *Waist Deep in the Big Muddy and Other
Love Songs*, a typical Seeger mixture of vintage folk and contemporary protest,
was one of his best. The title cut told the story of a unit commander during World
War II who ordered his men to ford a muddy river, not knowing how deep it was.
The disastrous result was predictable. The implied analogy to the Vietnam situation
was likewise immediately clear. LBJ kept ordering us in deeper ... and deeper ...
and deeper. Another notable song on this LP was Seeger's cover of Ed McCurdy's
pacifist anthem, "Last Night I Had the Strangest Dream," in which the world lived
out the message of Isaiah 2:4: "And God shall judge among the nations and repri-
mand many peoples, and they shall beat their swords into plowshares and their
spears into pruning hooks. No nation shall raise the sword against any other nation,
nor shall they learn war anymore."

Two hit singles praising San Francisco rode the airwaves this summer: "San
Franciscan Nights" by rough tough Eric Burdon and the Animals and "San Francisco (Wear Some Flowers in Your Hair)" by gentle folkie Scott McKenzie. Burdon
was from Walker, a working-class section of Newcastle in the north of England,
where the River Tyne enters the North Sea. Such a man might think that nights in
San Francisco are "warm." Few others would think so.

What exactly was the "new explanation" that John Phillips and Scott Mc-
Kenzie attributed to our generation in "San Francisco (Wear Some Flowers in Your
Hair)"? It was not simply the naive message of free and indiscriminate love. Nor
was it a fashion statement about hair and flowers. Rather, it was that the domain
of ethical action had ceased to be the family, the clan, the local community, the
nation, or the state, and had become the entire world. Ethical decisions would now

have to have universal application, i.e., they would now have to be equally valid in the United States, the Soviet Union, Vietnam, France, Sweden, Egypt, Cuba, and every other country in the world. San Francisco in the song served as a synecdoche for the world in which people of all kinds would come together in peace and harmony. Just as San Francisco would cease to thrive if everyone who went there were to fight with everyone else in town, so all we humans had damn well best be gentle with everyone in the world, or else the world would end in nuclear war.

In the nineteenth century to determine what was best for one's country and then to act accordingly was ethical, because international communication was awful and knowledge of foreign cultures was abysmal. But in the second half of the twentieth century, with international communication instantaneous and knowledge of foreign cultures excellent, such action was no longer ethical. Given this new access to enabling technology and to encyclopedic accounts of all cultures, religions, customs, languages, literatures, histories, cuisines, and artistic and musical traditions, the only ethical course for each individual was to determine what was best for humanity in general, then to act accordingly. If global or universal ethics would occasionally be consistent with national interest, then so much the better; but if the interest of humanity were ever to be found in conflict with the interest of any particular nation, even one's own, then, with the whole world available for us to know and love, our first duty must be to it rather than to our country.

Specifically, war is only ever in the interest of particular nations. It is never in the interest of humanity in general. Therefore, war can never be ethically justified, unless, as in the case of World War II, to save humanity from evils inflicted upon it by particular nations such as Nazi Germany and Tojo's Japan.

Ω

We in the east heard that something beautiful had happened from June 16 to June 18 at the Monterey International Pop Festival, but we did not know much about it, and would not until after the film *Monterey Pop* was released in December 1968. We either recognized or learned the names of the musicians who played there, but before the release of the film and several live recordings from the festival, we did not have access to the performances. Indeed, we had little interest in them until Eric Burdon's song, "Monterey," hit the airwaves in December 1967. Thereafter, the Monterey gigs fascinated us and we could not wait to learn more.

Insofar as many musicians played at Monterey who were not on the bill, and insofar as reconstructing set lists from conflicting memories and poor record-keeping has proved problematic, the following is only a partial list of all the songs, bands, and stage performances:

Friday evening, June 16:
  The Association: "Along Comes Mary" "Windy," "Enter the Young."

The Paupers: "Dr. Feelgood," "Let Me Be," "Magic People," "Simple Deed," "Think I Care," "Tudor Impressions."

Lou Rawls: "Love Is a Hurtin' Thing," "Dead End Street," "Tobacco Road," "Autumn Leaves," "On a Clear Day You Can See Forever."

Beverley: [set list undetermined]

Johnny Rivers: "Help," "Memphis."

Eric Burdon and the Animals: "San Franciscan Nights," "Hey Gyp," "Ginhouse Blues," "Paint It, Black."

Simon and Garfunkel: "59th Street Bridge Song," "At the Zoo," "Benedictus," "For Emily, Whenever I May Find Her," "Homeward Bound," "Punky's Dilemma," "Sounds of Silence."

Saturday afternoon, June 17:

Canned Heat: "Dust My Broom," "Bullfrog Blues," "Rollin' and Tumblin'."

Big Brother and the Holding Company: "Down on Me," "Combination of the Two," "Harry," "Roadblock," "Ball and Chain," "Coo Coo."

Country Joe and the Fish: "Not So Sweet Martha Lorraine," "I Feel Like I'm Fixin' to Die Rag," "Section 43," "The Bomb Song."

Al Kooper: "Wake Me, Shake Me," "Can't Keep from Cryin'."

The Paul Butterfield Blues Band: "Look Over Yonder Wall," "Mystery Train," "Born in Chicago," "Double Trouble," "Mary Ann," "Driftin' Blues," "Droppin' Out," "One More Heartache."

Quicksilver Messenger Service: "Acapulco Gold and Silver," "Dino's Song," "If You Live," "Too Long," "Who Do You Love."

The Steve Miller Band: "Mercury Blues," "Living in the U.S.A."

The Electric Flag: "Groovin' is Easy," "Wine," "Nighttime is the Right Time."

Saturday evening, June 17:

Moby Grape: "Fall on You," "Indifference," "Mr. Blues," "Omaha," "Sitting by the Window."

Hugh Masekela: "Bajabula Bonke / Healing Song," "Here, There, and Everywhere," "Society's Child."

The Byrds: "Renaissance Fair," "Have You Seen Her Face," "Hey Joe," "He Was a Friend of Mine," "Lady Friend," "Chimes of Freedom," "So You Want to Be a Rock 'n' Roll Star."

Laura Nyro: "Eli's Coming," "Poverty Train," "Wedding Bell Blues."

Jefferson Airplane: "Somebody to Love," "The Other Side of This Life," "White Rabbit," "High Flyin' Bird," "Today," "She Has Funny Cars," "The Ballad of You and Me and Pooneil," "Young Girl Sunday Blues."

Booker T. and the M.G.s with the Mar-Keys: "Booker-Loo," "Hip Hug-Her," "Philly Dog."

Otis Redding: "Respect," "I've Been Loving You Too Long," "Satisfaction," "Try a Little Tenderness," "Shake."

Sunday afternoon, June 18:

Ravi Shankar on sitar, Alla Rakha on tabla, Kamala Chakravarty on tamboura:

"Raga Bhimpalasi," "Tabla Solo in Ektal," "Dhun (Dadra and Fast Teental)," "Raga Todi in Rupaktal," "Raga Shuddha Sarang in Tintal," "Dhun in Pancham-se-Gara."

Sunday evening, June 18:

The Blues Project: "Wake Me, Shake Me," "Flute Thing."

Big Brother and the Holding Company (again): "Combination of the Two," "Coo Coo," "Ball and Chain."

The Group With No Name, led by Cyrus Faryar: [set list undetermined]

Buffalo Springfield, with David Crosby substituting for Neil Young: "A Child's Claim to Fame." "Bluebird," "For What It's Worth," "Nowadays Clancy Can't Even Sing," "Pretty Girl Why," "Rock and Roll Woman."

The Who: "Substitute," "Summertime Blues," "Pictures of Lily," "A Quick One While He's Away," "Happy Jack," "My Generation."

The Grateful Dead: "Alligator," "Caution (Do Not Stop on Tracks)," "Cold Rain and Snow," "Viola Lee Blues."

The Jimi Hendrix Experience: "Killing Floor," "Foxy Lady," "Like a Rolling Stone," "Rock Me Baby," "Hey Joe," "Can You See Me," "The Wind Cries Mary," "Purple Haze," "Wild Thing."

Scott McKenzie: "San Francisco (Wear Some Flowers in Your Hair)."

The Mamas and the Papas: "Straight Shooter," "Got a Feelin'," "California Dreamin'," "I Call Your Name," "Somebody Groovy," "Spanish Harlem," "Monday, Monday," "Dancing in the Streets."

$$\Omega$$

The King of Hearts portrayed in microcosm the whole world as if it were theater, not in the Shakespearian sense of "All the world's a stage," but rather in the sense that no human action is to be taken seriously and should only be used for amusement, as if it were merely play. A Scottish private, ordered to prevent the Germans from blowing up a strategic French town in the last days of World War I, discovered that all the town's inhabitants except the inmates of the local lunatic asylum had fled in fear. The private "freed" the loonies, joined them in their frolics, and almost fortuitously completed his mission to stop the demolition. The loonies in turn freed him from his world and took him into theirs — where he would live thereafter much happier as the unreal King of Hearts in an unreal world than as a real soldier in the real world. The loonies could not have been loonier, yet they made more sense than the warriors. Their insane little world was an island of sanity in the middle of the ocean of a greater insanity: war. To stick even a toe into that water meant horror, sadness, and death. To stay warily on the island meant happiness, life, and freedom.

The fifth Bond movie, *You Only Live Twice*, was as far removed from *Dr. No* and *From Russia with Love* as *Santa Claus Conquers the Martians* was from *Miracle on 34th Street*. It was the worst of the Connery Bonds. The fascinating repartee and character of Bond had given way to even more gadgets, fantasy, and unbelievable events. By now we had read all the Bond paperbacks. *You Only Live Twice* was an excellent book, one of Fleming's best, and as realistic as any of them. It dealt with S.P.E.C.T.R.E.'s exploitation of the Japanese cultural and religious predilection to suicide. More than any of the others, it showed Bond with a soul and normal human foibles. The filmmakers might have made a fine movie if they had only followed the plot of the book instead of concocting an implausible science fiction story based on premises that were counterfactual to human nature, geological and geographical reality, and the laws of physics. For example, where was the magic television camera that sent images of the interceptor rocket to the S.P.E.C.T.R.E. control room? What made that huge stream of lava appear so quickly when Blofeld blew up the crater? How farfetched was it to assume that no one among hundreds of Japanese fishing villagers would notice space rockets taking off from and landing on their tiny little island? Absurd, absurd, absurd. Connery was apparently disenchanted too. He quit the series after this film. Who could blame him?

In the early years of the Bond movies, they provided a few hours each of fairly intelligent escape from a rather dull world. But by summer 1967, besides all the good that was happening musically and culturally, so much evil was happening politically that we could not afford to ignore or try to escape from any of it. To do so might literally have meant our death in a Vietnamese rice paddy or a Mississippi street. We had to confront it head on. We wanted — and by that time needed — our movies to eschew fantasy and depict reality accurately. We needed them to help us understand and deal with whatever was trying to destroy us in the real world. We wanted our movie spies to be complex individuals like Harry Palmer and our movie heroes to be plain folk like Atticus Finch.

As if to answer this call for believability came a tremendous movie, *In the Heat of the Night*. In a Mississippi town not unlike the Alabama town in which *To Kill a Mockingbird* was set, a rich white man was murdered. Coincidence threw together a black police detective from Philadelphia, Virgil Tibbs (Sidney Poitier), an acknowledged homicide expert, and the local police chief, Bill Gillespie (Rod Steiger), a self-admitted novice at solving murders. Tibbs was in a bad situation: If he solved the murder, then he would seem like an uppity nigger who just had to show the white man up — "because you're so damn smart, you're smarter than any white man, you're just gonna stay here and show us all; you've got such a big head that you could never live with yourself unless you could put us all to shame," as Gillespie said — and if he did not solve it, then, through the bungling incompetence of the town police, an innocent person would be convicted and the murderer would remain free. In either case, Tibbs's life was in danger from the local rednecks. He had a limited choice to go home to Philadelphia, and Gillespie wavered between his racism wanting Tibbs to go and his sense of professional duty wanting Tibbs to stay. For Tibbs's part, maybe his reason for staying was only his own sense of professional duty and his moral desire to see the guilty person caught and punished, or maybe it was also tinged with his entrenched, racially motivated need to escape being the whites' "whipping boy" and to show them up indeed. The film left that point ambiguous, but, as Gillespie sarcastically told Tibbs, "I don't think you could let an opportunity like that pass by." Tibbs's plight showed how racism interferes with all justice, even those aspects of justice which have nothing immediately to do with racism, such as one white man murdering another. In the end, Gillespie came around to see Tibbs as a human being, invited him into his home for dinner, carried his bag to the train station, and even wished him well — sincerely. But the filmgoer could realistically surmise that, now that the townsfolk have branded Gillespie a "nigger lover," he would soon lose his job and perhaps also his life.

How could anyone remain a racist after hearing the wonderful contributions that black people have made to music? How could anyone believe in segregation after hearing interracial bands like the Jimi Hendrix Experience, the Electric Flag, or Booker T. and the M.G.s? Musicians, real musicians who really care about music, do not care about the color of other musicians' skin. They judge each other only by whether or not they have the chops, the licks, the pipes, i.e., by whether or not they are "the shit," "in the groove," or "in the pocket." If they can cut it, then they are in; if not, then not, regardless of skin color. Integrated bands were nearly unheard of before the sixties. Jim Crow laws and segregationist traditions had a terrible effect on music. Rock-and-roll — its shameful early exploitation of black music by white assholes like Pat Boone notwithstanding — was in general a godsend for racial harmony. How could any white person hate blacks after hearing black music, its white derivatives, or music made by blacks and whites together?

Compare the 1967 original "Some Kind of Wonderful" by the Soul Brothers Six with the cover done in 1974 by Grand Funk Railroad. Hyperion to a satyr! The original had bite, feel, soul. The cover was pale, bloodless, useless. Never existed a tighter, simpler, more seductive bass line than in "Some Kind of Wonderful." Even Grand Funk could not ruin it completely. Similar comparisons played out over and over and over and over again as white bands made inferior, but usually more popular and more lucrative, versions of exquisite black songs. Oh, we could talk all night about the Rolling Stones or Led Zeppelin ripping off Robert Johnson and other early African-American blues innovators, but more to the point would be Pat Boone ripping off Little Richard, Georgia Gibbs bowdlerizing Hank Ballard's "Work With Me, Annie" as "Dance With Me, Henry," the Beach Boys getting their licks from Chuck Berry, and everyone else and his brother ripping off Bo Diddley.

We were at last beginning to realize that the rock we loved had black roots. Accordingly, we began seeking out and listening to more and more black tunes.

Jackie Wilson, "Mr. Excitement" of the pop soul world, scored with "(Your Love Keeps Lifting Me) Higher and Higher," the last, and arguably the best of his crossover top-ten singles from the rhythm-and-blues charts to the pop charts. Whatever he and other black performers might have lacked in popularity among whites, they made up for it in raw vibrancy. The sheer positive energy of soul musicians like Wilson, James Brown, Sam and Dave, Otis Redding, Wilson Pickett, Arthur Conley, Joe Tex, Tina Turner, Edwin Starr, Junior Walker, Eddie Floyd, etc., was simply amazing. Few white singers — with the notable exception of Mick Jagger — could be so lively, so brisk, so untiring, night after night after night. For these rousing musicians, and increasingly for us listeners, dancers, and record buyers, music was better if you sweated for it. We whites had a lot to learn from the black community, not only about music, but also about basic human relations. Interracial bands like Booker T. and the M.G.s and the Mar-Keys, both of which featured white master instrumentalists Steve Cropper on guitar and Donald "Duck" Dunn on bass, were showing the way toward both better music and better human relations. Indeed, as we believed, better music and better human relations were inseparable.

In Janis Ian's "Society's Child," elders urged the interracial young lovers to stick with their own kind. Is such chauvinism universalizable? Is it defensible at all? Black with black, white with white, yellow with yellow, red with red, brown with brown. How dull! Ask the Kantian question: "What if everybody did it?" Black would get blacker, white whiter, yellow yellower, red redder, brown browner. The natural color divisions — minor biological differences — among humans would grow sharper, clearer, and would mutate into sociopolitical, geopolitical, and insidious ethnic hostilities. Sticking to one's own kind reverts humankind to tribalism. It makes walls and swords, not bridges and plowshares. Tribes are natural islands. To preserve themselves they must define themselves against all other tribes. This promotes ignorance, creates suspicion, and often leads to war. It can never foster peace. Local groups naturally separate themselves from others and eventually antagonize them; but the global group has no enemies. Let interracial marriage thrive!

The June 1967 *Mad* was its "Special Racial Issue." Returning to its standard vehicle, the Broadway musical, *Mad* presented "Stokely and Tess," in which Stokely Carmichael tried to lure Tess away from Martin Luther King, citing the anti-white ideology of black power against what he saw as King's Uncle Tom integrationist strategy.

Not only comedy about blacks was thriving, but also comedy by blacks. Bill Cosby continued telling wild stories of his childhood in Philadelphia on what many believe was his funniest album, *Revenge*. Richard Pryor appeared on *The Ed Sullivan Show* to present a bittersweet tale of African-American sailors being tricked into bunking in torpedo tubes so that the white sailors could jettison them from the submarine.

Meanwhile, the leadership of SNCC was passing over from Carmichael to H. Rap Brown. This did not bode well for the future of nonviolence in America. The high ideals with with SNCC had been founded in 1960 were being lost to mere criminals.

Yet, criminals were not without sympathy.

Warren Beatty's pet project, *Bonnie and Clyde*, which he produced and in which he starred, tried very hard to present a pair of bank-robbing killers as lovable victims of society, law, and the Great Depression. Part of his and director Arthur Penn's strategy to create this sympathetic view was comedic, part was sexual, and part was to juxtapose poor people and criminals together on the short side of distributive socioeconomic justice against the banks and police on the long side. Even if their attempt to show criminals as victims succeeded, even if this socioeconomic injustice was real, and even if the many, many victims of this injustice had the natural right to struggle against the poverty that society imposed on them, the film also showed that when these victims fail to organize themselves into coherent political resistance forces, but instead resort to simple crime and bank robbery, they thus become part of the problem, not part of the solution, however lovable they may be. Robin-Hood-ism may appear to be the instinctive recourse of the poor, but it does not contribute at all toward alleviating the conditions that create and sustain poverty in the first place. Robin Hood may be a folk hero, and Bonnie and Clyde and Woody Guthrie's Pretty Boy Floyd may be working class heroes, but the real heroes of class struggle are leaders and organizers like Martin Luther King, Samuel Gompers, John L. Lewis, and Eugene V. Debs. The film ultimately showed the moral hollowness of any values, criminal or lawful, that are based on money. Criminals have no home, not even among their families, friends, or admirers. They must always run, run, run, until society's law catches them and squashes them like bugs.

The law is only a suggestion. If it is ever obeyed, it should be obeyed, not because it is the law, but because it happens, in some particular case, to be right, i.e., because it is in accord with the universal moral duty that is known through conscience. The law is sometimes right, and it is often wrong. It was wrong when it persecuted Muhammad Ali.

Early in 1964, Cassius Clay, boxing gold medalist from the 1960 Rome Olympics, clobbered Sonny Liston for the heavyweight championship, proclaimed his Muslim faith, and changed his name to Muhammad Ali. From that time on, not because of his bombast, braggadocio, or even his bad poetry, but because of his Islamic faith, his association with Malcolm X and Elijah Muhammad, and what was perceived as his black militancy, white government authorities had it in for him. While Liston had been an acceptable champ from the white point of view, just a dumb, strong, quiet Uncle Tom, Ali, quite the contrary, was intelligent, brash, and outspoken — a real threat to white control.

Ali was a fine champion and a worthy ambassador for his barbaric sport, but he would not keep silent about injustices in race relations, religion, economics, politics, or war. Thus he was also a worthy ambassador to line up his white fans for leftist causes — and this the government could not tolerate. So, to get him out of the way, they drafted him into the Army. Having previously declared himself a conscientious objector on the basis of his reading of the Qur'an, which he interpreted as approving only religious war (*jihad*), but condemning secular wars such as that in Vietnam, he pointedly refused to report for induction, with these words: "I ain't got no quarrel with those Vietcong, anyway. They never called me 'nigger'." The several governing bodies of boxing promptly stripped him of all his titles. The federal government, with uncharacteristic speed, convicted him, fined him, sentenced him to five years in prison, and confiscated his passport so that he could not emigrate while he was out of jail on appeal. As he could no longer earn his living doing the only job he knew, fighting in the ring, he continued his fight in the courts. On June 28, 1971, the U.S. Supreme Court ruled eight to none that the Selective Service System should not have denied Ali's claim to conscientious objection to the Vietnam War. He was at last free and vindicated, but the government had robbed him of four years of his professional prime.

George Carlin would later joke that the government decided not to allow Ali to beat people up anymore because he refused to kill, but that joke was not far from the truth. Ali was not a peaceful man. He beat people up for a living. But he clearly saw that an American war against a sovereign, agrarian nation on the other side of the world was wrong, and he obeyed his conscience by refusing to be part of it. For that he deserved — and got — our lasting honor.

Ω

Hiroshima Day, 1967 — and Beyond

On August 6, 1967, my family and I were in Montréal visiting the World's Fair, Expo 67. It was Youth Day at the fair. I learned that the Jefferson Airplane was to play free concerts at Place-Ville-Marie that afternoon and at the fairgrounds that evening. I decided to go to both. I was fourteen and had never been to a rock show before. What better way to do my first one than with my favorite group? Opening both shows was another San Francisco band: the Grateful Dead.

On my way to Place-Ville-Marie I noticed a small, peaceful demonstration against nuclear warfare in general and against having dropped the bomb on Hiroshima in particular.

I thought at the time — and I still do — that Truman saved lives by dropping those two A-bombs on Japan. What else was he supposed to do? Kamikaze pilots were inflicting maximum casualties on the U.S. Navy. As the Japanese became more and more desperate with the fate of war turning against them in 1944 and 1945, we saw with increasing clarity that they would rather fight like cornered animals than surrender. The evidence at the time all pointed inexorably toward years of suicidal resistance to any invasion of Japan, with millions of dead on both sides. Three closely related events, the U.S. bombing of Hiroshima on August 6, 1945, the U.S. bombing of Nagasaki on August 9, and the Russian declaration of war against Japan on August 8, together led directly to Japan's unconditional surrender on August 15 and prevented all that extra carnage. To exchange a few hundred thousand lives for a few million is good rule-utilitarian logic.

If you are going to be a peacenik, be sure of your knowledge of history!

I watched the demonstration for a while then watched the roadies and locals set up the stage for the Dead and the Airplane. I had arrived early enough to get right in the front row, right in the middle, right in front of where Grace Slick would be. When she appeared on stage, I was no more than five or six feet away from her. She smiled at me once or twice.

I have never been able to decide whether Nick Auf der Maur's article, "'Flower Children' Gather: Hippie Love-Cry Fills Local Air," which appeared the next day in the *Montréal Gazette* and is here quoted in full, was condescending or merely bemused:

The love message flooded the heart of Montreal yesterday.
And with it, North America's hippie movement, and it's [sic] rallying

cry of "Make Love Not War," firmly established itself here with the city's biggest-ever love-in.

The youthful hippies gathered at Place Ville Marie plaza where California bands called the Jefferson Airplane and the Greatful [sic] Dead provided participants with "music to love by."

Thousands of hip-for-the-day tourists and ordinary citizens joined the "flower children," swelling the crowd to about 25,000, according to one PVM official. One of the numerous policemen assigned to keep the peace at the love-in put the figure at 20,000.

Hundreds of young persons, wearing garlands of flowers in their hair and with flowers painted on their hands, feet, legs and faces, listened passively as electronic music echoed through the plaza and the skyscraper canyon.

They wore beads, bangles and bells while their shirts carried assorted slogans exhorting everyone to "Love."

Some danced with their reflections in the building windows, but for the most part they just stood around, tossing flowers and streamers. Conga lines wended their way through the huge throng at intervals.

"This is the s t r a n g e s t thing," one elderly gentleman commented, " What happened to the hysterical teenagers who used to storm the Beatles and the Rolling Stones?"

The passivity of the crowd was remarkable, and one policeman appeared openly confused when a pretty teenaged girl offered him a flower.

Many of those at PVM yesterday participated in the Fletchers' [sic] Field love-in [on Mount Royal] two months ago, which was broken up when mounted police charged into the crowd.

Police were roundly criticized at that time, but the hippies advocated "flower power" to win them over to the cause.

That evening, after the day's second gig, I snuck backstage and hung out with the bands, their roadies, guests, and a few other sneaky fans for about two hours. No one tried to throw us intruders out or hassled us at all. If any awkwardness existed for me, it was not as a starstruck fan in the presence of admired celebrities, but as a fourteen-year-old in the presence of twenty-somethings. Despite the age difference, I felt right at home. The Airplane and the Dead were my people.

Our detractors said we were lazy, spoiled, grimy, and parasitic. White racist presidential candidate George C. Wallace would later counter our calling him a fascist by saying that we did not know what either work or soap were. To charges that we leftist activists were parasitic for our livelihood on the fruits and products of the solid hardworking citizens of the right, we retorted like good Marxists that these so-called "solid hardworking citizens" were in fact bigger parasites on the sweat and misery of the lower classes. The right accused us of being Soviet dupes, of hating America, of committing treason, and of not understanding that Jesus wanted us to win in Vietnam and keep the races separate. We accused them of systematic mass murder, of fomenting discord, of raping the people and the land, of the cynical manipulation of religious and moral values for material gain, and of profiteering at the expense of human dignity, decency, and individuality. Such exchanges created more heat than light and plainly are now best viewed as equally embarrassing to both sides. It was our fault. Rather than falling into their trap of contributing to polarize America (which helped their agenda, not ours), we should have strived more toward harmony, community, and reconciliation. But how we could ever have done that is difficult to imagine, given the deep-seated sociopolitical, socio-economic, and racial tensions that then permeated the country.

As if to point up all this discord in one fell swoop, Abbie Hoffman, Jerry Rubin, and several assorted hippies and Diggers successfully pulled off a startling guerrilla theater stunt in the heart of "enemy territory" and in the process garnered much free publicity — and notoriety — for the antiwar movement. Pretending that they had arrived for a tour, they gained access to the balcony two stories above the floor of the New York Stock Exchange. Preaching, chanting, yelling, they threw about 300 dollar bills over the rail. The crazed traders and brokers below did not know how to react. Some laughed, some cursed, some waved, and quite a few dashed for the money. Oh, how the right loved money! We could look forward to being entertained by the political street theater of these two wags, especially Abbie, for the next few years.

Fall 1967

Music = Truth

... and music / reached still further upward and surpassed us.
... und Musik / reichte noch weiter hinan und überstieg uns.
— Rainer Maria Rilke, "Seventh Elegy"

When I returned to high school that September and told of my experiences with the Airplane and the Dead in Montréal, my status among my peers immediately and unexpectedly went up. Before then, I had been regarded as what was then called a nerd and what is now called a geek. But suddenly I was cool. I've been cool ever since. I was no longer bullied; they gave me my space.

Music was the most effective bridge between people who would not otherwise communicate, and the best catalyst to create friends among those who would not otherwise be friends. If love was the only cement that would ever hold the world together,[49] then music was its applicator.

We were thankful when Jimi Hendrix assured us in "Third Stone from the Sun" that we would not have to endure surf music anymore. Surf music was fluffy, mindless, hedonistic crap. No substance. No meaning. The Beach Boys' "good vibrations" were not as good as a guitar hero's great vibrations.

Hendrix was the big news that fall. His music was full of substance and meaning as well as virtuosity, novelty, and power. As the liner notes of *Are You Experienced?* put it:

Used to be an Experience meant making you a bit older. This one makes you wider. ... Jimi Hendrix breaks the world into interesting fragments. Then reassembles it. You hear with new ears, after being Experienced. Those who've only seen him perform know only part of This Experience. They rave about a young

---

[49] Paraphrasing Woodrow Wilson, who said in a speech about the Red Cross on May 17, 1918, at the Metropolitan Opera House in New York City: "Friendship is the only cement that will ever hold the world together.

man who plays a guitar in more positions than anybody before him. Now, this debut album will put the heads of Hendrix' listeners into some novel positions.

Six of the eleven cuts on *Are You Experienced?* remained classic rock standards more than forty years after their first appearance on vinyl: "Purple Haze," "Manic Depression," "Hey Joe," "The Wind Cries Mary," "Fire," and "Foxy Lady." Two others, "Third Stone From the Sun" and the title song, sound just as trippy and fresh in 2009 as they did in 1967. As I write this, it still seems that no one wants to forget Hendrix.

"Purple Haze" was released as a single, but was practically ignored in that market. Could there ever be any better evidence that young people with taste for complex, innovative, revitalizing music had mostly abandoned singles for LPs?

The new Airplane single came out, but as we were not listening much to singles anymore, we waited for the LP follow-up to *Surrealistic Pillow*. So most of us did not hear "The Ballad of You and Me and Pooneil" until January.

Jim Morrison famously defied Ed Sullivan's attempt to censor "Light My Fire" for the Doors' live appearance on his show. Ed correctly thought it was a drug song. Thus he was afraid to let Jim sing the word "higher" on TV. Thank God that Morrison was no coward! The result was hilarious! As the fact became more and more obvious to everyone in the mid-sixties that the musicians whom we loved were almost all on illegal drugs and that much of their music was drug-inspired, our elders became fearful that we would be seduced into using these horrible narcotics, stimulants, psychedelics, and hallucinogens. Their fear was a self-parody as they sipped their martinis. Although their fear was justified in some cases, in general it was not. We were sensible enough to make our own decisions about personal lifestyle. We liked to think that we loved life while they loved only money, power, and — I suppose — us. What our parents failed to realize, and what may have eased their fears if they had realized it, was that these druggy musicians gave us listeners the vicarious experience of drugs, an experience so vivid and potent that, if we internalized the music, then we, on that account alone, had no need to use these drugs ourselves. *Sgt. Pepper*, for example, was an acid trip. Why take LSD when we could just listen to the Beatles and get much the same effect? Turning the volume up and shutting our eyes helped immeasurably. Music was a natural, more durable, more dependable high than drugs. We were not fools; we knew this — even if the musicians who created this beautiful trance did not.

Strange Days marked a quantum leap in songwriting over the Doors' debut album. There were no covers. As usual, Morrison's lyrics ranged from the ridiculous ("Love Me Two Times," "Moonlight Drive") to the sublime ("Strange Days," "When the Music's Over") to the pretentious ("Horse Latitudes"). We had to ask ourselves, "Is he a charlatan? When he writes good lyrics, is it only accidental?" Of course, we would not have asked these questions if he had not passed himself off as a poet, but because he had, we held him to a higher standard. Most rock lyricists did not claim to be poets, but among those who did, Lennon almost always passed the test, Dylan sometimes, and Morrison almost never. Nevertheless, the Doors' second album was probably their best, and much of this excellence must be attributed to Morrison's lyrics, especially in "When the Music's Over," an eleven-minute *tour de force* of rebellion, rejection, and disillusionment.

The title cut of *Strange Days* was a portent of imminent danger that would manifest itself not only physically, but also psychologically, socially, spiritually, environmentally, and in countless other ways. Regarding the psychological aspect of this overriding danger, "You're Lost Little Girl" advised her to look inside herself for answers to her deepest, most important questions. Similarly, "Unhappy Girl" asserted that her loneliness and sadness were her own fault and suggested that, if she would just recognize herself as the source of her problems, climb out of her self-created exile, and give herself over to the mysteries of life, then they might be happily resolved. If such dangers were not soon and decisively addressed, the result would be spiritual death, madness. Also similarly, "I Can't See Your Face in My Mind" was a gentle song of comfort for psychological distress.

"Horse Latitudes" was a stupid, discordant rant about the historical fact of sea captains ordering horses thrown overboard to lighten ships' ballast. "Moonlight Drive," best forgotten, was a one-dimensional tale of a teenage boy trying to seduce a teenage girl in an automobile. "My Eyes Have Seen You" was likewise just a simple song of seduction, and "Love Me Two Times" a simple example of sexual infatuation.

"People Are Strange" related the heartbreak of being a minority of one freak in a world of straights. We all want to belong, and to achieve this goal we have only two choices: either forsake each our own self and be accepted as a soulless entity by "them" and belong to "their" society, or be true each to our own self, continue naturally to belong each to our own self, and be rejected by the rest of the world. Be false to ourselves and be accepted, or be true to ourselves and be rejected — that was the predicament of shared individuality. This basic existential predicament was a common theme in literature from Shakespeare's *Hamlet* and *King Lear* through the more introspective nineteenth and twentieth-century philosophers and theologians and now even beyond, into the lyrics of popular music. Jean-Paul Sartre wrote much about the individual self being essentially nothing in the world of the perpetual scrutinizing gaze of "the other." Martin Heidegger wrote of *das Man* ("the them") as a stark, stultifying, merely physical, wall-like thing. Hell, as Sartre's character Garcin declared in *No Exit*, was indeed "other people." Belong to them or belong to yourself. That remains your only choice.

"When the Music's Over," Morrison's lyrical masterpiece, presented a multifaceted and, for him, an uncharacteristically unambiguous sociopolitical message. It was a song about various kinds of death. With an overall focus on the ephemeral, fragile nature of all life, Morrison's languid voice affirmed that music is life itself in many guises, so that, when any music ends, something has died. Life and music are both dangerous, but both necessary, equally dangerous, equally necessary, yet also both equally doomed. There is no hope after the end of either life or music. Both must end. Definitively. Thoroughly. Period.

One verse of "When the Music's Over" was pure apostasy, opening with a welcome rejection, in a single eloquent line, of the entire Christian promise of an afterlife. Such redirection toward the immediate affairs, pains, pleasures, trials —

and music — of this world, rather than the familiar din of fanciful and stupid cosmic plans for escape into some other world, was indeed music to our ears. True lovers of music were like the Rope Dancer in Nietzsche's Preface to *Thus Spake Zarathustra*: embracers of danger, lovers of fate, vigorous defenders of life, but placid accepters of death — when it came. True individuals, living every moment to the fullest, rejoicing, dancing, asking no special favors from God, that was us. We so aspired to this state. Neither Jesus nor anyone else nor anything else would save us. Maybe we did not need to be saved, but if any saving was to be done, we would each do it ourselves — by each turning our attention toward what mattered most: immediate life, love, and music. As another preeminent music lover, Nietzsche, said many times: "Be true to the earth!" Accordingly, another verse delivered a strong environmentalist message. The human race, rather than being loving, rejoicing, dancing stewards of the earth, instead assaulted, raped, and tortured the earth. This irresponsible, unsustainable plundering of the planet was essentially a political problem. Thus Morrison's demand for the world — Now! — recalled Judy Collins's unconditional plea for basic human rights and total political revolution — Now! — in "Marat/Sade" and her persona's slyly whispered command for the deaths of her oppressors — Right now! — in "Pirate Jenny," both on *In My Life*. Collins's and Morrison's impatience was quite reasonable. With people like LBJ ruining the world, we needed to take it over from them as soon as possible.

The other Morrison, Van, had quit Them earlier in 1967 and now re-emerged with his first solo album, *Blowin' Your Mind*, which contained his current hit single, "Brown-Eyed Girl." Van was a tremendous songwriter. If he had never written anything beyond the deceptively simple and frequently covered "Gloria," his place would still be assured in that regard. Critics loved his tunes, but he was too feisty to be successful in the studio, too reclusive to win audiences on the road, and too musically eclectic to gain much of a popular following. He did, however, have a steadily growing cult following, which would bring him wider acclaim later in the sixties and in the early seventies with such albums as *Astral Weeks*, *Moondance*, *Tupelo Honey*, and *Saint Dominic's Preview*, and such songs as "Into the Mystic," "Domino," "Wild Night," and "Jackie Wilson Said."

Buffalo Springfield's second LP, *Again*, was arguably the best of their three. Both Stephen Stills and Neil Young, but especially Young, had achieved great strides as songwriters. Stills's "Bluebird" and Young's "Mr. Soul" and "Broken Arrow" all proved to be durable standards of the folk rock genre.

Stills was a much underrated guitarist. He had a wicked crush on Judy Collins. "Bluebird," a vigorous, ringing, guitar-oriented tune with amazing riffs and solos, was the first of two hit songs that he wrote both for and about her, the other being "Suite: Judy Blue Eyes," which would be a huge single for Crosby, Stills, and Nash in 1969.

"Mr. Soul" had fairly difficult lyrics, but seemed to be just Neil whining about the wide variety of relationships that a rock star might have with his female fans. We would soon come to expect Neil to whine about almost anything. In "Broken Arrow," also with rather obscure lyrics, he whined about the tragic fate of Native Americans, a topic dear to his heart, and to which he would return many times throughout his long songwriting career.

The Rolling Stones, perhaps copying the Beatles, forayed into psychedelic rock with *Their Satanic Majesties Request*. The album cover was not unlike that of *Sgt. Pepper's*. It showed the five bad boys dressed in fanciful medieval costumes, Jagger like a sorcerer, all sitting cross-legged in a cluttered, surreal, almost extraterrestrial, mountain landscape framed in a wide blue and white border that resembled wispy, smoky, cirrus clouds against the brightest of bright blue skies. Some prints of the cover were even in three dimensions. A careful observer could discern the faces of all four Beatles hidden in the clutter. The color saturation of the whole phenomenon was fantastic.

The title was a pun on "Her Britannic Majesty requests ...", which was one standard way for the queen of England to say, "I want ..." It went far toward establishing two persistent reputations: Jagger's as a satanic influence and the Stones' as an evil band.

Unfortunately, most of the LP's music could not match its stunning visual effects. "She's a Rainbow" was the exception. The Stones' double-sided single from this period, "We Love You" / "Dandelion," was generally more interesting. The former, complete with jail sounds, was the Stones' "thank you" to their fans for supporting them through their various drug busts. Nicky Hopkins's distinctive piano riff would alone have made the tune worthwhile. The latter was a psychedelic ode to the playfulness of flower power, with Nicky on the harpsichord.

In a similar vein, Donovan's new single, "Wear Your Love Like Heaven," evoked a panoply of vibrant colors, an esoteric floral world, as a metaphor for universal serenity, harmony, and freedom. Moreover, his mention of Allah suggested the goal of religious tolerance. This song, above all of his, fed his image as a starry-eyed dreamer. Yet, just because those of us who were more realistic than Donovan recognized his dreams as unachievable was no reason for him not to dream them, beautify them with music, or express them in song.

Another prominent tune in the very large genre of late sixties songs about psychedelic colors was "SWLABR" on Cream's *Disraeli Gears*. The title was an acronym for "She Was Like A Bearded Rainbow." It was a heavier rocker than most others in this genre, and featured a lot of Cream's typical — and delicious — instrumental distortion. The lyrics did not disappoint. Indeed, they reminded us a bit of Marcel Duchamp's ready-made painting, *L.H.O.O.Q.*, which was just the *Mona Lisa* with a goatee and handlebar mustache inked on like graffiti. Duchamp's title, if pronounced in French, was a pun on *Elle a chaud au cul*, meaning "She has a hot ass" or "She's horny."

From "Lucy in the Sky With Diamonds" to "She's a Rainbow" to "Wear Your Love Like Heaven" to "SWLABR," in between, and beyond, lyrics about colors, especially radiant or unusual colors, were very popular in the latter half of 1967. Mostly these were serious, or semi-serious, lyrics about peace and love. But notably, in "Judy in Disguise," which some interpreters have taken as a parody of "Lucy in the Sky With Diamonds," John Fred and His Playboy Band used words about colors to comic effect.

Most of the lyrics in songs about colors were extraordinarily obscure.

One of the greatest failings of my generation was a tendency to equate ob-scurity with profundity. We assumed that any song lyrics that were difficult to un-derstand must be deep. We relegated transparent song lyrics to the realm of banality. Nowhere was this unfortunate tendency more evident than in attempts to decipher "I Am the Walrus."

Magical Mystery Tour, the Beatles' follow-up to *Sgt. Pepper's*, was dis-guised as a concept album, but it was really just numbers. Side one contained the title cut, four other new tunes, "The Fool on the Hill," "Flying" (the Beatles' only instrumental), "Blue Jay Way," and "Your Mother Should Know," plus their con-current single's B-side, "I Am the Walrus." Side two consisted of five collected singles: "Hello Goodbye" (the new single's A-side), "Strawberry Fields Forever," "Penny Lane," "Baby, You're a Rich Man," and "All You Need is Love."

"I Am the Walrus" is a wonderful song, one of the Beatles' very best. Its melody, rhythms, arrangement, and lyrics are all hypnotic. But, regarding its lyrics, many of us — myself included, I confess — were fooled by their very beauty and complexity into believing that they concealed deep meaning, buried for us to find. We were taken in by such features as subtle variations on lines within the song; apparent internal paradoxes and mysterious juxtapositions of images; references to Edgar Allan Poe, previous Beatles songs, Krishna, and the Eiffel Tower; and the inclusion of an excerpt from *King Lear*, IV, vi, 255-260. It seemed like a surreali-stic poem, an extended Zen koan, containing clues as to the nature of *samsara* and the Leibnizian interrelation of all worldly phenomena. We studied and searched and wondered and posited and tested. We read Shakespeare and Poe and the *Bha-gavad Gita* and anything else we imagined might have any connection with the words. At last we all had to admit defeat. "I Am the Walrus" was in fact inscruta-ble. It was, after all, just attractive nonsense.

Sometimes song lyrics *are* just plain nonsense. That is OK. What is not OK is when people try to inject reason into nonsense, or assume that reason is there when it clearly is not. When lyrics have no meaning, and when people try to find meaning in them anyway, interpretations produce immeasurable mirth for song-writers, who, more than anyone else, know perfectly well which of their lyrics are only nonsense. Moreover, some songwriters have deliberately exploited this pre-valent fault of their listeners. Some, such as Lennon, who were quite capable of writing important words, and often did, sometimes wrote pure nonsense just for fun. Our problem, as listeners, was that we typically could not tell the difference. The situation was even worse with lesser poets than Lennon, e.g., charlatan or quasi-charlatan poets such as Morrison or Dylan, who seemed able to write deep lyrics only accidentally. Our problem was only the lyricists who pretended or claimed to be serious. Inveterate rhyme-stretchers like McCartney, who would reach for rhyme at the expense of meaning, were no problem to interpret, because their words could seldom be taken seriously in any case. To express profound meaning accurately, writers must have the entire multilingual lexicon available, so that they can select precisely the right term to express each thought best. Being a slave to rhyme takes that advantage away.

"Homburg," Procol Harum's follow-up to "A Whiter Shade of Pale," was much less obscure. It depicted a dismayed businessman who was advised to give it all up because he had the wrong pants cuffs, shoelacing style, and overcoat length. We were back to the inconsequential conformist jerk whom Zappa had described in "Brown Shoes Don't Make It," albeit probably quite a bit less perverse. The homburg-wearer was hung up on stuff that was in no way worth getting hung up about. He was a paradigmatic victim of the middle-class-aspiring-to-be-upper-class shibboleth of our parents' generation: "Clothes make the man!" We already knew that "Clothes make the man!" and similar mottos were bullshit. This song only reaffirmed our knowledge that superficiality was not substance and could not contribute toward creating or maintaining anything either substantial or important.

Seventeen months after his near-fatal motorcycle crash, Dylan returned to active public musical life with a new LP, *John Wesley Harding*. It was not his best work, but yielded a few worthwhile songs, including the title cut about a legendary, Robin-Hood-type outlaw; "The Ballad of Frankie Lee and Judas Priest"; and "All Along the Watchtower," which Hendrix would later cover to great effect.

The liner notes of Byrds albums were some of the most interesting reading of the sixties. Dave Swaney's unbelievably hip liner notes for the Byrds' *Greatest Hits* were a neat summary and appraisal of rock history and the Byrds' impact on it since 1964:

Things are happening so incredibly fast.

Was it really three or four generations ago that The Byrds came along and helped turn the whole pop music scene around? Were they conservative then? Or now? Whatever, their thing was beautiful and heavy and will be as it is. Lasting. There will be this big nostalgia binge, and because so many people were part of what happened, and because they were an overwhelming part of a larger renaissance, The Byrds will be revered. It is too early for that now because The Byrds are still happening and very, very valuable. But it is good to be nostalgic, and necessary to find one's rung, and so much good was the start of so many better things happening and about to happen. So why not?

... all of West Coast hippiedom — which is to say Los Angeles, because San Francisco was yet to become as it is — was catalyzed by their sound. The Byrds brought them down from their canyon hideouts, in from their beach shelters, from Big Sur camps and Mexican communes, down from Sierra and Mojave anonymities, to dance and be together and realize how strong their numbers were. They came in rags and velvet, leather and denim, on foot and motorcycle and in Rolls, boots and chains and moccasins, and the LA press was exasperated and delighted.

The Byrds played loud, but with beauty and transcendent smoothness. ... Thousands showed up at The Palladium, where ... the rent-a-cops wondered how everyone could be so happy and have such fun on Coca-Cola and lemonade.

McGuinn made someone a lot of money by wearing those funny-looking Ben Franklin glasses; a wonderfully gentle, thoroughly human man named

Derek Taylor[50] began to gather a new circle of friends and admirers with his logical perspective on the nonsense swirling around them, and the Beatles were quoted as saying their favorite American group was The Byrds; Dylan got on stage with them at Ciro's to blow his harp straight into the dancing melee below as David Crosby smiled benignly at the whole scene; "Mr. Tambourine Man," for those who laughed up their sleeves and for those who dug it straight and would never be persuaded then that anyone could get away with that, made number one. Then there was the first album and a not-so-successful trip to England. The Byrds were *there*.

Someone in the label department at *Billboard* worked overtime to come up with the term "folk-rock" so that everyone would know what was going down in case they didn't want to think about it too much. And it stuck because no one ever had the time to try to change the words or pose an organized "Why?" There was just too much else important happening.

Off the hot streets of Los Angeles, even as other revolutions were finally gaining notice a few miles south in Watts, they would scatter themselves in a darkened studio and bend to the task of reaching into millions of homes, cars, dormitories, coffee shops, bars, bordellos, prisons, camps, insane asylums — minds.

Lots, some because of folks like The Byrds, has gone down since. With them and with us. The record herein, if you let it, will tell you a great deal. About The Byrds, about changes, about yourself. ...

Sometimes things happen so fast that we lose track of what is really the most valuable.

Well, what's wrong with just sitting and thinking? People don't want to do it because they have nothing in their minds. They're bored. They crave "action." Fuck action! Put something in their minds and they will gladly just sit and think! Educated people are seldom bored. The Byrds educated us. Their fans were seldom bored. The Byrds sparked interest in life. They put things in our minds that made us want to go exploring along all sorts of intellectual and spiritual pathways.

The Byrds' influence was indeed everywhere. Eric Burdon and the Animals quoted the last line of "Monterey," their memorable single about last summer's main event, from the Byrds' "Renaissance Fair."

The Who's first American tour was a ten-week affair in June, July, and August with highs like Monterey and lows like — in one of the most inexplicable pairings in concert history — opening for Herman's Hermits. That a heavy, innovative band of real musicians should open for a trifling bunch of super-clean teeny-bopper idols is just too bizarre for words! There were a lot of lows for the Who on that tour. Sets were short, money was barely sufficient, Hermit-loving audiences

---

[50] Press agent for the Beatles; public relations manager for the Byrds, the Beach Boys, Paul Revere and Raiders, and Captain Beefheart and His Magic Band; co-organizer of the Monterey International Pop Festival; and one of the friends whose tardiness inspired George Harrison to write "Blue Jay Way."

did not respond to the Who's work, and Townshend was angry about most of this much of the time.

Their second American tour made more sense. This time they shared the bill with the Animals, a more appropriate arrangement. A major high, and a major career booster, came on September 17 when they appeared on *The Smothers Brothers Comedy Hour*. This was a classic performance of "My Generation" and one of the most memorable television events of the sixties. Keith literally blew up his drum kit with a powerful explosive that — as we later learned — nearly set Pete's hair on fire. During the intros, he had told Tom, "My friends call me Keith; you can call me John."

The Who's brilliant sense of humor shone on their third album, *The Who Sell Out*, even more brightly than it had on *Happy Jack*. The songs were loosely themed around a pop radio premise, complete with airchecks, public service spots, and advertisements. Three of the songs, "Heinz Baked Beans," "Odorono," "Spotted Henry / Medac," and a few smaller bits were hilarious spoofs of product promotions that plugged things like deodorant, zit cream, and muscle building lessons. The makers of the non-musically related products may have shrugged, but Rotosound Manufacturing Limited must have been delighted when the Who told us to hold our groups together with Rotosound strings. Indeed, for many North American bass players, *Sell Out* was their first acquaintance with these fantastically dynamic English strings. We learned later that Entwistle himself had designed Rotosound's famous stainless steel roundwound Swing Bass strings in 1966, developing his idea from the heavy sound of piano strings.

The Who's ever-underlying sexual innuendo was alive and well on *Sell Out*: "Mary-Anne with the Shaky Hands" was a thinly disguised paean to a woman who was popular mainly because she gave great hand jobs. The innuendo pervaded the album, often quite subtly, and was even sometimes difficult to recognize. But it was there — and rewarded scrutiny. "Tattoo" portrayed two brothers who believed that they would be more manly with ink on their arms. "I Can't Reach You," a desperate cry of unrequited love, was a good example of how the Who were growing in musical intricacy without losing or compromising their raw heaviness. "Armenia City in the Sky," written by Townshend's roadie, John "Speedy" Keen, and containing cool squeaky sounds that we had never heard before, prescribed a dreamy way to escape worldly tension and just relax. Townshend's own "Relax" was more of the same. "Our Love Was, Is" and especially the gentle, melodic "Sunrise" were beautiful love songs. Entwistle's "Silas Stingy" made quirky and, in typical Entwistle fashion, rather morbid fun of a Scrooge-like miser.

"I Can See for Miles," their all-time highest charting U.S. single — it hit number nine in *Billboard* — was a tremendous, thundering, intelligent, hard-driving rock song. Townshend was pissed that it did not go to number one. For him it was the ultimate Who song to that point. Thereafter he disowned the singles market and concentrated instead on writing whole albums (or double albums like *Tommy* and *Quadrophenia*) as units.

As on *Happy Jack*, several guitar riffs on *Sell Out* were teasers that would resurface on *Tommy* in 1969. This was most notable in "Rael." Even though we had no idea what the future would hold, "Rael" seemed to be anticipating something beyond itself. Though six minutes long, it seemed somehow incomplete, not like a prologue, but more like a random excerpt. Its narrative was *in medias res*, and thus, without context, quite confusing.

Cream's second album, *Disraeli Gears*, demonstrated even better than *Fresh Cream* what tremendously versatile and interesting virtuosos the three were. Still based in the blues, they now ventured outward toward psychedelia, jazz fusion, hard rock, folk, and several other musical forms — excelling at them all. Besides each of themselves, they used a wide variety of songwriters, including producer Felix Pappalardi (who would later co-found Mountain with Leslie West), Pappalardi's wife Gail Collins, freelance lyricist Peter Brown (whom John Lennon would later mention in "The Ballad of John and Yoko"), and even Australian cartoonist Martin Sharp, who also did the psychedelic pink cover art for the album.

We remained keen to hear new sounds and new kinds of sounds from new voices and new instruments with new techniques. We were getting some of this from Hendrix, Procol Harum, the Beatles, the Airplane, the Doors, and a few other artists, but, with each new release, Eric Clapton's Stratocaster became more and more a source of wonder for us. Combined with Jack Bruce's instantly recognizable, high, peculiar voice, and Ginger Baker's powerful and imaginative drumming, Cream was simply astonishing.

The instant that we heard the first few notes of "Strange Brew," the first tune on *Disraeli Gears*, we just wanted to kick back and listen to Clapton play guitar forever. Not to detract from either *Fresh Cream* or *Wheels of Fire*, but, thanks to such magnificent licks, *Disraeli Gears* remains the apotheosis of Cream. In late 1967, Clapton was indeed God!

The varying blend and counterpoint of Bruce's vocals and Clapton's guitar in "World of Pain" and "Dance the Night Away" were particularly exquisite.

"Tales of Brave Ulysses" brought Homer's *Odyssey* into the world of psychedelic rock, complete with references to the innermost mysteries of the mind. Clapton's guitar effects fascinated, Bruce's voice evoked the perilous yet sensuous sea journey, and Baker's pummelling beats and cymbal accents suited it all perfectly. "Blue Condition" and "Outside Woman Blues" were plain, straight blues. "We're Going Wrong" was bluesy too, but a little more psychedelic than the others. Its combination of fast staccato drum riffs with slow, protracted vocals and occasional wails from Clapton's Stratocaster was mesmerizing. "Take It Back" was a rocking blues number with a solid, albeit understated, backbeat.

The lyrics of "Sunshine of Your Love," the hit single from the album, were just one big sexual innuendo, from the horny male point of view, about the man objectifying the woman. Love had nothing to do with it. The so-called "sunshine" of her love was just her pussy, the goal of his conquest.

The last song on *Disraeli Gears*, "A Mother's Lament," was pure comedy, an unexpected *a cappella* goof on an old British music hall tune. In this time of immoral war, racial injustice, and polarized communities, we truly appreciated bands with keen senses of humor. After all, part of our message was that the establishment took itself much too seriously.

Two other laments, one recorded, one our own, neither one comical, affected us profoundly. Johnny Rivers's pop single, "Summer Rain," came across as a lament for the Summer of Love. When his lyrics referred to *Sgt. Pepper's* in the past tense, we knew then, deep in our hearts, that our glorious summer was over, gone, lost, never to be recaptured. So soon, too soon, we had to confront the sobering fact that it was dead, like a fragile sunlit butterfly who could not stand the coming cold. The second lament we created ourselves from the appearance of a greatest hits LP from the Mamas and the Papas, *Farewell to the First Golden Era*. Its liner notes suggested that they would be back with more music, but somehow we did not believe it. They had lasted less than two years. We already missed them terribly.

Ω

On Saturday, October 21, the Student Mobilization Committee, which we affectionately called either the SMC or the Student Mobe, led between about 35,000 and 70,000 people in an antiwar march through Washington, across the Potomac, to the Pentagon. Contrary to what our prowar detractors said, there was no riot. Ed Sanders, Tuli Kupferberg, Abbie Hoffman, a bunch of Diggers, and many others participated in ceremonies to exorcize demons from the Pentagon and to levitate the building. Demonstrators planted flowers in the muzzles of soldiers' rifles. There was music. There was joy. There was peace. There was even some fear. Norman Mailer would write up the whole deal in his 1968 book, *Armies of the Night* — and for his efforts would win the 1969 Pulitzer Prize for General Non-Fiction.

The Fugs' next album, *Tenderness Junction*, fit perfectly into the aura that the October 21 march and other recent antiwar events had created. It was more "musical," i.e., more melodic and more professionally produced, than their previous releases, more folk-rockish than beat, and some might have said that, in it, the Fugs had lost a bit of their satiric edge. Its "Turn On / Tune In / Drop Out" was an upbeat extrapolation of Leary's notorious motto. "Knock Knock" sounded like ersatz doo wop or a goofy blend of psychedelia, blues, and crooning. "The Garden is Open" was a romantic interlude. "Wet Dream," which described nocturnal emissions sparked by lusting after a high school prom queen, was not quite as innocuous as the Who's "Pictures of Lily." After "Hare Krishna," the long-venerated Hindu chant, "Exorcising the Evil Spirits from the Pentagon, October 21, 1967," an excerpt from the very rites that the Fugs had performed onsite, reverently invoked various ancient Egyptian deities. "War Song" was an eerie dirge of burning mothers and other such niceties, and "Dover Beach," an evocative reading, to guitar accompaniment, of Matthew Arnold's classic mid-nineteenth-century poem about human misery mitigated by the hope of love. "Fingers of the Sun" used lyrics about the ancient Egyptian god/goddess of chaos and water, Nun, to comment on the dangers of nuclear waste. Finally, "Aphrodite Mass" parodied Roman Catholic Church music. The overall effect was typically Fuglike, though somewhat subdued.

On November 2 LBJ convened a meeting of his hand-picked "Wise Men," high-ranking patriotic advisers who would consider five questions: What should we do in South Vietnam? Should we mine the harbors and bomb the dikes in North Vietnam? Should we negotiate? Should we stop the war? How can we unite the American people behind the war? The only answers on which there was consensus were to the fourth and fifth questions — to the fourth, a resounding *No!*, to the fifth: Lie! Tell the people that everything is rosy. Give them nothing but optimistic reports about the war. Over the next few weeks LBJ, his staff, and his generals vigorously put this plan into action. No pessimistic word about Vietnam was allowed to emerge from the White House, Capitol Hill, or the Pentagon.[51] Washington officially reported "steady progress" in Vietnam, both militarily and politically. But we the people were not stupid enough to believe any of that bullshit any more.

Obviously inspired by Barbara Garson's *MacBird*, the cover of the October 1967 *Mad* was Norman Mingo's tableau depicting King Lyndon, Queen Lady Bird, Princesses Lynda and Luci, and their entourage being entertained at a banquet by the court jester, Alfred E. Neuman. All were in medieval dress. Hubert Humphrey was a humble friar. Robert McNamara was a belligerent knight in full battle gear with falling bombs and the Ford Model T emblazoned on his shield. LBJ scowled behind overflowing bags of gold marked "Viet Nam," "Anti-Poverty," and "Great Society." He ate with golden utensils and drank from a golden goblet while one of his beagles drooled on his golden plate. Attorney General Ramsey Clark, one of very few true liberals in LBJ's cabinet, lurked in the background with Chief Justice Earl Warren. United Nations Ambassador Arthur Goldberg peeked in through the window. Secretary of the Treasury Henry Fowler appeared as a bishop. Rakish George Hamilton laughed behind Lynda; jaunty Tommy Smothers laughed behind him. Secretary of State Dean Rusk looked especially thoughtful in spectacles. Next to him and behind Lady Bird was Sergio Aragonés, one of *Mad*'s regular contributors. Senator J. William Fulbright dispensed advice in the far corner. Bobby Kennedy skulked under the table.

LBJ needed advertising. He needed to sell his war. We were not buying it. These points were not lost on *Mad*'s Max Brandel, who in this same issue wrote "Hail to the Chief Copywriter Dept.: President Johnson on Madison Avenue," a scathing attack which implied that, since LBJ had so much experience selling the Great Society and the war, commercial advertisers would do well to hire him as a pitchman for everything from headache relievers to tranquilizers to candy to beer to whiskey to shampoo to toilet paper.

Country Joe and the Fish expressed what the people really thought about the war: Gimme an F! — Gimme a U! — Gimme a C! — Gimme a K! — FUCK! FUCK! FUCK! FUCK! FUCK! We were not fooled by the cleaned-up recorded version. The other songs on the *I Feel Like I'm Fixin' to Die* LP, besides this so-called "Fish Cheer" and the title cut, were bizarre, quintessentially psychedelic, and mostly unremarkable.

---

[51] See Chapters 7 and 8, "The Progress Report of November 1967" and "The Big Sell: The Tortoise of Progress vs. the Hare of Dissent" in Larry Berman's *Lyndon Johnson's War: The Road to Stalemate in Vietnam* (New York: W.W. Norton, 1989), pp. 93-138.

Perhaps the most enduring tale of sixties antiwar subversion was Arlo Guthrie's autobiographical "Alice's Restaurant Massacree," which, at over eighteen minutes, took up a whole vinyl side of his debut album, *Alice's Restaurant*, and soon became not only a countercultural phenomenon as a serious antimilitarism statement, but also a comedy classic. It was a talking folk blues story, a simple track with only Arlo's solo acoustic guitar for accompaniment. He used his Thanksgiving 1965 visit, as an eighteen-year-old, to his friend Alice Brock's home in Stockbridge, Massachusetts, as the basis of his extended satire on cops, the judicial system, the Vietnam War, and especially the draft.

The other side of the album likewise displayed Arlo's wonderful, wry, understated sense of humor. What was he? A folk singer masquerading as a comedian or a comedian masquerading as a folk singer? Who knew? Who cared? We loved Arlo from the start, whatever he was. Perhaps his most important achievement was his least well known: inspiring a whole new generation of listeners to seek out and become familiar with his dad Woody's music.

Jumping on the *Greatest Hits* LP-releasing bandwagon this fall was one of Arlo's favorite heroes, and one of Woody's favorite colleagues, Pete Seeger. By any measure, Pete was a freak. He may have denied it, but he was a real freak, even in some ways the arch-freak. He may have been old, but he was one of us. Freakdom vs. straightdom was not defined by birth year, hair length, musical taste, or even drugs; it was defined by politics. For example, Abbie Hoffman and Jerry Rubin were freaks, not because of the wide variety of illegal drugs that they did in large quantities, nor because of their shaggy hair, nor again because of their relatively young ages (born 1936 and 1938 respectively) or the music that they liked, but because they were wacko masters of street theater, purposeful comedy, and urban guerrilla movements who co-founded, along with Paul Krassner (born 1932) and several others, the Youth International Party (Yippies). Straight society did not want them. They were self-declared freaks. Or maybe freeks! And proud of it.

Young Republican stockbrokers who did drugs, happened to like the Grateful Dead, wore beads and flowers to parties, and let their hair stay uncombed on weekends were definitely ***NOT*** freaks!

Regarding drugs, many of us did indeed use them ourselves, but others among us just used our musicians to have our drug experiences for us. Given that rock musicians, by and large, with Zappa a noteworthy exception, were hardass junkies, they were a reliable and inexhaustible source of such vicarious thrills.

The problem was not that freak kids did drugs openly. The problem was that straight kids did them secretly. The problem was not drugs; it was hypocrisy. Right-wing kids sneaking drugs or alcohol were just the kind to impose Draconian drug laws and heartless drug enforcement on the rest of us when they grew up. Witness Republican New York Governor Nelson Rockefeller, popular Psi Upsilon party animal at Dartmouth College at the end of the so-called "Roaring Twenties" and great-grandson of notorious nineteenth-century narcotics hustler William Avery Rockefeller, founder of the family fortune.

Yet, whether we used drugs or not, we tolerated recreational drug use by others — mostly. Marijuana, LSD, peyote, mescaline, cocaine, morphine, heroin, opium, psilocybin, etc., all presented no real problems for us, users and non-users alike. Of course, you had to be careful with them. You did not want to die of an overdose. But that is true of aspirin, alcohol, and chocolate too.

Amphetamines were the exception to our general drug tolerance. We hated them. We actively discouraged using them. "Speed kills!" was a frequently heard slogan.

Filmed on May 3 but not broadcast until November 1967, "LSD: Lettvin vs. Leary" explored whether hallucinogenic drugs were benign means toward mind-expanding spiritual experiences or dangerous, psychosis-inducing, possibly even lethal, poisons. This 51-minute debate, between Massachusetts Institute of Technology (MIT) professor of physiology Jerome Lettvin and former Harvard University professor of psychology and current guru of psychedelia Timothy Leary, originated at WGBH-TV in Boston and was widely aired and re-aired on Public Broadcasting Service (PBS) stations for several months. Lettvin, the paragon of the uptight establishment, tried very hard to abide by and maintain the traditional forms and proprieties of debate. But Leary just did his thing, sitting crosslegged on the floor amid flowers and incense, paying no heed at all to Lettvin's obvious discomfort. The overall result was comical. Lettvin at one point grew so frustrated with Leary that he exclaimed, "Bullshit!" Leary had his opponent by the balls. Nearly everyone except Lettvin seemed to realize this. Even if the debate did not convince any of us to try LSD, we laughed, and that was enough.

$$\Omega$$

In the fifties nearly all network TV was in black-and-white. Gradually in the sixties the three major networks shifted over to color broadcasting. From about 1963 to 1967 this transition was a basic point of competition among them and each of them hyped it for all it was worth. NBC and ABC were about neck-and-neck, but CBS lagged pretty far behind. From 1957 until NBC won the color transition contest in the mid-sixties, the NBC peacock would appear before every NBC color broadcast with the voiceover proclaiming, "The following program is brought to you in living color on NBC." Excellent marketing tactic! Probably sold more color TV sets than any advertising campaign.

Another key element of sixties network TV was movies. Again NBC led the way. Starting in 1961, its *Saturday Night at the Movies* showed a recent movie every week, usually at about the same time that the third-run theaters were getting it, or, at the latest, within a few years of its original theatrical release. If the viewer was willing to endure frequent commercial breaks, the tiny screen, and the waiting, watching movies on TV was a lot easier and cheaper than schlepping out to theaters. NBC's *Saturday Night at the Movies* became incredibly popular and ran until 1978. The other networks followed suit, running *The ABC Sunday Night Movie* in 1962 and from 1964 to 1998, *The CBS Thursday Night Movie* from 1965 to 1968, *The CBS Friday Night Movie* from 1966 to 1977, *The ABC Wednesday Night*

Movie from 1966 to 1969, and *The ABC Tuesday Movie of the Week* from 1969 to 1970. NBC ran *Wednesday Night at the Movies* from 1964 to 1965, *Tuesday Night at the Movies* from 1965 to 1969, and *Monday Night at the Movies* in 1963 and from 1968 to 1997.

When *Tuesday Night at the Movies* offered the TV premiere of *A Hard Day's Night* on October 24, 1967, NBC did not miss the opportunity for a brilliant joke. Because the movie was in black-and-white, and because color TV broadcasts were by then the norm, NBC used, instead of its famous peacock, a fat, wobbly cartoon penguin. This silent bird, complete with top hat, waddled out into the middle of the screen, looked around, flapped its arms, set its top hat down, unzipped its front, and let all four cartoon Beatles, complete with instruments, leap out of its belly and begin playing. The voiceover announced, "*I Dream of Jeannie* and *The Jerry Lewis Show* will not be seen tonight. Instead, the following very, very special program is brought to you in lively black-and-white on NBC."

Throughout the summer the fact that John Lennon had cut his hair down to military length in order to play a World War II soldier had been well publicized. The movie, *How I Won the War*, was to be an antiwar comedy directed by Richard Lester, who had also directed Lennon in *A Hard Day's Night* and *Help!* and had recently scored two other tremendous comedic hits with *The Knack* in 1965 and *A Funny Thing Happened on the Way to the Forum* in 1966. We expected nothing less than a five-star classic comparable to *Dr. Strangelove*. In August a paperback reissue of Patrick Ryan's 1963 novel, *How I Won the War*, appeared with Lennon's face all over both covers and proudly proclaiming that he was to be the star of the movie. We bought this book — and loved it. It was sidesplitting! Why it has not come to be regarded as being nearly on a par with the greatest book in its genre, Joseph Heller's *Catch-22*, remains a mystery.

Seldom was any movie so eagerly anticipated or so disappointing when it finally arrived. Those of us who had read the book naturally expected that Lennon would be cast in the lead role of Lieutenant Ernest Goodbody. But Lennon only played a minor character, Private Gripweed. Judging from his cheeky performance as himself in *A Hard Day's Night*, he would have done a much better job than Michael Crawford as Goodbody. Moreover, it was a bad film, arguably Lester's worst. Lester took far too many liberties with Ryan's masterpiece. The book and the movie scarcely resembled each other. Lester's gimmick of having the killed-in-action follow their old platoon around, each as a different colored ghost, was just plain stupid.

Cool Hand Luke called into question the fairness and humanity of America's prison system. The movie opened with Paul Newman's character, Lucas Jackson, sentenced to two years on a chain gang for the drunken vandalism of parking meters with a pipe cutter. Given his nonviolent temperament, his clean prior record, and the nature of the act itself, the punishment seemed excessive. His inborn, smirky contempt for all rules and regulations immediately endeared him to us. He went through life heedless of consequences, with complete indifference. He neither celebrated when he won nor complained when he lost. He did not fear death. As "new meat," Luke could not gain the respect of either the guards or his fellow prisoners until he allowed the big, illiterate convict Dragline to beat the shit out of him. He appeared to do this quite willingly. Dragline gave him his nickname from the remark he made after bluffing his way to a big win at stud poker: "Sometimes nothin' can be a real cool hand." Nothing was all he had, but he made the most of it, accepting hardship with equanimity.

Luke had no thoughts of trying to escape until he was punished in solitary confinement just for mourning his mother's death. He then tried it, even with only a short time left in his sentence. His first time on the lam, he had a constant grin on his face. Was he insane? Probably not, allowing for the effects of prison stress. Was he suicidal? Perhaps. His tears for his mother, contrasted to his lack of emotion toward nearly everything else, suggested that he was not apathetic. To commit suicide would have required him to care about something, at least. Totally apathetic people do not kill themselves. Maybe he only wanted to see if he could escape, just as previously he had eaten fifty hard-boiled eggs in an hour just to see if he could. Maybe he wanted to extend his sentence because he knew that he had no prospects outside prison. But the second time, the grin was gone. Now he really wanted to get away. Maybe he had just had enough. When the guards finally succeeded in beating him into meek submission, his convict allies deserted him. But even after capitulating, he could only endure so much humiliation. Like the blind Samson between the Philistine temple pillars, he seized his last opportunity for dignity, stealing a prison truck for his third escape attempt. He died on his own terms, smiling with self-respect, mocking the prison captain.

Those of us who knew *The Myth of Sisyphus* by Albert Camus instantly recognized the parallel between Luke and Sisyphus. Both were absurd men thrown into absurd situations where they were forced to perform meaningless and even self-contradictory tasks. Sisyphus eternally rolled a boulder up a hill only to have it roll down again; Luke dug a gravelike ditch, filled it in, dug it out again, and collapsed. Yet both of these victims of absurdity seemed happy.

Absurdity was alive and well in San Francisco. Richard Brautigan's uniquely conceived and cleverly implemented environmentalist poem-disguised-as-a-novel, *Trout Fishing in America*, combined bittersweet lament, shrewd observation, silly comedy, biting satire, and leftist ideology into a lively, enthralling mishmash of craziness. Many of us took this to be Brautigan's *magnum opus*. In any case, it was certainly one of his most poignant. The chapter called "The Cleveland Wrecking Yard," attacking the commodification and commercialization of natural beauty, was alone worth the price of the book. *Trout Fishing in America* was an instant underground classic that also broke out into the mainstream.

Another idea that began in the underground but rather quickly found mainstream success was *Hair*. This soon-to-be-very-popular revue opened in October, off-Broadway, at Joseph Papp's New York Shakespeare Festival Public Theater. It was *not* your typical Manhattan musical comedy show. An interracial cast, frequent jabs at LBJ, pervasive irreverence, a dose of anarchy, and a bit of foul language all guaranteed that. Nevertheless, audiences treated it as if it were. Did they not understand it properly or was colorful leftist culture becoming trendy within the gray upper and middle classes? Would psychedelia hit Broadway? The answer, which would not be long in coming, was yes. *Hair* would lead the way.

Psychedelia was making strong inroads into AM radio too. The paradigm case this fall was "Incense and Peppermints" by the Strawberry Alarm Clock, which sounded like a shotgun marriage of spacy lyrics and LSD-laced bubble gum. Among the few other noteworthy or auspicious debut tunes that got more airplay on AM than on FM, at least for the time being, were "Different Drum" by Linda Ronstadt and the Stone Poneys, a Los Angeles folk rock band; "Itchycoo Park" by the Small Faces, a mod group from London; and the rollicking "Nobody But Me" by the Human Beinz, garage rockers from northern Ohio.

Two promising albums both gave and withheld great things. Except for "Down on Me," the tunes on the eponymous debut LP, *Big Brother and the Holding Company*, did not show their lead singer, Janis Joplin, at her best. After an undistinguished self-titled debut in 1966, Tim Buckley's second album, *Goodbye and Hello*, now established him as a versatile and fascinating songwriter, equally at home with jazz, folk, rock, funk, and several other musical styles.

Both Janis and Tim would die in their twenties, much too early, each from a heroin overdose.

"Get Together," the Youngbloods' song of hope, solidarity, and respect from their eponymous debut album of last January, was released as a single. It would soon become one of the foremost leftist political anthems and, in June 1969, would be re-released as a single, a very unusual development for a hippie song. It was sung at antiwar and civil rights events at least as often as "Kumbaya," probably more, but probably not as often as "We Shall Overcome."

The underground was expanding, in music, in politics, and in the natural relation between music and politics. WNEW-FM in New York City changed its format from middle-of-the-road pop to progressive rock, with DJs Rosko, Jonathan Schwartz, Scott Muni, and Alison Steele presenting a very eclectic and far-ranging mix. Tom Donahue brought progressive rock to KPPC-FM in Pasadena. Local underground presses were filling the cities with papers similar to the *Berkeley Barb*, the *Los Angeles Free Press*, or the *Village Voice*. Notably, in Philadelphia, the *Distant Drummer* began its three-year run. Perhaps most lastingly important of all, the debut issue of Jann Wenner's San-Francisco-based *Rolling Stone* magazine hit the national newsstands with Lennon in his *How I Won the War* garb on its cover. Wenner announced from the start that this publication would not be about only music, but about music in its full sociopolitical context. It was very successful.

Ω

Among the black tunes we enjoyed this fall were Sam and Dave's "Soul Man," the Fantastic Johnny C's "Boogaloo Down Broadway," the Impressions' "We're a Winner," and, direct from Africa itself, Miriam Makeba's "Pata Pata" — all quite danceable — if you were into dancing — or just as good for listening — if you were only into listening. An eighteen-year-old Scottish singer, Marie Lawrie, under her stage name, "Lulu," co-starred with Sidney Poitier in a movie about a black teacher of tough white kids in London's East End, and scored a hit with her recording of the title song from this film, *To Sir, With Love*. Not only music, but also now film, offered stronger and stronger support for the black cause.

Deservedly venerable movie stars of the thirties and forties, Spencer Tracy and Katharine Hepburn, teamed up with Sidney Poitier and Kate's real-life niece, Katharine Houghton, in *Guess Who's Coming to Dinner*, a chick flick about the insidiousness of racial bigotry, even among those who profess not to be bigoted. Poitier played an irreproachable 37-year-old widower physician engaged to marry the 23-year-old daughter of a white upper-class family complete with two black maids. One of the maids, Tillie, angrily rejected the very idea of their marriage: "I don't care to see a member of my own race gettin' above hisself." In other words, she entirely bought into the pervasive white racist notion that blacks were naturally inferior. Tillie was at least honest, but the white parents, especially the "fighting liberal" father, could scarcely contain their hypocrisy. The engaged couple soon won the mother's heart — indeed she summarily fired one of her employees who opposed the union on purely racist grounds — but the father, despite his avowed anti-racist stance, steadfastly objected. The doctor's parents responded analogously to the news. The only two characters in the drama who had no problem whatsoever with interracial marriage were the naively colorblind daughter, Joanna, and the genuinely unprejudiced Roman Catholic priest, a close friend of this non-Catholic family. The priest chastised the father's phoniness, suggesting that beneath his tolerant facade lurked reactionary bigotry and finding it "rather amusing, too, to see a broken-down old phony liberal come face to face with his principles." To top off his little sermon, the priest cited the Beatles' "We Can Work it Out."

The penultimate alignment of adversaries was the priest and the two mothers in favor of the marriage vs. Tillie and the two fathers against it. The irony that the black father and the white father saw absolutely eye-to-eye about the separation of the races underscored how groundless this separation would always be, both theoretically and practically. Racism was not only white bigotry against descendants of former slaves, but also black bigotry against descendants of former slave owners. As long as people thought of themselves as black people or white people, instead of just people, racism would persist. All that the fathers could see was that the interracial couple would have "problems." Joanna's father at last realized that he himself was one of those problems, so he relented; the doctor's father did not.

Guess Who's Coming to Dinner made another strong point about the nature of families that had nothing to do with race. During the huge, climactic argument between father and son, the doctor asserted that, even though he loved his father, he did not owe the father obedience and the father had no right to run his life. He was speaking philosophically, not only of his personal relationship with his own father, but of parents and children in general. Parents, because they choose to bring a new human life into the world, owe the child food, clothing, shelter, education, safety, moral support, and even love; but that child, because s/he did not ask to be born, and was in fact just thrown into existence, owes the parents nothing. Filial piety is antithetical to the human spirit. If the child loves the parents, then this love is given freely, not from any obligation, but as a natural and ingenuous expression of heartfelt gratitude.

In lambasting our parents' superficial middle- and upper-class values, *The Graduate* picked up where *Who's Afraid of Virginia Woolf?* left off. Mike Nichols again directed. It showed a bright but sullen and lonely young man returning home after four brilliant years of college to find himself an alien in his parents' world. Dustin Hoffman's title character, Benjamin Braddock, being taken for rides, first on the airplane then on the moving floor at Los Angeles International Airport, foreboded that forces outside his control would continue to push him along, trying to fascinate, assimilate, and dominate him.

Ben fretted about his future, feeling vaguely but profoundly uneasy about his expected role in the society that his rich parents, their rich friends and associates, and and their nationwide cohort of like-minded upwardly mobile go-getters had created for him, but he could not pinpoint either why he felt uneasy or what to do about it. He keenly felt "the guilt of the privileged," i.e., that he did not deserve his birthright and that his duty was to abandon it. He felt smothered. His elders' unexamined assumption that all Ben or any other decent young American man would ever want to do would be to climb the corporate ladder exasperated him. He had nothing in common with any of them. They were his parents' friends, not his, and their very presence, their cloying solicitations after his financial and social success, only intensified his alienation. The film's recurring image of a fish trapped inside an aquarium, on display for everyone else's enjoyment, aptly depicted Ben's plight. He did not know how to take charge of his own life — but at the same time he knew that somehow he had to do it.

When, in the instantly-famous-and-soon-thereafter-clichéd scene, Mr. McGuire told Ben to remember just one thing, "Plastics," he meant for Ben to get into the plastics business; but what we in the audience heard, who already knew the street meaning of "plastic" from Jefferson Airplane and the Mothers of Invention, was, "The way to get by, to be accepted, to get rich, to be successful, is to be phony." That was one of the most evocative *double entendres* in the whole history of film.

Those middle-aged adults were so insensitive, so wrapped up in only their own concerns, that all the while they thought they were praising Ben, they were in fact humiliating him. When his father forced him to demonstrate his birthday gift, a scuba outfit, Ben decided to be alone at the bottom of the swimming pool rather than come up and join the party. Why not? Who would want to celebrate his twenty-first birthday at a party full of his parents' friends and no one his own age?

Mrs. Robinson, the archetypal selfish bitch with utterly no regard for Ben or anyone else, was a metaphor of how her generation used ours for their pleasure. To her, other people existed only for her to use and then discard, like so many smoked cigarettes. No one in her generation, not even Ben's own parents, cared about Ben as a person. For her, he was a convenient sex toy; for his parents, he was a status symbol; for everyone else in their circle, he was a way to get in good with his parents. He was bombarded by their hypocritical, insincere, alcohol-fueled advice, not the least by Mr. Robinson's suggestion that he sow some wild oats, have a few flings, fuck a few chicks, and even date his daughter Elaine.

Ben resisted taking Elaine out as long as he could, but when finally black-mailed to do it, he took her to a strip club in a clumsy attempt to disgust her and thereby rid himself of at least this one of his parents' and Mr. Robinson's expectations. Yet at a key moment he realized that he had an ally in someone his own age. He discovered that Elaine was his kindred spirit, equally repressed by her parents' expectations, that she shared his fundamental resentment of their parents' world, and that she even felt the same "kinda compulsion ... to be rude all the time." After Mrs. Robinson sabotaged Ben's and Elaine's nascent relationship, Ben made a heroic decision to rescue both himself and Elaine by marrying her and running away from the two families of origin. He stalked her in Berkeley. She warmed up to him again only after she realized that her mother's tale of his raping her was a lie, but she was still caught between dwindling family loyalty and Ben's pushy maladroitness. She decided to break her minutes-old marriage and elope with Ben when she saw that the medical student whom her parents had forced her to marry would doom her to a lifetime in her parents' world. She wanted to be free, not like her mother, and freedom meant life with Ben.

The soundtrack revealed the psychological depth of the Simon and Garfunkel opus to date: "Sounds of Silence" over the opening and closing titles and as Ben succumbed to Mrs. Robinson's seduction, "April Come She Will" as he drifted into her world, "Big Bright Green Pleasure Machine" as he found a true friend in Elaine, "Scarborough Fair" as he sank into despair after Elaine learned about his affair with her mother, and "Mrs. Robinson" at various critical points.

In the late sixties and early seventies, you would have been hard pressed to find a college kid who did not in some way identify with Benjamin Braddock. To be free and whole, we would each, like him, have to break away from our parents and reject their values.

Spring 1968

I feel free!

> Does not each generation, by means of suppression, concealment and ridicule, efface what the previous generation considered most important?
> — Hermann Hesse, *The Journey to the East*, Chapter 1

LBJ had gall bladder surgery at Bethesda Naval Hospital on October 8, 1965. Upon returning to the White House on October 21, he lifted his shirt to show off his scar to reporters. The United Press International photo of his naked flabby paunch was widely circulated and soon became rather notorious. What better way to bring in the new year than for *Mad* to spread that photo across the back cover of its January 1968 issue — with the scar replaced by a map of Vietnam!

But 1968 really began with *After Bathing at Baxter's*.

Jefferson Airplane's third album, its masterpiece, unrelentingly attacked everything that LBJ and his generation had done to fuck up our lives: the Vietnam War, the draft, stupid sociosexual rules, socioeconomic hegemony, sociopolitical expectations, and, most of all, their damn hypocrisy.

"Streetmasse," the first section of *Baxter's*, opened with a hard, brilliant rocker, Paul Kantner's "The Ballad of You and Me and Pooneil," a song of love, hope, expectation, and a degree of doubt. Pooneil was Kantner's fanciful hybrid of A.A. Milne's character, Winnie the Pooh, and Fred Neil, the New York City folk rocker who wrote "The Other Side of This Life" and "Everybody's Talkin'." The next tune in this section, "A Small Package of Value Will Come to You Shortly," co-written by Airplane friend Gary Blackman, drummer Spencer Dryden, and manager Bill Thompson, was a farcical, spoken, mostly percussive spoof of the sanitized, shallow, ass-kissing, money-grubbing, gray conservatism of the nine-to-five business world. "Streetmasse" ended with Kantner's and Marty Balin's "Young Girl Sunday Blues," a simple but heavy psychedelic love song.

The second section, "The War is Over," consisted of two beautiful Kantner songs connected by an even more beautiful bridge. "Martha" told of a self-assured woman in the tradition of the Stones' "Ruby Tuesday" or "Complicated." It segued into the harder rocking, more upbeat "Wild Tyme (H)," which celebrated all the things that freaks love: freedom, innovation, freedom, zaniness, freedom, passion, freedom, love, freedom, transformation, freedom, unpredictability, freedom, peace, freedom, fun, freedom, revolution, and — oh, did I mention freedom?

The third section, "Hymn to an Older Generation," presented blunt and tactless criticisms. Jorma Kaukonen's "The Last Wall of the Castle" directly confronted our parents with their failures in raising us properly, i.e., failing to teach us how to love, cry, or be ourselves. Graham Nash would later more gently take up the same theme in "Teach Your Children."

When Grace Slick sang in "reJoyce" that she would rather have her country die for her, she was paraphrasing Stephen Dedalus's words of semi-comfort to Private Carr in James Joyce's *Ulysses*: "... this is the point. You die for your country. Suppose. ... Not that I wish it for you. But I say: Let my country die for me. Up to the present it has done so. I didn't want it to die. Damn death. Long live life!" Under what circumstances would one wish the end of one's country? Under what circumstances would its demise improve my lot? What would that loss entail for its citizens in general? Whatever the answers to these questions, countries dying for people generally benefit people more than people dying for anything benefit either countries or surviving people. Countries are not things that are worth dying for. Principles and people are sometimes worth dying for, but countries are neither principle nor person. Yet many nationalists and all jingoists routinely expect us to die for our respective countries.

The step from nationalism to jingoism is very short. It is difficult to discern. Even well-meaning nationalists who do not want to be jingoists often do not recognize when they have taken that step. It is thus best not to be a nationalist at all, but a world citizen, a humanist. People are more basic and more important than countries. Yet LBJ was a jingoist. The June 1968 *Mad* included a photo of him doctored to show him wearing a "War is good business, invest your son" button with a huge dollar sign on it. Grace's song apparently had had some effect.

Her lyrics in "reJoyce" attacked a wide range of targets beyond just jingoism — including conformity in general, conservatism in general, the draft, political polarization, mind control, and of course, the war. Her remedy seemed to be heightened individuality and defiance, even at the risk of despair.

"How Suite It Is," the fourth section, opened with Kantner's psychedelic love song, "Watch Her Ride," and closed with "Spare Chaynge," a dramatic, eerie, gripping, nine-minute instrumental crescendo co-written by Jack Casady, Spencer, and Jorma.

The last section, "Shizoforest Love Suite," began harshly with "Two Heads," Grace's nasty indictment of hypocritical, small-minded businessmen who embraced the sociosexual double standard, preached goodness but supported official killing, furthered their careers by conforming to whatever standards of dress, hair, and behavior the establishment dictated, and washed away with alcohol whatever guilt they may have felt. The closing medley, Kantner's "Won't You Try / Saturday Afternoon," was pure, almost stereotypical, soft psychedelia.

Music was a *sine qua non* of life itself for young white people in the anti-war movement. Eric Burdon's "Monterey" was an anthem through most of 1968, simply because in it he asserted that music is indispensable for anyone who seeks ultimate truth. Indeed, music is a vital component of any such truth. To ignore or despise music is to show contempt for truth. The 1967 "Summer of Love" might better have been called the "Summer of Music" — it was so close to this basic human truth.

"Monterey" continued in the tradition of the Lovin' Spoonful's "Do You Believe in Magic?" — suggesting that the best eras are those in which music matters. But Burdon pushed the argument several steps further than Sebastian. While the earlier song had only asserted that music was important because it could improve one's social life and general well-being, the later song declared that truth itself could not be grasped without music. Burdon saw music as tantamount to the true religion of peace, love, and tolerance. Burdon's exaltation of music is reminiscent of Schopenhauer's, and is indeed irrationalistic in a way that Schopenhauer might have endorsed, but his central claim is really a Hegelian move, insofar as art and religion must each be fully present and uncompromised in the final synthesis of art, religion, and philosophy.

1968 was a pivotal year for the relation between music and politics. The first "underground" FM radio station in America was KMPX in San Francisco in February 1967. WNEW in New York and KPPC in Pasadena began broadcasting progressive album rock later that year, but the movement did not really take off until 1968, when WBCN in Boston, WMMR in Philadelphia, KSAN in San Francisco, and KMET in Los Angeles all changed their formats. It was no accident that the song that WBCN played to break its classical format on March 15, 1968, was Cream's "I Feel Free." WBCN's first rock song being "I Feel Free" underscored the fact that, for us, freedom was the key to everything. All we ever wanted was freedom. It was likewise no accident that the DJs on these stations were uniformly antiwar. Since they programmed their own playlists, political content on each of their shows was assured.

Given that 1968 was pivotal for the relation between music and politics, it was *ipso facto* pivotal also for the general development of the youth culture of that era. The most important musical contributors to that sociopolitical culture in 1968 were Eric Burdon, Steppenwolf, Jefferson Airplane, the Doors, the Rolling Stones, Jimi Hendrix, Janis Joplin, Cream, Traffic, the Moody Blues, Tom Paxton, Pete Seeger, Frank Zappa, and the Beatles, especially John Lennon. Their influence was as much political as musical. In each of these cases, it was their songs with the most political content that had the greatest and most enduring impact. A song could be no longer just a song; it had to be a "statement."

Since its beginnings through Dylan, the Byrds, Buffalo Springfield, *et al.*, in 1965, American progressive rock had been intensely and increasingly political. In 1968 this intensity reached a milestone, as progressive rock became so intimately connected with the antiwar movement that the very boundary between music and politics was blurred. It seemed that that the lyrics of every FM rock song were somehow political, if not overtly then cryptically. Non-musicians in the movement listened to rock for political messages and musicians in the movement communicated their political messages primarily through music.

One of the biggest differences between 1968 and the present era — I am writing this paragraph in September 2006 — is that people then, and especially popular musicians, were expected and eager to wear their political hearts on their sleeves; but in 2006 nearly everyone in America is reluctant to say anything about any controversial subject that might disrupt friendships, family harmony, or any other social bond — not to mention careers. Peer pressure is the motivating force in both cases: then, to speak out, to be heard, to exercise one's freedom; now, to remain silent, to avoid rocking the boat, to keep one's negative feelings to oneself, to pretend that we still have as much freedom as we did in the sixties. Then, we were not afraid to speak; now, we seem to be scared shitless. Then, we did not care if we offended people; now, we tiptoe around issues, stifling ourselves, trying not to offend anyone. Songs were then scorned as "fluff" if they did not carry political or social messages. They had to make a "statement" in order to be respected. In the early twenty-first century, songs that have any political or social content are vilified along with their creators. The content of songs has become largely sex and violence, both of which now seem to be acceptable where political or social opinion is not.

One good principle is to detest major crimes such as murder, rape, and wanton destruction. Another good principle is to protect your child, sibling, or parent. Be thankful that these two principles seldom gainsay each other. What if they do, what then? If you ever have to throw one of these principles away in order to uphold the other, which will it be? If your brother commits rape, do you deny. belittle, or appear to condone the rape for your brother's sake, or do you condemn him just as you would any other rapist? If your son commits murder, do you say, "Oh, my little boy is a good boy. He would never do anything like that," or do you continue to love your son even as you hate his crime and approve the judgment of the court against him? If your father contributes materially to the unjust war against the Vietnamese, do you rationalize and forgive his collusion with the LBJ/Nixon regime, or do you distance yourself from him and work for peace?

Is it right to react to a crime differently according to whether the perpetrator is your friend, your lover, your family member, your enemy, or someone with whom you are unacquainted and toward whom your feelings are therefore neutral? Of course not! A crime is a crime is a crime. Justice is what restores balance to the social order after the crime has been committed. Justice is justice is justice. Yet, flying in the face of this consistent logic, gut instinct seems to be to protect our friends, lovers, and relatives from the legal or even moral consequences of their crimes, while at the same time seeking to punish our enemies even more than they deserve for theirs. Genuine justice thus can accrue only to those toward whom we feel neutral. — Instinct trumps principles. Emotion trumps reason. Prejudice trumps justice. This is all wrong!

If anyone kills, rapes, pillages, or otherwise disrupts life as it ought to be, then cut that person off, and do it uniformly, according to the nature and circumstances of the crime, not of the relationship. Be truer to your ethical principles than to your emotional leanings or blood ties! Breaking up a family or a friendship is bad, but complicity with ethical offense is worse. The very notion that if *we* do it, then it is OK, but if *they* do it, then it is not, must be eliminated from civilized thinking. Genuine ethics has no room for double standards.

So! Family harmony be damned! Say what you want! Rock the damn boat! What kind of "friends" would prefer you to stifle your free expression? As for social bonds: *Fiat justitia, pereat mundus! Fiat justitia, ruat coelum!* "Let justice be done, even if the world perishes! Let justice be done, though the heavens fall!" The New Hampshire state motto, "Live Free or Die!", would have fit us quite well in the sixties. It described our fundamental attitude very well. We would rather have been loudmouth fools in the streets than placid sheep in the boardrooms and country clubs. We saw injustice, immorality, useless war, and felt that it was our duty to speak out against them. In the twenty-first century our peer-pressured duty seems to be to keep silent and let the federal government do whatever it wants.

Music in the early twenty-first century has descended, or rather reverted, to being mere entertainment, as it was in the fifties. This is even true of rap. But from the early sixties to the late seventies or early eighties, music was the very reflection of life itself in all its depth and poignancy. It was communication, not just entertainment. Better said, entertainment then was substantial and important; today it is vacuous and trivial. In 1968 to call a song political was honorific; to call it so in 2008 was derogatory.

By 1968, culture and politics, at least for my generation, had become identical. The millions and millions of American fans that the Beatles had gained since their first appearance on *Ed Sullivan* had bifurcated from an apolitical or omnipolitical mass into a highly charged and polarized antagonism. The religious right had deserted progressive rock during and after the August 1966 Lennon incident, and the rest of the conservatives were not far behind. What you listened to, what you wore, what you looked like, what your politics were — these personal traits all mutually decided, indicated, and corroborated each other. The short-haired, neat, high-school-educated rightists were into Elvis, the Four Seasons, and top forty. The long-haired, sloppy, college-educated leftists were into Lennon, Hendrix, and underground rock. Songs had gone beyond just protest songs vs. non-political songs. *Every* new song, whether protest or not, was political. That is, regardless of the intentions of its songwriter, producer, or singer, we received and interpreted every new song politically. If a song was non-political, then we interpreted even that plain fact as a statement: "This is a non-political song, therefore none of the people responsible for this song are interested in justice, peace, or social change." Fairly or unfairly, we branded the songwriters, producers, and singers of deliberately non-political songs as conservative toadies of the establishment.

But the American right wing extols freedom too — and sometimes claims that we want to destroy theirs. We know that they want to destroy ours. Leftist and rightist concepts of freedom are quite different.

Freedom for the right is the Stirnerian freedom for each individual to exercise greed with impunity, to oppress, exploit, and compel anyone in the way. It is tantamount to unfettered selfishness and is not compatible with good citizenship.

Freedom for the non-anarchist left is the institutionalized protection of the people from the rich and powerful. Because no one who is chronically and involuntarily hungry can be free, ideal leftist freedom guarantees that everyone will have enough food to provide the nourishment necessary to begin to build each of their own lives the way they each want. In other words, there can be no "equal opportunity for all" unless each person starts off with a full belly. This universal "equal opportunity" should not, as the rightists want it, have to include the opportunity for starving people to try to get a full belly — and "Awww, too bad!" if they fail. There should never be any starving people. The full belly should be a given — an absolute precondition of humanity. Everyone must be fed. The right must be persuaded to cave in on this point.

Freedom for the anarchist left is just, well, anarchy — but, as Hegel clearly showed once and for all in the "Absolute Freedom and the Terror" section of the *Phenomenology of Spirit*, anarchy quickly and necessarily descends into tyranny and the Hobbesian war of all against all. It offers the people no protection from violence, no guarantees of sufficient food, no basic human rights, and no durable civil rights.

The institutionalized freedom of the non-anarchist left is internationalist, constructive, progressive, and inclusive. It entails a finely graduated income tax to ensure the fair distribution of wealth and the best use of natural assets and manufactured commodities. It guarantees to all citizens the peace, privacy, and freedom to think, raise families, and enjoy the benefits of the human commonwealth without having to worry about providing basic needs of food, clothing, shelter, or education. It develops systems and customs whereby the rich must take care of the poor, just as the poor already take care of the rich. Given that Hegel's master/slave dialectic shows that the rich and powerful would be neither rich nor powerful unless the poor and powerless did their work for them, employers accordingly owe prosperity to employees, as fair exchange for the prosperity that employees create for employers. The goal of all human interaction is civilization, and the goal of civilization is not gold, silver, or other physical possessions, but rather art, science, music, literature, and other truly spiritual possessions. Thus the intellectual left would develop and support education to the point of being able, at each successive level from prekindergarten to post-doctoral, to expunge credulity from thinking individuals and make them immune to religious fundamentalism, political propaganda, and commercial persuasion, however subtle. In this way, all the true sciences and free arts would thrive.

Millions for education! Not one cent for killing the innocent!

Such free spirit, bold vision, and unfettered individuality, with all needs supplied, all wants in sight, and happiness ever a real possibility on the horizon, is expressed metaphorically in the Byrds' "Wasn't Born to Follow." No conservative could either sing or appreciate that song. Its intrinsic joy and implied universalism are incompatible with the rightist notion of freedom, which is essentially Hobbesian. The freedom depicted here is quintessentially Rousseauian, i.e., romantic, not calculated; heartfelt, not bought.

Soulless conservativism vs. ensouled individualism was a frequent theme of protest songs. "If Six Was Nine," one of Hendrix's few protest songs, was also one of the true classics of the genre. It nailed perfectly the soulless, plastic, conservative oppression that the business community liked to dump on otherwise free people. Jimi's lyrics sent unyielding but peaceful threats of defiance to the gray, commercial, carbon-copy dullards who wanted to "run the show" and turn the naturally colorful, playful, diverse world upside down. His encouraging message was that they could never overcome the true, free, individualistic human spirit.

Every new song, whether protest or not, whether political or not, was also political in the sense that its reception further defined *us* and clarified who and what we were, at least in our own minds if not also in the minds of the establishment, as liberals against conservatives, hip against square, freaks against straights, peace people against warmongers, egalitarians against racists, internationalists against nationalists, feminists against chauvinists, and maybe even concerned citizens against rich bastards who did not give a shit. Anyone, with a little effort, could figure out who and what we were and what we believed just by listening to our music.

Steppenwolf's "Born to Be Wild" is a perfect example of a song that was *prima facie* neither political nor non-political but immediately became political by revealing an aspect of its audience and placing that aspect in stark relief. Every new song was in some way about us — and that one in particular.

For a rock band to name itself after the title character of a poignant psychological novel was a bold and brilliant move. It suggested, first, that to understand the band's music adequately one would have to read the book, and second, that Hermann Hesse was somehow the key to understanding *us*!

The very name of the band Steppenwolf was an advertisement for Hesse. Few of us already knew what a "Wolf of the Steppes" was and only a few more of us had ever even heard of Hesse. But we became immediately curious as to why a band that made such great music would call itself after a book. We searched out the book and read it. Many of us continued with Hesse to read *Demian* and *Siddhartha*. Some of us even slogged through *The Glass Bead Game*.

Thus John Kay's simple act of naming his band brought Hesse's entire corpus into play as an element of our new culture and led many of the more inquisitive among us to discover not only Hesse, but the whole powerful tradition of twentieth-century German literature. Reading Hesse, Thomas Mann, Franz Kafka, Rainer Maria Rilke, Bertolt Brecht, Friedrich Dürrenmatt, Günter Grass, Heinrich Böll, Stefan George, or Arnold Zweig naturally led back to a study of Nietzsche, Schopenhauer, Schiller, and Goethe. Moreover, Hesse's *Siddhartha* naturally led toward deeper appreciation of Buddhism and Hinduism.

Besides "Born to Be Wild," Steppenwolf's self-titled LP contained a disproportionately high number of instant musical and political classics, but also put out quite a bit of plain raw sex. The opening track, "Sookie Sookie," was a sexual song whose title meant something like "Hubba hubba!" or "Hot shit!" expressing a crass male admiration of female pulchritude, but it sounded enough like "sooey sooey" that we might have thought of calling a pig. What better way to start an LP in 1968!?! A freak trying to get a pig's attention! "Everybody's Next One" described a romantic woman who became a chronic sexual victim, and was clueless about how to remedy the situation. "Berry Rides Again" was an imitative ode to Chuck Berry. The title of Willie Dixon's frequently covered blues standard, "Hoochie Coochie Man," translates from black into white slang as "Cunt Man." Most of the early black blues artists, especially the Chicago men, were masters of sexual innuendo. Dixon was master of the masters. In "Your Wall's Too High" a guy tried to loosen up an uptight woman. Along a similar theme, the slower and gloomier "Desperation" offered tentative encouragement to her not to fall into depression. "A Girl I Knew" painted a portrait of an extraordinarily cheerful, uninhibited person. "Take What You Need" was a confession of monogamous devotion, but also stated his annoyance at her clinginess.

"The Ostrich" was the deepest political cut on the album. Each of its five verses pounced on a different aspect of the evil that America was then inflicting on itself and the world. The first verse pointed out how education did not really educate, in the sense of teaching kids how to think, but only prepared them to be pigeonholed into set careers and then left to die in superficial comfort. The second emphasized problems with the so-called "progress" that brought air pollution, water contamination, and the attitude that paved earth is better than green earth. The third condemned the citizens' feelings of futility, insignificance, and helplessness that prevented them from trying to take action to solve any of these problems. The fourth attacked the idea that keeping one's mouth shut and meekly obeying the censors and other authorities was the key to happiness. The last verse repeated the third, thus challenging the citizens to rise up, abandon social conformity and political acquiescence, and thereby save themselves. The image of the ostrich, of course, served as a metaphor for Americans who stuck their heads in the sand so that they would not notice the evil around them that was consuming and typifying their country.

Steppenwolf's cover of Hoyt Axton's "The Pusher" threw into sharp focus the ubiquitous drug pusher over against the friendly neighborhood drug dealer. Both were criminals in the eyes of the law, but only the pusher was a real crook. The pusher only craved the customer's money, and the customer be damned; while the dealer actually cared for the welfare, happiness, and satisfaction of the customer. The pusher's motto could have been, "Screw 'em all!" — but that of the dealer must have been, "Give the customers what they want!" Beneficence for the pusher meant beneficence only to self, friends, close associates, and family; but beneficence for the dealer meant altruism, or beneficience equally to all humankind, to whatever extent feasible. This contrast between pusher and dealer served as a synecdoche for the whole essential difference between commercial and humanitarian interests, or between rightist and leftist attitudes toward life in general.

The drug dealer in Traffic's song, "Dealer," was a different breed of cat. He was a gambler, dealing from the bottom of the deck, a smuggler, a selfish bastard, making sure that everything went his way, and killing when it did not. He was not like Steppenwolf's dealer at all; indeed he more closely resembled Steppenwolf's pusher — and may have been even more evil.

Traffic's *Mr. Fantasy* album was in many ways the pinnacle of psychedelia to date. Since *Sgt. Pepper's* and *Satanic Majesties*, the visual effects of albums had grown more important — not as important as the music itself — but still more important than before. Much could be done with a standard 12 3/8 inch x 12 3/8 inch album cover. Photographers, artists, and designers were gladly going apeshit with these new possibilities. The resultant cover of Traffic's debut LP was stunning! Its bright psychedelic pinkish orange or orangish pink, partially solarized, wraparound photograph of the band and their instruments beckoned the new listener. The black-and-white interior photos showed flutist Chris Wood and drummer Jim Capaldi just hanging out, multi-instrumentalist Steve Winwood winning wood by chopping it with an ax, and stringman Dave Mason sitting barefoot on the bare wood floor of a darkened, rustic room, playing the sitar, his back to the camera but his face in backlit profile.

Winwood's high, ethereal voice was perfect for psychedelia. Serious tunes like "No Face, No Name, and No Number," "Dealer," and "Coloured Rain" bear this out. Moreover, this LP was perfect "headphone music," with sounds shooting right through your head from side to side and all around as you listened in typically massive late sixties headphones that looked more like rifle range hearing protectors than the precision audio devices that they were. This was especially true of "Dear Mr. Fantasy" and even of its subsequent covers by other bands, notably the 1969 version on Mike Bloomfield's and Al Kooper's *Live Adventures*.

The album opened with the powerful bass notes of "Heaven is in Your Mind," with woodwind sounds soon superseded by Winwood's stellar vocals and the band's interesting vocal and instrumental harmonies. "Utterly Simple" was Mason's sitar contribution. "Hope I Never Find Me There," another Mason tune, was top-heavy with psychedelic effects. He would shortly become a better writer. "Berkshire Poppies" and "House for Everyone" were jocular knock-offs, and the finale, "Giving to You," sounded just like the band jamming and goofing around.

Traffic made music to think by.

Perhaps the most significant difference between my generation and the analogously aged generation of the early twenty-first century is that in the sixties we were readers. Reading the printed word was very popular and important in the sixties — not just among us, but among all generations — much more so than in subsequent eras of video anesthesia. You can read while listening to the radio, but not while watching the TV. Music opens the mind; images close it. The part of the mind that for us was taken up with books is for today's kids taken up with blogs, video games, online information of questionable reliability, downloaded texts, and other shortcuts to real engagement with issues and ideas. Sure, we watched our share of TV and movies too, but we loved books. We loved to fill our minds with thoughts, not just impressions. Images provide instant gratification, instant under-standing, and intense, thrilling, fleeting enjoyment, but they do not push the be-holder any further or deeper, i.e., they do not stimulate thought, analysis, or reflec-tion. They push the beholder only to seek the next image. The beholder can remain mentally passive. Words, on the other hand, may not provide gratification at all, and, if they do, it is seldom instant. They provide understanding only after active connection with the text and sometimes only after hard work. But the enjoyment that words provide is durable, more complex, more interesting, and more deeply re-warding than that provided by images. Words will always be the best stimulators of thought and reflection, and hence eventually of constructive action. We loved words. We will always have the advantage over the World Wide Web generation in that regard.

There was some great new stuff to read in 1968. Brautigan brought out two books, *In Watermelon Sugar*, a novel set in the surrealistic community of iDEATH, which may be pronounced either "i-death" or "idea-th"; and *The Pill Versus the Springhill Mine Disaster*, a volume of poetry. But the most important book for us that year was Black Panther leader Eldridge Cleaver's ideological autobiography, *Soul on Ice*. From 1954 to 1966, or from age eighteen to thirty-one, he was in prison for marijuana crimes, rape, and attempted murder. He began writing the essays and letters that would become *Soul on Ice* shortly after the murder of Malcolm X. By the time of his parole he was an articulate revolutionary, and soon joined the Black Panther Party as its Minister of Information, i.e., writer of most of its public statements. *Soul on Ice* offered sociological, empirical, and theoretical arguments for the close connection of pro-Vietnam-War and racist positions, thus implying that the antiwar and civil rights movements naturally belonged together, insofar as they shared common aims. Cleaver reduced class struggle and racial strife to sexual causes, identifying several racial-sexual stereotypes as key participants: the Omnipotent Administrator, the Supermasculine Menial, the Ultrafeminine, and the Subfeminine. The (white) Administrator, who ran the whole show, was physically weak and not sexually attractive. The (black) Menial radiated supreme sexual attractiveness. The white woman would thus naturally prefer the black man to the white man. The white man could not abide this, and so declared that the white woman must be Ultrafeminine, i.e., more effeminate than he already was, and that the black man and the white woman must be strictly off-limits to each other. The white man also declared that the black woman, being menially occupied and inclined, must be Subfeminine. Hence, in making the white woman more feminine and the black woman less so, he made the white woman even more attractive to the black man than she already was. Not allowed to have sex with the white woman, and no longer attracted to the black woman for sex, the Supermasculine Menial became the Black Eunuch — a very angry man! Thus the interrelated sexual frustrations of the white woman, the black man, and the black woman, all produced out of the sexual inadequacy of the white man, were the root of American colonialist or imperialist racism. Cleaver's revolutionary conclusion was: "We shall have our manhood. We shall have it or the earth will be leveled by our attempts to gain it." That seemed reasonable, given four centuries of unpardonable white crimes against blacks. If anyone disagreed with the threatened violence, at least now we could understand black rage, and see such violence as meager retaliation for the systematic kidnapping, transportation, slavery, rape, selling of kids away from their parents and spouses away from each other, lynching, Jim Crow laws, etc., etc., etc., that they had suffered.

No one was ever so disappointed, shocked, or disillusioned as we were in 1980 when Eldridge Cleaver — *Eldridge Cleaver, of all people!* — announced that he had become a conservative Republican and was supporting Ronald Reagan for president! We knew that he had converted to "born again" Christianity while living in France in the mid-seventies, and that in 1978 he had published a second autobiography, *Soul on Fire*, which had repudiated *Soul on Ice*. ***But this!?!*** A religious conversion is one thing; a political, philosophical, or ideological 180-degree turn is another. It is one thing to renounce one's former violence as a revolutionary, and to turn thereafter toward more peaceful, constructive methods of trying to effect sociopolitical change, as Malcolm X was trying to do when he was murdered, but it is quite another thing to renounce revolution itself. That is nothing else than abandoning one's principles. We wondered how he could have done it after having made so much plain common sense in *Soul on Ice*. There was no evidence that drugs had rotted his mind. But something had. The uncritical acceptance of the fundamentalist interpretation of any religion, particularly a vindictive missionary religion like Islam or Christianity, can rot minds as efficiently as any drug. It forces accepters to forswear the entire practice of thinking for themselves, and instead simply to believe whatever the founders and elders of the sect have decided is proper for them to believe. Most of the content of such faiths is contrary to common sense, natural deduction, impartial science, and rigorous logic. Yet, like Tertullian, they believe it either in spite of or because of its absurdity. Such people have abdicated their God-given reason and are ripe for conversion to any further absurdity. In short, if someone can accept the illogic of fundamentalism, then that person can accept any illogic. Conservative publicists, planners, and campaigners know this. That is why they are able to recruit so successfully among fundamentalists. As we saw it, Eldridge Cleaver becoming a conservative Republican and endorsing Reagan was analogous to a Jew joining the Nazi party, or perhaps better said, to George Washington grovelling up to King George III, begging forgiveness, admitting that the Boston Tea Party, the treasonable and murderous assaults on His Majesty's redcoats, the Declaration of Independence, etc., were all a big series of stupid, misguided mistakes. Cleaver's *Soul on Fire* was a declaration of *dependence*, and his endorsement of Reagan was spitting on the graves of Malcolm X, Martin Luther King, and centuries of lynched African-Americans.

We had a keen sense of history. Raised on Random House Landmark Books, we naturally developed this sense of history to an almost instinctive level. The idea that human history was or should be tantamount to human progress was firmly ingrained in us. The course of history was the course of civilization freeing, protecting, and enriching more and more people and creating stronger and stronger guarantees — like the American Constitution — to keep them free, safe, and enriched. Nothing comparable to the wonderfulness of Landmark Books exists for kids in the twenty-first century. If they have any sense of history at all, it is only a sense of the history of popular culture, and goes back at most a few decades.

We loved to think. Yes, just sit and think. Some of us believed that various substances helped in this venture, but others of us did not — and that was all very cool (unless the pusher showed up). About this time a cabal of feminists in New York City, including Anne Forer, Shulie Firestone, Anne Koedt, etc., coined the term "consciousness raising" to describe the educational process by which someone becomes so keenly aware of being oppressed that this person becomes motivated to take political action. Being natural thinkers, we took to this concept like fish to water as soon as we heard of it, which was typically in either 1968 or 1969.

Consciousness raising groups met not only for feminist causes, but also for gay liberation, racism, draft and antiwar issues, and indeed for any kind of injustice that we believed we might be able to do something about.

Ω

Comedy was solid in early 1968.

A brand new idea in comedy, *Rowan and Martin's Laugh-In*, replaced the popular but declining *Man from U.N.C.L.E.* on NBC. Insofar as the name "Laugh-In" was an obvious pun on "sit-in," "love-in," "teach-in," "be-in," and other anti-establishment sorts of events, we suspected even before we saw the show that its humor would be left of center. We were neither mistaken nor disappointed.

Yet, the appeal of *Laugh-In* easily crossed generational and political lines. Sitting around the TV watching *Laugh-In* on Monday nights was one of very few activities that American middle-class families were glad to do together anymore. Old straights and conservatives laughed just as hard as young freaks and liberals, though not always at the same jokes and probably for different reasons. Even our grandparents liked *Laugh-In*; it reminded them of Ole Olsen's and Chic Johnson's 1938 Broadway revue, *Hellzapoppin'*.

Tuxedo-clad hosts Dan Rowan (the beleaguered straight man *à la* Oliver Hardy, George Burns, Dean Martin, or Dick Smothers) and Dick Martin (the wacky, apparently obtuse, but insidiously clever sidekick *à la* Stan Laurel, Gracie Allen, Jerry Lewis, or Tom Smothers) presided over each eclectic, rapid-fire hour of skits, sketches, blackouts, cutaways, one-liners, sight gags, running gags, interruptions, and occasional musical numbers (precursors of the music video). Some of the bits were as short as two or three seconds and few were longer than a minute. Sex and politics were the subtext of nearly everything on the show, sometimes obvious, sometimes not, and sometimes probably even just imagined by the viewers. On a surreal, psychedelically colored set with trap doors, odd windows, and unexpected paraphernalia, characters romped through parties, dances, newscasts, street scenes, and other happenings. From 1968 to 1971, dozens of (not always original) catch-phrases from the show, such as "You bet your bippy," "Look it up in your Funk and Wagnalls," "Sock it to me," "Here comes the judge," "Ring my chimes," and "What you see is what you get," would become stock in American homes, schools, and streets. Frequent characters on *Laugh-In*, such as Ruth Buzzi's ugly, hypersensitive spinster; Henry Gibson's insipid poet; Arte Johnson's "very interesting" Nazi soldier, lecherous old bum, and Indian guru Rabbi Shankar; Judy Carne's robot doll; Lily Tomlin's snotty little Edith Ann and nosy telephone operator Ernestine; Jo Anne Worley's boisterous red-hot mama; Gary Owens's hammy announcer; and Rowan's jingoist General Bullright, became regularly imitated paragons of American pop culture. Lithe and gorgeous go-go dancers in bikinis and body paint could pop up anywhere at any time. Horny male viewers would look forward every week to reading the slogans on Goldie Hawn's gyrating, beautiful, near-naked body.

The eccentric, good-natured British satirical jazz rock troupe, the Bonzo Dog Doo-Dah Band, successors to the Goons, friends of the Beatles, and heralds of Monty Python's Flying Circus, burst into the *avant garde* comedy scene with their debut album, *Gorilla*, whose cover showed what looked like the cast of a Dada play frolicking with King Kong. Several tracks on this LP, including "Jollity Farm" and "The Intro and the Outro," became cult comedy classics.

Bill Cosby, as Captain Oh Wow, had a syndicated radio series from January to September 1968. That does not sound like much, but each show was only about five minutes long and there were about 350 of them. Mostly the good captain would just answer listeners' letters with wacko *non sequiturs*, but sometimes Bill would also play a comic superhero, the Brown Hornet.

Zappa's third Mothers of Invention album, *We're Only in It for the Money*, continued the satirical themes of his first two, and added a few new ones. From a distance, the cover looked just like that of *Sgt. Pepper's*, but closer inspection revealed the Mothers in drag; "Mothers" spelled out on the ground in carrots, watermelons, and tomatoes; and, in the background, a crowd that included Hendrix, LBJ, the Statue of Liberty, Lee Harvey Oswald, Eric Burdon, Gracie Allen, a very young Albert Einstein, Captain Beefheart, Nancy Sinatra, David Crosby, Max Schreck, and many others. Black rectangles, such as are typically used to prevent positive identification, obscured many of their faces across the eyes. The overriding theme of the album was appearance vs. reality. In particular, it lambasted those who affected fake appearances in order to present themselves as belonging to certain realities, to which they in fact did not and could not belong.

Opening with the musical question, "Are You Hung Up?" Zappa segued into "Who Needs the Peace Corps?" which added to his frequent attacks on phoniness within hippiedom with a devastating but almost didactic satire on the falsity of young people who had learned how to take drugs and how to look cool, but who were not really cool, because they still had not learned how to think freely, and because they did not understand that being hip had nothing to do with taking drugs. Was his identification with Los Angeles what made him want to send all such people to San Francisco? A friendly rivalry between the main cities of southern and northern California? Possibly, but we doubted it. Zappa did not seem to have any sort of a Harvard / Yale mentality. He would have dumped on San Francisco from wherever he lived, just as long as he perceived its phoniness, hypocrisy, and sleaze. The fact that Los Angeles itself was guilty of the same faults was beside the point.

In "Concentration Moon," Zappa described cops killing unarmed, peaceful, long-haired citizens just because the cops thought they were creepy. In its sequel, "Mom and Dad," he bitterly called attention to the pervasive conservative notion that if anyone looks weird, dresses weird, does not conform, then the proper response to that person is harassment, violence, torture, and eventually, murder. This notion was then alive and well in America, given how the cops, the plastic people, and even our parents treated us. Lennon would deliver a similar message a few months later in "Bungalow Bill" on the Beatles' White Album, criticizing the belief that killing is justified by the looks of the victim.

"Bow Tie Daddy" skewered the alcoholism and materialism of the middle-class establishment. "Harry, You're a Beast" deplored the difficulty, artificiality, and latent violence of heterosexual romance when the woman cares more about her appearance than about the man and when the man cares more about the merely physical sex act than about her. "What's the Ugliest Part of Your Body?" The answer: nothing physical, but just your filthy thoughts. "Absolutely Free" returned to the frequent psychedelic theme that absolute freedom comes only to those who want it, take it, and live it.

"Flower Punk" parodied "Hey Joe" with nasty lyrics, not about a jealous scumbag murdering his girlfriend and skipping off to Mexico, but about — you guessed it! — phony hippies. "Let's Make the Water Turn Black" told a story of perverse, violent, unloved, unsupervised little brats growing up to be soldiers and junkies. "The Idiot Bastard Son" continued this tale, emphasizing the violence and jingoism of the father, the lasciviousness and insensitivity of the mother, the mercenary hypocrisy of both, and the fact that, in this case at least, like breeds like. "Lonely Little Girl" condemned uncaring parents. "Take Your Clothes Off When You Dance" exhorted us to social freedom and the scrapping of conventions. "Mother People" defended life as freaks.

"The Chrome Plated Megaphone of Destiny" was only a six-and-a-half-minute instrumental, but the liner notes said:

THE CHROME PLATED MEGAPHONE OF DESTINY
instructions for the use of this material ... READ CAREFULLY
1. If you have already worked your way through "IN THE PENAL COLONY" by Franz Kafka, skip instructions #2, #3, #4.
2. Everybody else: go dig up a book of short stories & read "IN THE PENAL COLONY"
3. DO NOT LISTEN TO THIS PIECE UNTIL YOU HAVE READ THE STORY
4. After you have read the story, put the book away & turn on the record player ... it is now safe to listen (DO NOT READ & LISTEN AT THE SAME TIME).
5. As you listen, think of the concentration camps in California constructed during world war II to house potentially dangerous oriental citizens ... the same camps which many say are now being readied for use as part of the FINAL SOLUTION to the NON-CONFORMIST (hippy?) PROBLEM today. You might allow yourself (regardless of the length of your hair or how you feel about greedy wars & paid assassins) to imagine YOU ARE A GUEST AT CAMP REAGAN. You might imagine you have been invited to try out a wonderful new RECREATIONAL DEVICE (designed by the Human Factors Engineering Lab as a method of relieving tension & pent-up hostilities among the members of the CAMP STAFF ... a thankless job which gives little or no ego gratification ... even for the chief warden).
6. At the end of the piece, the name of YOUR CRIME will be carved on your back.

Zappa's fourth album, *Lumpy Gravy*, released a few months later, was just two side-long instrumentals.

Waiting for the Electrician or Someone Like Him, the debut album from the absurdist and superlatively good-natured comedy quartet, Firesign Theatre, contained just four long bits. As skilled at language games as Fibber McGee, as predisposed toward *non sequiturs* as Groucho Marx, as crazy as Franz Kafka, as intelligent as Jonathan Swift, as revolutionary as Lenny Bruce, as technically savvy as Stan Freberg, as daring as Richard Pryor, as mischievous as Oscar Wilde, and as unpredictable as Brownian motion, all four dudes on this bus were masters of topical and general cultural satire, poking friendly but pointed fun at just about everything. "Temporarily Humboldt County" lampooned white America's 400 years of abusing, cheating, exploiting, and slaughtering Native Americans. "W.C. Fields Forever" — the title a triple pun on "Strawberry Fields Forever," the song, "W.C. Fields," the comedian, and "W.C.," water closet — ridiculed hippiedom. "Le Trente-Huit Cunegonde" imagined the underground psychedelic culture as if it were mainstream. The title track, which took up all of side two on vinyl, was a wild collage of apparently disconnected bits that were probably connected after all, but we could not tell how.

Early in the national election primary season, deadpan comedian Pat Paulsen announced on *The Smothers Brothers Comedy Hour* that he was running for president as the choice of the Straight Talking American Government Party, i.e., the STAG Party. His campaign took on a life of its own outside the TV context. Actively stumping in primary states, his slogan was, "We cannot stand Pat." In one of his speeches he said:

> Censorship does not interfere with the constitutional rights of every American to sit alone in a dark room in the nude and cuss. There are realistic taboos, especially regarding political comments. Our leaders were not elected to be tittered at. For example, we're allowed to say Ronald Reagan is a lousy actor, but we're not allowed to say he's a lousy governor — which is ridiculous. We know he's a good actor. And we're not allowed to make fun of President Johnston [sic]. But if we praise him, who would believe it?

Finally, after censors relented, Pete Seeger got to sing "Waist Deep in the Big Muddy" on *The Smothers Brothers Comedy Hour*. It was almost anticlimactic by now, given the intense publicity surrounding the original ban. 1968 was a good year for Pete. He released three albums, *Pete Seeger Now*, *Pete Seeger Sings and Answers Questions at the Ford Hall Forum in Boston*, and *Pete Seeger Sings Leadbelly* (LP), and, largely thanks to the *Smothers* TV appearance, became much more visible outside just the social justice and antiwar movements.

The main attraction of Tom Paxton's fourth album, *Morning Again*, was a comedic gem, "Talking Vietnam Potluck Blues," which in one fell swoop savaged both the Vietnam War and American anti-marijuana postures. The first-person narrative followed an indolent pothead enlisted soldier in Vietnam whose pothead Yalie captain introduced him to the excellent wild marijuana growing native there. When a Vietcong soldier offered him some better grass, "Hanoi gold," the two enemy squads sat down, passed the joints around, and got peacefully stoned. Paxton's antiwar, anti-LBJ, and anti-racist credentials were already strong from his first three albums, but he was not a mere nay-sayer. On the contrary, perhaps more so than any other performer of the time, he actively promoted reconciliation on all levels and among all people.

Phil Ochs's new LP, *Pleasures of the Harbor*, was generally mellower and less protesty than his earlier work; but it had the advantage of containing "Outside of a Small Circle of Friends," one of the most trenchant shaftings of social hypocrisy ever recorded. Many of us bought the album just for that.

In what may have been the all-time peak of American irony, *Hair* made it to Broadway. Talk about the belly of the beast! Che Guevara had likened revolutionaries living in America to infiltrators or warriors in the belly of the beast, i.e., in the very middle of all that made revolution necessary in the first place. Broadway was a bastion of conservative values, ostentatious money, and fluffy performances. So along came James Rado and Gerome Ragni with a liberal, low key, serious sociopolitical message — albeit benign — disguised as musical comedy entertainment. Did Rado and Ragni sell out? Possibly. But we liked to believe instead that they were deliberately getting into the belly of the beast.

Part of the reason that protest was alive and well was that there was a lot to protest. For example, some idiot with a rifle murdered Martin Luther King. 'Nuff said. We were taking it to the streets. The various mobes, the SCLC, the SDS, various other groups and organizations, and even various individuals acting alone, all had something concrete and important to say, write, or do for civil rights or against the war. Their tactics, results, and side effects might not always have been laudable, but their motives, in general, were pure, heartfelt, and well-meaning.

Just nineteen days after the murder of Martin Luther King, a very surprising event occurred. The SDS took over Columbia University. Why? We wondered. It mystified us. We could have understood the SDS taking over a draft board office or performing some sort of civil disobedience against Dow Chemical — but we could not fathom why they would target a university. We had thought that the universities were on our side. With professors and intellectuals speaking out against the war, the draft, racism, imperialism, and even sometimes sexism, we were convinced that higher education was our ally. We were wrong.

I was nearing the end of my sophomore year in high school. My friends and I followed this story in the newspapers even more closely than we followed most stories. After all, college life would be our milieu before too long, so we wanted to know what was what. We gradually discovered that the SDS's intention had been to awaken the public to the fact that Columbia and other research institutions were in cahoots with the defense industry to develop and implement more and deadlier weapons. The SDS takeover was thus a gigantic, super-publicized teach-in, complete with guerrilla theater. Very effective! Well done! Its leader, recently expelled Columbia junior Mark Rudd, the SDS chapter president, became a sort of hero to us.

Ω

Judy Collins's new LP, *Wildflowers*, contained her noteworthy cover of Joni Mitchell's "Both Sides Now," a melancholy yet upbeat song about openmindedness, disullusionment, mystery, and patience. Joni would not release her own version until next year.

A Los Angeles psychedelic rock band, Spirit, fascinating because of its pervasive and eclectic jazz influences, released its self-titled debut album. The most significant track was the environmentalist anthem, "Fresh Garbage."

The Velvet Underground's second album, *White Light / White Heat*, passed by almost unnoticed.

The Vanilla Fudge performed "You Keep Me Hangin' On" live without incident on *The Ed Sullivan Show*. They were not nearly as obnoxious as the Doors, the Stones, or even the Byrds, and Ed was not his usual overbearing and condescending self toward them.

The Kinks released *Something Else*, but it meant little. They were in their nadir. We had forgotten them.

A flashy British blues band with nascent leanings toward psychedelia — and a very fast lead guitarist, Alvin Lee, released its eponymous debut album: *Ten Years After*. Blues aficionados might have discerned them early, but most of us did not get to know the first four Ten Years After albums until after their fifth, *Cricklewood Green*, and the Woodstock movie and soundtrack all appeared in 1970.

Blue Cheer, along with the Who, Led Zeppelin, and a few others, had the reputation of being one of most dangerously LOUD concert bands. They deserved this rep too. City traffic noise is about 85 decibels. Most rock concerts are between about 100 and 115 decibels. Ears hurt at 125 decibels. Ear tissue dies at 180 decibels. Blue Cheer routinely played at between 130 and 140 decibels, cranking ten separate Marshall amp stacks all the way up. Some have claimed that Blue Cheer was either the first heavy metal band or at least a precursor of heavy metal. But these claims could only be true if we equate heavy metal with sheer volume. Yes, heavy metal is loud, but true heavy metal also requires a great degree of finesse on guitar, such as real musicians like Jimmy Page were able to provide, but which Blue Cheer certainly could not.

Named for the popular laundry detergent (or maybe, some say, for one of Owsley Stanley's varieties of LSD), this mighty but rather bombastic San Francisco power trio hit the record stores with their debut album, *Vincebus Eruptum*, which means nothing — it is even worse Latin than *procol harum*, which at least can be seen to mean *something*. The album contained their current single, a thudding cover of Eddie Cochran's "Summertime Blues," and five more thundering songs.

Dick Clark was baffled, bewildered, quite at a loss. He did not have a clue how to deal with Blue Cheer. Asking the group his usual stupid questions between songs on *American Bandstand*, Dick was completely befuddled when they did not give the expected kinds of answers, but instead mentioned places like Kashmir — and the members of Blue Cheer were not even very smart!

"Wasn't Born to Follow" and "Goin' Back" were the highlights of the Byrds' new album, *Notorious Byrd Brothers*, which showed guitarist McGuinn, bassist Hillman, and drummer Clarke, now down to a trio, moving in a country rock direction. Their current single, "You Ain't Going Nowhere," which was even more countrified, would appear on their *Sweetheart of the Rodeo* LP next fall.

Other tunes besides "If Six Was Nine" on the Jimi Hendrix Experience's second LP, *Axis: Bold as Love*, included "Up From the Skies," which expressed general fascination with earthly phenomena, and "Spanish Castle Magic," which was so far inscrutable, but which we much later learned was a nostalgic song about a dance club, the Spanish Castle, where James Marshall Hendrix used to go as a high school kid in Seattle. "Wait Until Tomorrow" was a tragic tale of a young lover shot and killed by the father of the woman with whom he tried to elope. Among Jimi's love songs, "Ain't No Telling" was upbeat and percussive, "Little Wing" haunting and psychedelic, "You Got Me Floatin'" a solid rocker, and "Little Miss Lover" a straight ahead barroom pickup. "She's So Fine" was bassist Noel Redding's inclusion, a simple mod love song. Jimi's wistful "One Rainy Wish" evoked serene images of psychedelic colors and cosmic peace. "Castles Made of Sand" lamented the misfortunes of the world's downtrodden. "Bold as Love" equated colors with emotions and seemed to be about *samsara*, but its lyrics were very obscure. Perhaps clues to their meaning were to be found on the cover of *Axis*, which portrayed Hendrix, Redding, and drummer Mitch Mitchell as the three central deities of the Hindu pantheon.

The Moody Blues' second LP and their first in three years, *Days of Future Passed*, marked the beginning of what some would see as the pompous side of progressive rock. The Moodies used the London Festival Orchestra, conducted by Peter Knight, for much of their instrumentation. The Beatles, Procol Harum, and a few other bands had already used classical instrumentation, but not to this extent. Hence the charges of pomposity. But the fact was that the lyrics, especially those moronic poems spoken at dawn and at the end of "Nights in White Satin," were much more pompous than the music. The simple marriage of classical music and soft rock worked beautifully. *Days of Future Passed* was a gorgeous album. Its concept, to trace a single day — in this case an average Tuesday — from beginning to end, perhaps recalled Joyce's concept for *Ulysses*, to trace a single day, Thursday, June 16, 1904, in the life of Leopold Bloom.

Pink Floyd's debut album, depending on whether you had the British or an American release, and depending on which American release you had, was either called just *Pink Floyd* or *Piper at the Gates of Dawn*. The British version had neither "Arnold Layne" nor "See Emily Play," but one of the American versions had "See Emily Play." Any version was mainly a showcase of Barrett's psychedelia.

Barrett by no means had a monopoly on incoherent spaciness. It was certainly evident at the movies as well as in music:

Stanley Kubrick's *2001: A Space Odyssey* remains emblematic of much that is wrong with the relation between aesthetic and intellectual culture throughout the world, even in the most literate societies. It relied too much on visual representation, mental images, and what Hegel called "picture-thinking" (*Vorstellung*), but not enough on a clear, coherent, reasonable presentation of a story. Nearly every scene was stunningly beautiful, but at the same time almost completely meaningless. *2001* was the sort of mindless yet alluring entertainment that one might expect to find broadcast to the TV wall screens in *Fahrenheit 451*. Its gorgeous outer-space-simulating photography would serve civilization much better nine years later in the start of the *Star Wars* series, which at least had a plot. But in Kubrick's hands it gave the world nothing more than a vacuous yet formally attractive tableau.

According to the philosophy of art known as formalism, true art is purposeless beauty that cannot and should not express any specific emotion, thought, or tale. *2001*'s delicate synthesis of color, shape, texture, and music satisfied the aesthetic leanings of formalists in the tradition of Clive Bell, Eduard Hanslick, Edmund Gurney, and Roger Fry, but disappointed moviegoers who had come to expect a "message" from Kubrick, such as he had already skillfully delivered in *Paths of Glory* and *Dr. Strangelove* and would soon also in *A Clockwork Orange*. *2001* is just a Magrittean montage, a pastiche, a hodgepodge of impressions.

Future-speculative, space-oriented, flat-charactered science fiction is bad enough, but surrealistic future-speculative, space-oriented, flat-charactered science fiction that pretends through its sheer aesthetic appeal to be a profound, symbolic statement of ultimate reality is beyond the pale. Such statements ought to be made only by philosophers and other writers who deal in discursive reasoning. Photography and even music will be forever inadequate to this task, however much beauty they may add to our lives. If one picture is worth ten thousand words, then the trick is to know which ten thousand. Pictures lend themselves to a wider, more disparate, and less manageable range of interpretations than do discursive texts. All other things being equal — which they seldom are — keep your picture and give me the ten thousand words. I would rather exercise my imagination than just indulge my ears and eyes.

This preference for the visual over the discursive is a fault that my generation seldom recognized in itself and that subsequent generations have only made worse. The most constructive way to receive new ideas is by reading, because words are the best conveyors of these ideas. Listening to words is almost as useful, but in reading the reader controls the pace and thus is able to reflect at will and for as long as desired, while in listening the listener's ability to reflect is limited because someone else controls the pace. Looking at pictures, either still or moving, is the least constructive way, mainly because words need not be involved at all.

So we read books, comics, newspapers, and cereal boxes; we looked at all kinds of visual arts; and we did a lot of listening, not only to our friends', parents', and teachers' discourses and conversations, but also, and most enjoyably, to song lyrics. We actively sought radio stations that would provide broader varieties of remarkable new songs than what could typically be heard on AM.

There remained some — a little — good on AM radio this spring beyond the singles excerpted from the LPs to which we would rather have listened: The Fireballs' "Bottle of Wine" was a jubilant rocker celebrating the carefree life of a down-and-out wino. "Just Dropped in (to See What Condition my Condition Was in)" by Kenny Rogers and the First Edition was interesting music, but a clumsy attempt at psychedelic lyrics, an instant self-parody. "Dance to the Music" by Sly and the Family Stone was the ***real rock***! Manfred Mann's cover of Dylan's "The Mighty Quinn" showed how obscure and possibly meaningless lyrics could be presented without embarrassing oneself. Donovan's "Jennifer Juniper" was a gentle love song about George Harrison's sister-in-law, Helen Mary Boyd, who was known as "Jenny." The Beatles' "Lady Madonna," a mostly McCartney song, painted a heartbreaking portrait of an overwhelmed working mother. The Who released one of its few bits of pure commercial fluff, "Call Me Lightning," but it did not do very well, only going to number forty on the *Billboard* chart. Real life wife and husband Cathy and Jim Post, recording as Friend and Lover, gave us "Reach Out of the Darkness," a soft rock guide to winning friends, influencing people, and being influenced by them. "Angel of the Morning" by Merrilee Rush and the Turnabouts represented a woman who initiated sex with a guy, but expected him to respect her afterward. It was hard to believe that a protégée of Paul Revere and the Raiders could sing what might be interpreted as a liberated woman's anthem — but there it was. The lyrics of Richard Harris's splendid but melodramatic and perhaps overwrought "MacArthur Park" (which the Irish actor mispronounced as "MacArthur's Park") might at first have seemed ridiculous, but careful listening revealed an extended and coherent psychedelic metaphor for the impermanence of human relationships, the irrecoverability of lost love, and the beauty of fragility. A British mod quintet, the Status Quo, offered what some derided as "bubble gum psychedelia," but "Pictures of Matchstick Men" was really a finely crafted psychedelic tune with noteworthy blues influences and very interesting treble effects on lead guitar.

But FM was playing all these too, plus so much more!

In Philadelphia in the sixties there was a popular AM radio station called WIP, 610 on the dial, that played easy listening and soft pop. My mom listened to it. Most of WIP's programming was simulcast over its sister station, WIP-FM, 93.3. Both WIPs were owned by Metromedia. WIP-FM became WMMR. "MMR" stood for "MetroMedia Radio." In early 1968 the WIP brass, ironically under a Federal Communications Commission mandate, set out to find some different programming for its FM component. They hired an obscure New Jersey DJ, Dave Herman, to broadcast anything he wanted between 10:00 p.m. and 2:00 a.m. each night. Dave called his show the "Marconi Experiment." He had excellent taste in progressive rock and other underplayed music forms. Word of Dave's exciting new sound travelled among us with minimal advertising, and soon nearly every freak in the area was listening to WMMR, which quickly had a full schedule of free-form music, alternative news and commentary, and leftist politics. It had a huge transmitter: 50,000 watts. Within a few years it was the voice of underground and progressive rock throughout southeastern Pennsylvania, central and southern New Jersey, northern Delaware, and northeastern Maryland; and was one of the most influential radio stations in the country. Suffice to say that, if not for WMMR in the early seventies, Bruce Springsteen's career might never have gotten off the ground. Even though he was a north Jersey boy, he got more support from Philadelphia than from New York. WMMR was the reason in the seventies that so many rock bands began their North American tours in Philadelphia. They knew that they would get first-rate backing, knowledgeable DJs, and very enthusiastic audiences.

At the same time that Dave Herman, Luke O'Reilly (who later managed Al Stewart), Michael Cuscuna (who later produced Bonnie Raitt), Michael Tearson,

and other like-minded music experts were creating underground rock radio in Philadelphia, Tom and Raechel Donahue, Abe ("Voco") Kesh, Dusty Street, and their
crew were doing the same at another Metromedia station, KSAN, 94.9 in San Francisco. Under Tom's leadership KSAN became "The Jive 95." In its heyday from
1968 to 1972, KSAN was the pinnacle of its genre, the absolute best, the most blatant, outrageous, heavy, and unsettling stuff on the airwaves — nationwide, maybe
worldwide. Frank Zappa called it "the hippest station in the universe." Tom, as
the acknowledged inventor of free-form progressive rock radio, was inducted into
the Rock and Roll Hall of Fame in 1996, one of few DJs ever to be so honored.

The San Francisco Bay Area was a uniquely fertile area for the development of free-form progressive rock radio. It already had KPFA-FM, 94.1, in Berkeley. While WMMR, KSAN, and the rest nationwide were owned by Metromedia
or other for-profit corporations, and thus, despite their avowed leftist stances, were
beholden at least somewhat to commercial interests; KPFA was truly "underground." Pacifist activist Lewis Hill founded Pacifica, a not-for-profit organization,
in 1946 to create the nation's first community-supported radio station. His KPFA
(Pacifica) began broadcasting on April 15, 1949, frankly political and commercial-
free. It has always relied entirely on donations. It was preaching war resistance,
draft resistance, and civil disobedience as early as 1950. It broadcast Allen Ginsberg, Lawrence Ferlinghetti, Che Guevara, Bertolt Brecht, Dorothy Healey, Linus
Pauling, and many other leftist leaders and intellectuals. Alan Watts had a regular
program on KPFA from 1953 until he died in 1973. Pacifica has been harassed,
both violently and nonviolently, by the FCC, the FBI, the House Un-American Activities Committee (HUAC), the Senate Internal Security Subcommittee (SISS),
the Ku Klux Klan, and the American Nazi Party. KPFA's music programing was
— and, in 2009, still is — entirely eclectic, including folk, blues, rock, country,
classical, and a lot of live music. Compared to KPFA, KSAN was just plain commercial radio.

The Doors were unquestionably an AOR band. Throughout their five-year
career, their deep album cuts such as "Crystal Ship," "Break On Through," "Five
to One," "The End," "The Celebration of the Lizard," "Peace Frog," "When the
Music's Over," and "The Soft Parade" were generally far superior to their poppier
stuff that got airplay on AM radio. Singles like "Light My Fire" (especially the
abridged version), "Love Me Two Times," "Hello, I Love You," "Touch Me," and
"Love Her Madly" did not contribute to Morrison's mystique nearly as much as
did singles like "People are Strange" and "Riders on the Storm" and especially the
album cuts. So, when Elektra released "The Unknown Soldier" — a magnificent
antiwar song — as a *single* in March 1968, we were dumbfounded. This was four
months before its album, *Waiting for the Sun*, appeared. Needless to say, "The
Unknown Soldier" was the worst-selling single of the Doors career. Straights listened to AM radio; freaks listened to FM — and would wait for the album before
shelling out the bucks.

Another FM radio favorite was Laura Nyro, a twenty-year-old New York
City neurotic who was steeped in jazz, gospel, blues, pop, doo wop, and folk, as
well as light rock. The writer of such tunes as "And When I Die," "Wedding Bell

Blues," and "Stoney End" put out a new LP, *Eli and the Thirteenth Confession*, which contained "Sweet Blindness," "Poverty Train," "Eli's Comin'," "Stoned Soul Picnic," and nine other original compositions.

Bookends, the most recent LP by Simon and Garfunkel, was more experimental than their previous three. "Save the Life of My Child" was a simple narrative about a suicidal teenager. Similarly, "America" narrated the self-seeking journey of two Bohemians. "Overs," perhaps one of the most depressing songs ever, described a moribund relationship, probably a marriage. S&G actually sang it on the *Smothers Brothers* show, maybe as part of a "subversive Communist plot" to simultaneously dishearten the entire national CBS audience. (During the Cold War, people commonly saw "subversive Communist plots" where there were none. That was the premise of *Rocky and Bullwinkle* and many other satirical TV shows.) Almost as discouraging as "Overs" were Garfunkel's *vérité* recordings, "Voices of Old People," which made us want to run out screaming in search of the fabled Fountain of Youth. Reality sucked, but it sucked worse and worse and worse as we got older. The next song, "Old Friends," just sealed this pessimism about maturity, aging, elderliness, life in general. There was not much for us to look forward to. In our teens and twenties, our best days were already behind us.

The more upbeat and uplifting "Punky's Dilemma" was an enigmatic song, offering a choice between, it seemed, on the one hand, sanity, and, on the other hand, the blithe identification of the singer's persona with various breakfast foods. Of course, the mention of a cornflake reminded us of "I Am the Walrus," which we were still trying to decode. Were S&G making a deliberate connection with the Beatles here? We could not tell. Moreover, the song concluded with a few lines about draft evasion — evasion, not resistance. Where did that *non sequitur* come from? Is was unlike S&G to be so obscure. Yes, their lyrics were poetic and imagistic, but usually not so frustrating to try to understand.

"Mrs. Robinson," their hit single from *The Graduate*; "Fakin' It" and "At the Zoo," their year-old hit singles; and "A Hazy Shade of Winter," their year-and-a-half-old hit single, were also on *Bookends*.

Long-established Harvard Square folkie Tom Rush hit the big time with his sixth album, The *Circle Game*, chock full of beautiful, haunting, acoustic songs. His covers of Joni Mitchell's "Tin Angel," "Urge for Going," and "The Circle Game"; James Taylor's "Something in the Way She Moves," and "Sunshine, Sunshine"; Billy Hill's "The Glory of Love"; Jackson Browne's "Shadow Dream Song"; and Charlie Rich's "So Long" combined with his own "Rockport Sunday" and "No Regrets" to create a durable impression of New England serenity. If Tom had never released anything else, this album alone would have ensured his solid place of honor in the history of American folk music.

The self-titled debut LP from one of the premier San Francisco psychedelic rock bands, Quicksilver Messenger Service, contained a magnificent song, their current single, "Pride of Man," a no-holds-barred indictment of materialistic culture and its consequent warmongering. Its weakness was its "wrath of God" mentality. The lyrics suggested that if humankind did not soon straighten up and fly right, the divine day of wrath would engulf the world in the holy fire of eternal punishment.

What a crock of shit! We believed that imperialism, the nuclear threat, the rape of the planet, and other earthly, human problems could and should be solved on earth, by humans, with thisworldly action, not supernaturally, *ex caelo*, by the intervention of Yahweh or any other vengeful God. We could easily accept Quicksilver's attacks on materialism and militarism, but not from the fire-and-brimstone standpoint.

Ω

The king abdicated!

Sunday, March 31, at 9:00 p.m., Eastern Standard Time, Lyndon Johnson spoke from the White House on national TV, in detail and at length about the Vietnam War, American disunity, and related issues. Here are salient excerpts:

Good evening, my fellow Americans:

Tonight I want to speak to you of peace in Vietnam and Southeast Asia.

No other question so preoccupies our people. No other dream so absorbs the 250 million human beings who live in that part of the world. No other goal motivates American policy in Southeast Asia.

For years, representatives of our Government and others have traveled the world — seeking to find a basis for peace talks. ...

Hanoi denounced this offer, both privately and publicly. Even while the search for peace was going on, North Vietnam rushed their preparations for a savage assault on the people, the government, and the allies of South Vietnam.

Their attack — during the Tet holidays — failed to achieve its principal objectives.

It did not collapse the elected government of South Vietnam or shatter its army — as the Communists had hoped.

It did not produce a "general uprising" among the people of the cities as they had predicted. ...

They caused widespread disruption and suffering. Their attacks, and the battles that followed, made refugees of half a million human beings.

The Communists may renew their attack any day.

They are, it appears, trying to make 1968 the year of decision in South Vietnam — the year that brings, if not final victory or defeat, at least a turning point in the struggle. ...

There is no need to delay the talks that could bring an end to this long and this bloody war.

Tonight, I renew the offer I made last August — to stop the bombardment of North Vietnam. We ask that talks begin promptly, that they be serious talks on the substance of peace. We assume that during those talks Hanoi will not take advantage of our restraint.

We are prepared to move immediately toward peace through negotiations.

So, tonight, in the hope that this action will lead to early talks, I am taking the first step to deescalate the conflict. We are reducing — substantially reducing — the present level of hostilities.

And we are doing so unilaterally, and at once.

Tonight, I have ordered our aircraft and our naval vessels to make no attacks on North Vietnam, except in the area north of the demilitarized zone where the continuing enemy buildup directly threatens allied forward positions and where the movements of their troops and supplies are clearly related to that threat.

The area in which we are stopping our attacks includes almost 90 percent of North Vietnam's population, and most of its territory. Thus there will be no attacks around the principal populated areas, or in the food-producing areas of North Vietnam.

Even this very limited bombing of the North could come to an early end — if our restraint is matched by restraint in Hanoi. But I cannot in good conscience stop all bombing so long as to do so would immediately and directly endanger the lives of our men and our allies. Whether a complete bombing halt becomes possible in the future will be determined by events.

Our purpose in this action is to bring about a reduction in the level of violence that now exists.

It is to save the lives of brave men — and to save the lives of innocent women and children. It is to permit the contending forces to move closer to a political settlement. ...

I call upon President Ho Chi Minh to respond positively, and favorably, to this new step toward peace. ...

We and our allies can only help to provide a shield behind which the people of South Vietnam can survive and can grow and develop. ...

That small, beleaguered nation has suffered terrible punishment for more than 20 years. ...

We shall accelerate the reequipment of South Vietnam's armed forces — in order to meet the enemy's increased firepower. This will enable them progressively to undertake a larger share of combat operations against the Communist invaders.

On many occasions I have told the American people that we would send to Vietnam those forces that are required to accomplish our mission there. So, with that as our guide, we have previously authorized a force level of approximately 525,000. ...

I cannot promise that the initiative that I have announced tonight will be completely successful in achieving peace any more than the 30 others that we have undertaken and agreed to in recent years.

But it is our fervent hope that North Vietnam, after years of fighting that have left the issue unresolved, will now cease its efforts to achieve a military victory and will join with us in moving toward the peace table. ...

As Hanoi considers its course, it should be in no doubt of our intentions. It must not miscalculate the pressures within our democracy in this election year.

We have no intention of widening this war.

But the United States will never accept a fake solution to this long and arduous struggle and call it peace.

No one can foretell the precise terms of an eventual settlement.

Our objective in South Vietnam has never been the annihilation of the enemy. It has been to bring about a recognition in Hanoi that its objective — taking over the South by force — could not be achieved. ...

I think every American can take a great deal of pride in the role that we have played in bringing this about in Southeast Asia. We can rightly judge — as responsible Southeast Asians themselves do — that the progress of the past 3 years would have been far less likely — if not completely impossible — if America's sons and others had not made their stand in Vietnam. ...

One day, my fellow citizens, there will be peace in Southeast Asia.

It will come because the people of Southeast Asia want it — those whose armies are at war tonight, and those who, though threatened, have thus far been spared.

Peace will come because Asians were willing to work for it — and to sacrifice for it — and to die by the thousands for it.

But let it never be forgotten: Peace will come also because America sent her sons to help secure it. ...

Throughout this entire, long period, I have been sustained by a single principle: that what we are doing now, in Vietnam, is vital not only to the security of Southeast Asia, but it is vital to the security of every American. ...

I believe that a peaceful Asia is far nearer to reality because of what America has done in Vietnam. I believe that the men who endure the dangers of battle — fighting there for us tonight — are helping the entire world avoid far greater conflicts, far wider wars, far more destruction, than this one.

The peace that will bring them home someday will come. Tonight I have offered the first in what I hope will be a series of mutual moves toward peace.

I pray that it will not be rejected by the leaders of North Vietnam. I pray that they will accept it as a means by which the sacrifices of their own people may be ended. And I ask your help and your support, my fellow citizens, for this effort to reach across the battlefield toward an early peace.

Finally, my fellow Americans, let me say this:

Of those to whom much is given, much is asked. I cannot say and no man could say that no more will be asked of us. ...

Throughout my entire public career I have followed the personal philosophy that I am a free man, an American, a public servant, and a member of my party, in that order always and only. ...

So, I would ask all Americans, whatever their personal interests or concern, to guard against divisiveness and all its ugly consequences. ...

What we won when all of our people united just must not now be lost in suspicion, distrust, selfishness, and politics among any of our people.

Believing this as I do, I have concluded that I should not permit the Presidency to become involved in the partisan divisions that are developing in this political year.

With America's sons in the fields far away, with America's future under challenge right here at home, with our hopes and the world's hopes for peace in the balance every day, I do not believe that I should devote an hour or a day of my time to any personal partisan causes or to any duties other than the awesome duties of this office — the Presidency of your country.

Accordingly, I shall not seek, and I will not accept, the nomination of my party for another term as your President.

But let men everywhere know, however, that a strong, a confident, and a vigilant America stands ready tonight to seek an honorable peace — and stands ready tonight to defend an honored cause — whatever the price, whatever the burden, whatever the sacrifice that duty may require.

Thank you for listening.

Good night and God bless all of you.

The next morning was not a typical workday Monday. There was joy in the streets! Now we could look forward to a new president next January who would quickly and willingly end the war. Or at least that was what we thought at the time. Monday, April 1, 1968. April Fool's Day.

The front page of the Sunday, May 26, 1968 *Philadelphia Sunday Bulletin* had an Associated Press photo of LBJ giving a Nazi salute. For real! Unretouched! It is on the front cover of this book. The stiff-arm wave had happened the day before at the International Ladies' Garment Workers Union (ILGWU) convention in Atlantic City. OK, it was accidental. Yes, LBJ was not really a Nazi. But oh, how we relished that picture! Truth is not only stranger, but often, as in this case, *better* than fiction. The most effective satire is self-satire, especially when it is unintentional.

Ω

Summer 1968

The whole world's watching!

I will not be pushed, stamped, filed, indexed, briefed, debriefed,
or numbered! My life is my own!
— Patrick McGoohan as Number Six in *The Prisoner*

By 1968 the call for worldwide revolution that had been in slow crescendo since
about 1965 had become very loud. There were many reasons for this growing dissatisfaction with the *status quo* — most of which are beyond the scope of this book
— but let it suffice to say that these reasons ran the gamut from political to ethical
to religious to psychological to economic to emotional to aesthetic. Moreover, those
of us who wanted revolution could not agree on what kind of revolution we wanted.
Violent or nonviolent? Social or political? Anarchic or socialist? Tolerating capitalism or not? Destructive, to create room for the phoenix, or constructive, to build
on what little discernible good already existed in the system. Maoist or Marxist?
Gradual or immediate? This or that? *Ceci ou celui-là? Dieses oder das? Esto o ése?*

In America the revolutionaries were particularly disorganized. Sometimes
it seemed as if each revolutionary were each in a private camp of one. Yet, even if
only retrospectively, two general divisions could be identified: the nonviolent and
violent. Not all the nonviolent revolutionaries were pacifists and not all the violent
ones were Maoists. There were Marxists, anarchists, socialists, communists, and
even nationalists and capitalists on both sides. The nonviolent tended to want a
cultural revolution, i.e., just to change the way we lived, while the violent tended
to want a political revolution, i.e., to change or abolish the system itself; but these
tendencies were by no means universal.

Ah well, the enemy of my enemy is my friend — to a point.

One huge advantage that we cultural revolutionaries had over the political
revolutionaries was that we did not actually have to DO anything. All we had to
do was live, be ourselves, survive, act as if the revolution was already won, end
the war by refusing to participate in it and by persuading others not to participate
in it either, end racism and sexism by putting on our colorblind and genderblind

glasses in all our dealings with people, go to demonstrations to show our numbers and solidarity, and in all other matters just do our own individual things in the most civilly disobedient ways. They, on the other hand, had to get out into the streets and fight. That was tough on them, because they were an ill-armed minority; and tough on us, because they gave us a bad name. The newswatching public was generally not discerning enough to differentiate a Weatherman from a flower child or from anyone in between. We got tarred with the brush that should have been meant only for them.

Speaking of distortions:

Joseph Morgenstern began his review of one of Hollywood's all-time worst movies with these words: "Before you can decode and digest the contents of American International's *Wild in the Streets*, you must accept the notion that an abysmally crude, cheap, incoherent, dishonest, contemptible motion picture made for no other motive than profit can nevertheless also have enormous brute force and considerable significance."[52] I seldom agree with movie critics, but in this case, he hit the target spot on. American International specialized in patronizing teenagers with trashy exploitation films. *Wild in the Streets* was typical of this worthless genre, manipulating and distorting stereotypes in a way that seemed calculated to portray American youth as not only dangerous, but subversively and irresponsibly so — when in fact the truly irresponsible, subversive, and dangerous party was American International itself, for proliferating these counterproductive and generally false stereotypes.

The story centered on Max Frost, a teenage runaway who had become a zillionaire by age twenty-two from selling LSD and fronting a bubble gum horn band with about as much artistic merit as Gary Puckett and the Union Gap. Viewers could not tell whether the film was intended as serious or satirical. The plot was unbelievable, the dialogue was preposterous, and the one-dimensional anger was palpable, but, except for the hammy ridiculousness of Shelley Winters as Frost's despicable mother, *Wild in the Streets* was played in a deadpan style uncharacteristic of satire. First, using the power of his teeny bop celebrity, Frost organized successful street movements to get the voting age lowered to fifteen. Then, commanding his "troops," his huge but clandestine network of teenage supporters, he spiked the whole nation's water supply with LSD, but, while he and his inner circle remained straight, provided each unwitting adult tripper with a teenage guide to prevent bummers. In this way he railroaded through a constitutional amendment that lowered the age requirement for national elective offices, including president, to fourteen. With a youth-oriented platform not unlike the real-life ideology of Abbie Hoffman, he embraced the Republican Party out of sheer convenience, beat Nixon and Reagan in the primaries, ran against LBJ in the 1968 presidential election — and won in a landslide. As president, he declared that all the world's troubles were caused by old people, decreed thirty the national mandatory retirement age, and specified that everyone over thirty-five should be forced to take LSD. In this way,

---

[52] *Film 68/69: An Anthology by the National Society of Film Critics*, edited by Hollis Alpert and Andrew Sarris (New York: Simon and Schuster, 1969), p. 173.

peace, prosperity, and harmony would be assured. This was all enforced at gunpoint. Old people were interned in Auschwitz-like facilities called "Paradise Camps." As virtual dictator, he disbanded the armed forces but used goon squads as vicious as any storm troopers to build his "purely hedonistic society." Finally, shaken by a toddler telling him that at twenty-four he had become "old," Frost went insane.

This simplistic, absurd caricature of our youth movement, *Wild in the Streets*, being full of lies and distortions, did us a lot of harm.

Ω

There are many candidates for the one song that would epitomize 1968: "Born to Be Wild," "If Six Was Nine," "In-A-Gadda-Da-Vida," "People Got to Be Free," "Revolution," "Five to One," "Sympathy for the Devil," to name but a few. I would not want to have to pick it, but if I were forced, my choice would be "Sky Pilot."

"Sky Pilot" was a magnificent achievement for the Animals, musically, dramatically, and philosophically. It was as powerful an antiwar statement as any that was made in the sixties, and a distressing and eloquent reminder of the duplicity and perhaps self-deception of any religious leader who supports war. As such, it was the perfect song for its time, seven minutes and twenty-eight seconds of wracking our consciences.

Burdon's story concerned a military chaplain who was ordered to bolster the spirits of the troops just before a major battle. He gladly obeyed this order, encouraged the men, rallied them, and called the blessings of God down upon them. That done, they marched out. He seemed self-deceived, unaware that he was not really working on behalf of the Prince of Peace, as he may have believed, but on behalf of the demons of war, aiding and abetting killing and mayhem, not at all promoting the joyful message of the New Testament, which should have been his true calling as a servant of Jesus Christ. This priest had done what he saw as his duty, but Burdon, through the interior monologue of a bewildered, sickened, and terrified soldier, threw the words of the Sixth Commandment back into his teeth.

Priests, especially military chaplains, are called "sky pilots" not because they have anything to do with aviation, but because they conduct us to the afterlife,[53] i.e., to God's heaven, our reward, the eternal celestial paradise which is typically portrayed in a childish image as the realm of the "Old Man in the Sky." Burdon's exploitation of this image pointed up the central and unavoidable hypocrisy of Christianity, Christianity's "tragic flaw," namely, that Christians may commit any kind of evil, but as long as they say they are sorry, they may still go to heaven. In Christianity, unlike in secular systems of reward and punishment, there is no incentive for people to improve their ethical character. Christianity allows all kinds of scoundrels to thrive, always leaving open the possibility of repentance and for-

---

[53] In Iceland, the stone cairns that mark the edges of rural roads are called "priests," because "they show us where to go, but do not go there themselves."

giveness — but not of actual worldly amelioriation.

The song's sound effects — a cacaphony of bagpipes, marching feet, battle shouts, gunfire, and aircraft roars — avoided melodrama, but evoked life and death in the trenches of World War I, when, in the calculated war of dreadful attrition, generals literally regarded their troops only numerically, as so much cannon fodder.

With the full-side extravaganza, "In-A-Gadda-Da-Vida," getting so much attention, the flipside of Iron Butterfly's second album, *In-A-Gadda-Da-Vida*, was often overlooked. But some pretty good music was back there, especially "Most Anything You Want" and "Are You Happy." Nevertheless, the band was best known and is best remembered for "In-A-Gadda-Da-Vida."

As musicians, they were superior to their reputation: Erik Brann was a much underrated psychedelic guitarist, not in Jorma Kaukonen's league, but better than most. Bassist Lee Dorman was solid but not flashy, again, not in John Entwistle's league, but better than most. Drummer Ron Bushy was neither as fast as Keith Moon nor as creative as Ginger Baker, but his licks were a lot more interesting than, say, Ringo's. Then there were Doug Ingle's bombastic, churchy keyboards. Seldom was such a heavy band so dominated by keyboards. We could have put that down to Ingle's ego as founder, leader, and chief songwriter, but, with him, it worked. Not even more richly talented keyboardists like Gary Brooker of Procol Harum or Keith Emerson of the Nice could have anchored such a band as Iron Butterfly. Bombast was required. Even the name, "Iron Butterfly," testified to this. It meant that the music was heavy and thudding, but at the same time light enough to fly and be beautiful. Several heavy metal bands would follow this pattern, most notably "Le[a]d Zeppelin" (a Keith Moon coinage).

"In-A-Gadda-Da-Vida," i.e., "In the Garden of Eden" as pronounced by drunken Ingle, began with its signature keyboard riff, then bass, then fuzzy guitar, then Adam-and-Eve love song vocals, then a gigantic instrumental break with humungous solos on — in order — keyboards, guitar, drums, keyboards, and guitar, before resuming the vocals for the finale. "In-A-Gadda-Da-Vida" was also released as a *single*, cut down to 2:50. Was there ever anything so stupid!?! The whole point of the song was that it was made for people who loved seventeen-minute jams. Brann himself said it was bubblegummy without its fourteen middle minutes.

"People Got to be Free" was the decisive political, ethical, and socioeconomic statement of the Rascals, formerly the Young Rascals, even more formerly Joey Dee and the Starliters, purveyors of the "Peppermint Twist" in 1961. What a long, strange trip that must have been! From slaves to dance crazes to real freedom: free from corporate hegemony, from the draft, from stupid people trying to run our lives, from anyone trying to send us to war or force us away from peace. By 1968 popular song lyrics had for us largely assumed — or rather, usurped — the place of school-books, newspapers, TV, and barbershop chatter as sources and confirmations of information and opinion. These lyrics mattered. We paid attention to them, because they came from young cool people like *us*, not from old uptight people like *them*. So, when a band, who had up until now done only silly dance tunes, soft ballads, and love songs, and whom we had no reason to believe was anything but apolitical, suddenly leaped up with a no-nonsense "message song," we sat up and listened.

The liner notes of the Doors' third album, *Waiting for the Sun*, included a long poem by Morrison, "The Celebration of the Lizard," which was not half bad. One verse from this poem appeared as the lyrics of the third song on the album, "Not to Touch the Earth." We wished that we could have heard the rest of the poem as music too, but we would have to wait a few years for that. We were particularly curious about Jim's apparent identification of himself as "The Lizard King."

When the Doors did "message songs," they were mostly antiwar or, less frequently, environmentalist messages. Morrison did not seem very interested in too many other political or social issues. Most of his songs were about either (his own) drug use, (his own) libido, or no easily identifiable topic. Some, like the soft rocking "Love Street," were inscrutable. Others, like the mellow "Summer's Almost Gone" the waltz, "Wintertime Love," and the evocatively Iberian-flavored "Spanish Caravan" were quite transparent, almost simplistic. "We Could Be So Good Together," "Yes, the River Knows," and the *a cappella* "My Wild Love" were all melancholy love songs. "The Unknown Soldier," comprised of excellent, eerie music and bad, awkward poetry, nevertheless presented an eloquent antiwar drama.

"Five to One" obviously suggested a ratio of some sort. But what? That was anyone's guess. Speculation ran wild. The lyrics at first seemed to be just about sex, but the singer quickly involved the woman in political activity. Morrison would consistently deny that the song was in any way political, but we did not believe him. *Res ipsa loquitur*. The lyrics spoke for themselves. Opposing armed minorities to unarmed majorities in this age of fomenting revolution was certainly political — and that is exactly what this song did. Moreover, the lyrics were fatalistic, implying that the time for oblivious partying was past, and that now was the time to get serious about changing the world, to get what we wanted and what we knew the world needed.

"Hello, I Love You" was a pretty worthless AM pop song. Every Doors album, no matter how good it was, seemed to have at least one of those. Naturally it did very well as a single, spending two weeks in August as *Billboard*'s number one. Thank God it was superseded by the Rascals' "People Got to Be Free," which spent the last two weeks of August and the first three of September at number one, i.e., enveloping the Chicago Democratic Convention. What exquisite irony *that* was!

In July Dunhill released "Born to Be Wild" as a single. So what! We were not listening to 45 RPM records or AM radio anymore. We already knew the song from Steppenwolf's eponymous album that had been released in January. So to whom was Dunhill expecting to sell the single? Someone, certainly. They knew best. It went to number two on the *Billboard* singles chart. But who bought it? Phony pseudo-hippies and junior high school teeny boppers, I suppose. We serious rockers and genuine freaks bought the album.

Ω

The June 28, 1968 issue of *Life* magazine ran a special section of wonderful articles about rock. This section was mainly the brainchild of reporter Robin Richman, a rock insider who showed keen understanding of the whole scene when she wrote in the introduction, "Grace Slick vs. White Tie and Tails," on page 3:

> We wanted to get at the essence of each group. When we got to know them, we found each one was unique. And we had seven totally different experiences. They all share a compassion for people and they're reaching out directly with their music. The difference is mainly in their style. They will use whatever device seems appropriate. Any musical or literary form from the oldest to the newest is possible. So Grace Slick of the Jefferson Airplane has a way of commenting on society, using metaphor and allusion — like Joyce — to get her ideas across. Country Joe and the Fish have a kind of county fair burlesque way of attacking the system directly. And Jim Morrison of the Doors sings from a very private, tormented self and if you find a clear meaning in his lyrics, fine. If you don't, that is all right, too. These musicians don't make things easy for anybody — after all, they're serious about what they're doing. But then what they are trying to do isn't just casual entertainment, either. They put a lot into it and they demand a lot from us.

The issue's cover photo showed the Airplane posing inside transparent, probably Plexiglass, boxes. Marty and Spencer looked alert, Paul maybe semi-alert, but Jack, Jorma, and Grace obviously, totally, absolutely, catatonically, stone stoned — completely out of it. There in plain sight was our vicarious drug thrill!

The first of the four articles was Robin's pictorial essay on Janis and Big Brother, the Airplane, the Mothers, the Doors, Cream, the Who, and Country Joe and the Fish. Respectively, a few excerpts:

> Sound. Loud and heavy. The voice raw and tortured. Janis Joplin, a female Leadbelly ... They come alive when the audience stops listening and starts moving. ... Janis stomps. The band plays harder and faster. Faces twist. Janis screams. ... Her hair thrashes, and she picks up the bottle she keeps with her and belts down more Southern Comfort.

> The Jefferson Airplane flies the runways of the mind and the airways of the imagination. It arrives and departs at will, exploring surrealist landscapes. It wears transparent disguises ... Together they form a structure of thrust and counterthrust. Ballads of chance encounters in a stream of consciousness. Passenger, be free and easy. Go along with allegory.

> He is eager to have the young survive society's plague of plastic robots, ugly radio, false morality. He assumes the role of musicologist, psychologist and sociologist. ... Dolls are mutilated. A gas mask is displayed. A bag of vegetables is unpacked and examined. There are spaced intervals of "honks" and suddenly the Mothers perform "Dead Air." They stop, sit down and ignore the audience. ... They keep this going for as long as it takes the audience to become unsettled, uncomfortable and angry. Then Zappa calmly approaches the mike and says, "It brings out the hostilities in you, doesn't it?"

Doors open and close everywhere and nowhere. ... The sound of the Doors is primitive and mystical ... The music has no meaning, just mood.

Each man in Cream has something to say for himself with his instrument and competes fiercely to dominate the others. ... They play together but are almost incapable of playing together and so they drive against each other.

They play three-minute morality plays, mini-operas and spot commercials. To give the necessary traumatic melodramatic final finale to "My Generation" they are compelled to destroy on stage ... Then they take a moment for a nap after tea.

Climb on the funky Fish bandwagon and support Joe for President. His platform: Show contempt and don't vote.

The second article, Richard Goldstein's "Wiggy Words that Feed Your Mind," examined the lyrics of Leonard Cohen, Bob Dylan, Grace Slick, John Phillips, Pete Townshend, Mick Jagger, John Lennon, Donovan, Paul Simon, and John Sebastian — comparing them favorably with the words of Walt Whitman, William Wordsworth, and James Joyce, but unfavorably with the "graceless, primitive and unpoetic" rock lyrics of the fifties and early sixties.

The third article, by Jon Borgzinner, traced the aborted career of a jazz rock horn band called Ars Nova.

The section's last article, "The Oracle Has It All Psyched Out," was written by Zappa himself. That man could write! His main point was that good music, any good music, is essentially sexual, and that to repress sexuality effectively — as was done in America in the fifties — would entail strictly censoring the free expression of music. Zappa praised black people and their music for bringing America out of that repression and into the wider sexual freedom of the sixties. In this regard he was especially thankful to Hendrix, of whose fans he said on page 91: "The boys seem to enjoy the fact that their girl friends are turned on to Hendrix sexually; very few resent his appeal and show envy. They seem to give up and say: 'He's got it, I ain't got it, I don't know if I'll ever get it ... but if I do, I wanna be just like him, because he's really got it.' They settle for vicarious participation and/or buy a Fender Stratocaster ..."

Robin's article surely helped Janis's career. Janis had performed at Monterey in June 1967, but because the Monterey movie did not appear until December 1968, few people outside the San Francisco area knew about her before *Cheap Thrills* smashed a whisky bottle over our heads in July 1968. Our first introduction to her was likely either "Piece of My Heart" or "Summertime," but "Ball and Chain" was the gem of the LP. Recorded at a Fillmore gig, all seven tunes on *Cheap Thrills* conveyed the full power and energy of her live performance. As a backing band, Big Brother and the Holding Company were sloppy but funky, perfect for what was the greatest album Janis ever released.

Guitarist Sam Houston Andrew and Janis opened with an exhilarating vocal duet in "Combination of the Two," a vibrant number that dared you to sit in your chair and not dance. Janis then, in the most dominating and vigorous way, nailed four straight blues songs: She wailed, moaned, and shrieked through "I Need a Man to Love." Backed by minimalist guitar, she created the most compelling cover of George and Ira Gershwin's "Summertime" that you ever heard. She offered us her whole heart with "Piece of My Heart." She broke our hearts with her downcast portrayal of the brazen but lonely toughie in "Turtle Blues." Then she took a well deserved break while Sam sang lead in the psychedelic rocker, "Oh, Sweet Mary."

Incredibly distorted, loud psychedelic guitar chords introduced the finale, the nine-and-a-half-minute masterpiece, Janis's intricate but nuanced and subtle cover of Big Mama Thornton's "Ball and Chain." No words could ever describe this performance. Listen to it on the LP; watch it in *Monterey Pop*; give it to yourself any way you can.

Underground cartoonist R. Crumb did the cover art. His frankly sexual illustrations (complete with nipple pokies on the images of Janis) exposed the decadent sleaze and despondent squalor of the urban lower classes, zonked out hippies, and stifled blacks. In separate frames, he depicted each of the songs, each of the band members, and a few other incidentals, such as the Hell's Angels seal of approval, Bill Graham's Fillmore audience, himself as a phony Indian guru, and assorted tiny details, mostly quite funny.

Janis soon got into other things as well.

After directing light comedies such as *A Hard Day's Night*, *Help!*, *The Knack*, and *A Funny Thing Happened on the Way to the Forum*, and a bad dark comedy, *How I Won the War*, Richard Lester directed a good dark comedy, *Petulia*, which awoke those of us who had been ignorant of the violence inherent in marriage and forced us to confront the unfathomable motivations of abused women. In the unlikely opening scene of Janis Joplin and Big Brother playing a private party for a scowling crowd of jaded upper-class adults in tuxedos and evening gowns, Petulia (Julie Christie), in full sight of her architect husband (Richard Chamberlain), threw herself at an apparent stranger (George C. Scott). After she seduced him back to a fancy hotel, she refused to consummate the affair and, in effect, had simply wasted his time. But before we condemn her as a manipulative cockteasing cold selfish bitch, let us ask what made her this way, and see if we could place the blame there instead. The stranger, Archie, as we soon learned, was an orthopedic surgeon who had saved the life of a Mexican boy in her care. From her broken rib, he suspected and eventually confirmed that her husband beat her. Archie sympathized, yet he was far from honorable. With snide dismissiveness he psychologically abused his own wife, whom he was divorcing only because he was tired of her. He was full of suppressed hostility, thinly veiled misogyny, and probably misanthropy as well, yet he labeled Petulia a "kook." Her life was indeed one sad *non sequitur* after another. She stalked him, and he remained obsessed with her.

Lester showed himself to be a master of the incongruous juxtaposition of the tragic and the comic when, as Petulia's bloody, battered, and nearly dead body was being taken on a stretcher to a hospital, the entire Grateful Dead appeared in cameo roles as passersby. As she was put into the ambulance, Bob Weir cheerily waved, "Bye, bye, Mama." She would not name her attacker. Her rich-ass father-in-law (Joseph Cotten), from whom her husband obviously got his abusive disposition, naturally blamed Petulia for all that she had suffered. When she left the hospital prematurely and went home to her abuser, Archie appointed himself as her secret guardian angel, following them even into a club where the Dead were playing "Viola Lee Blues," and keeping an eye on her. At the end of the film, nothing was resolved.

Domestic abuse, whether psychological belittling or physical violence, can drive its victims insane, insofar as it is the ultimate betrayal of trust: hatred from the beloved, harm from a protector, cruelty from the most benevolent, villainy from a hero, fists from gentle hands.

The Grateful Dead's second album, *Anthem of the Sun*, showed significant movement away from blues and toward psychedelia, and began to establish them as the innovative jam band that would earn the loyal cultic following of legions of Deadheads. Besides their music on its own merits, the Dead were also well served by *The Electric Kool-Aid Acid Test*, Tom Wolfe's chronicle of the druggy, communal, psychedelic experiments of the Merry Pranksters. From 1964 until at least the publication of this book, the Pranksters, devoted to trying all manner of new drugs — in the most bizarre ways possible — existed as a loosely constituted group around the central figure of Ken Kesey. They included beats like Neal Cassady and Allen Ginsberg, younger druggies like Ken Babbs and Hugh ("Wavy Gravy") Romney, LSD zealots like Owsley Stanley, Yippies like Paul Krassner, and hangers-on like Carolyn ("Mountain Girl") Adams, who would later become Jerry Garcia's girlfriend and eventually his wife. From 1965 until 1967, the Warlocks, who, inspired by an Eastern European folklore motif, changed their name to the Grateful Dead in November 1965, were the Pranksters' house band, both absorbing and cultivating the hallucinogenic aura. The Dead lived all this and Wolfe documented it. The fifteen stories that made up Wolfe's other 1968 book, *The Pump House Gang*, likewise added to the countercultural California mystique.

Another drug-crazed California hippie band, Canned Heat, showed off its blues roots when the Blind Owl blew harmonica and sang lead on their new single, the rambling but hypnotic "On the Road Again." The Heat was an FM favorite, not least because of the Bear's and the Blind Owl's encyclopedic knowledge of blues, boogie, and folk rock.

Blues also got boosts this summer from many other bands, both British and American.

Fleetwood Mac, the Anglo-American five-piece group who, after many personnel changes, would become huge middle-of-the-road pop stars in the mid-seventies, started as a solid blues group in London in 1967. With all Britons — drummer Mick Fleetwood and bassist John McVie as the durable core, and fantastic but soon-to-depart guitarists Peter Green and Jeremy Spencer — their debut album, *Fleetwood Mac*, accurately reflected just what they were at the time: solid English bluesmakers.

With Mike Bloomfield on guitar and Buddy Miles on drums, the Electric Flag was almost a supergroup from the beginning. Its problem was that it encompassed so many different musical styles — blues, soul, funk, jazz, horn music — and the attendant egos, that it could neither stay together as a group nor achieve much musical cohesion even while it was together, despite its excellent individual musicians. Its debut album, *A Long Time Comin'*, featured the whole spectrum from blues treasures like Howlin' Wolf's "Killing Floor" to jazz fusion.

Ten Years After's second LP, *Undead*, was just as bluesy as their first, but, being live, was more raw and urgent. Its best track was Alvin Lee's composition, "I'm Going Home," which he would make famous next year at Woodstock. We wondered about the album's title. Did it refer to vampires? Was it a jab at the Grateful Dead? We could not tell.

As usual, we got a lot of blues from Cream on their most recent album, *Wheels of Fire*, a double set with another of those fantastic Martin Sharp covers, this one all silver on the outside but Disraeli-Gearsish pink on the inside. The LP had only thirteen cuts, nine from the studio and four live, but Cream made the most of them. Howlin' Wolf's "Sitting on Top of the World," Booker T.'s and William Bell's "Born Under a Bad Sign," Robert Johnson's "Crossroads," Willie Dixon's "Spoonful," and Jack Bruce's "Traintime" were all pure blues — but the LP had plenty else as well. Ginger Baker's and Mike Taylor's "Passing the Time" was a bit bluesy but more musically diverse and innovative, rather psychedelic and almost *avant garde* in places. Bruce's and Peter Brown's "Politician" was a basic twelve-bar blues tune that pointed up the greed, hypocrisy, amorality, and opportunism of our public servants. Baker's and Taylor's "Pressed Rat and Warthog" highlighted Ginger's spoken monologue of the surrealistic lives of working-class shopkeepers. Bruce's and Brown's "As You Said," an odd *tour de force* for Bruce on cello and twelve-string acoustic guitar, seemed to have been about the passage of time and the transitoriness of life. Baker's and Taylor's "Those Were the Days," Bruce's and Brown's "Deserted Cities of the Heart," and Bruce's and Brown's "White Room" were each solid psychedelic rockers, the last of which gave free rein to Clapton for one his most memorable guitar riffs. Finally, Ginger went apeshit for fifteen minutes on "Toad." God, how we loved that! Who ever would have thought that just an extended drum solo could be so enticing?

With their debut album, *Music From Big Pink*, the Band invented heavy organ-oriented progressive rock and took country rock into a new dimension. As Dylan's protégés and his former backing group, we might have expected to hear more of his influence on the LP than was actually there. Dylan did in fact either write or co-write three of the album's eleven tunes, but the Band really belonged to guitarist Robbie Robertson. All five members took turns on vocals, and each had a distinct voice. Pianist Richard Manuel sang "Tears of Rage," which he co-wrote with Dylan. Drummer Levon Helm sang Robertson's "The Weight." Garth Hudson's mighty organ introduced Manuel's and Helm's vocal duet in Robertson's "Chest Fever." Bassist Rick Danko sang his "This Wheel's on Fire," co-written with Dylan. Manuel's high, light tenor rendered Dylan's "I Shall Be Released."

Donovan released a live album, *In Concert*. The tunes and performances were not bad, but the bozo who introduced him tried to make the crowd believe that Donovan's mystical strength could control the weather. Yet it was a good LP to buy, mainly because of one previously unheard song, "Rules and Regulations," which, as you may imagine, came down against them. Accompanied by only a flute, small drums, and his own acoustic guitar, Donovan created interesting versions of familiar songs, notably "Celeste," "Fat Angel," and "Mellow Yellow." Also this summer, his new single, "Hurdy Gurdy Man," lamented the lack of love throughout humankind.

In Britain, folk rock took an interesting turn back toward the Renaissance with Fairport Convention's self-titled debut album. They were promising, but, with Judy Dyble and not yet Sandy Denny as their lead vocalist, their progress was analogous to that of the Airplane, which had begun with Signe Toly Anderson but after one album had the good sense to acquire Grace Slick. *Fairport Convention*, with Dyble, was their *Jefferson Airplane Takes Off*. Next year's *Liege and Lief*, with Denny, would be their *Surrealistic Pillow*.

Todd Rundgren led soft progressive rock out of Philadelphia with his band's self-titled debut LP, *Nazz*. Two of its tunes, "Open My Eyes" and "Hello, It's Me," got significant FM airplay from DJs who preferred gentler, synthesizer-oriented, Pink-Floydish psychedelia.

The Fifth Dimension's soft pop cover of Laura Nyro's "Stoned Soul Picnic" was about just what it sounded like it was about: a bunch of black people sitting around outside eating lunch and smoking dope. How could the usually overcautious AM radio censors have allowed such an insidious song to go to number three on the singles chart, infecting the impressionable minds of all those teeny boppers and leading them down the primrose path to marijuana addiction? How could they not have understood that title or those lyrics? Were they really that stupid or had they become apathetic? Score that one as a victory for our side. They missed it.

Three comedy or novelty records, Tiny Tim's stupid ultra-falsetto remake of the 1929 ditty, "Tip-Toe Through the Tulips With Me," and two versions of "Here Comes the Judge," the original by Dewey "Pigmeat" Markham, and the cover by Shorty Long, all of which had been popularized on *Laugh-In*, hit the charts.

Zappa's protégé Don Van Vliet, known as Captain Beefheart, scraped the bottom of the album charts with *Safe as Milk*, the debut release of Captain Beefheart and His Magic Band. Like Lou Reed, Beefheart was one of those musicians whom the public, at least at first, mostly ignored, but whom other musicians made sure to heed carefully, believing him to be a genius, a musical force ahead of his time. *Safe as Milk* was generally bluesy, but experimental and *avant garde* as well. Like Zappa's, Beefheart's lyrics were surreal, psychedelic, and political.

Nascent heavy metal took a giant step forward when Deep Purple's debut tune, "Hush," hit both the AM and FM airwaves. We had a feeling that we would be hearing more from these guys.

The Who's new single, "Magic Bus," which probably got more play on FM than on AM, was quintessentially British. Its lyrics were not just about visiting a girlfriend, riding public transportation, or complaining about bus fare inflation, but, beyond all that, they implied a happy-go-lucky, yet sneering, almost contemptuous attitude toward the powers-that-be, in this case, the bus authority. So our disgruntled rider, after the appropriate bantering and haggling, bought his own damn bus! With his newfound freedom and mobility, he was much happier. Again, and as we were coming to expect, Townshend's intelligent wit and humor shone through. Inspired by this song, we would typically call "magic buses" the psychedelically painted Volkswagen Type 2 Transporters, Minibuses, Microbuses, and Kombis that were common sights on American roads from about 1967 through the seventies.

The Rolling Stones released "Jumpin' Jack Flash," a swaggering, hyperbolic celebration of the life of a tough, self-reliant, disadvantaged, working-class hero. Wow! Did that tune ever rock!

Ω

A flag is a piece of cloth. A cross is two rectangular solids intersecting perpendicularly. A gold coin is a hunk of metal. A dollar bill is a piece of paper. To venerate any of these, or any other physical object, to give it special status among physical objects, to call down wrath upon anyone who would desecrate it — is idolatry, plain and simple. Use physical objects as symbols of greater entities if you wish, even of entities that you venerate and may even deserve veneration, but do not venerate any symbol itself. That is idolatry. Call us what you will. We were not idolaters.

One way that frustrated political protesters can attack what they should but cannot attack is to attack the recognized symbols of what they cannot attack.

That is why so many nonviolent protesters against the Vietnam War attacked the American flag. They could not attack America itself. That would have been violent, self-contradictory, and counterproductive, not to mention impractical. But attacking a piece of cloth, regardless of what that cloth might symbolize, can never be considered a violent act. Such acts do not harm anyone. But they make their point — visibly, unambiguously, dramatically.

Thus we in America applauded when we learned that keyboardist Keith Emerson had burned an American flag onstage at the Royal Albert Hall in London during the Nice's performance of Leonard Bernstein's "America." If that was only a publicity stunt to get radical freaks in America to pay attention to the Nice and buy their debut album, *The Thoughts of Emerlist Davjack*, it worked. But we were not so cynical. We believed that Emerson's action was sincere. Progressive rock was political. One did not get into progressive rock if one was not political. Keith was cool!

1968 was a good time to be burning, ripping, snotting into, pissing on, and otherwise attacking the American flag and other symbols of America. Not much that America *qua* America was doing was worth celebrating.

Some freaks complained that *Hair* was watered-down radicalism — and in many respects that complaint was justified. Nevertheless, *Hair* was, for all that, *our* intrusion onto *their* turf. As such we had to be aware of it, whatever its faults or shortcomings. Only a few of us ever got to see it on Broadway, but many more of us were exposed to its message after the original cast recording brought its songs to the whole nation in August. The music was bouncy and not especially heavy, but its lyrics dealt rather frankly with issues of racial bigotry and segregation, drugs, plasticity, hypocrisy, prejudice, premarital sex, masturbation, interracial love, the war, conservatism, environmentalism, casual encounters, religion, technology, lust, the space program, greed, street surviving, government waste, and, of course, personal freedom. *Hair* contained profanity and racial slurs, had a strongly interracial cast, made fun of the flag and flag-worshippers, exuded joy, quoted Shakespeare, and was occasionally funny. A minor problem was that it indulged in stereotypes and created a few. Its big problem was that it reduced us to "flower children," or made us out to be starry-eyed New Agers. The so-called "New Age" was a ridiculous syncretism of spacy religions, naive attitudes, and convenient mythologies. Some of us bought into it, but the logical among us wanted no part of it.

A far superior theatrical / musical / lyrical representation of radical causes in general and the black cause in particular was the work of the Last Poets. Of course, this was street theater, not Broadway or even off-Broadway. Specifically to honor Malcolm X and to help Eldridge Cleaver, who was in California, spread the Black Panther message in the east, three New York City black activists, Gylan Kain, David Nelson, and Abiodun Oyewole, founded the Last Poets at a poetry reading in Marcus Garvey Park, Harlem, on Malcolm's birthday. They would undergo several personnel changes and their first LP would not appear until 1970.

It almost seemed that, in the words of Jimmy Durante, "Everybody wants to get into da act." The political act, that is. People whom we never expected to be political ... were. But the time demanded it — demanded action. The situation in 1968 was serious.

Even straightlaced comedian Ray Stevens contributed a political song to the mix. "Mr. Businessman" did not sell very well (only three weeks on the *Billboard* singles chart topping out at number twenty-eight), but that did not matter. The fact that he had done it at all gained him a measure of credibility and respect among us freaks who would otherwise pooh-pooh his "Ahab the Arab" and "Gitarzan."

Most of us who were against the war and the draft tried very hard to keep our protests nonviolent — and therefore more effective. We were not uneasy about attacking property, objects, or symbols, but we worried about hurting any humans, including ourselves, in the process. A perfect example of a successful anti-draft protest was when nine Roman Catholics, both clergy and lay, acting purely from their Christian religious consciences, broke into the Selective Service office in Catonsville, Maryland, and burned draft records with homemade napalm. These heroes, the "Catonsville Nine," were Fathers Daniel and Philip Berrigan, Brother David Darst, Brother John Hogan, Thomas Lewis, Marjorie and Thomas Melville, George Mische, and Mary Moylan. This was how religion should be always used, in the service of peace, freedom, humanity, and life, not as the lackey of the state, conservatism, conformity, or death.

The civil rights movement tried equally hard to be nonviolent. After Martin Luther King's death, the Rev. Ralph David Abernathy and the Rev. Jesse Jackson were the *de facto*, if not also the *de jure*, leaders of the nonviolent side of the civil rights movement. Together they led a coalition of activists called the Poor People's Campaign, which marched on Washington and built a shanty town, Resurrection City, around the Reflecting Pool between the Lincoln Memorial and the Washington Monument. Among the participants' points was to emphasize that black people were overwhelmingly poor, not because of laziness, ambitionlessness, dullness, natural inferiority, or even bad luck, but because the white financial and social structures kept them down, denied them the ways, means, or opportunities to break out of poverty, and did this deliberately. The project failed to raise much consciousness about endemic socioeconomic injustice, but it did raise quite a few eyebrows about squalor, and quite a few legitimate concerns about public health. After six weeks the Civil Disturbance Unit of the District of Columbia Metropolitan Police Department peacefully closed Resurrection City and later bulldozed it. Between 1000 and 2000 police were involved. Over a hundred demonstrators, including Abernathy, were arrested. The National Guard was called in. No riot occurred.

Nevertheless, America remained gun-happy. Valerie Solanis tried to murder Andy Warhol. Sirhan Bishara Sirhan succeeded in murdering Bobby Kennedy, thus throwing the Democratic Party into more turmoil than it was already in. With LBJ out of the primaries, Bobby had led the race for the presidential nomination over two Minnesotans, Vice President Hubert Humphrey and Senator Eugene McCarthy. Rightly or wrongly, we believed that Humphrey would be four more years of LBJ. McCarthy offered a real alternative, but he was an opportunist flake. The party, and therefore the country, was in a lose-lose situation: either a lousy Democratic president or a Republican — or the jingoist racist George Wallace. Even with Wallace siphoning votes from the Republican nominee, whoever he might turn out to be, the Democrats without Bobby did not have a prayer of keeping the White House. It was not an ebullient party that went to Chicago late that August.

The ebullience was in the streets!

Thousands of antiwar protesters flocked to Chicago, vastly outnumbering the people who were there for the convention. They did not seek to influence the balloting at the convention, but rather to make sure that the nominee, whether Humphrey or McCarthy, would know that ending the war and the draft immediately upon taking office in January 1969 was what Americans wanted. The protests were large but peaceful.

The problem was the satrap of Chicago, Mayor Richard Joseph Daley, an ultrarightist holdover from the glory days of machine politics, a Democrat in name only, a key collaborator with J. Edgar Hoover's FBI, a cruel, militaristic, ruthless, intolerant, hateful, spiteful, sixty-six-year-old son-of-a-bitch.

Daley would be embarrassed if any antiwar activity were to happen in *his* city or if anything were to tarnish what he perceived as the pristine image of *his* convention. A macho man like Daley would have been embarrassed ever to be embarrassed, so he was determined not to be embarrassed. He called out his dogs.

With a zeal and efficiency that would have made the Gestapo proud, his Chicago police harassed, attacked, beat, gassed, kicked, bloodied, and brutalized peaceful, harmless, unarmed protesters every day and night of the convention. His big mistake was allowing this to happen on worldwide live TV! While the whole world watched, he and his police revealed not only themselves, but also the American prowar faction in general, as nothing but Nazis. In addition to their usual antiwar slogans, the beleaguered crowd chanted, "The whole world's watching! The whole world's watching! The whole world's watching!"

Officially sanctioned violence occurred inside the convention hall as well. While the whole world watched on Tuesday, August 27, Walter Cronkite called the security guards "thugs" who punched CBS TV floor reporter Dan Rather in the stomach. Deservedly well respected ABC TV newsman Howard K. Smith hosted his network's coverage of the convention. As a sort of coup over the other two national networks, Smith had booked the famous leftist intellectual Gore Vidal and the famous rightist intellectual William F. Buckley, Jr. to provide contrapuntal commentary on the unfolding events. Naturally Buckley was disgusted by the filthy, long-haired hippies in the streets, while Vidal was at least as disgusted by Daley's cops. The two ideological adversaries were mostly civil to each other, but Vidal often goaded Buckley. On Wednesday August 28, in the middle of prime time, 9:38 p.m. Eastern Daylight Time, Vidal, placidly defending the demonstrations outside, despite Buckley's constant attempts to interrupt, began:

> You must realize what some of the political issues are here. Many people in the United States happen to believe that the United States policy is wrong in Vietnam and the Vietcong are correct in wanting to organize their country in their own way politically. This happens to be pretty much the opinion of Western Europe and of many other parts of the world. If it is a novelty in Chicago, that is too bad, but I assume that the point of the American democracy ... [Buckley interrupted] ... is that you can express any point of view you want... [Buckley interrupted]

> Vidal: Shut up a minute.

> Buckley: No, I won't. Some people were pro-Nazi and the answer is that they were well treated by people who ostracized them, and I am for ostracizing people who egg on other people to shoot American Marines and American soldiers. I know you don't ... [Vidal interrupted]

> Vidal: As far as I'm concerned, the only pro- or crypto-Nazi I can think of is yourself. Failing that ... [Smith and Buckley both interrupted, Smith apparently to try to defuse the escalating anger]

> Smith: Let's stop calling names.

> Buckley: Now listen, you queer, stop calling me a crypto-Nazi, or I'll sock you in the goddam face and you'll stay plastered.

As Buckley quite lost his cool, calling Vidal a pornographer and introducing his own military record and several other irrelevant matters, Vidal sat calmly grinning, smug in his assurance that he had scored points. Bravo!

The same week as the Democratic National Convention in Chicago, the interracial Chambers Brothers band released its haunting, incisive, inflammatory anthem, "Time Has Come Today." Did we need any further reminders that now was the crisis, the *kairos*, the critical time, the right time for action, the fleeting opportunity, the waning moment, the due season, *our time*, soon to be lost forever?

Ω

For many of us the cultural highlight of the summer was *The Prisoner*, a British TV series that ran in seventeen hour-long episodes.[54] We were hooked even from the opening sequence of the first episode, "Arrival." We knew that this series was going to be extraordinary. Whatever we were doing that summer, we made absolutely sure to be free to watch it every Saturday night.

"Arrival" opened with a thunderclap and a stark scene of nature's sublimity in the looming storm. As an immediately unforgettable trumpet riff hit our ears, we saw Patrick McGoohan playing a character whom we instantly recognized as John Drake (although the identity of this character was never stated explicitly and remained a controversial point even beyond McGoohan's death in January 2009). Drake, driving the ideal secret agent car, better than James Bond's Aston Martin, a low-slung, sexy Lotus convertible, license plate KAR 120C, sped into the Westminster section of London and into an underground parking garage. He thundered down a long, Spartan corridor and into his boss's opulent office, where he made no attempt to restrain his fury as he slammed a sealed envelope marked "PRIVATE — PERSONAL   BY HAND" down onto his boss's desk. As he strode back out, robotic and mechanical arms were already updating his dossier and refiling it in the "Resigned" drawer. A sleek, black, limosine-like hearse, license plate TLH 858, tailed Drake home. As he packed his luggage, the driver of the hearse, an elderly formal man in frock coat and top hat, gassed him through the keyhole. The elegant hearse and undertaker-like gasser symbolized all the rich powers-that-be against the common man, who only wanted to be free, but had found that he had had to resign from service to that rich establishment in order to be so.

Drake awoke, groggy, but apparently believing that he was still in his own London flat. He looked out the window to see only a quaint, beautiful little village, colorful and ornate like something out of a child's storybook. Only very briefly shocked and bewildered, he at once mustered his secret agent training, resolved to use whatever strength or cunning he would need to get back to London. He did not yet realize that he was a prisoner. This fact dawned on him when he entered the thoroughly automated "Green Dome" to accept Number Two's breakfast invitation. He was in what was known only as "The Village."

Within the first six minutes, through Drake's encounter with an East Asian taxi driver who spoke to him in both English and French but thought that he may have been a Pole or a Czech, we were made to know that the Village was a microcosm of the entire world — an ideal world, on some views. Comfort was total, but

---

[54] The proper order of the episodes is very controversial. The order followed here is that of the original British broadcasts from October 1, 1967, to February 4, 1968. The 1968 CBS run was: "Arrival" (June 1), "The Chimes of Big Ben" (June 8 and rerun June 15), "A. B. and C." (June 22), "Free for All" (June 29), "The Schizoid Man" (July 6), "The General" (July 13), "Many Happy Returns" (July 20), "Dance of the Dead" (July 27), "Do Not Forsake Me Oh My Darling" (August 3), "It's Your Funeral" (August 10), "Checkmate" (August 17), "A Change of Mind" (August 24), "Hammer Into Anvil" (August 31), "The Girl Who Was Death" (September 7), "Once Upon a Time" (September 14), and "Fall Out" (September 21).

so was surveillance. Every citizen was cared for, but no one, except perhaps Number Two (the visible presence of government) and Number One (the invisible, unknown, but, we presumed, ultimate presence of government) had any privacy.

Number Two was friendly, welcoming, but unyielding. He frankly told Drake that the reason he had been brought to the Village was so that Number Two and his superiors could learn why he had resigned. They believed that the information inside Drake's head was too valuable to allow that question to remain unanswered. Drake told Number Two that his reasons were personal and that his life was his own, not to be meddled with or studied by anyone. Drake's refusal to cooperate with established authority, and his steadfast conviction that the essence of freedom is the absolute autonomy of the individual, was the overriding theme of the whole series.

The Village was bounded by impassable mountains on three sides and by the sea on the fourth. Escape was impossible. Its last, and most formidable, defense against escape was "Rover," an immense, bulbous, pure white menace, which could at any time be summoned to engulf any would-be escapee or malefactor. Those of us who had read *Moby Dick*, above all Chapter 42, "The Whiteness of the Whale," and Chapter 76, "The Battering-Ram," instantly recognized Rover's import: grim, faceless, mindless, cruelly efficient, and ineluctably mysterious.

We never learned who ran the Village. Perhaps the British Secret Service, perhaps the Soviets, perhaps some third group. Somehow that was never important. The important point was Drake's resistance to authority, whichever authority it was. God or Satan, it made no difference. His anger gradually subsided and transformed into an amused wiliness, so that, instead of raging and ranting against the Village, he began to play a sort of chess game against it. This transition was marked in the twenty-eighth minute of "Arrival," when he for the first time allowed himself to use the Village's standard farewell, "Be seeing you." Anger was tantamount to brute force. That would not work. Wiliness was the more subtle weapon of the free mind. With that he at least had a chance to preserve himself intact.

In the thirty-eighth minute our unnamed hero (whom for convenience heretofore we have called "Drake") learned that he not only lived in number six and had the phone number six, but that he also was to be called "Number Six." Numbering people is the nth degree of objectifying them. Governments cannot deal adequately with people, only with objects. Number Six reminded the new Number Two that he was a person, not a number, to which the new Number Two replied, "Six of one, a half a dozen of another." As we were to see throughout the series, the identity and strategy of Number Two, the main authority figure, changed frequently. The face of government changed, but the government itself remained the same. It had life beyond whatever humanity it may have had. The Village apparently numbered its citizens in order of their importance. Number Six was important, not for his authority, as he had none, except over himself, but for the information that he had and that "they" wanted.

At the beginning of the second episode, "The Chimes of Big Ben," the new Number Two, surveilling Number Six, was very impressed that he could "make even the act of putting on his dressing gown appear as a gesture of defiance." In this scene Number Two explained the overarching aim of the rulers of the Village with regard to Number Six: not to break or damage him, but to win him over — intact — to the Village's way of thinking. In that way the Village could use him for future practical purposes, putting to best advantage the zeal of a convert. Their fundamental question, "Why did he resign?" was thus tantamount to, "Why won't he conform?" If they had only each searched their own well hidden human souls, they could have discovered the answer without even asking him.

Number Six pretended to make a deal with Number Two, not disclosing the information that Number Two wanted, but agreeing to try to fit harmoniously into the tightly controlled Village life. In exchange, Number Two would quit torturing a Soviet woman spy, Number Eight, who, like Number Six, had resigned and had been brought to the Village to be asked why. Number Six and Number Eight at first did not trust each other, each apparently believing that the other was a guard rather than a fellow prisoner. But, gradually gaining each other's trust, they together planned and successfully executed their escape. The dénouement revealed that Number Eight, Number Two, and two of Number Six's former superiors in the British Secret Service were all in cahoots, plotting to trick Number Six — intact — into telling, of his own free will, why he had resigned. Number Six foiled the plot, but, given the collaboration across the Iron Curtain, we viewers were left in renewed wonder about who ran the Village, yet at the same time were more than ever convinced that East or West did not matter, that the Village was intended as microcosm or metaphor for the whole world community, bent on stifling individual dignity and freedom in the name of "order."

In the third episode, "A. B. and C.," Number Two and Number Fourteen used electroencephalography and a psychoactive drug to try to penetrate and decipher Number Six's mind, memories, and thoughts. By inducing him to dream, and by controlling and monitoring the content of these dreams, they hoped to learn why he resigned. From situation "A" they learned that he did not intend either to defect or to sell out his country to the other Cold War side. Situation "B," in which they tried to get him to confide in an old friend who was being threatened, failed because, even though he was unconscious, his powerful will resisted their probes and revealed this "friend" as a manipulated phantom. As he gradually remembered these two dreams, his capacity to resist the nightly invasion of his subconscious grew stronger. Suspicious of Number Fourteen, he followed her, discovered her laboratory, snuck into it, diluted the drug, then, that night, pretended unconsciousness and constructed his own dream "C" to thwart their inquiry. Mind over matter.

"Free for All" satirized the standard Western liberal democratic political process. In the Village it was impossible for any denizen to know with certainty who were the guards and who were the prisoners. Even those who believed themselves to be guards were sometimes, in fact, prisoners. Number Six had no doubt that he was only a prisoner, so he was quite surprised when the new Number Two invited him to run for the office of Number Two in the annual election. Number Two responded to Number Six's skepticism kindly, assuring him, "Humor is the very essence of a democratic society." Elections were depicted as a game, an extended *ad populum* fallacy. The illusion was democracy; the reality was dictatorship. The visible ruler (Number Two) was a figurehead; the actual ruler (Number One) remained unknown, unnamed, and invisible.

The so-called election was really an elaborate, carefully scripted and rigidly choreographed scheme to brainwash and debrief Number Six by inducing neurosis with Mickey Finns, hypnosis, modified shock therapy, and physical violence — in a way not unlike that employed against Harry Palmer in *The Ipcress File*. Yet, like Palmer, Number Six reasserted his individuality by sheer strength of will. He won in a landslide, but only because all the citizens had been ordered or forced to vote for him in a non-secret ballot. As he took on the role of Number Two, he found himself powerless, with even less power than when he had been an ordinary citizen. When he told the people to escape and be free, they ignored him. The irony and irreconcilable paradox of his desperate plea, "I am in command! Obey me and be free!" was apparently lost on him.

In "The Schizoid Man," the fifth episode, the new Number Two and his team of scientists used a combination of plastic surgery on Number Twelve and Pavlovian or Skinnerian conditioned reflex techniques on Number Six's subconscious to prepare a duplicate Number Six that would in many ways be more like Number Six than Number Six himself. The purpose was to make Number Six doubt his own identity, lose at least a portion of his sanity, and thereby become amenable to revealing why he resigned. But Number Six, just before he would have cracked, discovered the truth of the plot and took appropriate action, tricking Rover into killing Number Twelve, the phony Number Six. The point of the story seemed to be Cartesian, i.e., that true individual human identity lies in the inviolable, unitary, non-physical entity that Descartes would call "thinking substance" or that a Christian would call the "soul," and not, as the behaviorists believed, in any mere aggregation of physical characteristics.

"The General" was, philosophically, the most important episode in the series. A recurring theme in *The Prisoner* was that life could be happy for people who did not ask questions, but rough for those who did. The Village, guards and prisoners alike, actively discouraged its citizens, again guards and prisoners alike, from asking questions and constantly reminded them that docility meant happiness. Thus, to the Village's ideal citizens, obedient sheep, education would be only the memorization or absorption of lessons, not also the discussion or understanding of the conceptual content or implications of these lessons. On the memorization / absorption model of education, the teacher was a pourer and students were empty vessels waiting to be filled. Students sat in expectation of the teacher's gift, but the teacher had nothing to gain from the students. There was no exchange of ideas, but only the one-way dispensation of them, ready-made. Viewers of this episode were accordingly led to consider the difference, if any, between education, particularly the memorization / absorption model of education, and brainwashing, and to ask whether the relationship between teacher and student was necessarily analogous to that between lord and vassal, or whether it could be collegial, or at least less asymmetrical.

The General was a supercomputer jammed full of every known scientific fact and technique, as well as knowledge of literature, history, art, philosophy, and all the humanities. Number Two claimed that it could answer any question and teach any student three years worth of college-level material in three minutes. It could indeed do this — but without understanding. Moreover, the General failed to distinguish between factual and technical knowledge, on the one hand, and meditative or contemplative knowledge, on the other. It did not even recognize the latter. Even though it had "read" Aristotle's *Nicomachean Ethics*, including the section in Book VI on the five intellectual virtues, it had apparently not grasped them adequately. These virtues are: knowledge of how to do or make something (*technê*), factual knowledge (*epistêmê*), practical wisdom or "streetwise" political or social skills (*phronêsis*), philosophical wisdom (*sophia*), and overarching intelligence or pure contemplation (*nous*). Being an indefinitely powerful calculative thinker, the General could employ well enough the first two, and occasionally the third, but, not being sentient or self-conscious, it could not deal at all with the last two. It could not even comprehend the very existence of these last two. Indeed, the computer was probably called the General because the military teaches us facts, crafts, and skills, but not how to think, ask questions, or understand.

Number Six clearly saw the danger to the human spirit that the General posed. He succeeded in destroying it just by asking it the one insoluble question: "WHY?"

Number Six awakened in the seventh episode to find the Village deserted. Believing an attempt to escape over the mountains futile, he built a good, seaworthy raft from logs and 55-gallon drums, loaded up provisions from the abandoned store, took photos of the Village to serve as eventual proof that he was not dreaming, and set off. After twenty-five days at sea, the German crew of a small gunrunning boat discovered him as he slept and tried to rob and murder him, but in the nick of time he boarded the boat, overpowered the two scoundrels, and saved himself. He made land in Kent, near Dover, where Gypsies directed him to a road. He hopped a ride and found his way back to his own flat in London. He had become nervous, neurotic, almost paranoid, and his social skills had degenerated to confrontational abruptness. The middle-aged woman now inhabiting his flat was also driving his Lotus. His suspicion abated somewhat as she showed him only frankness, kindness, and care; but upon returning to his old superiors, he was greeted by hostile skepticism. Nevertheless, as true professionals in the Cold War espionage business, they investigated his report, calculated from his sea log the Village's possible location, and made plans to try to find it. Their aerial search was successful, but, just as Number Six spotted the Village, the pilot of his plane turned toward him, said "Be seeing you," and ejected him, thus forcing him to parachute back into the Village. That is why this episode was called "Many Happy Returns." Its point seemed to be that, no matter how we may try to escape the world, we are always in the world. The Village is the world and the world is the Village. Upon returning, Number Six found the Village no longer deserted, and the middle-aged woman from his London flat was the new Number Two.

The eighth episode, "Dance of the Dead," was among the most surrealistic and least satisfying of the seventeen. Number Six was subjected to electromedical torture by an overzealous physician with all the sensibilities of Josef Mengele, but was rescued when the new Number Two intervened. Subsequent events culminated in a morbid "carnival" during which Number Six, prosecuted by Little Bo-Peep, defended by Peter Pan, and calling a brain-damaged court jester as a character witness, was sentenced to death by a three-judge panel of Julius Caesar, Queen Elizabeth I, and Napoléon Bonaparte, for the crime of possessing a radio.

Chess was among the primary recurring metaphors of *The Prisoner*. In the ninth episode, "Checkmate," individuality was likened to chess pieces moving on their own, without direction from either player, thus rendering the game impossible. The issue was trust. Not being able to tell the guards from the prisoners, the prisoners from the guards, the white pieces from the black, or the black pieces from the white, how could Number Six ever know whom to trust in order to plan a successful escape? The implied wider question, in relation to our real Cold War world, was, "How could anyone tell, just by knowing a person, whether that person supported or opposed the current regime?" Any ostensible antiwar activist could in fact be an *agent provocateur*, a CIA plant, an LBJ dupe, a John Wayne ideologue. We could not tell. Politically, practically, against our better nature, we had to be suspicious, and suspicion was stifling, counterproductive, self-defeating. It played into the hands of the rulers, the warmongers, the backbenchers, the reactionaries, the entrenched oppressors of the free individual. Our peaceful revolution promised and promoted trust, but we had to be untrusting and untrustworthy in order to further that revolution. The Village was indeed global. It was our world. No escape from it was possible short of interplanetary travel — and escape velocity could not be achieved by anyone working alone. The paradox was complete. The pawns and pieces alike were all doomed. Checkmate was assured. ***They*** had already won.

Disgusted by the brutal interrogation techniques of the tenth episode's new Number Two, which had already driven a prisoner to suicide, Number Six vowed to avenge her death. The title of this episode, "Hammer Into Anvil," derived from Goethe's poem, *Ein Andres* ("An Other"):

Geh'! gehorche meinen Winken,	Go! Obey my signals,
Nutze deine jungen Tage,	Use your youthful days,
Lerne zeitig klüger sein!	Learn early to be more clever!
Auf des Glückes grosser Waage	On the grand scales of fortune
Steht die Zunge selten ein.	The tongue seldom matters.
Du musst steigen oder sinken,	You must rise or sink,
Du musst herrschen und gewinnen	You must prevail and win
Oder dienen und verlieren,	Or serve and lose,
Leiden oder triumphieren,	Suffer or triumph,
Amboss oder Hammer sein	Be either anvil or hammer

Number Two, as the hammer, threatened to beat on the anvil, Number Six, until the anvil cracked. Number Six was not cowed by Number Two's sadism or bullying, but noticed that Number Two lived in a world governed by fear, and that in particular Number Two trembled in fear of Number One. Playing on this fundamental flaw in Number Two's nature, Number Six put a sneaky plan into action. By concocting and performing a series of bizarre, meaningless, and seemingly illogical actions, though with just enough internal logic to suggest a meaningful connection among them, Number Six convinced Number Two that Number One had sent him (Six) to the Village specifically to spy on Number Two. Now believing that Number Six was not really a prisoner after all, but Number One's plant, Number Two's paranoia increased with each new incident. One of these incidents involved Number Six inserting, as a personal ad in the Village newspaper, a Spanish quotation from *Don Quixote*, First Part, Chapter XLVI, where Sancho told his master, "... hay más mal en el aldegüela que se suena," which means, "there is more evil in the Village than they tell you." Number Two apparently knew his Goethe better than he knew his Cervantes. He became the anvil, was broken by his own evil turned inward, and whimpered himself into total defeat.

The episode thus concluded on the optimistic note that intelligence in the end should always triumph over brute force. It led us toward identifying the free individual with the cultured thinker, the comprehensively educated person, while identifying the conformist, conservative, or apparatchik with the dullard, the ignorant brute. Perhaps those identifications would not always be accurate, but, for the time being, seeing ourselves as cultured while seeing LBJ, for example, as a brutish boor admired by goons, made us feel very good.

"Hammer Into Anvil" showed one of only a few clear victories for Number Six. Each of these victories further authenticated him as a champion — perhaps the Village's only champion — of humanity and civility against the overwhelming, intimidating, and well entrenched forces of inhumanity and crudeness. Number Six was a knight errant, but, far from the futile knight errantry of Don Quixote, the knight errantry of Number Six bore fruit, because it was grounded in lucid perspective, sound ideology, accurate observation, and realistic practicality.

Music played a large part in "Hammer Into Anvil." Number Six used Bizet in his psychological campaign against Number Two. Even the Village itself seemed in this episode to be promoting music. Among its visible slogans were, "Music makes a quiet mind," "Music begins where words leave off," and "Music says all."

"It's Your Funeral" was a confusing and rather incoherent episode. Number Six found himself wrapped up in a plot by the acting Number Two to assassinate the old Number Two, but why the acting Number Two felt any need to involve Number Six in the plot, or what this involvement might have had to do with the Village's general purpose in learning why Number Six resigned from government service, were not made clear. Indeed, the plot seemed more plausible or realistic without the complication of having added Number Six to it. We viewers could easily imagine a simpler version succeeding. In any case, Number Six, for no other reason than compassion for his fellow prisoners, whom he believed would be summarily, savagely, and indiscriminately punished if the assassination succeeded, foiled the plot and rescued the old Number Two.

Each of the new Number Twos throughout the series personified a different aspect of the way that social or political oppression typically occurs. Fat and oily, the Number Two of the twelfth episode, "A Change of Mind," personified peer pressure, one of the most insidious of these aspects. Ubiquitous "Your Community Needs You" posters showed Number Two in the beckoning posture of Uncle Sam on the "I Want You for U.S. Army" posters or of Horatio Herbert Kitchener on the

"Lord Kitchener Wants You" posters that, once answered, sent hundreds of thousands of young British men to their miserable deaths in the Battle of the Somme in 1916.

The plot revealed peer pressure as what it really is in any society, not just the Village: a vicious and powerful form of brainwashing. It proceeds as an inquisition, badgering otherwise free-spirited individuals into confession, conformity, complicity, or worse. Of course, Number Six was immune to such transparent and heavy-handed coercion, or so he thought. He found himself shunned, just as if he were *persona non grata* in a fundamentalist Christian community or cultic sect. He was hauled up before a citizens' committee of small-minded lemmings, consigned to social readjustment groups that resembled communist re-education cadres, branded with such labels as "reactionary," "disharmonious," and "unmutual," and threatened with "instant social conversion," which included the possibility of several behaviorist favorites: shock therapy, aversion therapy, or psychosurgery as a last resort. He also daily faced the unwanted intervention of cranky social workers. Finding himself between Scylla and Charybdis, i.e, between the psychological effect of solitary confinement, on the one hand, and conforming, on the other, he defied both, chose neither, and so was condemned. By a combination of drugs and play-acting, minions tried to trick him into believing that he had undergone psychosurgery, but he in turn tricked them into believing that their ruse had succeeded. He drugged and hypnotized one of the chief minions, then tricked her into denouncing Number Two himself as "unmutual." When Number Six spoke in support of her accusation, the lemmings, convinced that Number Six had been "socially converted" and was now one of them, attacked Number Two. The mob could not tolerate individuality, even in its leader.

The thirteenth episode revisited the topic of Cartesian mind/body dualism. A certain Professor Seltzman had invented a machine that could switch minds between two humans. The Village had obtained the machine, but Seltzman had escaped. The new Number Two, intent upon capturing the well-meaning neurologist so as to force him to work for the Village, switched Number Six's mind with that of one of the Village's high-level operatives and allowed Number Six to wake up in his old London flat. Number Two knew that Number Six would soon realize accurately what had happened to his mind and body, would then seek Seltzman in order to reclaim his own body, and, as resourceful as ever, would find him. He did find Seltzman, but within minutes the tail that Number Two had put on Number Six gassed them both and brought them back to the Village.

The episode's title, "Do Not Forsake Me Oh My Darling," was taken from the lyrics of the main theme music of the 1952 classic film, *High Noon*, in which Grace Kelly's character, Amy Kane, forsook her pacifist religious principles at the last minute to save the life of her gallant husband, Will Kane, played by Gary Cooper. What the connection between this episode and this movie might have been was not clear, except that it could have referred to Seltzman's pretending to forsake his principles and capitulate to Number Two's demands, so that he could not only save his own life and regain his freedom, but also restore the unified identity and original mind/body integrity of his friend, Number Six.

Granting separate or independent entity status to the non-physical "mind" is a touchy philosophical problem, and the fact that *The Prisoner* series in general granted such entity status may reveal its pro-Cartesian or perhaps even pro-Christian bias. Certainly its stance was anti-physicalist, anti-behaviorist, anti-reductionist, and anti-materialist; but one may reject all those positions without going all the way to the opposite extreme of substantialist mind/body dualism.

CBS censors, believing that the fourteenth episode, "Living in Harmony," was too near an allegory of the Vietnam War, refused to allow it to be broadcast during the original 1968 American run of the series. The reason they gave publicly for banning it was that it contained too many hallucinogenic drug references. We immediately suspected that that was a lie. TV spy dramas and thrillers, including several other episodes of *The Prisoner*, were full of evil drugs, and no one was ruling against them. We knew that censors, especially TV censors, and even more especially CBS TV censors, the scourge of the Smothers Brothers, were much more likely to rule against sex or politics than against drugs. Because there was very little of a sexual nature in *The Prisoner*, we suspected that the reason was politics. We were right. The first appearance in America of "Living in Harmony" was in syndication in 1971. As soon as we at last saw it, we recognized its pacifist political allegory, just the kind of thing that pro-Vietnam-War hawks would hate.

"The Girl Who Was Death" was the most palpably satirical episode. Indeed, it was quite silly, and could be taken as a comic interlude among the other sixteen. Its target was the spy movies, TV shows, and books that were popular throughout the sixties — not *The Spy Who Came in from the Cold*, *The Ipcress File*, or the other serious ones — but the semi-serious, *outré*, or downright goofy ones, like the James Bond series, *The Man from U.N.C.L.E.*, *The Avengers*, *Mission: Impossible*, *I Spy*, *Secret Agent*, *Get Smart*, etc. Familiar motifs from each of these could be discerned in this episode. For example, in one scene the girl, Death, used the same Turkish bath trick on Number Six that Bond used against Count Lippe in Chapter Four of Ian Fleming's *Thunderball* and in the 1965 movie; and at the end Number Six saved London from a rocket attack similar to that planned by Hugo Drax in the book, *Moonraker*.

A cricket match in a children's story book came to life. A cricketer was murdered by an exploding cricket ball. Number Six and other spies got involved. Unnecessary gadgets and improbable disguises abounded. Illogical communications triggered ridiculous events in absurd places. Number Six sported late nineteenth-century sideburns with a handlebar mustache and wore a deerstalker and tweeds to pass as Sherlock Holmes in late twentieth-century England. A car chase became surreal. Props were conjured out of nowhere as in a Road Runner cartoon. Fights seemed to have been choreographed for the Keystone Kops. Number Six battled a chief Napoléon and six subordinate Napoléons (in a possible reference to Arthur Conan Doyle's short story about Holmes). This episode would have been nothing but light entertainment if we had not learned one big, sobering lesson: There were very young children in the Village.

The last two episodes, "Once Upon a Time" and "Fall Out," should be considered as two parts of a single episode. We may be tempted to regard them both as nonsensical, but, given the underlying sense and logic — albeit often difficult to understand — of the most of the first fifteen, they deserve instead to be taken as allegorical and surrealistic, but no less sensible or logical.

As "Once Upon a Time" began, Rover occupied Number Two's usual chair, apparently signifying the facelessness and anonymity of ultimate, absolute power. The new Number Two, or rather, the returned Number Two from the second episode, "The Chimes of Big Ben," was angry and frustrated that he, all the other Number Twos, and Number One had all so far failed to find out what motivated the free spirit of Number Six. So Number Two asked him the direct question, "Why do you care?" to which Number Six replied with a smirk, "You'll never know."

At the last stage of desperation, Number Two requested and received from Number One the authorization for "degree absolute," a week-long, technologically aided psychological duel to the death between himself and Number Six, presided over by the fat little butler, who appeared silently in every episode and who may or may not have been either Number One or Number One's agent assigned to watch Number Two. The duel involved regression to childhood and partially followed the pattern of Shakespeare's famous division in *As You Like It* of a human life into seven ages: infant, schoolboy, lover, soldier, wise man, old man, and second childhood. Through all Number Two's proddings, torments, and temptations, Number Six retained his innate sense of honor, describing himself as "a fool, not a rat," and so in the end was able to make Number Two psychologically vulnerable to him, instead of, as Number Two had hoped, the other way around. Number Six won the duel; Number Two seemed to die; and Number Six, whom the butler and the supervisor now recognized as their boss, demanded to be taken to Number One. There the episode ended.

Its sequel, "Fall Out," even though the last episode, was not a dénouement. Little was explicitly resolved — yet, with some introspection, we could conjecture a few conclusions about the overall meaning of the series. The butler and the supervisor dutifully and without guile began to grant Number Six's wish. They gave him his own clothes back. As the three walked down a rocky, subterranean corridor, a row of jukeboxes played the Beatles' "All You Need is Love" in unison. The butler unlocked a massive medieval door at the end of the corridor to reveal a large, multipurpose room with soldiers marching, characters in stark black-and-white masks, banks of computers and other technological wonders, medical personnel, a wigged judge, and steaming holes not unlike those in Canto XIX of Dante's *Inferno*, but with victims upright instead of upside-down. A seeming chaos, but perhaps not. The judge presided over a large assembly of applauding bozos wearing white hoods and robes, looking rather like Ku Klux Klansmen, faces hidden by hideous black-left-white-right masks of tragedy, and each with a name plate to indicate his allegorical significance. While still asserting the right and value of any community to use extreme force to build itself and to bend the individual toward it, the judge warmly acknowledged that Number Six, through pure revolt, had succeeded in justifying the individual as an individual, and henceforth was no longer to be numbered, but simply addressed with respect as "Sir." The former Number Six was given the throne of honor. Throughout all this, the judge took direct orders from a giant, mechanical, steaming, light-flashing, one-eyed, white column with a big red number "1" on it.

At the judge's command, the medicos revived Number Two. The judge then announced that he would try three species of rebellion. First, the revolt of youth, the anarchic, purposeless revolt of sheer enthusiasm. He released its archetypal defendant from one of the steaming holes, a cheeky young rebel who immediately began singing, "Dem Bones," the traditional African-American spiritual based on Ezekiel 37:1-14. The whole assembly, despite the judge's disapproval, instantly got up and danced like spastics, apparently identifying with the dead, dry bones that were to be given new life. Ezekiel was the prophet of individual responsibility, as can be seen in Chapter 18, where he refuted the ancient Hebrew belief that the sins of the father would be visited upon the sons. Yet, for Ezekiel, despite the new accountability of each individual for his own moral fate, individuality remained subordinate, and morally inferior, to the needs of the community. The judge eventually joined in the dance, but found the young rebel guilty anyway, of defiance, asking questions, dressing oddly, sassing, and other sins against "social etiquette."

Second was the revolt of the conventional member of the community, the well reputed citizen who would manipulate the system from within for personal gain or aggrandizement. Its archetypal defendant was Number Two. He spat on the column, which he thought might be Number One. Guilty!

Third was the revolt of pure individuality on behalf of pure freedom, with no ulterior motives. Its archetypal defendant was the former Number Six. The court praised him and declared that he had earned the right to be recognized as a full and unique person. Moreover, they wanted him to volunteer to stay in the Village and become their leader, as either the new Number Two or perhaps even as the new Number One. He was free to go, and was given ample means to do so. He asked, "Why?" several times. Getting no satisfactory answer, he was briefly tempted to stay and lead them, presumably to teach them all how to be individuals themselves. But the true individual can neither lead nor be led. Truly free individuals can be neither slaves nor masters. The innate strength of will that is necessary to be any kind of an individual cannot be taught. He tried to tell them this in a speech but was shouted down. It thus became abundantly clear to the former Number Six that the judge, the assembly, and everyone else in the Village, except perhaps the two recently convicted rebels, just wanted to be sheep. They needed a leader. He needed none. Nor did he need to lead them. Also, being their leader would leave him just as unfree as when he was a prisoner. He decided to go.

The judge indicated that the former Number Six should enter one of the holes in order to meet Number One. He did so, descended into another, deeper subterranean corridor, metal-lined and heavily guarded. He proceeded past the tiny, transparent cells of the two convicts, and was conducted by the butler to the base of a spiral staircase inside the column. At the top he found Number One, a masked figure like a member of the assembly. He smashed the crystal ball that Number One offered him, then ripped off the mask. Beneath it was first the face of a chimpanzee — symbolizing the individual's brutish nature — then, beneath that, the leering, cackling, barely recognizable face of the former Number Six himself — symbolizing the individual's evil tendencies or inclinations. Both of these false visages must always be overcome — indeed must be constantly fought against — to get to the true individual.

The now enlightened former Number Six enlisted the butler and both of the other convicts to grab machine guns and fight their way out. They succeeded. Realizing that the column was really a rocket, he set it to launch and, with his companions, fought for an exit. As bullets were sending dozens to their deaths, "All You Need is Love" played again over the loudspeakers. The butler hijacked a semi truck, on whose flatbed escaped the three rebels in the prison cell kitchen from "Once Upon a Time." As the judge ordered the Village evacuated, and as its panicky citizens were doing so, the rocket blasted off. Rover shriveled and disintegrated.

The truck rolled along a six-lane highway toward London. The three rebels gleefully littered. A straightlaced motorist turned on his car radio and heard "Dem Bones." Passing the truck, he was shocked to see three goofballs merrily dancing in the open jail on the flatbed. The young rebel decided to get off and hitchhike. The former Number Two chose Westminster, where he apparently felt at home among the government buildings. The former Number Six went back to his flat. At the butler's silent command, the front door to the flat opened and closed automatically — just like the doors in the Village. As the former Number Six drove away in his Lotus, we saw him and the car in exactly the same attitude and position in which we had first seen them in "Arrival." So, was the whole story cyclical? Archetypal? Allegorical? Nietzschean eternal recurrence?

What had we learned? The individual is the only universal. Your only boss, i.e., the only one that matters, is yourself, your conscience, your inner being, your Kantian transcendental unity of apperception, your soul, your spirit, your "still, small voice," as Elijah called it in 1 Kings 19:12. In rational, free individuals, each of these voices would always counsel the same course, *mutatis mutandis* for specific empirical situations, i.e., would always instantiate the appropriate aspect of the same universal moral law; so, by each of us freely following the autonomous moral reason which is revealed to each of us in and by conscience, there would be peace.

Who is Number One? We are all, each of us, each our own Number One. This does not mean that each individual is ultimately selfish, isolated, or mean; that the world is ultimately Hobbesian; or that human society must necessarily be chaotic and never truly communal, harmonious, or unified. Recognizing the sovereignty of each individual alone, over only that particular individual self, does not entail having to recognize billions of equally legitimate points of view, in what might be called the "subjectivist egalitarian fallacy." Nor does it mean that there are as many Number Ones as there are people. Rather, there is only one moral point of view and only one Number One. We are each uniquely attuned to it through, and only through, our own particular individuality. We each have an accurate and immediate intuition of what is right or good and what is wrong or evil in any given situation. Our only duty is to respond to this intuition and to prefer the right to the wrong, the good to the evil. The "still, small voice" of conscience that each one of us privately hears is the same for everyone. Kant, in his *Groundwork of the Metaphysics of Morals*, got it right.

The German sociologist Ferdinand Tönnies coined the distinction between

Gemeinschaft, the form of social organization in which individuals are expected to conform to the will of the group for the sake of coherence and stability, and *Gesellschaft*, the opposite form of social organization, in which the group gains its support and unity by valuing and protecting the rights of individuals. The *Gemeinschaft* is a monistic "community." The community itself is the basic unit, and the individuals within it are seen as just replaceable parts, components, or cogs. Individuals have no importance in themselves, but only as the parts, components, or cogs that comprise or buttress the community. The *Gesellschaft*, on the other hand, is a pluralistic "society." Its individuals, i.e., its members or citizens, are each equally its basic units. It is not a unit in itself, but a loose and convenient association of individuals, with that convenience being determined only by its value to each individual, both in relation to other individuals within the society and in relation to the whole society, seen as an aggregate, not as an entity, goal, or deity.

The Village was an especially attractive but supremely oppressive *Gemeinschaft*. Number Six, of course, could not thrive in anything but a *Gesellschaft*. So he, alone of all the Village's denizens, treated the Village as if it were a *Gesellschaft*. He was free — and remained free, against tremendous odds — only because he deliberately lived as a free person, questioned the system, and made his questions stick. He just ignored the power structure. No one could be more heroic than that.

Freedom is not possible within a *Gemeinschaft*.

It is not necessarily actual within a *Gesellschaft* either, but at least there it is possible.

Therefore our duty as free individual Americans was to stop America from being a *Gemeinschaft*. But that, we realized, was an ideal duty. On a more practical level, we had to ask ourselves whether individual freedom was even possible in any well ordered community, society, or state? The Village was certainly a well ordered community, and we all knew many rightists, conservatives, militarists, and even some leftists who would have liked America to have been so well ordered.

The practical philosophical issue evoked by *The Prisoner* was the extent to which personal liberty might be possible within any given kind of political organization. This question, being practical, was as important to everyday people as to professional philosophers. Evidence of this general importance is the frequency with which it appears on all levels of culture: in novels like George Orwell's *1984*, Aldous Huxley's *Brave New World*, Ayn Rand's *Atlas Shrugged* and *The Fountainhead*, or Anthony Burgess's *A Clockwork Orange*; in music like Pete Townshend's rock opera *Tommy* or Quicksilver Messenger Service's "What About Me?"; in comedy like Monty Python's "Mrs. Premise and Mrs. Conclusion Visit Jean-Paul Sartre" sketch; in TV shows like *The Prisoner*; in motion pictures like *The Ipcress File* or *If ...* ; in photojournalism like Jeff Widener's AP image of a lone Chinese demonstrator staring down a line of tanks in Tiananmen Square, Beijing, in 1989; in popular psychology like the content of many of Thomas Szasz's books; in plastic artworks like Jean Louis Géricault's *The Raft of the "Medusa,"* Francisco Goya's *The Third of May 1808*, Edvard Munch's *The Scream*, Adrian Piper's *I Am the Locus # 2*, or Judy Chicago's *Dinner Party*; and in the book that Hillary Rodham Clinton wrote when she was first lady, *It Takes a Village*. But would it take *The* Village?

Hegelian thought offered a cogent response to this issue. Hegel was a conceptually greedy philosopher who did not regard the well ordered state and the full freedom of the individual as mutually exclusive alternatives. Whenever Hegel was offered any exclusive "either/or" disjunction as his only viable philosophical alternatives, he would always, instead of choosing either one of the other, take "both" — and then figure out how to do it. Hegel's four paradigmatic world-historical realms (Oriental, Greek, Roman, and Germanic) laid out a framework for dealing with the question of the free individual vs. the well ordered society. The Oriental Realm was an individual in itself, the state identified with the emperor, and the only free person in this state was the emperor. The Greek Realm was democracy, wherein everyone was free, but the society was chaotic and the state was weak. The Roman Realm was the Greek Realm mediated by law, so that each citizen had legally protected and enforceable rights, and so that the state was more stable, but at the cost of privacy and a certain amount of personal freedom. Hegel's Germanic Realm, a constitutional monarchy, was supposed to have solved all these problems by combining and reconciling the best aspects of the previous three, thus offering both leadership and social coherence while not restricting — but in fact guaranteeing — individual freedom. For Hegel it was possible in this mediated state for individual autonomy to co-exist with societal heteronomy and for the freedom of the individual to be guaranteed within the state (though not within civil society, i.e., the bourgeois world or the commercial marketplace). But Hegel expected citizens of this ideal state to be what we now call "team players."

The Hegelian state entailed several difficulties *vis-à-vis* realizing the autonomy of the individual. In some ways it resembled McGoohan's idea of the Village, where conformity and creature comforts reigned and the prisoners were generally indistinguishable from the wardens. Interpretations of the symbolism of *The Prisoner* vary widely, but one point upon which nearly all interpreters agree is that the Village was intended as a microcosm of the entire world. Some Hegelians, such as the anarchist Max Stirner, have held that freedom for the individual is not possible within any state, even Hegel's. Another notorious Young Hegelian anarchist, Edgar Bauer, did not move as far away from Hegel as Stirner did toward radical individualism, but saw anarchy as only "the *beginning* of all good things," i.e., as the natural precursor to any leftist egalitarian revolution.

This Hegelian dilemma was mediated by Paul Tillich, for whom, primarily in his three-volume *Systematic Theology*, the dialectical opposition between the Rousseauian autonomy of the individual and the heteronomy which any political system cannot avoid imposing upon the individual to some degree was *aufgehoben* (i.e., "preserved, cancelled, and raised to a higher level") and reconciled in what Tillich called "theonomy," or "autonomous reason united with its own depth." The abstract freedom *of* the individual, the individual's natural feeling of freedom, became concrete freedom *for* the individual only when mediated through both divine law and human law as actualized and harmonized in the state. Theonomy (the law of God) was not theocracy (the rule of God imposed from on high), but the governance of God rising up from each individual participating in *Sittlichkeit* (i.e., "coherent social morality" or the "ethical order of life") within the Hegelian state.

Some have compared the Village to the future global community in *Brave New World*, and the character of Number Six to that of the Savage in that book — but such comparisons are wrongheaded. Indeed, they demean *The Prisoner*. Number Six was subtle, intelligent, and equal or superior to the Village in almost every way. The Savage was, well, just that. He was helpless against the superior intellect and sensibilities of Mustapha Mond. Number Six, though often defeated, was never helpless against anything. He would never have surrendered, despaired, or, as the Savage did, committed suicide. Number Six adequately represented the true human spirit in most of its commendable aspects; but the Savage represented only what was pitiful about it. *Brave New World* has been successful only because the concept of hypothesizing a well ordered society opposed to the spirit, dignity, rights, and freedom of the individual has intrinsic appeal for thoughtful people. But while McGoohan took this same concept as his premise for *The Prisoner* and developed it into a multivalent and endlessly interesting depiction of the eternal struggle of the human spirit against its oppressors, Huxley made *Brave New World* just as blunt as could be, little more than a transparent rant.

The whole *Prisoner* series could be seen as an extended comment on the socialization process that must be the basis of any kind of civilization. We saw how this process broke the human spirit (in everyone except Number Six) and we asked ourselves whether it must *necessarily* break the human spirit. In other words, could anyone like Number Six really exist or survive in any civilized community, society, or state? If so, would that society *ipso facto* disintegrate? We did not know. But we knew that we cared more for the individual and freedom than for community, society, or order.

We were all prisoners — and yet we were all free. That was the point.

Fall 1968

Look for the best! Expect the worst! Take what you get!

Only when the vaulted ceiling booms with the sound
Do we truly feel the full power of the bass.

Wenn das Gewölbe widerschallt,
Fühlt man erst recht des Basses Grundgewalt.
                        — Goethe, *Faust*, Part I, 2085-2086

Jefferson's Airplane's *Crown of Creation* intensified and further defined the political flood into which we had been thrown and in which we had been awash all summer. Occupying the midpoint between *Baxter's* and *Volunteers* — the three of which should in retrospect be considered the Airplane's masterpiece trilogy of studio albums — *Crown* starkly mocked nearly everything it mentioned, and suggested new alternatives. While songs like "Lather," "The House at Pooneil Corners," "Crown of Creation," and "Greasy Heart" were bitter and damning, others like "If You Feel," "Triad," "Star Track," "Ice Cream Phoenix," and "Share a Little Joke" carried uplifting, positive messages.

What was the crown of creation? The album cover showed all six members of the band, each in a strangely juxtaposed double image, revealed as a multicolored hallucination within the giant nuclear fireball over Hiroshima. Was the crown then the atomic bomb, the universal sword that made us all feel like Damocles? The lyrics of Kantner's song, "Crown of Creation," stated that the crown was frustrated by finding itself at a dead end. It could, then, have been the bomb, the most obvious metaphor of death and finality. But he addressed the crown as "you." He would not have spoken to the bomb in second person. He might, though, have addressed the makers of the bomb with such familiarity, especially if they were our parents. All the lyrics of the album lent sense to interpreting the crown as a sarcastic metaphor of the generation that built, maintained, and profited from the bomb.

This song took up again the theme of the preferability of change to stability that John Phillips had sung about in "Look Through My Window." Grace, singing Paul's words, contrasted change to rocks and fossils, declaring positively that regularity, uniformity, or sociopolitical constancy could be achieved only through the death of the soul, the fossilization of life, and that real life required Heraclitean movement in order to be life at all. To conform was to die.

Grace's "Lather" not only portrayed, but actually celebrated, the generation gap. The song had several themes: selling out, censorship, aging, nudity, freedom, conformity, and societal expectations vs. individual self-respect. Why, for instance, should we no longer be allowed to play with toys after age thirty? Grace bemoaned that, as adults, we are expected to be dull and serious, task-oriented, and not at all spontaneous, uninhibited, or playful. She lamented that Lather's former playmates had sold out to the financial empire, the social establishment, and the false military promises of glory and honor. The song advocated not irresponsible hedonism, but simple, harmless, innocent freedom and fun. In that regard, Marty echoed its message in both "Share a Little Joke" and "If You Feel," both of which exhorted us to be free and therefore happy, happy and therefore free, and to share this joy with everyone. In other words, never forget how to laugh!

The lyrics of "In Time," a slow but uplifting song co-written by Paul and Marty, dabbled in synesthesia, identifying colors with emotions and creating a sensual environment of touch and sight as well as sound. Jorma's fuzzy guitar perfectly complemented this feeling.

David Crosby had failed to convince his old band, the Byrds, to record his seductive ballad, "Triad," but he apparently had little trouble persuading the Airplane to do it. Kantner and Crosby were close friends, both personally and musically. The Airplane / Crosby collaboration would prove very fruitful, eventually yielding such gems as the apocalyptic "Wooden Ships." Grace sang "Triad," her sexy voice enticing listeners to join in loving threesomes, no longer restricted by society's unwavering demand that sexual love must exist only in heterosexual twosomes. Warm, adventurous, affectionate insanity should always trump cold, intolerant, formal "sanity."

Jorma's "Star Track" (obviously a pun on *Star Trek*, the popular TV show) was a call to introspection. His lyrics celebrated love as the steadying influence on an otherwise out-of-control life. Similarly, his "Ice Cream Phoenix" admonished us to remain childlike.

"Chushingura" was an eerie instrumental written by Spencer. Of course, we just had to find out what Chushingura meant. We looked it up. The songs that we loved often inspired us to try to broaden our knowledge. We learned that in 1701 in feudal Japan, a certain lord, Asano, tried to kill another lord, Kira. The shogun sentenced Asano to death and confiscated his lands. Asano's forty-seven retainers thus became *ronin*, i.e., masterless, wandering *samurai* warriors. Still loyal to their dead master, they conspired, attacked Kira, killed him, placed his head on Asano's grave, then dutifully committed ritual suicide, *seppuku*. They are regarded as national heroes in Japan. Tales and legends that have grown about them are known collectively as Chushingura.

Grace's lyrics in "Greasy Heart" were among her most acerbic and most strongly anti-conformist. Ostensibly the song attacked women's culture as slaves to expensive fashion, but its connotations hit much deeper than that. She continued the theme of "Two Heads," proclaiming that whatever in any person's appearance, personality, character, dress, or speech was natural, spontaneous, and unaffected was genuine and sincere, while whatever was unnatural, preplanned, or phony was untrustworthy and probably evil. To be human meant to be oneself. To be oneself meant to obey only one's own conscience, in a Kantian way, and not to conform to anyone else's expectations, not to be beholden to anyone, but to be natural and therefore free, or free and therefore natural. Implied was the distinction between "ladies" and "women." Real down-to-earth women did not want to be ladies; they were content just being female. Ladies, on the other hand, were self-manufactured from social rules, bottles of goo, and accepted styles of dress. Fake this. Fake that. Nothing natural. Everything affected. Nothing human. Everything just "polite." The stuff of comedy. Why would anyone take it seriously?

For a human to pretend to be "automatic" was not only not real, it flew in the face of reality. For a human not to be human was what Jean-Paul Sartre labeled bad faith, what Martin Heidegger attacked as inauthentic existence, or what Grace lampooned as refusal to laugh at whatever needed to be laughed at. To be human was to accept change, to embrace life, to realize that life and change are one, and to laugh at anyone who would pretend otherwise.

Her mention of "grease" or "greasiness" was to remind us of the apolitical, amoral, unfree teen culture of the fifties, when Brylcreem, Vitalis, and other slimy concoctions were parentally approved means for boys to have stylish Elvis pompadours or duck's-ass (politely called "ducktail" or "D.A.") haircuts, and when girls were expected to lacquer up their hair into untouchable masses of curls and waves and to smear great gunky gobs of oily make-up on their faces, including cherry red lipstick. Most unnatural! It was no accident that the "greasers" of the fifties and early sixties had become mostly prowar. Greasing up one's hair and face was a very conservative thing to do.

Grace practiced what she preached. Look at her own hair. It just hung straight down — like many of us wore ours. That was not a style; it was a statement. It said, "Naturalness is better than artificiality. People should not be plastic."

Kantner's and Balin's jointly written apocalyptic dirge, "The House at Pooneil Corners" was much darker than its predecessor on *Baxter's*, "The Ballad of You and Me and Pooneil." Its graphically descriptive images of mass death and its gruesome aftermath made us think of nothing but nuclear war and its entailed universal annihilation. Was the crown of creation to be doomed to painful oblivion?

Jack was listed as playing the "Yggdrasil bass." Of course, as in the case of Chushingura, we just had to find out what Yggdrasil meant. Our search, for those of us who did not know it already, led us into the extensive and fascinating world of Norse mythology, where Yggdrasil was the "world ash," i.e., a gigantic, almost cosmic, ash tree growing from the center of the earth, with branches in heaven and roots in various supernatural wells. But what any of that might have meant for music remained anyone's guess.

The album had a printed lyrics sheet insert (which, by 2009, had become very collectible, even more so than the album itself). The insert included a huge photo of Bobby Kennedy's Newfoundland, Brumus, and a smaller photo of the Airplane's engineer, Pat Ieraci, known as "Maurice," at the eight-track tape machine. The insert is even more interesting because RCA, the record company, apparently was willing to let the Airplane *sing* dirty words but not willing to have them printed. Thus the lyrics show "bulsht" where "bullshit" is sung. The Airplane would continue this dodge on future albums, and would seem to have had quite a bit of fun with it. For instance, we would soon realize that whenever we read "Fred" in printed Airplane lyrics, we could expect to hear "motherfucker" in the song.

The Airplane performed "Crown of Creation" — uncensored, though awash in cheesy psychedelic visuals — and "Won't You Try / Saturday Afternoon" on *Ed Sullivan*. They also did "Crown" two months later on the *Smothers Brothers*, likewise uncensored — with Grace in blackface yet — but their appearance there was to be expected. I have never been able to figure out why Ed let "Crown" go by, especially after having enhanced his already lavish censorial credentials by hassling the crap out of the Byrds, the Doors, and the Stones. Was he asleep that day? Did he not understand the lyrics at all? Did he not recognize himself as one of the obstructionist fossils mentioned in the song? Or had he mellowed?

The Airplane embodied, typified, or personified disrespect. So, from the non-musical side of the movement, did Abbie Hoffman. Grace and Abbie were made for each other.

Do not believe whatever you might see in *Forrest Gump* about Abbie or the various peace marches in Washington. That movie is full of anachronisms.

The House Un-American Activities Committee (HUAC) — i.e., witch hunt central command — subpoenaed Abbie to testify on October 3 about events in Chicago and other leftist happenings. When cops on the U.S. Capitol grounds noticed him arriving for the hearings in a stars-and-stripes shirt, they attacked him, beat him, ripped the shirt, and arrested him for wearing a shirt made of an American flag. Abbie later claimed that the shirt was not itself a flag, but only designed to resemble a flag. He showed that it was commercially available. Of course, he was convicted, and given a suspended sentence of a $100 fine or thirty days in jail. Yet, surprisingly, given the flavor of the times, this conviction was overturned on appeal. The appellate court's judgment is worth reading.[55]

Abbie was often beaten — but somehow he did not seem to mind. He was not a masochist, but he always liked to bounce back smiling, because that frustrated his attackers. His resilience threw their thuggishness back at them, almost as if he were taunting them: "Your small-minded philosophy, your narrow-minded world view, your jingoistic politics, your anti-humanistic mentality, and your general attitude that only those who agree with you should be allowed their liberty, can be defended only by brute force, not by thought, logic, reason, human feeling, or common sense."

Here is a good place to point out that, in America, all arrests and convictions for flag desecration are motivated by ideological or sectarian politics, not by the plain, physical facts of the particular "crime." That is, when a leftist agitator

---

[55] Hoffman v. United States, 445 F.2d 226 (decided March 29, 1971, amended April 1, 1971).

like Abbie walked around in public minding his own business wearing an American flag shirt, he was arrested and persecuted, but when upright adherents of the established system, like Ted Nugent, Phyllis Diller, Mickey Mouse, Uncle Sam masqueraders, Catherine Malandrino, onlookers at Veterans Day parades, or customers of SawgrassBlossom.com, wore similar flag shirts, they were either hailed as patriots or just let be, even if, as Nugent often did, spewing hatred while wearing such clothes. Cover a dead soldier's coffin with the American flag, and you are a patriot; or drape the naked body of actress Charisma Carpenter in it, and no one will bother you; but use the flag as a bedsheet, pup tent, or blanket to keep a living leftist warm, and you could be arrested. There is no hypocrisy in America more obvious than flag etiquette and its ramifications. There is no American federal law more anti-freedom, more jingoistic, or more abhorrent through its selective application, than U.S. Code, Title 4, Chapter 1, § 8, "Respect for Flag." Anyone who would gladly obey such a law is a fitting slave such as Hitler would have been proud to call a Nazi.

I would never pledge allegiance to much of anything except principles, and certainly not to a *flag*! Not even to a flag that pretended to stand for freedom. The concept of freedom and the concept of allegiance are incompatible. I am free to enslave myself, and I may freely choose to do that, but if I exercise my freedom that way, I lose it, and end up a slave, even though a voluntary slave who believes that he is still free. So it is with pledging allegiance.

We saw ourselves as the legitimate descendants of the American revolutionaries of the 1770s and saw the supporters of the current American establishment as the descendants of the Tories of that period. We sought change; they sought the status quo. What irony that they and we alike honored those eighteenth-century revolutionaries! Yes, we would have fought in Washington's ragtag army in that necessary war; but they would have chosen the safer, more secure, more traditional path of remaining loyal subjects of the British crown.

Abbie's book about Chicago and related matters, *Revolution for the Hell of It*, appeared this fall. Few of us agreed with Abbie's communist-anarchist ideology, but we appreciated that the world was much more fun with Abbie in it. Humor was sorely lacking in law and politics. Abbie supplied it.

Whenever Abbie got in trouble, the YAF rejoiced.

The Young Americans for Freedom (YAF), the extreme conservative and — naturally — very well funded antithesis of the SDS, had been founded by about ninety ultra-obedient kids at William F. Buckley, Jr.'s estate in Sharon, Connecticut, on September 11, 1960. Its manifesto, the Sharon Statement, is as follows:

> In this time of moral and political crises, it is the responsibility of the youth of America to affirm certain eternal truths.
>
> We, as young conservatives, believe:
>
> That foremost among the transcendent values is the individual's use of his God-given free will, whence derives his right to be free from the restrictions of arbitrary force;

That liberty is indivisible, and that political freedom cannot long exist without economic freedom;

That the purpose of government is to protect those freedoms through the preservation of internal order, the provision of national defense, and the administration of justice;

That when government ventures beyond these rightful functions, it accumulates power, which tends to diminish order and liberty;

That the Constitution of the United States is the best arrangement yet devised for empowering government to fulfill its proper role, while restraining it from the concentration and abuse of power;

That the genius of the Constitution — the division of powers — is summed up in the clause that reserves primacy to the several states, or to the people in those spheres not specifically delegated to the Federal government;

That the market economy, allocating resources by the free play of supply and demand, is the single economic system compatible with the requirements of personal freedom and constitutional government, and that it is at the same time the most productive supplier of human needs;

That when government interferes with the work of the market economy, it tends to reduce the moral and physical strength of the nation, that when it takes from one to bestow on another, it diminishes the incentive of the first, the integrity of the second, and the moral autonomy of both;

That we will be free only so long as the national sovereignty of the United States is secure; that history shows periods of freedom are rare, and can exist only when free citizens concertedly defend their rights against all enemies;

That the forces of international Communism are, at present, the greatest single threat to these liberties;

That the United States should stress victory over, rather than coexistence with this menace; and

That American foreign policy must be judged by this criterion: does it serve the just interests of the United States?

The YAF first came to our attention in 1964 by their solid support of Barry Gold-water and their obsequious fawning over Ronald Reagan, but they did not really become a pain in our ass — or we in theirs — until the 1968 election. Many of them supported arch-segregationist George Wallace for president. They saw the world in terms of enemies. America vs. its enemies, both internal and external. YAF-ers were the ultimate ultranationalists. If they had been Germans in the thirties, they would happily have joined the Hitler Youth. Like the Nazis, they needed someone or something to hate, to rally against — otherwise they would have had no ideology at all. For Hitler, it was the Jews; for the YAF, it was the communists. They did not care about poverty as long as the few people that mattered had the opportunity (i.e., "political freedom") to get rich and/or stay rich (i.e., to achieve "economic freedom"). They favored the death penalty, wanted to abolish the minimum wage, enshrined "Victory in Vietnam" on top of their agenda, and generally supported anything that would make the rich richer and more powerful and the poor poorer and less powerful. Their focus on America, America, America revealed how parochial and insular they were, not realizing that countries are really very small things. Their *Cui bono?* was primarily "Does it benefit America?" and secondarily "My family?", "Myself?", "My faith?", "My school?", or "My business?", but never "Humanity?" They feared governmental power stealing their liberties, but they did not see that government becomes most powerful and therefore most dangerous when it most closely follows their own stated aims of preserving internal order, providing national defense, and administering justice. They did not see that following these aims without regard to the public welfare or general human rights would create a military or police state in which only the top levels of citizens, i.e., they and their cronies, would be "free." Or maybe they did see this. Maybe creating a military or police state with themselves on top was exactly what they wanted.

It was instantly obvious to us that the YAF did not have any idea of what freedom really was. For them, freedom was wealth, power, and the opportunity to achieve wealth and power. It was the freedom of the ruling class. Thanks to the American Revolution and conservative American economics, now any American, not just the sons and sometimes daughters of the already established ruling class, could be a member of the ruling class. The YAF saw America's big contribution to world history as making wealth and power no longer hereditary, but open to anyone who would be willing to play the game. The game had rules. Lots of rules. Break one and you would be justly condemned to poverty, powerlessness, discrimination, and ostracism. That was a rule too. That was their idea of "freedom."

One common slogan of American supporters of the Iraq War in the first decade of the twenty-first century is "Freedom Isn't Free." Well, that just ain't so! They misunderstand freedom in much the same way as the YAF did in the Vietnam era. The American Revolutionary War shifted power from a foreign hereditary monarchy to a resident but mobile elite of rich white males. The American Civil War abolished slavery and freed some blacks. World War II overthrew three evil dictatorships that directly threatened not only America, but the entire world. But no other war that America has ever fought has either enhanced freedom for average Americans or helped America to become a better country. Freedom is not won by war. True freedom is a state of mind as well as a political condition and a natural right. Freedom *is* free! Just live it! Free your mind and your ass will follow.

Real freedom had two new heroes, African-Americans, both alumni of San Jose State University (SJSU). At the Olympics in Mexico City, Tommie Smith won the gold medal and John Carlos the bronze in the 200-meter dash. At the awards ceremony, while the "The Star Spangled Banner" played, Smith raised his black-gloved right fist and Carlos his black-gloved left, showing the whole world the black power salute on live TV. Just a few weeks earlier, James Brown had released his anthem, "Say It Loud — I'm Black and I'm Proud." Many of us, black and white alike, would rather have heard that tune than "The Star Spangled Banner," because it was more appropriate, less militaristic, more humanistic, less about violence, and more about dignity. Both Smith and Carlos also bowed their heads to indicate that America should be ashamed of its historically consistent tyranny over people of color. Australian Peter Norman, winner of the silver medal, stood at attention on the podium in support of their protest. All three wore badges of the Olympic Project for Human Rights (OPHR), a predominantly black organization designed to use the Mexico City Olympics to publicize and advance the cause of civil rights around the world. The athletic community and the Olympic authorities immediately ostracized all three. Racists sent them death threats. Yet both Smith and Carlos were able to revive their careers in the seventies. Both played in the NFL and both became re-spected track coaches. In 2005 SJSU unveiled on campus, in their honor, a statue of their protest; and in 2008 both received the Arthur Ashe Award for Courage.

Americans who are proud to be American simply do not understand world history. What is there to be proud of? That America is the most self-righteous, ar-rogant, condescending nation in the world? It claims to have invented monarchless society, but it did not. Greece, Switzerland, Iceland, etc., beat America to that one. It claims to have invented republican government. Well, it might have a legitimate claim there, but surely it is no longer unique or preeminent in that regard. Are we to be proud that America has the mightiest military force on the planet? If so, then that is tantamount to the big bully challenging the other 200 kids in the schoolyard to try to knock the chip off his shoulder. Are we to be proud that America is, for the time being, the richest nation on the planet? All that means is that America is a successful grand thief and, by disproportionately dividing the world's wealth in its own favor, has been able to deprive other nations and peoples of the subsistence that they naturally deserve. The fact is that *every* nation from the dawn of civiliza-tion has contributed *something* to the development of civilization. Each has given its share — and has stolen its share. Why pick any one of them to be proud of, more than any other? Are our principles and priorities to be determined only by accidents of birth? If we can be proud of America for developing republican government, then we can for the same reasons be equally proud of France for abolishing monar-chy, of Italy for fostering Michelangelo, of Germany for birthing Beethoven, and of China for growing lots of rice. In the last analysis, it was people, living, flesh-and-blood individual humans, not nations or countries at all, that accomplished not only these things, but all non-natural, earthly things. Nations in general do not warrant pride, and no nation in particular warrants more or less overall pride than any other — unless we are making moral judgments on specific events in their respective and interrelated histories, e.g., praising Denmark, the Netherlands, and Sweden for rescuing some Jews from the Nazi holocaust, while at the same time condemning Germany for allowing Nazism to come into power and instigate the holocaust. Pride is a weird, sinister emotion anyway. If you are going to be proud of anything, be proud of your *humanity*, not your nationality, your ethnicity, nor especially your religion.

On a superficial, non-historical view, America can be reduced to its culture, and its culture can be reduced to its image, its products, or its obsessions. In "Living in the U.S.A.," the single from their new LP, *Sailor*, the Steve Miller Band depicted a plastic culture obsessed with careers, bravado, the banal trappings of materialism, handouts, transient pleasures, manipulating the system, auto racing, and of course, cheeseburgers. Hey! That tune would make a pretty accurate national anthem!

A parody poster for a non-existent movie called *Vietnam* showed LBJ relaxing smugly on a chaise lounge, drinking from a glass with the peace symbol on it. In the background was a collage of actual war photos, an image of Hitler, and a mini-poster of Nixon with the caption, "Sock It to Them Hard, Nix," a reference to Nixon's recent appearance on *Laugh-In*. The advertising copy was:

AN EASTERN THEATRE PRODUCTION
SEE ⋯ A Cast of Thousands!
SEE ⋯ Modern Atrocities in Full Color!
SEE ⋯ The Accounts of a Nation Destined to Save the World
        in Spite of Itself!
Gripping ... Moving ... A Film the Whole Family is Sure to Enjoy

VIETNAM

Filmed Thru the Courtesy and Cooperation of the Entire Military Forces of the World's Mightiest and Most Benevolent Nation
"A Truly Remarkable Portrayal of American Foreign Policy"
"Beautiful, Poignant"
Gross National Product
Filmed in Real Blood 'n Guts Color
Price of Admission: Your Son, Plus Taxes

The comedic assault on America's current world hegemony was complete when Henry Fonda — Henry Friggin' Fonda, of all people, the embodiment of propriety, sobriety, and rectitude, the guy who, albeit a liberal Democrat and the father of Jane and Peter, had played Abe Lincoln, Tom Joad, Wyatt Earp, Mister Roberts, and Brigadier General Theodore Roosevelt, Jr. — narrated "Pat Paulsen for President," a special campaign episode of *The Smothers Brothers Comedy Hour*. Pat was so self-effacing that he was almost believable, pledging, "If elected, I will win," declaring, "Issues have no place in a presidential campaign," and promising stiffer penalties for grammatical errors. He got a few write-in votes in the general election.

Ω

The Moody Blues' third album, *In Search of the Lost Chord*, used less classical inspiration and rocked a lot harder than did *Days of Future Passed*. It was also more

frankly psychedelic. The Moodies seemed obsessed in 1968 with using spoken poems on their LPs, but "Departure," the one that introduced this album, was not as
stupid as the two on *Days of Future Passed*, and its segue into the next song, "Ride
My See-Saw," was much cleaner, almost seamless, almost natural. "Legend of a
Mind" paid homage to Timothy Leary and thus revealed the band's interest in mystical, drug-induced expansions of ordinary consciousness. Yet "The Best Way to
Travel," while furthering this same theme, was ambiguous about whether mind-
expansion, which they still regarded as the greatest good, would depend upon drugs
or not. There were indeed many songs in late 1968 on both the FM and AM airwaves, such as the Temptations' "Cloud Nine," that blatantly advocated druggy
escapism. But — and this is a very important point — there were at the same time
many other songs that only *seemed* to be about drugs, but in fact were not. For example, Steppenwolf's "Magic Carpet Ride" was not about drugs, but about giving
free reign to one's imagination. "The Best Way to Travel" could be interpreted as
asserting that thinking alone, not drug use, would be the best way to reach the desired destination. Moreover, even "Cloud Nine" portrayed drug use as an act of
desperation and despair.

In Search of the Lost Chord finally found it! That is, it ended with a song
that called forth the serenity of the venerable ancient Hindu mantra, "Om" (which
would have more accurately been spelled "a-u-m").

British progressive psychedelia also advanced with Pink Floyd's *Saucerful
of Secrets* and Procol Harum's *Shine On Brightly*. The former, their last album with
the rapidly declining Syd Barrett, seemed appropriately embryonic. The classic
Floyd of David Gilmour on guitar, Roger Waters on bass, Richard Wright on keyboards, and Nick Mason on drums was just beginning to try to find its own feet.
The latter's title track, much in accord with the theme of "The Best Way to Travel,"
suggested that thinking, even insane thinking, was the only way out of confusion.
Procol's monumental "In Held 'Twas in I" on the second side was the first of many
meandering progressive rock suites that would soon become the stock-in-trade of
bands like King Crimson, Renaissance, Pink Floyd, and Genesis.

The Who's fourth U.S. album, *Magic Bus: The Who on Tour*, was really a
non-album. It was not a tour album; there was not a live cut on it. Rather, it was a
hodgepodge of singles, "Magic Bus," "Pictures of Lily," and "Call Me Lightning";
previously released album tracks, "Run, Run, Run" from *Happy Jack* and "I Can't
Reach You" and "Our Love Was, Is" from *Sell Out*; and only five new songs:
Townshend's "Disguises," Entwistle's "Dr. Jekyll and Mr. Hyde," "Someone's
Coming," and "Doctor, Doctor," and a cover of a Jan and Dean B-side car tune,
"Bucket T." We wondered about the apparent eclipse of Townshend. Little did we
know that he was off writing *Tommy*, which would appear early next year.

Better than *Magic Bus* was their *Direct Hits*, a simultaneous British compilation that was widely available underground in America. Overlaps with *Magic
Bus* were "Bucket T," "Pictures of Lily," "Doctor, Doctor," and "Call Me Lightning." Revisits from earlier LPs were "Happy Jack" from *Happy Jack* and "I Can
See for Miles" and "Mary-Anne with the Shaky Hands" from *Sell Out*. Collected
singles were "I'm a Boy," "In the City" (the B-side of "I'm a Boy"), and "Substi-

tute." New tunes were Townshend's quirky "Dogs," and a cover of the Stones' "The Last Time." "Dogs" alone was worth the price of the album, for a comic peek at the seedy side of lower-class British life at the dog track.

The Hendrix Experience's new double LP, *Electric Ladyland*, was jazzier, jammier, and more experimental than *Axis* and did not contain any songs as overtly political as "If Six Was Nine." Jimi seemed to have become gentler, subtler, mellower, and more melodic, especially in tunes like "Rainy Day, Dream Away," "1983," and "Have You Ever Been?" Of course, there were flat-out rockers too, like "Crosstown Traffic" and "Come On." "And the Gods Made Love" was a spacy intro to the whole set, in the same vein as "EXP" on *Axis*, but not as interesting. The obligatory Redding tune was there too, this time "Little Miss Strange." "Gypsy Eyes" was a very unusual love song with a fantastic backbeat. Jimi's slow, cool, lingering, fifteen-minute blues jam on "Voodoo Chile" [spelled with an "e"] was a delicious psychedelic ramble. His cover of Dylan's "All Along the Watchtower" was much praised, even by Dylan himself. But the most memorable bit was his riff at the beginning of "Voodoo Child [spelled with a "d"] (Slight Return)," which became not only his signature, but also the riff that thousands of young guitarists tried to learn so that they could impress their friends by being able to play like Hendrix.

The British version of the album art showed, appropriately enough, a photo of twenty naked women. The uptight American censors substituted a blurry red and yellow photo of Jimi's face.

Judy Collins's eighth album, *Who Knows Where the Time Goes*, made it easy to see why Stephen Stills was so deeply in love with her. Not as good as her landmark, *In My Life*, but still damn good!

Keyboardist Al Kooper, who had just left Blood, Sweat, and Tears after founding it and putting out their first LP, *Child is Father to the Man*, jammed with guitarists Mike Bloomfield from the Electric Flag for one album side and Stills from Buffalo Springfield for another album side. The result was *Super Session*, a big *tour de force* for all three. The Bloomfield and Kooper side featured the heavy blues instrumentals, "Albert's Shuffle" and "Really," and the bizarre riffs of a weird keyboard instrument, the ondioline (a sort of primitive synthesizer), in "His Holy Modal Majesty," a nine-minute jam. The Stills and Kooper side had an upbeat, country rock cover of Dylan's "It Takes a Lot to Laugh, It Takes a Train to Cry" and an eleven-minute psychedelic cover of Donovan's "Season of the Witch" that was just perfect for listening through headphones.

What did "holy modal" mean? We had no idea. But the phrase kept popping up. It seemed to have somehow originated with the Holy Modal Rounders, the New York City folk band that had been around for seven or eight years. They had a new LP, *The Moray Eels Eat the Holy Modal Rounders*, which was pretty good. It was their venture into psychedelic rock, but very much tongue-in-cheek, not serious at all. The Rounders and their tunes were very weird — using comic nasal vocals, jug band rhythms, falsetto harmonies, assorted shrieks, and a wide variety of unexpected effects to create "The Bird Song," "The Take-Off Artist Song," "The STP Song," and ten more little cuts.

The Rounders' cousins, or maybe parasites, the Fugs, also had a new LP, *It Crawled Into My Hand, Honest*. Indeed, the Rounders and the Fugs shared or exchanged so many members that they could easily be seen, not as two bands, but as two sides of the same band: Peter Stampfel and Steve Weber the musical side, and Ed Sanders and Tuli Kupferberg the poetic side. If you were looking for skullduggerous, subversive, self-indulgent, slap-happy semi-music, with song titles like "Johnny Pissoff Meets the Red Angel," "We're Both Dead Now, Alice," or "Tuli, Visited by the Ghost of Plotinus," how could you lose?

The third Country Joe and the Fish LP, *Together*, was, like most of theirs, uneven. At its best, it was either heavy psychedelia like "Susan" or "Mojo Navigator" or mordant sociopolitical humor like "Bright Suburban Mr. and Mrs. Clean Machine" or "Harlem Song." But most of it was ordinary, forgettable, not up to the standards that other California bands, notably the Airplane, Quicksilver, and the Dead, continued to set for themselves.

Phil Ochs dependably carried on against the war, decrying "White Boots Marching in a Yellow Land" and declaring "The War is Over" on one of his most adventurous LPs, *Tape From California*. Thematically more unified and internally more coherent than his other albums, this one probed with typically incisive lyrics the various aspects of the inevitable decadence of American culture.

Spirit's second LP, *The Family That Plays Together*, was not as interesting as their first, yet it spawned "I Got a Line on You," a hot, uptempo rocker.

Traffic's eponymous second LP showed a remarkable leap beyond the first in musicality, tunesmithing, lyrics, and general complexity. Indeed, the lyrics of some of these songs approached the level of surrealistic poetry. Most notably in this regard, the lyrics of Winwood's and Capaldi's "Pearly Queen" and "Forty Thousand Headmen" seemed like the narratives of dreams. Their "No Time to Live" was a pseudo-altruist's self-pitying lament that his having given so much of himself to others had left nothing for himself. But this is not the way that real altruism works. The fact is, the more love one gives, the more love one has. Their "Means to an End" continued the same self-pitying theme. Winwood's, Capaldi's, and Wood's "Who Knows What Tomorrow May Bring" seemed to be a call to druggy, *carpe diem* hedonism. We wondered where Dave Mason was on this one, either musically or thematically.

We were beginning to notice significant divergence between Winwood's (and Capaldi's) songwriting and Mason's. Steve (and Jim) seemed more imagistic and psychedelic, while Dave seemed more psychological and humanistic, but these are only generalizations. Mason's "You Can All Join In" presented the same message as the Airplane's "If You Feel" and dozens of other songs by dozens of other groups, i.e., that absolute freedom for anyone is determined only by that person's will to be free. His "Don't Be Sad" evoked deep feelings of genuine human empathy and sexual egalitarianism along the lines of Dylan's "All I Really Want to Do," which the Byrds had covered in 1965. His "Feelin' Alright" depicted a man trying to talk himself out of dejection and into positive action. It worked! At least for us. What a great tune! His tearjerking "Cryin' to Be Heard" was a song of hope in the midst of despair and loneliness. It could have been interpreted as a religious message, but not necessarily. It surely called for human solidarity. His and Wood's "Vagabond Virgin" related the damaging sexual and other misadventures of a thirteen-year-old country-to-city runaway, probably a groupie.

A true novelty, and a very interesting one — beyond the classically inspired progressive rock of the Moodies and Procol Harum, and beyond Peter Schickele's running classical music joke, the fictional composer, P.D.Q. Bach — was the idea to play Johann Sebastian Bach's music, just as he wrote it, on a Moog synthesizer. This was the brainchild of Walter Carlos, a classical pianist and composer trained at Brown and Columbia Universities. The resulting album, *Switched-On Bach*, was a surprise bestseller on both the classical and popular album charts. Walter would surgically become Wendy in 1972, but this fact would not be generally known before 1979.

Strictly Personal, the second LP of Captain Beefheart and His Magic Band, was more overtly psychedelic, more blatantly political, and rocked harder with punnier lyrics than their first. Still, few people noticed.

Zappa's and the Mothers' fifth LP, *Cruisin' With Ruben and the Jets*, was a mock doo wop album, at once parodying and honoring the harmonic styles of the late fifties and early sixties. Its cover art showed the band as a cartoon of lewd, leering, finger-popping doglike weasels or weasel-like dogs. Its tunes, like most of Zappa's work, were sexually charged, so much so that its overall purpose seemed to be to show what the doo wop hits of a decade earlier might have sounded like in their own time if they had not been so heavily censored.

Sweetheart of the Rodeo continued the country rock trajectory that the Byrds had begun with *Notorious Byrd Brothers*. With the band now consisting of McGuinn, Hillman, guitarist and keyboardist Gram Parsons, and drummer Kevin Kelley — and with very little original material — it sounded almost like a straight country album. Its highlights were two Dylan covers, "You Ain't Going Nowhere" and "Nothing Was Delivered."

Except for "The Loner" and the uneasy images and melancholy humor of "Last Trip to Tulsa," Neil Young's eponymous debut solo album was rather disappointing, given the high expectations we had of him after his wonderful contributions to Buffalo Springfield. This LP made us question whether he could make it on his own.

Van Morrison's second solo album, *Astral Weeks*, was what began to make him into a critical favorite and a persistent object of small-time cultic admiration.

With a musical approach similar to that of Fairport Convention — including even a female lead singer — though perhaps a bit jazzier and a bit more acoustic, Pentangle appeared with their self-titled debut LP. The name of the band reflected John Renbourn's fascination with medieval legends, chivalric mythology, and their attendant spiritual symbols, such as the five-pointed pentagram, which, pointed upwards, meant good, but downwards, boded evil. The quintet consisted of folkies Renbourn and Bert Jansch on guitars, bluesmen Danny Thompson on upright bass and Terry Cox on drums, and Jacqui McShee singing. They had to be fine musicians, because Pentangle was not about to get by on good looks! With the possible exception of Cox, they were five of the ugliest people who ever made great music.

Yet physical ugliness ought not to be taken very seriously. It never precluded great poetry, art, literature, or music. Indeed, the group who, ever since Sam Cutler's intro at one of their gigs in 1969, has been touted as "The Greatest Rock-and-Roll Band in the World" is also one of the ugliest bands in the world:

"Ladies and Gentlemen, the Rolling Stones!"

In *Beggars Banquet*, their first album after *Satanic Majesties*, the Stones returned to what they did best: basic hard-driving rock. The result was one of their best LPs ever. Bluesy, biting, and supremely musical, who could argue with it?

The original cover art of *Beggars Banquet* was to have been a photo of a filthy, graffiti-covered, public toilet stall. It was banned in both Great Britain and America. The LP was released on both sides of the Atlantic in a plain white jacket with fancy-schmancy script lettering to imitate an upper-class party invitation, complete with R.S.V.P. But we heard about the censorship. The Stones made sure that we heard about it.

The songs were instant classics — quintessential Stones. Jean-Luc Godard documented the writing, rehearsals, and recording of "Sympathy for the Devil," the album's masterpiece, but we in America would not see the film until 1970. The lyrics of "Sympathy" showed Jagger in his demonic excellence, judging the world situation and reminding us what real devils we all were. "No Expectations," a despondent blues tune featuring Brian's eerie slide guitar, portrayed a man who had lost everything, money, love, serenity, yet somehow managed not to let life defeat him. "Dear Doctor" was comic relief. "Parachute Woman," "Stray Cat Blues," and "Factory Girl" were all about raunchy sex. "Jig Saw Puzzle" was a psychedelic blues number with impossibly impressionistic lyrics. The anthemic "Street Fighting Man" was ever so timely, especially regarding events of the last several months in Chicago, Prague, Paris, Memphis, Los Angeles, Saigon, and many other cities around the world. We wondered, though, whether the song depicted a political fighter, an ideological urban guerrilla, or just a common, unprincipled street punk. "Prodigal Son" retold Jesus's cautionary tale from Luke 15:11-32. Continuing the biblical allusion, this time to Matthew 5:13, Keith praised the workers of the world in "Salt of the Earth."

Stonedhenge, Ten Years After's third LP in less than a year, was much like their first two, that is, mostly bluesy; but this one rocked a bit harder — plus its title had that cute allusion to marijuana.

The title of the Nice's second LP, *Ars Longa Vita Brevis*, meant "Art is long, life is short." It was a flipflop of the beginning of the standard Latin translation of an aphorism of the ancient Greek physician Hippocrates, "Life is short, art is long, opportunity is fleeting, experience is dangerous, and judgment is difficult." As we knew from Emerson's recent demonstration at the Royal Albert Hall, he believed that the world was sick and that America was the main cause of the present suffering. Hence we inferred that this reference to Hippocrates called upon everyone to become involved in political action and to use something analogous to the art of medicine, i.e., the knowledge and skill of the physician, to heal the world.

Musically, despite the band having lost its guitarist and being down to a trio of keyboards, bass, and drums, *Ars Longa Vita Brevis* was more complex than *The Thoughts of Emerlist Davjack*, more heavily dominated by Emerson's keyboards — and ego. In this new style of classically influenced progressive rock we were starting to hear the fascinating mix of finesse and bombast that would become Emerson, Lake, and Palmer in the early seventies.

Again the Kinks released a nondescript album, *Four More Well Respected Gentlemen*. Their nadir continued. They were still forgotten.

Ω

Singles extracted from previously released albums included Janis's "Piece of My Heart" and Cream's "White Room." A few other singles caught our attention.

Arthur Brown was *in-fucking-sane*! His one and only interesting tune was enough to imprint him in our minds forever, even if we only heard it or saw him perform it once. Both his lyrics and his stage act were beyond outrageous; they went all the way to wild-eyed fanatic loony crazy — which may be why he called his band the Crazy World of Arthur Brown. The full five-minute version of "Fire" began with a brass fanfare and a stupid autobiographical surrealistic poem, then leaped into a heavy psychedelic rock song built around a cheesy Hammond B-3 organ riff, peppered with brass, and notable for its lack of guitar. Singing in the persona of a malevolent deity, Brown, in satanic make-up and wearing a special costume hat that made his hair seem to be on fire, gleefully threatened universal immolation. If the song had not been obviously and intrinsically comic — not to mention overdone — we might have taken it as either a commentary on the real threat of worldwide nuclear annihilation or a reaffirmation of the Heraclitean idea of universal flux.

The extended funky jam in the middle of their eight-minute-thirty-seven-second cover of Dale Hawkins's "Susie Q" was what introduced most of us to Creedence Clearwater Revival, but those of us who delved into their self-titled first album found an even cooler tune, their cover of Screamin' Jay Hawkins's "I Put a Spell on You." We just had a good feeling about these guys. It was a travesty that the single version split "Susie Q" into two parts, one on each side of the 45, but then again, the singles world was full of travesties.

Eighteen-year-old Welsh folkie and McCartney protégée Mary Hopkin, one of the first artists signed to the Beatles' own record company, Apple, scored with her wistful cover of "Those Were the Days," Gene Raskin's English version of Boris Fomin's Russian song from the twenties. She was magic. She could actually make teenagers feel nostalgic for experiences they had not even had yet. But when we saw her on *Ed Sullivan*, we thought that her stage presence did not generate as much excitement as her voice did. She was no Janis Joplin! Nor was she up to the level of Grace Slick, Judy Collins, Mama Cass, or even Linda Ronstadt. She was cute but wooden. In the forties she would have been called a "canary," i.e., a woman singer who was talented enough to front a band by virtue of her vocals alone, but had little else to offer.

Max Frost and the Troopers, a phony, manufactured group, released a fairly heavy rocker, "Shape of Things to Come," written by Brill Building veterans Barry Mann and Cynthia Weil. Considered apart from its origin, the wretched exploitation movie, *Wild in the Streets*, it was not such a bad song. Naturally its title and future-oriented theme invited comparison with the Yardbirds' "Shapes of Things" from 1966. While the Yardbirds' lyrics were more psychological, hopeful, open, and a bit deeper, Frost's were more political, fatalistic, threatening, revolutionary, and — well, phony and manufactured. Yet, on a certain shallow level, it could be inspirational.

"Abraham, Martin, and John" by Dion DiMucci — yes, *that* Dion — was a soft pop or folk rock lament, a far cry from his doo wop days. It could have been called "Abraham, Martin, John, and Bobby," because it mourned the deaths of four murdered leaders, Abraham Lincoln, Martin Luther King, John F. Kennedy, and Bobby Kennedy. It was a genuine *Zeitgeist* piece, given that two of those assassinations had occurred within the last six months, and the nation was still very much in the grip of violence and street-level desperation — not to mention the war.

In "Love Child," the Supremes frankly tackled issues of premarital pregnancy, male libido, men's exploitation of women as sex objects, illegitimate children, dysfunctional families, and broken lives. For a Motown "girl group" who had previously garnered a string of AM radio hits singing about little besides broken hearts, cutesy relationships, and petty jealousies, this was strong stuff. We were impressed. We had not thought that Diana Ross had such bluntness in her, at least not in her public personality.

A Michigan rocker, Bob Seger, made his debut with "Ramblin' Gamblin' Man," which was not much of a tune. But we liked him because he called his band the Bob Seger System. It was, after all, systems against which we fought. We loved irony!

Canned Heat's new single, "Going Up the Country," was anti-American in the ironic and limited sense of suggesting that, despite America's boast of being "the land of the free," if one wanted to be truly free, one might have to live elsewhere than in America.

"Crimson and Clover" by Tommy James and the Shondells may have seemed like just another bubble gum song from this band — but listen to the words! It is a psychedelic hymn to freedom, serenity, self-determination, and tolerance.

The lyrics of "I Started a Joke" were the Bee Gees' most poignant. They evoked visions of unwitting victims of their own good intentions, the paradox of hilarity causing sadness, the cruelty of misery prompting laughter, and the irony of Jesus Christ and other martyrs sacrificing themselves for the world. We asked, "Does everything really grow out of its opposite?"

The Doors' new single, "Touch Me," was about as commercial as they ever got. The musical schizophrenia of this band continued to mystify us. On the one hand, they released complex, intelligent songs like "When the Music's Over," "Five to One," and "The End," but on the other hand, they spewed out AM radio crap like "Touch Me," "Love Me Two Times," "Hello, I Love You," and the short version of "Light My Fire." How could this be? In the Beatles' case, we could put such disparity down to the differences between Lennon and McCartney, but the Doors were Morrison's band, pure and simple, so any differences between one type of Doors song and another all originated from inside Morrison's own head. Was he a sellout pretending to be cool, or was he a cool guy who sometimes sold out?

Ω

The extraordinary musical event of the fall was the Beatles' untitled release, the so-called "White Album," four vinyl sides of the best, most varied, and most complex stuff that they had put out to date — and probably ever put out — and that is saying something!

Their double-sided single, McCartney's "Hey Jude" and Lennon's "Revolution" had appeared two months earlier and had served as a herald for their new album, their first in a year. Neither side of the single was really AM material, even though both, especially "Hey Jude," got plenty of AM airplay. At just over seven minutes, "Hey Jude" was much too long for AM, so AM DJs would cut the refrain off prematurely. That sucked! The refrain was nearly four minutes and had a full eighteen iterations of "na na ..." before fading out. We wanted to hear them all. Each was a bit different. We judged the relative coolness of radio stations according to how many of the eighteen they would typically play. Of course, FM stations always played them all.

"Revolution" was John's clearest political statement to date. He had previously only alluded in his lyrics to his political stance, but here, for the first time, he set it out plainly, in no uncertain terms. He was not only against the Vietnam War, but also against war in general — and violence in general, even revolutionary violence, even though he supported the ongoing political and cultural revolutions. He asserted all this with the zeal of the penitent convert. As a victim and former perpetrator of domestic abuse, he had had to come far in his own psyche to be able to reject violence sincerely. He had beaten his first wife, Cynthia, and had confessed these and other violent offenses in "Getting Better." He had thereafter worked hard to change himself. We must give Yoko Ono much credit for guiding him along his road to recovery and psychological redefinition, for awakening his spirit to universalism, pacifism, and feminism.

The White Album further identified and more sharply delineated the differences among the four, and especially between Lennon and McCartney. Where John was political, trenchant, edgy, imagistic, a bit angry, and a bit dark — but not always; Paul was soft, melodic, beautiful, uncontroversial, and given to "silly love songs" — but not always.

Paul's "Back in the U.S.S.R." opened the album. It rocked much harder than most of his tunes since "Yesterday," and suggested to us that the Soviets, the Russians, ought not to be objectified as the "enemy" or the "other side," but rather seen just as we see ourselves, as fellow humans.

John's "Dear Prudence" asserted the individual's integral harmony with the universe — and the natural beauty that emanates from that relationship.

"Glass Onion" was just Lennon toying with us. He knew that we were obsessed with digging for deep meanings in Beatles songs, so he deliberately threw out a bunch of dead-end "clues" to test our mettle. In effect, by revisiting several of his old songs, he was satirizing his fans' adoration of them.

"Ob-La-Di, Ob-La-Da" was typical — quintessential — McCartney, a meaningless, catchy, upbeat pop tune, a "silly love song" with a happy ending. One line, however, caught our attention, suggesting that Desmond may have indulged in a bit of transvestism after his idyllic marriage to Molly. In much the same vein, Paul's strident, staccato, almost discordant "Wild Honey Pie" conveyed a sense of the innately bizarre, but still managed also to convey approval of standard, old-fashioned, bilateral, heterosexual relationships.

John's "The Continuing Story of Bungalow Bill" condemned the tendency of rightists to want to kill — not just their supposed human "enemies," but all kinds of things. It portrayed the archetypal military mother, sending her oedipal, gun-loving son out to kill, then approving each little death that he caused, whether human or animal. We were reminded of sadistic but typical young boys shooting BBs at anything that moved while their mothers looked the other way and gave no more warning than, "Be careful, don't shoot anyone's eye out!" Lennon's pun on the name of the American wild west slaughterer, Buffalo Bill, was obvious and useful; but it was too bad that John could not have made an even more to-the-point pun on a name like Custer, Kitchener, Patton, Goldwater — or Johnson.

We may oversimply but heuristically discern four levels of human social organization: (1) the family, either nuclear or extended, a person's blood relations or adopted kin, to whom is felt the natural bond of love and the debt of life; (2) civil society, the people to whom one is not related but with whom one has acquaintance or does business in everyday experience outside the home: friends, shopkeepers, farmers, teachers, clerks, brokers, neighbors, casual encounters, etc.; (3) the state, the impersonal political umbrella organization, usually regarded as if it were itself an individual, which governs or regulates civil society; and (4) the international society of states, a loose, almost abstract confederation, at least so far in history. The often problematic distinction between right and left may be partially illuminated by examining our relationships with these four, especially the first two. Typically, both rightists and leftists love and are loved by their respective families. But the right stops there; the left looks beyond it. The right sees civil society as elements to be manipulated for one's own and one's family's own gain. The left sees civil society as comprised of humans like ourselves, who *ipso facto* deserve compassion and care, just as we and our families do. The right is willing to sacrifice civil society, indeed any human to whom one is not related, for the sake of one's family or one's self. The left, being more nearly egalitarian, is not willing to sacrifice any aspect of humanity for any insular or parochial gain, even family-oriented or self-oriented gain. Hence the rightist tendency to kill. Hence the leftist tendency to abandon one's family for the sake of humanistic principles.

George's "While My Guitar Gently Weeps" was surely his own greatest achievement and still contends for having been the best Beatles song ever, perhaps even better than Lennon's, McCartney's, or Lennon/McCartney's best, such as "A Day in the Life," "Hey Jude," "Eleanor Rigby," "Norwegian Wood," "Penny Lane," "Strawberry Fields Forever," "All You Need is Love," "Lucy in the Sky With Diamonds," "We Can Work It Out," "She Loves You," "I Am the Walrus," "You've Got to Hide Your Love Away," or "Let It Be." One of my friends was so impressed with the guitar part the first time he heard "While My Guitar Gently Weeps" that he exclaimed, "Wow! George is really getting good!" But soon thereafter he discovered that it was really Eric Clapton sitting in. The lyrics were just as inspiring as the music. The segue from the previous song was perfect, almost as if George were mourning the victims of Bungalow Bill's rifle. More broadly, with the zeal and eloquence of a Hebrew prophet exalting God's universal *hesed* ("loving kindness" or "steadfast love"), George lamented that the whole human world could not or would not show its God-given love to each other.

"Happiness is a Warm Gun" was John's sarcastic attack on the sappy but popular contemporary *Peanuts* catchphrase, "Happiness is a warm puppy." His inscrutable lyrics made it sound like a drug song. Maybe it was not, but it sounded like one.

Side two opened with Paul's piano rag, "Martha My Dear," a love song to his sheepdog. John's "I'm So Tired" immediately countered this upbeat effect and substituted a melancholy atmosphere of loneliness, despair, anger, and insomnia. Nevertheless, his suggestion that he would trade material possessions for serenity was uplifting. Back to Paul again for "Blackbird," the mood again became light, but not quite trivial, with its pervasive theme of natural freedom.

George's "Piggies" was a sarcastic damnation of anyone who would live by greed, the third of the seven deadly sins that have been standard in Roman Catholic theology since the sixth century.[56] George's words reminded us primarily of the lawless capitalists, the so-called "robber barons," of the American nineteenth century, who got rich by cheating, exploiting, blackmailing, and strongarming others, particularly their own employees and business associates. He suggested that humans preying on other humans in such fashion was tantamount to cannibalism.

Paul's narrative "Rocky Raccoon," a tale of the old American west, provided a bit of gentle humor by mocking a few stereotypes of American culture.

Ringo's "Don't Pass Me By" began as a simple story of loneliness, but in its last verse took a twist, implying that sometimes there are good reasons for people not keeping appointments. Trust is the foundation of being able to preserve any relationship.

---

[56] They are, in order: lust (*luxuria*), gluttony (*gula*), greed (*avaritia*), sloth (*acedia*), wrath (*ira*), envy (*invidia*), and pride (*superbia*). They were respectively opposed by one version of the seven cardinal virtues: chastity, temperance, charity, industry, patience, kindness, and humility. But a more nearly standard list of these virtues merges the four Platonic virtues, wisdom, justice, temperance, and courage, with the three Christian virtues, faith, hope, and love.

"Why Don't We Do It in the Road?" was so obnoxious and risqué that we naturally thought it must be one of John's. Imagine our surprise — and newfound [wink wink] respect for Paul — when we learned it was one of his. Just because he sang it did not necessarily mean that he had written it. But he had! We did not think he had it in him [wink wink]. Apparently it was about the ease, frequency, and innocence with which some animals, such as monkeys, have sex.

Paul's "I Will" was another of his "silly love songs."

John's "Julia" was an ode, not only to his mother, Julia Stanley Lennon, who was hit by a car and killed when she was forty-four and John was seventeen, but also to Yoko, whose name in Japanese means "Child of the Ocean."

Side three began with a true Lennon/McCartney collaboration, "Birthday," a catchy rocker which should replace the late nineteenth-century "Happy Birthday to You" as the usual song to be sung when annual candles are blown out and presents are opened.

John's "Yer Blues" was the heaviest song on the album. Its topic was the singer's contemplation of suicide. We assumed — hoped — that John was singing in a persona, not autobiographically. Given his hot young love affair with Yoko, then current, we had no reason to believe that it was autobiographical. Yet it was a powerful, heartfelt lyric. John must have felt this way at some earlier point, else he would not have been able to have written such despondent poetry, evoking the worst in just about everything. Again we silently thanked Yoko for rescuing him.

Paul's "Mother Nature's Son" suggested pastoral tranquillity, idyllic harmony, and the simple pleasures that would be available to anyone, regardless of age, race, gender, wealth, or social station. Of course, chief among these pleasures was music.

John's "Everybody's Got Something to Hide Except Me and My Monkey" was a humorous ditty about his relationship with Yoko. The word "monkey" was a *double entendre*, being both his nickname for her and a slang term for an addiction.

"Sexy Sadie" seemed at first like a dig at an unfaithful woman, in the tradition of "Runaround Sue," "Hey Joe," or the Syndicate of Sound's "Little Girl." In reality, as we would soon learn, it was not about a woman at all, but was John's bitter repudiation of what he had discovered to be the transparency and phoniness of Maharishi Mahesh Yogi's transcendental meditation, which he and several others had gone to India to study.

We had no idea what Paul's "Helter Skelter" meant. Rumors abounded that he had written it on a dare, just to prove that he could write something raucous. Some said that it was a response to the Who's "I Can See for Miles," but we could not fathom that connection. Because we did not understand the lyrics, we naturally assumed that they were about sex. As it would turn out next year, the mass murderer Charles Manson did not understand them either, but believed that he did. To him, "Helter Skelter" was a prophecy of universal race war, during which he and his followers would have to hide and kill in order to survive. We learned later that Ringo's anguished scream at the end about blisters on his fingers referred only to how many takes the recording had required and how long he had been drumming.

George's "Long, Long, Long" was a grateful song of found love.

Side four began with John's "Revolution 1," which had the same lyrics as the single, "Revolution," and nearly the same tune, but slower, jazzier, mellower.

Paul's "Honey Pie" sounded like a throwback to the twenties, a light, high-key, music hall number that could have been sung by Jimmy Durante and choreographed by Fred Astaire.

George's witty and charming "Savoy Truffle" attacked another of the seven deadly sins, gluttony.

"Cry Baby Cry" sounded like John's attempt to write a McCartney song. Indeed, we were surprised to learn that it was John's. It seemed so much like one of Paul's lesser efforts: airy topic, silly names, lousy rhymes, tacky sound effects, etc. We would learn later from John's 1980 *Playboy* interviews with David Sheff that he wanted to disown it.

John's and (uncredited but obviously there) Yoko's "Revolution 9" was an *avant garde*, eight-minute-twenty-two-second, apparently chaotic concoction of a wild variety of sounds and sound effects, some *vérité*, and some from the studio. Just barely musical, it contained oblique, obscure, or out-of-context references to such disconnected phenomena as religion, nudity, dance crazes, war, and American football. Some tried to find deep meaning in whatever words we could discern, and to decode whatever we could not, but to no avail. The track was played backwards, slowed down, speeded up, and subjected to many other kinds of technical tricks, all in order to delve into its presumed mysteries. Some would later think that it held clues in that idiotic "Paul is dead" business that surfaced in 1969. Some detractors even called it satanic. Manson would take it as pointing toward the ninth chapter of the New Testament book of Revelation. But some of us were merely amused by it, did not take it seriously at all. "Aw, it's probably just Lennon toying with us again," we said. Maybe we were right, maybe not.

Appropriately enough, John's gentle, soothing lullaby, "Good Night," sung by Ringo, ended the LP.

The White Album included four big color glossy portrait photos, one of each Beatle, and a huge folded lyrics sheet with montages of black-and-white and partially colored photos of all four in various phases, attitudes, and positions. One of these showed Lennon talking on the phone, sitting cross-legged, naked, in bed with Yoko, whose right arm was all over his left thigh. Uncensored! Amazing!

Ω

Peter O'Toole reprised his *Becket* role as King Henry II in *The Lion in Winter*, this time playing him at Christmas 1183 as an old man. Hence the title. Katharine Hepburn was Eleanor of Aquitaine. Their oldest son and heir, Henry, had just been killed in a rebellion with his younger brother Geoffrey against their father. The king, queen, their three surviving sons, and King Philip II of France convened to negotiate who would become the new heir to the English throne. In the father, mother, and their sons we saw five soulless, loveless wretches deciding the fate of nations. None of them possessed any of the human qualities necessary to govern any people wisely and well. Each was completely unqualified to understand the everyday interests of ordinary citizens. Their dysfunctionality as a family was matched only by their detachment from their actual vocation to govern. Yet such is the nature of the hereditary ruling class, to be aloof from real human concerns and to care only about power. Being the child of even a good ruler does not bestow any political aptitude; and being the child of a bad ruler, even less. In history, Henry was succeeded by his son, Richard I, Coeur de Lion, who frittered away his ten-year reign in foreign wars, and his last son, John Lackland, the notoriously cruel and incompetent king who was forced in 1215 to sign the Magna Carta.

Mel Brooks, who had honed his craft writing with Sid Caesar, Steve Allen, and Carl Reiner, jumpstarted his movie-making career by writing and directing *The Producers*. Others had made a few efforts, notably the CBS TV show, *Hogan's Heroes*, to find humor in Nazi atrocities, but none were nearly as funny as *The Producers*. Zero Mostel played Max Bialystock, a sleazy, bombastic, but lovable con man who fleeced rich little old ladies. Gene Wilder was Leo Bloom (not to be confused with James Joyce's Leopold Bloom), a neurotic accountant. When Bloom dreamily suggested that, with craftily maintained ledgers, a producer could make more money with a flop than with a hit, Bialystock, much to Bloom's surprise, seized upon the idea and immediately began to implement it, making Bloom his sidekick. They set out to find the worst play ever written, intending to produce it, see it close after one performance, and pocket all the backers' investments. They found *Springtime for Hitler*, an obsequious monstrosity devotedly written by a fanatic ex-Nazi who still wore his World War II helmet and medals. As Jews, they both naturally believed that any drama glorifying Hitler would flop on Broadway, but to ensure its failure even further, they hired a psychedelic wacko to play the title role. When the wacko camped it up with rock-and-roll anachronisms and hippie jive, sang the blues, and did Hitler strictly for laughs, the play, which the author wrote as straight drama, became a rollicking success as low comedy. The backers, the little old ladies who together owned 25,000 per cent of the profits, could not be paid and the producers went to prison — where they continued the same scheme with a new play, *Prisoners of Love*, bilking the other inmates, the guards, and even the warden.

Neither the 1975 campy cult classic, *The Rocky Horror Picture Show*, nor Douglas Adams's superior science fiction absurdity, his five-volume trilogy of *Hitchhiker's Guide to the Galaxy* books, would have been possible without first the movie, *Barbarella: Queen of the Galaxy*. There are some movies that we recognize as awful, yet we love them anyway — or maybe *because of* their utter lack of merit. *Barbarella* was just such a movie. It was not mindless fluff — we always hated that. Nor was it typical science fiction. It was groundbreaking, but not in a profound direction. The opening scene depicted the simple act of the title heroine removing her space suit as if doing a weightless strip tease. We saw Jane Fonda naked, even to the extent of pubic hair, before we heard a word of dialogue. Quickly the movie revealed itself as, not science fiction, but a sex farce masquerading as science fiction. Its tableaux owed as much to Hieronymus Bosch as to standard science fiction motifs. The music sucked and the plot reached new lows in contrivance, but the photography was stunning. For visual indulgence, *Barbarella* is still hard to beat. We could enjoy its vacuity, because it sought only to present visual beauty and did not take itself seriously, but at the same time we could regard *2001* as insufferable in spite of its breathtaking visual beauty, because it took itself much too seriously. Some of *Barbarella*'s self-parody was evident in its casting: Rolling Stones' paramour Anita Pallenberg played Barbarella's penultimate nemesis; Marcel Marceau had a speaking part; and David Hemmings, the antihero of *Blow-Up*, played an idiot insurgent aptly named Dildano. If the film had any theme at all, it was antiwar. From her distant future perspective, Barbarella was amazed that anyone would be interested in weapons and referred to warlike societies as "living in a primitive state of neurotic irresponsibility." Not as a whore, but as an innocent, Barbarella literally fucked her way to saving the universe.

On November 1, 1968, in response to several years of complaints from uptight parents about such "dangerous" films as *I Am Curious (Yellow)*, *Blow-Up*, and *The Graduate*, the Motion Picture Association of America (MPAA) instituted its infamous rating system. The original code, which has since been modified quite a few times, was: G = Anyone could see the film; M = Only "mature" people could see it; R = No one under seventeen would be allowed inside the theater unless accompanied by a parent or guardian; and X = No one under seventeen could see the film. This was cool, we thought, tongue-in-cheekly. This code would be a very useful guide to what films we wanted to see. To us it meant: G = This film sucks and is to be avoided at all costs; M = It might be OK; R = Probably a good flick; and X = Hell, yeah! Let's go see this one right away!

Greetings was rated X, so naturally we flocked to the theater. It was a disappointment, an absurd, plotless, slice-of-life comedy about three New York City draft dodgers — dodgers, not resisters — each trying to figure out the best way to avoid induction — and it was not even very sexy. Lloyd, who escaped the draft by pretending to be gay, was obsessed with conspiracy theories of JFK's assassination, was convinced that the FBI and the Warren Commission deliberately hid the truth, and must have been about to uncover these lies, because federal agents murdered him. Paul, who escaped the draft by pretending to be an ultra-rightist, frittered his life away with computer dates and other shallow sexual relationships. Jon also used the ultra-rightist ploy, but failed to escape and was sent to Vietnam. In New York he had been a voyeur who used trickery to get women to strip for him, but in Vietnam he found voyeurism easier because could force them to strip at the point of his gun.

Monterey Pop, being a documentary, somehow escaped being rated. That did not stop Jack Valenti's censors from rating the documentary *Woodstock* R in 1970 for "drug content, nudity, and language." Anyway, the Monterey movie did not show any druggy or naked scenes, and did not have any "foul-mouthed" dialogue (except for the word "bullshit" once), as did its Woodstock counterpart.

Photographically, it was the best concert footage we had ever seen. The marvelous close-ups of the singers, especially Janis, were sharper and more interesting than any we had seen on TV. The image of Mama Cass sitting in the audience completely enrapt by Janis singing "Ball and Chain" was priceless. Cass could have learned a lot from Janis.

Monterey's outdoor sound was state-of-the-art too. Five and a half minutes into the one-hour-twenty-minute film, as the opening titles and vignettes gave way and as a live version of Big Brother's "Combination of the Two" and the studio version of Scott McKenzie's "San Francisco" faded into the studio version of the Mamas' and the Papas' "Creeque Alley," we saw John Phillips giving set-up orders and David Crosby rejoicing over the unexpectedly high quality of the sound system. He knew.

Both the line-up and the audience were interracial. We saw people living in tents, just going about their daily business. Cameras sympathetically recorded the Native American influence on the peaceful culture of the happening. Despite the hard-ass metal folding chairs and the omnipresent cops, everyone seemed to be enjoying the time of their lives. We had glimpses of huge celebrities easily mingling with the crowd, even though recognized, not being hassled by gawkers or autograph-seekers, but being treated as just plain folks, like anyone else.

In the theater we were for the first time struck by the gentleness of the whole event, gentleness that went beyond mere tolerance of one another, all the way to love. We in the east wished we had been there, wished we had already known and felt what the people in San Francisco had known and felt for a year and a half. What we learned from this movie about just how to get along with one another would next summer become our spiritual blueprint for Woodstock.

The concert footage itself began with the Mamas and the Papas, all in glittering floor-length robes, singing "California Dreamin'" while Denny and Cass bantered with each other. Canned Heat's "Rollin' and Tumblin'," featuring Blind Owl Wilson's finger-pickin' slide guitar style, revealed why bassist Larry Taylor was called "The Mole." The starkly red and black night shot of Simon and Garfunkel singing "The 59th Street Bridge Song" then provided some contrast, but even more when they were followed by Hugh Masekela, whose African rhythms and phrases in "Bajabula Bonke / Healing Song" were at that time a novelty in America.

Marty and Grace presented a fantastic vocal duet in the Airplane's "High Flyin' Bird," but her voice mike did not function properly for their duet of "Today." Then appeared one of the high points of the whole film, Janis Joplin singing "Ball and Chain." After seeing and hearing that performance, could anyone doubt that a white chick could belt out the blues? Could anyone thereafter *not* be a fan of this lonely, tragic woman from Port Arthur, Texas?

With a funky psychedelic fiddle in the band, the Animals covered the Stones' "Paint It, Black," using new lyrics while the film interspersed shots of people in the crowd, including the peacock Brian Jones strolling the grounds. Over against the elegant "Prince Jones," Burdon resembled a stout plebeian gnome in his fringed peasant vest with broad horizontal stripes.

No less peacocks than Jones were the Who, in shimmering silk and satin at the height of their infatuation with mod fashions. We had never before seen as much energy behind the drums as Keith put out in that performance. At the end of their finale, "My Generation," John continued churning out his trademark bass riff while Pete smashed his guitar and attacked an amp, Roger twirled in his iridescent cape, Keith kicked over his kit, and roadies and security guys hustled onstage to rescue as much equipment as they could. No possibility of an encore.

Country Joe and the Fish were just plain weird. Joe McDonald wore a pink, blue, and green paisley shirt; brown pants with an American flag sticking out of his left ass pocket; beads; his stash; face paint; earrings; shades; assorted flowers; and a hardhat. Guitarist Barry Melton wore blue jeans and an old Army jacket; bassist Bruce Barthol a red and white striped tee shirt, dark gray pants, and a light gray vest; keyboardist David Cohen gray and white striped pants, a mottled red shirt, a black vest, a silver pendant, and a flat black hat with a wide wampum hatband holding a feather and a flower; and drummer Chicken Hirsch a Greek fisherman's cap and a black and gold shirt. They all looked semi-conscious, as did most of their audience. Yet their jam tune, "Section 43," mesmerized.

The only other performer in the film who exuded as much energy as Keith Moon was Otis Redding. With "Shake" he elicited the traditional African call-and-response then crooned a delicious "I've Been Loving You Too Long." We soul music fans were treated to glimpses of the already legendary Duck Dunn on bass and Steve Cropper on guitar.

Gum-chewing Jimi Hendrix was resplendent in a gold ruffled shirt, a purple headband, red pants, a black bolero vest trimmed in white, Beatle boots, and silver beads and chains. After coaxing never-before-heard sounds from his upside-down Fender Stratocaster, he segued into "Wild Thing," mimed sex with his guitar as both the penis and the partner, squirted lighter fluid on it like he was taking a piss, set it afire, and smashed it. Some in the audience looked disgusted, shocked, or disinterested with this display.

Director D.A. Pennebaker's insertion of the Mamas' and the Papas' "Got a Feelin'" into the film right after Hendrix's firestorm was like a douse of cold water. But from that rather low point, he built a culminating crescendo of enthusiasm. Masterfully, as disembodied, sporadic sitar notes wafted on the soundtrack, he showed audience members doing dull, mundane, automatic things: sleeping, resting, dressing, schlepping, smoking, eating, praying, etc., all in dull, mundane, automatic ways with dull, mundane, automatic looks on their faces. Gradually, beginning to realize what they might be hearing, these people turned to pay attention — to really listen — becoming more and more enthralled, happier and happier every second. After seven minutes of this, Pennebaker at last allowed us to see the source of these invigorating notes: Ravi Shankar.

Excluding the closing titles, the last nineteen minutes of the film, or about one fourth its total length, consisted of Shankar playing "Raga Bhimpalasi." He was magnificent! Seldom have faster or more dextrous hands charmed a more astonishing variety of exciting sounds from an acoustic stringed instrument! For sheer musicianship, on any instrument, he was by far the best we had *ever* heard or seen! The sitar is not easy to play — it is much more difficult to master than the guitar. Among Shankar's awestruck admirers that day was Hendrix himself, as indeed, many fine guitarists made themselves just part of the sitarist's audience, no doubt not only to enjoy the exotic Indian music, but also to learn.

Shankar's music, and the unforced standing ovation that followed it, underscored the highly civilized idea that the proper and ultimate goal of all human endeavor ought to be to make the world safe for musicians, and that progress in history can be measured by the extent to which we have neared this goal. Before the concert, as he revealed in the liner notes of his Liberty Records live Monterey album, Shankar had been worried that six-hundred-year-old Indian classical music would be underappreciated by an American pop music audience. He need not have worried. Beautiful, powerful music transcends all times and cultures. As he said in these same liner notes, "sound is God."

By the end of 1968 some of us had fallen into the trap of hating our opponents, treating them as if they were enemies rather than just political adversaries. With "Everyday People," Sly and the Family Stone gently chastised us for this essentially evil and counterproductive attitude, reminding us that we cannot serve the poor by hating the rich and loving the poor, serve cultural tolerance by hating the short-haired and loving the long-haired, or serve civil rights by hating white oppressors and loving all the colors that they oppress. Rather, we must accept all people for what they are, and deal with them only on those terms. Sly's interracial band, for the duration of its existence into the early seventies, would remain a persuasive voice for inclusiveness, tolerance, and a colorblind society. On the December 29 *Ed Sullivan Show* they performed "Everyday People," "Dance to the Music," "Ya Ya Ya," "M'Lady," and "Hey Music Lover," a variation of their standard medley that would later become famous at Woodstock.

Spring 1969

Hey, Dick!

You measure a democracy by the freedom it
gives its dissidents, not the freedom it gives
its assimilated conformists.
> — attributed to Abbie Hoffman

How to describe a torrent overreaching its furthest bounds? The emotions of those caught in the flood? The forces that drove it to crest and recede? If we could describe any of these things well, then we might be able to begin to describe 1969, the most tumultuous, schizophrenic, significant year of the entire period.

We were overwhelmed. We were at once as deliriously happy as we had ever been, sparked by that vague ghost, "Solidarity!" and as damnably pissed off as we had ever been: betrayed by Nixon, whom we had never trusted anyway; beslavered by straight society, which, after five years, had finally figured out a few ways to make a buck off us; and beleaguered by the same establishment that was flattering us, for they saw that the best way to exploit hippiedom for dollars was to keep the counterculture as "counter" as they could. The only ways to fight back against that sort of greedy condescension were either to sell out and be like them or to resolve to buy nothing at all and thus either steal or starve to death — Scylla and Charybdis! Or maybe corporate America would just leave us alone. As David Crosby would concisely put it on the August 19 *Dick Cavett Show*: "Fat chance!"

As in any situation, there were some whose focus was only on the transient spectacle of successive or overlapping phenomena. Such people would just sit back and enjoy, or get up and retch, and would derive little or no actual meaning from their experiences, however wide, long, or deep. But there were others who sought to configure phenomena into patterns of meaning, to discern meaning where it already existed, or to impose it where it did not. These latter people were not merely observers, but thinkers, philosophers, seekers after the overarching reason that their instinct told them must connect all otherwise disconnected phenomena. That included us. We wanted to make sense of it all — somehow.

To the extent that we were worldly, experienced, and self-assured, we could cope with the changes, but we were still mainly innocent, and in our innocence we were all deaf, dumb, and blind. Pete Townshend told us so — and we believed him, at least those of us who had read Rousseau. *Tommy*, the opera, the original blue album with doves, not any of its demeaning subsequent incarnations, immediately revealed to those of us who studied its implications seriously, philosophically, in their larger context, the genius of its creator, not just musical genius, but lyrical, speculative genius untainted by scholarly forms and dogmas, reflective genius in its primal state.

Townshend invented rock opera — singlehandedly, *ex nihilo*. Rock opera was not the unified music drama or *Gesamtkunstwerk* ("complete work of art") of Richard Wagner or Richard Strauss. Rather, it was just a loosely connected series of songs that, considered together, told a story. In that way it was not even as unified as the operas of Giuseppe Verdi or Giacomo Puccini, but, being more disjunct and impressionistic, more closely resembled the works of Gioacchino Rossini, Wolfgang Amadeus Mozart, George Frideric Handel, or Claudio Monteverdi. Instead of recitative holding the narrative together between the songs, as in these seventeenth and eighteenth-century operas, in rock opera there was nothing except the listeners' imaginations to fulfill this function. Hence rock opera, unless glossed by its composer — as Townshend often did, though not always consistently — would typically be open to a wide variety of plausible interpretations.

Before *Tommy* there was only one rock opera, "A Quick One While He's Away," and that was only a so-called "mini-opera." *Tommy* was the first full-length rock opera. Afterwards came a slew of them, notably the Kinks' *Arthur*.

In 1755 Jean-Jacques Rousseau published his *Discourse on the Origin of Inequality*, which asserted that humans in the state of nature were kind, peaceful, and basically good. In this he directly opposed Hobbes, for whom the state of nature was violent and hideous. Humans lost their natural innocence, compassion, and goodness only when some primeval person introduced the concept of property, ownership, or boundaries, and when other primeval people, perhaps too gullibly, accepted that concept. Rousseau's idea of "natural man" became a stock motif in European Romanticism for at least the next hundred years.

In the character Tommy, Townshend created the psychological natural man, i.e., someone who, only because of his own psychological blocks, was completely ignorant of civilization, society, or culture, and who was thus developmentally or morally equivalent to Rousseauian man in the state of nature. Whether Pete had read Rousseau or not, we did not know; but the similarities between his character and Rousseau's paragon were too obvious and too strong to ignore. We studied with great interest how Pete expanded upon the Rousseauian theme.

Nearly all that we each know about our particular civilization, society, or culture is learned through the senses of sight and hearing and through the act of communicating with other people. Imagine someone who possessed all these capabilities, physically, but at a very young age prevented himself, psychologically, from using them. There you have Tommy. What could he know of civilization, society, or culture? How could he interpret or apply whatever this knowledge might be?

Given that they were only self-directed, what were his thoughts and feelings?

"Overture / It's a Boy": Tommy Walker was born in 1914 while his dad was away in the British Army in World War I. He led a normal life for his first seven years, but Captain Walker did not return from the war. "1921" told of how finally and mysteriously he did return and caught Mrs. Walker *in flagrante delicto* with her new lover. The happily reunited married couple killed the lover. But there was a snag. Young Tommy had seen the whole thing. Desperate to suppress the witness and avoid prosecution, the pair told Tommy repeatedly and forcefully in "You Didn't Hear It" that he had not seen or heard anything. They commanded him never to tell anyone the truth. The boy, confused, terrified, and traumatized, convinced himself to believe his parents' words instead of his own senses. He shut down, becoming immediately unable to see, hear, or speak. Thus blind, deaf, and dumb, he set off upon a magnificent internal and perfectly private voyage of discovery, as portrayed in "Amazing Journey" and "Sparks." Therein, he experienced wonders that seeing, hearing, and speaking people could not possibly experience. It was they, not he, who were disadvantaged as perceivers.

Tommy grew and thrived, happy and healthy despite his self-imposed "handicaps." By age ten he had either forgotten or pushed into a remote corner of his mind not only the murder, but also any knowledge of his former civilization, society, and culture except the language. Apparently he could still think in English. Miraculously free of all undesirable knowledge, he had come to gain knowledge mainly through his sense of touch and marginally through smell and taste. Townshend explained that at this point Tommy perceived everything that he touched or that touched him as only vibration, or as "incredible, meaningless beauty."[57] In other words, nothing that Tommy experienced had any social stigma attached to it, so he could make up his own mind about it all, without any kind of interference.

Yet his parents, not realizing any of this, and believing that Tommy was "sick," were worried about their son. Evidently throwing caution to the winds with regard to their crime, they tried various ways to try to "cure" him. First, in a song called either "The Hawker" or "Eyesight to the Blind," they hired a huckster who claimed that his woman was so beautiful that she could restore sight. Of course, this ploy failed. Meanwhile, Tommy just continued to receive and enjoy tactile sensations devoid of any connotations or prejudices.

In "Christmas," we learned that his parents were also worried that, if Tommy could not recover sufficient sentience to become aware of Jesus Christ's promise of eternal salvation for those who became Christians, then he would have to go to hell. They cried that Tommy could neither hear their pleas nor learn how to pray.

In "Cousin Kevin," an Entwistle tune — obviously — Tommy became the victim of a sadist for a whole afternoon. In "The Acid Queen," his parents tried to "cure" him by hiring a gypsy to take Tommy on an LSD trip. In the ten-minute instrumental, the bass-heavy "Underture," we again could meditate on the mysteries of Tommy's unique way of experiencing the world.

---

[57] Rick Sanders and David Dalton, "[Interview with] Pete Townshend," *Rolling Stone*, 37 (July 12, 1969): 16.

In "Do You Think It's Alright?" his parents agreed that to allow Uncle Ernie to babysit Tommy would be safe, despite the fact that Ernie was already a bit drunk. Wrong! In "Fiddle About," Ernie raped Tommy, but Tommy liked it, not having any idea that incestuous homosexual rape was forbidden by society.

Tommy had been given a pinball machine for Christmas. Unable to see its flashing lights or hear its distracting bells and buzzers, he could therefore concentrate entirely on just feeling the machine, letting it become an extension or even a part of him, much like a race driver would ideally like his car to become. He had no knowledge of "rules," "points," or "scores," but by trial and error his body learned what to do to keep the machine vibrating just the way he wanted. Maintaining his vibrations was all he cared about. In this way he could even enjoy music without actually hearing it. He got to be so good at pinball that his parents took him on tour, exhibiting him like a sideshow attraction. He soon became a celebrity, beating every other pinball champion in England, as we learned in "Pinball Wizard" (the single from the double album set). Some kids, astounded by his sheer skill at pinball and that he could do it all without seeing or hearing, became his first disciples.

Meanwhile, the father came home one day exclaiming, "There's a Doctor I've Found." Tommy's parents' hopes for a "cure" were thus renewed.

Townshend's personae of the parents, the hawker, Kevin, the acid queen, Ernie, and the doctor each represented or symbolized a different aspect of the corrupting influences of civilization trying but failing to reach Tommy. Yet Tommy could sense the existence and presence of these other people. He knew deep down what sight, hearing, and speech were; and he knew that they possessed these powers. Thus he somehow sensed his abnormality and longed to become "normal," to regain these powers, and to restore communication with these others. In this connection it was very important to realize that Tommy's constant begging to be seen, felt, touched, and healed — which occurred first in "Christmas" — was directed only inward toward himself, not outward toward anyone else. He was happy and content being isolated; he only wanted to increase his own powers and so enhance his perceived vibrations. If any outside attempt failed to reach him, that was not because of any intrinsic failure in the attempt, but because Tommy did not want to be reached, and barricaded his psyche against intrusion. He was experiencing a sort of "identity crisis." He was not aware of his specific position or entity status. All he knew was that he was a thinking being who experienced beautiful vibrations, but to himself he was just another vibration. He was autistic, but even beyond that, he had no sense of self-identity. Being nothing but what David Hume called a "bundle of perceptions," he lacked what Kant called the "transcendental unity of apperception," i.e., he could not situate, reify, or delineate himself in the world, but only feel it in a self-decentralized way.

The doctor's "cure" consisted only of placing Tommy in front of a mirror and inducing him to gaze into it. In "Go to the Mirror Boy," we learned that the doctor had hooked up an electroencephalograph and was thrilled to notice much higher levels of brain activity as Tommy stared at his reflection. Still, neither the doctor nor the parents could communicate with him, and he gave no sign of having noticed them. The hypnotic effect of heightening self-awareness that he received from the mirror taught him that the ultimate source of all his knowledge was just himself. At this point he began to recognize and circumscribe his own identity. He was still not aware of anyone else and he had not yet regained his senses of sight or hearing, except for his uncanny ability to see himself, and nothing else, in a mirror. With his new awareness of his own position, he began to bifurcate himself from the rest of the world. Again, it was crucial for us LP listeners to realize that when Tommy addressed his reflection as "you," he was really talking only to himself. There was still no other "you" in his world. Whereas before he had been just pure subjectivity, he had now objectified himself.

In "Tommy Can You Hear Me," his parents still could not break through into his world. This angered his mother, who now suspected — wrongly — that he was deliberately, like a spoiled brat, refusing to communicate. The doctor had verified that nothing physically was wrong with Tommy's organs of sight, hearing, or speech, and had declared that science and medicine were powerless to penetrate the barriers of one who had closed his mind off from the world. From this she inferred that he was just being obtuse, disobedient, and obstructionistic. In "Smash the Mirror," she vented her rage. As her breaking the mirror suddenly robbed him of his focus, he snapped out of his reverie and began his "cure."

In "Sensation" we saw the untainted natural man as a missionary of goodness and light. Having recovered his awareness of other people, and having magnanimously decided to share the results of his "amazing journey" with them, he set out to give them nothing more or less than a pure example of a free, kind, loving human, just travelling about, letting himself be seen. Others, though not unreceptive, and though impressed by his aura, could not comprehend his message. Frustrated by his initial failure to achieve results, he began to give speeches on how to live and how to appreciate life, but this only created a multitude of "deaf," "blind," and "dumb" followers who could not "hear" him properly, "see" where they were going, or "say" what he meant. Aware that both his knowledge and his unique way of having acquired it were superior to anyone else's, he grew more full of himself. His newly inflated ego gave him a messianic delusion of himself as a spiritual hero and turned him into an unrealistic megalomaniac. He did not understand how communication in the real world worked. He did not appreciate that he could not just be their "vibration," as unnamed and unheralded vibrations had been for him during his "amazing journey."

Tommy's well publicized "Miracle Cure" was complete. He had again become just like any other person — with worldly ambitions and the whole kit and kaboodle.

"Sally Simpson" was a tragicomic interlude. She was a cult follower, a shallow groupie impressed only by Tommy's celebrity, not by either his substance or his message. Like many of her ilk, she was irrationally headstrong. She defied her father's direct order to stay home and instead tried to meet Tommy, who would have been about fifty by this time. She failed, and was maimed in the process. We sympathized with her, because she was the child of rich, restrictive parents, and she wanted only to be free.

Tommy himself, on the other hand, through his own devices, was quite free.

In "I'm Free," he described the exhilarating feeling of just living the life of pure freedom as if nothing else mattered. This was what his life had been like before the "cure," and he was fooling himself to believe that now, with civilization intruding upon him from every side, it could still be that way. Nevertheless, Tommy's mega-lomania had gotten the best of him. He believed that he could do anything, and he remained altruistic enough to want to share it all. People begged to follow him. He listened, he tried, but he could not reach them. He failed to realize that he could not make them free or even encourage them to make themselves free, if they insisted upon following him — or upon being followers at all. Tommy himself was never a follower. That was why he was free.

In "Welcome" we saw how Tommy, desperate that his message was not getting across, allowed his Uncle Ernie to institutionalize or routinize this message as an organized religion. That was Tommy's BIG mistake! He and Ernie built a huge temple-centered camp into which he and Ernie herded his followers.

"Tommy's Holiday Camp" showed how the forces of civilization, led and personified by Uncle Ernie, cared nothing for Tommy except to exploit him in order to make money.

Tommy had to impose rules on his followers so that they could resemble him and therefore have some hope to experience something like his "amazing journey." But Tommy himself had never had any rules to follow along his trip; hence his "amazing journey" was possible, but theirs was not possible, because it could not be free of restraints. He told them that they were not allowed to drink alcohol, smoke dope, or conform to society's norms. He further ordered each of them to be blindfolded, gagged, and earplugged, and to sit around doing nothing but playing pinball. Thus he tried to arrange that they would achieve enlightenment like his, in a way analogous to how he had achieved it.

But they rebelled. In "We're Not Gonna Take It," the finale, they refused to be commanded or to be deprived of what they considered their essential worldly pleasures. They trashed the camp and stormed out, leaving Tommy alone and de-jected. Through the shock of their violent desertion, he finally realized that the very fact of having followers made him less free, and the more of a leader he was, the less free he was. He again became blind, deaf, and dumb. This brought him to the third stage of his enlightenment. The first stage was his "amazing journey," when he became cognizant of the supreme natural beauty of pure vibration. The second began in the doctor's office, when he realized that this beauty came from himself. The third was now, as he discovered through bitter experience that no one can communicate such beauty to others, that no one can be led to enlightenment, but that each person must seek and find it completely alone. He was saddened to learn that humans had become so irretrievably involved in their respective civili-zations, societies, and cultures that they had become unwilling to relinquish any-thing, even for the sake or promise of greater good. Yet they would have to do so if there were ever to evolve any truly free society.

Tommy withered back into himself and died forgotten, but at peace with himself, in 1984.

The main point of *Tommy* was threefold: First, since followers are doomed to only partial or shallow fulfillment at best, do not be a follower or a servant. Second, even if you achieve great insight, do not presume to lead or dominate others and thus create followers, disciples, or servants, because they will get your message wrong, screw it up, and drag you down, as the servants, through no intention of their own, but simply by their servitude, drag the master down in Hegel's master/servant dialectic. Finally, because master and servant, teacher and disciple, leader and follower, all encumber each other so that the masters, teachers, and leaders are more dependent on their servants, disciples, and followers than the servants, disciples, and followers are on their masters, teachers, and leaders, do not allow others to help you toward enlightenment. Rather, as Zarathustra said, "If you want to climb high, use your own legs! Do not allow yourselves to be *carried*, do not ride on strange backs and heads!"[58] But, as you "follow" this advice, do not become Nietzsche's disciple. He did not want disciples — and he knew why. To be a true individual, one must guard more against becoming a master than against becoming a servant.

Ω

For too long my country, the wealthiest nation on a poor continent, failed to carry out its full responsibilities to its sister Republics. We have now accepted that responsibility. In the same way those who possess wealth and power in poor nations must accept their own responsibilities. They must lead the fight for those basic reforms which alone can preserve the fabric of their own societies. Those who make peaceful revolution impossible will make violent revolution inevitable.
— John F. Kennedy, speech at
the White House, March 13, 1962

The definitive, quintessential sixties film is Lindsay Anderson's *If...* No one can hope to understand the sixties who has not seen it. To call *If...* the allegory of the entire message of *Die at the Right Time!* would not be an overstatement. Nowhere in art, literature, or cinema are the basic motives of young anti-establishment revolutionaries made clearer. *If...* would certainly have shaken up anyone whose idea of the British "public school" (analogous to the American single-sex preparatory boarding school) was derived from *Goodbye, Mr. Chips* or *Tom Brown's School Days*. Far from being firm but fair, as depicted in those two classics, the administration, faculty, and all the social, political, and religious authorities, traditions, and policies that constituted the essence of College, the public school where *If...*

---

[58] *Also Sprach Zarathustra*, IV, 13, 10: "Wollt ihr hoch hinaus, so braucht die eignen Beine! Lasst euch nicht empor t r a g e n, setzt euch nicht auf fremde Rücken und Köpfe!"

was set, were firmer than firm and anything but fair.

College was a den of ingrained and officially sanctioned brutality. In the opening scene, as kids were returning for the fall term, and as new kids were arriving for the first time, we saw that its rules, traditions, and culture discouraged even simple friendliness and helpfulness among students. A wide-eyed innocent named Jute, politely asking a plain question such as any bewildered new student would ask on his first day in a new school, was instantly belittled, humiliated, scolded, and called "scum." In fact, all the new students were "scum," and were expected to serve as slaves to the upperclass "whips." The whips were the elite of the inveterate ass-kissers who had sucked up to the administration so long and so well that they had earned the right to practice their sadism upon any lower-ranking student they chose, without any fear of reprisal. One whip, Rowntree, habitually forced his scum to pre-warm his toilet seat for him every time he had to take a crap. Another, Denson, who did not even know what a mollusc was, routinely ordered boys to get haircuts even though their hair was scarcely longer than his own. In class, the whips were intellectually stupid and academically ignorant, whereas disobedient troublemakers like Mick Travis, the hero, played by Malcolm Mc-Dowell, were bright, well-read, and well-informed.

The boys were encouraged to form with fellow students, not friendships, but master/slave relationships determined by age, connections, and the caprice of the administration. The masters were encouraged to be mean; the slaves to fawn. The whips were masters of all; the scum slaves of all. In between, the rest of the students were masters of some and slaves of others. Students who did not instantly accommodate themselves within this hierarchy to each and every new situation that their respective masters might thrust upon them, each according to precisely his own particular station and its duties, were summarily and harshly punished. Lower masters were beaten if their slaves did not perform to the standards of the higher masters. The hierarchy was rigidly enforced. It taught nothing worthwhile, but only the militaristic virtues: how to obey orders, how to grovel, how to hate. It made the administration remote, unaccountable, and essentially inaccessible to any of the students except the whips.

Anger and fear governed. Human values were discounted. People were stereotyped, labeled, and pigeonholed. The individual was not recognized. Specific slurs, insults, and nicknames for specific categories of people were established, prescribed, learned by rote, and subject to oral examination. Peers bullying peers was neither encouraged nor discouraged — hence it thrived. No students except the whips had any privacy. Even the most personal bathroom activities were open to scrutiny by one's classmates, tattling by the whips' toadies, and subsequent punishment by the whips themselves. Some of the whips conspired to coerce homosexual favors from their scum. In other College settings homosexual contact and harassment was not uncommon, though well hidden.

College would not let the students simply live. It systematically sought to kill their natural spirits and replace them with its own hidebound culture of discipline, patriotism, and regimentation. Individuality was ferreted out and punished. Church leaders, military leaders, business leaders, schoolmasters, and all the powerful, perverted, diminished, de-individualized adult men in the film had allowed themselves while in school to succumb to the cruelty and spiritbreaking discipline that was the foundation of their so-called education. They had not in fact had an education, but only training in conformity — which they had passed with honors. They had surrendered their individuality in order to fit in.

The sight of young boys just trying to be themselves while gussied up in the standard school uniform — which resembled formal evening wear complete with vest, starched wing collar, and black tie — only underscored their repression, both social and sexual.

There was no female presence in College other than buxom, middle-aged Mrs. Kemp, wife of the fat, bald, elderly administrator Kemp, and the simpering, elderly matron; and hence no civilizing, mollifying, or conciliatory influence. The only choice was to either accept the macho way or be degraded, ostracized, and beaten. Mrs. Kemp was a classic case of marital bedroom frustration, while the matron appeared to take peculiar delight in her periodic flashlight inspection of the boys' genitalia — for medical and hygienic purposes, of course.

The mathematics teacher, an Anglican priest in dog collar, enjoyed slapping heads, twisting nipples, and other gratuitous physical abuse of students. We suspected as soon as we saw him that he was a sadistic homosexual pedophile rapist. We feared for Jute and others in the youngest class.

College associated religious ritual with pedagogical regimentation at every opportunity. The College song was set to the tune of the American Presbyterian hymn, "Stand Up, Stand Up for Jesus," and sounded like a high Anglican hymn. The chaplain, this same Anglican priest, declared in a sermon to the full body of students, all in military uniform:

> The Son of God goes forth to war, a kingly crown to gain. ... If a soldier doesn't do his duty, he expects to be punished. There are failures great and small and there are punishments great and small, but there is one failure, one crime, one betrayal, that can never be forgiven, and that betrayal is called desertion. The deserter in the face of the enemy must expect to be shot. Jesus Christ is our commanding officer, and if we desert Him, we can expect no mercy. And we are all deserters.

Such un-Christian, anti-Christian bombast, masquerading as Christianity, was typical of what was called "Muscular Christianity" in late nineteenth-century Britain. We recognized that its traditions were alive and well in America in 1969. This phony Christianity had sprung fullblown from the marriage of patriotism and the militant Calvinist idea that humanity must never enjoy itself, but, in order to be saved from itself, must see itself as depraved, unworthy of salvation. We doubted that Jesus, the Prince of Peace, the God of Love, would have approved of either Calvin, this cold militancy, or these unloving threats.

While the chaplain, now in military uniform but still in his dog collar, was leading everyone in College in military drills and war games, Mrs. Kemp took out her sexual frustrations by strolling naked through the boys' rooms, fondling their personal articles.

Fully in keeping with its military ambience, the film's title derived from Rudyard Kipling's militaristic poem, "If — ," an inspirational Stoic anthem that preaches sturdy resignation to the status quo. Among its lines are:

> If you can trust yourself when all men doubt you,
> But make allowance for their doubting too;
> If you can wait and not be tired by waiting,
> Or being lied about, don't deal in lies,
> Or being hated, don't give way to hating,
> And yet don't look too good, nor talk too wise

Kipling himself was a Muscular Christian, imperialistic and fascistic enough to have supported the establishment as depicted in *If…*

The main question of *If…* was the same as that of *The Prisoner*: Can the free individual survive, psychologically intact, under systematic government, within well ordered civilization, through well established institutions, or over against aristocracy? The culture in *If…* was not quite as well ordered as that of the Village, but it was more nearly recognizable as our own culture, and both analogies to our own lives were unsettling. Also, the *Gemeinschaft / Gesellschaft* distinction that we saw in *The Prisoner* was not as sharp in *If…*, yet it existed, and the point of the juxtaposition was the same: The free individual might be able to survive intact in a well ordered society (*Gesellschaft*), but never in a well ordered community (*Gemeinschaft*).

Only three students resisted this institutionalized cruelty, Mick and his two best friends, Johnny and Wallace. Rowntree branded them as "lunatic fringe" and "unruly elements" that "threaten the stability of the house," and thereby received *carte blanche* from Kemp for the whips to deal with them however they wished. The whole school listened to the whips gleefully slashing at the asses of Mick and the two other rebels with their canes, then Rowntree forced Mick to shake his hand and thank him for the beating. But soon thereafter Mick started pistol practice and the three performed the medieval Norse ceremony of blood brotherhood, pledging "Death to the oppressor," "Resistance," "Liberty," and "One man can change the world with a bullet in the right place."

In what was probably a dream sequence (although it was presented as if real), Mick and one of his mates escaped College one day during a rugby match and romped to the nearby town, which was off-limits. They annoyed passersby, stole a motorcycle, and, despite treating her rudely, Mick got to have consensual sex with a just-met waitress. The trio rode off on the motorcycle, with her standing up like a figurehead.

In the fifteenth minute color film gave way to black-and-white. Thereafter scenes alternated irregularly between black-and-white and color. We wondered if any significance attached to this shift, as in *The Wizard of Oz*, where Kansas was gray and Oz was colorful. Anderson later said that it was due to nothing other than his choosing to shoot some scenes in black-and-white because color was more expensive. Be that as it may, the audience of *If…* was frequently at pains to know whether a certain scene was real, a dream, or some of each. In one such scene, realistically shown, Mick seemed to have killed the cowering chaplain with two bullets and a bayonet. Next, the headmaster, who was made up to look as much as possible like Hitler without the mustache, opened from the wall of his office, as if from a mausoleum, a large drawer, in which the chaplain, apparently quite well, sat up, spoke not a word, shook hands with the three rebels, then lay back down and got shoved back into the wall, all as if the headmaster could just trot religion out whenever he needed it.

Assigned as punishment for their attack on the chaplain to clean out a long disused storage room, the three, with the waitress and another student, Wallace's gay lover, Bobby, discovered a large cache of World War II arms and ammo. They instantly grasped the possibilities.

In the final scene all the singleminded facets of the hypocritical aristocracy that had been College, its students, faculty, administration, parents, and alumni for centuries — generals, bishops, knights in armor, royals, whips, all their lot with all their ladies — gathered for a church service to celebrate "privilege." As the whip Denson's father, General Denson, was giving a rousing speech tenuously linking privilege to responsiblity to tradition to freedom to fighting to discipline to obedience, Mick and his allies set off smoke bombs under the floorboards. As the congregation fled the church, the five, from strong tactical positions in the battlements on the rooftops, opened fire on them with a mortar, grenades, Stens, and a Bren. General Denson ordered weapons distributed from the armory and returned the fire. The headmaster ordered cease fire and tried to plead with the five, but the waitress calmly put a pistol shot smack in the middle on his forehead. Anderson left ambiguous whether this last murderous segment was real or only Mick's wishful dream of reducing all the symbols and facilitators of the unholy union of militarism, religion, monarchy, and education to dust, putting into effect the eighteenth-century revolutionary vision that people would never be truly free until the neck of the last king was strangled with the bowels of the last priest.[59]

With regard to human values, aristocracy is always and necessarily hypocritical. It says that it respects the free individual and seeks a well ordered society, but what it really respects is only itself and what it really seeks is to create a well ordered community and to suppress all individuality except among its own.

The big point of If... was to illustrate how the establishment itself creates the revolutionaries who attack it. This is not to deny that revolutionaries each have free will and are each responsible for their own actions and especially for their own mistakes. Each person is and must always remain fully accountable for all her/his uncoerced choices, free decisions, or exercises of free will. Yet no sane person sets out to be a revolutionary without first having been humiliated, kicked, trampled, disgusted, or tormented by the establishment. If the establishment were sufficiently humane, there would then be no revolutionaries and no need for any revolutions. If the problem were taken to be only militarism, dictatorship, hereditary privilege, and religious hegemony, as it was in the *Ancien Régime*, then violence could be part

---

[59] This idea is often attributed to Denis Diderot, but more likely it derives from the posthumous *Testament* of the apostate Roman Catholic priest, Jean Meslier (1664-1729).

of the solution, as it had to be in the French Revolution; but if the core of the problem is recognized as institutionalized and systematic violence itself, then violence, even measured counterviolence, cannot be part of any solution, because violence can only perpetuate itself. To end any cycle of violence, the nonviolent alternative must be forcefully presented, as in the vigorous tactics of Mahatma Gandhi and Martin Luther King.

If ... portrayed how the right creates the left — or rather, how the establishment creates the conditions that goad people into rebelling against it, so that the rebels become the left and the establishment becomes the right. Again, if the establishment were decent, there would never be any rebellion against it, nor any need for rebellion. It is easier to live as a non-rebel than as a rebel — but each person can tolerate only so much abuse. No one can be a rebel unless there is something to rebel against. That is why the greasers, the Elvis fans, the James-Dean-style "rebels" or juvenile delinquents of the fifties and early sixties were not really rebels at all. They were not challenging any established values; they were just out to have irresponsible good times. From the conservative point of view, they were harmless. They did not threaten society as it was, but only occasional individuals. They had no vision for change. They grew up to be conservatives.

The system in *If ...* was such that any self-respecting human caught within it had no choice but to resist it, try to overthrow it, and replace it with a more egalitarian, respectful, humanistic means of educating eager young minds and civilizing eager young spirits. Nevertheless, Anderson wrote that Mick and his allies "are, without knowing it, old-fashioned ... They are not anti-heroes, or drop-outs, or Marxist-Leninists or Maoists or readers of Marcuse. Their revolt is inevitable, not because of what they *think*, but because of what they *are*. ... If his story can be said to be 'about' anything, it is about freedom. ... It doesn't look ... as though Mick can win. The world rallies as it always will, and brings its overwhelming fire-power to bear on the man who says 'No'."[60]

We did not emerge from seeing *If ...* thanking our lucky stars that our schools were not like College. On the contrary, we emerged angry that our schools, even to any small extent, resembled College. We were determined to ferret out any such resemblances, however tiny, and eliminate them. Preferably not by violent, counterproductive means, but by forceful and uncompromising means nonetheless.

We also recognized immediately that the kind of demeaning, entrenched sadism that we saw in *If ...* was not peculiar to British schools, but was alive and well in typical relationships between American adults and children — yet not so much in our schools as in our families. A paradigm case of our parents' generation's unexamined assumption of unanswerable power over their children was the long-running radio comedy, *Baby Snooks*, which starred Fanny Brice in the title role and Hanley Stafford as her father, Lancelot Higgins. The Snooks character was not a brat, just a normal, cheerful, decent child; but contemporary publicity described

---

[60] Lindsay Anderson, David Sherwin. *"If ...": A Film* (New York: Simon and Schuster, 1969), pp. 12-13.

her father as "long-suffering" at her hands, constantly provoked by her. The facts were opposite. He was mean, truculent, short-tempered, and unreasonable. His actions seemed almost calculated to discourage her from her natural developmental trajectory and to break her spirit, all for the sake of only his own convenience. He knew no way to relate to his daughter except to yell, insult, mock, threaten, and spank. He intended only his adult world, never her childish world, to be taken seriously or treated with respect. He squelched her curiosity and enthusiasm at every turn. For example, in the "Home Remodeling" episode of March 21, 1947, he accused her — falsely — of having a "subnormal intellect." She asked, politely and with perfect innocence, "What's an intellect?" He replied with typical unkindness, "Don't concern yourself. You'll never be bothered with one." Given his persistent psychological and frequent physical abuse, it was amazing that she was good-natured at all, or that she could retain her cheerful simplicity in his presence. Yet no criticism of his parenting methods was ever either expressed or implied. The show's listeners were apparently expected to side with him in his chronic humiliation of Snooks. Healthy parent/child relationships need to be asymmetrical in proportion to the child's age, but the parent must be sensitive enough not to enshrine this asymmetry, but to work toward gradually eliminating it, again in proportion to the child's age. This father showed no inclination toward any such beneficial change, which would, after all, have required taking his child seriously and treating her with respect.

If ... had a sequel, *O Lucky Man!*, which Anderson brought out in 1973. It put to rest once and for all the question of whether the armed rebellion at the end of *If* ... was real. It was not. Mick had survived, graduated, and was now in the mainstream of commercial society as a coffee salesman. Not only did McDowell reprise his role as Mick, but no fewer than eleven other actors from *If* ... played also in *O Lucky Man!*, most in new roles, many in multiple roles. This casting device of Anderson expressed one of the main points of the film, namely that, as individuals go through life, they encounter not other individuals, but types. The headmaster was now a factory manager and a prison warden; the history teacher now two different professors and a methedrine junkie; the general still a general but now also a judge; the chaplain now both a vicar and a bishop; the waitress serving coffee now packing coffee and participating in a porn party; and so on.

O Lucky Man! continued the same anti-establishment themes of *If* ..., but more particularly as a virulent indictment of global capitalism, its minions, and its class structure, in which justice was manifest as whatever way the affluent, powerful, privileged minority chose to oppress, torture, or murder the majority, who had to work for the minority just to survive. Mick was still a rebel and a risk-taker, but now he was a capitalist too, ambitious, quite willing to sell out. He soon learned how to fake sincerity and that money buys both justice and injustice. The object of his envy, the arch-capitalist, was presented as one who gladly allowed half a million peasants to starve for the sake of his clearing 50 millions pounds profit. Mick was impressed only by the 50 million pounds. Even though poor and desperate himself, he cared not a whit for other poor and desperate people, but thought only of schemes to get rich.

Surrealistic and self-referential, *O Lucky Man!* contained scenes in which Anderson was shown directing *O Lucky Man!* and casting *If...* He interspersed its narrative scenes with scenes of Alan Price's soft rock combo providing commentary in their songs like a Greek tragic chorus and sometimes even playing a part in the narrative itself. About half the lines in Price's theme song for *O Lucky Man!* began with the word "if."

Mick's ordeals in *O Lucky Man!* made about as much sense as those of Joseph K. in Kafka's *The Trial*, and for the same absurd reasons. Worldly power was simply arbitrary, self-serving, expedient, nonsensical, and dispensed no genuine justice. Corrupt police, as looters, fit right into the capitalist scheme of "Make it, take it, get it while you can, but don't get caught." The sexual perversions, militaristic natures, and exploitative tendencies of those in power were as strongly depicted here as they had been in *If...*

A prominent graffito in an East End London slum, "Revolution is the opium of the intellectuals," parodied Marx's dictum from the introduction to his 1844 *Critique of Hegel's Philosophy of Right*, "Religion is the opium of the people." This graffito expressed the whole cynicism of *O Lucky Man!*, that the common people, the lower classes, the workers, servants, and peasants, have all become so dependent on capitalism, so dispirited, obedient, religious, and infected with what Nietzsche called "slave morality," that they can no longer revolt, not even to better their own lot.

The film's overall message was that wealth is grounded in luck and only a few get to be lucky, while the rest of the billions of people in the world, thanks to the evils perpetrated by the lucky rich, must remain miserable, destitute, unlucky.

Ω

Lep Zeppelin! Thanks mostly to them, there was more musical difference in the five years from 1964 to 1969 than there has been in the thirty-eight years from 1969 to 2007 (when I am writing this). Steppenwolf may have coined the term, "heavy metal," and there may have been rumblings of it in the 1968 music of Blue Cheer, Cream, Hendrix, Jefferson Airplane, and a few others; but really, Led Zeppelin invented heavy metal. Nothing remotely like the first two Zeppelin albums had ever been heard before. That level of innovation seldom occurs in music, or in any other area. Led Zeppelin would have been completely unpredictable in 1959, ten years before they appeared; but just about any music that appeared in 2007 was predictable in 1997, or even 1987, or maybe even 1977. How much progress in popular music there was in the sixties! How little there has been since then! Not that the music since the sixties has been bad — indeed, much of it is excellent, even better than what we heard in the sixties — but it is just not very different.

The newness of the music, and the newness of its variety, woke us up then. The sameness of the music, despite its continued variety, puts us to sleep now. It is still great music, but we have heard it all before.

Britain spawned the debuts of several other groundbreaking bands in early 1969, most notably Jethro Tull, a progressive blues rock quartet fronted by a flute, of all things, and named after the eighteenth-century inventor of the seed-sowing drill. What kinds of seeds did we suppose they were sowing? Their first LP, *This Was*, proved impossible to categorize. Jazz-blues-rock-medieval-renaissance-folk-fusion-progressive. It was all there. In spades. And fun to listen to. We would pay attention to these guys.

The ultimate in British soul music began to emerge with Joe Cocker's first LP, *With a Little Help From My Friends*, which consisted of seven covers and three originals co-written with his keyboardist, Chris Stainton. His gutsy, dynamic voice was perfect for the blues and almost always made covers, even Beatles songs, sound more interesting than the originals. Some critics hailed him as a male Janis Joplin, but that might have been overstating the case. His klutzy, spastic way of dancing apparently embarrassed some people. When he performed Dave Mason's "Feelin' Alright" with the Grease Band on *Ed Sullivan*, the camera tried as much as possible to hide him behind his bandmates and dancers. That was not difficult to do, because he travelled with huge bands and entourages in those days. Nevertheless, his charisma shone through the crowd and he instantly acquired a sizeable cult following in America.

Also out of Britain came new works by familiar musicians. The Beatles launched *Yellow Submarine*, a cartoon film soundtrack album that repeated some good old tunes, introduced some good new tunes, but was mostly just their concession to the bubble gum caricature of psychedelia. More serious efforts came from John and Yoko. Their public nakedness, which we had glimpsed on the White Album's insert, proved to be no fluke when the pair released *Unfinished Music No. 1: Two Virgins*. Its totally nude photographs attracted more buyers than did its *avant garde* music. Their obvious statement was that sexuality should be easygoing and egalitarian. We got it. They were the hot couple that spring. After showing us their genitalia, they got married, honeymooned in public at the Amsterdam Hilton, promoted peace, love, and freedom — all to the good — but then had the bad judgment to release another *avant garde* album, the dismal *Unfinished Music No. 2: Life With the Lions*. Meanwhile, the Beatles scored another hit single with McCartney's "Get Back," a catchy tune with a mysterious but enticing lyric about marijuana, gender bending, and probably several other topics that we could not quite discern.

If ever just an album's title filled anyone with sadness, it was *Goodbye Cream*. Goodbye? Cream? No! That could not be. How could they break up after only two years and three albums? But they did. We wondered what Clapton, Bruce, and Baker — especially Clapton — would do next.

Donovan's *Greatest Hits* may have been his best album ever, next to *Sunshine Superman*, because it contained no crap. But Donovan still had plenty of crap to spread around, such as his new single, "Atlantis."

Pentangle's second LP, *Sweet Child*, staked out between jazz and folk music the uneven territory that Joni Mitchell would very soon come to dominate.

With its eye-catching cover photo of an incredibly ugly woman, we did not quite know what to expect from *English Rose*, Fleetwood Mac's second album. But it fulfilled and enhanced the promise of their first, serving up a tasty portion of solid blues tunes with virtuoso bass and guitar parts.

The Moodies' fourth LP, *On the Threshold of a Dream*, was spacier, but also more complex and diverse, than their earlier albums. Always a very tuneful band, their progressive leanings had now crossed over into a mellowness that may have estranged a few of their fans who preferred harder rock. They would not regain that edge until the release of songs like "Question" in 1970 and "The Story in Your Eyes" in 1971.

The Kinks are the Village Green Preservation Society was better than their last two albums, but, because we had forgotten the Kinks, we did not pay any attention to it. We would discover great songs like "Johnny Thunder" later.

After their stellar first two albums, Traffic's third, *Last Exit*, disappointed us. Probably the less said about it, the better.

A Salty Dog brought more excellent organ-driven tunes from Procol Harum. The title cut of the LP evoked the loneliness and preternatural terror of being a common seaman in the days of cloth-rigged ships. It gave us new respect for Samuel Taylor Coleridge's "Rime of the Ancient Mariner," Herman Melville's *Moby Dick*, and Richard Henry Dana's *Two Years Before the Mast*; made none of us want to join the merchant fleet or the navy; and gave us good reason to thank our lucky stars that we had not been born in the eighteenth or nineteenth century when roving press gangs might have forced us into those wretched ships. But then again — we still had the draft.

Ω

I Am Curious (Yellow) was finally released in the United States in March. It had been released in October 1967 in its native Sweden, but American customs officers had shortly thereafter seized and impounded it so that censors could determine whether its explicit nude sex scenes would preclude it from being shown in America. A similar fate awaited its sister film, *I Am Curious (Blue)*, which was released in Sweden in March 1968 but not until May 1970 in America. We had followed both censorship controversies all along in the press, and by now we knew not only the plots of both films, but also what body parts and whose we were likely to see if the censors ever let us. Like all censorship controversies, this whole affair was stupid. It reminded us of how a few arrogant, presumptuous, meddlesome, ignorant, philistinic American censors succeeded in banning one of the greatest novels ever written, James Joyce's *Ulysses*, for eleven years until Judge John M. Woolsey of the federal District of Southern New York ruled on December 6, 1933, that it was not obscene. What the hell do uptight sexual puritans know about art anyway? Their ideal of high art is *The Pilgrim's Progress* by John Bunyan! They should heed Plato's advice in the *Theaetetus* and Aristotle's in Book Alpha of the *Metaphysics* and abstain from involving themselves in matters which they do not understand, or of which they know little or nothing, for each person judges best what is within that person's own particular sphere of knowledge, and is not qualified to judge anything else.

So, at last, we got to see *I Am Curious (Yellow)* and — what was all the fuss about? There was plenty of full frontal nudity, male and female, but the greater part of the film was leftist political propaganda. Maybe this political aspect, and not the sex after all, was really what provoked the American censors.

Lena Nyman, a plain actress with hamster cheeks and a Kirk Douglas chin, played a 22-year-old working class woman afflicted with insatiable curiosity about politics and sex. To satisfy the former she used a tape recorder to ask random questions of passersby, and to satisfy the latter, she slept with twenty-four men. The movie was thus essentially, first, an exploration of the political and social tensions between nonviolence and violence, and second, of the sexual tensions between voluntary female adventurousness and typical male exploitation of women. Lena's curiosity was unsystematic, almost chaotic, and although she indulged it constantly, she seemed to learn little from her investigations. She was also a constant victim, primarily of her drunken father, who ripped her off and psychologically abused her, and her selfish, sneaky, and generally evil boyfriend, whose mistreatment and eventual rape of her seemed consistent with his conservative politics. We could scarcely blame her for dreaming of killing him with a shotgun and emasculating him with a knife.

I Am Curious (Yellow) was not only self-referential, but self-consciously, almost obnoxiously, so. Director Vilgot Sjöman haphazardly selected and confusingly truncated clips from his pseudo-documentary of Lena's random political interviews, then to this montage added his own more substantial interviews, which included Olof Palme, who later became prime minister of Sweden, and Martin Luther King. Yet it all seemed mostly pointless. The moviegoer might well have wondered whether Vilgot made this film just so he could fuck Lena. He probably could have anyway.

The two versions, *Yellow* and *Blue*, represented the two colors of the Swedish flag. *Blue* was even more self-consciously and obnoxiously self-referential than *Yellow*, more confusing, more chaotic, even sometimes to the point that *Blue* and *Yellow* flatly contradicted each other. *Blue*'s indulgences in curiosity seemed mainly like outtakes from *Yellow*, though emphasizing ecclesiastical more than secular politics. *Blue* portrayed the church and the prison system as analogous to each other and as both working against social reform, economic justice, and world-historical progress.

Much more authentically pornographic than either of these two films was Philip Roth's bestselling novel, *Portnoy's Complaint*, which, if it had not been so well written, so damn funny, and so full of worthwhile sociosexual commentary on American urban Judaism, would surely have been sold only in plain brown wrappers. But for some reason, the censors no longer hassled books as much as they hassled movies. Perhaps they figured that literate people were better suited than moviegoers to police their own morals. In any event, *Portnoy's Complaint* was the psychiatric autobiography of Alexander Portnoy, a middle-class Jew obsessed with sex — No. Not obsessed. "Obsessed" is too weak a word to describe Portnoy's

fanatical fixation on cunts, pussies, pricks, putzes, blowjobs, and jerkoffs. His entire life revolved around his own little penis, its possibilities, successes, failures,
and perversions. All this was exacerbated by two smothering influences: First, the
Procrustean traditions and legalities of Judaism repressed his fanatical fixation and
made it all the more unhealthy. Second, and probably more fatefully, his mother's
insensitive rules and expectations, combined with what he perceived as her own
steamy sexuality, stifled his emotional development and trapped it in permanent
hormone-raging adolescence. If *Portnoy's Complaint* had a message, it was just to
relax, relax, relax, don't be uptight about sex, but let emotions flow naturally, un-
assailed by religion, society, parents, or anything else except love.

Ω

On the American musical side, a new band from Chicago released its self-titled
debut, a double LP, *Chicago Transit Authority*. This band had guts. Not only for
releasing a double album as their debut, but for naming themselves after an actual
government agency. Well, the agency threatened to sue, so they shortened their
name to just Chicago. Apparently naming bands after cities, states, or countries
was OK, but not after bureaucracies. In the seventies they would degenerate into a
dull, pop, horn band, but for the time being, at least through their first two albums,
they were brilliant.
     We were not much into horn bands, especially white ones. That was forties
stuff. We preferred strings, percussion, and even woodwinds to brass. But we dug
the horn sections in Memphis soul music, the funky horns that accompanied James
Brown or Wilson Pickett, and the occasional trumpet accent in rock songs. Chicago
was different from most white horn bands. They had an edge, and did not seem
overly concerned with being mellow. They did not do short songs. Their extended
jazzy jams on their original tunes and especially on their cover of the Spencer Davis
Group's "I'm a Man" captivated us with spicy rhythms and fresh instrumentation.
But what really sealed our affinity for this band in its debut was that the entire
fourth side of the LP was a condemnation of the establishment's behavior at last
summer's Democratic National Convention in Chicago. The first three sides were
all from the studio, but side four began with "Prologue, August 29, 1968," a *vérité*
recording of demonstrators chanting "The whole world's watching!" as the Chicago
police beat the shit out of them. That segued into "Someday, August 29, 1968,"
which interspersed *vérité* with a studio song whose lyrics urged unity and suggested
that now was not too late to respond to the violence that was being done to us. The
album ended with "Liberation," a fourteen-minute live exploration of freedom.
     Creedence Clearwater Revival's second LP, *Bayou Country*, got the whole
country, on both sides of the political fence, into swamp rock. Everybody loved
Creedence. Maybe John Fogerty would lose a few of his rightist fans later after
recording such overtly leftist lyrics as "Fortunate Son" and "Who'll Stop the
Rain?" — but for now, at least, everybody loved him and his band. Catchy, loud,

funky, upbeat, solid tunes like "Proud Mary" and their new single, "Bad Moon Rising," ensured this. We kept right on chooglin', whatever that was.

Ed Sullivan kept right on pluggin', his uncanny knack for picking the best to showcase for three or four minutes intact. This spring, besides Creedence and Cocker, he had Janis, the Supremes (twice), the Chambers Brothers (twice), Sly and the Family Stone — who did "Love City" and "Stand!"; no way Ed would have let them do "Higher" — Vanilla Fudge, and Richie Havens, among others. His "shew" still condescended to "all you youngsters out there," but he was not slowing down in his effort to keep his wrinkly finger on the rapidly changing pulse of rock. Crotchety and censorial as he was, he nevertheless deserved much credit for bringing important new rock acts to wide, if not always appreciative, audiences. All things considered, he did as much for the promulgation of rock as did Alan Freed, Murray the K, Wolfman Jack, Cousin Brucie, Bud Ballou, and the whole slew of AM DJs.

The Airplane released a live album, *Bless Its Pointed Little Head*, with takes from October and November 1968 gigs at the Fillmores, West and East. Jorma was hot on the blues standard, "Rock Me Baby." Marty sounded strong and charismatic on "It's No Secret," "3/5 of a Mile in 10 Seconds," and "Plastic Fantastic Lover." Grace showed off a slower, funkier, jazzier arrangement of "Somebody to Love." Vocal polyphony between Marty and Grace soared on Fred Neil's "The Other Side of This Life." Kantner masterminded a self-indulgent cover of Donovan's "Fat Angel." They did an eleven-minute, Grateful-Deadish jam called "Bear Melt," whose title probably referred to Canned Heat's leader, Bob ("The Bear") Hite. As always, Jack's supreme musicianship held everything together. None of these tunes were as good as the Airplane's studio versions, but they all exuded tremendous energy and excitement. Marty's big hand was indeed grabbing and shaking us.

"MC5" meant "Motor City Five," i.e., the quintet from Detroit whose debut album, *Kick Out the Jams*, based on the lyrics inside, should have been called *Kick Out the Jams, Motherfuckers*. We did not know what "kick out the jams" meant, but we knew what "motherfuckers" were, so we could pretty much set the title in its proper context. The MC5 were hard rockers, *bona fide* punks, and, as we would learn in the mid-seventies, musical proto-punks. One of the two guitarists, Fred ("Sonic") Smith, married Patti Smith. You cannot get any punkier than that! We loved the MC5. They kicked ass! No holds barred! Their lyrics were pro-Panther, anti-oppression, pro-freedom, and anti-capitalist.

As a sort of Stills-less follow-up to *Super Session*, a double album appeared with the ultimate in All-American album cover art, a genuine Norman Rockwell painting. It full title was: *The Live Adventures of Mike Bloomfield and Al Kooper, Recorded at Bill Graham's Fillmore Auditorium, San Francisco, Sept. 26, 27, 28, 1968, Also Featuring Elvin Bishop, Carlos Santana*. Bloomfield's introductory speech, in which he very clearly explained "the thing of this gig," was a comedic gem that alone was worth the price of the whole album. Despite too many technical glitches and missed opportunities, the tracks included some amazing musical gems as well. "Dear Mr. Fantasy" would surely be a candidate for the greatest headphone cover version of any song ever, with Kooper's keyboard notes shooting through our brains like arrows.

As soon as *Retrospective*, Buffalo Springfield's greatest hits album, hit the record stores, we knew in our hearts that our suspicions had just been confirmed. That band was no more. Though we would miss them, we were not especially sad, because we were sure that all five would soon find other worthwhile musical projects to enchant us and enrich our lives. We were not wrong. Besides Neil Young's solo career with Crazy Horse, there would shortly also be Crosby, Stills, and Nash (and sometimes Young); Loggins and Messina; Poco; the Souther-Hillman-Furay Band; etc.

David Crosby of the Byrds, Stephen Stills of Buffalo Springfield, and Graham Nash of the Hollies got together and released their debut LP, *Crosby, Stills, and Nash*, whose cover showed Nash, Stills, and Crosby in blue jeans and scruffy old clothes sitting on a ratty old couch in front of a dilapidated old house, Stills playing guitar, Nash and Crosby with their filthy boots on the cushions. June Cleaver would have had a heart attack! The decorous era of album covers showing bands in neat new clothes and nice, clean poses was definitely gone.

The trio would soon become known for musical harmony and personal disharmony — and even more so when they became an occasional quartet with Neil Young. Their songs were beautiful, unprecedented, and the assorted blendings of their instruments and voices was unmistakably unique.

Stills's lyric fantasy, "Suite: Judy Blue Eyes," was his second romantic tribute to the perpetual object of his adoration, "Sweet Judy Blue Eyes," Judy Collins. His "You Don't Have to Cry" told of the emotion-stifling insanity of trying to live like a human in the nine-to-five plastic world of suits, neckties, and briefcases. His "Helplessly Hoping" was an alliterative portrait, in third person, of a loving couple and the innate problems of their relationship. His "49 Bye-Byes" seemed to be a continuation, in first person, of the tale begun in "Helplessly Hoping," but now the man was giving up on the woman. Forty-nine was the number of lines in the lyrics.

Nash's "Marrakesh Express" was just a pleasant, meaningless, little ode to tourism. His more serious "Pre-Road Downs" referred to the tearful farewells and other saddening events that a band would typically experience just before beginning a tour. His "Lady of the Island" was a love song from a postcoital perspective.

Crosby's "Guinnevere" was a gentle love song whose lyrics, full of images of the gorgeous, legendary, medieval queen, could have been written by Donovan, who, indeed, had his own "Guinevere" on *Sunshine Superman*. "Wooden Ships," which Crosby co-wrote with Stills and Paul Kantner of the Airplane, was a post-apocalyptic tale of a few desperate survivors of World War III, after the earth had been destroyed, after both sides had lost the war, and after countries, uniforms, flags, ideologies, and allegiances had ceased to have any meaning at all. The only way that these people could save themselves was to save each other, to share their humanity, to forget any differences among them. Then there might be hope. Crosby's "Long Time Gone" was a realistic song of hope, set in the present day. It seemed at first to be just about the pain of waiting and the drag of time — they did a lot of songs about the passage of time — but the second of its four verses turned sharply toward political meaning. By the third verse it was a full-fledged political song. It urged us to be true to our beliefs, not to compromise our principles, not to sell out, and to be vocal, resolute, attentive, obnoxious, and above all, patient, in our opposition to injustice.

Neil Young's second solo LP, *Everybody Knows This is Nowhere*, appeared the same month as *Crosby, Stills, and Nash*. This album, with heavier beats and brand new guitar sounds, was what made us sit up and take notice of Neil's solo career — indeed, it was what made him a superstar. Every song was a treasure, and three of them became absolute classics. No band could lay down as solid a groove as Crazy Horse. That is why Neil hired them — and he knew how to use it. From the very first note of the first track, "Cinnamon Girl," we felt that this album was special.

The "this" in the title cut referred to the urban rat race. It was nasty, cold, and "nowhere," but back home in the country would be nice, comfortable, and "somewhere."

"Round and Round" was what many people — fans and detractors alike — would consider a typical Neil Young song, a slow whiny ballad that made him sound like a wimp. Neil wrote a lot of such songs, but in reality he was much more versatile than that. At the core of his deepest soul he was a hard rocker, but a consummate musician and composer who knew how to use minor keys, discords, and modulations to his best advantage to express a subtle and wide range of emotions.

"Down by the River" was a haunting, allusive, elliptical tale of jealousy and murder, lacking narrative detail but packing emotional punch. The singer of "The Losing End" felt many of the same lonely emotions, but retreated into himself and did not resort to killing his lost lover. "Running Dry" continued the same theme: the difficulty of being alone, the guilt that we feel for our social mistakes, the pain of just being human. The tune reminded us of Country Joe's "Porpoise Mouth." But so what? It was still a new song.

The set culminated in the magnificent ten-and-a-half-minute "Cowgirl in the Sand," which, after a bit of light, tentative guitar noodling, suddenly thundered in with heavy chords and Neil's ringing electric guitar licks. The lyrics described an apparently quite wonderful woman who rejected suitor after suitor, but seemed not to know how to let them down gently. Or perhaps she did not care whether they were let down gently or not. Or again, perhaps she preferred to dump them roughly, just for her own amusement. We were left guessing on this point, as was the singer's persona. In an interesting twist, at the end she herself was rejected — yet we wondered whether she would take it seriously or just laugh it off and continue to play her cockteasing game. Neil knew his heart. He knew how to convey the full depth and destructiveness of unfulfilled desire. His guitar screamed, blasphemed, and moaned. Every heterosexual guy who has ever suffered unrequited love has felt these emotions.

Zappa's and the Mothers' sixth, *Uncle Meat*, a double LP, was wilder, more starkly *avant garde*, and showed more jazz and classical permutations than any of their previous work. It seemed inaccessible to all but the most zealous connoisseurs of the Zappanalian universe.

Yet another Velvet Underground LP, their eponymous third, passed by almost unnoticed. To the Velvets' lasting credit, Brian Eno is supposed to have said that very few people heard them in the sixties, but everyone who did either formed or joined a band. Their masterful work would bear much fruit in the seventies, not only through Lou Reed's solo career, but also through David Bowie, Mott the Hoople, the New York Dolls, Patti Smith, etc.

Nazz's second LP, stupidly titled *Nazz Nazz*, was just as stupid inside. After the promise of their first, we expected better.

Dylan's first new LP in over a year, *Nashville Skyline*, led in more of a country direction from his previous work. It yielded what would become at least three standards: the hit single, "Lay, Lady, Lay"; his duet with Johnny Cash, "Girl from the North Country"; and "Tonight I'll Be Staying Here with You."

The Byrds' new LP, *Dr. Byrds and Mr. Hyde*, continued in their country direction. Gram Parsons had gone. The band now consisted of McGuinn, guitarist Clarence White, bassist John York, and drummer Gene Parsons (no relation to Gram). Yet the highlight of the album was still one of Gram's songs, co-written with McGuinn, "Drug Store Truck Drivin' Man," which ridiculed the hypocrisy, inconsistency, and general idiocy of small-town Ku Klux Klansmen.

The David of Joan Baez's new LP, *David's Album*, was her husband, David Harris, a draft resistance activist who would soon be sent to federal prison. It was more of a country than a folk collection, with mostly traditional tunes, but one by U. Utah Phillips, one by Gram Parsons, and a few other originals. Joan very rarely wrote a song.

Joni Mitchell's second LP, her breakthrough, *Clouds*, established her not only as a singer, but especially as a songwriter. It was clearly a one-woman effort. She wrote everything on the album; her acoustic guitar was just about the only instrumentation; and she even did the cover art, a spooky self-portrait against a Saskatchewan landscape background. The recording showcased but did not show off her strong, three-octave voice. Two of the songs became classics: "Both Sides Now," which had already been a hit for Judy Collins a year ago, and "Chelsea Morning." Her "Songs to Aging Children Come" was noteworthy for its strange chord progressions. She made both her antiwar stance and her Canadian heritage unequivocal with "The Fiddle and the Drum," an eerie *a cappella* tune.

The highlight of Steppenwolf's third LP, *At Your Birthday Party*, was "Rock Me," in which we had a tough, gruff, macho-posing guy, John Kay, complaining that a woman was being objectified for sex. This was a surprising theme from an all-male band, and made us dudes reconsider our attitudes toward women and try to discover and overcome our prejudices against them. Maybe we should not call them chicks anymore, or babes, or even girls. Maybe we should just call them women. That is what they are, our social equal in every way. "Rock Me" was from the soundtrack of *Candy*, a lousy 1968 movie that pretended to be based on Voltaire's novel of the folly of unrealistic optimism, *Candide*. Eighteen-year-old Swedish bimbo Ewa Aulin starred as the ingenue, the title character. Co-stars in this sexploitation piece included Marlon Brando, Anita Pallenberg, Richard Burton, Ringo Starr, John Astin, James Coburn, Charles Aznavour, and Walter Matthau, all of whom just camped it up. The only good thing about this movie was Steppenwolf's song.

Sly and the Family Stone provided, not only in their music, but also in the very essence of their interracial band, a constructive, activist, upbeat vision of how good race relations could be. Their contagious optimism found clear articulation in the title cut of their fourth album, *Stand!* Their music was funkier, catchier, and even more danceable than usual. The antiphonal name-calling in "Don't Call Me Nigger, Whitey" offered a semi-comical view of racial bifurcation and racist stubbornness. "I Want to Take You Higher" was a bouncy, thumping, charismatic remake of "Higher" from their second album, *Dance to the Music*. "Sing a Simple Song" extended the theme of Burdon's "Monterey" and the Spoonful's "Do You Believe in Magic?", recommending music as the obvious but overlooked solution to the world's ills. "Everyday People" called for a fully egalitarian way of life, not judging anyone by color, gender, wealth, social position, or any other divisive criteria. "You Can Make It If You Try" urged us to work harder for peace and justice, identified plasticity as our main obstacle in this pursuit, and told us to hurry up.

Many black singles had sociopolitical implications. The Temptations' "Run Away Child, Running Wild" depicted adolescent frustration and alienation; the Isley Brothers' "It's Your Thing" promoted egalitarian concepts of personal freedom; and the Friends of Distinction's "Grazing in the Grass" was about marijuana. Even Edwin Starr's "Twenty-Five Miles," which at first seemed to be just a love song, implied a criticism of the low status that whites still imposed on black people in American society. The idea was that the singer was so devoted to his sweetie that he would gladly walk twenty-five miles to see her, no matter how tired he got or how much his feet hurt. He had to walk. There was no other way to reach her. Yet (we thought), poor whites who were separated from their sweeties would not have had to walk long distances to see them. They could have hitchhiked. We saw lots of hitchhikers in the sixties — but how many black hitchhikers? That mode of travel was not safe for them, and they knew it. Moreover, Starr's image of an optimistic young black man walking down the road reminded us of their ordeal expressed in civil rights marches.

Innocuous, middle-of-the-road pop bands doing songs from *Hair*, like the Fifth Dimension covering "Aquarius / Let the Sun Shine In" and the Cowsills covering "Hair," added to the sociopolitical message mix in the mainstream. A new vocal trio called Three Dog Night released a popular cover of Harry Nilsson's vivid portrayal of the pain of loneliness, "One." Even the conservative Elvis Presley delivered "In the Ghetto," a disturbing tale of how despair and desperation easily led to crime, violence, and death for young urban black men. But our parents' favorite, Frank Sinatra, did not contribute anything constructive to the growing world of sociopolitical message songs. His "My Way" picked up where "That's Life" left off, but added the dimension of selfishness to its theme.

"Darkness Darkness" by the Youngbloods was the most poignant antiwar song that spring. That is quite a compliment, because antiwar songs were everywhere in early 1969. Even little AM radio pop ditties like "Sweet Cherry Wine" by Tommy James and the Shondells were antiwar songs. Then, of course, Phil Ochs chimed in with his sixth LP, *Rehearsals for Retirement*, with his own gravestone on the cover and full of songs about death. The inscription on the stone said that he had died at the 1968 Chicago convention — which perhaps he had, in spirit. Some have speculated that the general morbidity of this album marked the beginning of Ochs's mental decline that ended with his suicide in 1976. In any case, he was increasingly concerned about FBI conspiracies against him. Songs like "I Kill Therefore I Am," "My Life," "Another Age," and the title track all seemed like reflections of a depressed, discouraged, and frightened mind.

Simon and Garfunkel's single, "The Boxer," was among their most sensitive and intelligent lyrics — and that is saying something! It told of a brave, honest man just trying, and failing, to make his way in the world. On one level it was only that. Yet the whole thing could also be seen as a metaphor for the young and innocent being sent off to war. The word "resistance" in the first verse was, of course, a *double entendre*. Literally it referred to the singer's struggles against the hard knocks of any poor person's life; but it also connoted political resistance, probably against the draft. "The Boxer" was a multifaceted literary work disguised as a simple song about a down-and-out loner. How high could culture rise?

The Guess Who's "Friends of Mine," a ten-minute track on *Wheatfield Soul*, was a shameless ripoff of Morrison's lengthy rants in Doors concerts and albums. A pop band imitating a charlatan! How low could culture sink?

Ω

Nixon began to wind the ground war down, but ever so slightly. We soon verified that his campaign promises to end the war and achieve "peace with honor" were nothing but lies. Thus the antiwar efforts continued unabated, even intensifying, because, unlike Nixon, LBJ had never said that he would end the war. This is not to say that LBJ had never lied to us, but only to assert that, of the two, Nixon was the bigger liar.

Under Nixon and like-minded governors, police power to harass peaceful leftists grew unchecked and unbalanced.

James Rector did not die at the right time. Like JFK, Martin Luther King, Malcolm X, Medgar Evers, Bobby Kennedy, and countless other political martyrs, he died too soon. The man who killed him did not die soon enough.

That man was Ronald Wilson Reagan, governor of California.

In 1967 the University of California acquired by eminent domain a block of land in Berkeley between Telegraph Avenue, Dwight Way, Haste Street, and Bowditch Street, but did not develop the land and allowed it to go derelict. In April 1969 a group of community members, tired of the eyesore and wanting to put it to good use, rolled up their sleeves, cleared the land, planted flowers, trees, and shrubs, and built a park — People's Park. These hundred or so activists claimed moral superiority over the university, and ownership of the land, by virtue of these improvements. The university did not agree, but Cal Berkeley Chancellor Roger W. Heyns and Vice Chancellor Earl F. Cheit each promised the community that they would take no action against the park without due warning. Reagan overrode the chancellors and broke these promises. Perceiving a direct leftist threat against the university's property rights, welcoming the chance to attack, and enjoying the support of his chief of staff, Edwin Meese, later his attorney general as president, he ordered shotgun-armed police to destroy the plantings and erect a chainlink fence around the block to keep the people out. On May 15, "Bloody Thursday," Charles C. Plummer's Berkeley cops murdered James Rector, blinded Alan Blanchard, and wounded over a hundred more. Thirty thousand people marched on May 30 in support of the park and against Reagan. Confrontations between the community and the university over the management of the park continued into the twenty-first century.

On April 7, 1970, in a speech to the California Council of Growers in Yosemite, Reagan endorsed the idea of murdering dissidents, antiwar activists, disobedient students, and hippies: "If it takes a bloodbath, let's get it over with. No more appeasement." At his retirement dinner as Alameda County sheriff on January 8, 2007, Plummer referred to his experience at People's Park: "I wish I would have hit some people harder during the riots. I regret that."

Reagan may have acted the part of the genial communicator to his constituents and may thereby have fooled millions of people, but he did not fool us. In reality, beneath that thin veneer, he was as mean as a snake. Like most arch-conservatives, he claimed to defend freedom, but, because he equated freedom with the right of conformists to get rich however they chose, while letting the chips fall where they may on the rest of us, he in fact defended only property, both private and public, never genuine human rights.

A group of African-Americans led by James Forman were convinced that, because America had been largely built by slave labor, America owed significant debts, back wages, as it were, to the descendants of these slaves. Believing that to ask either the government or industry for this money would be a waste of everyone's time and effort, Forman decided to ask the churches, playing upon their guilt and alleged morality. Accordingly he used the twenty-six-person Black Economic Development Conference (BEDC) to coordinate seeking these reparations. BEDC was entirely serious, and included among its members such eminent black leaders as Julian Bond, Vincent G. Harding, Muhammed Kenyatta, Fannie Lou Hamer, and J. Metz Rollins. On April 26 it issued Forman's Black Manifesto, which declared:

> We are demanding $500,000,000 from the Christian white churches and the Jewish synagogues. This total comes to 15 dollars per nigger. This is a low estimate for we maintain there are probably more than 30,000,000 black people in this country. $15 a nigger is not a large sum of money and we know that the churches and synagogues have a tremendous wealth and its membership, white America, has profited and still exploits black people. We are also not unaware that the exploitation of colored peoples around the world is aided and abetted by the white Christian churches and synagogues. This demand for $500,000,000 is not an idle resolution or empty words. Fifteen dollars for every black brother and sister in the United States is only a beginning of the reparations due us as people who have been exploited and degraded, brutalized, killed and persecuted. Underneath all of this ex-

ploitation, the racism of this country has produced a psychological effect upon us that we are beginning to shake off. We are no longer afraid to demand our full rights as a people in this decadent society.

BEDC's campaign began on May 1. Its strategy included disrupting white church services in order to bring attention to its cause by outraging complacent racists and attracting the media. In some ways this strategy worked, in some ways not. Naturally, it caused much backlash among whites who did not consider themselves racist but who considered the insides of churches sacred, not to be profaned or used for sociopolitical purposes. On May 4 Forman disrupted the communion service at Riverside Episcopal Church in New York City and throughout the rest of the year Kenyatta disrupted several church services in the Philadelphia area. Backlash! Counterproduction! Nevertheless, some white churches responded positively, and actually took up collections to contribute toward reparations.

Migrant Chicano field workers, as well as blacks, were getting a bit uppity at having been cheated for so long. César Chavez, on behalf of the United Farm Workers, declared May 10, 1969, as International Grape Boycott Day. We helped. We did not eat grapes for years after that. We knew that such refusals would help everything. We recognized that our main adversaries were the corporations, not the government, not even the rank-and-file jingoists, racists, and militarists. Under both LBJ and Nixon the Department of Defense became more and more the puppet of private industry. To defeat the moneyed interests, we did not want physical weapons like bombs or guns. Indeed, such weapons against such foes are worse than useless — they are counterproductive. They make us just like them — and our whole point was to make them more like us, i.e., less belligerent, more tolerant.

Our detractors said — and still say — that Lennon's idea that "all you need is love" was impractical, unrealistic, immature, and just plain silly. But our love of the people — expressed as solidarity with them in their political, social, and economic struggles — is not unworkable. Indeed it is the only way that human values can advance. It does not entail or promote hugging people, being promiscuous with them, or even touching them. It simply means sharing their values and aspirations and working to secure these values and achieve these aspirations.

Che was correct that the revolutionary is motivated by love — but he went about it all wrong. Love is never compatible with violence, will never tolerate violence, can never emerge from violence, and means renouncing violence. Guerrillas do not help us.

Rightists favor moneyed interests over the rights and well-being of the people; leftists favor the people over moneyed interests. That is about as good a definition of this basic political division as there is — and it is not much of an oversimplication. Given this definition, the attitudes and behavior of rightists and leftists alike become almost predictable. Rightists tend to be mean, judgmental, and selfish; leftists to be naive and disarrayed — those are their greatest disadvantages. Rightists tend to be well organized and unified; leftists to be motivated by ethics, mission, and a reasoned sense of history — those are their greatest advantages.

Summer 1969

Give peace a chance!

God, I'd like to fuck Janis Joplin!
— Abbie Hoffman, *Woodstock*
Nation (New York: Vintage, 1969), p. 118

Leave the goddam moon alone!

Here we were, trying to end the war, build social justice, and generally improve the planet earth, while our political opponents, the guys in power, were playing around on the goddam moon! What a stupid waste of time, money, effort, science, and resources! If the money that the government had poured into NASA had instead been poured into the National Institutes of Health, the Library of Congress, the National Endowment for the Arts, the National Endowment for the Humanities, or the National Science Foundation, then this country might well have been one for the whole world to emulate, "a light to the nations" (Isaiah 49:6).

But the country was caught up in this moon madness. Lunacy! Every TV station in the land was broadcasting the moon landing on July 20. My girlfriend and I drove around all day in the rain just so that we would not be near a TV set and accidentally see any of it.

Yet in a few places on planet earth there was sanity. Montréal, for instance, where, in suite 1738-1740-1742 of the Queen Elizabeth Hotel, newlyweds John and Yoko hosted their second "bed-in for peace." Together with Tim Leary, Tom Smothers, Derek Taylor, Petula Clark, Rabbi Abraham Feinberg, Allen Ginsberg, various Hare Krishna devotees, Yoko's daughter Kyoko Cox, and a wall-to-wall room full of others, comprising *ad hoc* the Plastic Ono Band, there, under a sign saying "Hair Peace," they wrote, rehearsed, recorded, and filmed their no-bullshit anthem, "Give Peace a Chance," which was released two months later. The Beatles had already recorded and would soon release "The Ballad of John and Yoko," a narrative of the pair's recent persecutions. "Give Peace a Chance" sought to reduce the world situation to its simplest elements, naming all sorts of distractions, characters, personalities, "-isms," "-ations," complications, as if to evoke and then purge them all, suggesting that merely living peacefully would bring peace. It fit in perfectly this summer, when songs of peace, unity, love, and forgiveness abounded. New ones included Jackie DeShannon's "Put a Little Love in Your Heart"; the Youngbloods' re-release of their stalwart anthem, "Get Together"; and Three Dog Night's cover of "Easy to Be Hard," from *Hair*.

Songs of revolution also abounded. The most interesting new one was Thunderclap Newman's "Something in the Air." Produced by Pete Townshend, this one-hit wonder band was built around Speedy Keen, jazz pianist Andy Newman, and guitarist Jimmy McCulloch, later to join Stone the Crows and Paul McCartney's Wings. "Something in the Air" asserted the necessity of strong, solid resistance in the face of opposing, counterrevolutionary force. Its lyrics also upheld the necessity of the revolution itself, and called upon revolutionaries to arm and defend themselves. In a way, its message was similar to that of "Get Together," but without the rejection of violence.

A gigantic setback for the antiwar movement occurred in June when the SDS splintered. One faction, the Revolutionary Youth Movement (RYM), opposed the Progressive Labor Party (PLP), which it accused of selling out. The RYM itself almost immediately splintered. Led by Mark Rudd, Bernardine Dohrn, and about a dozen others, RYM I dedicated itself to the violent overthrow of the American government and socioeconomic system, which they correctly perceived as unjust and violent. RYM I became known as the Weather Underground, the Weather Underground Organization (WUO), the Weatherman Faction, or simply, the Weathermen. Led by Mike Klonsky, RYM II consisted mostly of Maoists, and dedicated itself to promoting communist ideology. It soon faded into absorption by more general communist movements.

The Weathermen failed to perceive correctly that neither injustice nor violence can ever be defeated by more injustice or violence. If your enemy is unjust or violent, then you may likewise be unjust or violent, and may the best side win, but nothing will be resolved, and humanity will not advance. If, on the other hand, your enemy is either injustice itself or violence itself, then you should use neither injustice nor violence in your campaign, nor should you be either unjust or violent in your own life or actions. If you do, if you are, then injustice and violence have already won. LBJ and Nixon both said that they were fighting for peace, to which we would reply, "Fighting for peace is like fucking for chastity!" We could have applied analogous slogans to the Weather Underground. Fucking for chastity was also like bombing to end violence or attacking innocent people to end injustice.

The world was in a sorry state. The industrialists and polluters were ruining nature itself. We birds were shitting in our own nests. Even the water was burning. The Cuyahoga River caught fire in northern Ohio.

Ω

Midnight Cowboy was rated X. It became the first and only X-rated film to win the

Oscar for Best Picture. It certainly did not win this Oscar because of any prurient content it may have had. Rather, despite the censors' objections, the critics and theatergoers apparently overlooked its X-rating and noticed significant literary quality in it. Yes, there were some reprobates who went to see *Midnight Cowboy* only because they wanted to catch glimpses of Jon Voight's ass or Brenda Vaccaro's right tit, but most of us appreciated the film primarily for its psychological power.

As if *The Graduate* were not sufficient, *Midnight Cowboy* was the film that made a top star out of Dustin Hoffman, who played the crippled bum and street hustler, Enrico Salvatore ("Ratso") Rizzo.

The main theme of the film was the redemption of its title character, Joe Buck (Voight), a naive Texas bumpkin who came to New York to get rich as a prostitute for lonely upper-class women. Instead he found mostly just depravity, filth, despair, and swindling. He had little real human contact and made only one friend. Yet gradually and painfully he escaped this sordid, superficial, sexual Manhattan to find the meaning of true friendship and human warmth. The depth of his redemption was underscored by the fact that his new friend, Ratso, was ugly, unsavory, unworthy, and about the most unlikely man to become friends with him. We like to surround ourselves with attractive friends, but when we instead make friends of distasteful, disreputable people, we thereby show that we are able to see beneath the human surface to appreciate the inner beauty in each of us, even in those who at first would seem to have no inner beauty. Rizzo did not want pity, and Buck did not pity him. If he had, he never could have moved toward caring and friendship. When Ratso died of chronic respiratory disease brought on by his slovenly environment, Buck gave up prostitution and resolved to forge an honest, upright life for himself.

The movie made a hit out of Nilsson's cover of Fred Neil's "Everybody's Talkin'," Buck's main theme song.

Another X-rated movie, *Last Summer*, pushed outer beauty / inner ugliness vs. outer ugliness / inner beauty even further. Four vacationing middle-class teenagers — two average-looking boys; one gorgeous, cold, narcissistic girl, Sandy; and one homely, warm, sensitive girl, Rhoda — were on their adolescent voyage of discovery toward adulthood. Of course, they all wanted to be beautiful, cool kids. Only Sandy was already there, and she proved it by sneering at plain, klutzy, or ugly kids. The two boys sucked up to Sandy and, against their true natures, in order to gain her favor, became increasingly cruel to Rhoda. In the end, at Sandy's instigation, they raped Rhoda. The three apparently believed that their physical attractiveness justified their crime.

Robert Downey's *Putney Swope* was perhaps the funniest anti-racist farce ever made into a movie. Its premise was that a black man, the title character, by a sheer fluke became the absolute head of a big-time Madison Avenue advertising agency. His first words upon being elected chairman were to tell the son of the founder, "Your father was a horse's ass." At his first executive conference he declared, "The changes I'm going to make will be minimal. I'm not gonna rock the boat. Rockin' the boat's a drag. What you do is sink the boat, and there's no sense sinkin' nothin' unless you can salvage with productive alternatives, and brothers, you can't change nothin' with rhetoric and slogans ..." He immediately hired all black people for top-level positions and either fired most of the white employees or relegated them to menial jobs. The company's policy and corporate cultural changed 180 degrees. The ads it produced became funky and obscene. The whole business became cash-only. Swope's maid, chauffeur, and other servants were all white. But none of these racial role reversals in the corporate business world made any real difference. Black idiocy was no more idiotic than white idiocy. Nothing really changed. The fundamental greed of corporate executives remained intact. When the white chairman of the board dropped dead of a heart attack during the meeting at which Swope was subsequently elected chairman, the first thing the other white board members did was to steal his watch and pick his pockets; but Swope turned out to be just as bad. He stole ideas from his employees, whom he then summarily fired, and bandied their ideas about as if they were his own. The underlying cynical mood was set in the first scene, when a consultant from Mensa outfitted like a sleazy biker arrived in a helicopter flying a Jolly Roger and a Confederate battle flag to propose marketing beer, not as a "cool, soothing beverage," but as "pee pee dicky" juice for "men who doubt their masculinity." The movie's endless stream of malapropisms, *non sequiturs*, and other absurdities seemed calculated to underscore black anger at established society in general.

Easy Rider is much overrated as a window into the sixties. Of course, we did not think so at the time, but retrospect has made it so. If it depicted any of our culture accurately at all, and it probably did, then what it showed was only a very tiny aspect of that culture.

Dennis Hopper and Peter Fonda played Billy and Wyatt, a couple of small-time cocaine smugglers who made a big score with a little ratfaced kingpin played by Phil Spector. As Steppenwolf's "The Pusher" filled the soundtrack, they used part of their payment to buy a pair of fancy-schmancy motorcycles and the appropriate clothes to ride off in search of America, with no particular destination in mind, to the tune of Steppenwolf's "Born to Be Wild." Wyatt's bike, helmet, and leather jacket were all festooned with American flag designs. Billy was done up in fringed buckskins like a movie cowboy. Their longish hair, oddball clothes, and scruffy appearance alienated most of the people they met, so they took to the hills. There they found squalor, poverty, superstition, ignorance, and prejudice as disheartening as what they had seen in Mexico. The Byrds' "Wasn't Born to Follow" and the Band's "The Weight" accompanied their journey. They were kind to everyone. They picked up a hitchhiker. They smoked a lot of dope. They decided to go to Mardi Gras. Their hitcher brought them to a hippie commune about as far away from cities or civilization as you could imagine. Wyatt felt at home, but it made Billy suspicious, paranoid, impatient, and belligerent. They left. When redneck cops threw them in jail on trumped up charges, a drunken ACLU lawyer, played by Jack Nicholson, bribed them out. In gratitude they took him with them to New Orleans, as the Holy Modal Rounders did "The Bird Song," the Fraternity of Man did "Don't Bogart Me" (usually called erroneously "Don't Bogart That Joint"), and Hendrix did "If Six Was Nine."

After the three barely avoided redneck violence at a rural Louisiana diner, the lawyer pointed out to Wyatt and Billy that rednecks fear anyone who represents real freedom, which is why rednecks hate hippies. He further warned that rednecks would likely murder anyone who called their lack of freedom to their attention. That night, four rednecks snuck into the travellers' camp to club them as they slept, beating Wyatt senseless and killing the lawyer, but missing Billy. The idea of such an unprovoked attack was quite plausible to us, given all the lynchings and other murders of civil rights workers, Yankees, blacks, and freaks throughout the deep south. At last in New Orleans, to the tune of the Electric Prunes' "Kyrie Eleison," Wyatt and Billy visited an expensive whorehouse, but felt alienated by its sophistication. They and two of the whores decided to go out and enjoy Mardi Gras. In one of New Orleans' famous above-ground cemeteries, "cities of the dead," they took LSD, tripped, and fucked. The next day, accompanied by the Electric Flag's "Flash, Bam, Pow," they hightailed it out of the Big Easy and headed east. They disagreed on the outcome of their adventures: Billy thought they had it made; Wyatt kept repeating, "We blew it." By that he meant that their money had not made them free.

The next day, as Roger McGuinn covered Dylan's "It's Alright, Ma (I'm Only Bleeding)," the pair continued east along the Gulf coast. Two rednecks approached in a pickup truck. One pointed a shotgun at Billy and taunted him. Billy flipped him off. The redneck told him to get a haircut, then murdered him. When Wyatt tried to go for help, the other redneck murdered him. McGuinn sang "Ballad of Easy Rider" over the closing titles.

The still photo of Billy throwing the finger at the redneck — and, metaphorically, at everyone who hated us — became iconic.

The film, *Alice's Restaurant*, Arlo Guthrie's loosely autobiographical dark comedy, stretched the several anti-establishment themes of his song, "Alice's Restaurant Massacree," the eighteen-minute side of his 1967 LP, *Alice's Restaurant*. Like *Easy Rider*, it showed frequent conflict between bullying, goonish rednecks and long-hairs just trying to mind their own business. The difference was that *Alice's Restaurant* was less fictional, but at the same time less violent, less plot-driven, less contrived, more slice-of-life, and hence — even though sometimes deliberately exaggerated for comic effect in the good ol' American tall tale tradition — generally more believable. To his credit, Arlo presented himself, not so much as himself, but as Woody Guthrie's son, and willing heir to Woody's populism and folksy values. Pete Seeger put in a cameo appearance as himself and did an impromptu duet with Arlo at Woody's hospital bedside, where Woody was slowly dying from Huntington's disease. The film's two deaths, Woody's and especially that of Arlo's friend Shelly overdosing on heroin, brought the mood down to ugly reality. In the last analysis, *Alice's Restaurant* was a somber film that depicted the so-called "hippie lifestyle" more accurately and less romantically than did *Easy Rider*.

The first major film about the events surrounding the 1968 Chicago convention was *Medium Cool*, whose premise was that reporters covering violence or corruption can sometimes be caught up in violence or corruption themselves. It showed how the FBI and other government agencies could use the supposedly independent and unwitting news media to spy on dissidents. Such collusion certainly existed, but whether the media were deliberate participants or were duped, who could say? Sometimes it is difficult to know whether a film about recent or topical events is *bona fide* historical fiction or just exploitation. There were plenty of anti-hippie, anti-freak, anti-left exploitation films in that era, from *Wild in the Streets* to *The Strawberry Statement*, but there were also plenty of films, from *In the Heat of the Night* to *The Graduate* to *Easy Rider* to *Getting Straight*, that deserve respect for their attempted honesty in portraying the times.

Ω

Posters on telephone poles from Montréal to Virginia advertising the Atlantic City Pop Festival of August 1-3 showed a long-haired woman — who looked remarkably like Grace Slick but probably was someone else — staring off into space, her face painted in broad stripes of bright primary colors, red orange yellow horizontal on the left, green blue purple vertical on the right. Tickets for this "Music Carnival and 3-Day Exposition" were either $6.00 a day or $15.00 for all three. It is not to be confused with either the First Atlanta International Pop Festival, which was held in Hampton, Georgia, on July 4-5, 1969, nor with the Second Atlanta International Pop Festival, which, despite Governor Lester Maddox's attempts to kill it, would happen in Byron, Georgia, on July 3-5, 1970. The advertised line-up for Atlantic City was:

Friday, August 1: Iron Butterfly; Procol Harum; Crosby, Stills, and Nash; Booker T. and the M.G.s; Joni Mitchell; Chicago; Santana Blues Band; Johnny Winter.

Saturday, August 2: Jefferson Airplane; Creedence Clearwater Revival; Lighthouse; the Crazy World of Arthur Brown; B.B. King; the Paul Butterfield Blues Band; Tim Buckley; the Byrds; Hugh Masekela; the American Dream.

Sunday, August 3: Janis Joplin; Canned Heat; Frank Zappa the Mothers of Invention; the Sir Douglas Quintet; Three Dog Night; Dr. John the Night Tripper; Joe Cocker; Buddy Rich Big Band; Little Richard; the Moody Blues.

But a partial list of what the roughly 110,000 attendees actually heard would be:

Friday, August 1: Procol Harum; Joni Mitchell; the Chambers Brothers; Blood, Sweat, and Tears; Lighthouse; Iron Butterfly; Miles Davis; Mother Earth; Chicago.

Saturday, August 2: The American Dream; Tim Buckley; the Byrds; Booker T. and the M.G.s; Hugh Masekela; the Paul Butterfield Blues Band; B.B. King; Creedence Clearwater Revival; Jefferson Airplane; Dr. John the Night Tripper; AUM.

Sunday, August 3: Sir Douglas Quintet; Santana Blues Band; Canned Heat; Three Dog Night; Joe Cocker; Frank Zappa and the Mothers of Invention; Lothar and the Hand People; Buddy Miles; Janis Joplin; Little Richard.

Apparently it was difficult to book those bands dependably.

Santana, the album with the big black-and-white roaring lion on the cover, the self-titled debut LP of the six-piece band that had been named for its lead guitarist, Carlos Santana, introduced a large portion of the gringo world to Chicano soul. We liked it! Heavy on rhythm and percussion, with fascinating guitar licks, tasty organ runs, a progressive feel, and a dose of psychedelic rock, Santana delivered sounds like we had never heard before — but wanted to hear more of — in hot tunes like "Waiting," "Evil Ways," "Jingo," "You Just Don't Care," and "Soul Sacrifice."

The title track of Creedence Clearwater Revival's third LP, *Green River*, was their new single. It painted an attractive picture of simple, barefoot country life and urged everyone who had left the country for the city to change their minds and come back home if the city ever got them down — as it inevitably would. "Bad Moon Rising" harped on omens of impending catastrophe and perhaps, just perhaps, was meant as a comment on current events. "Lodi" told of the despair that could be felt by anyone just trying to make an honest living or find fortune in a backwater town like Lodi, California.

The eponymous debut Mountain LP contained a lot of loud, heavy music which, thanks to its dominating vocals and guitars, revealed it as really a Leslie West solo album. Felix Pappalardi, who produced the album, was reportedly so impressed with West's work in the recently defunct Vagrants that he promptly grabbed West and built a new band around him, with himself playing bass.

Spirit's third album, *Clear*, alternated between mellow psychedelia and what would later be called "soft rock," with just a hint of jazz, such as in "Caught." Their message was gentle, environmentalist, and conciliatory. Especially in trippy tunes like "Cold Wind," "Ice," and the title track, their musicianship, as always, was impeccable.

A supergroup is a band comprised entirely or mostly of famous members of previous bands. Cream, the first supergroup, spawned several others. The first of these was Blind Faith, with Clapton and Baker from Cream, Winwood from Traffic, and Rick Grech from Family. They were together from only February to August 1969, released only one album, and did only one tour, hitting Britain, Scandinavia, and North America from June 7 to August 24. On the American side, DJs touted them as "The New Cream, Rising to the Top."

When I saw them at the Spectrum in Philadelphia on July 16, in floor seats eight rows back from the revolving circular stage, two bands opened for them: Taste, an Irish power trio, with whom we were not familiar, but whom we later learned included guitarist Rory Gallagher; and Delaney and Bonnie and Friends, with whom Clapton soon formed a fruitful musical relationship. Blind Faith's own set was rather short — they did not have very much material — but included long improvised solos by each of the four. Baker's drums drove us apeshit!

Their self-titled album contained only six tunes: Winwood's "Had to Cry Today," "Can't Find My Way Home," and "Sea of Joy"; Clapton's "Presence of the Lord"; a cover of Buddy Holly's "Well All Right"; and Baker's fifteen-minute "Do What You Like," the lyrics of which were in the tradition of Traffic's "You Can All Join In" and the Airplane's "If You Feel." Perhaps the best way to describe the overall effect would be — psychedelic blues? — or bluesy psychedelia? There was a lot of virtuosity in that band! Maybe we should just call it music.

We loved Blind Faith for many reasons, mostly musical, but also because they gave the impression of being completely without inhibitions, i.e., completely willing to contravene straight society's expectations. In Britain, the LP cover depicted a naked teenage girl holding a toy airplane. Of course, that cover was censored in America (though it would become available here later). The American cover just showed a plain black-and-white photo of the band grinning and holding each other's instruments.

Exploiting blasphemy for comedic effect or sociopolitical commentary was not only fun, but stunningly efficient. To begin with, we did not believe in blasphemy. Nothing was taboo, nothing was off-limits for comedy or insults. But many of our adversaries, flag-waving Christians, the so-called "religious right," believed wholeheartedly in blasphemy and all its temporal and eternal implications. So our blaspheming was a great way to goad them. It was easy too.

At the Philadelphia Blind Faith gig I bought a huge black poster (that's Visual Thing B284 for you collectors), a bird's-eye-view photo of a beautiful young woman, naked, but with her long, disheveled, blond hair obscuring her tits and shadows obscuring her cunt; blindfolded and crucified, with ropes like the two thieves, not with nails like Jesus. Where "INRI" should have been, a nailed-up scroll said "Blind Faith." At the foot of the old rugged cross sat the band in half-light, amused, staring at the camera. The whole impact reminded us of one of Salvador Dali's crucifixion paintings, but, unlike his works, this poster was pure blasphemy. There should have been many more similar to it. Ridiculing stuffy, self-serving institutions like the church was, well — fun, harmless, and more invigorating than receiving the stigmata.

With his surprise number two chart hit, "A Boy Named Sue," penned by acerbic satirist Shel Silverstein, country star Johnny Cash offered an amusing but not controversial look at gender stereotypes. Yet the censors attacked it, blanking out "son of a bitch."

With *The Belle of Avenue A*, the Fugs continued to do what they did best, or rather, what they were the only ones to do at all: record minimalist, percussive songs of raw sex, urban squalor, chronic degeneracy, and anarchist politics. They remained as primitive, untalented, daring, and funny as ever.

Like a phoenix from the ashes of their lost career, the Kinks arose with *Arthur: or the Decline and Fall of the British Empire*. Now, impressed by the Kinks' revival, we took the time to discover their outstanding tunes of the past two years: "David Watts," "Waterloo Sunset," and "Johnny Thunder." *Arthur* was a concept album, telling the tale of a disillusioned but patriotic, elderly, working-class Briton, Arthur Morgan, whose family had had many of its members killed in wars, whose only surviving son was emigrating with his wife and kids to Australia, and whose other grandson, the war orphan, was a pain in the ass. Arthur wasted his life away in his comfortable suburban London home, Shangri-La, longing for the bygone days of Victorian empire. The opening song, "Victoria," expressed Arthur's jingoistic love for queen and country, and his willingness to die for both. "Yes Sir, No Sir" revealed his profound readiness to obey any command. "Some Mother's Son" was a lament for the war dead. "Drivin'," "Brainwashed," and "Shangri-La" each in its own way and from its own perspective exposed how far Arthur had sunk into the depths of believing that everything was OK, and that foreign wars and catastrophes had no adverse effect on his pleasant English suburban life. "Australia" described his son Derek's hopes for a rejuvenated life and a fresh start, as well as Derek's failure to convince Arthur of any of this. "Mr. Churchill Says" recounted how utterly effective the war propaganda of Winston Churchill, Fieldmarshall Montgomery, Lord Mountbatten, and other national heroes had been in shaping Arthur's world view. "She Bought a Hat Like Princess Marina" showed the great extent to which Arthur loved the very idea of monarchy and sucked up to the royal family, worshipping them almost as cultic deities. In "Young and Innocent Days," doubt at last began to creep into his mind. "Nothing to Say" implied the dissolution of his safe, secure, relaxed, family-oriented, old world. Finally, in the denouement song, "Arthur," he realized that his happiness was all pretense and his solid world was actually founded on lies, misunderstandings, and misplaced trust. But it was too late for him. The real world had passed him by. At the end he broke down crying over his lifelong loss. For some reason, the whole LP seemed to some of us to have been inspired by Dave Mason's "Cryin' to Be Heard" on the second Traffic album.

With "Bourée" [sic] on their second album, *Stand Up*, Jethro Tull added a larger portion of classical to their already eclectic mix of influences. The tune was in fact a cover of Johann Sebastian Bach's *Bourrée in E Minor*, the fifth movement of BWV 996, which he had scored for lute. In Tull's version Ian Anderson's flute was the lead instrument. *Stand Up* also included "A New Day Yesterday," lamenting a missed opportunity for love; "Look Into the Sun," which testified to the power of music to purge sadness; "Nothing Is Easy," a friendly plea to relax and stop worrying; and "For a Thousand Mothers," a hard rocker attacking self-righteous parents who insisted that they were right about us when we knew perfectly well that they were wrong. The album art resembled Renaissance woodcuts, with the inside of the gatefold popping up like the illustrations of some children's books.

American keyboardist Gary Wright got together in England with four Britons, guitarist Luther Grosvenor (later Ariel Bender of Mott the Hoople), bassist Greg Ridley, drummer Mike Kellie, and keyboardist Mike Harrison (not George's brother as is sometimes alleged) to form Spooky Tooth, a solid, heavy, progressive, hard-rocking band. Their first album in the U.S. was called *Spooky Two*. Their real first album, which had already been released in Britain as *It's All About Spooky Tooth*, would be released in the U.S. in 1971 as *Tobacco Road*. Their mighty riffs — organ in "Waiting for the Wind," guitar in "Evil Woman" — and powerful vocals all combined to create an intense, eerie, mesmerizing effect.

Ten Years After's fourth album, *Ssssh*, with its phantasmagorical cover art of several sides of Alvin Lee's entranced face, continued the band's solid British blues tradition. Nothing really new. No big changes. Just amazing music. TYA was a very tight band, always reliable for solid bass riffs and flashy guitar work.

The Stones did not seem to lose anything when Brian Jones drowned in his swimming pool on July 3. Indeed, as we later learned, he had already been out of the band for almost a month when he died. Drugs had ruled him since at least 1967, around the time that his girlfriend, Anita Pallenberg, had left him for Keith Richards. Brian had made no significant musical contributions to the Stones since 1968, and Jagger had fired him on June 8, ostensibly because Brian's drug convictions would prevent him from getting an American visa and participating in their next tour. If that were the actual reason, then Jagger would have been the world's biggest hypocrite, insofar as he and Keith had had their own share of drug problems with the police and the courts. The actual reason was a good one, namely, that drugs had ruined Brian's musical talent and made him moody and uncooperative. Mick Taylor gradually slid into the Stones as their co-guitarist with Keith. But oddly enough, Brian was included in the cover photos for this summer's Stones album, *Through the Past Darkly*, their second greatest hits compilation, a real rocker, covering the period from "Paint It, Black" through "Honky Tonk Women," their newest single.

With a new four-piece band, British bluesmaster John Mayall played the Fillmore East on July 12. *Turning Point*, the live LP of this gig, appeared just a month later. Without drums, but just guitars, bass, saxes, flutes, and harmonica, its sound was distinctive and riveting. Its lyrics were mainly political. The message of "The Laws Must Change" was self-evident from its title. The song asked demonstrators to be more tolerant of police officers, who, after all, were only trying to earn a living. It also pleaded for people to be sufficiently flexible to want to hear both sides of each argument, and cited Lenny Bruce as an example of someone who understood these issues. "Saw Mill Gulch Road" was a personal story of a strange encounter. "I'm Gonna Fight for You, J.B." eulogized J.B. Lenoir, African-American blues musician, political activist, and civil rights advocate, who had recently died at only thirty-eight. "So Hard to Share" attacked jealousy, particularly when it restricted a woman's natural freedom and frustrated the singer's attempt to get to know her better. "California" rivaled the Mamas' and the Papas' "California Dreamin'" or "Twelve Thirty," the Rivieras' "California Sun," Lesley Gore's "California Nights," Scott McKenzie's "San Francisco," Eric Burdon's "San Franciscan Nights," and any number of Beach Boys songs in promoting the Golden State as the land of fun, freedom, sunshine, and abundance. "Thoughts About Roxanne" was a wailing blues number, another very personal tale. "Room to Move," a rollicking, upbeat tune with a fantastic harmonica solo, closed the album in a celebration of individual freedom.

The Who's new single, "I'm Free," out of context from *Tommy*, could still be anthemic on a more general level. Seen in this way, the summer's three singles from Sly and the Family Stone, "Stand!", "I Want to Take You Higher," and "Hot Fun in the Summertime," could all be taken as promoting the same message of autonomy, authenticity, love, and hope.

Steppenwolf on *Ed Sullivan* did "Magic Carpet Ride" and, from *Birthday Party*, a song about overcoming guilt with hope, "It's Never to Late."

The Grateful Dead really hit their stride as the consummate, ultimate, definitive, archetypal, psychedelic jam band with their third LP, *Aoxomoxoa*. Jerry's voice was becoming a standard fixture in our music. The songwriting skills of Jerry the guitarist, Phil the bassist, and Robert Hunter the lyricist were becoming truly formidable. OK, no commercial potential. But so what? We found it! Here were a few tunes that would become Dead classics: "St. Stephen," "China Cat Sunflower," and "Cosmic Charlie." *Aoxomoxoa* was full of unusual rhythms and tonalities — and check out Rick Griffin's cover art. Does that fancy lettering really say "Grateful Dead"? Some thought it said "We ate the acid." Could drugs have been involved?

There were many songs about recreational drugs. Some were not *prima facie* about drugs, and for those one had to be "hip" in order to understand the real connotations of the lyrics (e.g., Bob Dylan's "Mr Tambourine Man" and the Beatles' "Got to Get You into My Life," "Norwegian Wood," and "Yellow Submarine"). Others were quite blatant (e.g., Lou Reed's "Heroin," the Rolling Stones' "Sister Morphine," and Leadbelly's "Take a Whiff on Me"). Still others were in fact not about drugs even though many listeners thought they were (e.g., the Byrds' "Eight Miles High," which was about a plane ride to London; Peter, Paul, and Mary's "Puff, the Magic Dragon," which was just what it said, with apparently no hidden meanings; and Steppenwolf's "Magic Carpet Ride," which was about music).

The sixties were especially rich in songs about marijuana. Most of these marijuana songs were incredibly funny. The funniest — and *ipso facto* arguably the best — pro-marijuana song of all time is Jaime Brockett's thirteen-and-a-half-minute mock epic, "Legend of the U.S.S. Titanic." One would be very hard pressed to find a bigger number of deliberate falsehoods, inaccuracies, inconsistencies, contradictions, anachronisms, absurdities, or impossibilities per word in this song than anywhere else in the history of music. Brockett was one funny dude — and in many ways epitomized the anarchic, joyful irreverence of the sixties.

Brockett was a much underrated folk singer and satirist from New England, really more of a regional than a national phenomenon. His best album, *Remember the Wind and the Rain*, contained not only "Legend of the U.S.S. Titanic," which, absurd and druggy as it was, was also a pretty good indictment of racism; but also, in the talking blues style popularized by Dylan and Tom Paxton, "Talkin' Green Beret New Super Yellow Hydraulic Banana Teeny Bopper Blues," which attacked Spiro Agnew, Dick Clark, militarism, patriotism, and several other butts related to the Vietnam War. "Blue Chip," "Nowadays," "Suzzane" (not to be confused with Leonard Cohen's "Suzanne"), "One Too Many Mornings," "Bag on the Table," and the title track were all gentle acoustic guitar ballads with sensitive lyrics. "St. Botolph St. Grey Morning Dulcimer Thing" was an appealing instrumental tune which, for many of us, was our introduction to the dulcimer.

We got high on music!

Drugs — if we freaks did them at all — were certainly not a great priority for us, except as a means of experimenting with new modes of merely sensuous perception. Our end, our final goal, on the contrary, involved the progressive development of better, more serious, more fun, more harmonious, more eudaimonistic, and more authentically human — but not necessarily new — forms and contents of awareness, communication, and interpersonal richness. This is what we accomplished at Woodstock.

$$\Omega$$

In medieval Scandinavia, a "berserk" was a warrior who was weak and useless when not in battle, but superhumanly strong, uncommonly skilled, terrifically lethal, and almost invincible when the frenzy of combat was upon him. Sometimes the battle alone was enough to hurl him into this ecstatic fit, or he might use extraordinary means to induce unnatural ferocity as he entered the fray. A smaller force with one berserk could easily defeat a larger force with none.

Janis Joplin was like that.

On the July 18 *Dick Cavett Show*, after singing just one song, a cover of Barry and Robin Gibb's "To Love Somebody" — brilliantly with her usual almighty intensity — Janis collapsed exhausted into the interview chair. Having caught her breath, she discussed with Dick the difference between herself and other "chick singers." She said that they only "float around on the top" of the music while she and other rock women who were not afraid to be unfeminine "get down on the bottom" of it. Music for her was raw emotion. The only way she could convey this emotion was to immerse herself in it entirely. She had to get "underneath" the melody to "get into the feeling." Melody was only superficial to music, almost epiphenomenal, not nearly as important as rhythm. She felt alive and happy only when her band was playing and she was singing. Little else mattered to her.

Dick reprised the same theme with her almost a year later on his June 25, 1970 show. He remarked how "shot" she was after just one number, "Move Over." Panting for breath, she replied, "I get so turned on by doing one that it's hard to stop." She meant that she derived her energy from her singing and derived her singing from her energy in a non-vicious circle just like a berserk in battle. Away from singing, Janis, and away from fighting, the berserk, were done in, but while singing or fighting Janis and the berserk could each go on indefinitely.

Jimi Hendrix was sandwiched between screenwriter Garson Kanin and dancer Gwen Verdon on the July 7 *Dick Cavett Show*. The eclectic, almost incongruous mix of guests was unusual for Cavett, indeed more typical of Johnny Carson. Hendrix seemed not to let it bother him, though he was obviously out of place in that group. He played only one song, "Hear My Train A-Comin'," solo with minimal backing from the house band, but Cavett showed the guitar-burning clip from *Monterey Pop*. During the interview Hendrix said that music has definite meaning:

It's got to be more spiritual or so than anything. Pretty soon, I believe that they're going to have to rely on music to, like, get some kind of peace of mind or satisfaction, direction actually, more so than politics, because, like, politics is really an ego scene. That's the way I look at it, anyway. It's sort of a big fat ego scene. Oh yeah, this art of words, which means nothing, you know. So therefore you have to rely on more of an earthier substance, like music or the arts, theater, you know, acting, painting, whatever.

Hendrix added that his reason for playing loud was to make his music enter people, not through their eardrums, but through their souls. For him, the electric nature of modern music was a key to spirituality. His goal was an "electric church" based on music, to wake people from their spiritual sleep. He criticized other musicians who played loud but "shrill," so that their music assaulted ears but did not enrich or penetrate souls. He distrusted compliments because they distract musicians, make them feel too satisfied, so that they forget about their talent and start living on compliments instead of on music.

Hendrix made his second appearance on the *Cavett Show* two months later, September 9, played "Izabella" and "Machine Gun" with the Experience, did not say much in the interview, but reiterated even more strongly his antipathy to compliments. The contrast between friendly, easygoing Hendrix and Dick's other guest, exceedingly cold and uptight Robert ("Jim Anderson" / "Marcus Welby") Young, was a stark reminder of the whole divide between the white-collar older generation and the paisley-collar younger generation. Young looked disgusted and did not offer to shake Hendrix's hand. Jimi, like a true gentleman, ignored the slight.

Our generation had shown much better manners to each other three weeks earlier at Woodstock than Young showed to Hendrix that night on *Cavett*.

The Woodstock Music and Art Fair was first supposed to have happened in a favorite haunt of *avant garde* artists and musicians, Woodstock, Ulster County, New York, then, after those plans fell through, in Wallkill, also in Ulster County; but instead it finally happened on Max Yasgur's dairy farm near Bethel, Sullivan County. Yasgur became a hero. After the Wallkill Zoning Board of Appeals acted on July 15 to ban the festival, he, urged by his son Sam and his friend Elliot Tiber, stepped in and allowed the unprecedented and unpredictably strange event to occur on his property. He was a hero who collected $75,000 rent.

The promoters and music insiders may have expected more — they probably did — but facilities on Yasgur's farm were set up for only about 100,000 people. The promoters had told Yasgur to expect only about 50,000. Somewhere between 300,000 and 500,000 showed up. Tickets cost $8/day or $24 for the whole shebang. Ticket sales netted about $1,500,000. The promoters lost a lot of money.

The full schedule and set lists at Woodstock were:[61]

Friday, August 15, starting just after 5:00 p.m.:

Richie Havens: "From the Prison / Get Together," "I'm a Stranger Here," "Minstrel from Gaul," "High Flyin' Bird," "I Had a Woman," "I Can't Make It Anymore," "With a Little Help from My Friends," "Strawberry Fields Forever," "Hey Jude," "Handsome Johnny," "Freedom / Motherless Child."

Swami Satchidananda: Invocation chant.

Sweetwater: "Motherless Child," "Look Out," "For Pete's Sake," "Day Song," "What's Wrong," "My Crystal Spider," "Two Worlds," "Why Oh Why," "Let the Sunshine In," "Oh Happy Day."

Bert Sommer: "Jennifer," "The Road to Travel," "I Wondered Where You'd Be," "She's Gone," "Things are Goin' My Way," "And When It's Over," "Jeanette," "America," "A Note That Read," "Smile."

Tim Hardin: "How Can We Hang onto a Dream?" "Susan," "If I Were A Carpenter," "Reason to Believe," "You Upset the Grace of Living When You

---

[61] This list is not authoritative, nor can it be. As there is an incredible degree of discrepancy among the literally hundreds of sources, it can be no more than a best effort.

Lie," "Speak Like a Child," "Snow White Lady," "Blue on My Ceiling," "Sing a Song of Freedom," "Misty Roses."

Ravi Shankar on sitar, Alla Rakha on tabla, Maya Kulkarni on tamboura: "Raga Puriya-Dhanashri: Gat in Sawarital," "Tabla Solo in Jhaptal," "Raga Manj Kmahaj: Alap Jor, Dhun in Kaharwatal, Medium and Fast Gat in Teental."

Melanie: "Close to It All, " "Momma Momma," "Beautiful People," "Animal Crackers," "Mr. Tambourine Man," "Tuning My Guitar," "Birthday of the Sun."

Arlo Guthrie: "Coming into Los Angeles," "Wheel of Fortune," "Walking Down The Line," "Oh Mary, Don't You Weep," "Every Hand in the Land," "Amazing Grace."

Joan Baez: "Oh Happy Day," "The Last Thing on My Mind," "I Shall Be Released," "Joe Hill," "Sweet Sir Galahad," "Hickory Wind," "Drug Store Truck Drivin' Man," "One Day at a Time," "Take Me Back to the Sweet Sunny South," "Warm and Tender Love," "Swing Low, Sweet Chariot," "We Shall Overcome."

Saturday, August 16, starting just past noon:

Quill: "That's How I Eat," "They Live the Life," "Waiting for You," "Driftin'."

Country Joe McDonald: "Janis," "Donovan's Reef," "Heartaches by the Number," "Ring of Fire," "Tennessee Stud," "I Find Myself Missing You," "Rockin' All Around the World," "Flyin' High," "Seen a Rocket," "Fish Cheer / I Feel Like I'm Fixin' to Die Rag."

Santana: "Waiting," "Evil Ways," "You Just Don't Care," "Savor," "Jingo," "Persuasion," "Soul Sacrifice," "Fried Neckbones."

John B. Sebastian: "How Have You Been?" "Rainbows All Over Your Blues," "I Had A Dream," "Darlin' Be Home Soon," "Younger Generation."

The Keef Hartley Band: "Spanish Fly," "She's Gone," "Too Much Thinkin'," "Believe in You," "Rock Me Baby," "Leavin' Trunk," "The Halfbreed," "Just to Cry," "Sinnin' for You."

The Incredible String Band: "Invocation," "Sleepers, Awake!" "Catty Come," "The Letter," "Gather 'Round," "This Moment," "Come With Me," "When You Find Out Who You Are."

Canned Heat: "A Change is Gonna Come / Leavin' This Town," "Woodstock Boogie," "Going up the Country," "Let's Work Together," "Too Many Drivers At The Wheel," "I'm Her Man," "I Know My Baby Loves Me in Her Own Peculiar Way," "On the Road Again."

Mountain: "Blood of the Sun," "Stormy Monday," "Long Red," "Who Am I but You and the Sun," "Beside the Sea," [untitled song later named "For Yasgur's Farm"], "You and Me," "Theme for an Imaginary Western," "Waiting to Take You Away," "Dreams of Milk and Honey," "Blind Man," "Blue Suede Shoes," "Southbound Train," "Mississippi Queen."

The Grateful Dead: "St. Stephen," "Mama Tried," "Dark Star / High Time," "Turn on Your Lovelight."

Creedence Clearwater Revival: "Born on the Bayou," "Green River," "Ninety-Nine and a Half (Won't Do)," "Commotion," "Bootleg," "Bad Moon Rising," "Proud Mary," "I Put a Spell on You," "Night Time is the Right Time," "Keep on Chooglin'," "Suzie Q."

Janis Joplin: "Raise Your Hand," "As Good as You've Been to This World," "To Love Somebody," "Summertime," "Try (Just a Little Bit Harder)," "Kosmic Blues," "I Can't Turn You Loose," "Work Me, Lord," "Piece of My Heart," "Ball and Chain."

Sly and the Family Stone: "M'Lady," "Sing a Simple Song," "You Can Make It If You Try," "Everyday People," "Stand!" "Love City," "Dance to the Music," "Music Lover," "(I Want to Take You) Higher."

The Who: "Heaven and Hell," "I Can't Explain," "It's a Boy," "1921," "Amazing Journey," "Sparks," "Eyesight to the Blind (The Hawker)," "Christmas," "Tommy, Can You Hear Me?" "The Acid Queen," "Pinball Wizard" [Abbie Hoffman interrupted; Townshend knocked him offstage], "Do You Think It's Alright?" "Fiddle About," "There's a Doctor," "Go to the Mirror!" "Smash the Mirror," "I'm Free," "Tommy's Holiday Camp," "We're Not Gonna Take It," "See Me, Feel Me," "Summertime Blues," "Shakin' All Over," "My Generation," "Naked Eye."

Sunday, August 17, starting about 8:00 a.m.:

Jefferson Airplane: "Somebody to Love," "The Other Side of This Life," "3/5 of a Mile in 10 Seconds," "Plastic Fantastic Lover," "Volunteers," "Won't You Try / Saturday Afternoon," "Eskimo Blue Day," "Wooden Ships," "Uncle Sam's Blues," "The Ballad of You and Me and Pooneil," "Come Back Baby," "The House at Pooneil Corners," "White Rabbit."

Break!

Sunday, August 17, starting about 2:00 p.m.:

Joe Cocker and the Grease Band: "Forty Thousand Headmen," "Delta Lady," "Something's Coming On," "Dear Landlord," "Just Like a Woman," "Do I Still Figure in Your Life?" "Feeling Alright," "I Don't Need No Doctor," "Let's Go Get Stoned," "I Shall Be Released," "Hitchcock Railway," "Something to Say," "With a Little Help from My Friends."

Gigantic thunderstorm! Crowd Rain Chant.

Country Joe and the Fish, *starting about 6:00 p.m.*: "Rock and Soul Music," "Barry's Caviar Jam" (i.e., "Gasman"), "Love," "Not So Sweet Martha Lorraine," "Sing Sing Sing," "Summer Dresses," "Friend Lover Woman Wife," "Silver and Gold," "Maria," "Thing Called Love," "The Love Machine," "Ever Since You Told Me That You Love Me," "Crystal Blues," "Fish Cheer / I Feel Like I'm Fixin' to Die Rag."

Ten Years After: "Spoonful," "Good Morning Little Schoolgirl," "The Hobbit," "Help Me," "I Just Can't Keep From Crying Sometimes," "I May Be Wrong, But I Won't Be Wrong Always," "Hear Me Calling," "I'm Going Home."

The Band: "Chest Fever," "Don't Do It," "Tears of Rage," "We Can Talk," "Long Black Veil," "Don't Ya Tell Henry," "Ain't No More Cane on the Brazos," "This Wheel's on Fire," "Loving You is Sweeter Than Ever," "The Weight," "I Shall Be Released."

Johnny Winter: "Tell the Truth," "Johnny B. Goode," "Six Feet in the Ground," "Leland, Mississippi Blues / Rock Me Baby," "Mama, Talk To Your Daughter / Six Feet in the Ground," "Mean Mistreater," "I Can't Stand It" (with Edgar Winter), "Tobacco Road" (with Edgar Winter), "Mean Town Blues."

Blood, Sweat, and Tears: "More and More," "Just One Smile," "Somethin' Goin' On," "I Love You More Than You'll Ever Know," "Spinning Wheel," "Sometimes in Winter," "Smiling Phases," "God Bless the Child," "And When I Die," "You've Made Me So Very Happy," "I Stand Accused."

Crosby, Stills, Nash, and Young: (acoustic set): "Suite: Judy Blue Eyes," "Blackbird," "Helplessly Hoping," "Guinnevere," "Marrakesh Express," "4 + 20," "Mr. Soul," "Wonderin'," "You Don't Have to Cry"; (electric set): "Pre-Road Downs," "Long Time Gone," "Bluebird," "Sea of Madness," "Wooden Ships," "Find the Cost of Freedom," "49 Bye-Byes."

The Paul Butterfield Blues Band: "Born under a Bad Sign," "No Amount of Loving," "Morning Sunrise," "All in a Day," "Driftin' and Driftin'," "All My Love Comin' Through to You," "Everything's Gonna Be Alright," "Love March."

Sha-Na-Na: "Sha Na Na Theme," "Get a Job," "Come Go With Me," "Yakety Yak," "Silhouettes," "Teen Angel," "Jailhouse Rock," "Her Latest Flame," "Wipe Out," "Book of Love," "Little Darlin'," "At the Hop," "Duke of Earl," "Sha Na Na Theme."

Monday, August 18, starting about 8:30 a.m.:

Jimi Hendrix: "Message to Love," "Hear My Train A-Comin' (Get My Heart Back Together," "Spanish Castle Magic," "Red House," "Master Mind," "Lover Man," "Foxy Lady," "Jam Back at the House (Beginnings)," "Izabella," "Gypsy Woman," "Fire," "Voodoo Child (Slight Return)," "Stepping Stone," "The Star Spangled Banner," "Purple Haze," "Woodstock Improvisation," "Villanova Junction," "Hey Joe."

The lesson of Woodstock was that our goal of human peace and universal love could indeed be achieved. But the negative result of Woodstock was the realization that this goal would be achievable only ephemerally. Human peace and universal love are together a charisma that thoroughly defies any attempt to routinize it. Only with great difficulty is such charisma possible, except in certain rare and extraordinary situations, like Woodstock. As this sobering realization gradually took hold even among the most rosy-eyed of us, the mentality which had given us so much progress in the past five or six years up to that point disappeared. The sixties faded away with our optimism.

The real tragedy was that this sobering and disappearance were generally interpreted to mean that the sixties had failed. But this post-Woodstock malaise was in fact only a transition, perhaps not foreseeably to a better world, but still, only a transition.

At this point, except for the 300,000 or half million or x-number of us who had actually been there, we did not know much about Woodstock beyond what we read in the papers or saw on TV. Most of us, especially in the northeast, knew someone who had been there, but even with this second-hand information, we who had not been there would not know much about it before the documentary movie appeared next spring and the soundtrack next summer. But rumors and legends grew in the meantime.

Tuesday, August 19, ABC broadcast *The Dick Cavett Show* with Jefferson Airplane, Joni Mitchell, Stephen Stills, and David Crosby, all just down to New York City from Woodstock. The show had obviously been recorded the day before, as there were several references to Hendrix having played that morning, now having to sleep it off, and thus being unable to be also among Dick's guests.

The set looked like it was intended to minimize or even eliminate the typical barrier between performers on stage facing audience in seats. It was kind of like theater in the round, but not quite. The audience sat or reclined on a hard terraced floor that took up about 300 of the 360 degrees of a circle. The Airplane's stage, about three feet high, was up center and Joni's was stage left. Dick did the interviews on a centrally located circular platform, about two feet high, with horrible little beige naugahide cube-shaped toadstool-like things in place of chairs. Dick to Grace: "Are you comfortable there?" Grace to Dick: "Uh, not really." Paul and Jorma preferred to sit on the floor using their naugahide doodads for armrests.

The Airplane, with the ubiquitous but unheralded Nicky Hopkins on keyboards, opened after Dick's monologue. Marty, thin and gorgeous in his usual dark blue blazer, never looked better. Grace and Jorma were in buckskin fringe, Paul in a purple muscle shirt to show off his lack of muscle, Jack resplendent in an iridescent gold silk or satin tunic, Spencer in his typical pseudo-cowboy garb. Paul was the only one who really looked wasted. Jorma had about a third of his hair up in a samurai topknot and was wearing a fat chunky swastika pendant, probably the same one he wore at Woodstock — who knows why?

The Airplane did "We Can Be Together" — uncensored — and "Volunteers," exploiting the national television opportunity to make a strong political point. Thank God for ABC letting them get away with it! This incident is generally taken to be the first instance of the uncensored word "fuck" heard on network TV. Then Joni did "Chelsea Morning," "Willy," and "For Free," about a real busker at 6th Street and 8th Avenue in New York — or was it 6th Avenue and 8th Street? She only said 6th and 8th. Grace led a standing ovation for "Chelsea Morning," but Paul seemed totally bored by it — as I was.

The video was fuzzy for the Airplane's numbers but sharp for Joni's. The sound was wimpy for the Airplane's voices and electronics but strong and clear for Joni's voice and acoustic instruments. I wish it had been the other way around. It looked like tampering with the Airplane's volume and crispness was ABC's cheap attempt to be "psychedelic."

Jorma, Jack, Spencer, and Marty never said a word in the interviews. Marty sat with his back to the camera the whole time. Dick was fixated on Grace. She called him "Jim" as some sort of private joke. Stephen and David arrived later as "unexpected(?)" guests. Joni, Stephen, and David were very talkative, Grace somewhat, and Paul not much. Stephen especially was quite witty and animated, pointing out the mud from Woodstock still on his jeans.

David said of Woodstock, "It's probably the strangest thing that's ever happened in the world." He described the helicopter's-eye view of the audience as looking like "an encampment of the Macedonian army on the Greek hills crossed with the biggest batch of gypsies you ever saw." Later he added, "about two nights ago, that place up there was the second biggest city in New York, and it had no violence."

Dick asked them all if they would ever endorse a political candidate. David said none were worth endorsing. There was general agreement until Joni said she would sing for Pierre Trudeau — then there was general agreement to that.

Dick suggested to Joni that her work was unpolitical. She went along with him to a point, but later sang *a cappella* to America the song that she wrote as an admonitory Canadian, a very political song equating America the fiddler with friendliness and goodness but America the drummer with belligerence and terror.

David grabbed a tambourine and joined the Airplane onstage for "Somebody to Love" and a fadeout jam. That was it. Joni danced with someone in the audience. Jorma's vibrato was perfect.

Fall 1969

Bring all the G.I.s home now!

The President is merely the most important among a large number of public servants. He should be supported or opposed exactly to the degree which is warranted by his good conduct or bad conduct, his efficiency or inefficiency in rendering loyal, able, and disinterested service to the Nation as a whole. Therefore it is absolutely necessary that there should be full liberty to tell the truth about his acts, and this means that it is exactly necessary to blame him when he does wrong as to praise him when he does right. Any other attitude in an American citizen is both base and servile. To announce that there must be no criticism of the President, or that we are to stand by the President, right or wrong, is not only unpatriotic and servile, but is morally treasonable to the American public. Nothing but the truth should be spoken about him or any one else. But it is even more important to tell the truth, pleasant or unpleasant, about him than about any one else.

— Theodore Roosevelt, guest editorial
in *The Kansas City Star*, May 7, 1918

We quickly noticed that the lyrics of the Rolling Stones' "Honky Tonk Women" scanned perfectly to the tune of "The Star Spangled Banner." This fact naturally changed our entire approach to sporting events.

The American national anthem is a war song, all about bombs, rockets, flags, ramparts, and other military things. The lyrics of "The Star Spangled Banner" make it just about the worst choice for a national anthem. We Americans should be more proud of our peaceful civilization than of our ability to make war, even to defend ourselves. The nationalistic spirit expressed in music should be celebratory and uplifting but not jingoistic. Thus Woody Guthrie's "This Land is Your Land" (seriously, because it pays tribute to natural, geographic grandeur and the positive, peaceful aspirations of everyday people); or "America the Beautiful," "My Country 'Tis of Thee (America)," or "God Bless America" (somewhat less seriously, given their references to God); or even Steve Miller's "Living in the U.S.A." (much less seriously, given its reference to cheeseburgers) would each have been better.

Music is a powerful, primal motivator. When repeated endlessly, it drives its point into the subconscious to affect both attitude and behavior. The powers-that-be clearly recognize this fact. That is why the ecclesiastical powers-that-be make believers sing hymns in church. That is also why the American political, civic, and commercial powers-that-be cram "The Star Spangled Banner" into our ears at every opportunity, especially at large gatherings where everyone has already come for a common purpose, such as to watch a ball game. This tactic has long been a key part of their plutocratic conspiracy to transform American citizens into automatic consumers of the standard message and supporters of the socioeconomic status quo. The powers-that-be fare better when we are automatons than when we are free to think and do as we each please. They would love to make a mockery of the First and Fourth Amendments, turn politics into sports and us into mindless sports fans, where we cheer for "Yew Ess Ay!" for exactly the same stupid reason that we cheer for our home team or our alma mater, i.e., just because America is ours, not because America is right. The constant din of the national anthem means that ethics, justice, and fairness do not matter, but winning — the flag being still there — means everything. "The Star Spangled Banner" has been meant to reprogram us to react to stimuli like Pavlov's dogs rather than think about situations like Aristotle's rational animals. We have not even been able to watch TV without hearing it over and over and over ...

The leaders inside the Beltway and on Wall Street would have liked nothing more than to turn us all into jingoes. That would have guaranteed their perpetual political and economic success. They did not care if they needed to make war, enslave minds, and violate basic ethical principles in order to get rich and powerful. Getting rich and powerful — winning — was all that mattered to them. In their view, Green Bay Packers coach Vince Lombardi, who infamously said, "Winning isn't everything; it's the only thing," was the consummate American.

In contrast to Lombardi's amoral emphasis on winning at any price, we ethical citizens preferred the more time-honored proverb: "It's not whether you win or lose; it's how you play the game."

We heard rumors that Hendrix had played "The Star Spangled Banner" at Woodstock as an antiwar song. We did not know for sure, because the movie and soundtrack would not be widely available until the following summer. We heard that he had done it as an instrumental and we wondered how, without rewritten lyrics, it could have been transformed into an antiwar song. We surmised that the muddy, spaced-out, drugged-up, hippie/freaks at Woodstock had just wishfully interpreted it as antiwar. That would not mean that Hendrix either intended or conveyed it as antiwar. People expected to hear antiwar songs at Woodstock.

Hendrix's national anthem became the most eagerly awaited scene in the movie and cut on the album. When those two Woodstock products finally appeared, we were delighted to learn that the rumors were true. Hendrix's "Star Spangled Banner" was beautiful! — and most definitely antiwar, despite being an instrumental. It articulated America's belligerence. With just his guitar, Hendrix shifted the song's emphasis away from the defended flag in Baltimore, of which many of us remained proud, and onto our country's aggressive policies in Southeast Asia, of which we were all ashamed.

Deconstructionist theory holds that the author of a text does not matter and that the text's meaning can be found only in the text itself, considered in the socio-political-sexual-economic context through which it is received and in view of its psychosocial subtext. Bullshit! Proper interpretation depends also on understanding the author's motivations. The author or creator — in this case the performer, Hendrix — matters a lot. He laid it out there. If anyone other than he, the most innovative guitar virtuoso of that time, had played the song in that style, no one would have taken it as antiwar. Only he could have made his guitar sound like an entire battle. Even without words, it was the most powerful antiwar message at Woodstock, more eloquent than Melanie, Joan Baez, Country Joe, and CSNY all put together. Also, the promoters, being antiwar themselves, made very sure that everyone on stage at Woodstock was likewise antiwar. This was a classic case of preaching to the choir. Hendrix was the presiding bishop. His "electric church" became a reality, if only for a few hours.

All things considered, I still wish that Woody Guthrie and not Francis Scott Key had written the lyrics. But maybe we should keep the same tune. There is a nice irony in using the eighteenth-century English drinking song, "To Anacreon in Heaven," as the anthem of one of the world's most belligerent nations. Fortunately, we can put just about any words to a slow waltz. Making just make few little adjustments to Woody's lyrics — and presto:

Say that you have an ideal, any ideal, call it x. Say that this ideal is realized on earth and established within an institution that we will call y. Say that y is justly honored for having furthered the cause of x. Yet, paradoxically, the more y is glorified for having brought x into being, the more x is overlooked. If y is consummately glorified, then x is forgotten. Say that z is a symbol of y. Say that z is honored alongside y. Say that the leaders of y require the members of y to worship z as a condition for remaining members in good standing. Say that the concept of worshipping anything is abhorrent to x. Then, to the extent that z is worshipped, x is lost.

The lesson is: To keep x safe, we must constantly focus on x, not on either y or z. Especially not on z.

Say that x = "individual liberty or personal freedom." Say that y = "the United States of America." Say that z = "the American flag."

Conservatives are obsessed with symbols, and typically elevate symbols to even greater heights of glory than the things that are symbolized. They honor the flag more than the country; the cross more than Jesus; the Constitution more than its guaranteed rights; and the pledge of allegiance more than its meaning. The shallow externals thrive; the deep internals wither.

One of the first projects that any government will undertake in order to establish itself as authoritarian is to convince citizens to worship its symbols. In the sixties (as probably in any era), to honor the external form of anything while ignoring its content was safe and easy; but to honor that internal content would have been more difficult, requiring courage, thought, and sometimes even self-critique. Hegel had complained in the "Hinrichs Foreword" about praising the frame more than the painting within it, but no one yet could read that text in English. The conservative denigration of the valuable and commendation of the worthless continued unchecked. The flag was the most extreme case. The lengths that the right wing took to honor that piece of cloth verged on the ridiculous. We were not blind to their folly in this regard.

Ultimately, any flag is a dead thing, a piece of cloth, a *caput mortuum*. Whatever it may symbolize may be vibrant, but it itself is not worthy of pretending that it has a life of its own. It is no more worthy of respect than Gessler's hat. Yet it grants to its venerators a large measure of stability. The right wing craves nothing so much as stability. But stability kills. Stability for its survival requires censorship, repression, conformity, and unfreedom. But what do the censors, repressors, conformists, and the unfree know? They are afraid of ideas. They are afraid of change. They are afraid of social or political progress. We had to ask: If all Americans in 1969 had been alive, at their same ages, in 1776, whose side would we each have taken in the American Revolution? We had to conclude that we young leftists and idealists would have been the rebels, the "patriots" of the new nation, and would have stood with Washington at Valley Forge; while the old rightists and realists of our day, the so-called "patriots" who pushed us into Vietnam, censored us, held the blacks down, cut our hair, and ridiculed our music, would have been the Tories who believed that we should have stayed with England. Like the true patriots of 1776, we had a vision of a better society and the boldness to bring it into existence;

but the lip-servicing "patriots" of 1969 had no such vision, and whatever boldness they may have had was directed toward keeping things just as they were.

The only symbols that interested us were the peace symbol ☮, the omega Ω (for resistance), and the ankh ☥, the ancient Egyptian symbol of life. We were never for a minute fooled into believing that any of these symbols was more important than the peace, principles, and life that they symbolized.

The omega was a very useful symbol. The last letter of the Greek alphabet and the standard symbol of the standard unit of electrical resistance, the ohm, named after German physicist Georg Ohm (1787-1854), it now had become the symbol of any kind of resistance, especially political resistance. It was also a natural frame. You could draw anything inside it: a clenched fist, an ankh, the peace symbol, the peace sign ✌ (two fingers raised in a vee, palmar side outward), the thumbs-up sign 👍, a cross ☦, a smiley face ☺, the third eye 👁, the yin-yang ☯, the woman symbol ♀, the infinity symbol ∞ — Resistance forever! — the hammer and sickle ☭, or whatever else may have struck your fancy.

Laws that demand respect for flag, ruler, country, religion, party, ancestry, wealth, status, dogma, Jesus Christ's blood, Mohammed's name, Lenin's corpse, or Gessler's hat are hallmarks of tyrannical regimes. Democratic, socialist, or egalitarian governments have no need of such laws. Respect cannot be demanded; it must be earned. Anything that is worthy of respect does not need a law to create or enforce that respect. Conversely, anything that boasts a law demanding that it be respected is, to that extent, not worthy of respect — *ipso facto*.

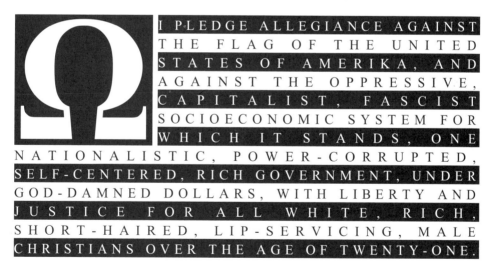

I PLEDGE ALLEGIANCE AGAINST THE FLAG OF THE UNITED STATES OF AMERIKA, AND AGAINST THE OPPRESSIVE, CAPITALIST, FASCIST SOCIOECONOMIC SYSTEM FOR WHICH IT STANDS, ONE NATIONALISTIC, POWER-CORRUPTED, SELF-CENTERED, RICH GOVERNMENT, UNDER GOD-DAMNED DOLLARS, WITH LIBERTY AND JUSTICE FOR ALL WHITE, RICH, SHORT-HAIRED, LIP-SERVICING, MALE CHRISTIANS OVER THE AGE OF TWENTY-ONE.

Jefferson Airplane was completely aware of all this topsy-turvy worship of the flag and other symbols by the right. To counter and satirize this tendency, the cover and interior art of their new LP, *Volunteers*, disrespected the flag at every opportunity. On the front cover, the group, black-and-white, masked, and goofy, posed in front of a huge, cracked, and tattered flag, in color. At the top the American eagle carried a flag and a marijuana leaf where the arrows were supposed to be. The back cover asked: "Question of the Day: What is Your Favorite Stripe on the Flag?" to which each of the six gave a flippant answer. A black-and-white photo on the back cover showed a man wearing a hat folded out of a newsprint flag (the only colored thing in the photo) that said, "A Flag for Your Window." Inside, after we got past the larger-than-life peanut-buttered slice of bread on one side of the gatefold and the equally larger-than-life jelly-covered slice on the other side, the lyrics sheet continued the comedy. The side with the lyrics on it was headlined, "Feed and Water Your Flag." The other side was a mock broadside newssheet, *Paz Progress*, whose logo was that same eagle with the flag and marijuana leaf. One of the headlines read: "Boy, 18, Accidentally Shoots Brother with a .22 Caliber Flag." An editorial by Tommy Smothers was heavily censored. The sports section listed the batting leaders in the Amerikan [sic] League. Jerry Garcia was quoted: "I broke a string so why don't you wait a minute & talk to each other. Or maybe talk to yourself, to your various selves. Can you talk to yourself? Do you even know you have selves to talk to?" A cartoon showed astronauts Neil Armstrong and Buzz Aldrin, with little flags sprouting all over them, playing on the moon like little boys in a sandbox while talking on the phone with a drooling Nixon. Eldridge Cleaver was hiding in one of the moon's craters.

The songs on *Volunteers* were no less part of the cultural and political revolutions. It began with Kantner's didactic rocker, "We Can Be Together," which boasted of youthful solidarity as obnoxious, subversive, anarchistic, outrageous, dodgy, illegal, motherfuckin' fun. The next track, "Good Shepherd," alerted us that *Volunteers* would be their most eclectic album. Jorma presented the traditional religious tune with all due respect, emphasizing the gentler side of Jesus and his followers. Next the Airplane took a joking stab at country rock with "The Farm"; yet its lyrics, though silly, had a serious Thoreauvian undercurrent, suggesting that maybe it was high time for urban and suburban rat-racers to simplify their lives. Grace's "Hey Fredrick," which we knew to translate as "Hey Motherfucker," continued in the vein of "reJoyce," "Two Heads," and "Greasy Heart," exposing hypocrisy, plasticity, and inhumanity wherever she found it. Jorma's "Turn My Life Down" was a song of frustration. The Airplane's version of "Wooden Ships" differed from that on *Crosby, Stills, and Nash* primarily by virtue of the added dimension of mentioning music as a savior of humanity. Grace's and Paul's "Eskimo Blue Day" assessed the damage that humans have done to the earth's whole ecology, observed how insignificant humans really are *sub specie aeternitatis*, and declared the industrial or post-industrial failure of humans to fit properly, meaningfully, or harmlessly into nature. Spencer's "A Song for All Seasons," another mock country song, took a comedic glimpse at the backside of the music business. Celebrating internationalism, "Meadowlands" was Jorma's instrumental version of the 1934 Soviet military tune. Marty's and Paul's "Volunteers" honored and applauded all the street demonstrators, antiwar protesters, cultural warriors, joyful dancers, and political revolutionaries of America.

The album's name derived from the fact that, whereas some of the people on the pro-Vietnam-War, anti-civil-rights side were either draftees or otherwise compromised, there was no one on the antiwar, pro-civil-rights side who did not want to be there. One hundred per cent of us were volunteers! We could have taken the easy way out and gone with the government and the conservative tradition, but we chose the harder, principled path.

Speaking of principles:

Middle-of-the-road, predominantly white churches were polarized over the war and social issues, mainly along generational lines. Few attempted internal reconciliation within these denominations. One noteworthy exception was Episcopal Bishop Robert L. DeWitt of the Diocese of Pennsylvania. He supported draft resistance and encouraged his ministers to be trained in draft counseling, ordered dialogue with BEDC when it angered most whites by demanding financial reparations for slavery, brought teenagers into the diocesan convention as delegates, and later, in 1974, defied the entire Anglican communion by ordaining women as priests.

Bishop DeWitt was one of us volunteers! Other prominent Christians were with us too — William Sloane Coffin, Daniel and Philip Berrigan, Paul Moore, *et al.* — polarizing the white mainstream Protestant churches and the Roman Catholic Church into dovish liberal vs. hawkish conservative, tearing congregations apart. The polarization of these churches only reflected the polarization of the whole country — no more, no worse, no better, no different.

From September 24 to next February 20 in Chicago, the kangaroo court of Judge Julius Hoffman, Mayor Daley's former law partner — hardly impartial — tried leftists on trumped-up charges connected with demonstrations at the 1968 convention. Led by Abbie Hoffman (who spared no effort to point out that he was no relation to the inquisitor on the bench), the defendants treated their trial as it deserved to be treated: as a farce. First known as the Chicago Eight, they became the Chicago Seven on November 5 when Julie denied Black Panther Bobby Seale adequate legal counsel, had him bound and gagged, severed him from the case, and sentenced him to four years for contempt. The Seven's trial, played out in the press and on the TV news, was the funniest guerrilla theater of the year! The world was so much more interesting with Abbie in it!

From October 8 to 11, the Weather Underground provoked violence in the streets of Chicago. Quite the opposite of what had happened at the Democratic National Convention in August 1968, this time the demonstrators were deliberately violent and the police were restrained. The point of these so-called "Weatherman Days of Rage" was to show that affluent Americans, just minding their own business and going about their everyday capitalist lives, were *ipso facto* doing violence against the people of Vietnam — or, ultraparadoxically, to show that being passive, i.e., *not* using street violence to attack government violence, was in fact violent. Their slogan was "Bring the War Home!" They did. Temporarily.

The Weathermen were an embarrassment. They were to the New Left as LBJ was to the Democratic Party: unilateralists who gave their respective larger movements bad reputations. Their "Days of Rage" were worse than ridiculous; they were counterproductive.

The Weathermen killed the SDS — on purpose. The SDS was by and large committed to nonviolence, but the Weathermen wanted armed struggle and violent revolution. So a handful of them did away with the SDS. But, in January 2006, responding to the Iraq War and other abuses of the Dubya administration, high school and college students refounded the SDS. Shortly thereafter, some former

SDS-ers from the sixties founded the Movement for a Democratic Society (MDS) as a sort of "Old Farts Auxiliary" for the second SDS. At the first national MDS conference at the New School in New York City on February 17, 2007, in an extraordinary act of courage and repentance, Mark Rudd, one of the original Weathermen, publicly confessed his role in the demise of the first SDS:

> I come before you this morning as one of the principal authors, almost forty years ago, of a totally failed strategy. In the course of things, my little faction seized control of the SDS national office and several of the regional offices. We then made the tragic decision in 1969, at the height of the war, to kill off SDS because it wasn't revolutionary enough for us. I am not proud of this history.
>
> So there is no reason in the world why you should want to listen to me, except for the fact that over the last thirty seven years I've reflected continually about the complex of errors that led to the death of SDS and also on my part in this historical crime. As a result I've come up with some hard-won conclusions.
>
> I often read references in historical literature and commentary to SDS "self-destructing." This seems to refer to a constellation of generalized forces including Maoist sectarian infiltration, the development of various brands of Marxist dogmatism among the "regulars," the drive toward hyper-militancy, violent confrontation, and ultimately "armed struggle," all within a bitter context of government repression. In some renditions of the death of SDS story there is the consoling air of historical inevitability, no matter what we in the national leadership would have done, SDS was destined (by the God of History, I suppose) to implode.
>
> But I don't agree. I remember a certain meeting with no more than ten people present, out of a national membership of 12,000 and perhaps ten times that many chapter members, at which we in the Weatherman clique ... decided to scuttle SDS. I remember driving a VW van with Teddy Gold from the New York Regional Office in the basement of 131 Prince Street to the Sanitation Department pier at the end of West 14th Street, just a few blocks from here, and dumping the addressograph, mailing stencils, and other records from the Regional Office onto a barge. These were insane decisions which I and my comrades made unilaterally, to the exclusion of other, much better, choices. We could have, for example, fought to keep SDS in existence so as to unite as many people as possible against the war (which is what the Vietnamese had asked us to do) while at the same time educating around imperialism. I often wonder, had we done so, where we would have been a few months later, in May 1970, when the biggest student protests in American history jumped off. Or today, when imperialist war rages yet again, would we have had to reinvent the anti-imperialist movement almost from scratch?
>
> Alas, with all the best intentions of promoting revolutionary solidarity with the people of the world, the Weatherman faction by killing off SDS

did the work of the FBI for them. Assuming we weren't in the pay of the FBI, we should have been.

Obviously this is a harsh critique. But it gets even worse: Our hyper-militancy and armed struggle line created a deep division which weakened the larger antiwar movement and demoralized many good people. This was totally unnecessary. Also, we provided a gold-plated gift to the media and the government, enabling them to characterize the entire movement as violent and therefore deranged. As a tragic coda, three of our own beloved comrades were accidentally killed by bombs they were making just two blocks from here, in the townhouse on West 11th Street.

The subsequent Weather Underground did not, of course, lead to the growth of a revolutionary movement in this country. It led to isolation and defeat. The guerrilla focus did not help build either a revolutionary army or a mass movement. One thing I'm absolutely certain of, having learned the hard way, is that political violence in any form can never be understood in this society.

No amount of rhetoric around revolutionary heroism and solidarity with the Third World can mask the Weather strategy as anything other than sure revolutionary suicide. Revolutionary suicide may serve some psychological or existential function, but politically it produces nothing.

So the greatest lesson I draw from my disastrous history is that the left must absolutely stay away from violence or any talk of violence. The government is violent; we oppose their violence.

Rudd's admission is among the most encouraging signs I have seen for the future of post-sixties leftist revolution. We may well speculate what may have happened if violent leftist organizations like the Weathermen and the Black Panthers had not stolen the national spotlight in the late sixties and early seventies from nonviolent leftist organizations like the SDS, the NAACP, and the Southern Christian Leadership Conference.

The only two SDS meetings I attended were in the fall of 1970 in Portland, Maine, and Boston, Massachusetts. I did not learn until many years later that the SDS already no longer existed and that these were not meetings of the real SDS, but covert Weather Underground recruiting sessions. The content of these meetings surprised and alarmed me and my friends. It did not jive with what I had heard of the SDS. In short, the Weathermen tried to dupe us. They indeed did the FBI's work very well.

A coalition of the various Mobes and other antiwar and draft resistance organizations called for a completely nonviolent nationwide series of silent protests, consciousness raising events, work stoppages, and other constructive activities to happen on Wednesday, October 15. Millions, mostly high school and college students, participated. This "National Moratorium Day" was the closest we achieved toward a European-style general strike. It should have lasted longer.

On November 7, eight protégés of Philip Berrigan, including two priests, a nun, a seminarian, a staffer of the National Council to Repeal the Draft, and three others, burglarized Selective Service offices in Boston. This was their statement, mimeographed and circulated underground:

> We, the Boston Eight, claim responsibility for the destruction of draft files at Jamaica Plain, Dudley, Uphams Corner, and Copley Square in Boston on November 7. Through this offence to good taste and to law and order we make ourselves responsible for our lives and for the lives of our brothers.
>
> We destroy some of these files today [i.e., November 15] in Washington because we believe that the Peace Movement must seriously consider its responsibility to MOVE. We, as you, have marched, written letters, conferred with officialdom, spoken against the war, capitalist materialism, and military control. Mr. Nixon responded to our and your pleas in his November 3 speech, and we responded to these same pleas in Boston on November 7. If you feel as we do that marching and demonstrating are unproductive, we encourage you to take responsible action to secure peace and to end injustice.
>
> We have fashioned hope with our bodies, as free people must do. We oppose with our lives genocide in Viet Nam and the arms race, exploitative investment abroad, rape of foreign manpower and resources, domestic racism, environmental ruin, and militarism in any form — Selective Service, lottery, or volunteer army.
>
> We attack Selective Service because it illustrates the powerlessness of all Americans, as well as the arrogance of power. It is to return control to the one, and to check the other, that we have acted. We believe that it will be impossible to reconstruct the draft records in Boston. All 1-A and 1-Y files were destroyed, as were files for resisters, delinquents, non-registrants. Chronological ledgers, alphabetical cross reference systems and minutes of draft board meetings were also destroyed.
>
> Our action demonstrates that non-violent civil disobedience can effectively halt injustice. To us, such action is a profound moral and political duty, necessary to exalt life and secure peace. To these ends we deplore terroristic attacks which endanger life and engender fear.
>
> Peace,   William Au
> Mary Cain, S.N.D.
> Paul Couming
> Darrell Dewease
> John Galvani, S.J.
> Claudette Piper
> Barbara Shapiro
> Anthony Scoblick, S.S.J.

The message of these activists was the same as in Buffy Sainte-Marie's "Universal Soldier": MANPOWER MAKES WAR POWER: REPEAL THE DRAFT!

Ω

March on Washington, November 15, 1969, to Bring All the Troops Home Now!

Around 5:30 a.m. my friend Heidi picked me up in her Ford Maverick. Half an hour later at the University of Delaware we boarded one of several large buses chartered by the Newark New Mobe, the Delaware chapter of the New Mobilization to End the War in Vietnam. On each bus were two New Mobe marshals. I think they were Quakers. Their job was to spend the trip training the riders in the nonviolent principles and tactics that we would need to know and use in Washington that day in order to make an effective antiwar statement. Given that the Weather Underground had dumped a ton of terrible publicity on the whole antiwar movement less than six weeks ago with the senseless "Days of Rage" in Chicago, the avowedly and typically peaceful New Mobe was especially careful to ensure that this day would be peaceful enough to garner us some good publicity for a change. For those of us in the Student Mobe (SMC) with whom I discussed the various splinter groups internal to the movement, the Yippies were cool, the Diggers were cool, the original SDS was cool, and even the Lower-East-Side-Collective-Up-Against-the-Wall-Motherfuckers had their points in a Sansculottish sort of way, but we considered the Weathermen as much our enemy as Nixon. They each did us about as much damage.

When we got to Washington we walked to the Mall from where the buses parked a few blocks north of Pennsylvania Avenue. The air was bitter cold. Most of the morning we just huddled on the Mall, shivered, and waited. Singers and speakers presented their schticks from near the Washington Monument, but from where I was, between 4th and 7th Streets N.W., I could not hear them very well or see them at all. Finally the marshalls began organizing the march itself, from the Capitol up Pennsylvania Avenue to encircle the White House, then to disperse peacefully back to the buses to go home. The march was fun. We chanted, sang, yelled slogans, and generally had a great time. At least we were moving instead of standing and freezing. We could not get close to the White House because of the perimeter barricade of buses, cops, and Secret Service agents. Rumors flew that Nixon was not there anyway, or if he was, he was watching football and not paying attention to us. Heidi and I lost track of each other.

Toward the end of the march, in the vicinity of the White House, I heard someone say that some of us were going over to the Justice Department to show support for Bobby Seale. I had plenty of time to get back to the bus, so I decided to go. When I got there, I realized that I was a latecomer. Thousands of people who had already surrounded the building were chanting, "Free Bobby Seale! Free Bobby Seale!" There was no violence. I could not get very close to the action, but on a little rise across Constitution Avenue from the southeast corner of the building, I could see the whole scene pretty well. I noticed a handful of guards between the crowd and the building, mostly near the flagpole. No one was attacking anyone.

Some demonstrators tried to lower the U.S. flag. The guards pushed them back and reraised the flag. More people then tried to lower the flag. Again the guards intervened, but our side managed to get it down. Someone threw what might have been a water balloon filled with blood-red dye at the building. It hit and burst about twenty feet up the wall. That did not hurt anyone. It was just a symbolic act. It did not break a window. Two skirmish lines of D.C. cops in full riot gear advanced with batons at the ready, one from the north, the other from the east. There may have been more, but those two were all I could see from where I was. When they had blocked our possible escapes on Constitution Avenue and 9th Street N.W., they lobbed at least three tear gas canisters into the middle of the crowd, all the while maintaining their slow, deliberate advance. No one had attacked them first! They attacked us!

The stinging, searing effect of the gas was immediate. I would endure bleeding, open sores in my nose and mouth for the next two weeks.

Coughing like crazy, nearly blinded, and scared that I was about to get my skull bashed in, I pulled the front of my coat collar over my face with my left hand and the back of the collar over my head with my right hand, leaving only a slit for my eyes. Images of savage beatings that other cops had inflicted on other innocent and unarmed people at other antiwar events flashed through my mind. Desperate to avoid suffering any such harm myself, I ducked and sprinted like a halfback between two cops and got the hell out of there. I do not know what happened to anyone else nearby. Besides being just barely able to see, pure survival instinct had taken me over. I made it back to the bus on time. The marshalls and others with cold compresses and assorted makeshift remedies helped those half dozen or so of us who been gassed. Heidi dropped me off at home around 10 or 10:30 p.m.

It so happened that the various prime time TV programs that Saturday — movies or football or something — ended at staggered times. This meant that the three 11 o'clock network news broadcasts ran consecutively instead of concurrently. I seized upon this unusual opportunity to watch all three. ABC, NBC, and CBS each told a slightly different story, but each got it wrong. Each blamed the violence at the Justice Department on the marchers. Each said that we attacked the cops before they used the gas on us.

"It wasn't like that!" I blurted out.

"How do you know?" my parents both asked.

"Because I was there!" I snapped. I had not told them that I was going to Washington, because, if I had, then they might not have let me go.

The Sunday, November 16, *New York Times* headline was: "250,000 War Protesters Stage Peaceful Rally in Washington; Militants Stir Clashes Later." The rally was indeed peaceful, but there were probably closer to half a million of us, and it was not any "militants" who had stirred the clashes. It was the District of Columbia Metropolitan Police Department.

Ω

Maybe rumor, maybe fact, maybe some of each, but we got the word that Spiro Agnew's thirteen-year-old daughter Kim was one of us. She was supposed to have smoked dope, worn an antiwar armband, and tried to join our demonstrations. Of course, Spiro was supposed to have come down on her like a ton of bricks and isolated her. Thus, among our usual chants, bumper stickers, and button slogans of the time was "Free Kim Agnew." We meant it too. We knew exactly what she was going through. Spiro was the spitting image of our own parents. They liked him. They elected him. He spoke for them.

Nixon's war against humanity continued. Agnew was its designated orator.

One thing that America is no good at is putting itself in other people's shoes. There would not be nearly as many wars if prospective aggressors and invaders could first more easily imagine how they would react if they were the victims rather than the perpetrators of aggression or invasion. America believes that it can just traipse into sovereign nations like Vietnam or Iraq and tell them how to live — but then America, in all its arrogance, simplicity, tactlessness, and confusion, wondered why the Vietnamese and Iraqis fought back. Why should they resist these improvements that America had so magnanimously and unilaterally decided to bestow upon their backward lands? They should be grateful! America either could not or would not imagine the reverse situation. Would not everyday Americans resist, defend, and fight back even harder than the Vietnamese and Iraqis did, if a Vietnamese or Iraqi army were to come uninvited into Peoria, Santa Fe, or Mayberry and try to tell us how to live? You bet your ass we would! And our cause would be just! By exactly the same token, the Vietnamese and Iraqi anti-American causes were just. There are none so blind as those who refuse to see.

So America instituted its draft lottery, and made either murderers, criminals, evaders, or resisters out of all young boys born on September 14, 1950. Its police murdered twenty-one-year-old Fred Hampton in cold blood in his bed in Chicago just because he was an eloquent Black Panther. By printing Ronald Haeberle's photos of the American army's slaughter of unarmed civilians in My Lai, Vietnam, *Life* magazine presented irrefutable evidence that America was not the goody-goody that it claimed to be. America committed in war the same kind of atrocities for which it had always condemned the Nazis — and moreover, it had already covered this massacre up for a year and a half.

Yet the fascists marched on: "My country, right or wrong!"

The message of Merle Haggard's "Okie from Muskogee" was "My country, right or wrong, and who cares whether or not it's right!" To paraphrase the lyrics:

> We obey every law and rule we hear of,
> We conform just like U.S. Marines,
> We never ever question what we're doin',
> We have no idea what freedom means.

> And I'm proud to be a patsy from the Heartland,
> Where we suck up to Nixon like he's pope,
> We still adore a piece of cloth a-flappin',
> And we get drunk instead of smokin' dope.

> We exploit women and treat 'em like we own 'em,
> We flatter and are chauvinistic too,

Our hair is short and neat just like God wants it,
And unlike the hippies, we don't have a clue.

And I'm proud to be a patsy from the Heartland,
Where we suck up to Nixon like he's pope,
We still adore a piece of cloth a-flappin',
And we get drunk instead of smokin' dope.

We also wear whatever clothes God tells us,
Never mind that Jesus was a freak,
Brutal sports are a great substitute for thinkin',
And each kid's a grovelin' little geek.

And I'm proud to be a patsy from the Heartland,
Where we suck up to Nixon like he's pope,
We still adore a piece of cloth a-flappin',
And we get drunk instead of smokin' dope.

We still adore a piece of flappin' cloth — by jingo!
In the fascist Heartland of the U.S.A.

Haggard was a convicted shoplifter, burglar, robber, and assailant, a serial felon pardoned by — who else? — Governor Ronald Reagan. Ain't it odd how criminals tend to embrace patriotism, even while victimizing the citizens of the country that they say they love, and even if they are not pardoned by the reigning jingoist? Haggard kept at it too. In January 1970 he released "The Fightin' Side of Me," which explicitly threatened bodily harm against anyone who did not agree with his ultra-American point of view.

On the opposite side from Haggard, Steppenwolf's fourth album, *Monster*, likened America to an out-of-control fiend. The title cut laid the case out in detail, attacking Christian complicity with warmongering, citing genocide against Native Americans, and decrying class warfare in the fat rich man's exploitation of the urban poor. "Draft Resister" praised people who refused to allow the government to use them as weapons. "Power Play" was not about hockey; rather, it depicted the hatred that compulsory inequality provokes among people who would probably not hate each other if society allowed them their natural equality. "Move Over" was a plea for ethical national leadership and "What Would You Do (If I Did That to You)?" a plea for human understanding. "From Here to There Eventually" condemned the hypocrisy of priests.

Luchino Visconti's *The Damned* began with what looked at first like a flaming vision of hell, but as the camera panned, we saw that it was really the furnace fires of a steel mill. The owners of those steel works, the family of Baron Joachin von Essenbeck, were worried about the effect of the new Nazi regime on their business. The movie opened on the night of the Reichstag fire in 1933,[62] when, to placate the Nazis, the Baron transferred executive power over the company to his

---

[62] Visconti got the date wrong. It was February 27, not, as the movie states, February 18.

son Konstantin, a prominent member of the Sturmabteilung (S.A.). Instantly the whole extended family, some willingly, some not, became entangled in the nascent deadly intrigues among the S.A., the general staff of the regular army, the Schutz-staffel (S.S.), and the Gestapo. These intrigues grew more tortuous and deranged the more the S.A. fell out of favor.

Imagining a more decadent and perverted clan of wealthy industrialists than the von Essenbecks would be difficult. To exhort an ambitious future in-law toward further pro-Nazi crimes beyond the murder of his future father-in-law that he has already committed, one cousin misquoted Hegel out of context: "The state cannot but crush the innocent little flower — if the flower obstructs its path."[63] The back-stabbing, interfamilial hatred, and Nazi toadying continued. Konstantin died at Wiessee in the Night of the Long Knives purge against the S.A. on June 30, 1934. Soon after, the most depraved member of the family, Martin, the Caligula of the story, a transvestite, child molester, incestuous rapist, and matricide, took control of the steel company, survived the intrigues, and emerged as the Gestapo's pet.

Anything that is depicted in any form of art, from painting to music to TV shows, receives *ipso facto* a certain level of validation. This is true even if what is depicted is depicted as disgusting, foul, detrimental, and evil. The very fact that it is presented at all validates it to some extent. Whether its creator intends or not to validate it, it will be validated. If it is depicted realistically, then the beholders of the artwork will take the validation seriously; but if unrealistically, then not so much. That is why propaganda movies like *Reefer Madness* and implausible TV shows like *Leave It to Beaver* typically fail in their original intentions, because they are manifestly unreal. No family like the Cleavers ever existed — or could exist. Human emotions are just not that carefree or one-dimensional. *Reefer Madness* failed to deter marijuana use because it depicted marijuana as disgusting, foul, detrimental, and evil. That was not only unrealistic; it was ludicrous.

The relation between artistic realism and social validation is also why realistic artworks that try to edify people, preclude certain kinds of beliefs, or prevent certain kinds of behavior frequently also fail. No matter how disgusting, foul, detrimental, and evil something is depicted, if it is depicted realistically, then someone, somewhere, is going to want to emulate what is shown. *The Damned*, even though its clear intention was anti-Nazi, and even though it accurately showed Nazism as thoroughly disgusting, foul, detrimental, and evil, surely encouraged some viewers to become Nazis. Its very accuracy was its undoing in this regard. A good but unrealistic family like the Cleavers would not generate emulators, but an

---

[63] G.W.F. Hegel, *Introduction to the Philosophy of History*, translated by Leo Rauch (Indianapolis: Hackett, 1988), p. 35: "A world-historical individual is not so circumspect as to want this, that, and the other, and to take account of everything; rather, he commits himself unreservedly to one purpose alone. So it happens that such individuals treat other interests, even sacred ones, in a casual way — a mode of conduct certainly open to moral censure. But so great a figure must necessarily trample on many an innocent flower, crushing much that gets in his way." As usual, Hegel is speaking descriptively, not prescriptively.

evil and realistic family like the von Essenbecks would. That is just human nature — what Edgar Allan Poe called "the imp of the perverse."

Oh! What a Lovely War! was a surreal musical comedy revue about World War I, a potpourri of juxtapositions, mostly between the perspectives of the upper and lower classes. It was didactic and obvious as antiwar propaganda, but its songs were fun. Juxtaposition recurred throughout between the Brighton carnival euphoria of the British home front and the horrors of the war itself in France and Belgium. Purely visual as well as conceptual juxtapositions abounded, always in a bittersweet way. Crosses for graves and cross-shaped communication poles resembled each other. The act of digging trenches was seen as digging graves. The process of enlistment was depicted as General Sir Douglas Haig selling tickets to the "World War One" amusement park at Brighton Pier. (Yes, we recognized the anachronism.) The impromptu truce on Christmas 1914 between German and British enlisted infantry underscored the fact that their real enemies were not each other, but the coldhearted upper classes and royals who had started the war. The miserable reality of duped enlistees stood constantly in sharp contrast to the unreality of kings and generals playing war games and having no more regard for the lives of their men than they would for pawns in a chess game. While corrupt British staff officers waltzed through the war as if it were one big party, thousands of troops died each day in the trenches that stretched from Switzerland to the North Sea. The highest echelons of command were shown as willfully ignorant of the actual toll of war on the millions of lesser human beings in those trenches. They had convinced themselves that the wounded and dying were cheerful and just itching to get back to the front for another good crack at the Boche. Haig ordered his soldiers to advance into enemy fire and, under threat of court-martial, not to take cover, but just "walk through the enemy lines." He did not care how many of his own men died, just as long as the German casualties were larger. The goal of his war of attrition was to finish as soon as possible with the Germans having 5,000 troops to the British 10,000, so that he could declare victory before the Americans arrived. The film ended with four women picnicking after the war in a vast military graveyard, as that was the only way they could still socialize with five of their beloved men.

Bonnie and Clyde may not have succeeded to the fullest possible extent to make a couple of serial felons seem lovable, but *Butch Cassidy and the Sundance Kid* certainly did. Even forty years after its appearance, it remains the standard by which both the tragicomic outlaw film and the so-called "buddy film" are measured. Why should this be? Perhaps Paul Newman and Robert Redford were simply more charismatic than Faye Dunaway and Warren Beatty — or Geena Davis and Susan Sarandon in *Thelma and Louise*, for that matter. That interpretation would readily be supported by their repeat juxtaposition four years later as con men in *The Sting*. Moreover, Newman's and Redford's joint charisma seemed greater than the sum of its two parts. Unlike the pairing of Dunaway and Beatty, which was based on sex and pathos, the pairing of Newman and Redford in both *Butch Cassidy and the Sundance Kid* and *The Sting* was based on wit, intelligence, and charm. The Cassidy and Sundance characters were in themselves much more interesting than the Bonnie and Clyde characters, who, after all, were rather dim — and that makes all the difference.

On Her Majesty's Secret Service was the last straw for our film connection to James Bond. Even as disappointed as we were with *You Only Live Twice*, we went to see this sixth Bond movie for three reasons: First, out of curiosity, to see if George Lazenby could play Bond as well as Sean Connery — He could not. Second, because we loved Diana Rigg in *The Avengers*. Third, because everyone loved Telly Savalas, whatever he did.

Despite Lazenby's un-Connery-like appearance, un-Bond-like demeanor, self-conscious delivery of key lines, and generally wooden acting, *On Her Majesty's Secret Service* was a very good film, a genuine love story with interesting characters. Its gadgets were minimal and believable. If Connery had been its star it would have been excellent.

Nevertheless, we were done with Bond — and with all escapist distractions that made no political or social statements. Those of us who still chose to escape reality did it with drugs, not with movies. The rest of us, who were brave enough to face reality without surrendering to drugs, wanted to change it by any means necessary: political, psychological, religious, social, economic, legislative. A few — even though most in the antiwar movement preached tolerance and nonviolence — wanted to change it by force or violence. But for all of us, nonviolent and violent alike, music, books, and political street action were our main connections to reality now.

Bob and Carol and Ted and Alice, i.e., Robert Culp and Natalie Wood and Elliott Gould and Dyan Cannon, was a stupid movie about a stupid activity, spouse swapping. Ah well, free love was free love, and the best plan was probably to get it out of its closet and avoid its pretense. Even so, this movie was not really about free love. It was about superficial, loveless, meaningless, but harmful sex among upper-class — Bob drove a Jaguar XK-E, hardly plebeian transport — swingers indulging in pseudopsychological, touchy-feely, New Age trendiness. We freaks, even those of us who were free-love freaks, could not relate to it. We felt alienated from these people, not in any kind of sociosexual or psychosexual solidarity with them. Their sexuality was shallow, a caricature of real sexuality, reducing the best aspects of the human spirit to the merely physical. In other words, they were phony, plastic, hedonistic, and quite uncomprehending of what humanity was really all about. The film exposed the voyeuristic hypocrisy of psychobabblers and facilitators who sought through perverse group therapy to break down the private intimacy of loving couples and air it in public for their own amusement, thus creating a communal and naturally misunderstood squalor of raw, formerly personal, delicate emotions. Contrast this to David Crosby's "Triad," which really was about love as love, pure, unforced, honest love. But these four idiots tried to force each other to be what they considered honest. Forced honesty is insincere honesty and thus, even if its content is honest, not genuine honesty at all. Genuine honesty is determined both by its content and its unforced spontaneity. They never got that point. Their hollow facade of hipness was underscored at the end by Jackie DeShannon's "What the World Needs Now is Love" on the soundtrack.

Maybe we filmgoers could be generous and interpret *Bob and Carol and*

Ted and Alice as an elaborate or extended satire on pseudopsychology in general. God knows such folly was rampant in 1969, and a ripe target for such barbs.

Ω

Peggy Lee asked, "Is That All There Is?" No! There was a lot more.

Mainly because of the songwriting of departing guitarist Peter Green and new guitarist Danny Kirwan, Fleetwood Mac's third LP, *Then Play On*, radically expanded their range, moving them a bit out of the blues toward progressive rock and even psychedelia. Its most progressive number was Green's "Oh Well," almost nine minutes of mind-boggling chords, virtuoso musicianship, and the lyrical blasphemy of belittling not only one's humanity, but also the love of one's God. Green had a sense of humor too. His "Rattlesnake Shake" was obviously about male masturbation.

The Rod Stewart Album, the auspicious debut of a great solo singer, opened with Rod's cover of the Stones' "Street Fighting Man," in which Nicky Hopkins's piano riff from the Stones' "We Love You" resurfaced, thus cleverly connecting the themes of the two songs, perhaps suggesting that street fighters end up in jail. The second tune, "Man of Constant Sorrow," obviously referred to Judy Collins's "Maid of Constant Sorrow," "Joan Baez's "Girl of Constant Sorrow," and ultimately Dick Burnett's "Man of Constant Sorrow," but did not sound much like any of them. It was much closer to the version on Dylan's first album. The other six songs included solid rocking blues, blues laments, moderately hard rockers, and a soft ballad, "Dirty Old Town," all nourished by expert session musicians like Ian McLagan, Keith Emerson, and Ron Wood.

The Band's eponymous second LP contained twelve original tunes, all written or co-written by Jaime Robert Robertson. Highlights included "Rag Mama Rag"; "Across the Great Divide"; "Up on Cripple Creek," which they did on *Ed Sullivan*; "The Night They Drove Old Dixie Down," an antiwar lyric; and "Look Out Cleveland." Their peculiar blend of country rock, jug band music, organ riffs, and horn, woodwind, violin, and mouth harp accents continued to be unique.

The Byrds were now McGuinn, White, Gene Parsons, and, playing bass, York on his way out and Skip Battin on his way in. Their ninth album, *Ballad of Easy Rider*, featured Arthur Reid Reynolds's "Jesus is Just Alright," the fountainhead of what would become the huge genre of Christian rock. It also included, besides the title cut from the movie soundtrack, a painfully slow cover of Dylan's "It's All Over Now, Baby Blue," and a poignant cover of Woody Guthrie's and Martin Hoffman's "Deportee," which Pete Seeger had already covered, complaining about the cruelty and racism of American immigration and naturalization policies.

Abbey Road was very important to us this fall. Serene and reassuring, it gave us a mellow feeling that the world was still a joyful, human place, despite all the miserable, inhuman crap that was happening in it. Every song on the LP was upbeat and optimistic. "Come Together," despite its inscrutable lyrics, was an encouraging call to unity. "Something" was George's most sensitive love song and his "Here Comes the Sun" assured us of future brightness. "Maxwell's Silver Hammer" and "Octopus's Garden" were just plain silly. The harmonies in "Oh! Darling," "I Want You (She's So Heavy)," and "Because" were among the Beatles' best ever. The medley, "You Never Give Me Your Money" / "Sun King" / "Mean Mr. Mustard" / "Polythene Pam" / "She Came in Through the Bathroom Window," reminded us that people should not be avaricious, dishonest, or plastic, took a stab at the privileged, and assumed the proletarian side in the class war. The further medley, "Golden Slumbers" / "Carry That Weight" / "The End," formed the perfect thematic coda, both musically and lyrically. The LP ended with a little irreverent goof, "Her Majesty," twenty-three seconds of fun.

John and Yoko released *Wedding Album*, a dreadful *avant garde* LP recollecting their honeymoon in Amsterdam. Lennon and the Plastic Ono Band continued their antiwar efforts with their new LP, *Live Peace in Toronto*, which included "Give Peace a Chance," "Yer Blues," "Cold Turkey," and Yoko's screaming "John, John (Let's Hope for Peace)."

America's greatest singles band, Creedence Clearwater Revival, became unmistakably political with the two-sided 45: "Down on the Corner" / "Fortunate Son." The former implied that the best music, i.e., the most heartfelt, is free and comes up from the people. By extrapolation, it likewise implied that little of cultural value comes down from the top. The latter more explicitly attacked the whole notion of privilege. Its sun-clear message was not only that inherited wealth, its accompanying status, and its associated flag-waving jingoism are unjust by their very nature, but also that the children of powerful politicians, military leaders, and millionaires are not innocent of their parents' sociopolitical or socioeconomic crimes and are themselves unjust unless they openly and unambiguously reject their families' bloodsoaked heritage. In other words, every human should be judged only on his or her own merits, and if an otherwise innocent child chooses to hang on palpably guilty parents, then that kid shares that guilt. Both these tunes were on Creedence's fourth LP, *Willy and the Poor Boys*, along with "It Came Out of the Sky," which satirized mass frenzy over UFOs, and "Effigy," which likened the burgeoning anti-authoritarian movements to a wildfire threatening not only the oligarchy and its traditionalist, militarist, and capitalist policies, but also the entire nation, and maybe even the world.

Country Joe and the Fish cranked out two more albums, *Here We Are Again* and *Greatest Hits*, neither of which, except for "Doctor of Electricity" on the former and a slew of old tunes on the latter, was of much interest. Similarly, the Doors just marked time with *Soft Parade*, whose meager highlights were "Running Blues," "Wild Child" and their AM pop hit, "Touch Me."

The revamped Blood, Sweat, and Tears, without Al Kooper but with new vocalist David Clayton-Thomas, was now completely different from Kooper's original vision for the band. They now only pretended to be hip, while in reality they had become, with Clayton-Thomas's distinctive gritty voice, nothing more than a pop singles group with a string of number two hits on AM radio: a cover of Brenda Holloway's "You've Made Me So Very Happy," Clayton-Thomas's own "Spinning

Wheel," and most recently, a cover of Laura Nyro's "And When I Die."

Joe Cocker's eponymous second LP continued his usual *modus operandi* of delivering high-energy cover tunes, such as Leon Russell's "Delta Lady," George Harrison's "Something," Lennon/McCartney's "She Came in Through the Bathroom Window," John Sebastian's "Darlin' Be Home Soon," and Leonard Cohen's "Bird on the Wire."

Keyboardist Gregg Allman and co-lead guitarists Duane Allman and Dickey Betts leaped into the blues rock scene with their debut album, *The Allman Brothers Band*, which contained the original studio versions of what would soon become concert classics, "Whipping Post," "It's Not My Cross to Bear," and their cover of Muddy Waters's "Trouble No More." This LP marked the invention of what would become tremendously popular in the seventies as "southern rock."

When the group Smith, with Gayle McCormick singing lead, covered the soft old Burt Bacharach / Mack David / Barney Williams tune, "Baby, It's You," which had previously been covered by the Beatles and the Shirelles, it became nothing but raw sex. That is exactly what a rock song ought to be. Gayle made it hard, wild, and edgy. Better looking than Janis Joplin and louder than Grace Slick, she just exuded pure vaginal power. When she sang it during Smith's appearance on the October 19 *Ed Sullivan Show*, probably millions of horny young heterosexual men creamed in their pants. She was that good! Why she never became as popular as Janis or Grace, I cannot imagine. It certainly was not for lack of either talent or charisma. In the mid-seventies she voluntarily gave up the music business and returned to obscurity in her native St. Louis.

Meanwhile Janis herself was adrift. She even went so far as to submit herself to the ultimate incongruity: singing "Raise Your Hand" as a duet with middle-of-the-road pop star Tom Jones on his ABC TV show, *This is Tom Jones*. To grasp the full absurdity of this pairing, imagine a duet between punk rocker Patti Smith and gentle crooner Perry Como (which never really happened) or between young, androgynous David Bowie and old, macho Bing Crosby (which did).

At least two other female singers were doing very well fronting their respective bands. Jacqui McShee contributed strong, confident, versatile, and sometimes soaring vocals to Pentangle's third album, *Basket of Light*, arguably among their best. In a similar vein, but a bit edgier, Sandy Denny made an even greater impact on Fairport Convention's fourth LP, their breakthrough, *Liege and Lief*, which was not the origination of British electric folk music, but certainly its elevation to its highest pinnacle. She had pushed the band away from covers of recent tunes and toward original material and electric versions of traditional British folk tunes. The result was stunning. Even in a sextet of vocals, violin, two guitars, bass, and drums, her voice stood out as the most musical element in the mix. She would become a much sought duetist, notably with Robert Plant in "The Battle of Evermore" on the fourth Zep album. Whether the fall downstairs that killed her at thirty-one in 1978 was due to substance abuse or a brain tumor, we will never know — but the point is that the untimely loss of Sandy Denny was a setback for music.

On *The Sons*, the Sons of Champlin reached new and glorious heights in jazz-rock-psychedelia fusion. Even those of us who did not like jazz liked this San

Francisco band, who were sort of akin to Chicago, but mellower. Their "You Can Fly" was such a feel-good tune that it almost convinced us.

Zappa's and the Mothers' seventh, *Burnt Weeny Sandwich*, was pretty much more of the same, but his first solo album, *Hot Rats*, featured one of his best known tunes, the jazz rock instrumental "Peaches en Regalia." Captain Beefheart contributed the sleazebag vocal to "Willie the Pimp," a dirty, dirty song with dynamite guitar work. The other four tunes, "Son of Mr. Green Genes," "Little Umbrellas," "The Gumbo Variations," and "It Must Be a Camel," were all instrumentals. Even though it was crazy jazz, *avant garde*, fusion, post-classical, or whatever you want to call it, *Hot Rats* had good, strong beats and was quite accessible.

King Crimson's first album, *In the Court of the Crimson King*, introduced pretentious, ponderous bombast to classically-influenced progressive rock. Robert Fripp, the band's leader, guitarist, and theorist, knew his stuff. He was a fine musician with groundbreaking ideas in art rock, *avant garde* music, instrumentation, and harmony. Under his tutelage, Crimson sounded good, but it also gave progressive rock's detractors a lot of ammunition. Eventually these detractors would invent punk rock, i.e., bare-bones, hard-driving simplicity as an antidote to overblown concert music masquerading as rock.

In a similarly grandiloquent but somewhat more humorous vein, Pink Floyd's third album, the four-sided *Ummagumma*, offered trippy tunes like "Grantchester Meadows" and "Several Species of Small Furry Animals Gathered Together in a Cave and Grooving With a Pict" on the studio half; and "Astronomy Domine," "Careful With That Axe, Eugene," and "Set the Controls for the Heart of the Sun" on the live half. Floyd was not popular yet, and would not be until their eighth LP, *Dark Side of the Moon*, appeared in 1973, but in the meantime they enjoyed a substantial cult following, a small but dedicated clique of spaced-out fans worldwide.

The Moody Blues' fifth album, *To Our Children's Children*, just continued their previously established mellow patterns, as if it were *Threshold, Part II*.

The second Led Zep album, *Led Zeppelin II*, was just as loud and innovative as their first, but a bit more commercial — and therefore not quite as wonderful. A condensed version of "Whole Lotta Love" (3:10 instead of 5:34) was even an AM hit, going to number four. "Heartbreaker" and "Living Loving Maid" rocked our asses off, but "What Is and What Should Never Be," "Thank You," "Ramble On," and "Bring It on Home" were softer and more lyrical. "The Lemon Song," though attributed to all four members of Led Zep, was in fact a shameless ripoff of Howlin' Wolf's "Killing Floor." "Moby Dick" seemed like the now obligatory drum showoff piece, post-"Toad."

Zep II's cover art by David Juniper included the famous 1917 photo of some of the pilots in Manfred von Richthofen's Flying Circus, but with faces either pasted over the real ones or altered: *back row, left to right:* original pilot with beard and bushy eyebrows added, Blind Willie Johnson, original pilot with beard added, original pilot with beard and sunglasses added, Mary Woronov, Neil Armstrong, John Bonham; *middle row, left to right:* Jimmy Page, Robert Plant; *seated:* John Paul Jones.

"THIS RECORD SHOULD BE PLAYED LOUD" — so proclaimed the

liner notes of the Stones' new LP, *Let It Bleed*. Good advice! The louder we played
it, the better it got. Its cover art expressed the anger and frustration that many of us
were beginning to feel with the political world: a beautiful cake, tire, pizza, clock
face, film reel, platter, and record turntable on the front, all smashed to hell on the
back. Its nine tunes ranged from from the saddest of blues to the hardest of hard
rock and pushed the boundaries of several different genres: "Gimme Shelter," "Live
With Me," and "Monkey Man," hard rock; "Love in Vain," old-time blues; "Country Honk," country rock; the title track and "You Got the Silver," modern blues;
"Midnight Rambler," blues rock; and "You Can't Always Get What You Want,"
classically influenced progressive rock accompanied by the London Bach Choir.
With Brian gone and Mick Taylor just coming aboard, *Let It Bleed* was mainly an
effort of Mick, Keith, Charlie, Bill, and excellent session musicians like Al Kooper,
Nicky Hopkins, Leon Russell, Ry Cooder, Bobby Keys, and Merry Clayton. Was
the title a pun on "Let It Be"? Of course not! That would have been anachronistic.
Maybe McCartney's "Let It Be" was a pun on "Let It Bleed" [wink wink].

The Stones toured America in November and December to promote *Let It
Bleed*. Uncensored for a change, they were allowed to perform "Gimme Shelter,"
"Love in Vain," and "Honky Tonk Women" on *Ed Sullivan*. Two days later, on
November 25, B.B. King opened for them at the Spectrum in Philadelphia. As if
anyone could have opened for the Stones! Yet the Stones somehow always seemed
to bring out the best in their opening acts — showcasing black acts, soul acts, and
blues acts for fans to get to know and appreciate.

On December 6 the Stones, the Airplane, CSNY, Santana, and the Flying
Burrito Brothers gave a free concert at the auto racing track in Altamont, California.
In order to avoid the cops, who naturally had acquired a bad rep in northern Cali-
fornia after last May's incidents in People's Park, someone suggested substituting
Hell's Angels. The Angels had caused no problems in 1967 at either the Be-In or
Monterey, and were well known around the Bay Area, so there was no cogent or
overpowering reason for the organizers to suspect that they would bring any trouble
if they were hired to provide security at Altamont. The organizers guessed wrong.
Angels stabbed, kicked, and beat an eighteen-year-old black man, Meredith Hunter,
to death right in front of the stage as the Stones played "Under My Thumb" (not
"Sympathy for the Devil" as legend claims). Subsequent investigation acquitted the
Angels and proved that Hunter was brandishing a gun and high on methampheta-
mines when the fight started. But that is not the point. Trained security guards would
have known how to handle the situation without resort to deadly force. There was
plenty of other violence too, some caused by Angels, some by drugs and alcohol,
some by opportunists. The 300,000 who attended, expecting another Woodstock,
did not have a good time.

Altamont illustrated the Hegelian dialectical truth that anarchy, e.g., the
anarchy of Woodstock, however well-intentioned and however successful in the
short run, quickly and inevitably descends into the Hobbesian war of all against
all. Anarchy is so fragile, so full of contradictions, that, from it, the Hegelian dialectic must nearly start all over again. It does not satisfy the depths of the human
spirit, measure up to human nature, protect the weak from the strong, provide se-

curity from want, or constitute an adequate basis for harmonious community. By levelling society, it ensures universal poverty, torpor, and dullness. Altamont laid bare the ugly truth that the spiritual solidarity and peace that — just because we had chosen for three days to be completely tolerant and forgiving — we had enjoyed at Woodstock would not be sustainable.

Some of us had already sold out.

Selling out was — and is — a big problem. When we grew up we wanted to be good citizens and ethical people making honest livings and neither knocking ourselves out nor sacrificing our principles to get rich. This was our collective praiseworthy ambition. We had nothing but contempt for middle American kids whose ambitions centered around money, who wanted to get rich in any way possible, whose success would be measured in big houses, beautiful silverware, fancy cars, and other trappings of gilded shallowness. For us success meant doing what we loved and getting paid for it enough to live on. For them success meant excess. They wanted to be masters of war when they grew up, but would be satisfied as rich mercenaries. We would not sell out for *anything*! In "Thank You Falettinme Be Mice Elf Agin," Sly Stone declared that even though dying young is horrible, it is better to die young than to sell out.

There was an incorruptible democracy in our general approach to life, culture, and the human world. The Family Stone proclaimed this in "Everybody is a Star." The Kinks would affirm it in 1975 on *Soap Opera* with "Everybody's a Star (Starmaker)."

God Save the Kinks! After the Kinks released "One of the Survivors" in 1973, we began calling "survivors" those few of us who still had not yet sold out. I saw a cartoon once, probably in the late seventies or early eighties, which showed a young woman introducing her long-haired fiancé to her scowling father. The uptight old fart said something like, "My daughter tells me you're a survivor. I'm not sure I approve of that."[64]

Ω

At the end of the fall 1969 semester, the Princeton Triangle Club (PTC) toured a dozen U.S. cities with *Call a Spade a Shovel*, a student-written revue that satirized what they saw as the precarious and rather unpleasant contemporary American political, military, and social situation. This show was brilliantly conceived, written, and performed, as one would naturally expect, because, unlike many college theater troupes, PTC not only considered itself to be of professional caliber, but also actually deserved this reputation. With sketches like "God at the Unemployment Office," "My Favorite Assassin," "The Great Black Hope," "Gay Gourmet," "The Wonderful World of War," "The Prime of Miss Jean Bircher," "The Generals," "Nazi and Cop," "Agnew Press Conference," and "Julie and David"; and production numbers

---

[64] My apologies for not citing this cartoon properly. I just do not remember where I saw it.

like "D-Day is Over," "Dying Duck Ballet," and "Don't Let the Rain [i.e., violence] in on Me"; *Call a Spade a Shovel* was deliberately obnoxious — and riotously funny! It did not aim to please, praise, salute, or even tolerate the bigots, jingoists, or rich Princeton alumni who then typified the "establishment." On the contrary, it confronted reality directly, forced its audiences to do likewise, and made uncomfortable those theatergoers who wished to escape or ignore the harsher facts of that reality, which they themselves either had helped to create or to which they acquiesced. Its purpose was to awaken, for the good of the country, those who wished to remain asleep. It succeeded at this task, albeit on too small a scale. Its power over its audiences in this regard earned it the right to be called "art."

Of course, conservative Princeton alumni were furious. In Grosse Pointe, Michigan, the home of many top executives of the automobile industry, the audience at the Fries Auditorium was particularly enraged. Many walked out. Well, fuck 'em if they couldn't take a joke! Why walk out of anything? Sit through it. Keep your mind open. Try to understand it. You will have plenty of time later to worry about whether you agreed with it or not.

If *Call a Spade a Shovel* was characterized by offended alumni and other older audience members hating it, it was characterized just as much by current students and other younger audience members, by and large, loving it. It was entertainment, but it was not *mere* entertainment. Whether one agreed with its antiwar, anti-establishment message or not, one had to agree that it was not just fluffy like most revues. It had real meaning. That was one more good reason to call it "art."

But political satire was a departure from PTC's general or traditional repertoire. After the Grosse Pointe incident, the Princeton administration came down on PTC like a ton of bricks. Citing "budgetary" and "logistical" concerns, the powers-that-be sharply curtailed the next year's tour and forced PTC to return to bland, harmless forms of comedy that would not jeopardize the annual giving campaign for the alumni fund.

Exactly ten years later, PTC toured with another revue, *Academia Nuts*. In sharp contrast to *Call a Spade a Shovel*, *Academia Nuts* was sanitized, bowdlerized, and almost entirely contentless. It contained few sketches but many production numbers, among which were "Let's Take An Exam," "I Want My Candy Now," and "The Subtle Charm of a Good Ale." It was specifically designed to be inoffensive. It was so fluffy that it would have been perfectly forgettable — if not for the fact that it had all the appearance of an implicit but pointed disavowal of the world view that PTC had expressed in *Call a Spade a Shovel*, an apology to the alumni for the impression that *Call a Spade a Shovel* had left upon them, and an act of contrition to woo their donations back into Princeton coffers. The whole purpose of *Academia Nuts* seemed to be to reassure the most conservative faction of the alumni that the current students at Princeton would no longer criticize the government in public, would not deviate from the standards of filial obedience and ivory tower innocence expected of them during their "best four years," and probably would not even interest themselves in any event that happened off campus. *Academia Nuts* seemed to promise the alumni that the students would no longer turn anything political or otherwise important into the subject of a PTC show. If this was the plan, it worked. For example, at the 1979 show, because he sat only two seats down the first row from me, I was able to observe closely the reaction of the then governor of Delaware, Pierre S. ("Pete") du Pont IV, a Republican and a member of the Princeton class of 1956. He was thoroughly charmed. *Academia Nuts* kept its promise of pure diversion and escape from reality. It was neither a picture of reality nor a critique of reality. It did not engage reality in any way. It was pure, meaningless fantasy, very well executed, a pleasant form, but with no real value. It did not point toward anything beyond itself. It was entertainment, and indeed it was *mere* entertainment. It only diverted the audience from reality, and thus failed to be any kind of "art."

This little vignette from 1979 shows how, even as early as the late seventies, America was returning, almost galloping back, to the repressive era of politically motivated censorship that had characterized the fifties. In the early twenty-first century, that return is complete. The sixties, after all, were not the herald of a new era of free speech and expression, but only a brief bright light in the darkness of conformity. In the sixties, i.e., from about 1965 to 1974, if a musician took a shit on LBJ or Nixon, it would actually *help* that musician's career. The bigger the shit, the bigger the career boost. But that *Zeitgeist* disappeared. By Reagan's era, it was gone, and it has stayed gone. In 2003, for example, Natalie Maines, a singer from the Texas-based crossover country music trio, the Dixie Chicks, took a minor shit on George "Dubya" Bush, a comparably terrible and arguably worse president than LBJ. She said to an audience in London (hardly pro-Bush territory), "Just so you know, we're ashamed the president of the United States is from Texas." That was hardly even a shit at all; it was barely more than a fart on him, but it nearly ruined their career. If a Texan such as Monkee Mike Nesmith had said in 1967 that he was ashamed to be from the same state as LBJ, his career would have soared even more than it did. But the Dixie Chicks were forced to apologize to save their asses. Nevertheless, it was too much for them to stomach. In 2006, Maines apologized for apologizing: "I apologized for disrespecting the office of the president, but I don't feel that way anymore. I don't feel he is owed any respect whatsoever." *Bravo! In the end, she put conscience ahead of career!*

The big, and most important, difference between the two PTC shows was that *Call a Spade a Shovel* was funny and *Academia Nuts* was not. By their very nature, political satire is funnier than Broadway-style musical comedy. Even when political satire is disguised as musical comedy, it is still funnier than straight musical comedy. By abandoning — or having been forced to abandon — political satire, PTC turned 180 degrees, stepping out of the rollicking and unrestrained comedy of the late sixties and back into the tightly controlled, carefully supervised, and ruthlessly censored comedy of the Depression, World War II, and early Cold War eras.

In the thirties, forties, and fifties, as we can still hear by listening to "old time radio" stars such as Edgar Bergen and Charlie McCarthy, George Burns and Gracie Allen, Jack Benny, and Fibber McGee and Molly, typical humor consisted of representing miscommunications, misunderstandings, or missteps. In other words, white middle-American conformity was the norm, and comedy could be wrought just by depicting any departure from this norm as somehow goofy. This would include tongue twisters, puns, tall tales, outright lies, and gratuitous insults, all with no substance. Indeed, comedy was then intended as escape from substance, not as means to confront it.

If the old comedy was escapist, then the new comedy was confrontational. If comedians of the thirties, forties, and fifties did not like FDR, Truman, or Eisenhower, then they typically would not even mention him on stage, or, if they did so, then they would do it only in perfunctory and inoffensive ways. But if comedians of the sixties, post-Lenny-Bruce and post-Mort-Sahl, did not like LBJ or Nixon, then then would confront him directly on stage, and would not pull any punches. David Frye's album, *I Am the President*, a sometimes gentle, sometimes savage, mockery of Nixon, was a case in point.

Before Sahl, Bruce, and George Carlin, comedy was laughter at deviations from the normal; after them, it was laughter at the normal. Before them, jokes centered on the style of one's dress, the cut of one's hair, the conventions or accents of one's speech, the ethnicity of one's family, and things of that nature. After them, any comedian who objectified, reified, or belittled any such thing in light or fluffy ways was a throwback to the fifties. Our parents wanted their comedians to be silly, harmless decorations; we wanted ours to be the most serious of serious sociopolitical commentators, the most subversive of subversive citizens, the most offensive of offensive sociopaths — but we wanted to laugh uproariously at them at the same time. Sahl and Bruce reinvented comedy just this way in the early sixties, making it not only funny, but also serious, and thus even funnier.

In this comedic frame of mind we read Abbie Hoffman's new book, *Woodstock Nation: A Talk-Rock Album*. Damn! It was funny! But serious too — between its lines. Marcuse's new little booklet, *An Essay on Liberation*, obviously written to inspire street revolutionaries, not, like most of his other books, to impress scholars, was also funny in places. We found them. We laughed. Good old Marcuse!

In contrast to Marcuse's little gem, Theodore Roszak's *The Making of a Counter Culture: Reflections on the Technocratic Society and its Youthful Opposition* was a turkey, an outsider's attempt to do what only an insider should ever want to do, and could ever have the means, feelings, and knowledge to be able to do. He had no authority, no credentials, no credibility, to write this book. Henri Bergson claimed in *An Introduction to Metaphysics* that analysis kills, i.e., that to analyze anything is to treat it as if it were stiff. That is what Roszak did. He studied a dead thing. His own murder victim. Perhaps he even studied it accurately. But he never got at the living phenomena. He never developed any Bergsonian "intuition" of his subject matter or "intellectual sympathy" with it. He never intuited the *durée* of the sixties. Abbie's books were much more to the point.

By 1969 *Mad* was losing its grip on the pulse of the contemporary life of its main constituency, the young. It no longer had the incisive satirical edge that had made it magnificent in the early and mid-sixties. Things in the streets seemed to be moving too fast for its writers to keep up. Its political satire became less and less frequent, less and less perceptive. One of its few worthwhile political bits was "The Mad Primer of Bigots, Extremists, and Other Loose Ends" in the September 1969 issue, but the general content of the magazine had mostly become just plain silly.

I let my subscription lapse.

Firesign Theatre's second album, *How Can You Be in Two Places at Once When You're Not Anywhere at All?*, consisted of only two tracks, the title track on side one, and "The Further Adventures of Nick Danger" on side two. Using their trademark rapid-fire clutter of puns, *non sequiturs*, logical illogic, musical absurdities, and outlandishly relevant sound effects, they evoked the comedic spirits of W.C. Fields, Groucho Marx, and even James Joyce in satirizing commercialism, racism, the Weather Underground (via its slogan, "We're Bringing the War Back Home"), the middle class, jingoism, drug use, the Beatles, and anything else that popped into their crazy minds, all from a leftist perspective. Side one was loosely woven around sleazy Ralph Spoilsport, a car salesman, while side two sent up the hard-boiled private detective genre of movies and radio dramas that was popular in the thirties and forties.

Almost three years before *National Lampoon*, No. 22 (January 1972) hit new heights of cool blasphemy with "Son o' God Comics," Rip Off Press in San Francisco published *The New Adventures of Jesus*, a sacrilegious underground comic by Foolbert Sturgeon, *nom de guerre* of Frank Huntington Stack, professor of art at the University of Missouri, Columbia. Some historians believe that *The Adventures of Jesus*, Sturgeon's fourteen-page privately circulated photocopied booklet, originated the underground comics movement in 1962.[65] In any case, *New Adventures* was a big underground winner, not only among anti-religious types, but even with some prominent liberal Christians. Bishop Robert L. Dewitt of the Episcopal Diocese of Pennsylvania kept a copy on his desk.[66]

On the cover of *New Adventures*, Jesus and his French poodle contemplated Halo shampoo in a discount drug store window. In the first of seven "Stories From the Good Book," Jesus turned three-days-dead Lazarus into a loaf of bread then added yeast to make him rise. In "Jesus Gets a Ride," he materialized — Zing! — in the back seat of a Roman Catholic priest's car and scolded him: "You guys give me a pain in the ass! Why can't you decide whether you want to **be superstitious or** reasonable?" As the scolding continued, the exasperated priest finally yelled out, "No wonder they crucified you!!! You're just a troublemaker!" In the last panel Jesus gave him the finger. In the second "Stories From the Good Book," Jesus in Gethsemane endured a lecture from Yahweh like an embarrassed adolescent, then got busted by the Romans for practicing medicine without a license. In "Somebody We All Know Rides Again," Jesus assumed the role of the Lone Ranger. In the third "Stories From the Good Book," Jesus told a modern-day crowd how he once turned himself into a camel so that he could survive in the wilderness while waiting for the devil to tempt him. In "A Momentous Event is About to Take Place ... and Here It Is ... the Long-Awaited Rockem-Sockem Second Coming of Jesus Christ! Pause

---

[65] A strong case can be made for Don Dohler's *Wild*, with its central character Projunior, in 1961.

[66] I never actually saw it there, but, as a member of his church, I heard him mention it in a sermon sometime during my senior year in high school, 1969-1970. Shortly thereafter I went down to Sansom Street in Philadelphia and bought a copy.

for a Moment of Silent Amazement," an extra-meek and bewildered Jesus fell in with flower children and later was severely beaten by two cops just for having a beard. He lost his temper, turned the cops into pigs, and sicced his French poodle on them. In the fourth "Stories From the Good Book," after informing a rich man that it would be easier for a camel to go through the eye of a needle than for him to get into heaven, Jesus obliged him by turning him into a camel and telling him to look for a needle. In "Jesus and his Gang on a Hot Day," the apostles all went swimming but Jesus just bounced on the surface of the stream. In the fifth "Stories From the Good Book," after saving the whore from the stoning mob, Jesus lamented, "The problem isn't sin, it's stupidity."

In "Jesus Goes to the Movies," he and John the Baptist were each depicted in *The Greatest Story Ever Shown* as musclebound Steve Reeves / Hercules heroes embroiled in a jealous rivalry over John's fiancée, Mary Magdalene. They agreed to a truce, committed themselves to nonviolent political action, and set up a Jules-Jim-Catherine sort of threesome. After Herod killed John and raped Mary Magdalene, Jesus renounced nonviolence and declared war on the establishment. Shouting the standard military slogan, "God is on my side!", Jesus, the brand-new action superhero, swinging his cross like Babe Ruth at the plate, singlehandedly defeated the entire Herodian guard and Roman army. He overthrew the state, freed the slaves, and established peace. The last scene showed Jesus and Mary Magdalene posing in triumph with his cross on top of the world. The real Jesus, in the theater audience, agreed with the rest of the moviegoers that the film was better than the book.

In the sixth "Stories From the Good Book," Jesus mocked John the Baptist as a fanatic nuisance. In the seventh, Jesus, the little kid with the temple elders, sassed them mercilessly and got in trouble with Mary and Joseph for yelling in public, "My mom's a virgin!" In "Some Other Comings," the returning Jesus got run over in traffic, rose three days later, got caught in a crossfire between cops and gangsters, rose again three days later, got blown up by a hydrogen bomb, then rose yet again three days later to discover that the planet was gone. The back cover showed an eager Virgin Mary leading a reluctant Jesus by the nose to a wedding. She loved it there, but he was bored. He turned his water into wine so that he could get drunk. Other bored attendees noticed this and asked him to turn their water into wine too. As he got them all shitfaced, they sang "What a Friend We Have in Jesus" while Mary proudly exclaimed, "My boy's popular wherever he goes!"

This is the way to approach religion — and all self-important traditions and institutions. Laugh at them! Prick holes in the stuffed shirts! Show your contempt!

The cumulative effect of *New Adventures* was just one more bit of evidence that laughing at even the most serious subjects satisfies the human spirit more deeply than taking these subjects seriously. Taking serious subjects seriously enslaves us to them; laughing at them frees us.

Ω

Spring 1970

We ain't gonna party no more!

Mr. Natural: You're **lost**, my boy! It's a simple matter of getting your self under control!

Flakey Foont: What should I do, Mr. Natural? Sob.

Mr. Natural: When you arise in the morning, you should do last night's dirty dishes ... then you should sing a simple melody (of your own choice) ... then you should call somebody up (not me) ... then go to the store ... buy some asperagus! [sic]

Flakey Foont: Yes? Yes?

Mr. Natural: Then meet a new person, go home, take LSD, say a prayer, breathe ten times, stand on your head, set your watch, take a shit, pick your nose, squeeze a tit ...

Flakey Foont: Gee ... all that's kind of hard to remember ...

Mr. Natural: **TAKE IT OR *LEAVE* IT!**

Flakey Foont: Yeh ... right ... Why do I keep thinking you can tell me anything?

> — Robert Crumb, "Mr. Natural in Death
> Valley," *Zap Comix*, No. 0, pp. [10-11]

> Keep on truckin' ...
> Truckin' on down the line ...
> Hey hey hey ...
> I said keep on truckin' ...
> Truckin' my blues away!
> — Robert Crumb
> *Zap Comix*, No. 1, p. [20]

Zap was part of the whole scene now, but awareness of R. Crumb had travelled slowly. His first trickle toward fame was when *Zap Comix* (No. 0) appeared in San Francisco in early 1968, but for most of us, our earliest introduction to him was the

July 1968 cover of Big Brother's *Cheap Thrills* LP, not his underground comic art. *Zap* (No. 0 through No. 5) crept across the country from Haight-Ashbury in San Francisco to St. Mark's Place in New York City, Sansom Street in Philadelphia, and other big urban "head shop" locales or "hippie hangouts." Crumb added *Big Ass* and *Motor City* comics to his portfolio in mid-1969, the *San Francisco Comic Book*, *Despair*, *Mr. Natural*, and *Uneeda Comix* in 1970, and *Home Grown Funnies* in 1971. His characters, the archetypal phony guru Mr. Natural (an ex-cab driver from Afghanistan), his disciple Flakey Foont, Uncle Uh Uh, the sewer Snoids, Smelly Old Cat, Whiteman, the vulture demonesses, the over-endowed primeval negroid sexpot Angelfood McSpade, Shuman the Human, Bill Ding, Cheesis K. Reist, Dale Steinberger the Jewish cowgirl, Meatball, Dirty Dog, Joe Blow, Mr. Goodbar, Itzy and Bitzy, Horny Harriet, Fuzzy the Bunny, Lenore Goldberg the girl commando, Eggs Ackley, Mr. Meat, Mrs. Quiver, Fritz the Cat, Artsy Fartsy, Bo Bo Bolinski, Dora Zockman, Honeybunch Kaminski the drug-crazed runaway, Pud, Lark Clark, Maryjane, Merciful Percival, Sy Klopps, Ruff Tuff Creampuff, Boingy Baxter, Big Baby, Savannah Foomo, *et al.*, offered an intimate "stream of consciousness" view of the seedy, depraved side of everyday life. He tackled racism, capitalism, macho posing, militarism, drugs, bigotry, random violence, urban squalor, paranoia, neurotic sexual hang-ups, and the connections among them all, thus revealing the essential morbidity of LBJ's Great Society and the vulgar, piss-skank, unwiped — but well covered — ass of Nixon's America.

Crumb was William Hogarth, George Cruikshank, James Gillray, Thomas Rowlandson, Honoré Daumier, both Pieter Brueghels, Hieronymus Bosch, Rube Goldberg, Francisco Goya, John Tenniel, Al Capp, Alberto Vargas, and Salvador Dali all wrapped up into one with your favorite pornographer. Soaked in his own sexual perversity, his realistic but grotesque nudes with outrageous genitalia depicted blatant, unrestrained sexuality of all stripes, even incest, pederasty, bestiality, and sexual mutilation. Not far below the surface was the damaging rage, frustration, and emotional immaturity that he held over from his abused childhood in a wretched Philadelphia family that drove both of his brothers to madness and one to suicide. He accurately and unflatteringly drew himself as Mr. Sketchum, a skinny, leering, sex-obsessed, masturbating nerd with bad teeth and big, round, hyperopic glasses. His bitterness blurred and mocked the boundary between satire and pornography. His drawings of losers straddled the line between commiseration and misanthropy. The change of artistic style that derived from his LSD experiences in San Francisco illuminated the fundamental differences between freak society and straight society. Besides social criticism, revolutionary politics, and sexual obsession, he diddled with "kozmic trooth" — and probably could have become a very rich man ... but ...

Crumb never sold out!

The underground comics industry in San Francisco in the late sixties and early seventies was run as a collective. Many other graphic artists rode on Crumb's coattails. S. Clay Wilson scored with two sicko classics in *Zap* No. 2, "The Hog Ridin' Fools," in which the Checkered Demon ("Nice day for somethin'.") fomented rape and violence between lesbian and greaser motorcycle gangs and ended up getting tumbled three miles down the road, and "Head First," in which one pirate chopped off and ate another's glans penis. In *Zap* No. 3 Wilson offered "Come Fix," in which lesbians shot up semen like heroin, and "Captain Pissgums and His Pervert Pirates," about a horrific, sexually deviant sea battle between the captain's gay, male, sadomasochistic pirates and Captain Fatima's dyke pirates. Wilson's work got sicker and sicker. His "A Ball in the Bung Hole" and "Star-Eyed Stella" in *Zap* No. 4, and "Lester Gass, the Midnight Misogynist," "Ruby the Dyke Meets Weedman," and "Snake Snatch Tale" in *Zap* No. 5 were hallmarks of sexual evil.

Wilson presented hardly anything else except cruel sex and unjustified violence, but other underground comic artists, including Crumb, were mainly political, social, and cultural commentators, of course from a leftist, often nearly anarchist, perspective. Gilbert Shelton's jingoistic superhero, Wonder Wart-Hog ("Believe it or leave it!"), appeared in *Zap* Nos. 3, 4, and 5 and his Fabulous Furry Freak Brothers showed up in No. 5. Shelton was the *primus inter pares* among the underground political cartoonists.

Shelton, Crumb, and a few other cartoonists put together *Hydrogen Bomb and Biochemical Warfare Funnies: Apocalyptic Apocrypha for Apoplectic Apostates*, which they stamped as "Rated X by the Puritan Fascists." The cover showed Shelton's caricature of "America's Three Most Popular Men." Spiro Agnew looked like a microcephalic bullet. Drawing Nixon with his nose like a dick and his jowls like balls was common in the underground press, but this caricature instead made his nose look like ass cheeks. Billy Graham appeared as a hollow-eyed, screaming, raving, cross-waving lunatic. All three were dressed in identical blue pinstriped suits. In one of Shelton's contributions, "Wonder Wart-Hog and the Invasion of the Pigs from Uranus," the Uranian Empire attacked Earth because the Uranians felt that theirs was "the greatest planet of all" and that their duty was to save Earth from itself. Being greedy, slovenly, conspicuous consumers, i.e., real pigs, they were alarmed when their spies told them that Earth was full of conservationists. The implied analogy of porcine Uranus to human Earth as capitalist America to communist Vietnam was obvious. The pig invaders killed as many humans as they could, but spared Agnew because they thought he was handsome. They dressed him up in a fancy-schmancy military uniform, complete with oversized polkadot bow tie, and made him dictator of Earth because they wanted "to run a tight ship." Wonder Wart-Hog tried to save Earth, but the Uranians destroyed it with H-bombs. As the lone survivor of Earth, he sought refuge on Uranus, but the pig bureaucrats there told him, "you might be a 'wonder' wherever you **came** from, but **here** you're just another **foreigner**! You can apply for immigration at the Ministry of **Labor**." He ended up with a job shovelling shit. Again, the implied analogy of Wonder Wart-Hog to Uranus as Vietnamese refugees to America was obvious.

Also in *Hydrogen Bomb and Biochemical Warfare Funnies*, Foolbert Sturgeon (i.e., Frank Stack) presented "Jesus, Saviour of the World" and Gregory Rodman Irons offered "Raw War Comics." In the former, even Jesus's direct intervention could not prevent world leaders from unleashing nuclear war. In the latter, Irons tried to tell a simple war story, but kept having to restart because his drawn characters kept getting killed in the war. Finally he just admitted defeat. In the last panel he shrugged, "Ahh ... fuck it!!" and blew up the world with an H-bomb.

The violence and misogyny that typified many of the underground comics disturbed many readers, yet the overriding purpose of these publications was clearly political. By exposing the horror and futility of inner city existence, and by occasionally injecting leftist propaganda, the cartoonists seemed to intend to spark socioeconomic change. Or perhaps not. Perhaps they were already resigned to misery as it was. Perhaps their whole enterprise was just a dare to the censors. After all, if the censors would not censor Wilson, then they could not censor anyone.

Crumb described his basic project in "Definitely a Case of Derangement" on the inside front cover of *Zap* No. 1:

> I've been called an evil genius by cities of assholes ... but I know who those people are! And they're on my list! I may be nuts but a speedfreak I ain't! The truth is, I'm one of the last great medieval thinkers! You might say I'm a mad scientist, for my plans have all been worked out quite methodically ... logically ... but the ends justify the means ... heh heh. This comic book is part of that plan ... but you've read too much already ... I have you right where I want you ... So, kitchee-koo, you bastards!

All of which jived with Mr. Natural's basic hedonistic and nihilistic message that the whole universe is insane, absurd, and chaotic. We did not believe this all the time, yet often it seemed to be true.

Ω

When Vintage Books released Associate Justice William O. Douglas's *Points of Rebellion* in paperback in February 1970, we recognized this book immediately as a manifesto by one of our most productive infiltrators of the opposition's ranks. A Supreme Court judge on our side! How amazing! He said that our protests were protected by the Constitution, that the content of our message was reasonable, that society needed to be fundamentally restructured to accommodate our demands and to prevent violence, and that both politics and the non-partisan bureaucracy that actually ran the country were so frustrating that "an overwhelming sense of futility possesses the young generation" (p. 54). He was perfectly correct. Yet we did not want to feel futile. Already we were nostalgic for the tremendous hope, joy, and power that we had felt in 1967. The Chicago convention and the Days of Rage had sobered us. Just having Douglas on our side was not enough. We were losing our optimism, becoming cynical — even before the murders at Kent State.

In 1970 Nixon had about 200,000 fewer troops in Vietnam than LBJ had had in 1968, but still he showed no sign of wanting to end the war. The troops he was bringing home were ground troops, but he was escalating the air war, which required fewer personnel. Republicans are not elephants. They are wolves, loving their own small circle very much, providing for these loved ones very well — and killing everyone else.

A commonly heard prowar slogan of the time was "Support Our Boys in Vietnam." To satirize this, a psychedelic Day-Glo black-light cartoon poster showed a pink, blue, and green battle-ready tank manned by four scowling, heavily armed U.S. troops, coming right at you. Its caption was, "Support Our Boys in Vietnam, Korea, Germany, Japan, England, Italy, Canada, Sweden, Denmark, Berkeley, Watts, Boston, Cuba, Argentina, Pakistan, Laos, Congo, Thailand, Acapulco, India, Lebanon, Chicago, Dominican Republic, Ecuador, Hong Kong, Woodstock, D.C., Columbia, Greenland, Puerto Rico, Tijuana, Kowloon, Chapel Hill, Russia, Haiti, Indonesia, Bermuda, Australia, Conshohocken, Cicero, Princeton, Liberia, Biafra, Norway, Okinawa, M.I.T., Philippines, Scotland, Greece, Iceland, Guam, Afghanistan, Brazil, Turkey, Spain, Harlem, Burma, Cambodia, Peru, Nova Scotia, Azores, Panama, Crete, Costa Rica, Austria, East Village, Bolivia, Iran, Honolulu, Tahiti, Sicily, Ireland, Corsica, Dubuque, Israel, Spain [sic], Netherlands, Uruguay, Venezuela, Shanghai, Glendale, Aruba, Fire Island, Chile, Canary Islands, Guatemala, Antigua, Iwo Jima, Nigeria ..."

Antiwar poster slogans proliferated. Among the most trenchant was, "Join the Army, see the world, meet fascinating people, and kill them."

Our growing despair about this never-ending war was vented in bitter song lyrics, mostly deep tracks that got airplay, if at all, only on underground FM and college radio. Probably the best example was the Turtles' "We Ain't Gonna Party No More." Buried as the B-side of a stupid pop single, it was nearly five minutes of markedly poignant antiwar protest. A few of us freaks discovered it, but it never received the airplay or the adulation it deserved. Better known lyrics of early 1970 that were openly contemptuous of American military policy, sociopolitical order, or cruel morality included Simon and Garfunkel's "The Boxer," Creedence Clearwater Revival's "Who'll Stop the Rain?", the Guess Who's "American Woman," and about half the songs on the Doors' *Morrison Hotel*, notably "Peace Frog" and "Ship of Fools." Also in this category is Jethro Tull's "Teacher," if we accept its double metaphor that the narrator of the song, the student, the protagonist, represents young men who follow the rules, do their duty, but get cheated out of what they deserve; while the teacher represents old men who make the rules, take the credit, and glorify themselves.

The lyrics of "We Ain't Gonna Party No More" were blunt and tactless assertions of governmental lying about its determination and capability to end war, of pacifist resolve, of resistance to the draft, of the hypocrisy of hiding behind flags and pretending on that account to be moral, and of refusal to either kill or be complicit in killing. The song forced serious listeners to confront whether young people were going to be mindless hedonists while the world crumbled around them or face the reality of contemporary moral evil and try their best to fix it. Don Henley would reprise this theme in 1984 with "All She Wants to Do Is Dance," whose author, ex-Fug Danny ("Kootch") Kortchmar, wrote or co-wrote several songs in that vein, including "Johnny Can't Read."

Lennon took up the Hindu idea of karma as retributive justice in "Instant Karma," which threatened warmongers and other evildoers with divine wrath.

Richard Brautigan published his best poetry collection, *Rommel Drives on Deep into Egypt*, which expressed, in his characteristically absurd terms, the futility of war and his skepticism that there might really be anything at all that we could ever do about it.

This pessimistic spirit in music and literature had, of course, arisen out of 1968, the year that had shattered our naive San Franciscan optimism. The Summer of Love was followed, not by another, but by a summer of riots. 1969 compounded the violent failures of 1968. Woodstock was a brief bright moment, but Altamont had superseded Woodstock. With Tricky Dick at the helm, 1970 promised to be no better.

1968 had been a watershed year for the symbiosis of rock music and leftist politics. Jean-Luc Godard had apparently perceived this fact — and made a movie about it: *One Plus One* — which we in America did not get to see until a year and a half after its release in England — and then only with a new title — *Sympathy for the Devil* — and edits and additions that reportedly infuriated Godard. In either version, it is a terrible film — a lost opportunity that a more coherent director such as Lindsay Anderson, D.A. Pennebaker, or Mike Nichols — or a consummately intelligent documentary producer such as David L.Wolper — would not have flubbed. Its concept was to intersperse a straight unnarrated documentary of the Rolling Stones writing, rehearsing, and recording a song — which turned out to be "Sympathy for the Devil" — with a fanciful allegory of contemporary black, anarchist, and communist revolutions. But the allegory was too obscure to be poignant — and the acting was terrible. "Collision of Ideas" — the anonymous review in the May 18, 1970 issue of *Time* — implicated the stultifying formality of the non-Stones portions of the film. If Godard had restricted himself just to spying on the Stones in the studio, *One Plus One* would have been among the most important rock films ever — a rare historical witness to the evolution of creative process in a seminal band. — Notice how far out of the loop poor Brian already was! — If you are annoyed by the excess of em dashes in this paragraph, consider that Godard's abrupt disjunctions in *One Plus One* were even worse.

Despite Godard's self-indulgent ruining of his own documentary on the Stones in the act of creation, 1970 was a splendid year for the cinematic depiction of the marriage of music and politics. Filmed later but released earlier than *Sympathy for the Devil* was Antonioni's *Zabriskie Point*, which included a soundtrack by Pink Floyd and sound clips from the Grateful Dead, the Stones, the Youngbloods, Patti Page, and several others. Contemporary critics hated this film, but retrospective critics seem to appreciate it slightly better. Theatergoers either loved it or hated it. It was too blatant for anyone who saw it to remain neutral. Opinion about it did not divide along political lines. Some American leftists hated it because they saw Antonioni's underinformed European stereotypes of Americans as affected. Other American leftists loved it precisely because his stereotypes were so underinformed and affected that they were funny. Some American rightists hated it because it was vulgar, disrespectful, and unintelligible. Other American rightists loved it because it made the left look silly. Thus, perhaps opinion about this film actually divided along lines of whether or not one had a sense of humor.

Whether one liked it or not, appreciated its comedy or not, agreed with its amorphous politics or not, one had to admit that *Zabriskie Point* was essentially bullshit. Its two central characters, Mark, fed up with college campus revolutionary bullshit, and Daria, fed up with corporate commercial capitalistic bullshit, met by chance when both bolted to the California desert to escape. Mark's case was a bit more serious. A Los Angeles cop had murdered a surrendering black demonstrator. As an impulsive act of vengeance, Mark had intended to shoot the cop in the back, but someone else shot first. Nevertheless, Mark was tagged as the cop-killer.

Antonioni portrayed the cops as unbelievably primitive. As a demonstrator was being booked, this conversation ensued: "Occupation?" "Associate professor of history." "That's too long, uh, I'll just put down 'clerk'." Not-yet-revolutionary Mark was arrested for the crime of trying to bail out his friend. When asked for his name, he snottily replied, "Karl Marx," at which, without so much as raising an eyebrow, the ignorant booking cop dutifully typed, "Carl Marx."

Mark's escape was a tad more flamboyant than Daria's. She just tooled out in her own car. He stole a plane, a pink and white Cessna 210 four-seater named "Lilly 7." He showed himself to be a darn good pilot when, seeing her car as the only one for miles on a lonely desert highway, he buzzed her just for fun, sometimes just a few feet above the ground. Naturally this pissed her off, but she had nowhere to hide. Gradually she realized that he was only playing a harmless game. A while later, seeing that he had landed by the side of the road, she voluntarily pulled over just to make his acquaintance, even though by now she had heard on the radio news that the plane had been stolen. The plane had run out of fuel, so together they continued in her car on their aimless journey. At Zabriskie Point they parked, romped, bantered, and fucked.

They refueled the plane and painted it in psychedelic colors with slogans such as "No War," "Suck Bucks," "No Words," "Thankx," and "She He It" all over it. He decided to return it to its airfield and take his chances on the lam in the streets of Los Angeles. She tried to talk him into abandoning the plane and riding with her to Phoenix, but he would not hear of it, declaring instead that he preferred to take risks. When she heard on her car radio that the cops had summarily executed him in cold blood as he landed the plane, she, until that moment the paragon of nonviolent life, was overwhelmed, not only by sorrow and disgust, but also by visions of retaliatory violence. The last seven minutes of the film were a montage of her unbridled fantasies of destroying everything that represented the society that had killed him, particularly the moneyed developers who had employed her.

Zabriskie Point juxtaposed the barren beauty of the desert with the urban proliferation of gaudy advertising, shiny corporate headquarters, decrepit factories, derelict warehouses, and neglected storefronts. Somehow, through this, the innocent, forsaken desert seemed more alive than the teeming but depraved city.

Ω

Déja Vu from Crosby, Stills, Nash, and Young began with Stills's "Carry On," which carried on where Crosby's "Long Time Gone" had left off, inspiring hope and promise for the future, but in a more personal than political direction, with the main focus on love rather than on protest. Stills's "4 + 20" told the despondent tale of a young man so tortured by guilt, loneliness, and spiritual bankruptcy that he was considering suicide — but there the song ended. We did not learn what happened to him. Stills's and Young's "Everybody I Love You" was a song of forgiveness. We hoped that the protagonist of "4 + 20" heard it and felt released.

Young's "Country Girl" was a whiny, morose, almost morbid attempt to win a woman's love. She would do best to run the other way. Why would she want to take up with such a pessimist? Nor did Neil's "Helpless" do anything to dispel his reputation among his detractors — and even among some of his fans — as a wimp. Its title alone was enough to make us cringe. We did not relish feeling helpless. We were vigorous, motivated, empowered, invincible — and we wanted to rejoice in all that, not moan about any lack of strength, hope, power, or life.

Nash's "Teach Your Children" not only saw life as a series of journeys, but also took each of the two major stages of life, youth and adulthood, as balancing aspects of any worthy life, so that, in their respective journeys, children would teach adults as much valuable stuff as adults would teach children — if and only if the adults allowed it. The lyrics pleaded for openness among adults and for compassion among children. This ideal of intergenerational reciprocity could be realized if adults would give up their ages-old idea that children were mere clay to be molded in the adults' image, and if children would give up their natural smugness and actually listen for any sign of wisdom, from anywhere, anyone, any source. On a similar, almost corollary theme, his "Our House" was a hymn to domesticity, comfort, security, and lifelong marital accord, implying the evenly shared nature of happy marriage, rather than the traditional husband-centered arrangement. Yet perhaps the tranquil bliss of this couple was because they had cats, not kids.

CSNY's cover of Joni Mitchell's "Woodstock" proved to be the definitive among many, many versions. After all, it should. They were there. She was not.

Crosby's "Déjà Vu" was another of his many songs about time. Not quite as hopeful as "Long Time Gone," it toyed with vague notions of learning through reincarnation, recalling past lives, and *amor fati*. His "Almost Cut My Hair" was probably his most important political song. It celebrated individualism, pure freedom, the courage not to succumb to conformity, the will to improve oneself and to make all things better, and the absolute resolve to resist injustice, even in the face of terrifying realities. Crosby set himself up as a lone freak against the mustered forces of straight society. That was easy enough. The straights looked straight and the freaks looked like freaks. You could tell the politics of most Americans under thirty just by looking at them. Crosby got it exactly right in "Almost Cut My Hair" when he sang about flying his freak flag. But he was dead wrong about owing it to anyone. Conformity was only on one side. The straights dressed like other straights, tried to look as much as possible like other straights, did not want to stand out, did not want to have different views, and did not want to rock the boat. Conformity in dress and appearance entailed acceptance of the established sociopolitical order in general and support of the Vietnam War in particular. Young people who dressed like their parents thought like their parents. But we freaks did not set out to dress like other freaks. We each dressed just however we damn well pleased — and if we ended up looking like other freaks, well, that was only coincidence. The point was to be and to look like free, real individuals.

Hair was political. The following year, in one of most slyly political LPs of the era, the New Riders of the Purple Sage would proclaim in "Last Lonely Eagle" that forgetting one's dreams was equivalent to cutting off one's hair. In order to get a job in the straight, conservative world, one had to sell out. Some of us succumbed to wanting to get rich through straight, conservative jobs. One week we were marching against the war, the next week we were working for the gigantic corporations that built the weapons.

We recalled that when the founding fathers were selecting the national bird, Ben Franklin suggested the wild turkey, which is industrious, self-sufficient, and native to the soil. However, they selected the bald eagle, which is predatory, dangerous, violent, carrion-feeding, and destructive. We came to see the terrible logic of choosing the eagle as the symbol of this country.

Joni Mitchell continued her inexorable stride toward superstardom with her third album, *Ladies of the Canyon*. It consisted of twelve original songs, at least eight of which would soon become classics of folk rock, soft rock, or jazz rock: "Morning Morgantown," "For Free," "Conversation," "Rainy Night House," "Big Yellow Taxi," "Woodstock," "The Circle Game," and the title track, which referred to Laurel Canyon in Los Angeles, a hippie hangout.

With his second album, his breakthrough, *Sweet Baby James*, James Taylor established a new fusion of folk and blues that would become the benchmark for soft rock musicians in the seventies. Specifically, his "Fire and Rain" crowned him the king of wimp anthems and ushered in the early, pre-disco seventies as the brief era of the vulnerable, moody acoustic singer-songwriter.

Morrison Hotel,[67] the new Doors album, went far toward redeeming them from *Soft Parade*. Morrison wrote or co-wrote with Robbie Krieger all the songs — including some of his best work. "Roadhouse Blues" was a celebration of the degenerate life, drinking beer for breakfast, fucking whenever we wanted — all the things that would soon kill Jimi, Janis, and Morrison himself. "Waiting for the Sun" was a fuzzy anticipation of imminent freedom. "You Make Me Real" was a hard-rockin' love song — not much more to it than that — i.e., less than we had come to expect from the Doors at this point. Much more interesting was "Peace Frog," which told a downhearted, alarming, but cryptic tale of bloody urban street fights, then segued flawlessly into "Blue Sunday," another love song, an eerie, cloying one. "Ship of Fools," a pale reflection of Crosby/Stills/Kantner's "Wooden Ships," used a curious pessimism to attack our contemporary obsession with NASA's moon missions, to decry air pollution, to satirize human dejection, and to imagine a savior who would herd us alienated earthlings onto a spaceship, lace us all with

---

[67] Side one of *Morrison Hotel*, called "Hard Rock Cafe," was apparently the inspiration for the successful chain of bars and restaurants that began in London on June 14, 1971.

LSD, and take us away. Following this mock seriousness, "Land Ho!" blithely related an old salt's tale of joyful life at sea. "The Spy," a song of skulking love, was even eerier than "Blue Sunday." "Queen of the Highway" described the bizarre marriage of two American nomads, maybe bikers. Two more love songs ended the LP, "Indian Summer," simplicity itself, and "Maggie M'Gill," about a groupie who got knocked up by a rock star in the back of his car — suggesting that casual sex was all routine.

Even in our bleak milieu of despair about the never-ending war some notes of hope were sounded. Melanie, supported by the Edwin Hawkins Singers, burst into the singles scene with her uplifting "Lay Down (Candles in the Rain)." Ray Stevens's latest single, "Everything is Beautiful," expressed the naive but seductive hope that people would eventually see things as they really are. Five white guys from Detroit — not Motown's first white act, but its first *successful* white act — recorded a hit single, a cover of the 1966 Temptations song, "Get Ready," on the Motown label named for themselves: Rare Earth. In its album version "Get Ready" delivered twenty-one and a half minutes of live, steaming soul, urging preparedness and determination against any contingency, and even the two-minute-forty-eight-second single version was pretty inspiring. Creedence's new single, "Up Around the Bend," promised that people would listen to us. That was important. If only it were true.

The Temptations, maybe unwittingly, embarrassed themselves and us with "Psychedelic Shack," which set up phony hippiedom as if it were the real thing. Zappa had already shown that he perceived clearly and understood accurately in his unceasing disparagement of such phoniness, but the Temps seemed to see white youth culture only dimly and superficially. Just as Jimmy Gilmer's "Sugar Shack" had caricatured, misrepresented, and insulted beatniks and folkies, "Psychedelic Shack" now did the same and worse to true freaks.

The two centerpieces of Van Morrison's *Moondance* LP were the title track and "Into the Mystic." The former was upbeat and fun, but the latter — a perennial favorite among soft rockers — was just a pretty tune with a catchy rhythm, a seductive, acoustic song whose melancholy yet oddly hopeful lyrics could be heard as a schmaltzy or pseudo-ethereal metaphorization of a Celtic sea voyage. Less pretentious nostalgia appeared in Marmalade's haunting, grief-stricken, progressive rocker, "Reflections of My Life."

Even though it included "The Boxer," *Bridge Over Troubled Water* added a hefty dose of silliness to Simon's and Garfunkel's usually serious psychological repertoire. Three of Simon's songs on this album, "Cecilia," "Baby Driver," and "Why Don't You Write Me," were just "silly love songs" such as we had come to expect from shallower lyricists like Paul McCartney. Even worse, S&G covered the Everly Brothers' "Bye Bye Love." Simon neatly summed up his newfound pandering in "Song for the Asking." Nevertheless, the album was redeemed by each of its other six songs. We had become used to Simon's lyrics making us think. We liked it. We expected it. Those six tracks, at least, did not disappoint us in this regard: The title cut, simultaneously a single with "Keep the Customer Satisfied" on its flipside, extolled unconditional loyalty to a beloved person, presumably one worthy of such love and loyalty. "Keep the Customer Satisfied" expressed the frustration that we freaks all felt from not being accepted by straight society — not that we were likely to compromise our principles or change in any way in order to gain such acceptance. "El Condor Pasa" was an ode to possibility, to the glories to nature, and to optimism, as "So Long, Frank Lloyd Wright" was to modern architecture. "The Only Living Boy in New York" suggested that life should be relaxed, unhurried, unfettered, that we should beware of getting caught up in urban stress, and that we should not try to do things in a "New York minute."

The poster that was included with the LP showed an ınto-the-sun dawnlit color photo of the 59th Street Bridge, which seemed to be growing out of a black-and-white photo of Simon and Garfunkel — or maybe the black-and-white photo of S&G was growing out of the color photo of the bridge. A sprig of flowers from nowhere floated over Garfunkel's left shoulder. Almost naturally the superimposition of men-on-bridge, bridge-on-men recalled one of Nietzsche's lines: "What is great about humans is that they are a bridge and not a goal."[68]

Ω

World War II was a just war, i.e., the Allies' cause was just. This does not mean that it was a good war. There are no good wars. The Allies committed atrocities to win it, just as the Nazis and the Japanese committed atrocities to provoke it. The so-called "heroes" of war should be regarded as only what they were: necessary evils, professional killers who rose to the occasion at the right time, not larger-than-life, not heroes *simpliciter*. To present any war hero as an example of what a human could or should be is to do a disservice to humanity. Allied World War II veterans deserve to be thanked for saving us from the Nazis and the Japanese — sincerely and wholeheartedly thanked — and they each deserve state-of-the-art lifelong free health care at the finest possible facilities, but they do not deserve honor. Nothing they did as fighters was honorable, because nothing connected with war is ever honorable, unless it has to do with negating, abrogating, denying, outlawing, or overcoming war. General William Tecumseh Sherman was right: "War is hell." He, above all, knew this. He was neither a hero nor a lover of war, but the very devil who brought hell to Atlanta in 1864. To the Atlanta city government he wrote, just before he burned them out: "You cannot qualify war in harsher terms than I will. War is cruelty, and you cannot refine it; and those who brought war into our country deserve all the curses and maledictions a people can pour out." Fight cruelty with harsher cruelty. That's the way to advance civilization! Way to go, Bill!

Anyone who loves war is sick. To portray any lover of war as a hero is sick. Lovers of war, if they are portrayed at all, should be portrayed only as what they are: sick.

Of all the World War II American generals that Hollywood could have de-

---

[68] *Also Sprach Zarathustra*, Preface 4, 4: "Was gross ist am Menschen, das ist, dass eine Brücke und kein Zweck ist."

cided to biographize on film at the height of the Vietnam War era — decent humans like Eisenhower, George C. Marshall, Omar Bradley, Skinny Wainwright, or even questionable characters like Douglas MacArthur — it chose instead a murderous scumbag of whom America should be forever ashamed, George S. Patton, the moral equivalent of Himmler, Goering, or any other Nazi leader. While probably every other Allied general would pray for peace, Patton alone would more likely pray for more war. (He did indeed suggest that America should invade the Soviet Union after the fall of Berlin in 1945.) Thus we could only regard *Patton* as a propaganda film in line with the LBJ/Nixon prowar policies.

That both the real Patton and the Hollywood Patton were lovers of war is not open to question. In the film's first scene George C. Scott, as Patton, declared, "Americans traditionally love to fight. All real Americans love the sting of battle. ... the very thought of losing is hateful to Americans. ... This individuality stuff is a bunch of crap." Later he said, "Compared to war, all other forms of human endeavor shrink to insignificance." At one point Bradley reproached Patton for being too cavalier with common soldiers' lives: "There's one big difference between you and me, George. I do this job because I've been trained to do it. You do it because you love it." Patton confirmed this many times, notably in France in late 1944 when, strolling through the carnage of a hand-to-hand battle, he told his aide-de-camp, "I love it. God help me, I do love it so. I love it more than my life." A Nazi officer called him "a pure warrior," unable to thrive outside the milieu of war. This officer accurately recognized that Patton, after the war, would at once become "a magnificent anachronism," quite useless in any world that would not allow him to kill.

But all that said, *Patton* was a very well written, well acted, and well constructed film. It showed Patton and Montgomery as vain, pompous glory-seekers, but Bradley as a warm, sympathetic man with genuinely admirable human qualities. It did not shy from portraying Patton as a natural killer or from detailing his many faults and flaws; yet, in the end, it also portrayed him as a hero — and for that reason alone we rejected this film as prowar propaganda.

Hollywood did not leave the militaristic implications of *Patton* unanswered. It also offered *M*A*S*H*.

Along with Lew Ayres's 1930 *All Quiet on the Western Front*, *M*A*S*H* was probably one of the two most eloquent and perceptive antiwar movies ever made. We recognized *M*A*S*H*'s antiwar importance instantly with the opening sequence of helicopters bearing grievously wounded men over a hostile landscape into a makeshift hospital camp, all under the main theme song, "Suicide is Painless." We loved it! Vietnam hawks hated it! Most of us young antiwar activists saw it in theaters more than once, if only to try to catch more punchlines in the blur of dialogue. But by the time it had become a CBS TV series in 1972, its handlers had watered it down so much that even the most hawkish rightists could enjoy it and not see it as politically offensive. It was widely and durably popular throughout the seventies, and its last show, on February 28, 1983, is among the highest rated TV events ever, with 50,150,000 households, 105,900,000 viewers, a Nielsen rating of 60.2 per cent of households, and a 77 per cent share of households that were watching TV at the time. By contrast, the record-breaking rating of the Beatles' first *Ed Sullivan* appearance on February 9, 1964, was 23,240,000 households, 73,000,000 viewers, a 60 per cent Nielsen, and a 45.3 per cent share. But I submit that those who preferred the *M*A*S*H* TV show to either Robert Altman's movie or Richard Hooker's book would prefer their Shakespeare bowdlerized, their food pureed, and their whole environment air conditioned. The TV show had no meaning! It had no bite! Donald Sutherland is the only genuine Hawkeye Pierce; Alan Alda is *not* Hawkeye. Sutherland portrayed him as a resilient man nearly ruined by war; Alda portrayed him as a wimpy goof, just right for saccharine American TV.

As dull as the *M*A*S*H* TV show was, the movie remains luminous and underappreciated. Giving the Best Picture Oscar that year to the explicitly prowar *Patton* instead of to *M*A*S*H* was a travesty. It said nothing to us except that the Academy of Motion Picture Arts and Sciences was firmly in the back pocket of commercial interests and was not a good judge of what was truly important in filmmaking.

The Adventurers, set in a fictional South American country plagued by continuous armed insurrection, laid bare the fundamental evil and futility of all war. The film's antihero, Dax, a ten-year-old boy who had recently witnessed and barely survived soldiers pillaging his home and another hacienda, murdering his mother, and raping and murdering his sister and many other women, turned immediately to execute seven unarmed men himself. Thus — his comrades said — he became a man. He confided to a girl even younger than he: "I don't want a wife and family, because the soldiers will come and kill them." By war's perverse criteria of masculinity, even the most idealistic, intelligent, and sensitive young men, such as Dax, lose their childhood too early for healthy psychological development.

The moviegoer followed Dax from age ten, through his rich playboy life in Italy and America, to his being killed at about age thirty-five by a misguided but fanatic revolutionary. Just as war transformed decent young boys into cold-blooded killers, so unrestrained wealth transformed them into arrogant, hollow, sexist boors. Through both of these causes, natural human feelings and the capacity for love, friendship, trust, honor, and sincerity all died. Dax desperately but mostly wrongheadedly tried to recover his lost humanity.

The dictator Rojo, the war's victor, not only secretly employed the loser Gutierrez who had murdered both Rojo's and Dax's families, but also secretly ordered the murders of Dax's father and other friends who had stood by him in the war. Treachery was his watchword. He warned Dax: "Until you've learned that evil and politics must tolerate each other, there's no place for you here." Rojo tricked Dax into financing further oppression of the already miserable people.

How anyone could watch all two hours and 57 minutes of *The Adventurers* without coming away as an antiwar activist is difficult to imagine.

Mart Crowley's *The Boys in the Band* was for many straight kids their first realistic introduction to gay male urban life. In this mordant dark comedy we met eight gay guys and one straight gentleman at various stages of emotional growth, various levels of self-acceptance, and in various kinds of relationship trouble. The pretext was a birthday party for Harold, "a thirty-two-year-old, ugly, pockmarked Jew fairy" who hated himself but accepted his homosexuality. The party's host,

Michael, was at least equally self-hating but did not accept his homosexuality at all. Rather, he regularly, almost fanatically, attended St. Malachy's Roman Catholic Church near Times Square and prayed to be straight. We gradually saw that while Harold was an emotional wreck, he was much better adjusted than Michael.

The eight gays ran the gamut of stereotypes. Besides Michael and Harold were: Emory, a pronoun-challenged prancing queen, who could not possibly pass for straight in any situation; Bernard, a self-effacing, passive black queen; Donald, anxiety-ridden and mired in psychoanalysis; Tex, stupid and merely physical, a male prostitute whom Emory bought for $20 as Harold's birthday present; Hank, a beer-drinking, macho jock, a "regular guy" who could easily pass for straight and who had as little patience with Emory as most straight guys would; and Larry, terminally horny, reluctant to give up the gay bar cruising scene despite his professed love for his "roommate" Hank. Their conversation consisted mainly of insults designed to expose the inborn neurosis of the homosexual. When Michael disclosed his adherence to Pascal's Wager, the idea that one believes in God only to get into heaven, Emory called him Harriet Hypocrisy. The only time they seemed to have genuine fun was when they played music and danced. Into these four dysfunctional pairings, Michael-Donald, Emory-Bernard, Harold-Tex, and Hank-Larry, stumbled Alan, Michael's old college roommate, upper class, snooty, straight as an arrow, but severely conflicted about some deep secret.

As Michael and Donald were preparing for the party, Alan, whom Michael had not heard from in ages and whom Michael did not even suspect was in New York, called Michael out of the blue, insisted that he had to see him immediately, and uncharacteristically broke down sobbing on the phone. Alan did not know that Michael was gay. When Michael simply told Alan that he already had other plans, Alan apologized to Michael and said that he would *not* come over. But Alan *did* come over, like a party crasher, also apparently a departure from his usual well-mannered character. Michael leaped to conclude that Alan was on his way out of the closet and that that was why he had cried on the phone. This *idée fixe* poisoned everything.

Some of the guys, including Michael, tried to persuade Alan to leave before he figured out that they were all gay. Larry strongly and coldly resented Alan barging in. Others, particularly Donald, wanted Alan to stay, but maybe only out of morbid curiosity to see what Michael would do to him. Michael, after five weeks on the wagon, resumed smoking and drinking as soon as Alan showed up. Alcohol heightened his hostility.

Alan tried politely to insinuate himself into the party and instantly took a shine to Hank. Alan was shocked to learn that Hank, the married father of two, had recently come out of the closet and had left his wife to try to start a domestic relationship with Larry. In Alan's world, a husband leaving a wife for another woman was normal, but not for another man.

Taking advantage of the spiteful campiness and sniping cattiness that was second nature to urban gays, Michael devised a cruel game to pry loose Alan's secret. The game backfired horribly, humiliating everyone except the aloof Harold, the clueless Tex, and the impervious Larry. Alan went home to his wife, Fran.

"If we could just not hate ourselves so much!" lamented Michael, chastised and shattered. The movie solidly held that gayness was a natural human trait, like lefthandedness, and suggested that gay self-hatred was not intrinsic among gays, but rather emerged from gays taking upon themselves the persecution that straight society inflicted upon them. As long as well-meaning and decent citizens like Alan mechanically puked whenever in the presence of homosexuality, the need would exist for Gay Pride movements of the kind that burgeoned in the seventies.

Allen Funt became famous in the fifties and sixties by playing practical jokes on people, filming them secretly, then broadcasting their reactions on his TV show, *Candid Camera*. *What Do You Say to a Naked Lady?* brought this hidden camera concept to the movies. All its jokes involved either nudity or frank sexuality in unexpected situations. The camera caught fully clothed men, just going about their daily business, suddenly confronted by naked women getting out of elevators, asking directions, or hitchhiking. It caught fully clothed women reacting to replicas of Michelangelo's *David* that either talked or had spinning fig leaves, to a nude male model breaking his pose and striking up a conversation, or to a nude woman lecturer; plus fully clothed students of both genders finding themselves in a class taught by a nude woman professor; as well as fully clothed people of both genders having to defend their sexual hypocrisy in discussions of public interracial kissing, eleven-year-olds screwing, or general social decadence. Unfortunately, only three or four of the film's 85 minutes were funny. Funt too seriously presumed for himself the role of a Masters, Johnson, or Kinsey, spending too much time interviewing, explaining, and pseudopsychologizing, but not enough on the simple gags. Yet, he did here take a small step to bring full frontal nudity into big screen comedy.

Set in the early days of the ancient Roman Empire, *Fellini Satyricon* was one long orgy of omnisexual debauchery, homosexual perversity — not that homosexuality itself was perverse — and general wantonness. It apparently had little point, but then pure sensuality seldom does. Its scenes were gaudy, grotesque, bestial, surrealistic, and sometimes anachronistic, gradually bloating into a squalid carnival of prurience and purulence, a gratuitous display of flabby tits and farting asses, almost as if Fellini had calculated to make nudity itself seem ugly to the filmgoer. Its profusion of misshapen bodies, mutilated limbs, hideous faces, ridiculous costumes, routine cruelty, and rapacious lust may have signified some message, but we could not tell what. Whatever its meaning, if it had any, its disconnected representation owed more to Hieronymus Bosch than to Petronius.

The Fugs played the Fillmore East in 1968 and now, over a year later, released a live album of that gig, appropriately called *Golden Filth*. It would be their last album. They had some pretty good musicians with them that night, so this LP rocked a bit tighter and harder than most of their others. I guess Bill Graham had standards! The cover art, a cartoon of several overflowing or tipped-over garbage cans on a disgusting urban sidewalk, perfectly heralded the album's nine nasty tunes, including "Slum Goddess," "I Couldn't Get High," "Saran Wrap," and "Coca Cola Douche."

Besides "Teacher," Jethro Tull's third LP, *Benefit*, included "Son," which attacked tyrannical fathers; "Nothing to Say," which called on each of us to be just ourselves and not to intrude with criticism into others' privacy or freedom; "A Time for Everything," which urged us to experience as much as possible before we get old; "Inside," which expressed inner resolve to be joyful in friendship and love; "Play in Time," which celebrated the excitement of life and regretted that there are not enough hours in a day to do everything that we would like to do; "With You There to Help Me," which asserted that love and sharing are the way out of despair; and "To Cry You a Song," a song of impatience. *Benefit*'s overall effect was of receiving fresh, useful wisdom in the presence of an unmistakably unique sound.

With raspy vocals, minimalist arrangements, mostly percussive instrumentation, constant provocation, and wacko presence, Captain Beefheart and His Magic Band finally achieved an *avant garde* masterpiece, *Trout Mask Replica*, almost seventy-nine minutes of sheer insanity. Song titles like "Hair Pie," "Bill's Corpse," "Ant Man Bee," "Frownland," "China Pig," "She's Too Much for My Mirror," "Dachau Blues," and "Old Fart at Play" accurately indicated the double album's lyrics, tone, and impact. It tried to be surrealistic, but was sometimes just obnoxious.

The Grateful Dead's fourth album, their first live one, *Live Dead*, showed a bare-breasted nymph rising from a coffin on the front cover and an American flag with its stripes rearranged to spell "Dead" and resemble jail bars on the back cover. The four sides contained only seven tunes! The extended jams on "Dark Star," "Turn on Your Love Light," and "Death Don't Have No Mercy" were like nothing we had ever heard! Magnificent! We were mesmerized. The legend of the Grateful Dead as the ultimate live band began *right here*! Subdued, understated, low-key, unhurried, easygoing, but supremely powerful — that was the Dead. They out-Fudged the Fudge, out-Fished the Fish, and even sometimes outflew the Airplane.

Woodstock replaced *Monterey Pop* in our collective imagination as the definitive video statement of our generation's highest ideals. Michael Wadleigh's director's cut of the *Woodstock* movie, released for the festival's twenty-fifth anniversary in 1994, was forty-one minutes longer than the version released to theaters in March 1970. It added the Airplane's "Won't You Try" and "Uncle Sam's Blues," Janis's "Work Me, Lord," Hendrix's "Voodoo Chile," CSNY's "Find the Cost of Freedom," and some extra interview and documentary footage. The original version was good enough, but the director's cut is the one to watch if you can find it.

Most of our knowledge of whatever occurred at Woodstock and whatever those occurrences may have meant was based on the documentary movie. Its split screen on the wide screen format was perfect for compressing accurately as much information as possible into a naturally small amount of time — and, above all, its theater sound was the best then available. Its first run was mostly just to big theaters with excellent acoustics and state-of-the-art sound systems. Knowing how indispensable music was to us, the producers obviously worked very hard to honor and accommodate our love of the defining sounds of our lives.

Scene 18, "In Search of," on side one of the director's cut DVD, showed an illuminating interview with two kids who saw themselves just as two humans, male and female, who loved each other, had sex with each other, and obviously enjoyed each other, but who were not "in love." They laughed at the very idea of jealousy. Their love, though bilateral, had not descended to the base level of bilateralism that would have excluded all other sides. Their love was a unifying force for all humanity, not something that divided them as a unified pair from the rest of the world. Such "free love" fosters universal respect and cooperation; but being "in love" divides, builds walls, cuts off people from one another. "Free love" does not necessarily mean orgiastic hedonism. Rather, it suggests, within the context of multilateral erotic relationships, each participant's full respect for all other involved persons as free, autonomous individuals, eschewing the inherent possessiveness and inequality of the "great American romance." Above all, free love, true love, entails what the early Christians called *agapê*, universal love and genuine, deep respect for *every* other person. Such love gives us no reason to be afraid. At Woodstock many women walked around naked amid thousands of men without fear and without incident.[69] Such fearlessness, grounded in love, is true freedom.

Also on side one, in Scene 25, "What's It All About?", the laid-back, grinning co-producer Artie Kornfeld told an NBC interviewer, "Financially this is a disaster," to which the clueless interviewer responded, "But you look so happy?"

Well of course Artie was happy! Real happiness comes from human solidarity, from smiling, from random acts of kindness, and indeed from freely accepting the serene message of music, not from amassing riches or from outdoing others. The interviewer, apparently well representing mainstream America by not being able to see anything except in terms of money, seemed incapable of fathoming this point. But it can be clearly shown by comparing this original Woodstock with the 1994 and 1999 Woodstocks, where commercial interests were allowed to run wild. Commercialism ruins everything. It alone differentiated the considerate, sharing attendees of the first Woodstock from the mean-spirited, selfish attendees of the next two. Moneyless anarchy can work only if well-meaning citizens all work together to make it work.

Like all anarchies, Woodstock was parasitic on ordered society and necessarily short-lived. It depended for basic goods and services upon non-anarchists outside the collective community. In another few days dysentery would have broken out. It was not a blueprint for any reform of society at large, but only a giant expression of good will.

Trust is also necessary for anarchy to work, but trusting makes the trusters vulnerable. Eventually some selfish goon will take advantage of the general good will in any anarchistic situation, and there will then be profiteering, rape, child molestation, theft, murder, and other such crimes and counterproductive occurrences — of which there were none at Woodstock.

In the movie we saw Grace Slick introducing Nicky Hopkins. Until then, few of us had ever heard of him. Shame on us! But curiosity got the best of us and we looked him up. Turns out he was one of most prolific keyboardists and one of the most important session players in rock. Besides the Airplane, he recorded with the Who, the Kinks, Quicksilver, the Beatles, Steve Miller, the New Riders, Joe

---

[69] Cf. Eric v.d. Luft, *A Socialist Manifesto* (North Syracuse, New York: Gegensatz Press, 2007), Principle 22, "Ownership of One's Own Body," pp. 60-61. Cf. the description of two Woodstocks in Principle 21, "Decriminalization of Marijuana," p. 59.

Cocker, Donovan, etc.; and, for all intents and purposes, he was the sixth Rolling Stone from 1966 to 1979. He is on *Sgt. Pepper's*, *Tommy*, *Imagine*, *Brave New World*, *Beck-Ola*, *My Generation*, *Arthur*, fourteen Stones albums, and hundreds of other rock albums. Much of his session work was done with bassist John Paul Jones and guitarist Jimmy Page before they formed Led Zeppelin. He was fairly reclusive, but we could see him playing piano in *One Plus One*.

Mountain, who had achieved stardom at Woodstock despite not having appeared in the movie, released their second album, their breakthrough, *Climbing*, with a balance of explosive tracks like "Mississippi Queen" and "Never in My Life" and dreamy tracks "Theme for an Imaginary Western" and "For Yasgur's Farm." Mountain was a collaborative project between gigantic guitarist Leslie West (whose own nickname named the band) and skinny bassist Felix Pappalardi. They looked like Laurel and Hardy next to each other. But their music was stunning. The back cover of the LP insisted "THIS RECORD WAS MADE TO BE PLAYED LOUD" and showed the pair slapping hands.

Ten Years After, who really lit up their career with Alvin Lee's lightning guitar wizardry when the *Woodstock* movie appeared, released their fifth album, their best yet, *Cricklewood Green*, consisting of all Lee originals. Still essentially a blues band, heavy cuts like "Working on the Road," spacy cuts like "50,000 Miles Beneath My Brain," and riff-driven cuts like "Love Like a Man" moved them ever further toward psychedelia. Damn, they rocked hard! Often overlooked but just as fascinating as Lee's proto-speed-metal guitar was Leo Lyons's frantic, ferocious, often one-fingered bass attack, also visible in *Woodstock*.

Ω

We gradually realized that *Abbey Road* had begun the Beatles' long swan song that continued through their compilation LP, *Hey Jude*, their last studio album, *Let It Be*, and ended in their last single, "The Long and Winding Road." When Paul's semi-official announcement of their break-up appeared in April, we were shocked but not surprised, for it had only confirmed rumors and suspicions that had been building for months. We still could not believe it. We were in denial. We blamed him. That's it! Stupid fans! Shoot the messenger! A better reason to get mad at him might have been the crass timing of his announcement to coincide with the release of his first solo album.

The *Hey Jude* album prompted us to relive gems like "Can't Buy Me Love," "I Should Have Known Better," "Paperback Writer," "Rain," the title cut, "Lady Madonna," and the three-minute version of "Revolution," and to revel in newer tunes like "The Ballad of John and Yoko," "Don't Let Me Down," and "Old Brown Shoe." Unlike most compilation LPs, this one had its own soul and character.

The *Let It Be* album was another story. Our emotions about it were mixed. When it came out, the Beatles were already history. Phil Spector had monkeyed with it, some said for the better, some not. There seemed to be as many opinions of that album as there were copies of it. Contrast, for example, its title track to the non-Spectorized version that had been been released as a single two months earlier. One was obviously better than the other. But which one? We argued.

But the Beatles had left us with good advice:

Let it be, indeed! Do it! Yes! Just let it be!

Was this a call to passivity? Not at all. Rather, it was a call to immerse ourselves in the whole breadth and depth of life and thus to let it show itself to us on its own self-preserving terms, not the terms of either our death-dealing analysis of it or our ulteriorly motivated ambitions for it. Do it!

Jerry Rubin's prescriptions in *Do It! Scenarios of the Revolution* were so crazy and were stated in such hyperbolic language that I doubt if even he believed most of them, but his overall message was clear: If you want to be free, really free, then don't fight for freedom. Fighting is not liberating. If you want to be free, just live it! Live freely! No matter what. Just do it!

That was how Abbie and (at that time) Jerry lived. They just did it!

Abbie, for one, thought: Fuck the flag! Worshipping a flag ain't freedom. I'm not gonna haul it up a pole and grovel underneath it. I'm gonna wear it for a shirt. So he did. He wore it on Merv Griffin's popular talk show, but CBS blurred it out so that no one at home could see it. Never mind that mainstream Americans could wear flag shirts with impunity, even for commercial purposes. A month later, Grace Slick, armed with a genuine invitation to the White House from Nixon's daughter, asked Abbie to be her "date." They plotted to put LSD in the drinks, hoping, against hope, for success and their own safety, and even more against hope, that Nixon himself would drink some. Guards would not let them inside because they were both on the FBI's "list."

Abbie was lucky that the Secret Service did not just plunk him that day.

The right wing's solution to any problem that vexes them seems to be to kill whomever they perceive as having caused it, as being part of it, or as perpetuating it. In May 1970 they began murdering unarmed students in cold blood: Allison Krause, Jeffrey Glenn Miller, Sandra Lee Scheuer, and William Knox Schroeder at Kent State, Ohio, on May 4; Phillip Lafayette Gibbs and James Earl Green at Jackson State, Mississippi, the night of May 14-15. Immediately after the Ohio National Guard committed its four murders, students and faculty at many universities, colleges, grad schools, and even some secondary schools nationwide either shut down their respective institutions completely or drastically altered their regular routines, including cancelling final exams and commencement ceremonies, in order to conduct, arrange, or attend teach-ins to address emergent existential concerns that not we, but lethal force called up by Republican Governor Jim Rhodes — who was already well known as a hater of student radicals — in support of the Nixon regime and its pursuit of LBJ's imperialist policies, had in effect destroyed the American higher educational process, at least for the time being. Ten days later there were two more slain students, this time the victims of a combined force of Jackson City Police, Mississippi State Police, and the Mississippi National Guard, who peppered two dorms and a crowd with hundreds of rounds of ammo. But few noticed, even the press. We wondered: Were the Jackson State murders discounted and underreported because the victims were black? Were we so jaded that more killings of innocent blacks in the deep South no longer seemed newsworthy?

This all happened on — Lynch Street!

Overnight on May 19 about a dozen students, college dropouts, and recent graduates, mostly in their early twenties, burglarized four draft board offices in the Philadelphia area, destroyed the records, and clogged the toilets. Calling themselves "We, the People," they issued a manifesto, which stated in part:

> It is not great talents, no unique political ideology, nor heroic grace that brought us to this action. We are just everyday people who believe in love, in justice, and in the human rights of our brothers and sisters. ... WE, THE PEOPLE have been labeled vandals and robbers because we have taken a militant non-violent action against the War Machine ... but who has vandalized life more than the industries with their napalm, defoliants, scatter bombs and unjust capitalistic contracts! Who has robbed young men of their right to choose their own destinies and robbed babies of their right to live but our leaders who insist on technological death.

Many of us believed in *wu wei*, the Taoist ideal of non-action. We wanted, with the Beatles and Martin Heidegger, just to "let it be," but, after Kent State, we could not. Those of us who had read J.R.R. Tolkien's *Lord of the Rings* may have wondered when a Frodo Baggins would arise from among us to throw the one ring into the fires of Mount Doom and thus end militaristic insanity forever. We are still waiting. Dubya's America became more like Tolkien's Mordor with each new invasion, incursion, escalation of hostilities, or judicial, legislative, executive, or martial curtailment of essential human rights or basic constitutional guarantees. Dubya's success at strident militarism owed much to LBJ's and Nixon's failed attempts at it. Top American rightists in the meantime have learned to erode the people's rights and liberties first, make them expect to be unfree, have them call their unfreedom "freedom," then and only then fabricate a common enemy and rally them against it. The USA-PATRIOT Act had to come before the invasion of Iraq. The people needed to be cowed into letting the federal government make its own decisions without the input of democratic reason. The USA-PATRIOT Act accomplished this cowing. Citizens in LBJ's and Nixon's time were not afraid of the government. In Dubya's time and beyond, they are. Dubya's domestic surveillance and control minions have proved more powerful, feared, subtle, and clandestine than either the fifties' HUAC or J. Edgar Hoover's FBI ever were.

Let it be! Let Vietnam be! Let Black America be! Let us be!

Ω

Summer 1970

Wake up, niggers!

I do not know exactly when the Yippie Manifesto was written, but I picked up a full-color newsprint poster copy of it in July 1970 in Greenwich Village. I assume that Abbie and Jerry wrote it. It could not have been very old, since it refers to events that occurred in late 1969. It reads in full:

Youth International Party Manifesto!

WE ARE A PEOPLE
We are a new nation.
We believe in life.
And we want to live now.
We want to be alive 24 hours a day.
Nine-to-five Amerika doesn't even live on weekends.

Amerika is a death machine. It is run on and for money whose power determines a society based on war, racism, sexism, and the destruction of the planet. Our life-energy is the greatest threat to the machine.

So they're out to stop us. They have to make us like them. They cut our hair, ban our music festivals, put cops and narcs in the schools, put 200,000 of us in jail for smoking flowers, induct us, housewive us, Easy-Rider murder us.

Amerika has declared war on our New Nation!

WE WILL BUILD AND DEFEND OUR NEW NATION
But we will continue to live and grow.
We are young, we have beautiful ideas about the way we should live.
We want everyone to control their own life and to care for one another.
And we will defend our freedom because we can't live any other way.

We will continue to seize control of our minds and our bodies. We can't do it in their schools, so we'll take them over or create our own. We can't do it in their Army, so we'll keep them from taking our brothers. We can't make it in their jobs, so we'll work only to survive. We can't relate to each other like they do — our nation is built on cooperation not competition.

We will provide for all that we need to build and defend our nation. We will teach each other the true history of Amerika so that we may learn from the past to survive in the present. We will teach each other the tactics of self-defense. We will provide free health services: birth control and abortions, drug information, medical care, that this society is not providing us with.

We will begin to take control of drug manufacture and distribution, and stop the flow of bad shit. We will make sure that everyone has a decent place to live: we will fight landlords, renovate buildings, live communally, have places for sisters and brothers from out-of-town, and for runaways and freed prisoners. We will set up national and international transportation and communication so that we can be together with our sisters and brothers from different parts of the country and the world. We will fight the unnatural division between cities and country by facilitating travel and communication.

We will end the domination of women by men, and children by adults.

The well-being of our nation is the well-being of all peace-loving people.

WE WILL HAVE PEACE
We cannot tolerate attitudes, institutions, and machines whose purpose is the destruction of life, the accumulation of "profit."

Schools and universities are training us for roles in Amerika's empire of endless war. We cannot allow them to use us for the military-industrial profiteers.

Companies that produce waste, poisons, germs, and bombs have no place in this world.

We are living in the capital of the world war being waged against life. We are not good Germans. We who are living in this strategic center of Babylon must make it our strategic center. We can and we must stop the death machine from butchering the planet.

We will shut the motherfucker down!

WE WILL MAKE OUR NEW NATION FIT FOR LIVING THINGS
We will seize Amerika's technology and use it to build a nation based on love and respect for all life.

Our new society is not about the power of a few men but the right of all humans, animals, and plants to play out their natural roles in harmony. We will build our communities to reflect the beauty inside us.

People from all over the world are fighting to keep Amerika from turning their countries into parking lots!

WE WILL BE TOGETHER WITH ALL THE TOGETHER PEOPLES OF THE EARTH
Pig Empire is ravaging the globe, but the beautiful people everywhere are fighting back.
New Nation is one with the black, red, brown & yellow nations.

Che said: "You North Amerikans are very lucky. You live in the middle of the beast. You are fighting the most important fight of all, in the center of the battle. If I had my wish, I would go back with you to North Amerika to fight there. I envy you."

The expected symbolism abounded. The manifesto was printed in white text on a black background, symbolizing anarchy. Centered on the poster was an extra-large version of the usual Yippie emblem: a bright green marijuana leaf, symbolizing joy, superimposed on a red star, symbolizing communism. Yeah, Abbie's communism and anarchism were tiresome, but his *joie de vivre* was fascinating, and that was what drew us to him.

During that same trip to New York City I saw a poster of a black-and-white photo, a full-length frontal view of two pedestrians waiting at a traffic light to cross a city street. On the right was a well-scrubbed, well-dressed, portly, middle-aged businessman, complete with briefcase, *Wall Street Journal*, and self-important, arrogant sneer. On the left was a filthy, sleazy, skinny, scruffy, long-haired freak who, looking with contempt out of the corner of his eye at Mr. Self-Importance, whips out his gigantic cock and pisses on him sidelong. The funniest thing was that Mr. S.-I. remained completely unaware of the stream of piss hitting his leg. I loved it!

It seemed in 1970 that legal authorities all over were determined to ban our festivals on any pretense. We in the Philadelphia area were eager to attend the Harmonyville festival in Chester County, Pennsylvania, which was scheduled for August 4 to August 9, but was cancelled before I could even buy a ticket. The Powder Ridge festival in south central Connecticut, sponsored and produced by Middletown Arts International, was to have included from Friday, July 31, to Sunday, August 1, at least Sly and the Family Stone, Mountain, James Taylor, Ten Wheel Drive, Jethro Tull, Joe Cocker, Grand Funk Railroad, Melanie, John Sebastian, Van Morrison, Ten Years After, Janis Joplin, Delaney and Bonnie and Friends, Spirit, the Allman Brothers, and (rumor had it) Neil Young, the Band, and Led Zeppelin. On Monday, July 27, Judge Aaron Palmer of the Middletown Superior Court issued an injunction banning the festival as a "public nuisance." Fans began arriving on Tuesday. Perhaps they had heard about the injunction, perhaps not. Promoters considered putting the festival on anyway, but backed down when Palmer threatened them with imprisonment and seven-figure fines. They contacted all the musicians and told them not to come. Among the musicians, only Melanie defied the ban. Police erected roadblocks on Thursday to try to stop the influx of fans. To no avail. By Thursday there were about 15,000 and by Friday, over 30,000. Melanie was among those who snuck in. Because any musician who stepped onto the main stage would be arrested, she hooked her microphone up to a Mr. Softee ice cream truck generator and played as long as she could. But with no other music, the scene quickly got ugly. William Abruzzi, M.D., told his story to Robert Stokes in the August 14 issue of *Life* magazine:

> At Woodstock everybody was determined to make it a peace and love thing. I think the kids were still hopeful that our society would make it — and wanted to help. So Woodstock was a benign, gentle drug scene. We had 800 bad trips there, but that many among a half million kids was small. At Powder Ridge with only 35,000 kids, we treated 985 bad trips, 400 of them on Friday night alone. The acid was heavily laced — up to 30% — with dangerous chemicals like strychnine, which give a faster and better high. Half of the bad trips we treated were from mixing acid with methedrine — tripping and speeding at the same time. We even saw some animal tranquilizers used for downers. It's truly a miracle that we didn't have any deaths. ...
>
> There is no doubt in my mind that the lack of music at Powder Ridge contributed to the heavy drug scene. On Friday night, when there was no music, we had hundreds of bad trips. On Saturday night, when local rock groups finally arrived, we had only 57 bummers from 6 p.m. to 8 a.m. The whole spirit of the place changed. The kids walked around with smiles on their faces, and they weren't dropping everything in sight.
>
> The kids at rockfests are saying, "You don't want us. We're really not a part of what you are. You've never really listened to us or taken us into your society." These kids want to be a part of something where everyone cares about everyone else. We didn't treat a knife wound or a punch in the 5,000 kids we treated there. The kids at Powder Ridge turned their hostility and frustration inward. They arrived in relatively good faith, but filled with doubt, questions, uncertainty, boredom, futility and resentment. Gradually, they felt they'd been taken, co-opted, utilized for financial reasons, for political reasons. Because of this they did a lot of things they wouldn't have done otherwise. There were a lot of kids who had never tried heavy drugs before. They lost their sense of discrimination in the drugs they used. They lost their sense of self-protection.

The pigs accomplished nothing except making about 35,000 people miserable and disappointing thousands of others.

I had a ticket to Powder Ridge. On Thursday morning I hitchhiked from Philadelphia to Greenwich Village, crashed there that night, and set out the next morning to hitch the rest of the way to the festival. Two women from New Hampshire picked me up on the Cross Bronx Expressway and asked where I was going. I said Powder Ridge. They said they had just come from there. They told me about the injunction and the roadblocks. With their original plans for the weekend abandoned, they had decided to visit New York City, which neither of them had ever seen before. I offered to show them around. We drove back down to the Village. We shopped at St. Mark's Place, looked at the outside of the Fillmore East, strolled through Washington Square, and saw *Catch-22*. They decided they did not like New York City much and would rather go "up the country," as Canned Heat put it. We drove up the Taconic State Parkway about as far as Millbrook (hoping to find some leftover Timmy Leary vibes). Late that night we pulled over to sleep in a secluded rest area. The weather was perfect. Dale slept across the front seat, I across the back, and Linda, who was rather short, rigged up a sort of nest with several blankets and slept in the open trunk.

The next day we continued north, meandering through the Berkshires and ending up in southern Vermont. We could not find a rest area, so we coughed up $2.00 to spend the night in a campground. We tried the same sleeping arrangement as the previous night, but an officer interrupted us to say that we were not allowed in the campground without a tent. We did not have a tent, but we managed to hide that little fact from him. We told him we would set it up right away. Linda, with her flair for engineering, jerry-rigged a serviceable pup tent from her blanket nest and a few other odds and ends. She stayed the night in there while Dale and I slept on our respective car seats. The officer passed by a few times but did not bother us again.

Sunday we drove to New Hampshire. Dale and Linda both had to be at work on Monday morning. They envied me because I was seventeen and unemployed. Dale dropped Linda off first then took me to her home. After her family fed me a great lunch, I thumbed down I-95 to Boston, where I had never been before. I found a free crash pad called Project Place in Cambridge, hung around Boston for two days, was lucky enough to be on Cambridge Common when Peter Schumann's Bread and Puppet Theater was performing, then hitched back to Pennsylvania.

Things were free and easy like that in those days. Men and women simply respected each other as people. There was no sexual tension. There was little danger. From the mid-sixties to the late seventies hitchhiking was common and usually unproblematic for both genders. We were in more danger from cops and rednecks than from perverts and murderers. Of course, it was best for women to hitch in pairs and best for lone women drivers not to pick up male hitchhikers, but generally everything was cool. Those in my generation with cars were happy to help those without. Hitching was a great way to meet new people and have some innocent fun. But the joy of hitchhiking disappeared in the seventies as rapists and serial killers began to take greater advantage of our trust. Also, as my generation broke into our twenties and thirties, we almost all acquired cars of our own. Where there had been safety in numbers, there was now danger in sparseness. By the early eighties hitchhiking had become truly dangerous, with opportunistic criminals on the deliberate prowl for young meat.

There was a lot of very heavy music this summer.

The Who at last realized their full power on vinyl with the release of what was then acknowledged as the greatest live rock album ever made, *Live at Leeds*. Despite pops, hisses, and other technical faults that were then common enough on live records, its amazingly energetic, imaginative, and authoritative performances of "Summertime Blues," "Young Man Blues," "Shakin' All Over," "Substitute," "Magic Bus," and especially the medley and jam around "My Generation" solidified the Who's position as the hardest rocking of all progressive bands — and one of the loudest.

With new vocalist Ian Gillan and new bassist Roger Glover, Deep Purple achieved a much heavier sound and finally broke through with their fifth album, *Deep Purple in Rock*. Yet the album cover, showing five young British musicians in place of four old American presidents on Mount Rushmore, was a monument of irony, even more interesting than the tunes inside.

A London group called Free had a hit single in the U.S. with "All Right Now," a wicked rocker about amoral seduction. Later Free would be better known for spawning half of the supergroup Bad Company, with one quarter coming from Mott the Hoople and the other quarter from King Crimson.

Joe Cocker had cobbled together at the last minute a humongous band for an American tour that spring. The resulting eponymous double live album, *Mad Dogs and Englishmen*, recorded in March at the Fillmore East, unleashed what we called "Cocker Power," vibrant, contagious, and spontaneous musical energy. The band was amazing — about thirty people just milling around onstage, with Cocker, the star, not really at the center or in the front of any of it. They were so uninhibited. They made fun of Easter. There were so many of them. They seemed so disorganized, and yet they exuded such pure joy in their music. Little did we know how fragile they were, both as a band and as individuals. Many of them, including Cocker himself, would burn out on drugs within the next few years. Jim Gordon, one of the drummers, would murder his mother with a hammer in 1983.

Another huge, amorphous band was Delaney and Bonnie and Friends, whose third LP, *On Tour with Eric Clapton*, a toe-tapper full of hot boogie tunes, provided refuge for Clapton after the demise of Blind Faith. Clapton had met Bonnie and Delaney Bramlett during the Blind Faith tour, and had quickly taken to jamming with them and their band. Many of these Friends were also Mad Dogs or Englishmen, and three of them, Bobby Whitlock on keyboards, Carl Radle on bass, and Gordon on drums, would soon form Derek and the Dominos with Clapton.

For some reason the rock critics hated the Doors' four-sided *Absolutely Live* LP. Why? Who knows! Maybe they were just idiots. Obviously the selections were heavily edited, but still bursting with energy. Morrison's incredible stage persona shone through with humorous brilliance. He bantered with the audience, teased them, berated them, yelled at them — and generally had them in the palm of his hand. To imagine any other rock singer who could so effortlessly establish such solid rapport with his front-row fans would be tough. His sixteen-minute rendering of "When the Music's Over" was definitive, evoking apocalyptic visions of dying, polluted, unnatural, music-starved civilizations. Other highlights included a particularly strident version of "Five to One"; "Petition the Lord with Prayer," which summarily sent up fire-and-brimstone preaching; "Universal Mind," a melancholy hymn to freedom; and the entire seven-part "Celebration of the Lizard," a rare treat, despite Morrison's uneven poetry.

Zappa and the Mothers released their eighth album, *Weasels Ripped My Flesh*, their funniest in quite some time. The cover showed a businessman shaving with an electric weasel, which was tearing his face apart. This juxtaposition of the artificial business world and the natural world was heavy-handed but hilarious. As usual, Zappa's humor was sexually charged. Songs like "Didja Get Any Onya," "Toads of the Short Forest," "Prelude to the Afternoon of a Sexually Aroused Gas Mask," and "My Guitar Wants to Kill Your Mama" kept us howling.

King Crimson's second LP, *In the Wake of Poseidon*, presented more bombast and more jazz but less art. They were clearly a one-shot deal. Fripp, Lake, and their bandmates would soon break up and go on to other things. The eight tunes wove loosely around the "Peace" trilogy and usually sounded more like a cross between lounge lizard music and a church cantata than rock.

Rod Stewart's second LP, *Gasoline Alley*, continued in the blues and soft rock direction of his debut — and really added not much new to the mix.

I do not remember the first time I heard most bands, but I distinctly remember the first time I heard Black Sabbath. In a mostly dark dorm room with about ten or twelve other people, some of whom were smoking dope, I and three others were playing bridge on a tipped-over cable spool. We had a terrific stereo system, and a great variety of music enveloped us at full volume. Then out of nowhere came the rainstorm. Then the eerie church bell. Then the thunder. Then those magnificent three notes: The big sonorous G, its octave, and its tritone, the C# in between. We were already blown away by the time the drums and vocals kicked in! It was the first time most of us in the room had heard it. The guy who had put it on the turntable instantly became our hero of the evening. The album was the eponymous first Black Sabbath album, and we were hearing the title cut, its first tune. After six minutes of that, even a great song like "The Wizard" seemed anticlimactic.

With the possible exceptions of Led Zeppelin, Deep Purple, Blue Cheer, Hendrix, and *Live at Leeds*, Sabbath was the heaviest music that any of us had ever heard. There are some who say that Black Sabbath invented heavy metal, but let's not go that far. Led Zeppelin invented heavy metal. Period. Yet Sabbath certainly extended it quite a lot with this debut album. Ozzy Osbourne's tormented voice was perfect for heavy metal, and Geezer Butler, the soul of the band, was charting unexplored territory in bass distortion. Among bass players, John Entwistle may have surpassed Geezer in virtuosity, John Paul Jones in raw power, Phil Lesh in musicianship, Bill Wyman in solidity, Larry Graham in funkiness, Jack Casady in versatility, and Paul McCartney in creativity, but none of them used distortion to more powerful effect than Geezer did on the first two Sabbath albums.

Some said that Sabbath was a satanic band and that their music would lead fans into satanist cults. Well sure, we recognized satanism as their schtick, but we did not take it seriously. We figured that neither did they. Their music, not their phony stage religion, was what was important. Our immortal souls were no more in peril of eternal damnation from Black Sabbath than from the Rolling Stones' "Sympathy for the Devil" or Mitch Ryder's "Devil with a Blue Dress On." To us satanism was all a big joke.

We went to see *Performance* because Mick Jagger was in it, but when we did we were mystified. We had no idea what it was about. Something about the sleazy underside of London, a small-time criminal on the lam holed up in a druggy artsy-fartsy den. Lots of apparently gratuitous sex, nudity, perversion, and violence. It might have been about the ephemerality of personal identity, the mutablility of humanity, the meaning of life itself, or maybe it was just a stylish way to present odd camera angles on naked nipples and other kinky, *avant garde* cinematographic conceits. Maybe the whole key was in the stuffed warthog head on Turner's wall. Who knew? We heard a rumor that at one showing the projectionist accidentally ran the reels out of sequence, but no one in the audience noticed. Maybe that was true, maybe not, but it certainly captured the chaotic essence of the film. The music was suitably eclectic, but not bad. The Last Poets' "Wake Up, Niggers," Jagger's own acerbic "Memo from Turner," and some very spacy, eerie sounds were all on the soundtrack.

The Last Poets invented rap music! Drawing upon African rhythms and traditions, they worked hard, not only in their music but also in their community, to stir up their black brothers and sisters to take control of their own lives. Part of their rhetorical strategy toward this goal was to refer to their black brothers and sisters relentlessly as "niggers," a provocative insult calculated to get attention, response, and action. Their eponymous first album contained spoken-word numbers with titles like "Run, Nigger," "Niggers Are Scared of Revolution," "Black Thighs," "Wake Up, Niggers," "Black Wish," "When the Revolution Comes," and lyrics to match. No bullshit, just the ugly truth as they saw it. The Last Poets pulled no punches.

Other black groups may have been just as angry as the Last Poets were about racism and other injustices, but in general they did not express their anger quite so forcefully. A case in point would be the Temptations' new single, "Ball of Confusion," which complained in a fairly gentle way about the world's ills.

Creedence Clearwater Revival's fifth LP in two years, *Cosmo's Factory*, showed the band at higher levels of musical intensity and sociopolitical activism. It not only rocked harder than any of their previous four, it also exposed more raw nerves. Their cover of Bo Diddley's "Before You Accuse Me" attacked hypocrisy — an easy target, but some of Fogerty's own lyrics were more subtle. "Lookin' Out My Back Door" was a cheerleading song of leaving trouble behind and keeping hope alive. "Run Through the Jungle" recounted the horror of trying to escape being caught in — or drafted into — an immoral, senseless war. "Up Around the Bend" expressed a similar theme of desperate escape, preferring a bucolic life of song and story to an industrialized, urban life which would lead eventually, perhaps imminently, to war and ruin. Also similarly, "Long as I Can See the Light" urged us to keep moving.

The most important song in Creedence's history was "Who'll Stop the Rain?", in which Fogerty criticized the whole political enterprise and questioned the value of its fruits. With extensive metaphors and allusions in just twelve iambic hexameter lines, he implicated not only, though primarily, America, but also the U.S.S.R. and all other oversized, overbearing leviathans. What did he see in Virginia? Was the "tower" the Pentagon, the biblical Tower of Babel, or some third thing? What-ever it was, it was against the best interests of the people, the real people, as he made clear in the third verse. The rain would not wash the tower away, would not save us, but would only make it wet, slippery, and more dangerous.

Rain was a metaphor for violence. The idea was that violence spares no one. When it rains, everyone gets wet; when anyone is violent; everyone gets hurt. This usage went back at least as far as Dylan's "A Hard Rain's A-Gonna Fall" in 1963, but it really caught on with Creedence's "Who'll Stop the Rain?" Lyrics aside, the haunting three-note closing riff, B - low G - high G, was sufficient to get the point across. Fifteen years later on his solo album, *Centerfield*, John Fogerty used the same three-note riff to close his nostalgic song about the fifties, sixties, and early seventies, "I Saw It on TV." No three notes were ever so evocative. They told the whole story of how little progress we had made since the sixties toward ending violence. The first time I ever heard "I Saw It on TV," I could not help bursting into tears as soon as those three notes sounded.

"Who'll Stop the Rain?" presented us a challenge. The first verse depicted a longstanding world of disorder and illogic wrought by violence and suggested that its remedy would lie at the end of a neoplatonic quest for ultimate goodness and bounty, the *summum bonum* of logic and coherence, represented by the sun. In the second verse Fogerty revealed the self-delusion, self-corrosion, and self-enslavement that we suffer by believing the rulers' lies, from Stalin to FDR to the Vietnam War mongers. The third verse surely referred to Woodstock. The chal-lenge was to bring from among ourselves a Woodstock-inspired *Zeitgeist* to over-come the belligerent dissembling that had formed the dangerous contemporary world and create instead a peaceful world based on honesty and truth.

People want to "belong," so they join gangs and clubs, develop mecha-nical loyalties to their countries and religions, remain true to their families, clans, and tribes, and do other stupid, self-contradictory things that absolutely guarantee that they will never "belong." Anyone who is born human already, automatically "belongs." To align yourself with any smaller subset of humans thereby cuts you off from whatever portion of humanity is not in that subset. Just be yourself, a true individual, answering only to your own conscience, and you will always "belong" to the greatest possible group: the universal set of humans. Your essential humanity is more precious than being part of the Ummah or the Roman Catholic Church, the American or the Soviet citizenry, the white or the black race, the male or the female gender, or any other domineering subset that insists that you must "belong." Do not reject your humanity. If you join or otherwise find yourself a member of any group, do not take it seriously. Remember always that you are human first. If you let that be your guiding principle, then you will always "belong." Dave Ma-son's album, *Alone Together*, especially the songs "Look at You Look at Me," "Only You Know and I Know," and "World in Changes," underscored this point of universal human "belonging."

Alone Together may have been the most warmly and deeply human album of the era. Each of its songs emphasized, described, or advocated an attractive hu-man trait. "Only You Know and I Know" told of the purity of honest love. "Can't

Stop Worrying, Can't Stop Loving" urged hard inner struggle so as not to forsake one's dreams. "Waitin' on You" alluded to the value of trust. "Shouldn't Have Took More Than You Gave" attacked greed. "World in Changes" promoted lifelong learning. "Sad and Deep as You" suggested the importance of discovering each other's emotions in order to get to know and understand each other. "Just a Song" stressed the power of music as the natural human unifier. "Look at You Look at Me" endorsed serenity as a worthy goal and encouraged active participation in the world as a means to achieve it.

Now down to a trio without Mason, Traffic released *John Barleycorn Must Die*, which may have been their best album. It was certainly their most political. "Glad," a jaunty six-and-a-half-minute instrumental, segued perfectly into "Freedom Rider," celebrating the steadfast optimism of the American civil rights workers who risked, and sometimes lost, their lives in the struggle for justice, equality, and human solidarity. "Empty Pages" reminded us of how friendly emotional support can revive our spirits when we feel lost, overwhelmed, or frustrated. "Stranger to Himself" described a tormented soul, apparently alone, without either purpose or friendly emotional support. "John Barleycorn" was Traffic's remake of a centuries-old English folk song. It was either pro-alcohol or anti-alcohol, depending on how the listener heard it. "Every Mother's Son" (not to be confused with "Some Mother's Son" on the Kinks' *Arthur*) was a song of persistence, hope, and expectation.

If any of the flower children deserved to be taken more seriously — much more seriously — than they were, it was Melanie. Her little-girl-innocent looks did not always serve her well. She was an astute psychosocial and political observer, a fine poet, and an accomplished musician with a beautiful voice. She was not the cutesy pop star that many took her to be. Even her cutsiest songs had deeper, often Freudian, meanings. "Brand New Key," for example, was about discovering sex. The zenith of her antiwar and social revolutionary credentials was achieved in her third album, *Candles in the Rain*, for which she wrote seven of the nine songs. The other two were sensitive covers of James Taylor's "Carolina in My Mind" and the Jagger/Richards classic, "Ruby Tuesday." The very fact that she, a woman, covered a Rolling Stones song went far toward redeeming the Stones in the eyes of feminists. Granted, she did not cover a misogynist lyric like "Stupid Girl" or "Under My Thumb," but rather a tribute to a strong, independent, uninhibited woman. Among her own songs, the metaphor of "Candles in the Rain" / "Lay Down (Candles in the Rain)" was clear enough. Light, illumination, and enlightenment are delicate and can easily be extinguished by violence, ignorance, or apathy. Better to light a candle than curse the darkness, and better to come in out of the rain than let violence either kill you outright or poison your spirit. "Leftover Wine" was her plea for people to share life's bitterness as well as its joys, and thus more profoundly develop their humanity. "What Have They Done To My Song, Ma?" decried the ill effects of various sides of society monkeying with individual freedom. Her libertarianism was showing early. Her new single, "Peace Will Come" — which she originally wanted to call "According to Plan" and which is sometimes listed as "Peace Will Come" ("According to Plan)" — quickly became an anthem. In October she would sing it on *Ed Sullivan* and in December it would become the centerpiece of her next album, *Leftover Wine*, the only studio cut on what was otherwise a live recording of a Carnegie Hall performance. "Peace Will Come" regarded peace on earth as in tune with the natural forces of cosmic harmony.

Three funny singles struck our fancy, providing harmless little fantasies of the gentle, lighthearted side of life: "Gimme Dat Ding" by the Pipkins was a crazy dance tune built around a hot boogie woogie piano riff. "In the Summertime" by Mungo Jerry recounted in jug band style the pleasures of happy-go-lucky working-class seaside party boys cruising for women, drinks, and food. Randy Newman's "Mama Told Me Not to Come," covered by Three Dog Night, depicted a naive bumpkin caught up in the ultrasophisticated phoniness of the urban *nouveaux riches*.

Blues Image's "Ride, Captain, Ride" was a song about freedom. Its message — ably given in the extended metaphor of the seventy-three sailors entering the Pacific from San Francisco Bay — was that only small fraction of humanity would ever be capable of finding the true enlightenment and perfect freedom of love and friendship, the rest being too slavishly entrenched, too occupied with the mundane concerns and minutiae of material existence, to notice their unique spiritual opportunity just to pick up, leave it all behind, and escape to a happier, more meaningful, more satisfying life. Again, to be free, all you have to do is — be free! Be bold! Live it! Do it! Don't ask permission now; ask forgiveness later.

"The Long and Winding Road," the single from the *Let It Be* album, was sufficiently sad to reflect our feelings about the end of the Beatles. Yet also, in an uncanny way, it was a song of hope, hinting that, because of the Beatles, things had become somehow better, and could even stay so for a while.

Dylan's four-sided *Self Portrait* was difficult to take seriously. Whether he was enjoying a private joke at our expense or just jerking us around, we, fans and critics alike, found little that we ourselves could enjoy here. We knew that Dylan was a shape shifter, but we could not reconcile this new, frivolous, affected country singer and tune coverer with the thought-provoking antiwar troubadour and poet of the early and mid-sixties. Maybe he was a charlatan after all.

The Grateful Dead's fifth LP, *Workingman's Dead*, was full of gems like "Uncle John's Band," "Dire Wolf," "New Speedway Boogie," "Cumberland Blues," "Black Peter," and "Casey Jones" that no self-respecting Deadhead would not love. Of course, these songs were about drugs, deception, lowlifes, and sleaze — but all done with high musicality and good humor. That is what the Dead did. They were not the best at what they did; they were the only ones who did what they did.

But the summer's most eagerly awaited album was the *Woodstock* soundtrack — and it did not disappoint. Much music from the movie was not on this six-sided album, and some from the album was not in the movie; so, altogether, the movie and the album were two quite different experiences. The album even contained some contrived segues, clever edits, and other brilliantly manufactured stuff that had not even been heard at the festival itself, such as the bridge from CSNY's "Wooden Ships" to the Who's "We're Not Gonna Take It."

One particularly motivating segment on side two of the album had Joan Baez's sideman, Jeffrey Shurtleff, giving a little talk about draft resistance while he introduced their next tune, "Drug Store Truck Drivin' Man," which, appropriately enough, he dedicated to "Ronald Ray Guns." Shurtleff claimed that the draft resistance movement was unique in the sense that it had "no enemies." While Shurtleff himself may indeed have had "no enemies," he obviously remembered with some bitterness Reagan's coldblooded reaction against the People's Park initiative and his complicity in the murder of James Rector.

Little bits and pieces of more and more recordings of Woodstock music, such as 1971's four-sided *Woodstock Two*, with selections by Hendrix, the Airplane, Butterfield, Baez, CSNY, Melanie, Mountain, and Canned Heat, soon began to dribble out — and continue to do so even to the present, more than forty years after the fact, September 2009! — but this first LP, the six-sided soundtrack, was from the outset the definitive, iconic, canonical anthology of Woodstock audio.

Whatever our detractors might say, Woodstock was about music, freedom, solidarity, shared humanity, and shared vision, not drugs. It was a spiritual event, not a soulless, self-congratulatory, hedonistic carnival like the two subsequent so-called "Woodstocks" in 1994 and 1999.

Perhaps our best argument against drug use was the obvious deterioriation of Sly Stone. In just two years we watched him publicly decline from the bright, upbeat young man whom we had seen on *Ed Sullivan* and at Woodstock into the paranoid, undependable, unsympathetic turd that he was throughout the seventies. The Family Stone was no good after this. They released a *Greatest Hits* LP and re-released "Higher." Because of Sly's drugs, they were finished.

The Kinks' classic single, "Lola," about an innocent lad who got seduced by a drag queen — and liked it, marked their re-entry into the top echelon of important rock artists. With albums like *Lola Versus Powerman and the Moneygoround*, *Muswell Hillbillies*, *Preservation: Act 1*, *Schoolboys in Disgrace*, *Sleepwalker*, *Misfits*, *Low Budget*, and *State of Confusion*; and with songs like "Apeman," "20th Century Man," "Skin and Bone," "Alcohol," "Celluloid Heroes," "One of the Survivors," "Everybody's a Star (Starmaker)," "Education," "No More Looking Back," "Life on the Road," "Life Goes On," "Rock and Roll Fantasy," "Permanent Waves," "Attitude," "Catch Me Now I'm Falling," "(Wish I Could Fly Like) Superman," "Little Bit of Emotion," "Around the Dial," "Destroyer," and "Living on a Thin Line," they would stay solidly there until the mid-eighties. In that period we could always depend upon them for incisive satire, intelligent lyrics, driving rock, subtle harmonies, clever arrangements, and sincere emotion. They did not have consistent commercial success during these fifteen years, but we consistent and serious rock music fans paid consistent and serious attention to them — and that was what mattered.

Access to all this music and more grew by leaps and bounds in the Philadelphia area after Michael Tearson, a University of Pennsylvania alumnus who had cultivated his extraordinarily wide and deep knowledge of music by playing underground rock at WXPN since 1967, became the music director of WMMR-FM. MMR, as we affectionately called it, had the coolest station promos, many of them parodies of popular songs. For example, to the tune of "Don't Let It Bring You Down," we heard a wailing, whining voice reminiscent of Neil Young: "Old man lyin' by the side of the road with a radio in his paw-aw / Listenin' to WMMR in

Philadelphi-aw-aw / He's sick of those AM DJ boys and he's sick of their music too-oo / He got himself an FM set and he'll show you what to doo-oo / Don't let it bring you down, it's only AM radio / So get yourself an FM, and you will come around."

Ω

Patton notwithstanding, in 1970 we were as awash in antiwar movies as we had been in prowar movies in 1963. Two of the most interesting were *Kelly's Heroes* and *Catch-22*, both dark comedies.

So far known mainly for cowboy roles like Rowdy Yates in 217 episodes of CBS TV's *Rawhide* and various heroes in Sergio Leone's so-called "spaghetti westerns," and not yet known for Dirty Harry, Clint Eastwood starred in the title role of *Kelly's Heroes* as a renegade private who had been busted down from lieutenant because the top brass needed a fallguy for their mistake. His platoon saw itself as "tourists" in France and preferred to use Michelin guides rather than military maps or orders to plot its course. For three months his division, the 35th Infantry, had slogged its way inland from Omaha Beach, always in the front lines, and now, in September 1944, was pushing toward Nancy. He and his comrades in arms were angry because they were in harm's way more often and more urgently than Patton's Third Army, which had come in later but was getting the lion's share of the glory, prostitutes, booze, and loot. Kelly's out-of-touch captain, the general's nephew, looted an entire yacht while blithely reminding his men that the penalty, if they were to loot anything, would be death.

Kelly captured and interrogated a Nazi colonel and learned from him of a $16,000,000 stash of gold bullion. Kelly convinced his platoon, his sergeant (Big Joe, played by Telly Savalas), and two other sergeants (Crapgame, the greedy quartermaster played by Don Rickles, and Oddball, the Sherman tank enthusiast anachronistically played as a hippie by Donald Sutherland) to follow him AWOL and steal this gold. They figured that there would be no more danger to their lives in robbing a bank behind enemy lines and hightailing it to Switzerland than in what they had already been doing — and this time they would be doing it for themselves rather than because they were ordered.

By a series of subversions in defiance of the Allied chain of command, Kelly and Oddball succeeded in breaking past the Nazis, thus creating a salient then a breach through which bombastic Major General Colt (played by Carroll O'Connor as a foreshadowing of his famous Archie Bunker character) led the entire 35th. Kelly's feat was thus the ironic ultimate in "private vice, public virtue," as Bernard Mandeville put it in *The Fable of the Bees*. Colt believed that Kelly *et al.* were true war heroes. He had no idea of their actual intentions, or that by collaborating with a Tiger tank commander, they had succeeded in stealing the gold and had made good their escape and desertion.

Mike Nichols directed his third film, *Catch-22*, in a markedly different way from his first two, playing fast and loose with chronology to create a sur-realistic fabrication of unexpected flashbacks and cut forwards, repeated scenes, dreamlike sequences, and illogical tableaux, all of which together presented the impression of uncontrolled yet intelligible chaos in the waning months of World War II. The obvious influence of Fellini and Antonioni on Nichols became more pronounced as the film proceeded. His overarching theme was the absurd contra-diction between natural humanity and unnatural military fixations on power and money. This theme was intimated in the opening vista, a beautiful, serene, Medi-terranean sunrise shattered by the deafening snarl of war machines. The military-industrial complex's love of money and its attendant indifference to human life was illustrated in greedy entrepreneur Lieutenant Milo Minderbinder (Jon Voight) and greedy customer Colonel Cathcart (Martin Balsam) not interrupting their busi-ness conversation — or even batting an eye — as one of their own planes crashed in a fatal fireball within a stone's throw of them. Milo routinely endangered his fellow soldiers by stealing parachutes, morphine, diesel engines, and other essen-tials from the army so that he could trade these items as commodities to make — money. For him, human life itself was just another commodity whose significance paled beside that of — money. He called an air raid on his own base as part of a business deal with the Nazis. Cathcart ordered his squadron to bomb innocent Italian civilians in a town that he knew to be non-military, just because his superior, Ge-neral Dreedle (Orson Welles) wanted to enjoy "a nice tight bombing pattern" in the aerial reconnaissance photos. But the real power was held, not by staff officers like Cathcart and Dreedle, but by the wheeler-dealer lieutenant who controlled the — money. Deaths were nothing to Milo as long as he and his shareholders got rich. At the end of the film, the planes, the vehicles, the MPs, the uniforms, etc., of the most powerful Americans in Europe bore the insignia, not of the U.S. Army, but of Milo's syndicate. "*What's good for* M+M *Enterprises* **IS GOOD** FOR THE **WORLD**" said the sign over the bed of Nately's whore (Gina Rovere) in the slums of Rome. *Geld über Alles!*

The opening song, "Question," on the Moody Blues' sixth LP, *A Question of Balance*, frankly blamed greed for all the world's ills. The singer admitted utter confusion about how to abolish greed and thus save the world from war and hatred. Many leftists at that time equated greed with capitalism, and thus resolved to abolish capitalism and fulfill Marx's prophecy. Yet to make that equation, or even to reduce capitalism to institutionalized greed, was politically oversimple and historically inaccurate. There are many kinds of greed that have nothing to do with capitalism. Also, not everything about capitalism is bad. It is, for example, an excellent way to fund the startup and maintenance of businesses and innovations. Everyone could benefit from such a system. Nevertheless, it is true that greedy people can thrive more easily in a capitalist system than in any other kind of financial or economic system, impoverishing the many, enriching the few, and eventually tearing society apart, instead of providing the means to comfort and financial security for all. For that reason alone, capitalism must always be closely monitored, carefully scrutinized, and strictly regulated, in order to keep the greedy in check and protect the people.

Liberal activist and current heartthrob Elliott Gould played an inveterate cunt man, or in "polite" but less accurate terms, a skirt chaser, in *Getting Straight*, a real downer of a film about disillusionment among leftist college students. Gould's character was an impoverished Vietnam veteran (a draftee), who had been active against the war, had been a spaced-out druggie, and claimed to have marched with King in Selma in 1965, but was now trying, not very hard, to get an M.A. in English and professional credentials so that he could teach. He did not really want to teach, and had no calling for it, but perceived a void in his spirit that he needed somehow to fill. Old enough to be trusted by the plastic people who ran the university, but still young enough and perhaps hip enough to be trusted by the student radicals, he got caught up in campus protests, riots, and police clashes, and had a chance to exercise his conscience for the good of all, but in the end failed to negotiate this middle ground, and turned out to be nothing more than an arrogant, amoral, self-righteous, misogynist asshole. Nevertheless, he won the heart of Candice Bergen's character. We could only assume that, with him, she would live miserably ever after.

Meanwhile, back in the real world, the Nixonians held the second draft lottery, with boys born on July 9, 1951, winning all-expenses-paid trips to Vietnam. The catch? They only had to risk their lives, shrivel their souls, and compromise their honor to participate in an immoral, futile, and disgusting war.

The persistence of the draft continued to inspire (or incite) grassroots antidraft activities. This summer, nationwide, local resistance and antiwar groups hosted what we called "resistance picnics," i.e., free block parties that brought people together for consciousness raising, counseling, and education about the draft — and fun. A typical advertisement for such an event was a psychedelic yellow, orange, brown, and black poster for the August 22 picnic at 36th and Hamilton in the Powelton Village section of Philadelphia, just north-northwest of Drexel University. It showed a huge omega framing a clenched fist — Power to the People! — and proclaimed, "Resistance Celebration, Fun, Corn on the Cob, Films, Food, Watermelon, Music, Games!" I do not recall there having been any films, but everything else was as advertised. It was free, peaceful, orderly, well attended — and fun!

Why would anyone ever want to look like everyone else? Why would anyone ever put up with being made to look like everyone else? That is not freedom! The reasons for not wanting to be in the armed forces were aesthetic as well as moral. Moral first, indeed, but also aesthetic. Uniforms! Ugh! That is why I hated tie dye and blue jeans. I wanted to look like myself, not like everyone else.

Edwin Starr's "War" was a stark, blunt, unequivocal statement of the utter futility, counterproductivity, evil, and irrationality of trying to solve any problems at all by resorting to war. We were heartened to know that a black man had leaped so fully into the antiwar movement. Generally, heretofore, the civil rights activists had been black and the antiwar activists had been white. Overlap was growing. The more of that the better.

The Strawberry Statement was a dreadful mess of a movie, the worst cinematographic exploitation of the so-called "counterculture" since *Wild in the Streets*. It pretended to be a docudrama, or rather, the film of James Simon Kunen's autobiographical account of student protests at Columbia University from March to

May 1968, but was so full of inaccuracies and anachronisms that it was practically worthless as a representation of historical events. The story was transposed to San Francisco and set subsequent to the Sharon Tate murder of August 9, 1969. Its characters were exaggerated, stereotyped, or cartoonish. The filmmakers plainly wanted to show leftist college students in the worst possible light, but they did this in such a klutzy, unrealistic, and sensational way that they succeeded only in making laughingstocks of themselves. To begin with, we knew that the title was derived from Columbia University Vice Provost Herbert Deane's remark that students' political opinions meant as little to him as their opinions of strawberries. Therefore, to set the plot in California was ridiculous. The very title shouted, "Columbia!" The screen might have been showing fall 1969, but we were seeing spring 1968.

The Strawberry Statement was to accuracy about student protests as *Reefer Madness* was to accuracy about marijuana. Both were essentially just inept, idiotic, wrongheaded propaganda films. *The Strawberry Statement* should either not have been made at all or made specifically about Columbia, as in the book.

So, there we were, sitting in the theater, minding our own business, watching the film, when all of a sudden those kids started singing "Give Peace a Chance." We were at once amazed, amused, and angry: "Hey, fuck this! That song wasn't even out yet in spring 1968!" We all knew the Beatles, and which of their songs came out when. To be off by a few months was forgivable, but to be off by over a year just plain sucked. *The Strawberry Statement* lost at that point any credibility it may ever have had. How could we trust the historicity or insight of any film that contained such a gigantic and obvious mistake? Anachronism is just plain sloppy, and never speaks well of its perpetrator.

That was not *The Strawberry Statement*'s only musical anachronism, but just the most glaring.

From a more levelheaded and true-to-life perspective, CSNY responded quickly and angrily to the Kent State murders of May 4. Young wrote "Ohio" around May 14 after Crosby showed him graphic photos of the event; CSNY recorded it on May 15; and it was available for airplay and sales nationwide within seven weeks. Its lyrics relayed the horror of finding innocent, unarmed citizens murdered by government troops in full battle gear, and strongly suggested that Nixon himself condoned such horror. When some commercial AM radio stations banned it as being too negative, too radical, too antiwar, too anti-Nixon, too honest, or whatever, this censorship only enhanced for us the credibility of college radio and underground FM stations, which were unanimously proud to play it.

Fanatics never understand the value of the marketplace of ideas. They would rather just kill and have done with it. They do not listen to anything that they do not want to hear, lest it may change their minds. Even worse, they do not let their kids hear anything that does not serve the cause of indoctrinating them into this same fanaticism or that might make them question the indoctrination they have already received. Kill the opposition and teach your children to kill the opposition. Preserve the patriotic purity of narrow-mindedness.

Joe was *Easy Rider* seen from the other side. Susan Sarandon took the role analogous to Peter Fonda's, a wide-eyed innocent runaway, a stereotypical flower child, a rich business executive's daughter, who had fallen in with a mean, sleazy heroin dealer. We easily saw why she had run away. Her parents were nothing but empty promises, shallow priorities, materialistic values — and they did not even love each other very much. She was only searching for a better life, not governed by money, but her desperation had just led her to a worse one. Her naïveté should have been disarming, but it had little effect on anyone.

Her father burglarized her apartment, murdered her junkie boyfriend, then took refuge in a bar where at once he began to make friends with Joe, a loudmouth, middle-aged, beer-swilling, blue-collar bigot bragging about how much he would enjoy killing nigger-loving, queer, America-hating, liberal, hippie bastards. Their shared hatred made them soulmates despite their intractable class differences. Joe admired the father, Bill, as a true American hero because, whereas Joe only talked and fantasized about killing a hippie, Bill had actually done it. Joe embodied the intimate relationship among hatred, conformity, and hypocrisy. He railed against the drugs, wild parties, and casual sex of the hippie lifestyle, but then gladly indulged in all three as soon as the opportunity presented itself. Joe and Bill hung out like old buddies, discussing the futility of their respective lives. They went hunting together, first for Bill's daughter in Greenwich Village, then upstate for the three hippies who stole their wallets. On the prowl, the gun-loving World War II Pacific Theater veteran Joe was in his element. Joe had loads of fun killing five hippies in cold blood, shooting three of them in back. Then Bill got into it, killing four more. The last one, shot in the back, was his daughter.

The film was populated with caricatures, yet strong caricatures, from whom lessons could be drawn. Despite their various drug dependencies, amorality, and general decadence, the film's hippies, mainly because of their non-belligerence, made more sense than Joe, Bill, and the film's other establishment types. They were indeed sneaky, selfish, and sly, but categorically unwilling to use force, even when cornered by deadly adversaries.

Regular guys like Joe, on the other hand, are always willing to use force, for any reason, or for no reason at all. They enjoy using force. Physical violence, as the most immediate, visceral expression of the prearticulate, universal hatred they naturally feel because they cannot understand, is all they understand. Their whole life's logic revolves around the *ad baculum* fallacy, the idea that if they are willing to use force, then they must be right. Such people are so illogical, so subhuman, that they cannot construct, follow, or even recognize a genuinely rational argument. They spontaneously gravitate toward the political right, where instinctive militarism provides an obvious haven for their seething hatred of anything better than they are, encourages their basest fears, and approves their violent dispositions with clear purpose, regimented support, and definite targets.

Joe was a very important film from a sociological perspective. It showed how the rich right, which is generally contemptuous of the working class, manages to attract working-class men to support its political agenda. Given that the ultimate goal of the rich right in every single one of its endeavors is solely to maximize its own financial gain, it must necessarily see the working class as its tool, not as either humans or natural allies. But, given that it needs allies outside its relatively small circle to swell its constituency — but not its numbers — in order to secure its position of wealth and power; and given its natural pragmatism, cynicism, and self-righteousness; it pretends not to be against the working class, or pretends to believe that the working class consists of humans; and it invents issues, fabricates crises, and starts wars, all calculated to appeal to the primal male instinct to attack and kill, and thus to attract to its side the strong working-class men who revel in this instinct. Even though it itself abhors merely physical action, fancying itself too civilized for such mindless pursuits, it recognizes that having goons to support it is essential for its own survival as a privileged class, so it panders to the goons. It counts on the working class never figuring out what its true agenda is. History so far has shown the rich right almost entirely successful in this beguiling of the working class. Yet the fact is that the working class has nothing substantial to achieve by supporting the rich right. Even though the very idea that further enriching the rich helps the working class by creating jobs is illogical, mean-spirited, and condescending, the rich right has been quite successful in promulgating and implementing this idea. The so-called "trickle-down" economics that union-busting Ronald Reagan established in the eighties was nothing other than the standard capitalist strategy that had already been in effect for centuries. What "trickle down" really means is that the rich right stands on top of the heap and pisses, so that everyone below them gets pissed on and eventually those at the bottom of the heap find themselves wallowing in piss.

Reactionary Neanderthals like Joe in real life accused us peace freaks of hating America, because we did not support the war in Vietnam. We did not hate America. We did not hate much of anything except war, violence, intolerance — and LBJ for having gotten us into this mess in the first place. Hatred was the province of more militant groups like the Weathermen. We were not Weathermen. Nonviolence was our strength. Analogous to Shakespeare's Brutus, who defended his part in the murder of Caesar by asserting that he did not love Caesar less, but loved Rome more, we acted against the war not because we loved America less, but because we loved humanity more. The Weathermen were more like Shakespeare's Cassius.

Fall 1970

Power to the people!

> Progress, far from consisting in change, depends on retentiveness. When change is absolute there remains no being to improve and no direction is set for possible improvement: and when experience is not retained, as among savages, infancy is perpetual. Those who cannot remember the past are condemned to repeat it.
> — George Santayana, *The Life of Reason* (1905)

Some members of my generation believed that, because our freaky new way of life was so obviously superior to that of our elders and our straight contemporaries, all we had to do was tell them, show them, make them understand, and they would instantly drop all their old traditions and join us. Yes, some of us really were that naive. The problem, in their starry little eyes, was not that there might be legitimate counterarguments to our way of life, but only that straight America was too pigheaded to listen to us. If straight America ever did listen to us, it would, as if suddenly enlightened, see the error of its former ways and become part of freak America. Or so the Pollyannian flower children among us supposed.

There was some truth, but not a lot, in what these latter-day Candides and Panglosses believed about the natural ability of our message to present itself and create converts without much effort on our part. Their artless assumption that our new way was the only way to peace, freedom, and harmony; their uncritical and generally insufficient appreciation of history; and their inability to discern legitimate counterarguments — these defects were their undoing, and contributed much to the gradual undoing in the seventies and eighties of our open-minded leftism. People began to laugh at us for our shallowness.

Yes, some of us were shallow, very shallow, and those shallow ones gave our movement a bad name. They blew themselves out with drugs, astrology, the occult, or wacko religions, and did not comprehend practical politics, practical philosophy, or any other discipline that might have helped to bring the world around to our peaceful, musical, poetic, tolerant way of thinking.

But most of us were not shallow at all. Our "Make Love, Not War" alternative way of life was rational. We lacked only a clear means to communicate it. We knew what it was ourselves, but we could not easily express it for others. Perhaps it is more honest to say that we did not really know what it was, because, if we had really known, then we would have been able to communicate it — and convert the world. Unless one can express what one knows, and communicate it widely, clearly, and in all its depth, then one does not really know; one only intuits. Intuition is not enough on which to base a society.

Our principles needed to be written down. Unwritten, they were too fragile. Documents like the Port Huron Statement and the Yippie Manifesto were insufficient because they were too specific. We were more concerned to change humans themselves than particular political situations. Ethical codes tended to be tied to particular systems or religions. We needed a simple, universally appealing, transcultural declaration. Why it was never written I cannot imagine. Among its listed principles would have been:

Be a citizen of the world before being a citizen of any particular country.

Be a human before being a member of either gender, any race, any organization, or any other group, whether naturally or artificially defined.

Be a child of God before being a member of any particular religion.

Elevate your own self-respect and human dignity in general by refusing to dress, act, think, talk, write, eat, walk, or live as anyone else tells you.

Do anything you want, as long as it hurts no one else and does not detract from the general welfare.

Maintain healthy skepticism toward authority.

Never obey a person, but obey only and always the dictates of your own conscience. A useful tool for developing the skill of recognizing and heeding the voice of conscience is Kant's categorical imperative, which, in two of its five formulations, says: "Act only so that you treat humanity as an end and never as a means." "Act only according to the maxims of the universal lawgiver in the potential realm of ends."

Be honest in all your dealings.

Judge people by their intellect, aesthetic sensitivity, and ethical character, not by their wealth, color, gender, position, age, nationality, ethnicity, sexual orientation, or social status.

Respect music as the universal language.

Promote all the creative, literary, intellectual, and practical arts.

Above all, the Golden Rule: Do unto others as you would have them do unto you.

These twelve principles, if put into effect, would prevent war, promote international, interracial, intergenerational, and intercultural understanding, and ensure cooperation and prosperity. That is what we meant by "Power to the People!"

The slogan "Power to the People!" originated as "All Power to the People!", coined by either Huey Newton or Bobby Seale shortly after they founded the Black Panthers in 1966. Soon white leftists were using it too. By the time Lennon did his song, "Power to the People," in early 1971, the phrase had become a tenet for anyone who opposed the racist, militaristic, plutocratic oligarchy. Power naturally belonged to the people, not to the confrontational pigs who routinely harassed the people. Pigs were not only subordinate functionaries like the police who brutalized Huey and other African-Americans in the streets of Oakland and attacked peaceful demonstrators in Selma, Chicago, and Washington. The real pigs, as Black Sabbath forcefully reminded us in "War Pigs," were the oligarchs themselves, the rich white men at the very top. As an antiwar anthem, "War Pigs" was especially effective in equating warmongering with satanic rituals and suggesting that God would judge and damn all the leaders who start wars, who send the poor and the powerless to fight and die, but who stay safe at home themselves, usually just getting richer.

The second Black Sabbath album, *Paranoid*, made clear that, in the minds of the band members, it was not they themselves who were satanic, evil, occultist, or deathmongering, but large industrialized nations like the United States, which — apparently just because they enjoyed it — made war on small agrarian nations like Vietnam. Equating America with Satan was Black Sabbath's stroke of satiric brilliance. They were not geniuses, but *idiots savants*. Their poetry was awful and their world view simplistic, but their message came through clearly enough. "War Pigs," driven by Ozzy's mighty lungs, was the gem of the album. Each of the other songs was at least as dark. The title cut told a harrowing story of a rejected lover's gradually losing his ability to feel emotion and thereby descending into madness. Musically, "Iron Man" resonated as an instant heavy metal classic, with amazing guitar licks from Tony Iommi and thrilling bass distortions from Geezer, but lyrically, it was just an insipid tale from a moronic comic book. "Electric Funeral," about nuclear holocaust, and "Hand of Doom," about death in general, added so much to the ghoulish ambiance that, by the end of side two, the semi-serious "Fairies Wear Boots" came almost as a relief.

Neil Young's "Southern Man" attacked the American South for its slave-holding past and racist present. But Neil made a mistake. He implied that the Bible prohibits slavery and racism. It does no such thing. That is all the more reason to treat the Bible as nothing special, to read it as a book like any other book, written by humans, a historical document, a record of its times, and nothing more.

"Southern Man" hit its anti-racist mark. The only rebuttal that the defensive children of the Confederacy could ever come up with was Lynyrd Skynyrd's pointless *ad hominem* attack in 1974's "Sweet Home Alabama." There has been speculation that Skynyrd's jibe at Young was a joke. Maybe we should give Skynyrd the benefit of the doubt. After all, they were from Florida, not Alabama, and Ronnie Van Zant would have had to be very stupid to think that he could refute the idea that Southern heritage is racist just by sneering at a Canadian who only mentioned it.

None of the other songs on Neil's third solo album, *After the Gold Rush*, rocked as hard as "Southern Man." Indeed, most of them were whiny ballads, with Neil's voice even higher and more quasi-falsetto than usual, again providing evidence for detractors who would brand him a wimp. "Tell Me Why" whined about loneliness. The title cut told a science fiction story of a human remnant fleeing our planet after a global environmental disaster. Within the relatively new genre of songs about escape from secular apocalypse, "After the Gold Rush" was less eloquent than "Wooden Ships" but more eloquent than "Ship of Fools." "Only Love Can Break Your Heart" was a mitigated song of diminished hope. "Don't Let It Bring You Down" was slightly, ever so slightly, more hopeful. "When You Dance You Can Really Love" explained itself in its title, and suggested that a bit more hope could be found in love. "I Believe in You" continued the crescendo of increasing hopefulness. Did "Cripple Creek Ferry" refer to the Band's "Up on Cripple Creek"? Why was that little Colorado town getting so much free publicity anyway?

While walking across the campus of Syracuse University in 1995 I heard *After the Gold Rush* blasting out the window of one of the undergraduate dorms. I was immediately struck by how powerful our generation's music is, to have such persistent appeal for those who were not yet born when it was recorded and released. Our parents' music could not match that power. Theirs was soft, pleasant, fluffy, melodic, and forgettable; ours was hard, edgy, substantial, rhythmic, and — evidently — memorable. I could not imagine the parallel situation of any undergraduate in 1970 blasting popular music from 1945 out the dorm window. We might have gone back as far as *Meet the Beatles*, but that would have been it.

Here is a corroborating anecdote: I know a person, born in 1990, who at sixteen was at least as savvy about contemporary music as I had been about my contemporary music when I was sixteen. His favorite song then was Metallica's "Master of Puppets," which came out in 1986, four years before his birth. I could not imagine either myself or anyone in my generation having a favorite song that had been released four years before any of our births. That is the power of rock! It is too energetic ever to get old.

Yet Jimi and Janis both died — at the wrong time — from drugs.

. Perhaps in part because of these early deaths, more fatalism was turning up in our music. The very title of George Harrison's triple solo album, *All Things Must Pass*, was a case in point. The title probably referred mainly to the demise of the Beatles, but surely it also had wider, more ominous, implications.

It surprised us somewhat that George, not John or Paul, created the best of the ex-Beatles' early solo works. Apparently he had stockpiled a wealth of material which, for whatever reasons, he did not record with the Beatles. Again, as he had already shown in "Think for Yourself," "Piggies," "Within You Without You," "While My Guitar Gently Weeps," and other songs, he proved himself quite capable of writing deep, incisive, and often witty lyrics. Among these nuggets of intelligence and sensitivity on *All Things Must Pass* were "Isn't It a Pity?", a lament that inhumanity and spiritual blindness form a vicious circle which prevents us from seeing the natural beauty in one another; "What is Life?", an optimistic promise of active, constant love; "Behind That Locked Door," an encouragement to let cheerfulness overcome sorrow; "Let It Down," a call to love, perhaps corollary to Paul's "Let It Be"; "Run of the Mill," an appeal to individualism and true freedom over against society's expected conformity; "Beware of Darkness," an epitome of the equanimity of Hindu philosophy; "Let It Roll," a jaunty reminder just to go blithely on about one's business, regardless of obstacles or disillusionments, again perhaps corollary to "Let It Be"; "Awaiting on You All," a statement of just how very simple true religion can be; "Art of Dying," an implicit invocation of Montaigne's essay, "To Philosophize is to Learn How to Die," and Socrates's antecedent declaration in the *Phaedo* of the same belief; and the title cut, which suggested that we could find happiness just by recognizing and quietly accepting the universal flow. Sides five and six were just for fun, full of crazy jams and weird licks.

John Lennon's new semi-solo album, *Plastic Ono Band*, contained his most blunt sociopolitical statements to date. His "Working Class Hero" took a clear position in the age-old class war, telling of how established society is a playground for aristocrats, plutocrats, and toadies, but hell for everyone else. Society is based on beating people down, bullying them both psychologically and physically until they conform, forget their natural inclinations toward kindness and sympathy, twist their human logic so that they see the upside-down world as right-side-up, and thus become willing to sell their souls for a few comforts. The idea of "equal opportunity" is only a bullshit myth with which the already-rich console themselves, or trick themselves into believing that their society is just and fair. It would be, if everyone were allowed the same start and forced to play by the same rules. But imagine, for example, six people playing Monopoly, but only two of the six being allowed to collect $200 salary whenever they pass Go, the other four getting only $50 each. Or imagine a fifty-yard dash in which some of the participants have to run seventy yards and a few ninety. That is the reality of "equal opportunity" in advanced industrial or post-industrial capitalist nations. Yes, anyone can make it, anyone can win, but some have farther to go than others. Yes, John himself was a very rich man, but an honest one who never forgot his working class roots.

His song, "God" was a keen little bit of theology. Defining God as a concept by which pain is measured was a stroke of genius. Indeed, if humans had never felt pain, loss, or melancholy, no need would have arisen for them to perceive, experience, or — as some say — invent God. This is not to say that God would not have "existed" without human pain, loss, or melancholy; but, without these feelings, humans would not have become emotionally or spiritually aware of God and, if they knew God at all, would have done so only intellectually, e.g., through Thomas Aquinas's five ways, Anselm's ontological argument, or Spinoza's *amor intellectualis Dei*.

John's litany of things in which he did *not* believe culminated in his having to believe at least in himself. Like Job, who lost everything else, he could not also lose himself as long as he was still alive. Lennon's song thereby reminded me of a sermon I heard in the mid-sixties by the Reverend Canon James Gillespie Birney of the Episcopal Diocese of Delaware. Birney argued progressively that if God, fate, bad luck, or any other agent were to take from him his home, his possessions, his family, his security, and even his happiness, then, in the end, he would still have himself as that which could not be taken from him — and then, miraculously, deep inside himself, he would find the vestige of God that would enable him to go on. Shades of Meister Eckhart's divine spark (*Fünklein*) and René Descartes's innate idea of God in the *Meditations*! Echoes of the "still small voice" that Elijah heard in 1 Kings 19:12! God was not in the earthquake, the fire, or any other gigantic, majestic, intimidating thing, but in the friendly voice of conscience. Similarly, God was not in the grandeur of Pope Paul VI, the bromides of Billy Graham, or the hellfire-and-brimstone bombast of fundamentalist preachers, but in the serene intuitions of mercy, truth, justice, goodness, and nonviolence as received privately through meditation, *satori*, prayer, or happenstance.

Culture critic Paul Swift believed the Beatles, especially "Dangerous John," to be philosophers in the Nietzschean sense, i.e., underminers, tunnelers, moles:

> Unlike the widely prevalent view that considers anyone who has a philosophy Ph.D. to be a philosopher, Nietzsche thought there was a dignity in philosophy to which thinkers needed to measure up. His view distinguishes philosophy scholars from genuine philosophers, as the latter frequently are not sanctioned by the ruling establishment (dominant state or religious powers). This type of philosopher is often perceived as dangerous, since this type of thinker frequently undermines accepted authorities in the quest for truth. ... By undermining the idea that institutionalized religions have a privileged access to divinity (above and beyond the individual), John Lennon suggested a new path in the quest for knowledge of God and self.
>
> As someone who embodied courage, strength, reflection, and personal freedom, John Lennon was a dangerous philosophic force ... Insofar as political and religious leaders are accepted authorities who want to rule over others and make them obey, this special type of philosophic individual poses a legitimate danger.[70]

The greatest among us were those who lived as if the revolution had already been won. They were the only ones who knew how to win the revolution. It could never be won by force, violence, confrontation, debate, or diplomacy. The superficial revolution might be won at the ballot box, but the deeper, more important revolution, i.e., the fundamental changing of human nature into a gentler, more civilized, more cooperative essence, could only be won by each individual freely and voluntarily changing her/himself into such a person. We could stimulate this change by each setting examples of how to live better, happier, more fulfilling lives. Then those on the other side would see us just living simple, happy lives, would come to envy our happiness, and would eventually want to abandon their stultifying, conservative, conformist, status-seeking traditions, all in order to be like us. They would at last realize that complex economy based on greed, exploitation, and war can never give them the happiness they seek. Only simple, fair, socialist economy based on respect for each other, for the arts, and for the world's natural beauty can do that. In other words, true happiness is spiritual, not material; contemplative, not calculative, meditative, not manipulative, and aesthetic, not commercial. It empowers and is empowered by the ethical character, not the instinct to dominate. It is not entirely passive, but is more yin-like than yang-like. It can never be correlated with wealth-based power. This idea is not part of the naive flower child syndrome. On the contrary, it is practical politics. It is that greatest of all oxymorons: honest

---

[70] Paul Swift, "The Beatles as Nietzsche's Music-Playing Socrates," in: *The Beatles and Philosophy*, edited by Michael and Steven Baur (Chicago: Open Court, 2006), p. 213.

politics. Just live the way you want to live, sit back, and see who joins you. Just be happier than they are. That is the way to win.

Nietzsche's will to power is the will to high cultural creativity and to the greatest possible realization of this creativity in the world-historical future. It is not the will to political, military, or economic power, or to any kind of domination, authority, or mastery over anyone else. It is the will to mastery of self.

Self-mastery included not being tempted by money. We identified success with happiness and redefined success as personal fulfillment rather than prosperity. It was grounded in the warmth of society, not in acquisition.

Changing human nature would be essential to eliminate fear from the school environment, the workplace, and everyday life in general. Everyday life is arranged in hierarchies of authority, and such hierarchies naturally breed fear because they naturally create distance and distrust between humans. We needed environments that would be more open, more friendly, and more flatly arranged, so that students, employees, and underlings of all sorts would actually have a say in what goes on in those environments. No one should have to live in habitual fear of one's boss, teacher, principal, parent, spouse, ruler, priest, or deity. No one should have to see any of these figures as absolutely authoritative. No one should have to cringe like the antiheroine of the forties-fifties radio comedy and fifties TV comedy, *Our Miss Brooks*. High school English teacher Connie Brooks lived in near poverty and in constant fear of her autocratic boss, principal Osgood Conklin, who controlled almost every aspect of her existence. She was utterly powerless. Yet she was brilliant and he was incompetent. The whole school would have gained if she had had more power and he less. Sad to say, *Our Miss Brooks* in its time was a rather accurate reflection of American secondary public schools. Their teachers and students in general needed to have more power and their administrators less.

But practically speaking, how would we have gone about trying to change human nature to a more benign, less selfish temperament? Were we after the best possible result or the best result possible? The more starry-eyed among us preferred the former, but the more realistic chose to restrict our expectations to specific changes in human nature that had already occurred in individuals. Because some individuals had already existed who had put lust, gluttony, sloth, wrath, greed, envy, and hubris behind them in favor of love, generosity, fruitfulness, equanimity, moderation, fellow-feeling, and self-respect, it was not unreasonable to expect more such individuals to come. To create conditions under which a higher percentage of humankind would consist of such individuals was an achievable goal. We needed more Gandhis and fewer Stalins; more poets, artists, writers, and musicians and fewer politicians; more gentle souls and fewer hardass business tycoons; and more people willing to accept everyone else as equal and free and fewer people stuck in the counterproductive and essentially violent mentality of master/servant, parent/child, employer/employee, or leader/follower hierarchies.

We also needed more comedians and fewer pontificators, more people who pretended to be stupid and silly, but were really intelligent and serious; and fewer people (mainly politicians, priests, military officers, and suit wearers) who took themselves oh-so-seriously and believed themselves to be oh-so-logical, oh-so-brilliant, and oh-so-valuable, but were really absurd and useless. Firesign Theatre helped in this regard. With their usual methodical chaos, these four loonies ridiculed militarism, our parents' generation's meddlesomeness, commercialism, paranoia, radio comedies such as *The Aldrich Family*, high school rivalries, evangelism, and many other American phenemena in their third LP, *Don't Crush that Dwarf, Hand Me the Pliers*. We did not know what the title meant, though we would speculate with reasonable certainty that it translated as something like, "Don't trash that last little bit of the joint, but hand me those needlenose pliers that I can use for a roach clip." Often spontaneously quoted in the street, at parties, and in dorms, this album became an even richer source of subcultural catchphrases, cliquish greetings, and in-jokes than their first two.

Jim Bickhart wrote in his liner notes to the Byrds' tenth album, the double *Untitled*:

> The problems of society are grossly large and painful, but the sickness is perhaps the healthiest agony yet endured by a modern civilization. There remains, at least, the chance that the best of all heretofore existing worlds may come out of it, and an important awareness, subconscious if not conscious, has already shown signs of becoming a permanent part of us. Awareness is an important term because it implies the beginnings of understanding. And awareness, as positively as it can be applied to today's youth (the people who have made the longer-than-you-think trek from John Kennedy's death through Monterey and the Haight-Ashbury Summer of Love to Orangeburg [South Carolina, February 8, 1968, murder of three protesters by police], People's Park, Woodstock, Altamont, Kent State and Jackson), owes one Hell of a lot to this rock and roll band called The Byrds.

Untitled marked their turn back from their country period again toward psychedelia. The first two sides were live; the last two in the studio. McGuinn co-wrote four of the songs with Jacques Levy, a very odd duck: a Ph.D. in psychology; a clinical psychoanalyst; the director of the nude revue, *Oh! Calcutta!*; a songwriting collaborator with McGuinn, Dylan, and a few others; and later a professor of English at Colgate University. Their "Chestnut Mare," a tall tale about one man's love affair with a horse, was a big hit. Their "Lover of the Bayou," with its haunting bass line, challenged Creedence's supremacy in swamp rock. Their "Just a Season" asserted that life lived without purpose would not be worth living. Their "All the Things" grieved that some people are so involved in their work, business, or other gray artificialities that they develop spiritual myopia or tunnel-vision and never learn to love, or even notice, the natural world. Battin's and Kim Fowley's "You All Look Alike" condemned the violence that conformity does to both the individual and society. Battin's, Fowley's, and McGuinn's "Hungry Planet" imagined what might happen if the earth struck back against the industrialists who were raping it and plundering its resources. The group's cover of Leadbelly's "Take a Whiff on Me" sounded like it should have been a mainstream advertisement for cocaine — if there were such ads. Their sixteen-minute jam on "Eight Miles High," especially Skip's bass solo, was alone worth the price of the album.

The Kinks' concept album, *Lola Versus Powerman and the Moneygoround*, was a worthy follow-up to *Arthur*. Generally, in the tradition of the Stones' "Under-Assistant West Coast Promo Man" and the Byrds' "So You Want to Be a Rock 'n' Roll Star," it was an extended attack on the business end of the music industry, each song criticizing a different aspect: "The Contenders," the greed; "Strangers," the artists' surrender of ideals and principles; "Denmark Street," the music publishers; "Get Back in Line," the unions; "Top of the Pops," the ass-kissing; "The Moneygoround," the beancounters; "This Time Tomorrow," the rigors of the road; "A Long Way From Home," the loneliness and social alienation; "Rats," the backstabbing; and "Powerman," the boss. A few of the tunes did not quite fit this mold. "Lola" was about transvestism. "Apeman" went further than the Airplane's "The Farm" to suggest that the only way to be happy might be to abandon civilization and live a natural animal life in the woods. "Got to Be Free" needs no explanation. It was what it was and it said it all.

The title song of Quicksilver's *What About Me?* expressed what most of us by now clearly felt: alienation from and frustration with straight America. From several standpoints — environmentalist, pacifist, egalitarian, anti-corporate, and just plain rebellious — "What About Me?" harked back to the Yardbirds' "Over, Under, Sideways, Down" and a host of other rock songs to restate their common theme, namely, that what our parents saw as our failure to meet their expectations was in fact our success. Quicksilver's current single, "Fresh Air," was an environmentalist anthem that likened the experience of a clean outdoors to the intoxication of psychoactive drugs.

The overriding message of Spirit's fourth LP, *The Twelve Dreams of Dr. Sardonicus*, was environmentalist. "Nature's Way," "Nothin' to Hide," and "Animal Zoo" conveyed this message eloquently. The dirgelike "Soldier" could be heard as a rebuttal of Bobby Vinton's "Mr. Lonely" and was definitely antiwar. "When I Touch You" and "Morning Will Come" were hard-rocking love songs. "Love Has Found a Way," "Life Has Just Begun," and "Space Child" featured trippy *avant garde* experimentation. "Why Can't I Be Free?" was a soul-searching lament for one's apparently lost self. "Street Worm" was the first-person braggadocio of an urban working man. "Mr. Skin" was full of pop hooks and, along with "Nature's Way" and "Soldier," was soon released several times in 45 RPM format. The overall mood of *Sardonicus* was eclectic yet coherent and alluring.

Canned Heat's new single from *Future Blues*, a cover of Wilbert Harrison's "Let's Work Together," was a hard-hitting call to unity, solidarity, and cooperation.

The Stones brought out an energetic live album, *Get Yer Ya-Ya's Out*, which they recorded just eight and nine days before Altamont. It featured quite a bit of sexual banter between Jagger and the Madison Square Garden audience and included landmark versions of "Midnight Rambler," "Jumpin' Jack Flash," "Sympathy for the Devil," and "Street Fighting Man."

Out of its original context in *Tommy*, where it signified Tommy's self-revelation, the Who's "See Me, Feel Me" as a single seemed like just a wimpy cry for help. It was still great music, but, extracted from its dramatic setting, no longer asserted that ultimately one is and ought to be dependent only upon oneself. Rather, it now seemed — inaccurately — to portray a feeble soul floundering for deliverance among his fellows.

Nazz's third album, *Nazz III*, included "Loosen Up," a hilarious parody of Archie Bell's 1968 number one dance hit, "Tighten Up." They loosened up on the drums until they sounded like cardboard, on the bass until it sounded like rubber bands, on the guitar until it sounded like paper clips, and on the organ until it sounded like toy whistles — all while eating a tuna fish hoagie like good Philadelphians. They really got loose on that one, but the rest of the album was not much improved over the first two.

New Morning got Dylan back on track and redeemed him from *Self Portrait*. Its twelve songs revealed Dylan more soulful, heavy, and gutwrenching than he had been in a long time, with serious lyrics such as the *memento mori*, "Day of the Locusts," but with comic interludes too, such as "If Dogs Run Free."

With Country Joe himself and Barry ("The Fish") Melton as the only remaining original members, *CJ Fish*, the new LP from Country Joe and the Fish, was melodic but meandering and not especially memorable. It did not rock. The band did not last much longer.

In general, Pink Floyd's fourth LP, *Atom Heart Mother*, continued in the pastoral direction that, especially with tunes like "Grantchester Meadows," they had begun on *Ummagumma*. The main exception was "Alan's Psychedelic Breakfast," a minimally connected collage of *avant garde* sounds. We did not know who Alan was, but we later learned that he was one of Floyd's roadies, Alan Stiles.

In his second solo LP, *Chunga's Revenge*, Zappa was even more fixated on sex than usual and showed some movement away from satire toward raw comedy. This album marked the debut of Flo ("The Phlorescent Leech") and Eddie, i.e., Mark Volman and Howard Kaylan, respectively, from the Turtles, who used these stupid monikers because shysters prevented them from either using their own real names or even mentioning the Turtles.

The fourth Velvet Underground LP, *Loaded*, arguably their best, still achieved no commercial success. That such excellent work as this would fail to crack even the top 200 on the *Billboard* album charts boggles the mind and nearly causes one to lose faith in the intelligence and discernment of the American record-buying public, even then, when we were more savvy about music than we are in the twenty-first century. Lou Reed wrote all the songs on *Loaded* but Doug Yule sang most of them. Great hooks! "Who Loves the Sun," a pop ditty, sounded like the AM radio hit that it never was. "Sweet Jane," a vignette of urban perversion and loneliness sung by Lou, would ironically make posthumous stars of the Velvets when Mott the Hoople covered it on *All the Young Dudes* in 1972. Lou also sang "Rock and Roll," which explained in clear terms the central role of music in making life worth living. "Cool It Down" was about poverty and prostitution. "New Age" satirized groupies, fans, and ravers. "Head Held High" used dancing as a metaphor to suggest the futility of being unrealistically optimistic. "Lonesome Cowboy Bill" (which Zappa would parody as "Lonesome Cowboy Burt" in 1971 on *200 Motels*), painted an amusing portrait of a rodeo rider. "Train Round the Bend" rejected rural life for urban existence. "I Found a Reason" and "Oh! Sweet Nuthin'" were soft ballads.

Led Zeppelin III, their third album in less than two years, featured twirly rotating cover art that stoners could play with like little kids. Excepting "Immigrant Song" and a few others, its songs were generally less heavy and more melodic than those on the first two albums. This group had depth, versality, and dynamics!

Santana's second album, *Abraxas*, not only continued to develop the band's unique fusion of jazz influences, Latin rhythms, and Chicano culture, but also even more solidly established Carlos Santana as a guitar hero, particularly through their current single, "Black Magic Woman." The word "abraxas" seems to be a common misspelling of "abrasax," which denotes any of several occult motifs in Greek Gnosticism and medieval mysticism. Carlos was apparently quite taken with that sort of stuff.

Still in their very listenable pre-disco days, the Bee Gees offered "Lonely Days," an evocative and exceptionally well constructed pop song. It twice moved from a listless, melancholy verse into a rousing chorus, simulating the range and progress of emotions in crescendo from abject loneliness, even amid material prosperity, to the natural joy of human company and romantic encounter.

The Dead kept getting better and better. Just four months after they released *Workingman's Dead*, they topped it with *American Beauty*. Who would have thought that they could top *Workingman's* at all, let alone so soon?! All ten tunes were original, and at least seven became classics: "Box of Rain," "Friend of the Devil," "Sugar Magnolia," "Candyman," "Ripple," "Brokedown Palace," and "Truckin'." Topics included despair, free love, bigamy, lust, revenge, jealousy, hatred, poverty, gambling, loneliness, police harassment, and of course, drugs. The title metaphor of "Ripple" referred to music's uncanny power to alter stillness, invade minds, and create unpredictable results.

The Allman Brothers' second LP, *Idlewild South*, was noteworthy for the emergence of Dickey Betts as an entrancing melodic guitarist. His "In Memory of Elizabeth Reed" would prove to be a greater memorial to her than her gravestone in Rose Hill Cemetery, Macon, Georgia, where, just over a year later, Duane Allman would also lie.

Jorma and Jack splintered from the Airplane to do some acoustic blues. A story circulated that they had wanted to call their duo and their album Hot Shit, but RCA would not let them, hence Hot Tuna. We did not know whether this story was true, but we liked to believe it was. Anyway, *Hot Tuna* appeared with only minimal foreshadowing from what we had heard in the Airplane. It was a live gig, ten tunes recorded in Berkeley over a year prior. Highlights included "Hesitation Blues," a song of lust; "Uncle Sam Blues," a sarcastic recommendation that any man who wants to kill, loves war, or hates his own life should join the U.S. Army, where he would feel right at home; "Death Don't Have No Mercy," an eloquent, straighforward lament; "I Know You Rider," a virtuoso rendering of the frequently covered traditional tune; and "Mann's Fate," which, though an instrumental, surely referred to Thomas Mann.

As it turned out, *Volunteers* had been the last Jefferson Airplane album, at least for a while. With Spencer gone to drum for the New Riders, Jorma and Jack off doing Hot Tuna, Marty barely contributing, and Joey Covington recruited as the new drummer, the band had become effectively Paul's and Grace's, or, more accurately, just Paul's. He renamed it Jefferson Starship and recorded what was really a solo album, *Blows Against the Empire*, with primarily Grace and secondarily a horde of musicians like Jerry Garcia, David Crosby, Bill Kreutzman, Graham Nash, Jorma's younger brother Peter, Mickey Hart, and David Freiberg sitting in. From the title on down, it was even more frankly political than anything the Airplane had put out. Based loosely on Robert Heinlein's 1941 novel, *Methuselah's Children*, it was somewhere between a concept album and a rock opera, a science fiction tale of hijacking a spaceship to escape the corrupt Earth and begin a new, better life elsewhere in the galaxy.

Blows was didactic, so much so that in general its lyrics suffered from the reciprocal flaw of all didactic poetry, i.e., in the words of Edgar Wind in *Art and Anarchy*, reason got in the way of art and art got in the way of reason. "Mau Mau (Amerikon)" noted the sharp differences in attitude between Nixon's and Reagan's generation and ours. The stern morality that they tried to impose on us emphasized sexual and social prohibitions, but tolerated many forms of violence. The joyful morality that we tried to impose on them emphasized abstaining from exploitation, violence, and killing, but tolerated a wide variety of sexual and social activity. Kantner likened them to fierce, old, huge, self-confident dinosaurs, and us to the playful, new, little mammals who ate the dinosaurs' eggs and thus hastened their demise. "The Baby Tree" suggested that our parents would want us only if we were pleasant and did not cause any fuss. "Let's Go Together" suggested that, if we wanted to be truly free, happy, and authentic, then getting out of the United States might be the way to do it. "A Child is Coming" was an optimistic anti-draft lyric, a refusal of new parents to train their child to kill other parents' children. "Sunrise" was Grace's curse upon the entire two millennia of Christian arrogance and militarism. "Hijack" explicitly rejected biblical accounts of reality, promoted cocaine and other hard drugs, and referred to an unnamed event that happened, perhaps in Chicago, on some November 23. We could not discover what that event might have been. Kantner metaphorized his fanciful ideals of omnifaceted freedom in a future arklike starship that would allow 7000 to escape the solar system to a hedonistic world beyond. Following the psychedelic instrumental bridge, "Home," "Have You Seen the Stars Tonite" celebrated the freedom of a destinationless journey. Another instrumental bridge, "XM," sounded like rockets blasting off and brought us to the finale, "Starship," which reprised the idea that the United States embraces only those who conform or at least present the image of psychological mediocrity, as determined from the top down. It also alluded to Bobby Kennedy as someone too outrageous for the United States to tolerate. Poor choice! It might better have alluded instead to a genuine, subversive, destabilizing, happy-go-lucky loony, like Abbie, whom mainstream America truly detested. Obviously, from the point of view of mainstream America, anyone must be crazy who thinks that being free entails doing the opposite of what America wants or expects us to do! But, if you choose America, then you choose to obey America, and obedience is not freedom. If you want to be free, then choose always to be able to continue choosing.

We naturally admired Kantner's disgust with America, yet we mostly had to admit that his prescriptions for bettering the situation, as he expressed them in *Blows*, were a low point of leftist imagination. Sheer hedonism, like sheer anarchy, might bring temporary relief, but could never be a realistic basis of any meaningful reformation of society, politics, or public policy.

Ω

Five Easy Pieces, a cross between a dark comedy and a deep character-study drama, was the film that made Jack Nicholson a major star. He played a selfish, mean, irresponsible womanizer, an oil rig worker who treated his white trash girlfriend like crap and seemed to enjoy stereotypical working-class pleasures like bowling and drinking beer. We gradually learned that he was not a member of the working class at all, but a spoiled rich kid, a self-imposed exile from the sterile, cold environment of his childhood and adolescence. He had serious musical inclinations, was an accomplished pianist, and came from a musical family, but a dreary family who knew just the formality of classical music and not the real spirit of any music. We never gained any sympathy for him — he was too heartless, spiteful, and manipulative — but we understood why his restless nature had led him away from his origins in search of authentic life and genuine emotion. We blamed his malice, egocentricity, and general lack of love or any other redeeming human quality on his unchosen upper-class heritage, not on his chosen lower-class environment.

Andy Warhol's *Trash* starred real-life street hustler Joe Dallesandro as, essentially, himself, a slum-scavenger so strung out on heroin that he could not get an erection. Filmed in an almost *vérité* style, if Warhol's name had not been prominently displayed in its opening credits, *Trash* would have been dismissed as softcore porn. The first thing we saw was an ugly close-up of Joe's naked zitty ass. As the camera pulled back, we perceived that a beautiful woman was giving him a blowjob, but to no avail. His dick just would not get hard, whatever she did. The movie's whole plot consisted of Joe, his amorality, his heroin, and his limp dick.

Documentary film or *cinéma vérité* works much better without any admixture of fiction. Albert and David Maysles and Charlotte Zwerin succeeded in creating with *Gimme Shelter*, their Altamont documentary, everything that Godard had failed to create with *One Plus One*. The sound quality was better — you could actually hear what the Stones were saying — the camera angles were more interesting, and, best of all, the social commentary was real and implicit, not phony or superfluous. Truth is enough to satisfy us if it is accurately recorded. We can supply our own didactic allegory, thank you very much, Monsieur Godard.

Altamont could have been a peaceful, exemplary, and inspiring event like Monterey or Woodstock, but instead became the prime case in point for anyone who would demean the so-called "hippie subculture." The film revealed that the reasons why Altamont did not become another Monterey or Woodstock were mainly physical. Whereas Woodstock had a huge, high stage with a wide pit and a gigantic fence in front of it, and whereas Monterey had the natural separation formed by seating in orderly rows of folding chairs, Altamont had only a small, low stage, with the audience standing right there in the middle of the action, within easy grabbing distance of performers' ankles. The only thing between the performers and the audience was a cadre of Hell's Angels. If the atmosphere had been intimate and the audience few and friendly, as for example in a club setting, such proximity would not have mattered, but with any large crowd, especially an outdoor or stadium crowd, the stage needs to be a certain height and distance from the audience to ensure calm. Also, whereas at Woodstock the concertgoers felt that the promoters and producers were one with them, and that they all shared the same "disaster," at Altamont the concertgoers quickly perceived that the promoters and producers themselves had caused the problem by allowing the development of the adversary relationship that led to violence.

Historical fiction should be, first of all, accurate. Its fictitious characters should be interwoven through actual events with as little falsification and as much care for facts as possible. The thematic credibility of novels, plays, or movies is diminished if they pretend to be historical fiction but instead are full of anachronisms, compressions, out-of-sequence events, misrepresentations, or just plain blunders. *Forrest Gump* and *Little Big Man* are two such flawed movies.

Even though *Little Big Man* was bad historical fiction, it was a brilliant dark comedy that might have worked better if we could have regarded it as only fiction — but unfortunately, it was full of historical characters to confuse this issue. Its main point was to show Native Americans, particularly the Cheyenne, as sincere believers in a fair, just, holistic, moral universe, and to contrast them to Christian whites as hypocritical purveyors of a perverse, cruel, despotic, but fragmented world order. Whites, in all their various stations and guises throughout the movie, were less human than the Native Americans whom they objectified as animals, heathens, or savages. "Garry Owen" and Christian hymns alike were the musical accompaniment of the genocide that they perpetrated against these indigenous peoples. For all its underlying seriousness about murder, evil, and inhumanity, *Little Big Man* was generally a farcical — not serious — exposition of the plain truth that there are always plenty of white men, but never enough human beings. The Cheyenne chief's encapsulation of that truth was priceless. Yet, at the same time, his language's calling only his own tribe "human beings" revealed the tragic parochialism of his world view.

$$\Omega$$

Epilogue

Them hippies was right!

My clothes are not expensive but they are friendly and neat and my human presence is welcoming. People feel better when they look at me.
— Richard Brautigan, *The Abortion* (New York: Simon and Schuster, 1971), p. 13

During the children's revolt of the sixties and seventies, I was just old enough to understand what these kids had in mind — they meant to turn the world upside down — and just young enough to believe they might actually succeed. ... I won't apologize for my naïveté; you only have to listen to the songs to know that I wasn't alone. ... The revolt [was not] put down, it ... just dwindled away into a fashion statement.
— Daniel Quinn, *Ishmael* (New York: Bantam, 1995), pp. 4-5

Things fall apart; the centre cannot hold.
— William Butler Yeats
"The Second Coming"

Why do adolescents rebel? It is not only out of restlessness, bravado, or natural propensity toward delinquency, but also, and chiefly, because no group ever sees another group better than children see their elders. Just as no one, including the employer, knows the employer better than the employee does, and no one, including the master, knows the master better than the servant does, so no one, including the parent, knows the parent better than the child does.

The child knows the parent better than the parent knows the child because, while parents are beset with myriad cares and distractions, children really have very little else to do except to observe the big people who control their lives.

We rebelled because we sincerely believed that we were more competent than our parents to build a good world. The fact that we rebelled at all showed that we were better motivated than they to build that world. They wanted us to take, hold, and cherish everything they gave us. When we rejected some of it, they accused us of rejecting all of it. They said that we were tearing down tradition and society without having anything to put in its place. That accusation was not true for most of us. We were more discerning than that. We were selective. We wanted to reject and discard a lot of their tradition and society, but not all of it. We saw what was good and we wanted to keep it.

To say to any person, "I would do anything for you," is to compromise oneself morally, because it leaves open the possibility of abandoning principles, discriminating unjustly, dealing unfairly, and even perpetrating crimes or frauds. But to say of any ethical principle, "I would do anything for this," is to commit oneself to honest moral action, regardless of consequences.

In order to be true to what we saw as universal principles of justice and peace, we sometimes had to abandon our families of origin and reject their values. To remain with them and endure their patriarchal, condescending hegemony of the old over the young would have made hypocrites of us. Yet that situation could not last. It was not an adequate resolution to the natural conflict between adult conservatives and adolescent liberals. The biological tie between parents and children is, after all, a plain fact. Neither it nor its emotional ramifications can be discounted in any worthy social order. Nor can the universal principles of justice and peace that our elders largely ignored in the sixties. Given that an ethical order of life, the coherent social morality that Hegel calls *Sittlichkeit*, is an ideal to which every rational person can aspire, both sides must agree that no such goal can be reached until family ties and universal principles are reconciled. What Hegel says about faith vs. reason in the first two paragraphs of the Hinrichs Foreword applies as well to most other essential bifurcations that could be healed dialectically, including the opposition between loyalty to family and loyalty to principles:

> For that opposition is of such a nature that the human spirit can turn away from neither of its two aspects; each shows itself rather to be rooted in spirit's innermost self-consciousness, so that, if they are conceived to be in conflict, the stability of spirit is shaken and its condition is one of the most unfortunate bifurcation. However, had the conflict of [families] and [principles] disappeared and been changed over into a reconciliation, then it would be essentially dependent on the nature of this reconciliation itself to what degree it should be congratulated.
>
> For there is also a frivolous, barren, peace, indifferent to the depths of spirit; in such a peace the annoying problem can appear removed, while it is only set aside. However, that which is only overlooked or looked down upon is not thereby overcome. On the contrary, if the deepest genuine needs were not satisfied in the reconciliation, if the sanctuary of spirit were not to obtain its right, then the bifurcation in itself would remain, and the enmity would fester all the more deeply within; the harm, itself neither acknowledged nor cognized, would only be all the more dangerous.

To oversimplify, our parents' generation believed that those who thought the same, looked the same, and acted the same should be privileged, and anyone who was different should be shut out; while we, on the other hand, believed that everyone should be fed, but that those who were different should be admired, and anyone who tried to think, look, or act the same as everyone else should on that account be scorned. Both sides were wrong: theirs for its self-righteous cultural elitism, ours for its shortsightedness, naïveté, and shallowness.

Yet the Western world was briefly a better place because my generation re-invented and exalted good, clean fun in the sixties. But our moment fell apart and descended into the early twenty-first-century Hobbesian world of selfishness, lies, cruelty, unilateralism, and arrogance. How did this happen? Did we blow it? Perhaps. If so, it was because of our greatest flaw and failure: our lack of self-discipline.

Some of our detractors called us hedonists. There was plenty of evidence for their opinion. For example, they may have taken seriously as an indication of our culture one of our favorite humor LPs, *A Child's Garden of Grass: A Pre-Legalization Comedy*, which made fun of all sides and effects of the marijuana culture only, i.e., just a small and rather dispensable part of our whole freak culture. While marijuana was never central to our culture, it was a frequent focus of our comic lines and music lyrics, and was always good for a laugh. Case in point: NRPS:

The New Riders of the Purple Sage were a low-key sort of supergroup. Several of the original musicians regarded the band as a side project, because in their own bands (the Dead and the Airplane) they could not play enough of the country music that they loved. With songwriter John Dawson on guitar and vocals, David Nelson on guitar and vocals, Dave Torbert having replaced Phil Lesh of the Dead on bass and vocals, Spencer Dryden of the Airplane having replaced Mickey Hart of the Dead on drums, and Jerry Garcia of the Dead not yet having been replaced by Buddy Cage on pedal steel guitar, NRPS released its first album and quickly became the epitome of countrified rock — or rockified country. This album, self-titled and consummately political, drug-laced, and drug-induced, nevertheless began with a simple, catchy, pop song, "I Don't Know You," a paean to the infatuation of new love. There were a few other love songs on the album, but the memorable, important ones were the workers' lament, "Dirty Business," the marijuana-celebrating "Henry," the environmentalist "Last Lonely Eagle," and the rather revolutionary "Garden of Eden."

Even though we valued fun more than our parents' generation did, we were not hedonists. Hedonism is the belief in having fun regardless of what happens in the world. *Fiat laetitia, pereat mundus*. But we believed that the way to save the world was to have fun. That is quite different. We were more interested in saving the world than in having fun — and we saw the connection between the two. The British satirist Douglas Adams, who was born the same year I was, put it best in Chapter 23 of *The Hitchhiker's Guide to the Galaxy*:

... man had always assumed that he was more intelligent than dolphins because he had achieved so much — the wheel, New York, wars and so on — while all the dolphins had ever done was muck about in the water having a good time. But conversely, the dolphins had always believed that they were far more intelligent than man — for precisely the same reasons.

If we had not seen fun as the way to improve the world, fun would not have been so important for us. This constructive attitude, connecting our fun with the fate of the world, was definitely a generational peculiarity. My generation had it and lost it. Neither my parents' generation nor my kids' generation ever had it. Neither ever knew how to have fun. They were too serious about making money and fighting wars. But my generation could teach any generation that ever lived how to have fun in the most illuminating and beneficial way — and have fun doing it. We grew up on Dr. Seuss, whose Cat in the Hat taught us: "It is fun to have fun, but you have to know how." We were the masters of fun. We were Nietzschean higher humans. We had learned to laugh — at anything. But our fun was never mean.

Our comedy was kind. We did not enjoy "insult comics" like Don Rickles. Impressionist David Frye's second anti-Nixon satirical LP, *Radio Free Nixon*, hit its targets (not only Nixon) just as accurately as did his first, but again, gently. The Youngbloods' new LP, *Good and Dusty*, included the parody, "Hippie from Olema," which answered Haggard's "Okie from Muskogee" and put it smack down in its place. They treated him much more good-naturedly than he would have treated them.

The Mothers' ninth, a live LP, *Fillmore East, June 1971*, was mostly an extended satire of sexual bantering between groupies and rock stars. Showcasing the comedic talents of Flo and Eddie, it was their funniest, raunchiest, dirtiest album to date, and maybe ever. The prurient context of songs like "Bwana Dik" (extolling the huge penis) and "Latex Solar Beef" (referring to a hot cock wrapped in a condom) gave entirely new meaning to the Turtles' old pop single, "Happy Together."

Fritz the Cat, billed as the world's first X-rated full-length cartoon movie, presented the sweaty underside of urban depravity in ways that the creators of Top Cat, Mr. Jinks, Felix the Cat, Krazy Kat, or even the wicked Oil Can Harry never even imagined. Set in the late sixties around Greenwich Village, it followed a down-and-out pseudo-intellectual "cat" — *double entendre* intentional — through chaotic adventures of drugs, orgies, sleaze, violence, auto theft, stupid cops, racial strife, doublecrosses, Harlem nights, lechery, ignorant revolutionary demagoguery, riots, murder, hustling, phony religion, naive delusions, neo-Nazism, a road trip to L.A., gratuitous cruelty, streams of piss, and the desecration of an orthodox synagogue. The film character Fritz was director Ralph Bakshi's major alteration of R. Crumb's original Fritz. Crumb hated it, disavowed the film, and later killed his Fritz in one of his comic strips. Crumb was just being a grouch, perhaps jealous; both Fritzes were pretty damn funny.

Brautigan's *The Abortion: An Historical Romance 1966* glorified the library as a center of culture, learning, sex, and fun. With the craziness that we had come to expect from him, he tantalized our minds, tickled our libido, teased our sense of the bizarre, and left us wondering what the fuck it was all about. We had no idea, but we loved connecting his *non sequiturs*, scrutinizing his impressions, decoding his insinuations, and inventing possible meanings.

We valued our brains.

Intelligence can comprehend stupidity, but stupidity cannot comprehend intelligence. That is why stupid people bow down to the prevailing regime and gladly send their young to be cannon fodder, because they cannot comprehend that anyone might come up with a better solution to an international problem than they themselves have come up with — which is typically brute force. They want their leaders to be like them, not smarter. They understand brute force and trust the government because it can deliver brute force. Their entire lives are extended *ad baculum* fallacies. Intelligent people, on the other hand, see quite clearly just how stupid the prevailing regime is, how unproductive in the long run brute force usually is, and how gullible the uncritical supporters of government warmongering usually are.

So we, the intelligent, have to work very hard to prevent the governments of the world from giving in to the baser side of human instinct. That requires freedom, vision, hope, self-knowledge, *kairos*, and sometimes, revolution.

One thing we never were was frustrated — at least not for long. Of course we experienced minor, episodic frustrations, but nothing like the chronic, endemic frustration that characterized post-Reagan first-world revolutionaries and drove Abbie to suicide.[71] On the contrary, we were joyful. Our joy was the joy of creators. We could not have fun in our parents' world, so we created our own. Because we had to go outside their world to be true to ourselves and to preserve ourselves as integral, sincere, whole beings, and because they had provided no world for us outside theirs, we had to create one of our own.

Nothing is more joyful than creation. We expressed this creative joy mostly as music.

Led Zeppelin released what would become their greatest classic, though not necessarily their greatest music, their untitled fourth album, usually known as either *Lep Zep IV* or *Zoso*, containing "Stairway to Heaven" and seven other tunes.

The Moody Blues put out their seventh LP, *Every Good Boy Deserves Favor*. (*Seventh Sojourn* in 1972 would actually be their eighth.) *EGBDF*, named after the standard mnemonic for the lines on the treble clef, contained one of their best songs, "The Story in Your Eyes," a rocker, but broke little new ground apart from that.

The Stones kept getting better and better and better. With every new album from *Beggars Banquet* to *Let It Bleed* to 1971's *Sticky Fingers* to 1972's *Exile on Main Street* to 1973's *Goat's Head Soup*, they would uncompromisingly reinvent progressive, blues-based, hard rock. *Sticky Fingers* was chock full of not only drug songs like "Sister Morphine," but also sex songs like "Dead Flowers" with obvious mentions of drugs. "Wild Horses" may have been about heroin, freedom, or any number of things — or all of them. We did not care. It was just a powerful song. "Brown Sugar" and "Bitch" became stock party dance tunes, despite their misogyny. Andy Warhol's cover art was a photo of pants with a working zipper, which, when opened, showed ... what?

With rough tunes like "Maggie May," "That's All Right," "I'm Losing You," and the title cut, Rod Stewart's third LP, *Every Picture Tells a Story*, rocked much

---

[71] Abbie Hoffman overdosed on phenobarbitol on April 12, 1989. His alleged last words were, "It's too late. We can't win, they've gotten too powerful."

harder than either of his first two, and almost made him a reputation as a rocker instead of a balladeer. But each of his subsequent LPs would undo this new, hard image to some extent.

L.A. Woman turned out to be the Doors' last real album, as Morrison died three months after its release. It contained the usual Doors mix of useless pop, such as "Love Her Madly" and the title track, and fascinating progressive rock, such as "The Changeling" and "Riders on the Storm." Given that he had nowhere else to go and was getting more and more miserable, Jim probably died at his right time.

Spooky Tooth's fourth American LP, *Tobacco Road*, was three years old, as it was really their first LP overall, released in 1968 in Britain as *It's All About Spooky Tooth*. The whole business was confusing. The band had already broken up, so there would be no tour. Ah well, some suit-wearers got a bit richer.

The Dead's second live album, a double set officially called just *Grateful Dead*, but usually called *Skull and Roses* because of its cover art, showed the Dead moving in a more narrative or at least thematic direction. Songs included "Bertha," about a man trying desperately to escape a broken love affair; "Mama Tried," their cover of a Merle Haggard tune about prison; "Playing in the Band," Bob Weir's *tour de force*; "The Other One," an extended jam; "Me and My Uncle," a tale of robbery, treachery, and murder; "Big Boss Man," a litany of a working man's valid gripes; "Wharf Rat," a dirge of waterfront despair; and the cathartic final medley, "Not Fade Away" / "Goin' Down the Road Feeling Bad." The Dead also kept the teeny bopper side of their fan base satisfied by releasing "Truckin'" as a single.

Who's Next was flipflopped. Side one should have been side two and side two should have been side one. The first song on side two was "Gettin' in Tune" and the last song on side one was "The Song is Over." Whether this was deliberate, we could not say — but we sure all noticed it.

The expertly crafted "Baba O'Riley" — not, as it is commonly miscalled, "Teenage Wasteland" — opened the LP in this order of entrances: Townshend's synthesizer, Townshend's piano, Moon's drums, Entwistle's bass, Daltrey's vocal, Townshend's guitar, Townshend's vocal, Dave Arbus's violin. Baba O'Riley was a made-up name that referred to two of Pete's main influences at the time: Meher Baba, Pete's spiritual guru, and Terry Riley, the American minimalist composer. It was a song of hope, resolve, and courage.

Another spiritually oriented song on *Who's Next* was Pete's deep-searching "Behind Blue Eyes," a lyric about using one's ideals, aspirations, and introspective ideas to overcome despair, self-doubt, a guilty conscience, or feelings of personal worthlessness.

The end of "The Song is Over" quoted a Townshend solo song, "Pure and Easy" — but we did not know that yet. Pete's version came out on his first solo LP, *Who Came First*, in 1972 and the Who's version was on their 1974 compilation LP, *Odds and Sods*. Of course, when we heard "Pure and Easy" in 1972, we immediately thought back to *Who's Next*. "Pure and Easy" contained some of Pete's most eloquent and perceptive lyrics. It deserved to be heard loud and often.

"Won't Get Fooled Again" raised the question of Townshend's political leanings. Conservatives loved and frequently quoted it, and continue to love and frequently quote it. Well, why not? It's a great song! Let them interpret it any way they choose. It could just as easily be interpreted as a leftist hymn about the need to continue revolution despite its apparent futility. We did not believe for a second that Pete was conservative. So what if he thought hippies were "daft"? A lot of us did too, from Zappa on down. So what if he had thrown Abbie off the stage at Woodstock? A lot of us would have thrown *anyone* off *any* stage who was interrupting our show. Pete was cool. The man who wrote that his dreams seemed less empty than his conscience could not be a pig.

Politically inclined music in general did not diminish. If anything, at least through the first few years of the seventies, it intensified. Creedence's "Have You Ever Seen the Rain?", their sequel to "Who'll Stop the Rain?", asked whether listeners really heard, lookers really saw, or thinkers really understood. In that sense, it reminded us of Old Testament prophets preaching against the complacent, widespread ignorance that typically signified impending disaster. In "Sweet Hitch-Hiker" they noted both the free joys and the lurking dangers of hitchhiking, which, for us, was as much a political statement as a mode of easy transportation. The heretofore apolitical Motown crooner Marvin Gaye surprised us with a black power anthem, "What's Going On." In all fifteen cuts on their second LP, *This Is Madness*, the Last Poets continued pulling no punches. These earliest of rappers were intelligent, sensitive, realistic, nuanced, egalitarian, loud, proud, and entirely political.

Lennon continued to lead the way in political music and, perhaps because of Yoko, in political action as well. His "Power to the People" supported feminism, working class struggles, individual freedom, and street activism. In "How Do You Sleep?" he not only attacked McCartney personally, but also challenged him to put more meaning into his lyrics. (Paul would later become more political, espousing various causes and writing songs like "Give Ireland Back to the Irish.") John's much gentler "Imagine" provided a vision of a peaceful, secular, cooperative, unified, egalitarian, worldwide utopia. The Lennons made themselves available for extended stints on American talk TV, doing two long late-night shows for Dick Cavett in September 1971 and five daytime co-hosting gigs with Mike Douglas in February 1972. Their agenda in so doing was entirely self-promoting and political.

Then, of course, there was always Pete Seeger, whose *Young vs. Old* continued his antiwar and social justice struggles. The liner notes urged Uncle Sam to be more willing to pick up hitchhikers.

CSNY's live double LP, *4 Way Street*, contained a few gems, a few duds, some good banter, and quite a lot of wit. Highlights included Young's long jams, especially on "Southern Man"; Crosby's "Triad" and "Long Time Gone"; Stills's "Carry On" and "Find the Cost of Freedom"; and Nash's "Teach Your Children" and "Chicago." Stills proclaimed in "49 Bye-Byes / America's Children" that Jesus invented nonviolent revolution. That may have been an overstatement, yet it well made his point that anyone who would use Christianity in general or Jesus in particular to justify militarism, foreign adventurism, or class oppression is *ipso facto* holding a self-contradictory position. Jesus was no right-winger.

Jethro Tull stormed forth with their masterpiece, *Aqualung*. Its title character was a down-and-out bum, the victim of not only his own lechery, pessimism, and dissipation, but also society's class structure, prejudice, and institutions.

The entire second side of *Aqualung* was a ferocious, overdue, and most welcome attack on organized religion in general and Anglican Christianity in particular. It reminded us of the role of religion in *If...*, as Tull presented church, state, business, and conformity all bundled together, antithetical to freedom. Listening to side two would not convert anyone away from organized religion who was not already leaning away from it, but its lyrics would surely inspire any freedom-loving listener to think about these issues.

"My God" related how church and society have twisted the spiritual and ethical message of Judaeo-Christian revelation to fit their own material ends. "Hymn 43" harked back to the Beatles' "Bungalow Bill" in pointing out the hypocrisy of using religion to justify genocide, imperialism, or other forms of money-driven violence. "Locomotive Breath" alluded to the pointlessness of glomming onto religion, expecting to be saved — from what? "Wind Up" nailed down what we had suspected for years, i.e., that the leaders of church and state were pompous asses who were so terrified for both their worldly positions and their eternal souls that they toadied up to death itself. Their world view entailed some winners and many losers; we could not all be just survivors — or even contented. A few, if they played the prescribed game and kissed the right asses, would be privileged to power, prosperity, happiness, and the favor of the lords, both earthly and heavenly; while anyone who refused to play the game, kiss ass, or acknowledge the reality or legitimacy of lords would be doomed to ostracism and misery. The bishops *et al.* would see to that. But fuck the bishops! "Wind Up" reminded us that it is the rebels, those who refuse to play society's money-and-status game, who are closest to God. Indeed, Jesus himself was a rebel, Gethsemane notwithstanding. Being godly and moral is not achieved by performing rituals, following conventions, or groveling before God and God's ministers, but, as the prophet Amos says in 5:21-24, by spreading joy, justice, and good will.

We were impatient with the metaphors of ages past. For us, it was no longer sufficient merely to accept, either tentatively or devotedly, recourse to the will or providence of God. We now required scientific, systematic, or *wissenschaftlich* explanations of what had been called "will," "providence," and "God." We were no longer pleased with the sort of apologetic exegesis of these matters which had typified Western religious thought since Philo, with all too rare exceptions. We expected our God, if we had one at all, to be our friend, enabler, source of moral authority, or inspiration for change and progress, not our boss, dictator, tyrant, or inspiration to keep things as they are. Yet the American Christian right still expects to be bossed, dictated to, tyrannized, and inspired, for the sake of the other world, to stifle anything that might be of value in this world. They appear not to realize that they would have been Tories in 1776 and persecutors of Jesus Christ in the first century.

Even songs that probably were not intended to make us think made us think. The title song of Mountain's *Nantucket Sleighride* album, for example, was probably intended just as a melancholy whaling ditty with fine guitar hooks, bass lines, organ fills, and drum licks — which it was — but, a level above all that, it was also a stark comment on the heartbreak and loss of human values that men suffer when they attack nature in quest of commercial gain. The Nantucket sleighride itself, i.e., the wild and uncontrolled career of a whaleboat stuck fast by its own harpoon to the back of a still lively whale, is the perfect metaphor for how men are dragged along, often to their spiritual or actual doom, when they surrender to commercial interests and attach themselves to the moneyed leviathan.

In the late sixties and especially the early seventies, commercial America made many attempts to stereotype hippies, i.e., to reduce them to their appearance: long hair, love beads, slogan buttons, Nehru jackets, bell bottoms, etc. But hippies could not be stereotyped. We were, after all, not really hippies, but freaks, each an individual freak. We did not buy into the commercial mass-production of our clothes. We wore only whatever we each damn well wanted. Whenever we noticed anyone wearing hippie garb from the chain stores, we knew immediately that they were not freaks, but those same pseudo-hippies that Zappa had complained about as early as 1966. Yet the suit-wearers expected us to follow trends like good little consumers.

The irony was that *they* started to follow *us* — at least superficially. *They* started to grow their hair long. Wow! What natural sheep they were!

Long hair on conservatives did not appear until the early seventies. I am rather at a loss to explain why it ever happened at all, given the right wing's obsession with conformity, which had rendered men's business attire and hairstyle essentially unchanged since beards disappeared from the approved canon in the 1890s. Here are three possible explanations: 1. Right wingers are mechanical followers of whatever prevailing fashion is set by others, for example, the sideburns on George Bush the Elder when he was Nixon's ambassador to the United Nations in the early seventies. 2. The libertarian individualist streak that transcends political affiliation took hold of them. 3. They had something to hide.

Ovid wrote in Book II of *Ars Amatoria* that art succeeds when it is concealed. LBJ and Nixon tried to hoodwink us, and succeeded to some extent, but in general we saw through their schemes, because we had created in ourselves a finely tuned leftist skepticism of anything emerging from the right. George Bush the Younger, on the other hand, succeeded in this sort of subterfuge at nearly every turn, because American youth during his terms, far from being leftists or skeptics, were credulous, anesthetized, overloaded rightists who were quite willing to believe any lie he told them. If the government wants to restrict our freedom, as is typically its aim, it cannot succeed by coming out bluntly and saying, "We want to restrict your freedom. Be good citizens and give us more of what is rightfully your power." If the government were that artless, we would simply tell them to go to hell and that would be the end of it. We would then keep our freedom. But if, with the same aim, the government were to say, "We want to protect and enhance your freedom. Here is some important legislation that will enable us to do just that. Be good citizens and lend your support to this bill," and if it then were to trot out the USA-PATRIOT Act, then they could — *and in fact did* — restrict our freedom to their stony hearts' content, and we, completely duped, would blithely traipse along believing that our freedom had thus been expanded. *What exceptional masters of deceit!*

America's sharp turn to the right began in reaction to Roe v. Wade and continues in the twenty-first century. Francis Fukuyama's proclamation of the end of history, along with Bill Clinton's inauguration, both in 1992, lulled us leftists to sleep. Fukuyama argued that classical liberalism had finally triumphed against monarchy, dictatorship, and controlled economies, so that all that remained in history to be done was a bit of mopping up — in Iraq, for instance. Leftist apathy after the end of the Cold War allowed the right to sweep into even more power than it already had under Reagan-Bush. The climate that Fukuyama partially created was responsible for Newt Gingrich's 1994 rightist revolution. But Fukuyama was wrong. History has not ended. The new overarching world-historical battle is between fanaticism, fundamentalism, prejudice, intolerance, religion, rudeness, superstition, and willful ignorance, all on one side, and reasonableness, open-mindedness, respect, tolerance, secularism, civility, science, and impartial education, all on the other.

On college and school campuses and anywhere in America at large where young people had any influence, there was more cultural, social, and attitudinal change from 1960 to 1970 than from 1970 to the first decade of the twenty-first century. There are many, many reasons for this, but the main one is that generations younger than ours have been progressively — and probably deliberately — anesthetized with sound bites instead of full sentences; action movies instead of multivalent films; video games instead of chess, bridge, or other thinking pastimes; and, above all, the basic shift in the nature of public sociopolitical discourse. Republicans and Democrats used to call each other "the loyal opposition" and, despite their disagreements, would be courteous enough to listen to each other and allow each other to speak. Yet such dialogue takes time, its benefits are not immediate, it can be soporific, and the general public has been conditioned to crave instant gratification, even if mindless. Calm, respectful, intelligent dialogue between opposing factions is not exciting, especially on radio, but rudeness is. Hence the popularity of radio demagogues such as Rush Limbaugh and Bill O'Reilly, who do not allow anyone whom they perceive to disagree with them to finish uttering a single idea; do not countenance original, reflective, or individual points of view on issues, but seek only "ditto" thinking; and truncate the whole thought process even to the point of labeling anyone who disagrees with them as "un-American," "traitor," "leftist," "liberal," "socialist," etc. Because of their goonish tactics — in which the left will not indulge — the left has lost its audience and the political center in America is much further to the right than it was in the sixties. Wacko rightists have become mainstream. Polite respect for ideological opponents has disappeared. Interrupting, because it is quick and exciting, has replaced considerate listening as the norm in radio. In short, these younger generations have surrendered to the god "Excitement" and no longer in general care about politics, social justice, unselfish goals, or moral causes — because all that connected, coherent argumentation takes too long.

Indeed, peace is not exciting; it is merely rational, proper, and necessary.

Information presented visually in pictures, either still or moving, is immediate in the Hegelian sense and complete in itself. It does not foster its own transformation into concepts in the mind of the beholder. But information presented visually as printed or written words necessarily entails this transformation into concepts, else it would not be understood at all. Without concepts, we fall into mere acceptance of the most convenient prefabricated ideologies, usually in the form of religious dogma or societal prejudices. To persist in following any social, political, economic, or especially religious ideology that history has clearly shown to have become obsolete or just plain wrong is one-dimensional in the Marcusean sense. Stubbornness in the face of evil is a virtue; but in the face of the facts, a moronic vice. The real tragedy of America is that we have ceased to be readers — and therefore thinkers. Former readers of serious nonfiction have been ployed with video games, graphic novels, action movies, and pulp fiction. We need more teenage school movies like *If...*, providing lingering concepts, and fewer like *Fast Times at Ridgemont High*, providing instantaneous flash and thrills. Yes, one picture is worth ten thousand words. You keep the picture; give me the ten thousand words.

The young leftist revolutionaries of the twenty-first century are motivated too much by anger and hatred, and through this poison they will ensure the destruction of their own spirit. Why do they hate? Why are they consumed by anger? These are difficult questions, and history may not yet have progressed far enough for us to answer them. But this much is clear: They are frustrated. Frustrated as hell! Their frustration stems from the monolithic, nebulous nature of the behemoth that they have declared their enemy; their small numbers; their merely dim, visual, not yet clear or conceptual, perception that something is wrong; their lack of unified ideology; and their alienation from their *own* generation.

We also felt alienation keenly, but only from our elders. We never felt alienated from people our own age. Even those of our generation who disagreed with us understood us to a tolerable extent. Anti-intellectualism and religious fundamentalism were not yet as rampant as they became subsequent to Roe v. Wade. The biggest problem within our generation was the ideological polarization between freaks and straights our own age, which needed to be overcome or reconciled to the full satisfaction of both sides, but not resolved in favor of either one side or the other. Unfortunately we did not take this problem seriously in its time, and it never was adequately settled. Rather, the polarization increased, and continues today.

The cultural sixties were a dream. We woke up from it — or rather, we were awakened, roughly. Our dream was hopeful, gentle, and inspired. Above all, the sixties were characterized by a glimmering and pervasive hope among the youth of America. That hope was dealt a vicious but nonlethal blow in Dallas in 1963, and was gradually squashed to death by LBJ and Nixon. Hope, when frustrated, descends into either apathy or anger. If formerly hopeful people cease to care, they become apathetic. If they continue to care, they become angry. Both apathy and anger are socially, politically, and culturally poisonous. Our apathy would spell victory for the conformist conservatives. As Edmund Burke is supposed to have said, "The only thing necessary for the triumph of evil is for good men to do nothing." Anger, in contrast, leads to street violence, to other counterproductive actions, and eventually to repression in reaction to it.

Larry McMurtry's and Peter Bogdanovich's *The Last Picture Show* reminded us that, however much joy we had wrought in the last seven or eight years, much of America was still mired in the miserable culture of the fifties. The movie was set mostly during the 1951-1952 school year in a bleak north Texas town so remote from the excitement of urban culture and so uninvolved with any kind of innovative thinking that everyday life there was more likely to produce resignation or despair than creative social transformation. The town's values were so superficial that boys were judged either upright or disgusting by how well they played football. Its desolation was searingly exemplified in a reasonably decent and attractive high school senior succumbing to a merely physical affair with the terrified, sniveling, forty-something, maritally frustrated wife of his football and basketball coach. Life offered so few options that just about all the local people could do to make it seem worthwhile was indulge in booze, pills, gossip, and tawdry sex; listen to country music; dance; play dominoes; or join the army and get shipped off to Korea.

A similar, but not so morbid, movie was *Summer of '42*. It was supposed to be a light comedy, but was really quite ugly as it portrayed the male adolescent roots of adult America's pervasive oppression, objectification, and exploitation of women. In desperation as much from loneliness as from hormones, two typical, socially maladroit, sex-obsessed fifteen-year-old boys conspired to seduce or date rape — whichever would turn out to be more convenient for them — any female who seemed available. The kink in their plans was that one of them actually felt respect for his object of lust, a gorgeous married woman whose loving husband was away fighting in World War II. Ironically, only after her husband was killed in action did she and the boy each find the depth of human emotion and sincerity to approach each other as equals and make love naturally, silently, without shame, guilt, or tension.

In *Carnal Knowledge* director Mike Nichols continued to attack the values of his own generation, specifically his society's expected sexual roles as they were manifest in the typical consequences of trying to choreograph human relations via artificial and unavoidably phony preplanned social events, like college mixers, in this case between Smith and Amherst Colleges. He reused one of his stars from *Catch-22*, Art Garfunkel, and managed to cop Jack Nicholson and Candice Bergen as well. Art (Sandy) and Jack (Jonathan) respectively played the good and evil angels of womanizing. Sandy was a decent, sensitive human who sought true companionship. Jonathan was a primitive male animal who only wanted to fuck. They and every woman involved with them got hurt. How much better everything could be if social conventions did not force people into unnatural roles of predator and prey, or into situations in which they must objectify and use each other instead of just being honest, natural, and open about their sexual feelings — and indeed, about their humanity itself!

The dark comedy, *Harold and Maude*, showed the ultimate bridging of the generation gap: a teenager falling in love with a seventy-nine-year-old woman. Harold was an unloved but pampered upper-class kid, obsessed with death and all its trappings, even to the extent of repeatedly play-acting his own suicide, dressing like an undertaker, driving a hearse, listening to Cat Stevens, and going to funerals for fun. Maude was a serial auto thief, eccentrically and effervescently living in an ornately, bizarrely, and eclectically furnished railroad car, obsessed with life and all its ephemeral joys, so much so that she went to as many funerals as she could, just in order to celebrate it. Harold saw death as the end of suffering; Maude saw it as just another welcome step in the process of universal life. With her, for the first time in his life, he was happy. When she died, he abandoned his former existence completely, and instead honored her by resolving to carry on her defiant, spontaneous, musical way of life as full, unbroken festivity. The point was that she was not typical of her own generation. With her irrepressible *joie de vivre*, she was more typical of *ours*. Harold, by contrast, in his initial fascination with death, seemed more like how we often imagined those older ones, the World War II glorifiers and the Vietnam War promoters. The bond of the older generation to systematic death was stunningly brought out in two antiwar scenes, in which Harold's amputee jingoist uncle tried to sell Harold on the virtues of fighting for "peace" in America's military. But, as Maude said, "What sense in borders and nations and patriotism?"

Those of us who knew Kant's *Groundwork of the Metaphysics of Morals* saw in *A Clockwork Orange* a special significance that was evident enough in Stanley Kubrick's film but even more so in Anthony Burgess's book. Those who attended or, God forbid, enjoyed the film just for its "action," its "ultraviolence," or any of its other merely sensory aspects missed its point entirely. This was a very cerebral film — and book — whose main points were philosophical, particularly as regards moral philosophy or ethics, considering the relation of the moral or amoral individual to society, self, and art. It culminated in a complete rejection of utilitarian, consequentialist, behaviorist, or society-based ethics.

For Kant, the *sine qua non* for any rational being is freedom. If any being is not free, then it cannot be either rational or, by extension, human. Freedom is expressed in and as free will. Nothing at all is good except good will, i.e., any will which has freely chosen to be good, regardless of consequences.

A Clockwork Orange considered what happens when society becomes too concerned with results, even to the point of creating "goodness" by reducing the free, organic, but problematic to the programmed, mechanical, but unproblematic. By the biological and physiological means of the Ludovico treatment, a young thug and murderer, Alex, was transformed into a nonviolent paragon, a "model citizen," but a miserable, suicidal, soulless shell of a person. Hence the metaphorical title: clockwork = mechanical; orange = organic. This paradox of the "clockwork *Groundwork*" was repeated in other metaphors throughout the book and film, notably in the name "Ludovico," a corruption of "Ludwig," referring to Beethoven, whose music Alex loved. The overall message was that the utilitarian social engineering that creates the conditioned reflex is not true to the human spirit, human nature, or human values. An evil person with full free will is more human and therefore "better" than a "good" person with limited free will who has been taught, trained, or conditioned to conform to whatever idea of "goodness" is in the mind of the teacher, trainer, or conditioner. A person with no free will is not a person at all. A "good" automaton is not as "good" as a whole person who freely chooses evil.

One of the last movies with a genuine sixties feel, even though released in 1972, was *The Ruling Class*, a dark comedy depicting a British privileged family's intrinsic perversions — political, social, sexual, autoerotic — that rendered them not only unfit to rule, but also even to be called human. Rather, they and their upper-class cohorts were revealed to be, by and large, criminally insane. Peter O'Toole played the looniest one af all, a paranoid schizophrenic who believed himself to be, first, Jesus Christ, then himself, the Fourteenth Earl of Gurney, and finally, Jack the Ripper. The closing irony was that it was the Ripper's skills, attitudes, and general psyche that were deemed most suitable for any successful aristocrat. Not universal love or compassion, but ruthless cruelty, murderous instinct, and the ability to produce fear were what they wanted. Monarchic dictatorship was their ideal.

All dictatorships are rightist. There is no such thing as a leftist dictatorship. The very concept is a contradiction in terms. Sometimes practical politics prevents ideologues, even sincere ideologues, from remaining true to their principles. Sometimes leftist populists degenerate into rightist tyrants — usually via the influx of nationalism into their thinking. Stalin is a case in point. The left is concerned with establishing and maintaining the rights and welfare of the people, and does not care if it has to break laws or disrupt order to achieve those goals. If a leftist revolution becomes a dictatorship, then *ipso facto* it has changed into a rightist government. The right is concerned with establishing and maintaining law and order, and, in its dearest incarnation, being the government of the few. It does not care if, in that process of establishing and maintaining safety for itself, it tramples the rights or saps the welfare of the many. All people try to gain rights for themselves. The left tries to do it by securing rights for everyone; the right by taking rights from others.

Among the many ironies in the tension between left and right is that, if the right restricts the left, the left thereby gains power. The restriction becomes counterproductive for the right, as it only drives the left underground and strengthens its will. Conversely, if the right gives the left free rein, the left thereby loses power. Preach revolution from the U.S. Capitol steps, be arrested or beaten, and you will have done much to help the revolution. But preach the same revolutionary message from those same Capitol steps, as occurred on April 24, 1971, be allowed to do so unmolested, be ignored by everyone except the hundreds of thousands in the assembled choir to whom you are preaching, and you will have done the revolution a disservice. After all, what are you preaching against? A government that gladly allows you enough freedom to challenge it at its very core? What a wonderful government that must be! You would be crazy to preach against it, if it lets you preach against it. Why should anyone revolt against such benevolent paternalism? Marcuse's analysis of repressive tolerance was spot on!

You can proclaim revolution from the Capitol steps, even from the Oval Office itself, but if the government allows it, then you will not be taken seriously and the revolution will not succeed.

Dissent is good for any body politic. It gets all the viable solutions to a problem aired in the marketplace of ideas. It is enshrined in the U.S. Constitution, a liberal document, a pinnacle of political intelligence. But conservatives piss on the Constitution, especially the First and Fourth Amendments, all the while they pretend to be praising it.

The hypocrisy of America knows no bounds! It preaches freedom while denying it in order to preserve it. America's Statue of Liberty and its accompanying poem by Emma Lazarus unequivocally welcome immigrants, yet America systematically excludes immigrants and, if it lets them in, herds, exploits, and beats them. It preaches self-determination for all, yet it systematically undermines the self-determination of any other nation that dares to disagree with it.

Because we criticized America, the American establishment accused us of hating America. We did not hate America. We did not love it as a political entity or a military power, as they did. We loved it as our home. As such, we naturally wanted to maintain it properly and make a few home improvements now and then.

Under what circumstances ought one to be proud of one's country? Surely not automatically. One can be justly proud of one's country whenever it fosters the interest of humanity in general. But when it fosters its own narrow self-interest at the expense of other nations, then one should be ashamed of its actions and should work to change it, to make it ethical.

Our cause against the war was increasingly bolstered by revelations in the press about the government's unethical conduct in a variety of areas. The army's official scapegoat, Lieutenant William Calley, was convicted of the My Lai murders, though many higher-ranking but probably at least equally guilty officers escaped justice. Daniel Ellsberg stole incriminating, war-related files from the Pentagon and had them published in the *New York Times*. The draft lottery continued with its third drawing in 1971, but ended after the fourth in 1972. The number of American ground troops in Vietnam decreased ever more rapidly. As the American public turned more and more against Nixon, his policies, his ideology, his inherited war, and his ugly, immoral soul, he became more paranoid than he already was. Some of his most fanatical sycophants burgled the Watergate building in Washington to try to find some dirt on the Democrats with which to improve his sagging chances for reelection. Apparently his general strategy of filthy political trickery worked — at least on Ed Muskie — as he won the 1972 election in a landslide, beating George McGovern, our last hope. But Watergate would soon catch up with him, and his actual malevolence would soon be revealed to the whole nation.

Many events of 1971 and 1972 added to the seal of closure on the era of hope. Many symbols of the sixties disappeared. Bill Graham closed both Fillmores. Jim Morrison died. *The Ed Sullivan Show* and *Life* magazine both ended. Don McLean's "American Pie" marked and cryptically described his perception of the end of an era, the death of joy, the death of music.

After it became apparent in 1973 that the Vietnam War would eventually wind down into a pyrrhic victory for the Vietnamese, most of my generation lost their idealism — which apparently had been situational for many of them all along — and sold out.

Some of us chose careers in the arts or humanities rather than the sciences — even though we had aptitude for science — because we believed that, in the big picture of world-historical progress, science had already come too far, but ethics, morality, and humanity had not yet come far enough. Science had given us horrible weapons, pointless space travel, and superfluous gizmos, but history had not yet given us the good sense not to use these things. We were wrong. Science was not the problem. Science was innocent. The real problem, the real culprits, that we only more slowly recognized, were the corporations, entrepreneurs, and politicians, who used science to maximize their own profits rather than to help people. Most of the basic sociopolitical and socioeconomic problems are essentially scientific problems: hunger, for example. We need only to keep the profiteers away from science, if science is to live up to its proper calling; i.e., we need to regulate and keep under constant legal scrutiny all the corporations, entrepreneurs, and politicians.

Besides our own sell-outs, we had four major types of political and cultural opponents: segregationists, traditionalists, capitalists, and fundamentalists. They were our "opponents," not our "enemies." Part of our ideology was to have no enemies. We won against the segregationists. Even George Wallace saw the light eventually. The fundamentalists did not become a significant force until after Roe v. Wade in 1973. They had been humiliated by the Scopes trial in 1925 and its depiction in Jerome Lawrence's and Robert E. Lee's play, *Inherit the Wind*, in 1955. In the sixties they were generally and correctly regarded as credulous, undereducated, emotionally underdeveloped, psychologically desperate, and spiritually childlike conservatives. Until Roe v. Wade they had no central political issue around which to rally. Quickly they drew together in opposition to the natural right of every woman to maintain control over her own body, and soon added anti-gay, anti-science, anti-intellectual, and anti-freedom issues to their retrogressive agenda. It is no accident that the fideistic revolution, which led in America to Jerry Falwell founding the so-called "Moral Majority" in 1979 and to subsequent creationist attempts to curtail solid biomedical research, began with an anti-feminist crusade. Religious people — even women themselves — have always hated women.

But in the sixties the greatest threat to our freewheeling way of life came from traditionalists and capitalists. We enjoyed some small victories against the traditionalists, and they enjoyed some against us, but we won nothing against the capitalists. They held and still hold all the cards. In general, as I write this in mid-2007, our struggle against the traditionalists and capitalists has not gone well and still is not going well.

Capitalists believe that business exists for only one purpose: to make a profit. They do not see any part of their mission as being to provide essential commodities, products, and services to their customers. If an essential commodity, product, or service turns not to be profitable, they will stop providing it, and let the community do without. They allow themselves to worry about social issues and human needs if and only if their ledger is in the black and their bottom line is secure. We have never made any headway against them.

Traditionalists believe that students, children, employees, and all other persons in lowly positions should just follow like sheep, obey without question, and not seek to become part of the decision-making process that affects their present lives. Traditionalists support business interests over human values, property rights over human rights, stability over justice, order over freedom, and socioeconomic privilege over attempts to achieve socioeconomic fairness. The arch-traditionalist of the sixties was California governor Ronald Reagan, a thoroughly mean, simple, and narrow-minded man. That he eventually sweet-talked his way to becoming president was a cultural and political disaster for America. He, his administration, and his personality cult, including the "Moral Majority," worked very hard to erase as much of the egalitarian progress of the sixties and seventies as possible. Their vision of an ideal world consisted of a global American empire and an intolerant, regimented, obedient, "patriotic" society.

A too fine line exists between flag-waving patriotism and fascism. A true patriot is more concerned to guard principles than to wave the flag or defend the country. To declare, "My country, right or wrong!" exalts the parochial above the universal, or elevates a contingent human construct over absolute ethical principles. It gives a person the wrong loyalties. The phrase originated as a misquotation — but not a misrepresentation — of a toast offered around 1816 by Commodore Stephen Decatur, "Our Country! In her intercourse with foreign nations may she always be in the right; but right or wrong, our country!" Better said was Carl Schurz's correction of Decatur's motto: "My country, right or wrong; if right, to be kept right; and if wrong, to be set right."

Curse Stephen Decatur! Attitudes like his reduce patriotism to the amoral level by which we cheer for our favorite football team just because it is *ours*. Whether or not we cheer for our country ought to be determined by whether or not it is *ethically upright*, not by whether or not it is *ours*. When our country is wrong, and their country is right, we ought to point that fact out, and support theirs — while striving vigorously and urgently to put ours right.

We "nattering nabobs of negativism," as Spiro Agnew called us,[72] turned out to have been right all along, about Vietnam and about a ton of other divisive issues. We were also something that Agnew himself never was: honest. He and his ilk were the negative ones. All they ever wanted to do was to use America for their own personal gain. We actually and sincerely wanted to improve it, to be its good citizens, to celebrate its occasional righteousness, to decry its frequent ethical lapses, to share in its wealth, and to make sure that there was plenty to go around. We could still look ourselves in the mirror and each other in the face with clear consciences while he was chanting "*Nolo contendere.*"

The United States of America is indeed a wonderful country! I say that with complete sincerity. But — and this is the crux of the whole matter — we must remain ever vigilant to keep it wonderful and make it better. That is an internal process of citizen activism. It does not entail competing with other nations, and especially it does not involve abusing them, bullying them, or invading them. Every goodhearted American citizen will work hard to prevent the government from grabbing power, restricting freedom, misusing authority, or suppressing dissent. The country will not stay the same if we rest. The slumber of citizens gives governments the opportunity for tyranny. The president, courts, and Congress will surely grab that opportunity the instant they detect it. It *can* happen here! Our complacency would be the death of everything we hold dear.

But what is America?

America is where citizens can come and go as they please without fear of

---

[72] In a speech written by William Safire and delivered at the California State Republican Convention in San Diego on September 11, 1970, Agnew said: "In the United States today, we have more than our share of the nattering nabobs of negativism. They have formed their own 4-H Club — the hopeless, hysterical hypochondriacs of history." In the "Talk of the Town" column in *The New Yorker*, July 10, 2006, David Remnick accurately characterized Agnew as the "White House Torquemada" and his style as "surrealist-alliterative."

being spied upon. It is where they can freely, overtly, and with impunity, dissent from the government. It is the land where consenting adults can do whatever they want as long as they do not harm anyone else. It is the land of the First Amendment, the Fourth Amendment, the Gettysburg Address, the Marshall Plan, the Freedom of Information Act, and the National Institutes of Health. It is not the land of the Alien and Sedition Acts of 1798, the slaveholding tradition that lasted far too long, Jim Crow laws, Prohibition, sodomy laws, J. Edgar Hoover, the Gulf of Tonkin Resolution, the USA-PATRIOT Act, the Vietnam War, the Iraq War, or the Department of Homeland Security's Automated Targeting System. No government has any right to keep any secret files on any of its own citizens, unless a specific and legal warrant to allow it has come into existence through due process.

The problem is not the system. The problem is greed.

Tom Wolfe was quite correct to label the seventies "The Me Decade." How did the sixties, a decade of youthful idealism, collapse into the seventies, a decade of selfishness? Pat answers include the temptation of greed, the cynicism of Watergate, the tiresomeness of protesting, and the plain fact that young people living off their parents now grew up and found that they had to make their own livings. There is some truth in each of these, but a better answer would involve an analysis of the natural aging process. Not only do individuals age, but also groups, movements, and indeed, life itself. People born after around 1956 or 1957 did not remember JFK or his idealism very well. They were now fourteen or fifteen and had been raised on a steady diet of LBJ and Nixon. What a dreadful way to raise kids! The leftist *Zeitgeist* of the sixties had originated in a post-JFK concern for sociopolitical ethics, social justice, and individual freedom. But, because the sixties had expressed this concern in fresh music, bright clothes, flashy art, and other new, attractive forms, these phenomena naturally led, among those who did not remember JFK well, to a shift from the ethical toward the aesthetic. That is, they saw what was around them, they saw that it was new, and they liked it, but they did not remember or know why it had arisen. A paradigmatic illustration of this shift would be the common sixties slogan, "Do Your Own Thing!", whose original meaning had been ethical, but now meant something in the aesthetic sphere. It had come to refer to matter, no longer to spirit. There was our lack of discipline! Thus, following the standard Hegelian dialectical patterns that ably inform our understanding of historical change, idealistic, moralistic individualism became selfish, amoral individualism. Once the ethical had been lost or subsumed in the aesthetic, it was then just a small step down from the most honorable libertarian motives into pure selfishness. Even some sociopolitical movements that remained ethical and altruistic in the seventies were wrongly perceived as aesthetic or selfish. For example, anti-feminists saw the Equal Rights Amendment as an item on the selfish agenda of a special interest lobby, not as what is really was: an attempt to legalize the natural equality of both genders.

We can never know what transpires in corporate boardrooms or in the highest echelons of business or finance. Their decisions are more secret — and ultimately more powerful — than those made in the highest echelons of politics, even in the White House. Yet we can imagine what the business leaders of the late sixties and early seventies thought about the record industry. On one hand, many suit-wearers were getting filthy rich from music that they did not like or understand. On the other hand, they could not continue to allow radical bands like the Airplane to make subversive political statements under their corporate aegis. The achievements of music-as-politics, or more specifically, of popular-music-as-leftist-politics, had not gone unnoticed or uncountered — quite successfully— by our opponents. Music had united the listeners, created bridges. For example, the black civil rights movement had to a large extent been strengthened by white kids who had learned to love black music. But as soon as the vested-interest suit-wearers became aware of what was really happening in music, they invoked the ancient conservative oligarch's watchword: "Divide and conquer!" They would divide the listeners, invent "narrowcasting," create new radio formats such as "classic rock" to segregate the audience into manageable blocs. They probably also began refusing to sign new artists whose politics were outside the acceptable mainstream — but we outside the corporate realm cannot prove that assertion. Records in the late seventies, eighties, nineties, and into the new century became more exciting, louder, more violent, and less evocative, featuring rhythms, tunes, and hooks that kids would buy, but without many subversive leftist lyrics. Rather, their typical lyrics were either meaningless or promoted violence, hatred, cop-killing, misogyny, sexual predation, or some aspect of the rightist agenda. Peace and love no more! DJs and musicians remained typically on our side, at least into the nineties, but their bosses remained, for the most part, "them": the tools of the conservative order.

Here are three counterfactual consequences that I am sure would have ensued if their respective antecedents had occurred:

1. If JFK had not been assassinated, the United States would not have become so entangled in Vietnam. JFK was too shrewd, prescient, and prudent to let that happen. LBJ was more arrogant, less intelligent, less diplomatic, and less well informed about foreign affairs than JFK. JFK would not have rushed into war after the Gulf of Tonkin incident. He would have used diplomacy, brinkmanship, and consummate skill to keep us out of war while yet maintaining our national integrity and protecting our legitimate interests in Southeast Asia.

2. If Bobby Kennedy had not been assassinated, he would have been elected president in 1968. That would have been disaster! The reaction of both the right and the center, not to mention foreign powers, to his brash, devious, and hypocritical leadership would have made the actual 1968 Democratic Convention seem tame compared to the mayhem that would have characterized it in 1972.

The worst thing that JFK did in his presidency was to elevate his brother Bobby to any position of power. Bobby, unlike his brothers Jack and Ted, was an unprincipled opportunist. Among his first jobs as a lawyer fresh out of the University of Virginia School of Law was on the staff of Senator Joseph McCarthy, "Tail Gunner Joe." He stayed with McCarthy, the godfather of his first child, through the main years of the McCarthy Era. When the prevailing winds of public opinion and political savvy began to blow away from McCarthyism in 1953, Bobby quickly resigned and went to feather his nest elsewhere. Seldom in all history has there been such a master of deceiving the public in order to create and ensure his own popularity. By the mid-sixties he had convinced a large and influential fraction of the American people that he was sincere about his opposition to the Vietnam War. Ha! Bobby Kennedy was never sincere about anything except his own self-aggrandizement. He wanted to be president. He took advantage of LBJ's decreasing popularity by embracing positions contrary to LBJ's. If LBJ had been antiwar, Bobby would have been prowar. It is just that simple.

3. If McGovern had been elected president in 1972, he may have served two productive terms and might have prevented Reagan's right wing takeover in 1980, which succeeded in large measure because of the broad reaction against Jimmy Carter's ineptitude in practical politics. McGovern had an asset in 1972 that the two major antiwar candidates of 1968, Bobby Kennedy and Eugene McCarthy, did not have: the respect and friendship of Barry Goldwater. McGovern was both a good man and a practical politician. That contrasts him with Carter, a good but impractical man.

Without regard to respective ideologies, a quick-and-dirty comparison of the ethical characters and political skills of the presidents and some of the near presidents from the fifties to the eighties might be useful:

Dwight D. Eisenhower: good man, middlingly practical politician
JFK: good man, very practical politician
LBJ: evil man, practical in domestic politics, impractical in foreign policy
Bobby Kennedy: evil man, impractical politician, expert self-promoter
Hubert Humphrey: good man, practical politician, but too subservient to LBJ
Eugene McCarthy: good man, impractical politician
Nixon: thoroughly evil and sneaky man, very practical politician
McGovern: good man, practical politician
Carter: very good man, conscientious but impractical politician
Reagan: amoral and violent man, practical politician, masterful demagogue

On April 24, 1971, a bright, warm, sunny Saturday, about half a million nonviolent antiwar activists marched on Washington under the aegis of the National Peace Action Coalition (NPAC). From my own vantage point on the slope of the Capitol west lawn I observed the demonstrations to be entirely peaceful. But the following Monday, April 26, and lasting until Thursday, May 6, a few thousand violent antiwar activists, believing that nonviolent means would not end the war or improve American society, staged destructive protests and provoked confrontations with police. We wished that they had either emulated us or stayed home.

Why did we march? Was it an empty gesture with no practical political significance? Yes, probably. Our marching did not change LBJ's, Nixon's, or any senator's or representative's mind who might have actually had a hand in ending the war sooner. But not marching would have emboldened them to escalate further. Our non-action would have been interpreted as assent to their warmongering. So, negatively, our marching had a positive effect.

But make no mistake: **WE** ended the war! We did it! We ourselves! How? By convincing Nixon and his successor, Gerald Ford, that the young people of America were so overwhelmingly against the war that the government would soon no longer be able to either draft or recruit enough new soldiers to fight it. Whether or not the majority of our parents' generation continued to support the war did not matter. That we had alienated many of them made no difference. They were too old to fight anyway. A critical percentage of military-aged men would simply refuse.

Yet overall, our political revolution was a failure. If it had been a success, George McGovern would have won the 1972 election, America would have continued along FDR's path toward true socialism, the Equal Rights Amendment would have become part of the Constitution, and American foreign policy would thereafter have prohibited the American military from invading other countries, launching pre-emptive strikes against them, or meddling in their affairs unless America was first severely provoked — as it had been in 1941 at Pearl Harbor.

Three of the factors that contributed to the failure of our political revolution were:

1. We were responsible for too much violence. Fighting for peace is indeed, as we commonly said at the time, like fucking for chastity. We generally recognized that nonviolence was the only way to build a better country, a better society, and a better world, but we should have paid more attention to our nonviolent role models such as Gandhi, King, Tolstoi, Staughton Lynd, the Society of Friends (Quakers), and many other wonderful people. It was absolutely essential to occupy always the high moral ground. We failed miserably at this. By either starting violence ourselves, as the Weathermen and the Panthers did, or by retaliating in kind when others used violence against us, as most of the rest of us did, we descended toward — maybe not all the way down to — but toward the low moral level of our violent adversaries. Retaliating with violent force to the attack on Pearl Harbor was necessary and justified, and World War II from the Allied point of view was as just as any war ever is, yet entering even that war brought the United States down a few moral pegs toward, but not all the way to, the level of Tojo.

2. We indulged in too much ego-driven ideological competition among ourselves. One of us might brag, "I'm farther left than you." To compete with one's own political allies to see who is ideologically purer is narrow-minded and counterproductive. The point is not to see who is farther left, but to make a better world. If making a better world occasionally means taking a centrist or even a rightist position on some issue, then so be it. We leftists must always keep our minds open, decide each issue on its ethical merits, and act accordingly. To do so is neither situational nor unprincipled, but pragmatic.

3. We failed to articulate our fundamental positions clearly and to criticize them objectively. We talked and wrote a great deal, but much of what we said and wrote began *in medias res* and had no substantial empirical, ideological, or even commonsensical foundation. It lacked thorough scrutiny, intellectual rigor, and even everyday levels of exactitude. We did not doublecheck facts before we built castles in the air on their basis. There was a tendency — by no means universal, but significant — to assume in the case of class struggle that the poor, the have-nots, or the workers were always right and that the rich, the haves, or the bosses were always wrong. We did not analyze the roots and causes of particular situations, but only the present realities in which the poor, the have-nots, or the workers were plainly oppressed, suppressed, firebombed, rounded up, or shot at. Our argu-

ments in these situations were seldom *ad rem*, addressing the true matter-at-hand, but typically *ad misericordiam*, appealing to pity and attempting to motivate action to relieve the perceived immediate, existential suffering of the poor, the have-nots, or the workers, regardless or whether they were ultimately right or wrong in any particular situation. Of course we were correct to act against such oppression, suppression, firebombing, rounding up, or shooting, but we were generally wrong not to try first to learn some history. We treated the tactics of the rich, the haves, and the bosses as their grand strategy; we equated their outward violence with their inward spirit; and we saw the symptoms of injustice as the essence of injustice. Thus we left ourselves vulnerable — and the rich, the haves, and the bosses relatively impervious — to philosophical criticism. Our critics accurately claimed that we were very good at recognizing injustice and tearing systems down, but not good at establishing justice or inventing new systems to protect justice. We did not ruminate hard enough, broadly enough, or in sufficient depth.

But the outcome of our cultural revolution was better. Thanks to us, dress codes were relaxed in schools and workplaces; censorship in comedy, music, and film was relaxed; black music, leftist-message music, and innovative rock music in general, all became part of the mainstream; overt feminist and gay initiatives became part of the national fabric; pressure to conform decreased; school administrations became less authoritarian; the whole Western world, even despite the Vietnam War, racial strife, and assassinations, became temporarily much more fun; and perhaps a few bosses even became less bossy.

If we failed at all, we failed to articulate or communicate accurately and properly our vision of what the world could and should be. We expended little effort on this task, which, in retrospect, should have held the highest priority. But it all seemed just so obvious to us. We knew, saw, and understood each other all implicitly, or so we thought at the time. To try to articulate this knowledge, vision, and understanding would have ruined the moment, or at least made it awkward and artificial. It would have routinized our shared, leaderless charisma (to borrow and mangle a concept from Max Weber's *Theory of Social and Economic Organization*).

Our revolt was mainly against stodginess, priggishness, meddlesomeness, conformity, chauvinism, bigotry, jingoism, severity, and the attitude that adults are entitled to dictate what their children are and do. Our weapons were tolerance, humor, irreverence, joy, and music. We won! Our cultural revolution was a success!

$$\Omega$$

Our victory, however, seems to have been short-lived.

$$\Omega$$

Bibliography

Abbott, Keith. *Downstream from Trout Fishing in America: A Memoir of Richard Brautigan*. Santa Barbara: Capra, 1989.

Adler, Nathan. *The Underground Stream: New Life Styles and the Antinomian Personality*. New York: Harper Torchbooks, 1972.

Ahmad, Muhammad. *We Will Return in the Whirlwind: Black Radical Organizations, 1960-1975*. Chicago: Charles H. Kerr, 2007.

Ali, Tariq; Watkins, Susan. *1968: Marching in the Streets*. New York: Free Press, 1998.

Ali, Tariq. *Street Fighting Years: An Autobiography of the Sixties*. New York: Verso, 2005.

Allyn, David Smith. *Make Love, Not War: The Sexual Revolution: An Unfettered History*. New York: Routledge, 2001.

Alpert, Jane. *Growing Up Underground*. New York: Citadel, 1990.

American Film Institute Catalog of Motion Pictures Produced in the United States: Feature Films 1961-1970, edited by Richard P. Krafsur. Berkeley: University of California Press, 1997.

Anders, Jentri. *Beyond Counterculture: The Community of Mateel*. Pullman: Washington State University Press, 1990.

Anderson, Lindsay; Sherwin, David. *"If…": A Film*. New York: Simon and Schuster, 1969.

Anderson, Terry H. *The Movement and the Sixties*. New York: Oxford University Press, 1995.

Anthony, Gene. *Summer of Love: Haight-Ashbury at its Highest*. San Francisco: Last Gasp Eco-Funnies, 1995.

Archer, Jules. *The Incredible Sixties: The Stormy Years That Changed America*. San Diego: Harcourt Brace Jovanovich, 1986.

Aristotle. *Nicomachean Ethics*. Should have been more widely read and heeded in the sixties, as indeed in all eras.

The Ballad of John and Yoko, edited by Jonathan Cott and Christine Doudna. Garden City, N.Y.: Rolling Stone Press, 1982.

Barber, John F. *Richard Brautigan: An Annotated Bibliography*. Jefferson, N.C.: McFarland, 1990.

Barrie, Bill, *et al.* "We, The People." Philadelphia: [s.n.], 1970. Public claim of responsibility for destroying draft records in Lansdale, Pennsylvania, on May 19, 1970.

Bates, Tom. *Rads: The 1970 Bombing of the Army Math Research Center at the University of Wisconsin and its Aftermath*. New York: HarperCollins, 1992.

The Beatles and Philosophy, edited by Michael and Steven Baur. Chicago: Open Court, 2006.

Beauvoir, Simone de. *The Ethics of Ambiguity*, translated by Bernard Frechtman. New York: Philosophical Library, 1949.

Beauvoir, Simone de. *The Second Sex*, translated by H.M. Parshley. New York: Knopf, 1953.

Bell, Inge Powell. *CORE and the Strategy of Non-Violence*. New York: Random House, 1968.

Berger, Dan. *Outlaws of America: The Weather Underground and the Politics of Solidarity*. Oakland: AK Press, 2005.

Berman, Larry. *Lyndon Johnson's War: The Road to Stalemate in Vietnam*. New York: W.W. Norton, 1989.

Berman, Ronald. *America in the Sixties: An Intellectual History*. New York: Free Press, 1968.

Bhagavad Gita. A poetic essay on devotion, obedience, and one's station and its duties.

Bloom, Allan. *The Closing of the American Mind*. New York: Simon & Schuster, 1987.

Bondurant, Joan V. *Conquest of Violence*. Princeton: Princeton University Press, 1958.

Boyer, Jay. *Richard Brautigan*. Boise, Idaho: Boise State University, 1987.

Brautigan, Ianthe. *You Can't Catch Death: A Daughter's Memoir*. New York: St. Martin's, 2000.

Brautigan, Richard. *The Abortion: An Historical Romance*. New York: Simon and Schuster, 1971.

Brautigan, Richard. *All Watched Over by Machines of Loving Grace*. San Francisco: Communication Company, 1967.

Brautigan, Richard. *A Confederate General from Big Sur*. New York: Grove Press, 1965.

Brautigan, Richard. *The Galilee Hitch-Hiker*. San Francisco: David Sandberg, Cranium Press, 1966.

Brautigan, Richard. *In Watermelon Sugar*. San Francisco: Four Seasons Foundation, 1968.

Brautigan, Richard. *The Pill Versus the Springhill Mine Disaster*. San Francisco: Four Seasons Foundation, City Light Books, 1968.

Brautigan, Richard. *Revenge of the Lawn: Stories, 1962-1970*. New York: Simon and Schuster, 1971.

Brautigan, Richard. *Rommel Drives on Deep into Egypt*. New York: Delacorte Press, 1970.

Brautigan, Richard. *Trout Fishing in America: A Novel*. San Francisco: Four Seasons Foundation, City Light Books, 1967.

Brick, Howard. *Age of Contradiction: American Thought and Culture in the 1960s*. Ithaca: Cornell University Press, 2001.

Brightman, Carol. *Sweet Chaos: The Grateful Dead's American Adventure*. New York: Simon & Schuster, 1998.

Brokaw, Tom, *Boom: Voices of the Sixties*. New York: Random House, 2007. What a piece of crap! Condescending, snide, name-dropping, self-serving fluff.

Bromell, Nicholas Knowles. *Tomorrow Never Knows: Rock and Psychedelics in the 1960s*. Chicago: University of Chicago Press, 2000.

Buckley, Christopher. *Sleepwalk: California Dreamin' and a Last Dance With the '60s*. Spokane: Eastern Washington University Press, 2006.

Burgess, Anthony. *A Clockwork Orange*. New York: Ballantine, 1962.

Burner, David. *Making Peace With the 60s*. Princeton: Princeton University Press, 1998.

Burns, Ron. *The Suicide Club: A Dark Comedy About Surviving Sex, Drugs, Rock & Roll*. Online at <101hollywood.com/3suicide/>.

Camden (N.J.) Lutheran Youth Ministry. *Do-It* 1, 6 (August 21, 1970). Typical of the plethora of antiwar journals spontaneously published by Christian teenagers with their church's money and with or without their church's approval; contains plenty of poetry, music reviews, open letters, and slogans.

Carroll, James. *An American Requiem: God, My Father, and the War that Came Between Us*. Boston: Houghton Mifflin, 1996.

Case, Clarence Marsh. *Non-Violent Coercion: A Study in Methods of Social Pressure*. New York: Century, 1923.

The Cash Box Singles Charts, 1950-1981, edited by Frank W. Hoffman and Lee Ann Hoffman. Metuchen, N.J.: Scarecrow, 1983.

Cavallo, Dominick. *A Fiction of the Past: The Sixties in American History*. New York: St. Martin's, 1999.

Chénetier, Marc. *Richard Brautigan*. London: Methuen, 1983.

Circus. New York: Circus Enterprises, 1967-1978.

Cleaver, Eldridge. *Soul on Fire*. Waco, Texas: Word Books, 1978. A travesty, a repudiation of all the good he ever did.

Cleaver, Eldridge. *Soul on Ice*. New York: Delta, 1968. Essential for understanding the motivations of the Black Panthers.

Clergy and Laymen Concerned About Vietnam. "Vietnamization: Some Facts and Figures." New York: [s.n., ca. 1970]. Well researched and tightly argued information sheet, mailed in great quantities to resistance chapters nationwide.

Coleman, Ray. *Lennon*. New York: McGraw-Hill, 1985.

Coleridge, Samuel Taylor. "The Rime of the Ancient Mariner." A classic of ecological awareness.

Cowie, Peter. *Revolution! The Explosion of World Cinema in the Sixties*. New York: Faber and Faber, 2004.

Cox, Harvey. *The Secular City: Secularization and Urbanization in Theological Perspective*. New York: Macmillan, 1965.

Crawdaddy. New York: [s.n.], 1966-1978.

Creem. Detroit: [s.n.]; Los Angeles: Cambray, 1969-1991.

Davidson, Eugene. *Reflections on a Disruptive Decade: Essays on the Sixties*. Columbia: University of Missouri Press, 2000.

Davies, Ray. *X-Ray*. Woodstock, N.Y.: Overlook Press, 1995. Among the most entertaining and informative of all rock biographies or autobiographies.

Davis, Angela. *An Autobiography*. New York: International, 1989.

Davis, R.G. *The San Francisco Mime Troupe: The First Ten Years*. Palo Alto, Calif.: Ramparts, 1975.

Deighton, Len. *The Ipcress File*. New York: Simon and Schuster, 1963.

DeKoven, Marianne. *Utopia Limited: The Sixties and the Emergence of the Postmodern*. Durham: Duke University Press, 2004.

Dickens, Charles. *A Tale of Two Cities*. Sydney Carton is a prototypical hero of the human revolution.

Dickstein, Morris. *Gates of Eden: American Culture in the Sixties*. New York: Basic Books, 1977.

The Disobedient Generation: Social Theorists in the Sixties, edited by Alan Sica and Stephen Turner. Chicago: University of Chicago Press, 2005.

Donovan, John C. *The Politics of Poverty* — 2nd edition — Indianapolis: Bobbs-Merrill, 1973.

Douglas, William O. *Points of Rebellion*. New York: Random House, 1969; Vintage, 1970.

The Drummer [sometimes called *The Distant Drummer*, *Thursday's Drummer*, etc.]. Underground weekly or biweekly newspaper that ran 568 issues in Philadelphia from November 1967 until August 1979.

Dunaway, David King. *How Can I Keep From Singing: Pete Seeger*. New York: McGraw-Hill, 1981.

Echols, Alice. *Shaky Ground: The '60s and its Aftershocks*. New York: Columbia University Press, 2002.

Ellsberg, Daniel. *Papers on the War*. New York: Simon & Schuster, 1972.

Episcopal Peace Fellowship. *EPF Newsletter* (Summer 1970). Probably the best issue of a very good series; a vision of what the church could and ought to be.

Episcopal Peace Fellowship. "Which Way Are You Going? Counsel for Men Facing the Draft." New York: [ca. 1968-1969]. An informative pamphlet which was in general use among both clergy and lay draft counselors.

Episcopal Year, 1969, edited by Philip Deemer. New York: Jarrow, 1970. An encyclopedic chronicle of the turbulent polarization of this church as it was at last forced, through confrontations with the Black Economic Development Conference (BEDC) and with federal policy, to struggle with ethical issues whose obvious solutions flew in the face of its traditions.

Erikson, Erik H. *Gandhi's Truth: On the Origins of Militant Nonviolence*. New York: Norton, 1969.

Farber, David R. *The Sixties: From Memory to History*. Chapel Hill: University of North Carolina Press, 1994.

Farber, Jerry. "The Student as Nigger," *Los Angeles Free Press*, vol. 4, no. 9, issue 137 (March 3, 1967): 8, 18-19. Widely mimeographed for free general distribution. A professor's eloquent call for students to seize power over the classroom.

Farley, Chuck U. [pseudonym]. *Tattoo Charlie: Teaching a New Generation of Cannon Fodder What Not to Do, and How Not to Do It*. Historical novel online at <justsopress.typepad.com/tattoo_charlie/>. "Chuck you, Farley" was a classic sixties spoonerism for "Fuck You, Charley."

Farmer, James. *Lay Bare the Heart: An Autobiography of the Civil Rights Movement*. Fort Worth: Texas Christian University Press, 1998.

Farrell, James J. *The Spirit of the Sixties: Making Postwar Radicalism*. New York: Routledge, 1997.

The Fellowship of Reconciliation. "A Father's Day Message: It Time to Stop Killing Fathers — and Sons, Time to Disarm America." Nyack, N.Y.: June [1968]. Broadside issued in the immediate wake of the madness surrounding the murder of Robert F. Kennedy, calling for abolition of all small arms.

Film 68/69: An Anthology by the National Society of Film Critics, edited by Hollis Alpert and Andrew Sarris. New York: Simon & Schuster, 1969.

Findlay, John Niemeyer. *Hegel: A Re-Examination*. New York: Oxford University Press, 1976; London: George Allen and Unwin, 1958.

Finn, James. *Protest: Pacifism and Politics*. New York: Random House, 1967.

Fischer, Klaus P. *America in White, Black, and Gray: The Stromy 1960s*. New York: Continuum International, 2006.

Foster, Edward Halsey. *Richard Brautigan*. Boston: Twayne, 1983.

Free History Project. *The Weather Underground* [video recording, 92 minutes]. DVD: Waterville, Maine: Shadow Distribution, 2003

Friends Peace Committee. *A Perspective on Nonviolence*. Philadelphia: Friends Peace Committee, 1957.

Furst, Peter T. *Hallucinogens and Culture*. San Francisco: Chandler and Sharp, 1976.

Gallagher, R[obert]. "Institutional Racism and Reparations." Philadelphia: Crisis Forum, [1969]. A white man's support for BEDC's demands, privately mimeographed and circulated within the Episcopal Diocese of Pennsylvania.

Gandhi, Mohandas K. *An Autobiography: The Story of My Experiments with Truth*. Boston: Beacon, 1929.

Garson, Barbara. *MacBird*. New York: Grove Press, 1967.

Gibran, Kahlil. *The Prophet*. New York: Alfred A. Knopf, 1952.

Gitlin, Todd. *The Sixties: Years of Hope, Days of Rage*. New York: Bantam, 1987. So far, the standard history.

Goldman, Albert Harry. *The Lives of John Lennon*. New York: Morrow, 1988.

Goldman, Eric Frederick. *The Tragedy of Lyndon Johnson*. New York: Knopf, 1969.

Goldstein, Richard. "Wiggy Words That Feed Your Mind," *Life* 64, 26 (June 28, 1968): 67-70.

Goldstein, Toby. *Waking from the Dream: America in the Sixties*. New York: J. Messner, 1988.

Goodman, Paul. *Growing Up Absurd: Problems of Youth in the Organized System*. New York: Random House, 1960.

Gosse, Van. *The Movements of the New Left, 1950-1975: A Brief History with Documents*. Boston: Bedford / St. Martin's, 2005.

Gowan, Susanne; Lakey, George; Moyer, William; Taylor, Richard. *Moving Toward a New Society*. Philadelphia: New Society Press, 1976.

Greenfield, Robert. *Timothy Leary: A Biography*. Orlando: Harcourt, 2006.

Gregg, Richard Bartlett. *The Power of Nonviolence* — 2nd edition — New York: Schocken, 1966.

Grene, Marjorie Glicksman. *Dreadful Freedom: A Critique of Existentialism*. Chicago: University of Chicago Press, 1948.

Guthrie, Arlo. *Alice's Restaurant*, drawings by Marvin Glass. New York: Grove Press, 1968. The epic tale of the happy-go-lucky freak's confrontation with a ridiculous social system.

"Hairsplitting," *Time* 87 (May 27, 1966): 55-56.

Haley, Alex. *The Autobiography of Malcolm X*. New York: Grove Press, 1965.

Harris, David. *Dreams Die Hard*. New York: St. Martin's / Marek, 1982.

Harrison, George. *I Me Mine*. New York: Simon & Schuster, 1980.

Hayden, Tom. *Trial*. New York: Holt, Rinehart and Winston, 1970.

Hegel, G.W.F. *Introduction to the Philosophy of History*, translated by Leo Rauch
  Indianapolis: Hackett, 1988.

Hegel, G.W.F. *Phenomenology of Spirit*, translated by A.V. Miller. Oxford:
  Clarendon, 1977.

Hegel, G.W.F. *Philosophy of Right*, translated by T.M. Knox. Oxford: Clarendon, 1952.

Heineman, Kenneth J. *Put Your Bodies Upon the Wheels: Student Revolt in the
  1960s*. Chicago: I.R. Dee, 2001.

Heirich, Max. *The Beginning: Berkeley 1964*. New York: Columbia University Press,
  1971.

Heller, Joseph. *Catch-22*. New York: Simon and Schuster, 1961.

Hersey, John. "1968: America's Worst Year Ever," *The Philadelphia Inquirer, Today
  Magazine* (Sunday, December 3, 1978): 14-41.

Hesse, Hermann. *Beneath the Wheel*, translated by Michael Roloff. New York:
  Farrar, Straus, and Giroux, 1968.

Hesse, Hermann. *Demian: The Story of Emil Sinclair's Youth*, translated by Michael
  Roloff and Michael Lebeck. New York: Harper and Row, 1965.

Hesse, Hermann. *Gertrude*, translated by Hilda Rosner. New York: Farrar, Straus,
  and Giroux, 1969.

Hesse, Hermann. *The Glass Bead Game (Magister Ludi)*, translated by Richard and
  Clara Winston. New York: Holt, Rinehart, and Winston, 1969.

Hesse, Hermann. *The Journey to the East*, translated by Hilda Rosner. New York:
  Picador; Farrar, Straus and Giroux, 1956.

Hesse, Hermann. *Narcissus and Goldmund*, translated by Ursule Molinaro. New
  York: Farrar, Straus, and Giroux, 1968.

Hesse, Hermann. *Siddhartha*, translated by Hilda Rosner. New York: New
  Directions, 1951.

Hesse, Hermann. *Steppenwolf*, translated by Basil Creighton and Walter Sorell. New
  York: Modern Library, 1963.

Hill, Laban Carrick. *America Dreaming: How the 60's Changed America*. New York:
  Little, Brown, 2007.

Hinckle, Warren. *If You Have a Lemon, Make Lemonade*. New York: Putnam, 1974.

Hoffer, Eric. *The True Believer: Thoughts on the Nature of Mass Movements*. New
  York: Perennial Library, 1989.

[Hoffman, Abbie]. *Fuck the System*. [New York: s.n., 1967]. Anonymous
  underground anarchist pamphlet later revealed as Hoffman's work.

Hoffman, Abbie. *Revolution for the Hell of It*. New York: Dial Press, 1968. A tongue-
  in-cheek *Mein Kampf* for a moneyless society, written under the pseudonym, "Free."

Hoffman, Abbie. *Soon to be a Major Motion Picture*. New York: Putnam, 1980. His
  fanciful autobiography.

Hoffman, Abbie. *Steal This Book: A Handbook of Survival and Warfare for the
  Citizens of Woodstock Nation*. New York: Pirate Editions, 1971.

Hoffman, Abbie. *Woodstock Nation: A Talk-Rock Album*. New York: Vintage, 1969.

Hoffman, Abbie, John, Florence, Jack, Phyllis, Anita, *et al.* "Hoffman Family
  Papers," Archives and Special Collections at the Thomas J. Dodd Center, University
  of Connecticut, Storrs, Connecticut.

Holland, Gini. *A Cultural History of the United States Through the Decades: The 1960s*. San Diego, Calif.: Lucent, 1999. Simplistic and superficial.

Hollingshead, Michael. *The Man Who Turned On theWorld*. London: Blond and Briggs, 1973.

Hooker, Richard. *M*A*S*H*. New York: Morrow, 1968.

Hopkins, Jerry; Sugerman, Daniel. *No One Here Gets Out Alive*. New York: Warner, 1980.

Howard-Pitney, David. *Martin Luther King, Jr., Malcolm X, and the Civil Rights Struggle of the 1950s: A Brief History with Documents*. Boston: Bedford / St. Martin's, 2004.

Huxley, Aldous. *The Doors of Perception*. New York: Perennial Library; Harper & Row, 1954. Our main vicarious mescaline trip, a manifesto of the idea that altering our sensations of the physical can affect our intellection of the non-physical. Jim Morrison named his band after this book.

Isserman, Maurice; Kazin, Michael. *America Divided: The Civil War of the 1960s*. New York: Oxford University Press, 2003.

It Did Happen Here: Recollections of Political Repression in America, edited by Bud Schultz and Ruth Schultz. Berkeley: University of California Press, 1989.

Jacobs, Harold. *Weatherman*. Berkeley: Ramparts Press, 1971.

Jacobs, Ron. *The Way the Wind Blew: A History of the Weather Underground*. New York: Verso, 1997.

Jenkins, Philip. *Decade of Nightmares: The End of the Sixties and the Making of Eighties America*. New York: Oxford University Press, 2006.

Jezer, Marty. *Abbie Hoffman: American Rebel*. New Brunswick, N.J.: Rutgers University Press, 1992.

Kafka, Franz. *Amerika*, translated by Edwin Muir. New York: New Directions, 1962.

Kafka, Franz. *The Castle*, translated by Willa and Edwin Muir. New York: Alfred A. Knopf, 1954.

Kafka, Franz. *Metamorphosis*, translated by Albert Lancaster Lloyd. New York: Vanguard, 1946.

Kafka, Franz. *The Trial*, translated by Willa and Edwin Muir. New York: Alfred A. Knopf, 1957.

Kaiser, Charles. *1968 In America: Music, Politics, Chaos, Counterculture and the Shaping of a Generation*. New York: Grove Press, 1988.

Katsiaficas, George N. *The Imagination of the New Left: A Global Analysis of 1968*. Boston: South End Press, 1987.

Kaufmann, Walter. *Hegel: A Reinterpretation*. New York: Doubleday, 1965.

Kennedy, John Fitzgerald. *Profiles in Courage*. New York: Harper & Brothers, 1956.

Kent, Stephen A. *From Slogans to Mantras: Social Protest and Religious Conversion in the Late Vietnam War Era*. Syracuse: Syracuse University Press, 2001.

Kercher, Stephen Edward. "The Limits of Irreverence: 'Sick' Humor and Satire in America, 1950-1964" (Ph.D. dissertation, Indiana University, 2000). An analysis of editorial and political cartooning during that era.

Kitchell, Mark, *et al. Berkeley in the Sixties* [video recording, 117 minutes]. VHS: San Francisco: California Newsreel, 1990; DVD: New York: First Run Features, 2002.

Kleps, Art. *Millbrook: The True Story of the Early Years of the Psychedelic Revolution*. Oakland, Calif.: Bench Press, 1977.

Krishnamurti, Y.G. *Independent India and a New World Order*. Bombay: Popular Book Depot, 1943.

Kunen, James Simon. *The Strawberry Statement: Notes of a College Revolutionary*. New York: Random House, 1969.

Kurlansky, Mark. *1968: The Year that Rocked the World*. New York: Ballantine, 2004.

Lakey, George. *Non-Violent Action: How it Works*. Wallingford, Pennsylvania: Pendle Hill Pamphelets, 1963.

Lakey, George. *Revolution: A Quaker Prescription for a Sick Society*. Philadelphia: Quaker Action Group, 1971.

Lakey, George. *Training for Nonviolent Responses in Social Conflict: A Manual for Trainers*. Philadelphia: Friends Peace Committee, 1969.

Lang, Michael. *The Road to Woodstock: From the Man Behind the Legendary Festival*. New York: HarperCollins, 2009.

Lattin, Don. *Following Our Bliss: How the Spiritual Ideals of the Sixties Shape our Lives Today*. San Francisco: HarperSanFrancisco, 2003.

Leary, Timothy. *Flashbacks: An Autobiography*. Los Angeles: Tarcher, 1983.

LeCarre, John. *The Spy Who Came in from the Cold*. New York: Coward-McCann, 1963.

Lee, Martin A.; Shlain, Bruce. *Acid Dreams: The Complete Social History of LSD: The CIA, The Sixties, and Beyond*. New York: Grove Weidenfeld, 1992.

Lehrer, Tom. *Too Many Songs by Tom Lehrer With Not Enough Drawings by Ronald Searle*. New York: Pantheon, 1981.

Lennon, Cynthia. *John*. New York: Crown, 2005.

Lennon, John. *In His Own Write*. New York: Simon and Schuster, 1964. Taught us how to think and speak like sharp-witted freaks.

Lennon, John. *A Spaniard in the Works*. New York: Simon and Schuster, 1965. Not as good as *In His Own Write*.

Levitt, Cyril. *Children of Privilege: Student Revolt in the Sixties: A Study of Student Movements in Canada, the United States, and West Germany*. Toronto: University of Toronto Press, 1984.

Lingeman, Richard R. *Drugs from A to Z: A Dictionary*. New York: McGraw-Hill, 1969.

Loewenberg, Jacob. *Hegel's "Phenomenology": Dialogues on the Life of Mind*. La Salle, Illinois: Open Court, 1965.

Long Time Gone: Sixties America Then and Now, edited by Alexander Bloom. Oxford: Oxford University Press, 2001.

Louis, Debbie. *And We Are Not Saved: A History of the Movement as People*. New York: Doubleday, 1970.

Luft, Eric v.d. *A Socialist Manifesto*. North Syracuse, New York: Gegensatz, 2007.

Lukas, J. Anthony. *Don't Shoot — We Are Your Children!* New York: Random House, 1971.

Lynd, Staughton. *Intellectual Origins of American Radicalism*. New York: Pantheon, 1968.

Lynd, Staughton. *The New Radicals and "Participatory Democracy."* Chicago: Students for a Democratic Society, 1965.

Lynd, Staughton; Hayden, Tom. *The Other Side*. New York: New American Library, 1966.

Lytle, Mark Hamilton. *America's Uncivil Wars: The Sixties Era: From Elvis to the Fall of Richard Nixon*. New York: Oxford University Press, 2005.

Mailer, Norman. *The Armies of the Night: History as a Novel, The Novel as History*. New York: New American Library, 1968. "Nonfiction novel" account of the October 21, 1967 march on the Pentagon.

Mailer, Norman. *The Naked and the Dead: A Novel*. New York: Rinehart and Company, 1948.

Malley, Terence. *Richard Brautigan*. New York: Warner Paperback Library, 1972.

Marcus, Daniel. *Happy Days and Wonder Years: The Fifties and the Sixties in Contemporary Cultural Politics*. New Brunswick, N.J.: Rutgers University Press, 2004.

Marcuse, Herbert. *Eros and Civilization: A Philosophical Inquiry into Freud*. Boston: Beacon, 1955; New York: Vintage, 1962.

Marcuse, Herbert. *An Essay on Liberation*. Boston: Beacon, 1969.

Marcuse, Herbert. *One-Dimensional Man: Studies in the Ideology of Advanced Industrial Society*. Boston: Beacon, 1964.

Marcuse, Herbert. *Reason and Revolution: Hegel and the Rise of Social Theory*. New York: Oxford University Press, 1941; Boston: Beacon, 1960.

Marijuana: Chemistry, Pharmacology, and Patterns of Social Use, edited by Arnold J. Singer. New York: New York Academy of Sciences, 1971.

Markoff, John. *What the Dormouse Said: How the Sixties Counterculture Shaped the Personal Computer Industry*. New York: Viking, 2005.

Marqusee, Mike. *Chimes of Freedom: The Politics of Bob Dylan's Art*. New York: New Press, 2003.

Marqusee, Mike. *Redemption Song: Muhammad Ali and the Spirit of the Sixties*. New York: Verso, 2005.

Marqusee, Mike. *Wicked Messenger: Bob Dylan and the 1960s, Chimes of Freedom, Revised and Expanded*. New York: Seven Stories Press, 2005.

Marsh, Dave. *Before I Get Old: The Story of the Who*. New York: St. Martin's Press, 1983.

Martin, Bradford D. *The Theater is in the Street: Politics and Performance in Sixties America*. Amherst: University of Massachusetts Press, 2004.

McGee, C. Douglas. *The Recovery of Meaning: An Essay on the Good Life*. New York: Random House, 1966. A very dear and tragic book.

McNamara, Robert Strange. *In Retrospect: The Tragedy and Lessons of Vietnam*. New York: Random House, Times Books, 1995.

McWilliams, John C. *The 1960s Cultural Revolution*. Westport, Conn.: Greenwood Press, 2000.

Meltzer, Richard. *The Aesthetics of Rock*. New York: Something Else Press, 1970; New York: Da Capo, 1987.

Merton, Thomas. *Zen and the Birds of Appetite*. New York: New Directions, 1968.

Miller, Arthur. *The Crucible*. New York: Viking, 1953.

Miller, Douglas T.; Nowak, Marion. *The Fifties: The Way We Really Were*. Garden City, N.Y.: Doubleday, 1977.

Miller, Timothy. *The Hippies and American Values*. Knoxville: University of Tennessee Press, 1991.

Miller, William Robert. *Nonviolence: A Christian Interpretation*. New York: Association Press, 1964.

Monhollon, Rusty L. *This is America? The Sixties in Lawrence, Kansas*. New York: Palgrave, 2002.

Mungo, Raymond. *Famous Long Ago: My Life and Hard Times with Liberation News Service, at Total Loss Farm, and on the Dharma Trail*. New York: Citadel, 1990.

Naha, Ed. *Lillian Roxon's Rock Encyclopedia*. New York: Grosset & Dunlap, 1978.

National Black Economic Development Conference. "The Full Text of the Black Manifesto." Detroit: [BEDC], 1969. Privately printed and mimeographed by BEDC for circulation among several major religious denominations in an attempt to secure payment of at least $500,000,000 — "15 dollars per nigger" — in reparations for four centuries of white crimes against blacks.

The New Student Left: An Anthology, edited by Mitchell Cohen and Dennis Hale. Boston: Beacon, 1967.

Nietzsche, Friedrich. *Thus Spake Zarathustra*, translated by Alexander Tille. New York: Macmillan, 1896.

1968: A Student Generation in Revolt, edited by Fraser, Ronard, *et al.* New York: Pantheon, 1988.

Nonviolence in America: A Documentary History, edited by Staughton Lynd. Indianapolis: Bobbs-Merrill, 1966.

Oldham, Andrew Loog, *Stoned: A Memoir of London in the 1960s*. New York: St. Martin's Press, 2000. Bizarre autobiographical sketches of the Rolling Stones' manager.

O'Neill, William. *Coming Apart: An Informal History of America in the 1960's*. New York: Random House, Times Books; Chicago: Quadrangle, 1971.

Ono, Yoko. *Memories of John Lennon*. New York: Harper, 2005.

Olson, James S.; Roberts, Randy. *My Lai: A Brief History with Documents*. Boston: Bedford, 1998.

Oppenheimer, Martin; Lakey, George. *A Manual for Direct Action*. Chicago: Quadrangle, 1965.

Orwell, George. *Nineteen Eighty-Four*. New York: Harcourt, Brace, 1949.

Oswald, Andrew. "The Hippies Were Right All Along About Happiness," *Financial Times* (January 19, 2006).

Partridge, Elizabeth. *John Lennon: All I Want is Truth: A Biography*. New York: Viking, 2005.

Peck, Abe. *Uncovering the Sixties: The Life and Times of the Underground Press*. New York: Pantheon, 1985.

Pendergast, Tom and Sara. *Sixties in America: Primary Sources*. Detroit: U.X.L, 2005.

Pendergast, Tom and Sara. *The Sixties in America: Biographies*. Detroit: Thomson Gale, 2005.

Perone, James E. *Music of the Counterculture Era*. Westport, Conn.: Greenwood Press, 2004.

Perry, Charles. *The Haight-Ashbury: A History*. New York: Random House, 1984.

Perry, Helen Swick. *The Human Be-In*. New York: Basic Books, 1970.

Philadelphia New Mobilization Committee. "March on Washington, November 15, for the Immediate Withdrawal of all 500,000 U.S. Troops." Philadelphia: [s.n., 1969]. Flyer to publicize the March Against Death and to sell bus tickets.

Playboy. Not to be overlooked as a primary source of the sixties *Zeitgeist*. The cartoons and articles are much more interesting than the pictures.

The Playboy Interviews with John Lennon and Yoko Ono, conducted by David Sheff, edited by G. Barry Golson. New York: Playboy Press, 1981.

The Portable Beat Reader, edited by Ann Charters. New York: Penguin, 1992.

The Quiet Battle: Writings on the Theory and Practice of Non-Violent Resistance, edited by Mulford Quickert Sibley. Garden City, N.Y.: Doubleday, 1963.

Raines, Howell. *My Soul is Rested: Movement Days in the Deep South Remembered*. New York: Penguin, 1983.

Raskin, Jonah. *For the Hell of It: The Life and Times of Abbie Hoffman*. Berkeley: University of California Press, 1996.

Ravan, Genya, *Lollipop Lounge: Memoirs of a Rock and Roll Refugee*. New York: Billboard, 2004. Not just tits and ass.

Richman, Robin. "The New Rock," *Life* 64, 26 (June 28, 1968): 51-64.

Rielly, Edward J. *The 1960s*. Westport, Conn.: Greenwood Press, 2003.

Riggenbach, Jeff. *In Praise of Decadence*. Amherst, N.Y.: Prometheus Books, 1998.

Riley, Charles A. *The Art of Peter Max*. New York: Harry N. Abrams, 2002.

Rodnitzky, Jerome L. "The Sixties Between the Microgrooves: Using Folk and Protest Music to Understand American History, 1963-1973," *Popular Music and Society*, 23 (1999): 105-122.

Rolling Stone. San Francisco: Straight Arrow, 1967- . Slick and mainstream since the 1980s, but in its earliest years was the voice of the musical underground.

Rolling Stones: An Unauthorized Biography in Words, Photographs, and Music, edited by David Dalton. New York: Amsco Music, 1972.

Roskind, Robert A. *Memoirs of an Ex-Hippie: Seven Years in the Counterculture*. Blowing Rock, North Carolina: One Love Press, 2001.

Rossman, Michael. *New Age Blues: On the Politics of Consciousness*. New York: Dutton, 1979.

Roszak, Theodore. *The Making of a Counter Culture: Reflections on the Technocratic Society and its Youthful Opposition*. New York: Doubleday, 1969.

Roth, Philip. *Portnoy's Complaint*. New York: Random House, 1969.

Rousseau, Jean-Jacques. *The Social Contract and Discourse on the Origin and Foundation of Inequality Among Mankind*, edited by Lester G. Crocker. New York: Washington Square Press, 1967.

Roxon, Lillian; Naha, Ed. *Lillian Roxon's Rock Encyclopedia*. New York: Grosset and Dunlap, 1978. Full of typographical errors and conspicuous omissions, but truly indispensable.

Rubin, Jerry. *Do It! Scenarios of the Revolution*. New York: Simon and Schuster, 1970.

Rubin, Jerry. "Positively the Last Underground Interview with Abbie Hoffman ... (Maybe)," *High Times* 54 (February 1980).

Rudd, Mark. *Truth and Consequences: The Education of Mark Rudd*. New York: Grove Press, 1990.

Rudd, Mark. *Underground: My Life with SDS and the Weathermen*. New York: William Morrow, 2009.

Ryan, Patrick. *How I Won the War*. New York: Ballantine, 1963.

Sale, Kirkpatrick. *SDS*. New York: Vintage, 1974.

Salinger, J.D. *The Catcher in the Rye*. Boston: Little, Brown, 1951.

Sanders, Rick; Dalton, David. "[Interview with] Pete Townshend," *Rolling Stone*, 37 (July 12, 1969): 16-18.

Sann, Paul. *The Angry Decade: The Sixties*. New York: Crown Publishers, 1979.

Sayre, Nora. *Sixties Going on Seventies*. New York, Arbor House, 1973.

Schuchter, Arnold. *Reparations: The Black Manifesto and its Challenge to White America*. Philadelphia: Lippincott, 1970.

Schulz, Charles M. *Snoopy and the Red Baron*. New York: Holt, Rinehart and Winston, 1966. Quintessential pathos in the face of war.

The Scribner Encyclopedia of American Lives: The 1960s, edited by William L. O'Neill. New York: Thomson, Gale, 2003. Generally a solid biographical reference work, with excellent bibliographical hints, but also with occasional glaring errors, such as claiming that Abbie Hoffman coined the slogan, "Don't Trust Anyone Over Thirty!" (it was really Jack Weinberg during the 1964 Berkeley Free Speech Movement), and that Signe Anderson left Jefferson Airplane in September 1968 (it was really 1966 — quite a difference!).

Seeger, Pete. *Where Have All the Flowers Gone: A Musical Autobiography*, edited by Peter Blood. Bethlehem, Pa.: Sing Out, 1997.

Seeger, Pete. *Where Have All the Flowers Gone: A Singer's Stories, Songs, Seeds, Robberies*. Bethlehem, Pa.: Sing Out, 1993.

Shaw, George Bernard. *Man and Superman: A Comedy and a Philosophy*. Baltimore: Penguin, 1952. Contains, as an appendix, "The Revolutionists Handbook and Pocket Companion, by John Tanner, M.I.R.C. (Member of the Idle Rich Class)." Tanner is a character in Shaw's play, styled after Don Juan.

Shelton, Robert. *No Direction Home: The Life and Music of Bob Dylan*. New York: Beech Tree, 1986; Cambridge, Mass.: Da Capo, 2003.

Sherman, Allan. *The Rape of the A*P*E*: The Official History of the Sex Revolution, 1945-1973: The Obscening of America*. Chicago: Playboy Press, 1973. Although inaccurate on many key facts, especially dates, and although Sherman is notoriously unfamiliar with rock music and unappreciative of its significance, nevertheless, this book is keen insight thinly disguised as raucous comedy, and should be required reading for all sociologists.

The Sixties in America, edited by Carl Singleton. Pasadena: Salem, 1999.

The 60s Without Apology, edited by Sohnya Sayres, Anders Stephanson, Stanley Aronowitz, and Fredric Jameson. Minneapolis: University of Minnesota Press, 1984.

Slaven, Neil. *Electric Don Quixote: The Definitive Story of Frank Zappa*. London: Omnibus, 2003.

Slick, Grace, with Andrea Cagan. *Somebody to Love? A Rock-and-Roll Memoir*. New York: Warner, 1998.

Spann, Edward K. *Democracy's Children: The Young Rebels of the 1960s and the Power of Ideals*. Wilmington, Del.: Scholarly Resources, 2003.

Staller, Karen M. *Runaways: How the Sixties Counterculture Shaped Today's Practices and Policies*. New York: Columbia University Press, 2006.

Steigerwald, David. *The Sixties and the End of Modern America*. New York: St. Martin's, 1995.

Stevens, Jay. *Storming Heaven: LSD and the American Dream*. New York: Atlantic Monthly Press, 1987.

Stone, Robert. *Prime Green: Remembering the Nineteen Sixties*. New York: Ecco, 2007.

"Takin' it to the Streets": A Sixties Reader, edited by Alexander Bloom and Wini Breines. New York: Oxford University Press, 2002.

Tamarkin, Jeff. *Got a Revolution: The Turbulent Flight of Jefferson Airplane*. New York: Atria, 2003.

Templin, Ralph T. *Democracy and Nonviolence: The Role of the Individual in World Crisis*. Boston: Sargent, 1965.

Thompson, Thomas. "The New Far-Out Beatles," *Life* 62, 24 (June 16, 1967): 100-106.

Thoreau, Henry David. *Walden and Civil Disobedience: Authoritative Texts, Background, Reviews, and Essays in Criticism*, edited by Owen Paul Thomas. New York: Norton, 1966.

The Times Were A-Changin': The Sixties Reader, edited by Irwin Unger and Debi Unger. New York: Three Rivers Press, 1998.

Tollefson, James W. *The Strength Not to Fight: Conscientious Objectors of the Vietnam War in Their Own Words*. Boston: Little, Brown, 1993.

Unterberger, Richie. *Eight Miles High: Folk-Rock's Flight from Haight-Ashbury to Woodstock*. San Francisco: Backbeat Books, 2003.

Unterberger, Richie. *Turn! Turn! Turn!: The '60s Folk-Rock Revolution*. San Francisco: Backbeat Books, 2002.

Viorst, Milton. *Fire in the Streets: America in the 1960s*. New York: Simon and Schuster, 1979.

Vogel, Steve. "Once More to the Pentagon: Demonstrators Evoke Historic Confrontation In Planning March, Rally Opposing Iraq War." *Washington Post* (March 16, 2007): B01.

Vonnegut, Kurt. *Slaughterhouse-Five; or, The Children's Crusade: A Duty-Dance With Death*. New York: Delacorte, 1969.

Washington Square Memoirs: The Great Urban Folk Boom, 1950-1970. Santa Monica, Calif.: Rhino. 2001. Indispensable three CD set for anyone who wants to understand the early sixties.

Watts, Alan W. *The Joyous Cosmology: Adventures in the Chemistry of Consciousness*, foreword by Timothy Leary and Richard Alpert. New York: Pantheon, 1962. Applicable to some of us, i.e., only to those of us who are not yet sophisticated enough to realize that consciousness does not have a chemistry. Beautiful photographs.

Weinberg, Arthur and Lila. *Instead of Violence*. New York: Grossman, 1963.

Weiner, Rex; Stillman, Deanne. *Woodstock Census: The Nationwide Survey of the Sixties Generation*. New York: Viking, 1979.

Weissman, Dick. *Which Side Are You On? An Inside Story of the Folk Music Revival in America*. New York: Continuum, 2005.

White, Matthew; Ali, Jaffer. *The Official Prisoner Companion*. New York: Warner, 1988.

Wiener, Jon. *Come Together: John Lennon in His Time*. New York: Random House, 1984.

Wilkinson, Paul. *The New Fascists*. London: Pan, 1983.

Witcover, Jules. *The Year the Dream Died: Revisiting 1968 in America*. New York: Warner, 1998.

Wittner, Lawrence S. *Rebels Against the War: The American Peace Movement, 1933-1983*. Philadelphia: Temple University Press, 1984.

Wittner, Lawrence S. *Rebels Against the War: The American Peace Movement, 1941-1960*. New York: Columbia University Press, 1969.

Wolff, Robert Paul; Moore, Barrington, Jr.; Marcuse, Herbert. *A Critique of Pure Tolerance*. Boston: Beacon, 1965.

Wolin, Sheldon S.; Schaar, John N. *The Berkeley Rebellion and Beyond: Essays on Politics and Education in the Technological Society*. New York: New York Review / Vintage, 1970.

Woods, Randall Bennett. *Quest for Identity: America Since 1945*. Cambridge: Cambridge University Press, 2005.

The World the Sixties Made: Politics and Culture in Recent America, edited by Van Gosse and Richard Moser. Philadelphia: Temple University Press, 2003.

Youth International Party. *Manifesto*. [broadside: s.l.: s.n., s.d.].

Zap Comix. Berkeley: Print Mint; San Francisco: Apex Novelty Company, 1967- .

Zappa, Frank. "The Oracle Has It All Psyched Out," *Life* 64, 26 (June 28, 1968): 82-94.

Zaroulis, Nancy; Sullivan, Gerald. *Who Spoke Up? American Protest Against The War In Vietnam 1963-1975*. Garden City, N.Y.: Doubleday, 1984.

Zinn, Howard. *Postwar America, 1945-1971*. Boston: South End Press, 2002.

Zwigoff, Terry; Lynch, David; *et al. Crumb* [video recording, 119 minutes, 1994]. VHS: Culver City, Calif.: Columbia TriStar Home Video, 1995; DVD: Culver City, Calif.: Columbia TriStar Home Video, 1998; Culver City, Calif.: Sony Pictures Home Entertainment, 2006.

Ω

Index